HEARTS
ON FIRE

HEARTS ON FIRE

SIX YEARS THAT CHANGED

CANADIAN MUSIC

2000–2005

MICHAEL BARCLAY

Published by ECW Press
665 Gerrard Street East
Toronto, Ontario, Canada M4M 1Y2
416-694-3348 / info@ecwpress.com

Editor for the Press: Michael Holmes
Cover design: David A. Gee
Front cover photograph copyright © Kathryn Yu

All quoted lyrics appear by permission of the rights holders.

LIBRARY AND ARCHIVES CANADA CATALOGUING
IN PUBLICATION

Title: Hearts on fire : six years that changed Canadian
music, 2000-2005 / Michael Barclay

Names: Barclay, Michael, 1971- author.

Identifiers: Canadiana (print) 20210389788 | Canadiana
(ebook) 2021039000X

ISBN 978-1-77041-587-4 (hardcover)
ISBN 978-1-77305-904-4 (ePub)
ISBN 978-1-77305-905-1 (PDF)
ISBN 978-1-77305-906-8 (Kindle)

Subjects: LCSH: Popular music—Canada—2001-2010—
History and criticism. | LCSH: Popular music—
Canada—1991-2000—History and criticism.

Classification: LCC ML3484 .B244 2022 | DDC
781.64/0971—dc23

This book is funded in part by the Government of Canada. Ce livre est financé en partie par le gouvernement du Canada. We acknowledge
the support of the Canada Council for the Arts. Nous remercions le Conseil des arts du Canada de son soutien. We acknowledge the support
of the Ontario Arts Council (OAC), an agency of the Government of Ontario, which last year funded 1,965 individual artists and 1,152
organizations in 197 communities across Ontario for a total of $51.9 million. We also acknowledge the support of the Government of
Ontario through the Ontario Book Publishing Tax Credit, and through Ontario Creates.

PRINTED AND BOUND IN CANADA

PRINTING: FRIESENS   5   4   3   2   1

For Helen and Leonard

TABLE OF CONTENTS

INTRODUCTION
GET IN OR GET OUT

This book was originally going to be about the entire first decade of the new century. Ten is a nice round number. This book's predecessor, *Have Not Been the Same*, covered a decade. But this time I soon realized I had way too much to talk about, and most of the really important moments happened in the first half of a decade; the six following years were a continuation, not as transformative.

Part of the central thesis here is that the years 2000 to 2005 are when the rest of the world actually gave a shit about Canadian music: not just our somewhat random chart-toppers, but the groundswell of creativity that was happening en masse at the time, in many genres of music, using many different metrics of success. Evolving technology and media helped facilitate this in ways old models could not.

I grew up in alternative culture and have a degree in Canadian history. Therefore I've always thought external validation is nice but by no means necessary: if the music made around the corner moves you, it is therefore important—whether or not the rest of the country or the rest of the world hears it. It's a tired truism that Canadian media often ignores its artists until they get covered in the U.S. or U.K. It's been true for as long as Canada has been a country. Every arts writer has used that hook to pitch stories to reluctant Canadian editors, shaming them into playing catch-up. We rarely celebrate our own until someone else celebrates them first. That's a national embarrassment.

And yet this book is primarily about those who broke through borders. In another era, that would just mean the superstars—you know who they are. This time period, however, was when weirdos and innovators were more likely to break internationally than anyone aiming for commercial radio.

Applying an international filter to my thesis was one easy way to further narrow my focus—and frankly, people outside Canada might now actually read this book. That meant excluding many of my favourite artists, some of my friends and likely many of yours, too. But you're holding this book right now: Can you imagine it being longer? Me neither. I'm well aware who's missing from this book; I'm sure I'll be hearing about it. Don't assume it's because I'm not a fan: sometimes that's true; often it isn't. Buy me a drink and I'll tell you the reasons—and give you a list of 50 other great Canadian records from this time period that aren't found in these pages.

Every review of this book will quibble about who's in and who's out. Every musician who put out records during this time period is going to jump to the index[1] to see how many times they're mentioned, if they are at all. Readers across the country will complain it has too much Toronto. Readers in Toronto will complain there's not enough. Residents of every province and every metropolis will feel underrepresented. That's the story of Canadian history. Because Canada is not a thing. Any attempt to represent Canada will be an abject failure. That's the story of this book as well.

There are so many stories about this period of time, inside and outside these pages, that could be spun into books of their own. I want to read them. I encourage you to write them—and to take this book for what it is, not what it isn't.

Now, dive in. These are deep waters.

---

1   Spoiler: there isn't one, so download your free e-book that comes with your purchase, and do your own search.

CHAPTER 1
VISUALIZE
SUCCESS

THAT NIGHT IN TORONTO

This book began on December 14, 2001. Toronto was blanketed in the first heavy snowfall of the year: the warm, insulating kind that makes the city look beautiful, the kind that makes the coming winter feel welcome. The band Royal City was headlining Lee's Palace for the first time, to launch their second album, *Alone at the Microphone*, on Three Gut Records. Also on the bill was a brand new act called the Hidden Cameras, an unruly orchestra that looked like a group of queer camp counsellors, with underwear-clad go-go dancers, playing perfect '50s-style pop melodies set to four-on-the-floor disco thumps and violins.[1]

It was one of the most beautiful nights of music I'd ever seen in my life. The Hidden Cameras were a complete surprise; though I had a few friends in the band, that was my virgin experience. Royal City was not a surprise. I'd played on a solo record by bandleader Aaron Riches, who in turn had played drums in my band when we needed a fill-in. Royal City drummer Nathan Lawr was a former roommate. That week I'd given *Alone at the Microphone* a five-star review in *Eye Weekly*. Nepotism? Sure. But if I hadn't written that review, someone else would have: the album was a critical favourite across the country that year and still gets mentioned as a classic of the era. It was on an entirely different level from other records that happened to be made by friends in my musical orbit.

---

1   First on the bill that night at Lee's Palace was a guy Royal City had met at a show in Brooklyn: an unknown singer-songwriter named Sufjan Stevens. Rounding out the bill was Deep Dark United, a band featuring Alex Lukashevsky, whose earlier band opened Godspeed's first Toronto show.

It eventually got Royal City a record deal with the U.K.'s Rough Trade Records, with the man who'd signed both the Smiths and, more recently, the Strokes; the label signed the Hidden Cameras at the same time. The idea of either signing seemed ridiculous on that cold December night.

When the show was over, I lingered at the bar. I ran into Stuart Berman, my editor at *Eye Weekly*, and we shared our rave reactions. "Mark my words," he said. "This is the start of something. In a couple of years, everyone will be talking about Toronto."

I was highly skeptical. Two months earlier, in the same venue, had been the launch party for a book I co-wrote, *Have Not Been the Same*. That book was about Canadian music between 1985 and '95 that was beloved at home but, with some notable exceptions, barely registered anywhere else. Tales of Canuck under-achievement had been hammered into me to the point that I believed, just like one of my favourite (non-Canadian) songs of 2001 said, "Mediocrity rules, man."

"I don't want to burst your bubble," I told Berman, "but the rest of the world doesn't give a shit about Canada, no matter how good our music is. People care more about indie music from New Zealand or Iceland than they ever will about Canada. Canada will never be cool."

In 2001, I believed the Nickelbacks of the world would likely be our greatest export, not the Royal Cities. Not the Hidden Cameras. Not the Feists. Not any other genre of music, either, especially not our hip-hop.

That night, Royal City covered Iggy Pop's "Success." I should have listened. I should have known. Another Three Gut act had already warned me.

NINE MONTHS EARLIER, I first heard the Constantines. I was living in Guelph and had just finished co-writing *Have Not Been the Same*; I'd barely left the house in a year. The week before, Berman had written about them with the most hyperbolic prose I'd ever read. Before I knew it, my friends at Three Gut Records had signed them. It turned out that one of the greatest new Canadian bands was living liter-ally around the corner from me, 100 metres away, and I'd been too suffocated by history to even notice.

That weekend I went to see them play. The show was in a bright grad lounge on the fifth floor of Guelph's University Centre, a building akin to a shopping mall with office space. It was the most unappealing venue possible, a benefit show for some loosely knit campus club of some kind, which meant that most people were there to talk disinterestedly to colleagues and chain-smoke. (You could still do that indoors then.)

None of that mattered to the four blue-jeaned boys who plugged into their amps on the ersatz stage. By the end of their first song, every ear in the room was fixated on the ferocious sound coming from the corner. In no time, singer/guitarist Bry Webb was climbing his large Marshall stack, perhaps because it seemed the correct move to make over such a gigantic sound, or maybe he just felt liberated playing somewhere that wasn't a basement with a five-foot ceiling. Bassist Dallas Wehrle closed his eyes meditatively, his left fist raised in a rock'n'roll salute while his right hand plucked pulsing open strings. Guitarist Steve Lambke stood relatively in place, legs apart, his occasional barked hardcore vocals the antithesis of his quiet, offstage speech. Drummer Doug MacGregor commanded the beat with a rare balance of force, precision and grace.

Interviewing them in their living room a week later for *Exclaim!*, their landline kept ringing with requests to speak to "a Constantine." In the background, Webb had put on a very early album by fellow rock'n'roll believer Springsteen; "Rosalita" competed with our conversation. All four were humble and polite and, with the exception of the gregarious MacGregor, soft-spoken. Their normalcy was surprising. Not because I'd expected the Constantines to be arrogant hipsters, necessarily. But for performers known to dangle from ceilings and strip down to their underwear, screaming for the death of rock'n'roll while simultaneously tapping into everything glorious about the art form—well, you'd expect them to have bigger heads than four nice small-town men who grew up playing in hardcore bands.

That first show I saw shouldn't be totally glamorized. The performance was far from perfect. They stammered awkwardly between songs, stalling any momentum. Webb's raspy voice was inaudible, with only faint traces of poetry distinguishable in the din. The rubbery rhythm section tied everything together, as the Sleater-Kinney-esque guitar interplay between Webb and Lambke was often lost underneath sheets of distortion and volume. And while they suggested transcendence, they didn't yet deliver.

Soon, of course, they would. Night after night, howling at the moon. In the next few years, I saw them everywhere short of a stadium: rock clubs, folk festivals, outdoor university frosh gigs, farmers' fields, 150-year-old hotels, the CBC studios, in New York City, and in their Guelph basement.

And Stuart Berman was right: the rest of the world *did* care. Peaches was already becoming one of the most influential musicians in pop, and non-Torontonian acts as musically diverse as Godspeed, Kid Koala, the New Pornographers, the Weakerthans and the Be Good Tanyas had been getting international attention for the past two years. The Constantines signed to Sub Pop after a set at South by Southwest in March 2002.

LESS THAN A YEAR LATER, Berman was right again: in October 2002 he wrote a five-star review of *You Forgot It in People*, made by friends of his, Broken Social Scene. His review openly fessed up to the nepotism, negated immediately by the perfect or near-perfect scores that record got from Berman's peers in Toronto and far beyond.

You Forgot It in People was released four months before I moved to Montreal to work at CBC Radio's *Brave New Waves*. On December 1, I was there to scout out apartments, and Broken Social Scene, with Leslie Feist in tow, happened to be playing La Sala Rossa. Royal City was the opening act. I had dinner with them across the street at Casa del Popolo, where we ran into Broken Social Scene's Kevin Drew. I'd met him once before: two years ago, on a Toronto patio where he was eagerly eavesdropping on the *Have Not Been the Same* co-authors discussing our work-in-progress. I liked him immediately, and not just because he was a schmoozer who courted critics. That night in Montreal, he good-naturedly needled me on the chances that *You Forgot It in People* would make *Exclaim!*'s year-end list.[2]

That night I met Tim Kingsbury, with whom I had many mutual friends from Guelph, including the members of Royal City. Tim had just joined the band first on the bill that night. That band was called Arcade Fire.

I can't lie: I missed Arcade Fire's set to hang out with an old friend across town. When I arrived at the venue, everyone was raving about Tim's band. A lovely and engaging woman with wild curls and lace gloves was working the merch table, peddling a two-song cassette tape that came in a standard letter envelope, on the front of which was written in marker: "With ♥ from Arcade Fire." Her name was Régine. I bought the cassette for two dollars. I brought it back to Guelph and played it every week on my campus radio show. In the next two years, I made sure I didn't miss a single Arcade Fire show. I became an evangelist.

I also got to know them. We shared dinners, soccer games, random adventures. I was at the EP release show at Casa del Popolo where they broke up on stage. I saw them regroup in several incarnations. I repeatedly saw rooms full of people fall in love with them: at their first show in Toronto, in Hamilton, in Chapel Hill, in New York City.

When they were working on *Funeral*, they became socially scarce, all holding down shitty jobs and spending every spare moment recording. One day Tim invited me to their apartment studio where they were going to record gang vocals

---

2   It didn't. It came out so close to the deadline that few critics outside Toronto had heard it. But it landed on plenty of lists in 2003.

on "Wake Up." They wanted to get all their friends on the track, including all of Wolf Parade, but only Tim's roommate, Matt Brown, and I showed up.[3]

By the late summer of 2004, advance copies of *Funeral* had been floating among critics for a few months. The band's North American tour in June, opening up for their friends in the Unicorns, made a huge impression on all who witnessed it. Like Berman with Broken Social Scene, I indulged in nepotism and wrote an Arcade Fire cover story for *Exclaim!* the month of *Funeral*'s release. (The album came out the same day as Stars' *Set Yourself on Fire* and Tegan and Sara's *So Jealous*.) The language I used in the story would have read as ridiculous hyperbole if my peers across the continent didn't already agree with me. This band was not just people I happened to know. This band was going to be huge.

And yet I still doubted my own instincts. If I knew anything about commercial appeal, I'd be marketing music instead of writing about it. But I didn't, and I don't.

North Carolina's Merge Records thought they were being ambitious when they pressed 10,000 copies of *Funeral*, an unusually high number for an obscure indie band's debut album. But it sold out of its first pressing in a week and went on to sell more than one million copies worldwide. In the pre-Napster era, it likely would have sold at least three times that amount. Maybe 10 times. A curious thing for historians writing about this time is that there's no real metric for an artist's popularity in the pre-streaming era, during the decline of physical media.

A month after its release, my girlfriend at the time, Helen Spitzer, and I drove some of Arcade Fire down to New York City for the CMJ festival in October 2004. Their tour hadn't started yet, but between the demand for the suddenly hard-to-find album and the glowing reviews—including a game-changing one in *Pitchfork*—the hype was now huge. The money wasn't, though. To paraphrase the Constantines' "Some Party," the season's new rock hopefuls were still just hoping to get paid. That's why they were hitching a ride to their official New York City launch with two music critics. They didn't even have a manager yet. (They did, however, have a New York lawyer.)

Win Butler, one of the most tenacious people I've ever met, was seeing his vision come true; he was probably more prepared than the others. Violinist Sarah Neufeld, who came from the world of modern dance and electroacoustic music, picked my meagre brain during the drive back to Montreal: What might all of this mean in terms of actual numbers? How many copies might they actually sell? I knew that American indie stalwarts like Yo La Tengo might be lucky to sell

---

3   We did several takes. The hook, as every fan can tell you, is insanely high; it's way out of my limited range. Wolf Parade drummer Arlen Thompson told me later he too was part of an earlier group vocal take on the song, which got cut. I highly doubt my voice is on the final version, though the very generous Tim assures me it is—and that's what I tell my child.

100,000, newer acts like Bright Eyes might sell half that, but I didn't really have any more of a sense of it than she did. My lifelong love of Canadian underdogs had lowered my expectations considerably. Expectations changed after that week.

While Arcade Fire were slaying New York City, the Constantines were likely on a stage somewhere, spreading a gospel, Bry Webb testifying and howling, "Can I get a witness?"

By the dawn of 2005, for him and everyone else in this book, witnesses were no longer hard to come by.

CHAPTER 2
NATIONAL
HUM

SETTING THE STAGE

"More and more neglected hands
Judgment ripe, they're starting bands
Working on a new solution"
—Constantines, "National Hum," 2003

O n stage at Toronto's Massey Hall in 1904, prime minister Wilfrid Laurier boldly declared that "the 20th century shall be the century of Canada." The political entity of Canada was still very new; Laurier had been 25 years old at the time of Confederation. Canada was still very much a colonial outpost that looked to Britain for guidance. Laurier's promise for the new century was trotted out in ensuing decades as either perpetually postponed potential or as hilarious hubris from a country of underachievers. Canadians spent the next 100 years waiting in vain for Laurier to be proven correct, for the country to stake its place in the world, for its culture to thrive.

But maybe Laurier's pronouncement was just ahead by a century.[1]

DISCOVERY CHANNELS

It's strange now to recall the excitement people had in 1999 over a flip in the calendar. Everyone said "the year 2000" in ways no one ever said "the year 1994" or "the year 1971." "The year 2000" was a fantasy of the future for kids raised on *The Jetsons*, whose parents read Alvin Toffler and Buckminster Fuller. A year of rebirth,

---

1   Citing Laurier is more than a bit complicated: his vision of Canada was also behind by a century, and downright racist: he imposed the Chinese Head Tax and deemed "the Negro race unsuitable to the requirements of Canada."

of renewal, of potential. The new millennium! "Let's all meet up in the year 2000!" Y2K, it turned out okay! "Two-thousand-zero-zero, party over, oops, out of time!"

The music industry was at a crucial turning point in its history, which rolled out over the next five years. In 2000, record companies had just had their most profitable year ever, riding high on teen pop and CD sales. Independent artists still made money from sales of physical product, even though peer-to-peer file-sharing was exploding, due to software like Napster and LimeWire. In 2000, print media and terrestrial radio were still crucial ways to learn about new music, soon to be complemented by message boards, blogs, satellite radio, and internet radio. The iTunes store launched in 2003, and MySpace a few months later. The latter became a major discovery engine for listeners, and easy for artists to use without middlemen. YouTube appeared in 2005, as did Pandora's algorithm-based, paid-subscription streaming model, the basis of the music industry in the 2020s. It's fitting that a Swedish band emerged called the Soundtrack of Our Lives at a time when it was never easier to soundtrack your life: to discover new artists from around the world, and for music to be a huge part of your identity.

Since the days of Wilfrid Laurier, Canadian music had difficulty being heard beyond its home and native land. Canada was (and is) a small market. No one else cared how popular you were in Canada. The country itself was not "exotic" enough to be interesting. No radio programmer or journalist in the world would ever open a package promising a hot new artist from Canada. There's a reason the phrase "worthwhile Canadian initiative" is a long-standing joke in American newsrooms as the least enticing headline ever.

To successfully attract an international audience, Canadian musicians usually needed foreign record label support and ideally foreign radio and press—not to mention savvy management, a lot of luck and dogged determination to tour constantly and slowly build a fan base. It also helped to make music that sounded like everything else already popular in the world.

In the latter half of Laurier's century, Canada had reliably managed to produce global superstars, the best of which were unique and groundbreaking (Joni Mitchell, Rush); others merely captured the zeitgeist with grand gestures inside an accepted commercial sphere (Bryan Adams, Céline Dion). Either way, those international success stories were occasional flare-ups from a country often ignored. Outside their home turf, the artists in question were rarely understood to be Canadian.

Arcade Fire's Will Butler—born in California in 1982, raised in Texas, and whose mother idolized Joni Mitchell—didn't know anything about Canada when his brother, Win, moved to Montreal in 2000. "I could probably have told you it was in Quebec and they spoke French," he laughs. "I probably didn't know

Leonard Cohen was a Montreal figure; I might have been able to tell you he was Canadian, but probably not."

Meanwhile, Canadians didn't even know what exists inside their own borders. "The people who tell us what Canadian culture is are oftentimes missing our best exports," says Dan Boeckner of Wolf Parade. He grew up a big fan of Skinny Puppy, pioneers of industrial music. Skinny Puppy won't ever get a tribute at the Junos or be included in a coffee-table book about Canadian music. "They are internationally famous," he says. "When you go to Europe and ask about Skinny Puppy, [people there] think they're American, and Americans think they're European. No one knows they're Canadian, or that they're from Vancouver. We do this over and over again, decade by decade: produce this music that impacts on a global level." And yet Canadians were the perpetual cultural underdogs of the Western world—without having a geographical excuse, like Australia or New Zealand.

That all changed starting in 2000, the year Dan Bejar of Destroyer sang, "There is joy in being barred from the temple." A Canadian artist's fate was no longer superstar or bust, thanks in large part to new methods of music discovery, ones not predicated on national media. You could be a weirdo making a record in your bedroom and disseminating it online, and you might get a rave review from afar before most people in your hometown had even heard of you. If the stars aligned, you might even sell hundreds of thousands of records without any real radio support. It didn't matter if you were one woman with a synth and a drum machine, a turntablist with an absurd sense of humour, three folk-singing tree-planters or a nine-member art-rock collective. And if your neighbours are doing something equally innovative or interesting, then suddenly Canada as a whole looks a lot more intriguing to the rest of the world—for the first time in its musical history.

Vancouver band the New Pornographers put out their debut album, *Mass Romantic*, in November 2000 on a local indie label, Mint Records. Within weeks, the *New York Times* picked it as one of the best records of the year—something that hadn't happened to any indie Canadian act ever, especially one that was barely known at home beyond the cover of *Exclaim!* magazine. The acclaim for *Mass Romantic* continued to spread at the same time that Toronto artist Peaches was becoming one of the biggest buzz acts in Europe—again, before most Canadians knew who she was.

The New Pornographers' Carl Newman recalls, "Somebody came up to me at [Manhattan club] Brownies in February 2001 and said, 'Hey, you know, Canada's kinda hip now. It's getting a rep for music. You guys and Peaches.' None of the other [Canadian] bands had shown up [in the U.S.] yet; we were the only two with any profile. That comment sticks in my head because it just seemed weird to me: us and Peaches. It doesn't quite seem like a scene, but it's cool."

Meanwhile, hometown bringdown was still real. "I remember in 2001, Peaches had just started to be a thing," says singer-songwriter Owen Pallett. "I was reading [U.K. mag] *Mojo*, where they were interviewing people at some industry party, and asking what was the best thing that came out that year. Everyone named various records, then someone would run back over and say, 'Oh, I forgot something: Peaches is amazing!' The person next to them would be like, 'Oh, yes, Peaches!' Whereas in Toronto, people were like, 'Who wants to listen to fucking Peaches?!'"

Take a look at what else came out in Canadian music in 2000: Godspeed You! Black Emperor's *Lift Your Skinny Fists Like Antennas to Heaven*, the Weakerthans' *Left and Leaving*, the Dears' *End of a Hollywood Bedtime Story*, the Be Good Tanyas' *Blue Horse*, Kid Koala's *Carpal Tunnel Syndrome*, Tegan and Sara's *This Business of Art*, Sarah Harmer's *You Were Here*, Destroyer's *Thief*.

That same year, Win Butler moved to Montreal, hoping to find people to play in his band, Arcade Fire. Kevin Drew and Brendan Canning started recording as Broken Social Scene. Joel Plaskett started his eponymous band. Leslie Feist was touring her first solo album across Western Canada, playing to a few people sitting on the floor in Medicine Hat. The Hidden Cameras played their first gig at a Toronto art gallery. Montreal's inaugural MUTEK festival secured the city's place at the forefront of innovative electronic music in North America.

The question was no longer "How did this come from Canada?" It quickly became, "How come there are so many great Canadian acts right now?"

"Everywhere we go," said Kevin Drew in November 2003, "people are always asking what kind of city [Toronto] is and [whether] we know this band or that band. It feels wonderful to know that the 32-block radius that you live in is being analyzed in Louisville, Kentucky, and Berlin." That same month, Broken Social Scene's picture ran beneath a headline in *GQ* that read, "Is Canada cooler than us?"

In February 2005, both *Spin* and the *New York Times* ran big profiles of the Montreal scene; the full-page photo leading off the *Spin* piece was of a band yet to release their debut album: Wolf Parade. By June 2005, *Spin*'s review of British Columbian band Hot Hot Heat joked about the "Buy Canadian!" movement in music. By that point—especially after the runaway success of Arcade Fire's 2004 debut, *Funeral*—international media were turning their eyes and ears north like never before. In October 2005, BBC Radio 2 aired a two-hour special called *The Maple Music Revolution*, featuring interviews with Arcade Fire, Kathleen Edwards, Sarah Harmer and—yes—Nickelback, who in December 2009 *Billboard* declared the bestselling group of the decade, beating out Destiny's Child.

Arcade Fire's real breakthrough moment—when they proved to a large U.S. audience that their live show could deliver on six months of hype—was at the 2005 Coachella festival in California, where six other Canadian acts joined them on the all-star bill, including Tegan and Sara, k-os, and Buck 65, and only one of which, Sloan, came from a previous generation. "I felt there was some magic at that Coachella '05," says Buck 65. "It was one of the few times in my life where I felt, 'It feels kinda badass to be a Canadian right now.' For a few years that's all people would talk about in interviews. 'How do you explain this Canadian thing that's going on?'"

This arose from a generation of kids born in the 1970s, who were raised on the pride and cultural protectionism of Pierre Trudeau and on the entrepreneurship and free trade policies of Brian Mulroney. A musically curious generation raised on MuchMusic, a Toronto-based broadcaster invested in myth-making from various regions of the country and where genres of music collided in a pre-poptimist context: Voivod next to the Rankin Family next to Michie Mee next to Tom Cochrane. A generation who grew up watching *Degrassi High* and *The Kids in the Hall*, two internationally successful shows beloved *because* they were dorky and unique and Canadian, not in spite of it. This generation learned to build up their own community, shake off any potential inferiority complex and then take their mission to the world, no matter how weird it might seem.

LET'S NOT PARTY LIKE IT'S 1999

To understand 2000, dial it back even just one year, to 1999. Live music was in peril: dance clubs thrived, DJs ruled, and bubblegum pop ruled the charts. Hip-hop was eclipsing rock music, and pop as well, but the Canadian industry was woefully (wilfully?) underequipped to figure it out. Something called electronica cast its shadow everywhere, even though no one knew what it meant—or they didn't want to, despite the international success of Plastikman from Windsor, Ontario. Third-rate grunge ruled rock radio and nu-metal was on the rise. The underground was abandoning songwriting and becoming obsessed with post-rock that appealed primarily to eggheads (not that there's anything wrong with that). The indie boom of the early to mid-'90s had gone bust: joyless audiences sat on the floor, if they showed up to gigs at all. Dave Matthews was a thing. Live, raw rock'n'roll was as niche as jazz. Only the garage-rock underground was thriving—and largely preaching to the converted.

Almost every musical genre seemed to be in a state of flux. An old-school major label deal seemed impossible, and likely not worth the trouble anyway.

That said, major labels had a lot of money from the CD era and were throwing it at anything they could: Ska! Lounge! Trip-hop! Swing! Nothing wrong with a hodgepodge of styles defining a scene, of course. As Canadians are constantly told, "Diversity is our strength." But there's a big difference between a landfill of assorted refuse and a flourishing ecosystem.

Canada's major musical exports throughout the '90s were solo women. Alanis Morissette was the first Canadian to win the Grammy for Album of the Year.[2] Shania Twain was the bestselling female country artist of all time. Diana Krall was the last jazz superstar of the 20th century. Loreena McKennitt sold millions of copies as an independent Celtic folk act. Sarah McLachlan had enough star wattage to commandeer one of the most historically significant ventures in mainstream music, the Lilith Fair.

Rock groups did not fare as well, with only Barenaked Ladies (belatedly) making any impact at all outside the country, with a No. 1 Billboard hit in 1998. Sloan, Blue Rodeo and the Tragically Hip were resigning themselves to cult status at best outside Canada. One of the biggest Canadian pop bands in the domestic market was literally a cartoon (Prozzäk), while another looked like one (the Moffatts). Homegrown hip-hop had been entirely invisible, even to most Canadians, since the days of Snow and the Dream Warriors—and there are plenty of structural reasons to blame for that. The Rascalz' 1998 single "Northern Touch" was in part so epochal because so little had changed in the 10 years since the breakthrough of Maestro Fresh Wes.

In 1999, unless it was one of the aforementioned solo female superstars, you would never see an upcoming Canadian artist on the cover of an American or British music magazine—or, for that matter, even find one of their records reviewed inside. *Rolling Stone* was more likely to put a Canadian actor (Jim Carrey, Pamela Anderson) on the cover than a Canadian musician. The acknowledged influence of underground figures fared better, like D.O.A., NoMeansNo, Skinny Puppy, Mecca Normal—all Vancouver or Victoria acts of the '80s who made more inroads down the West Coast and in Europe than they ever did in Toronto or Montreal. Winnipeg's Propagandhi and Halifax's Sloan were two of the only exceptions in the '90s. Toronto acts were usually left in the dust, other than Cowboy Junkies. While all those acts received some attention, there were certainly no breathless hyperboles being doled out. In 1999, you could have polled the average music listener—or even most critics, whose job involves musical discovery—and not find a Canadian album in their top 10 of the year. That includes critics at Canadian publications.

---

2   One could argue it was David Clayton-Thomas, in 1970, as singer of Blood, Sweat & Tears, or David Foster for his key role in 1994's *The Bodyguard* soundtrack—but why bother?

Whether you made mainstream music or not, the rest of the world wasn't waiting to hear more from Canada, and Canadians barely knew how to market themselves beyond even our interprovincial borders. You had little chance of pleasing anyone else. Might as well make music to please yourself.

"I'm learning to survive," sang the Constantines, "on earthworms and houseflies."

The history of Canadian music is that of independence. Until the 1970s, artists almost certainly had to leave the country to have any kind of career: hence Nova Scotian Hank Snow's "I'm Movin' On," a song that spent 21 weeks atop the Billboard charts in 1950. Proper recording studios weren't built here until Jack Richardson's Nimbus 9 Soundstage Recording Studio in 1972; he famously remortgaged his house to finance the first Guess Who album. Stompin' Tom Connors ran his own label, Boot Records, which released regional favourites from across the nation, including Indigenous artists and a fair amount of Jamaica-to-Toronto reggae as well. Rush started their own label because no one would sign them and licensed their albums out to majors as they became more popular. Superstar Corey Hart was signed to Aquarius Records, a Montreal indie that first struck gold with April Wine in the '70s (and later with Sum 41 in the 2000s). Punk rockers like to think they invented DIY, but if punk and DIY are inextricably linked, then every Canadian musician has always been a punk.

But in 1999, punk was dead—or, at the very least, beyond meaningless. Five years after Kurt Cobain's suicide, the Woodstock '99 lineup was filled with punks, and MuchMusic VJ Sook-Yin Lee described it as "the total breakdown of 'civilized society,' where corporate greed and a clash of college bros and idyllic hippies devolved into a throng of shit-throwing, raping and pillaging ravagers." She wasn't remotely exaggerating. New definitions were needed on every level, in every genre.

Artists could spend a lot of energy trying to second-guess trends—or they could just turn off the noise and do whatever they want. "In Toronto on Queen Street at the time," says Hawksley Workman, "with people like Spookey Ruben and John Southworth, it was, 'How weird can we get? How niche? How oddball?' [EMI Publishing's] Mike McCarty was handing out $10,000 publishing deals to a lot of bands back then, and that felt like a million dollars. Only a couple of bands, like Sum 41, ever became anything. None of us had any money, so it was an easy time when Toronto was kind of grungy and grimy and we could all live really cheap and entertain ourselves by passing around cassette demos and trying to blow each other's minds. Because that's all we had."

The time was ripe for a seismic shift, one that would have ripples for decades to come.

SHAKING THE STIGMA

Every five years in popular music—the amount of time it takes someone to get from grade 8 to grade 12—there's an inevitable generational shift: a teenager in 1990 will reject Rush and Rough Trade; a teenager in 2000 will reject the Tragically Hip and Blue Rodeo; a teenager in 2020 will think Drake is an old man. Meanwhile, Canada's strong continuum of groundbreakers and non-mainstream artists have often been written out of history, a blight that's only been rectified in recent years, helped by a wealth of obscurities resurfacing either online or in official reissues. Canadians make a choice—conscious or otherwise—to be swamped by American and British culture. It's very easy for young Canadians of every generation to believe everyone knows this is nowhere—whether or not they know the Neil Young song in question.

"I've always hated Canadian music," Joel Gibb of the Hidden Cameras said in 2004, citing proto-riot grrrls Mecca Normal and Fifth Column as two lonely exceptions. "Especially in the '90s, the music scene was not good—but it's typical for Canadians to say that it's good. It's like having a magazine policy where you're not allowed to give bad reviews to Canadian bands. It doesn't help the culture." Gibb's own band, perhaps naturally, appealed to people who had zero interest in the Tea Party or Our Lady Peace, if they even knew who those artists were. "We played a show at Shepherds Bush Hall in England," he said, "and there were these fans who actually said, 'I don't want to be rude or whatever, but I just can't believe you're from Canada!' They were going on and on about it, and it was supposed to be a compliment."

Joel Carriere, who started Dine Alone Records and has managed Alexisonfire since they formed in 2001, worked at a record store when the Constantines' self-titled debut came in a hand-assembled cardboard sleeve with an actual match inside it, urging the listener to start their own metaphorical fire. Intrigued—and frustrated that it didn't fit in display cases—Carriere listened to it and was blown away, recommending it to regular customer Dallas Green, who also fell in love. "Then I found out they were Canadian," says Carriere. "At the time, in the '90s, things would sound 'Canadian.' Then, in the 2000s, nothing sounded 'Canadian'—everything just sounded good or bad."

Basia Bulat is a Toronto singer-songwriter who signed to U.K. label Rough Trade in 2007. Five years earlier, she was a campus radio DJ in London, Ontario, energized by her playlist. She'd grown up as a massive fan of Sloan and Hayden, and now dozens of new Canadian records were showing up at the radio station every month, which inspired her to pursue her own musical path. "The radio station's guidelines were to play at least 40% Canadian content, but we'd end up playing almost 100%," she says. "There was so much we loved. It wasn't even hard. Everything that was coming into the station, we'd get so excited."

Black Mountain's Stephen McBean recalls going to see a very early New Pornographers show, with Dave Wenger of Daddy's Hands. They knew some of the band through friends of friends. "We were watching them play and were trying to make fun of them," says McBean, "but then we realized, Oh wait, this band is *really fucking good.*"

About the New Pornographers in 2002, one Houston magazine wrote, "Despite the obvious benefits that the Band, Neil Young, Daniel Lanois and others have heaped upon the world, few word pairs evince an instant smirk like 'Canadian rock.'" In 2003, the Universal Records exec who signed Sam Roberts told *Maclean's*, "We have a saying [in the U.S.]: if you're from Canada you're either going to become one of the world's biggest acts or you won't be able to get arrested. There's no middle ground—either you're Céline, Alanis, Sarah, Avril [Lavigne] or Nelly [Furtado], or you're the Tea Party, Matthew Good, Sloan, the Tragically Hip."

Except that *of course* there's a middle ground, and only a narrow-minded corporate suit with blockbusters on their mind would think otherwise. While the mega-merger-minded industry ignored that middle ground, a whole lot of Canadian music came out of nowhere, often rewriting the rules of their supposed genre boundaries. Kid Koala was a turntablist who didn't make hip-hop. Caribou had more in common with psychedelic jazz than electronic music of the day. The Weakerthans were a punk band with folk songs and a poet at the core. Peaches flipped all kinds of scripts. Broken Social Scene rewrote the rules of what defines a rock band.

Only the most minuscule minority of musicians could ever hope to be within close proximity of mainstream success. By definition, "the mainstream does not include everybody," says Peaches. "It just includes a traditional path. We all need to find out who we are and find a path, and if you look to the mainstream, then you're going to have a lot of problems understanding who you are. Because 99% of the time, you're not really going to be included in the way you want to express yourself."

Everything changed in July 1999, when a decidedly non-mainstream Montreal band almost no one had heard of—weirdos who purposely avoided ties to industry capital—somehow ended up on the cover of Britain's most influential music publication.

THE BIG BANG

"The first indication that something different was going on was when Godspeed You! Black Emperor appeared on the cover of the *NME*," says Howard Bilerman, who partnered with members of that band to create the Hotel 2 Tango studio in 2000. "No one in Montreal had ever seen someone from here on the cover of that magazine—or even written about. If something that was Canadian was written about in a U.S. or U.K. publication, it was like, wow, we penetrated a fortress. But to be on the cover of those magazines? Never. That I'd never seen in my lifetime."

And yet ironies abound. Yes, a story about Godspeed was on the cover—but the band wasn't, because they refused to be photographed. It was the first *NME* cover story in history not to feature a photo of the artist: instead it was an image of a storm with text from the spoken-word intro to "The Dead Flag Blues." Godspeed has only ever given maybe 10 interviews in their history, mostly railing about how they're portrayed in the press (after being goaded by journalists complaining about unrequited love). So it's more than a bit amusing that the one magazine this Canadian anticapitalist band would agree to talk to would be a British music tabloid—which is why they did it, precisely because it seemed so absurd.[3]

What's even funnier is that the Godspeed issue was one of the lowest-selling in the magazine's history; an editorial later that year even lamented the choice to put them on the cover. But the effect was galvanizing. "I'd seen Godspeed at the Fleece and Firkin in Bristol a couple of weeks earlier," one *NME* reader told the *Guardian* years later. "It was an incredible set: cramped, sweat dripping from the ceiling, ridiculously noisy, two drummers. To then see them on the cover of the *NME*, which seemed to be an endless procession of the usual Britpop faces, was amazing."

Ro Cemm is a British journalist and show promoter who, as a teen, felt alienated by the boorish lad culture of '90s Britpop and found himself drawn to Swedish and Canadian music instead. Godspeed's *NME* cover was a life-changing moment for the future Canuckophile. "I was 17 in 1999, and it was a massive deal for me to have this [obscure Canadian] music that I had discovered and loved held up alongside the biggest bands in the world," he says. "I think I had that cover on my wall for about three years. It was gloriously strange, and folks were still talking about it years later."

---

3   Godspeed were odd bedfellows: they were sandwiched between issues featuring cover stars Marilyn Manson, for the second time that calendar year, and proto-Coldplay band Travis; Oasis appeared on the cover five times in 1999 alone.

Once Godspeed cracked that door open, perceptions of Canadian music were forever altered—if any perception of it had existed before. It was a pretty low bar. For non-Canadians, says Arcade Fire's Will Butler, "Canada was a coherent unit. They didn't know how goddamn big it is. Of course, people in Montreal only identify as being from Montreal. But there was this weird thing where the border matters more than you think it would: there's more back and forth between Montreal and Toronto, or even Montreal and Vancouver. It's the same swirl of ideas. And it wasn't like the Avril Lavigne moment or the Nickelback moment. There was a DIY-ness to it; it was a scrappy moment."

"There were all these mini scenes with people in them all trying to do the same thing," says Stars' Torquil Campbell. "I didn't know anyone in Arcade Fire or the Weakerthans or Godspeed. We all felt very different from each other then, but if you listen to that music now, it's so similar—all of it. The spirit of it, and the fact we weren't afraid to use horns and violins and orchestral instrumentation. We'd all come through an education system where you had to be in band or in orchestra. There was this epic aspect to all of it that was of a kind, even though we didn't all hang out with each other."

Stephen McBean of Black Mountain says, "Things started to change from, 'Oh hey, you're from Canada: do you know a guy named Fred?' To, 'Hey, you're from Canada: do you know Godspeed?'" The question didn't seem that strange, with nine people in the Montreal band. And besides, McBean actually *did* know the band from the other side of the country: in 2009, his side project Pink Mountaintops made a record with violinist Sophie Trudeau of Godspeed. They met at a mutual friend's wedding.

Because of Godspeed's 20-minute instrumental songs, it was obvious they were going to exist outside normal rock paradigms. But even in experimental circles, they were outliers. "Everything was post-rave in the U.K. and Europe," says Godspeed's Efrim Menuck when talking about their early tours there. "When we'd do interviews, it wasn't just odd to [Europeans] that we had string instruments: there was this idea that [in the future] there would only be DJs. So the idea that we played instruments *at all*, for German journalists, was fascinating." The late '90s was the era when there was a minor moral panic over the idea that turntables might be outselling guitars.

Godspeed also set the template for what would soon become a cliché: the co-ed Canadian band with six or more people, at least one of whom has to play the violin and/or cello. Arcade Fire and Broken Social Scene didn't sound like Godspeed or each other, but all three embraced the Big Sound—all three bands, in their own way, defying every expectation of what rock music had settled for at that point in its history, and very different from the new wave of rock bands in the

U.S., primarily from New York City. The American bands were stripped down to bare basics: the White Stripes and the Black Keys were duos. The Big Sound was a very Canadian thing: New Pornographers, Hidden Cameras, Black Mountain, Hey Rosetta! The more people on stage, the better. Hell, even our best-known punk band, Fucked Up, had six people in it. Everyone had side projects; concentric circles enveloped dozens more. Federalism at work. That literal representation of community embodied the explosion of talent and ambition coming out of every corner of the country.

Godspeed referred to itself as a collective and would often issue press releases written in the first-person plural. Some other bands got labelled a "collective," like Broken Social Scene, a band founded by two men but featuring multiple lead singers and a large pool of players, any of whom may or may not be on any given tour. That doesn't mean every large band is a collective. That certainly wasn't true of the Hidden Cameras, where bandleader Joel Gibb considered everyone inter-changeable—and as a result, most of his band started their own.

When the New Pornographers became one of the first breakthroughs of the new era in 2000, they were half-jokingly referred to in the indie press as a "super-group." Yet principal songwriter Carl Newman had led Zumpano, one of the least successful Sub Pop bands of the last decade, whereas secondary songwriter Dan Bejar released obscure indie records championed by nobody who didn't work at Scratch Records or at *Exclaim!* Only singer Neko Case, who released her second solo album earlier that year, was remotely recognizable, even though drummer Ryan Dahle had radio hits and *Big Shiny Tunes* with his bands Age of Electric and Limblifter. The idea that this combination of people would constitute a hot, hyped supergroup was laughable even to the New Pornographers themselves—except that as their popularity grew, the phrase was repeated, non-ironically, in every mention of the band.

Soon every Canadian ensemble with more than one singer or who had active side projects was either a "collective" or a "supergroup" or both. Meanwhile, the American trios Yeah Yeah Yeahs, Sleater-Kinney and the Gossip didn't even have bassists.

How did a country with a sparse population spread across a massive geo-graphical distance produce so many large bands? "I've always felt there were some material reasons for the Canadian mainstream music success—like [public] health care," says the Weakerthans' John K. Samson. "My theory is that you don't have a Broken Social Scene in America because a giant group of people on stage is not feasible if you have to pay for health care."

BAY OF FUNDING

The other obvious answer is arts funding, which made Canadians the envy of their American peers—their European peers, less so. Funding is an incredibly complex and fraught issue. It doesn't explain the success of many artists in this book, many of whom didn't access funding until they were well established, if they ever did at all. Labels like Constellation and Three Gut made a splash without any funding. The system is usually rigged in favour of people who've already proven themselves by one measure or another.

"Grants are a big part of this story, for how this all happened," says Vancouver singer-songwriter Geoff Berner. "Independent people started to figure out how to game the system the way the majors had been doing. [The system] was a filter to keep poor people and real independent musicians out. That was the whole spirit of the rules. But if you could meet the letter of the rules, you could get some of the money."

Since the Massey Commission's report of 1951, there has been arts funding in Canada—though its effect on what can loosely be called pop music didn't kick in until decades later. In 1971, CanCon regulations came into effect requiring radio stations to play a minimum of 30% Canadian content—which led to more Anne Murray, Gordon Lightfoot and Guess Who on Canadian radios than anyone could bear. Ten years later, private radio broadcasters decided—not entirely altruistically —to found FACTOR (Foundation to Assist Canadian Talent on Record), with the intention of further developing the domestic music scene. Frankly, they wanted more selection to fulfill CanCon requirements: it was in their best interest to invest in more domestic music. VideoFACT, funded entirely by MuchMusic, arrived in 1984 (and ended in 2017). FACTOR itself got a boost in 1986 when the federal government stepped in as a funding partner.

"It was easy to get touring grants then," says Trish Klein of the Be Good Tanyas, who became an artist manager later in her career. "You just needed to have a distribution agreement in hand, and an album finished, and a couple of show contracts—the rest could be made up, like 15 shows but only two contracts. You'd get 50% of your shortfall up to a certain amount. You'd rely on your merchandise to fill the gap. Our first couple of years, the FACTOR grants enabled us to do low-level touring: hotels, vehicles, food. The tour wouldn't have paid for itself without the FACTOR money. But you can't get FACTOR touring money now without getting a sound recording grant first."

The new kid on the block was the Radio Starmaker Fund, founded in 2000, again by private broadcasters, with a focus on marketing Canadians abroad— because, of course, Canadians are far more likely to listen to snowbirds who succeed elsewhere first. It offered to match, or exceed by a maximum of twice as much, the money the artist (or, more likely, the artist's management and/or record company) was planning to spend on marketing and/or touring. (Marketing can include videos, publicity, website design, photo shoots, digital media distribution, etc.)

Touring is a different story. As of 2021, Radio Starmaker offered a subsidy of $2,500 per domestic or foreign gig, with the number of gigs capped per territory. That's cash on top of guarantees or box office receipts; in other words, even if no one comes to your shows, your expenses will have been covered by the Radio Starmaker grant. Little to none of that money goes into an artist's pocket: it goes to tech crew, tour manager, transportation, accommodation, etc. This fund was key for Canadian artists touring in the U.S., Europe and beyond.

Radio Starmaker's arrival in 2000 coincides with the trajectory of many artists in this book—although only about half of them benefited from it, and to varying degrees. Broken Social Scene—a band everyone assumes must be funded—only got it six times (of 42 opportunities) between 2001 and 2011, just as often as Propagandhi and fewer times than Owen Pallett, Feist or the Dears. Broken Social Scene did, however, get the most in dollars ($600,653) during that decade, followed by Metric ($553,671, not including $91,663 for Emily Haines's solo efforts), Dallas Green's solo project City and Colour ($513,320) and his original band, Alexisonfire ($509,158). Again: that money does not go to the artists; it goes to crew, tour expenses, video productions and more. It certainly makes U.S. musicians intensely jealous, especially when combined with public health care.

Did Radio Starmaker make or break any of its most funded acts? Not to the point where the fund can be solely credited for any artist's success, no, not at all. With the exception of Feist, no artist in this book had a breakout international video hit, or became successful solely through clever marketing that might have been assisted by funding. But Radio Starmaker did make touring—especially abroad—a more feasible venture for many, assuming the act in question had already sold enough records to qualify and had capital of their own to invest. Some more popular bands (like Broken Social Scene and Stars) clearly benefited; others, like the Hidden Cameras or Black Mountain, never got its funding at all. And there are many names on Radio Starmaker lists that are real head-scratchers, either for their obscurity (Stabilo, Kazzer) or their popularity (Bruce Cockburn, Sum 41).

Most important, Radio Starmaker was yet another pool of money to draw from. There's FACTOR money for everything: recording an album or demo, touring, showcasing, operational grants for labels and festivals, etc. It's all a huge investment in the very existence of Canadian music that can't be understated. That doesn't mean it's easy to get funding, especially early in one's career. All of these programs don't foster innovation: they support something that's already working. Which is important and valid and essential, even if it's easy to poke holes in specific funding decisions from any side of the political spectrum.

"It's insane. The impact cannot be dismissed," says Carl Newman. "As absurd as it might sound, a lot of this is just to handle losses. You get touring grants so you don't lose your shirt on tours. We get so used to them, but when I talk to musicians in the U.S., I realize how lucky we are. That's the reason I got to tour in Australia, New Zealand or Japan. If you don't get as big as Arcade Fire, it's hard."

Also overlooked is the difference between loans and grants; a lot of FACTOR money was a loan. "I got a recording loan for my first solo album," says Newman, "and I felt cheated when I actually had to pay some of it back. It's like, 'Oh no, this backfired, it sold! Are you kidding me, FACTOR? I have to give you 15 grand?!'" That changed in 2014, when FACTOR became a grant-only body.

Danko Jones's career has largely been in Europe, where he has No. 1 hits on rock radio and regular main-stage slots at large festivals. That's in part been possible because of FACTOR touring grants. It's also made the band a punching bag for those who think repeat grant recipients are a leech on the system.

"Absolutely, we benefited from that; we were a success story," says Jones. "A lot of the criticism is levelled at people taking advantage of the system. We became successful due in large part to the help it gave us. Of course, nothing might have come of it if we sucked as a band. But we were a good band that connected with an audience abroad. Sometimes you need a step up. We don't come from wealthy backgrounds, and touring grants helped us directly.

"I remember seeing Avril Lavigne, who already had platinum records, getting grants, and thinking [that] would ruin [the perception of funding] for bands like us, who have never had a gold record," Danko continues. He says funding critics "have some good points, but please don't include us in that. We paid back every penny of our loans. Maybe we got grants, but we didn't use them to spend 80% on alcohol, 20% on the recording budget and the producer is my brother. You know? Though I'm 100% sure that has happened—which sucks for real musicians."

Geoff Berner tells the story of a Vancouver promoter who figured out ways, in the late '90s, to get his roster of non-commercial punks and odd folkies over to Europe on FACTOR's dime: "He would [tell FACTOR] things like, 'We've received an invitation to play an international festival of independent alternative music in Ljubljana, Slovenia. If you will pay for us to go and play this showcase, we might tack on a European tour after that.' That would cover your airfare. Then his buddy Bobo on the ground in Ljubljana would make sure a website existed.". The "festival" would be half Canadian acts booked by the one manager, the other half were Slovenian acts. FACTOR eventually realized they were bankrolling an entire festival in eastern Europe. And yet stunts not unlike this have helped dozens of Canadian artists get a foothold in Europe.

Godspeed You! Black Emperor got a FACTOR touring grant to subsidize their first European tour in 1998, an event that arguably facilitated many things in this book. But they didn't go back to the well—or, at least, not until much later. "The moment our tours started breaking even, we stopped because it seemed immoral to take money out of that fund when we didn't need it," says Efrim Menuck. "After we got back together [in 2012], we got FACTOR funding to play China, because we would have lost money otherwise." Menuck's other band, A Silver Mt. Zion, founded in 1999, applied for and got FACTOR touring grants in the early 2010s. "We used it to subsidize a tour nanny, because we were travelling with a kid," he says. There's a documentary about that tour, 2013's *Come Worry with Us!* "Mt. Zion was categorized as an 'emerging artist.' I don't know what we were, but we weren't emerging—we were filling rooms."

Joel Carriere's company, Dine Alone Records, and his clients (including Alexisonfire and City and Colour) have benefited enormously from funding over the years—but not at the outset, and it's never something he builds into a business plan. "We didn't [apply] early on because I just didn't have the patience to deal with it," he says. "The way we look at funding is that it's gravy. Don't rely on it. Don't do anything you can't do without it. If we're going to take a loss, we'll take a loss and use money from a [big Toronto] show. Alexisonfire wasn't living large and paying themselves a lot; I wasn't making a lot. We had a trajectory and knew how we needed to do it. When we get [funding], we're not going to waste it. If you give it to us, we'll show you that we used it wisely and it's for growth." Dine Alone is now one of the biggest indies in Canada.

You've Changed Records is one of the smallest indies in Canada. It's run by the Constantines' Steve Lambke, whose experience with funding bodies, as a musician and as a label owner, has been unusually minimal. "We never got a dime," he says. "When Three Gut [Records] folded [in 2005], management stuff fell to me. I applied for FACTOR funding for a [Constantines] tour and some other things, and we were denied. Maybe my grant-writing chops weren't up to snuff; that's possible. But we were a legitimate band with a history and a future and we couldn't get funding. Even now, 10 years into running You've Changed, it's only recently that I've got FACTOR money. A few individual projects have got grants and significant funding from various public bodies, but [the label] didn't even have a [FACTOR] profile until [2019]. It's not been my reality."

Baked into Canada's music funding philosophy is that the artist has to have some financial skin in the game. It rewards entrepreneurship as much, or likely even more, than artistic merit. "It was a good time for entrepreneurs," says

Carriere, of the period when Dine Alone was joined by Arts & Crafts, Paper Bag, Six Shooter, Last Gang and other labels in the Toronto area. "It was an exciting groundswell of these young people creating something left of centre from what had been happening the past few years. Knowing that major labels were a bit behind on tech allowed us to do stuff ourselves that didn't require giving away creative control."

He cites American punk labels like Epitaph and Dischord as models. The lesson learned from those venerable, artist-run indies was clear: fair contracts, low overhead, niche marketing. But American labels have the benefit of a large domestic market, which Canadians don't; it's harder to scale up in Canada. This became even more of a problem after 2005, when sales of physical product plummeted, and labels like Mint and Constellation finally started applying for grants.

Amy Millan of Stars is clear about the benefits of funding. "The investment comes back," she says, "because what happened after we got those grants? We were taxed incredibly high numbers." Stars' 2004 album *Set Yourself on Fire* sold more than 100,000 copies in Canada alone—after which, says Millan, "I had the highest tax bill I'd ever paid. We paid three times what we made in grants. So it's okay, everybody relax! It's not something to be embarrassed about. It's something to be proud of as a country, that we invest in art. In Germany or France, they treat art and theatre like libraries and schools. I remember that really clearly about the [1990s federal] Chrétien government having posters for culture, saying, 'We have grants for you. Come and get the money. Make music. Let's make this a viable place.' Because guess what? When you do that, you fill the bars, you fill the clubs, you pay the bartenders, people are out. Let's have a beautiful platform to create art and culture. Which we all did, which put Canada on the map for the rest of the world."

The economic benefit of arts funding is a story seldom told—or not told well enough, in a North American political culture that's become more and more openly hostile to artists. A 2013 report by the Canadian Independent Music Association claimed that "every $1 in federal or provincial music program support yields $1.22 back in taxes."

CHEAP THRILLS

Public funding is hardly the only catalyst for the creative explosion of the early 2000s. Many point to Montreal's insanely cheap rent—a historical truism, but particularly true in the wake of the nail-biter 1995 referendum on Quebec sovereignty —as a significant factor in the city being a magnet for musicians from coast to coast.

Spencer Krug of Wolf Parade lived for a while at 100 Sided Die, a loft run by artists Chloë Lum and Yannick Desranleau. It's where Wolf Parade recorded much of their debut album and where that 2005 photo of them was taken for *Spin* magazine. "The physical infrastructure for that kind of thing just wasn't possible in B.C.," says Wolf Parade's Dan Boeckner. "The fact that a bunch of people working minimum or sub-minimum wage jobs could put their money together and rent the corner suite of an industrial building 20 floors up that looked over the entire city and turn it into a factory for screen-printing and recording albums and housing a tattoo artist? That's what 100 Sided Die was, and that would be unimaginable in Vancouver."

That said, as hard as it is to believe now, Toronto and Vancouver were also cheap at the time. "This was the tail end of a time in B.C. when you could live the welfare musician lifestyle," says Geoff Berner. "You'd get a cheque every month that would cover your rent, and you'd play for cash. This is highly uncredited in what makes a music scene happen: generous welfare. The British Invasion was caused by free art school for working-class kids. They didn't have to pay tuition and they got a stipend to live on, and a thousand bands came out of that. All those punk rockers on the dole in the '70s; you could actually live on the dole. They didn't check in on you every five minutes to see if you got a job at a coffee shop. If the four of you were in a band, you could rent a shitty house with a practice space in the basement. The Be Good Tanyas had a house like that. They were on EI because they were seasonal workers."

"I was paying $237 for a room in a shared house," says Trish Klein of the Be Good Tanyas. "I had part-time, low-paying jobs that still provided me with enough income that I could live a life completely devoted to creative output."

Owen Pallett lived on the outskirts of Toronto's Kensington Market, paying $350 a month for one room of five. Residents of the Three Gut Records house, spitting distance from the MuchMusic building, paid something similar, depending on the room size; Jim Guthrie paid $50 a month for a renovated closet there, where he built a bunk bed with a home studio underneath. A bit earlier, Stephen McBean of Black Mountain recalls paying $75 a month when he lived in Victoria in the late '90s. In Vancouver, he says, "I lived in a house in Strathcona, an amazing heritage house that was $1,000 a month. Three of us lived there, so $333 each. When it was being sold, they offered it to me and my girlfriend at the time for $220,000—which we thought was so much money." Twenty years later, a similar house in that neighbourhood might sell for $2 million, and musicians make even less money than they did then—even before adjusting for inflation.

Real estate wasn't the only thing that was cheap. Studio technology was becoming much cheaper and accessible—and it sounded a lot better than the

TASCAM four-track that had launched the lo-fi movement in indie rock 20 years earlier. In the mid-'90s, Jim Guthrie put out a cassette called *Home Is Where the Rock Is*, a phrase he adopted as his motto. But it wasn't only true for indie rockers inspired by Ween and Sebadoh: the arrival of recording software for home computers allowed people like Dan Snaith of Caribou to develop complex, sample-based electronic compositions. Pro Tools replaced expensive tape technology. And while the industry was shifting toward digital, a lot of once-valuable old analog equipment could be snapped up inexpensively.

It became possible to record radio hits in your basement, which is what happened to Hawksley Workman in 2001 with his first hit single, "Striptease," made on an eight-track machine. "I didn't have any digital equipment," he says. "All my stuff was cobbled together from the '60s, '70, '80s. Hayden was also doing that. People could assemble an interesting collection of gear in their own homes and make interesting records without going into a studio. Back then, studios could still charge $3,000 a day." Workman charged clients $100 a day to record and mix one song, including his own services on any instrument. He made early records for Tegan and Sara, Sarah Slean, Serena Ryder and others.

"People just started taking risks, including engineers, because there was nothing to lose," says Kevin Drew, who had been playing around with four-tracks since high school, and recorded Broken Social Scene's debut album, 2001's *Feel Good Lost*, largely in his basement apartment. Tony Dekker of Great Lake Swimmers illicitly recorded his band's stunning debut album in an abandoned silo near the shores of Lake Erie.

Professional studios were hardly irrelevant, but there was a new crop of artist-run rooms like Hotel 2 Tango in Montreal, the House of Miracles in London, Ontario, JC/DC or the Hive in Vancouver that provided an affordable alternative to either basements or bigger rooms. Andy Magoffin's House of Miracles had a 1975 tape machine that was $80,000 when it was first on the market; he got it for $2,500. It's part of the reason that records he made for the Three Gut label and others sounded so good. Young musicians had no shortage of options, and their engineers started getting calls from international artists wondering how to capture the same magic heard on Canadian records. In other words, even on a technical level, Canadian music simply sounded better than it ever had before.

And it was easier for people to find it. The early 2000s marked an explosion of music discussion on message boards and the then-new concept of blogs. *Pitchfork* was one of five or six that became the most popular. By no means was it a professional operation—the site's early writing could be awkwardly hyper-personal, sexist, shamelessly hyperbolic or dismissively snarky, sometimes all at the same time. But a good rating could launch a career; that was certainly true for Broken

Social Scene, the Unicorns and Arcade Fire, among others. For better or worse, *Pitchfork* and its peers—including Brooklyn-via-Montreal's *Vice*—were crucial in developing modern hipster culture: people obsessed with knowing about a hot new trend—or band—before anyone else. With the glut of music available through file-sharing came the cultural currency of being able to champion the unique and unexpected. Like, say, Canada.

On an even more amateur level, "message board culture was a real thing for the counterculture scene," says Joel Carriere, who came up in the punk community of the Niagara region. "Kids were connecting, feeling they were a part of something. Every city had a message board, and I would go on each of them and talk about Alexisonfire, just saying, 'You gotta check this out.' It was also the time of Napster and MySpace, so we had tech behind us."

Hamilton's Junior Boys launched their career simply by posting an MP3 of their song "Birthday" on the Hyperdub message board in Britain in 2004. After sending demos to record labels and meeting radio silence, the band was soon barraged with requests from journalists and fans requesting more music because of Hyperdub. Within months, they had a British record deal.

Frank Yang, a photographer in Toronto, started *Chromewaves*, one of the world's first MP3 blogs, in September 2002, focusing mostly on show reviews and rare live tracks. Sean Michaels, a writer in Montreal, followed with *Said the Gramophone* in March 2003, writing poetically about new tracks from everywhere. Both were key to inserting Canadian bands into an international conversation between music geeks looking for the next big things. By 2004, Canada itself was the next big thing.

DIGITAL WITNESSES

In October 2004, Arcade Fire played their first U.S. show after *Funeral* came out. Taking the stage at the Mercury Lounge in New York City—as part of the CMJ Music Marathon, where the media crowned them the prince of buzz—Win Butler stepped to the mic. In an affectation of an award recipient, he said, "I'd like to thank the internet."

Only four and a half years earlier, in April 2000, Leslie Feist held a launch party for her *website*, designed by her friend Tyler Clark Burke, with a demonstration at the gig of how it looked and worked. It seems absurd now, but in 2000 not a lot of indie artists had their own website, and this was a pretty big fucking deal.

Stars' first media supporters in 2000 were at L.A. radio station KCRW, which reached not only Hollywood tastemakers—the kind of industry people who place songs in film and television—but also a wider audience listening via then-new internet radio. Through KCRW support online alone, Stars gained a foothold up and down the west coast of the U.S., allowing them to tour there before they could fill clubs in their native Ontario.

But it's not like Stars' Torquil Campbell was tech savvy—far from it. After the band first met the Michigan indie label that would put out their debut record, the owner called Campbell.

"I want to sign you guys, but there's one thing: your name," said the label head.

"What about our name? It's amazing."

"Well, I like the name, but have you heard of the internet?"

"Yeah, kinda. I'm vaguely familiar."

"There's this thing on the internet that's just come out, it's called Google. You type things into this box and it tells you everything you need to know about what you've entered. If you write 'stars' in this box, it will only show you astronomy websites and astrology and nobody will be able to find you."

Campbell laughed out loud. "Dude, nobody is going to find out about *music* from something called *Google*. That is the lamest shit I've ever heard! You find out about *music* from reading the *Village Voice*, man. That's how *cool* people do it."

Telling this story 20 years later, Campbell can only laugh about it. "I actually said that to him! That was my business acumen kicking in." But can you blame him? Before 2000, it was near impossible for Canadian artists to build any kind of international interest without the support of major labels, press and radio, which is one thing that made Godspeed such an anomaly.

By the time Arcade Fire's *Funeral* came out, it had been five years since file-sharing and illegal downloading reshaped the music industry; if a listener didn't have the option of buying a physical copy of a poorly distributed record, they could surely find it online for free. Long gone were the days of reading about an album in a print magazine weeks after its release and then gambling $20 on whether it was any good. Now, listeners could download the Arcade Fire album they'd read about on *Pitchfork* two days *before* its release. They could also poke around and find the band's first EP, which was otherwise only available at their live shows. Audiences started calling out requests for "Cars and Telephones," a song that appeared on the very first demo Win Butler ever recorded, circulated only among a few friends.

Even weirder, the supremely curious could find other oddities, like something called "A Very Arcade Xmas," which didn't even qualify as a demo tape, or as an Arcade Fire recording at all. It was made at the band's loft during a party, when microphones were left on and a bunch of friends—not even necessarily members of the band—goofed off and murdered some carols. *The Basement Tapes* it ain't. But it still became part of early Arcade Fire lore.

Arcade Fire became the poster children for internet success stories, Canadian or otherwise. But they were hardly the only ones, nor the first. In early 2003, Broken Social Scene also got a *Pitchfork* rave before *You Forgot It in People* was even available in the U.S., which cemented that website's reputation as a global taste-maker far more on the cutting edge than print magazines in any country. "The internet broke us as an international band, nothing else," said Kevin Drew in 2003. "We were [on tour] in Glasgow and Berlin, meeting people who read about us on *Pitchfork*. Or we'd meet girls at an all-ages gig in New York, and we'd ask them how they heard about us, and they'd say, 'I heard about it on a Coldplay chat site.'"

"Who knows if Social Scene would have had that kind of reaction if they were reviewed by *Rolling Stone* first," says Stars' Amy Millan, who often toured with the band. "There was a power being given to the *Pitchfork*s that was just starting. There was no YouTube. It was a completely different beast. In some ways, it was amazing, because you could reach Taiwan. [Stars] became really big over there. In Singapore, we felt like the Beatles." And they didn't need a major label to do it. When Stars first started taking label meetings in 2000, Millan recalls, "All those [A&R] guys were like, 'We were afraid our [security] cards weren't going to work today because we thought we might be laid off.' Because of everything that was happening already."

"The takeovers were happening," says Steve Jordan, who worked A&R for Warner Canada until 2001—the year of the AOL Time Warner merger. "What were before mildly annoying publicly traded pressures to turn over hits at a rapid rate, those pressures were multiplying with each new takeover of a music company. Around the AOL time, we were getting all sorts of comments like, 'Don't even think of signing [an act] unless you think you can sell 100,000.' And when you're dealing with a band like Stars, when there is no route to actually developing an audience over time, you're just hitting a brick wall. The other side is that the artists themselves were getting savvy, and saying, 'Screw the majors in Canada. There's no future here.' All the musicians who mattered were talking to each other and saying, 'Yeah, [the A&R reps] get it, but why would we sign with them? Our audience isn't just in Canada. Let's go to Europe and the States.'"

It was becoming clear that a traditional label route was not the ticket out. Which was as frustrating for Canadian A&R reps who were music fans as it was for artists. "The ripeness of the artistic fruit was so incredible, and I couldn't do anything," continues Steve Jordan. "There was something happening right underneath our noses, and all these artists were making amazing shit—and none of them sound like each other either. Metric doesn't sound like the Dears who don't sound like the Weakerthans who don't sound like Sam Roberts who doesn't sound like Sarah Harmer who doesn't sound like k-os—you could fill a book! It was a dark time to be a major label A&R person, sitting amongst a field of gems, of bountiful talent and originality and creativity. The development that we trick ourselves into thinking happened with Fleetwood Mac or Springsteen or Prince, with artists getting a chance to have some sorta okay-selling albums before a big one— that wasn't there."

Meanwhile, file-sharing on peer-to-peer (P2P) networks was laying waste to major label jobs. Listeners entered a search term (the artist, song or album) and found every person online at that moment who had made it shareable from their hard drive. Sure, everyone had Radiohead or Jay-Z. But if the two people in the world who had some rarity were online, that rarity was instantly available to the whole world. It was the end of scarcity. Among other things, the notion of "only available on import" became a joke.

Buck 65 developed an early fan base through file-sharing—certainly not by his own design. In 1999, he started working on an album and was shocked when his collaborator Sixtoo told him it was already on the internet and being shared. "I was like, 'How?!'" he says. "It had only been heard by three people at that point. I was really upset about it, which was ridiculous because I was a nobody—but now people in Australia were hearing my music. It didn't take me too long to realize that it was helping me."

He decided to conduct an experiment. "I approached a friend of mine to teach me how LimeWire works," he says. "I made a couple of folders to share. One had rarities of popular indie bands; I thought there would be an appetite for that. Another folder had superstar pop acts. And the last one had my stuff. When someone was downloading your files, you could watch it on your screen. My stuff was being downloaded constantly, and no one touched Madonna or whatever." The reason, of course, was that the rapper's own computer was one of the few places in the world to house his music; people could find Madonna anywhere.

That same year, young Victoria band Hot Hot Heat were breaking up after the departure of their singer. Andy Dixon, who ran a small Vancouver record label that had put out singles by the band, was using a file-sharing service to poke around the files of keyboardist Steve Bays, just for kicks. He found some demos that were more melodic than the prog-punk Hot Hot Heat played at that point. Excited, Dixon offered to put them out. The band decided to make Bays their new singer and change their musical direction entirely, and Hot Hot Heat became a big buzz band three years later.

Of course, file-sharing meant that artists were losing income they might have gained from record sales. There's no question that it opened the door to the wide-scale devaluation of not just physical product, but music itself, as played out in the streaming models of the 2010s. But for a lot of new unknown acts who weren't getting played on the radio or getting coverage in dying print media, file-sharing brought a lot more people out to shows. By 2010, first Drake and then the Weeknd had proven that giving your music away for free at the outset could pay huge dividends. Between the launch of Napster in 1999 and the launch of the iTunes store in 2003, the roots of that idea took hold, when file-sharing became a primary source of music discovery.

Not that CDs were dead yet. "There were still robust sales," says Hawksley Workman, whose first three records were released independently; the third, in 2001, had major label distribution. "If I did well at a festival, even on a side stage as a curiosity, I could still sell 200 or 300 CDs—which sounds insane now."

"At [Toronto] stores like Rotate This and Soundscapes, CDs just started flying out the door," says Kevin Drew. "People wouldn't have that hometown bias any-more: 'Oh, it's just a hometown band, I don't know if I need to buy it.' The local indie section in any store [was] so vibrant and eclectic, there [was] everything you could ever want."

Steve Lambke of the Constantines worked at Soundscapes from 2002 to 2005. "During those years, the difference in the way people responded to and bought Canadian music was massive," he says. "At the beginning, in '02, people wouldn't care or would avoid Canadian music. [Soundscapes owner] Greg [Davis] was always very supportive of local musicians, and there was a big consignment sec-tion. But in terms of front-row, marquee stuff, people weren't buying it. But by ['05], it was massive, and of the front section maybe a third of it was new Canadian releases that people were actually buying. There was a shift in consciousness in how people related to Canadian music."

Some pioneering Western Canadian indie labels were still around to be part of this story: Nettwerk, Mint, Stony Plain. Many artists, starting in 2000 with Peaches, Kid Koala and Caribou, went right to international indies first—there simply were no Canadian labels able to promote their style of music properly. But there were also new domestic labels to build this new wave. Some, like Toronto's Three Gut, were complete labours of love, with no capital investment; others, like Constellation and Paper Bag, started with no more than $10,000 in their pockets. Winnipeg's G7 Welcoming Committee got a loan from American punk star Fat Mike. Arts & Crafts, started by EMI A&R rep Jeffrey Remedios, was nurtured by that corporate parent because they didn't want to lose him. Last Gang was started by Chris Taylor, a Toronto lawyer who represented many people in this book at one time or another.

Others were corporate funded: MapleMusic was an online merch site that became a label in 2002, after Universal Records was forced by the federal gov-ernment to invest in Canadian initiatives once its international parent company merged with Polygram. Maple had a No. 1 radio hit with its first single, "Brother Down," by Sam Roberts; in its first year it signed Kathleen Edwards, the Dears and Joel Plaskett. "I look back at that time now," says Maple co-founder Kim Cooke, "and, man, talk about low-hanging fruit. But remember: [in 2002] there was no Arts & Crafts, no Dine Alone, no Last Gang, no Paper Bag. Maple was the first of that wave of new millennium Canadian indies." With few exceptions—like Buck 65 signing to Warner—the major labels were increasingly conservative, as they watched their profit margins crumble in the wake of file-sharing. "Launching a record company in that environment," says Cooke, "made you either a hero or a fool."

On a micro-indie level, "people were still making money," says Owen Pallett, who recorded for the Blocks Recording Club in 2003, a small Toronto co-op that focused on hand-assembled art projects to encase their artists' CDs. "If you put out a shitty CD and folded it together yourself, you could easily make $2,000 by selling 200 of them. It was a reliable source of instant gratification and income. In 2004, Blocks was having discussions about if we should put our stuff up on iTunes, and I was a vociferous no! I believed the packaging was part of it. I couldn't foresee that 10 years down the line there would be no CD drives on laptops."

Stephen McBean of Black Mountain says, "I don't think our [2005 debut] record came out on iTunes for at least six months [after the CD]. Back then, [the way people felt about] iTunes was like, 'Oh my god, this is fucked.' Now, of course, I would love it if people bought our record on iTunes for $8. That sounds fucking awesome."

"We stayed out of iTunes for a long time, on principle," says Ian Ilavsky of Constellation Records. "The quality of audio compression, the divorce from the physical object and the sheer corporatization—Apple was the dominant player. We spent a couple of years with [independent MP3 stores]. We thought if people wanted digital they could support these places—which did not happen at all. It was nothing. We kept waiting for one of those platforms to build, but no. Quarter to quarter, iTunes numbers were blowing the roof off."

In the first part of the decade, however, business was booming for Constellation and other indies. "P2P file-sharing was a boon for music discovery and indie labels," says Ilavsky. "CDs were outselling vinyl four to one, and the margins were higher. There was a weak Canadian dollar. All kinds of factors made it very good for Canadian indies. To say nothing of having low recording budgets and spending almost nothing on marketing or internet presence."

The coming end of physical product had large repercussions for every level, from superstars to avant-garde musicians. It was certainly a confusing time for the more corporate side of the industry. The CD for Hawksley Workman's 2003 major label debut *Lover/Fighter* was packaged with a three-inch mini-CD, featuring the single "Anger as Beauty" and snippets of three other songs, which the buyer was instructed to share with a friend: a form of legal file-sharing in a physical format. Dumb idea. Nobody cared. And it wasn't the music's fault. The week after the album came out, Universal A&R rep Allan Reid told Workman that it had been the most illegally downloaded record that week—not a prize anyone really wanted to win in 2003.

"We were able to track the traffic of records being downloaded," says Reid. "It was always a good-news-bad-news story: 'Everyone's listening to your record—but the majority have not bought it.' It wasn't an official chart, luckily. The irony is that if you *weren't* getting illegally downloaded, you're like, 'Oh, the record isn't happening. There's no buzz.'"

Universal had already resisted Workman's other ideas. "I said, 'Why can't we package this CD with a T-shirt?'" he recalls. "Then a chorus of people would say, 'How are they going to stock it at stores?' Fast-forward a few years, and packaging merch with physical product became a thing. I was trying to mitigate what I could see was coming. The labels did what a lot of big entities do when faced with adversity, which is put their head in the sand. *Lover/Fighter* didn't do the numbers they expected, considering the amount of money they put into it."

For Stars' 2007 album, *In Our Bedroom After the War*, they pioneered the instant digital drop that became industry norm years later for Beyoncé and others—remarkable for a band whose founder didn't know what Google was eight years earlier. Singer/guitarist Amy Millan was frustrated by albums being leaked, and reviewed, three months before anyone even had a chance to buy it. She convinced her label to release the album on iTunes the day after it was mastered, with physical copies in stores several months later (the usual lag time between completion and official release). "But it was too soon for something that radical to happen," she says, "because then the dinosaurs at HMV and Tower Records punished us. We got a lot of flak from people who said, 'You're making this harder for us. Now people won't come buy a physical CD.' But people were going to steal it anyway!"

Ultimately, the new playing field benefited Canadians, especially those with limited international distribution, and particularly those who had a live show to back up any hype (which was most of them). The music didn't have to jump through old industry hurdles in order to get heard. That came at a long-term cost: nothing short of the devaluation of music. But weathering that initial storm prepared many well for the future. In 2020, during the global pandemic, Kathleen Edwards said, "Right now I've been asked a lot of questions like, 'What's it like to put out a record during this time? It must be so challenging.' I say when I signed my record deal in 2002, there wasn't even a component in the contract that included digital sales. If you want to talk about having to navigate a whole new set of circumstances every few years in which you're putting out music, that's it. Covid is just par for the course. It's not fun."

YOU CAN ONLY DRIVE DOWN MAIN STREET SO MANY TIMES

In 1998, Gord Downie sang about the things one can accomplish when an artist refuses to allow things like "the nation" to obstruct their vision. His band, the Tragically Hip, became poster boys for culturally insecure peanut-gallerists, who either a) loved the band even more because they were superstars only at home in Canada, or b) saw them as an example of Canadian mediocrity that couldn't cut it in the larger world. Any working musician knew then that cracking the American market was always a crapshoot, one that usually involved an intense amount of luck and timing on top of incredibly hard work. (That's still true, though instant internet sensations like Justin Bieber and Ruth B are now possible, albeit rare.)

Jason Beck moved to Berlin in 1999 and rebranded himself as "Chilly Gonzales, musical genius." His hubris—which flopped in the crab bucket of Canada—helped him become a minor media sensation there and later in Paris. Mainstream European success came in 2004. He had grown up in Toronto and went to university in Montreal, two cities where Canadian musicians usually migrate to begin their careers. But for him, those familiar surroundings contained too much baggage. And so just as someone in Saskatoon might move to Vancouver to reinvent themselves, Beck answered what Joni Mitchell called the "urge for going" and left Canada altogether.

"Detachment is important to becoming yourself," he says. "I had an instinct to conform in Toronto. Going to Berlin freed me from that. But it could also be someone conforming in Berlin would need to come to Canada. It's more about [the act of] leaving. You strip yourself of the markers that make you conform. You want to go into the equivalent of those sensory deprivation tanks that John Cage talked about, where you hear the sound of your own blood vessels. Then you know who you are. There's a great French word *depayssage*, to 'de-countrify' yourself."

"In Canada in 1997, the dream was still to move to New York or L.A. or London or Paris," says Stars' Torquil Campbell, whose band members all grew up in Toronto and moved to Montreal together. "But when Montreal 'happened,' people who lived in Saskatchewan or Alberta realized they could move within their own country and be in the coolest place in the world. That changes a culture, when people feel like they can be at the centre of the conversation within their own country. That's when you build a real generational artistic scene."

An unusual number of musicians in this book have non-Canadian parentage (Feist, Stars, Be Good Tanyas, Billy Talent's Ian D'Sa, Metric, Broken Social Scene, Destroyer, Caribou, Kardinal Offishall, k-os, Sam Roberts—you get the idea) or were born outside Canada themselves. They come from families unburdened by Canadian humility. "I was an outsider who didn't know anyone in Toronto and felt free to embarrass myself," says Tyler Clark Burke of Three Gut Records, who was born in Kentucky but grew up in Winnipeg. "Because I'm American and lived in Canada all my life, I grew up with stories about how different and less bold Canadians were. That informed who I was. I really felt when we started that I wasn't working on a Canadian record label: I was building a label that happened to be in Canada."

Punk band Fucked Up got a write-up in Toronto's *Now* magazine after they'd already been featured in *NME*. Before that, they hadn't even been included in weekly club listings. "We weren't setting our sights on being popular in Toronto," says guitarist Mike Haliechuk. "From the get-go, we wanted to be popular in England and the States and Japan. We don't care about going to Regina or what-ever the fuck. When we came back from England and were being written up in local papers, we were scornful and treated it like a joke. It's a very Canadian thing, to cover something because it's got coverage somewhere else, and we were not interested in catering to that."

For an artist like Arcade Fire, led by Texan Win Butler, impressing Canadian audiences and peers was important, but engaging with the Canadian industry was not. "Win knew nothing about the Canadian music industry and didn't care," says Arcade Fire's Tim Kingsbury. "He wasn't trying to impress anyone in Toronto. Whereas for me, playing with the Constantines at the Horseshoe [in October 2003] was exciting." That was also true in particular of artists on the West Coast, who had long felt excluded from the Toronto- and Montreal-based industry. "Even when I had no popularity, I wanted to break out," says New Pornographers' Carl Newman. "There was a part of me that wanted to get out of Vancouver, out of Canada. We're not just a Canadian band; we're a world band."

One should never underestimate the geographic distance between Canada's major population centres in decisions to look abroad. "We never, ever wanted to drive across Canada," says Mauro Pezzente of Godspeed You! Black Emperor. "You read about the Tragically Hip and bands like that playing all these tiny towns across Canada—I never wanted to do that. I have nothing against Wawa or Thunder Bay, but the idea of playing there is not exciting to me. The times we'd drive across the continent, we were always in the South. We would play Vancouver, Victoria, and all the Midwest towns. But we'd skip the Mountain time zone altogether."

Meanwhile, Europe always beckoned. "Coming from Canada," Leslie Feist told NPR, "America is enormous, 10 times as populated, tons of cities, and yet somehow [there are only] those two enormous iron doors: one in New York City and one in California. Those are the ways you can get into America, as a musician. Europe, though, you just squint and imagine that there's hundreds of these little colourful Hobbit doors, you know? A little red one in Sweden and another little orange one in Spain; there's more places where you can begin." Feist chose Paris, where she signed a major label deal before she had anything in North America.

Geoff Berner appeared on national radio in Norway, on a show similar to John Peel's on the BBC, before he ever got national radio play in Canada. "The first time I got on [a] CBC Radio morning [show], I was on my way to Norway—that was the story," he says. "That's how Canadians are: you have to show that other people give a damn about you first." And the U.S. isn't always the best option. "It's expensive and it's a lot of trouble," says Berner. "You gotta get a dog licence to go down there. If you're having a crap day and a crap show and you're in Copenhagen—well, hey, you're still in Copenhagen. If you have a bad show in Cleveland, you're also in Cleveland, you know?"

Do Make Say Think was one of the first Toronto acts of this era to gain a foothold in Europe, where they found a huge contrast to their North American experience. "Our first tour of the U.S. was mostly basements, other than one venue that was maybe the size of [Toronto's 240-capacity] Rivoli," says guitarist Justin Small. "It was hardcore-style touring. Then we went to Europe, and our first show was at a venue that was like [Toronto rock club] the Opera House, sold out, 900 people, with a full stage and people who worried about us: 'What do you need? How are your monitors?' You don't feel famous, you just feel appreciated."

Do Make Say Think built an audience the old-school way: through good press, word of mouth and their association with a hip label, Constellation Records. Acts that followed benefited directly from online exposure. In the summer of 2005, Wolf Parade booked a tour of Scandinavia before their debut album came out—because promoters there had heard their early demos streaming on the CBC Radio 3 site, which had created a MySpace-like template for artists to create a profile and upload tracks. "We were getting played on Swedish public radio," says drummer Arlen Thompson. "We played the Øya Festival in Norway. Helsinki was totally insane: small club, totally sold out. We met a bunch of people we've all kept in touch with. When indie rock was becoming a thing, we were one of the first North American bands to play there. Even though we were ramshackle, it was a big show for people there."

By 2003, some Canadians had been signed to leading American indies like Matador, Merge, Epitaph and Sub Pop. And yet it was still surprising when the

Hidden Cameras signed to Rough Trade, the landmark U.K. label of early '80s post-punk, including the Smiths. Rough Trade's Geoff Travis had recently revived the label—and his tastemaking reputation—by signing the Strokes before that New York band even had an American deal. The label had never signed a Canadian act, despite being named after the Toronto band of the '70s. "When the Cameras signed to Rough Trade, it was like, what?" says the band's early violinist, Owen Pallett. "No Canadian bands ever signed to Rough Trade, or [other hip U.K. labels] Too Pure or Beggars or 4AD. To just have that happen was exciting. To later realize [Rough Trade] literally signed every idiot wandering around the Lower East Side was a little dispiriting, but at least there was a moment when they saw what Joel [Gibb] was doing and thought it was good enough to sign for a couple of albums."

In the four years since Gonzales left for Berlin, it became possible for Canadians to stay home and have international careers. Kevin Drew of Broken Social Scene never felt the need to leave his hometown of Toronto, primarily because of all the local industry and media support for Arts & Crafts, the label he co-founded with Jeffrey Remedios, which was backed by EMI Canada. "You don't have to live in L.A. or New York or London to make this happen," says Drew. "You can do it from [your] hometown. We had all these people who wanted us to do well."

THE MOUSE THAT ROARED

For the first time in history, Canada was an exotic curiosity geopolitically, which may well have led to curiosity about its culture. American hegemony in the George W. Bush era was in question, if not in outright decline. Consider:

In 2001, Canada legalized medical cannabis; at that time, only eight U.S. states had done so (10 more would do so over the next 10 years).

In 2002, Canada ratified the Kyoto Protocol on climate change; the U.S. never did (though Canada eventually pulled out in 2012).

On March 17, 2003, prime minister Jean Chrétien declared that, unlike the U.K., Canada would not be joining the U.S. in the invasion of Iraq, which took place three days later.[4] It was an exceedingly rare disagreement in the North American alliance, one that came with a backlash from the Fox News crowd—which in turn twigged the interest of George W. Bush's opponents, many of whom, for the next five years, openly mused about moving to Canada.

Three months later, in June 2003, an Ontario court decision made that province the first North American jurisdiction to sanction gay marriage; in the Western

---

4   It was, however, heavily involved in the Afghanistan war, which had begun 18 months earlier.

world, only the Netherlands and Belgium preceded it. A British lesbian couple who got married in Vancouver later in 2003 sparked a legal challenge in the U.K. about whether their marriage would be recognized in that country, where gay marriage wasn't fully legalized until 2014. The U.S. did it state by state, starting in Massachusetts in 2004, and finally federally in 2015. In Canada, it had been federal law since 2005.

All of this was clearly on the minds of at least some U.S. listeners, as manifested in music writing at the time. In a May 29, 2003, review of Kathleen Edwards's *Failer*, future *New Yorker* critic Amanda Petrusich wrote in *Pitchfork* that "Edwards seems firmly rooted in a very specific kind of guilty, gritty American longing, despite hailing from a tidy, peaceable country with unarmed policemen and free health care." (Canadian police are, in fact, armed. She's thinking of Britain.) A 2005 cover story in *Magnet* magazine about the New Pornographers spent an inordinate amount of time talking about Canadian health care and grants, getting many facts laughably wrong—no doubt fed to the writer by pranksters in the band.

This all followed the weird late-'90s trend of U.S. and U.K. acts naming themselves after Canadian geography: Scotland's Boards of Canada, Georgia's Of Montreal, the Indiana record label Secretly Canadian, and others. Now actual Canadians were part of the conversation.

Unless Drake is depicted sitting atop the CN Tower, it's usually not obvious that an artist is Canadian. Godspeed may have been an instrumental band, but they made it clear in their liner notes and visuals that they were a product of Montreal. Broken Social Scene's Kevin Drew is a very different lyric writer than his friend Gord Downie, but he made sure everyone knew that he was from Toronto. Destroyer's Dan Bejar never put much stock in being a Canadian artist, but he's unapologetically a Vancouverite, which is reflected in his lyrics. Feist's first hit was named after a tiny town in Nova Scotia. Alberta's Corb Lund, Ontario's Sarah Harmer and Nova Scotia's Joel Plaskett were not as internationally successful as some of their peers, but it wasn't because of their regionally specific lyrics.

"It's important to embrace regionalism in art," says Corb Lund, who wrote specifically about Alberta while touring Texas, Australia and the U.K. "No matter who you are, if you're expressing your own reality well, it will have universal appeal. My whole career—like Geoff Berner's, like Carolyn Mark's, like Tanya Tagaq's, like the Sadies', like all my friends'—it's been based on honest expression, and making art for people who want to hear it, regardless of what's on the radio. And speaking of regionalism, all my American friends are obsessed with *Letterkenny* and *Trailer Park Boys*."

John K. Samson of the Weakerthans endeared himself to thousands of American and German listeners precisely because of the specificity of his songwriting. "I'm more interested in regional writing," says Samson, "those people who explore the places they're from and distort them in a way that allows us to hear those places in different ways and understand our own communities in fresh new ways. In an accelerated culture like ours, localities are the most valuable tool for exploring the world. The centres of culture are so difficult for me to get a handle on, and the people writing about the world from the margins—either marginalized places or marginalized positions—are, to me, having the most insight into who we are right now. The idea of a Canadian identity is a bit troubling to me, but it's certainly there."

Ah, yes, the "Canadian identity," the subject of a thousand *Toronto Star* op-eds and a million more academic papers that wrestle themselves into defeatist knots. Buck 65 thinks it doesn't exist—which is to Canada's advantage in many ways. "I go to all these other parts of the world and I find that people feel really shackled or constrained by the identity they have there," he told *Exclaim!* "If you're a musician and come from a place with a very distinct sound, you're likely to [either] have that sound or have difficulty escaping it. Really, we don't have any of that. What we have is this amazing filter through which we receive the world." And then reflect it back, infused with whatever intangible elements are specific to either this country or one neighbourhood in it.

Almost everyone in this book is a child of the 1970s: very few are born before 1970 or after 1980. They were the first generation of kids raised by the hippie generation. A surprising number of them are also children of Vietnam War draft dodgers. Their collective vision of Canada was and is very different than generations before them. "Toronto was a big social experiment when we were growing up, about how progressive a city could be," says Torquil Campbell. "We were living in a time where it moved from being a very stultifying, very conservative place, to being a very dynamic, multicultural, forward-thinking community-based place. There was a huge amount of money put into the education system. If you wanted to play trumpet, you could play trumpet—whatever you want." This was the first Canadian generation raised with real creative opportunity: locally, nationally, and with the chutzpah en masse to take it to the world.

FIRESTARTER

The unquestionable peak of the period was Arcade Fire's *Funeral*, released on September 14, 2004. Hype had been building since the beginning of 2004, but no one expected *Funeral* to be that good—not even their friends. Jim Guthrie, who gave the band their first Toronto show in January 2003, had heard some rough mixes he'd been sent by guitarist Tim Kingsbury. "I loved what I heard, but at the same time it was just another record in a sea of other crazy good records being made in that scene," he says. "I'm not sure anyone thought it would go on to be as huge as it was—including them."

The first pressing of the album sold out that first week. Carl Newman was lucky enough to get a copy. "I was in San Francisco," he recalls. "The day that *Funeral* came out, I'd read something about this band from Montreal who were supposed to be good. I had nothing to do and my girlfriend was at work, so I walked 45 minutes to Amoeba [Music] on Haight Street to go buy this album and then go home and listen. I was so floored. Two months later they played in Vancouver and I happened to be there. I loved the record, but when they came on stage at the Commodore and played 'Wake Up,' I thought, Holy shit. I'd never seen a [new] band where I thought, This band will be fucking monstrous. You could put this band in front of anybody, and they are going to destroy. We had the same booking agent and she brought me backstage. I talked to a few of them: 'Do you guys know you're going to be huge?' They were all, 'Aw shucks, this is the biggest show we've ever played.' Which was 1,200 people. I knew they were going to be playing places 10 times that size."

Buck 65 was living in New York City the week *Funeral* came out. As he was walking to his record company's office, "I swear to God, a total stranger stopped me on the street and said, 'Have you heard this Arcade Fire record?!' I thought, Holy Jesus, people were losing their shit. I got to the office and told my publicist what had just happened. She said, 'Oh yeah, I love that record, too. You'd love it. You should go buy it if you haven't already.' The office was right across the street from Other Music, so I did. Shortly after, I did a photo shoot with *Spin* magazine, and the photographer said, 'Hey, man, you want to play any music to get you in the mood while we're shooting these photos?' I put the Arcade Fire record on. These people from *Spin* were like, 'What the fuck is this?!'"

Buck 65 found himself playing the same festivals as Arcade Fire throughout 2005, including Coachella in California and many of the major European festivals. "It was the most exciting shit I've ever seen, just bananas," he says. "Every show they played was like their last night on earth. They played until they collapsed. One guy would be incapacitated for two songs and just not play, lying prone on the stage trying to recover from the exertion. I remember being in either the Netherlands or Switzerland, and the main stage was a tent. Will Butler climbed one of the beams that supported the tent, carrying that parade drum they had, with a strap over the shoulder. He climbed to the top of the tent, so high. Once he got up there, he steadied himself and started banging the shit out of this drum. Everyone was right there with them. I was watching a lot of these shows from the stage, and feeling the energy in the room rise. It seemed like there was this rapture and danger involved and they were putting it all on the line. It was really something. I mean, it was cool to watch what was going on with Broken Social Scene and Stars and everyone else, but that particular run after *Funeral* was just wildly exciting—and cool to see it happening in these far-flung parts of the world. I probably saw them play 20 times that year in different cities, and I felt this overwhelming sense of pride watching them just kill it. It was really special. It felt like the world was changing before my eyes."

Though a *Pitchfork* review set things in motion, it was a large *New York Times* profile by Kelefa Sanneh in October 2004, set during the CMJ festival, that put Arcade Fire into a more mainstream conversation—before radio started playing them, before old-guard magazines had reviewed the record. From that point onward, the hype was overwhelming. Luckily, both the record and the band's live show more than lived up to it, otherwise they'd be in the dustbin of history alongside Clap Your Hands Say Yeah. (Look 'em up.)

The world turned its eyes toward Montreal, writing about it like it was the next Seattle or Manchester—in other words, a geographical trend piece that writes itself. Constellation Records would usually be contacted for comment from Godspeed, and someone there would laugh and hang up the phone. "Older" acts like the Dears and Stars, who were busy touring the world while the next generation came up in the clubs, didn't know their younger peers at all. The Unicorns had already broken up before Arcade Fire made it to the West Coast. Kid Koala and the thriving electronic music scene around the MUTEK festival was usually omitted entirely, as of course was every single francophone artist in the city. It wasn't a Montreal "scene" as much as it was different peer groups who all blossomed at approximately the same time—not unlike Toronto or Vancouver, but those cities simply aren't as sexy or "exotic" to English-language media outside Canada. For non-Canadians, Arcade Fire was the ideal entry point to Montreal and by extension Canada: influenced by British new wave and American indie rock, fronted by two Texan brothers and a francophone woman of Haitian parentage who played accordion.

LEAN ON YOUR PEERS

In 2000, Gord Downie looked at the outline for a book project called *Have Not Been the Same*, about his peers in Canadian music from 1985 to '95. He turned to co-author Jason Schneider and me and said, "The more it happens, the more it happens more," a variation on an old idiom, one that plays into sociologist Pierre Bourdieu's influential "field theory." It's one thing to be inspired by artists from afar; it's another to be lifted up by the person down the street from you—and a matter of time before you become an inspiration to someone else. For anyone in a major urban Canadian centre during 2000 to 2005 (and beyond), there was a good chance that a 100-mile musical diet was almost sustainable (though never a valid excuse for myopia).

"When you witness peers, just a bit further down the road from you, who are achieving what you strive for, it is then in reach," says Howard Bilerman, who recorded Arcade Fire's *Funeral*. When that band's Win Butler saw Wolf Parade's first show, he had been wondering if his band had any future at all. Seeing a new band of neighbours come roaring out of the gate was the galvanizing force he needed. Butler recalls, "Just being in the same physical space as other bands that are doing stuff that's better than what you're doing—that's so important, to be around contemporaries who are making you feel like, 'Yikes, I gotta get back to work.' To see an artist write a song one day and play it live the next week and you're there to see it, that's a whole different can of worms from listening to someone's recorded output. You're seeing it being made in real time."

It didn't matter if it was happening on the other side of the city or the country. Kevin Drew, when filling out an early grant application for Broken Social Scene in 2002, described the band as "the East Coast version of the New Pornographers." A year later, the New Pornographers were in New York City to play on David Letterman's TV show and met Broken Social Scene outside Other Music, where the Toronto band had just done an in-store appearance. "We literally ran into each other in the street, like two gangs meeting," says Newman. *West Side Story* jokes ensued. "There were eight of them and six of us. Feist was with them. We didn't know them, but there was this sense of 'Check us out, we're two Canadian indie rock bands here in New York!' That bonds us together."

"Any kind of creative thing happens out of friends exciting friends," says Stephen McBean, who grew up in Victoria's productive punk scene and launched Black Mountain and Pink Mountaintops in Vancouver. "A lot of times, there will be a bunch of bands hanging out together and say, 'The scene sucks, man. No one is supportive.' Well, guess what, dude? *Your* band fucking sucks. Start better bands, and people will be stoked. That happened then: New Pornographers. Destroyer. Hot Hot Heat. Daddy's Hands. Ladyhawk moved from Kelowna. Venues were opening. Every once in a while a new group of young kids would come in. The first Pink Mountaintops show, we sold out Richard's on Richards and I couldn't believe that many people came out. There were more people there than there were for the release of D.O.A.'s *Hardcore 81*. That excites you. It keeps your fire inside. Then you go to see Dan Bejar play, and it's like, 'Man, Dan's got a killer new tune called "Canadian Lover." What a stupid but amazing title!'"

Globe and Mail music critic Carl Wilson, a huge Destroyer fan, would normally write a year-end top 20 list of his favourite records—from everywhere. In 2003, he wrote, "The world's been laying wet smackers on our artists all year. So instead of a general best-of-the-year list, I offer an all-Canadian list. Its flaw is that it's too short. Except for No. 1, the albums could easily be replaced with 20 more nearly as good." His No. 1 pick was *The Golden River* by Dan Bejar's friends in Frog Eyes.

By 2004, half of *Exclaim!*'s top 10 rock records of the year were Canadian; the same was true of their R&B and electronic picks. None of it felt like tokenism or CBC flag-waving or government-mandated CanCon. Two years later, former A&R rep Steve Jordan launched the inaugural Polaris Music Prize, an annual critics' prize that—unlike the Junos—was not remotely concerned with commercial success but with artistry and, often, innovation. The prize's first winner was former Hidden Camera Owen Pallett, a solo Toronto violinist in a tiny independent artists' co-op, who wrote pop songs about the CN Tower and his occasional employers, Arcade Fire. Almost everything about that last sentence encapsulates what was happening in Canada at the time.

This new movement—which wasn't a short-lived trend but continues today—wasn't just so-called indie rock, chart pop or any music traditionally associated with Canada's cultural output. It was everything. This was music made by unclassifiable iconoclasts and mall-punk teens. It was artsy curmudgeons and commercially minded careerists. It was artsy, aggro metallic punk and Inuit throat singers. It was ghostly singer-songwriters and psychedelic country bands. It was electronic music, both EDM and more experimental. By the end of the decade, it was even hip-hop (finally), and one Toronto rapper went on to be the biggest pop artist of the next decade, shattering all kinds of records.

At some point, it stopped being unusual. It wasn't just one amazing artist in your hometown; it was several. It wasn't just one Canadian album a year you were falling in love with; it was a new one every few months, each filled with romance and power and the ability to connect, each one the sound of this generation, each one about being alive in the now. It wasn't just one genre or one commercial sphere of music. And it wasn't just your city or even your country taking notice: these bands, these albums, they were everywhere. Fans in Chicago, L.A., London, Paris, Berlin, Prague: they all wanted to know what was happening in Montreal, Toronto, Vancouver. Maybe even Hamilton, Winnipeg, Calgary.

Carl Newman says, "We weren't the best, or the most popular, or the most influential, but I feel like, 'We were there, man!' It's like an LCD Soundsystem song: 'I was there when Broken Social Scene put out *You Forgot It in People*! I was there when Arcade Fire put out *Funeral*!'"

By the time Arcade Fire won the Grammy for Album of the Year—for a 2010 album that also won the Polaris, the Juno and even the Brit Award—it didn't feel like validation or recognition. It just felt right. Ten years earlier, it would have been a momentous occasion for the country, like Olympic hockey gold or an NBA championship. Yet this was merely yet another WTF moment in a game-changing decade of Canadian music, before which most artists would never have considered a Grammy to be a feasible—or even a desirable—career goal.[5] That night, just before their big win, Arcade Fire took to the Grammy stage singing a lyric about how "businessmen drink my blood / just like the kids in art school said they would." They avoided that fate. Canadian music had won—on its own terms.

Cumulatively the stage had been set. There was no turning back. We owned the podium. We the North.

"It wasn't the moment that was so wonderful," says Aaron Riches of Royal City. "It was the expectation that anything could happen."

---

5   The news did make the cover of the *Montreal Gazette* the next day, though below the fold,
     underneath stories about an injured hawk and a municipal rail study.

CHAPTER 3
DEAD FLAG
BLUES

GODSPEED YOU! BLACK EMPEROR, CONSTELLATION RECORDS

A bunch of people in a band is not a collective. Lazy writers look at any rock group with more than five people in it and cry, "Collective!" Which happened far too often in the 2000s. But Godspeed You! Black Emperor actually *were* a collective. There were nine of them. They made all decisions by consensus. No one person spoke for Godspeed. They wanted the music to speak for itself.

Which it did: Godspeed was one of the most influential international bands of the 2000s, inspiring young musicians, artists, filmmakers and activists in ways that seemed impossible for a ragtag bunch of hippie punks from Montreal's Mile End neighbourhood on a fiercely independent record label.

The city itself was a character in their music and their visuals, creating a mystique that the world found enchanting. And whether the band liked it or not—spoiler: they didn't—Godspeed is directly responsible for making Montreal the subject of international attention as a bohemian ideal, alongside Brooklyn and Berlin. Non-Canadians were fascinated by the city's francophone and separatist history. Canadians were mostly fascinated by the cheap rent. Either way, Montreal became a mecca for British Columbian punks, Brazilian electronic musicians on British record labels, wandering Texans and no shortage of Ontarians and Americans looking to live in the most European metropolis in North America. Montreal was a hotbed of anarchists and the antiglobalization movement, for which the 2001 Summit of the Americas in nearby Quebec City became a galvanizing moment—and for which Godspeed was the ideal soundtrack of resistance. (Montreal-born *No Logo* author Naomi Klein also helped.)

This next generation knew little of Leonard Cohen or the Quiet Revolution. They weren't moving there because of Céline Dion or even Rufus Wainwright. They were drawn to Mile End—because of Godspeed. Whoever that might be.

That said: Godspeed was started by one guy, Efrim Manuel Menuck, who alone recorded the first cassette credited to Godspeed You! Black Emperor in 1994. Menuck was born in Montreal but raised in Toronto. Two of his high school friends and one other Toronto expat formed the initial core of the band, which expanded to include francophone string players and two drummers. At one point there were 15 people loosely associated with Godspeed. By the time they went on their first tour in 1997, there were nine.

By the time they finished touring their third record and went on hiatus in 2004, they'd changed the course of Canadian music—and how it was seen around the world.

———

EFRIM MENUCK WAS RAISED in the shadow of Toronto's Upper Canada College, the private boys school for Canada's English elite. He didn't attend: he went to first a Hebrew day school and then Forest Hill Collegiate, alongside future bandmates Mauro Pezzente and Mike Moya. (Other Forest Hill alumni: Drake, Lorne Michaels, Neve Campbell.) Menuck grew up "middle class, the other side of the tracks from Forest Hill in a Protestant, two-storey neighbourhood," he says. "None of us were rich kids. We were going to this high school with children of wealthy orthodontists. We glommed onto each other because we were weirdos."

Menuck and Moya eventually ended up at the alternative school SEED; though the curriculum was largely self-directed and loose, Menuck dropped out. "The ages of 17 to 21 were heavy years, with a lot of temporary homelessness," he says. "It sucked. Hard times." He briefly had a punk band with Moya that played two gigs at the Slither Club (on the southwest corner of Queen and Bathurst streets). He went to see five-band bills at the Rivoli, with the likes of UIC, Jellyfishbabies, NoMind and Heimlich Maneuver. He was too young to see trance-rock local legends A Neon Rome, but he had their record. In 1991, he applied to Concordia as a mature student to study film. "It was the only university I could get into," he says. "I mostly wanted access to lectures and a library, and that's what I got out of it. They mostly left you alone to do what you wanted." Pezzente moved to Montreal the same year, following his girlfriend, Kiva Stimac, who also went to Concordia. Moya followed shortly afterwards.

Menuck and Pezzente started a grunge trio called Pud. Like the character in the Dubble Bubble comics? "No," says Pezzente, "post-urinal drip. We then

changed it to Bueno Pud Bueno because we didn't want to be a one-word band."
One-word bands were a '90s trend: Nirvana. Soundgarden. Sloan. Slint. Stereolab.
Low. One night, Efrim came to practice after his film class had screened a Japanese
documentary about motorcycle gangs. It was called *God Speed You! Black Emperor*.
"We were like, That's perfect, that's the name," says Pezzente. "It's long and no
one will remember it." But the days of Bueno Pud Bueno were numbered regardless. Menuck didn't want to be in a grunge band. Nor did anyone else. "We had a
last show at Bifteck," says Pezzente. "It was really depressing. I never wanted to
do that again."

That scene seemed over anyway. Before Menuck left Toronto, he had gone to see
Dinosaur Jr. at the Concert Hall and watched jocks in Sub Pop T-shirts mercilessly
heckle one of his favourite bands, Die Kreuzen. Menuck was reading the fanzine
Forced Exposure and getting into dark, droning bands like New Zealand's the Dead C,
music that helped him heal what he describes as "a heavy deal, when you have your
first adult breakup and it knocks you on your ass for a year." He hung out at the St.
Laurent bar Miami (between Bifteck and Schwartz's), got drunk with friends who
worked there, then went home and would "just record whatever came to my head,"
he says. "The next day, hungover, I'd try and turn that into a song."

That led to a solo tape called *All Lights Fucked on the Hairy Amp Drooling*, credited to Godspeed You! Black Emperor. He made 33 copies and figured that would
be the last musical thing he did. "A friend who knew I wasn't doing good, to whom
I'd given the cassette, had a show and invited me to open," he says. "I asked Mauro
and Mike if they wanted to do it. That's how it all started."

Pezzente was in. "I was listening to a lot of Spacemen 3," he says. "The idea of
playing drone-y rock was my ideal plan."

The next show took place in a used clothing store in Moncton, by invitation
from an old friend. The third show added another Toronto expat, Dave Bryant, on
drums; he soon switched to third guitar. He'd played in a Toronto grunge band,
Soulfly, and a somewhat popular crust-punk Montreal band, Bliss. Pezzente brought
in two sisters who played French horn and violin, as well as another violinist. He
also supplied the venue that would shape the rest of Godspeed's career.

He and Stimac had moved to a loft above an auto shop at 173A Avenue Van
Horne, between Parc and St. Urbain, to open Gallery Qui Va (translation: who's
going?). This was as far north of the nightlife scene as anyone thought imaginable, adjacent to a set of train tracks that act as an unofficial municipal border.
Though the building is only three kilometres away from Bifteck, the Anglo arts
scene in Montreal was so geographically centred on the lower Plateau—or southwest of downtown, near Concordia, in St. Henri—that Van Horne might as well
have been Ungava Bay.

Pezzente and Stimac only lasted there for six months—the fumes from the downstairs auto mechanic were too much—and were succeeded by Menuck, drummer Aidan Girt and bassist Thierry Amar, the latter two being new additions to Godspeed. Visual artist John Tinholt and cellist Norsola Johnson were also briefly residents. They dubbed the loft Hotel 2 Tango, shortwave radio lingo for Mile End's postal code. Godspeed started playing shows at the Hotel, inviting other local bands to play as well. Menuck and Pezzente were working as movers at the time; they'd drive their van down to Bifteck to pick up anyone who wanted to go to the show. That made Hotel 2 Tango the only punk rock venue in Montreal to have shuttle service.

This was all very word of mouth, removed from even the underground. Howard Bilerman, who later co-managed the Hotel 2 Tango studio, says that before 1997, Godspeed was a mysterious presence. "I had a recording studio in Old Montreal, recording a bunch of bands who didn't sound like that," he says. "I heard there was a group of people who had their own practice space and their own venue and they were a nine-piece band. All the bands I was recording were begging, or paying, to play places. I didn't know anyone in this band; they seemed like this self-contained, insular thing. I definitely had never *heard* a band like that."

Godspeed was one of the few rock bands using orchestral elements at a time when grunge quartets ruled. In Montreal, *Brave New Waves* employee Gen Heistek played violin in Pest 5000, one of a few non-Celtic rock bands to use the instrument, along with U.S. bands the Dambuilders, That Dog and Geraldine Fibbers. By the mid-'90s, instrumental Australian trio Dirty Three, featuring fiery violinist Warren Ellis, was establishing a beachhead in North America via rapturous live shows. The more subdued indie rock chamber-music ensemble Rachel's was from the Louisville, Kentucky, scene that spawned Slint and other Godspeed influences. The Beach Boys' critical reputation had a renaissance, which led to the neo-psychedelia of the Elephant 6 collective in the U.S. and British chamber pop. In Scotland, the instrumental band Mogwai was on a similar wavelength as Godspeed, but the two bands were not yet aware of each other—and Mogwai didn't have strings. Mogwai's Glaswegian neighbours Belle and Sebastian did, but that's a whole other kettle of haggis. Both Mogwai and Belle and Sebastian released their proper debut albums the same year Godspeed did, in 1997.

Menuck had been taping modern classical music from friends' CDs, notably Henryk Górecki's Symphony No. 3 (also known as *Symphony of Sorrowful Songs*), which was used widely in films and was a rare modern classical work that became a bestseller. Arvo Pärt's *Tabula Rasa* was another favourite. But it was the *way* Menuck heard that music that had as much of an influence on Godspeed as the music itself. "Whenever I'd tape people's CDs, I'd put the input into the red," he says. "It made rock and punk music in my van sound better. It would be compressed and would cut through the cheap speakers. When friends were turning me on to modern classical stuff, I'd do the same thing. All these weird harmonics came out. I had that in my head. But honestly, we only had strings because Mauro knew [early members] Jessie [Pratt] and [the man only ever credited as] Christophe, and then we met Norsola. [Violinist] Sophie [Trudeau] came later on. It was an accident."

Everything about Godspeed was an accident—including the fact they ended up with two bassists and two drummers. "When we got asked to play our first show, we didn't have any songs," says Pezzente. "The idea was to just jam on two notes—F# and A#—because Efrim and Mike had tuned their guitars in the F# open tuning. I tuned my bass strings to F# and A# so that I could play open strings." Hence the name of Godspeed's debut album: *F# A# ∞*. When second bassist Thierry Amar joined, he sometimes played upright bass, often melodic lines. "We can trade off on who gets to play the root note," says Pezzante, "which ends up being me."

One night, Menuck and Bryant were drinking at the Miami and talking about next steps. "We came up with the idea that anyone who didn't have a career or anything that was tying them down, we should get them to join the band, even if they didn't play an instrument, and then we'll make a record and go on tour," says Menuck. "That's when the band became 15 people at its height."

Describing the period of "proto-Godspeed," Constellation Records' Ian Ilavsky compares it to what he imagined early Velvet Underground performances were like at Andy Warhol's Plastic Exploding Inevitable, "in the sense of sensory overload, wall of sound. The first show I saw was not at the Hotel; it was in a concrete space, an upstart gallery, very DIY, not a good-sounding room. They just played a scale, up and down, mostly in unison, drenched in distortion. They had this cross-shaped wood, and suspended from that were two sheets also making a cross, so that as it was spinning you had four quadrants making 90-degree angles. That was set up in front of them, spinning very slowly, with two 16-millimetre projectors hitting it at different angles. It was much more abstract and musically more of a smear. Over those two years, from '95 to '97, every show was different. They were composing a bit more. The lineup was clarifying and gelling."

Backdrop projections became a key element of Godspeed's live set. A recurring visual theme was the riveted metal water tower atop a warehouse near the Hotel on Van Horne, built in the early 20th century. It seemed to symbolize a decaying industrial past, much like the train imagery (and sounds) also employed.

The films were blurry and grainy, largely depicting Mile End as a bleak, imper-sonal, cold landscape of the postindustrial age.

"Originally the films were all mine," says Menuck. "The movie I made in my last year at film school, I cut it up and turned it into loops. I also shot new stuff. Mark Littlefair was our projectionist [at first]; Jean-Sébastien Truchy from Fly Pan Am was our projectionist for many years." Later on, American filmmaker Jem Cohen also contributed footage. Shows often opened with a flickering image of the word *HOPE* scrawled in Menuck's distinctive handwriting. For a band without lyrics or stage banter, that was the message they wanted to convey before expos-ing audiences to an equally punishing and exuberant set of urban industrial blues adorned with classical, noise and rock overtones.

Easily—and understandably—misconstrued as misanthropes, Godspeed believed in hope, a decade before a poster for a U.S. presidential nominee became a mean-ingless mainstream meme. "We felt that anything we were able to accomplish, as a crew of fuckups, was hugely great," says Menuck. "We were committed to doing it collectively; we were also proud of it—and still are. There are all types of people in the band, so I'm generalizing, but most of us were really broke with no famil-ial wealth. Things were dark. We all found each other, and that was our idealism." Unfortunately, he admits, "our starting point was alienating for a lot of people. I don't think that would be the case today." In the exuberant 1990s, you were mocked if you were a bummer. In the 2020s, it's totally understandable.

F# A# ∞ was recorded at the Hotel 2 Tango, where the band rehearsed. It features one of the most striking openings of any album released in at least that decade. On "The Dead Flag Blues," over a low pulsing rumble, a man's deep voice intones the following:

> *The car's on fire and there's no driver at the wheel. And the sewers are all muddied with a thousand lonely suicides. And a dark wind blows.*
>
> *The government is corrupt, and we're all so many drunks with the radio on and the curtains drawn. We're trapped in the belly of this hor-rible machine, and the machine is bleeding to death.*
>
> *The sun has fallen down and the billboards are all leering and the flags are all dead at the top of their poles.*
>
> *It went like this: the buildings toppled in on themselves. Mothers clutching babies picked through the rubble and pulled out their hair. The skyline was beautiful on fire, all twisted metal stretching upwards. Everything washed in a thin orange haze.*
>
> *I said, "Kiss me you're beautiful. These are truly the last days." You grabbed my hand and we fell into it like a daydream or a fever.*

The second movement of the song, "The Cowboy," features train sounds and cascading slide guitars, before becoming a languid Morricone-ish spaghetti western soundtrack. The outro is a surprisingly jaunty fiddle waltz with glockenspiel. "East Hastings" opens with an African street preacher and the sound of bagpipes, then slowly evolves into a rock epic over the course of its 17 minutes, concluding with what sounds like an electronic mosquito. The 21-minute "Providence" moves through a delicate 7/8 intro before opening up into a dual-drum attack and ascending guitars, then evaporates into an ethereal folk song, followed by an uplifting march that falls into another scratchy folk song loop before ending in drones and decaying tapes. Prefacing all of that, the track opens with the following exchange with what appears to be a retail clerk: "Do you think the end of the world is coming?" "No. So says the preacher man, but I don't go by what he says."

As they were getting ready to mix the record, the band had no idea what to do next. Large indie distributor Cargo—which also employed many Montreal musicians—was in dire straits and soon went under. Godspeed didn't make remotely commercial music, and didn't aim to. The band considered putting out F# A# ∞ on a double seven-inch single.

One day Dave Bryant heard through mutual friends that two guys were looking for a venue to host Dub Narcotic Sound System, led by indie icon Calvin Johnson of Olympia, Washington. The show ended up happening at the Hotel 2 Tango. The two promoters, Ian Ilavsky and Don Wilkie, had just started a record label called Constellation Records. They agreed to put out a full-length vinyl record of F# A# ∞ and joined the band in the studio to help mix the record. Everyone on deck. All hands on the faders. So began their collective journey into sound.

LIKE HALF OF GODSPEED, Ian Ilavsky and Don Wilkie were also transplants to Montreal. Ilavsky left Winnipeg to attend McGill; after graduation, he worked for years at Fairmount Bagel, an experience that bestows honorary Montreal citizenship. Wilkie was a Cape Bretoner who got a business degree and worked a corporate job in Toronto. There, he had an epiphany: he came out of the closet, realized he had to change everything in his life and moved to Montreal. Ilavsky played in a dour grunge band called Sofa. They moved in together and made big plans.

"We all felt we were outside the mainstream francophone culture," says Ilavsky. "It was very much a hunkered-down, small-scene mentality. We had the intent to build something. We thought it would be a venue. We had the Knitting Factory in mind, even though that was a received idea: neither of us had ever been to New York City, never mind the Knitting Factory. But we read in zines about this cool club that put on shows and also had a label and recorded sessions. That was our idea."

They started with the label, equally inspired by the ethics of Fugazi's Dischord, the community of Chicago's Touch and Go and the design of 4AD and Kranky. Constellation's first two releases were a seven-inch and a CD from Sofa. In 1996, most CD cases were discardable plastic. This CD looked like an art project. Artist John Tinholt, with Wilkie and Ilavsky, cut notches into tiny hardwood sticks and glued them together into a three-sided frame, then glued paper around each one. "It was a very artisanal craft project," says Ilavsky. "Three people working collectively for a ten-hour day could make 100 of them." It was obvious from the outset that Constellation would be different, even from other arty indies like Chicago's Thrill Jockey.

Wilkie had $10,000, savings from his Toronto corporate job, to invest in the venture. "He and I lived on his [unemployment insurance] cheques, which went a long way in Montreal," says Ilavsky. "We lived comfortably on those for the first year, $1,300 a month. I got to quit my job. We shared rent." They leased a space across from Leonard Cohen's house at St. Laurent and Marie-Anne, with the intent of opening a vegan café and live venue as well as office space, until realizing the plumbing hadn't been used in 30 years and required extensive renovations. "They were looking for someone to make leaseholder improvements, and we didn't even understand that language," he says. "Instead we got a loft."

That loft was the ground floor in a building co-owned by Patti Schmidt, host and producer of CBC Radio's Brave New Waves, and her former workmate and Pest 5000 bandmate Kevin Komoda. In 1997, the rent was $700 a month. "A 16-foot ceiling, 1,500 square foot, 1860s loft in Old Montreal," says Ilavsky. "But heat wasn't included, and it was absolutely brutal in the winter. It was 14 degrees [Celsius] in there and even that cost us another $500 a month—which was still incredibly cheap." Old Montreal did not have night life; it closed up shop once the tourists and businesspeople went home for the day. Constellation started hosting a music series there called Musique Fragile. "It was a destination venue, because no one lived down there," says Ilavsky. "People would get off at the Victoria metro station, and we'd do these intimate soirees and make sure they were done in time so people could catch the last metro home. That series was a bit of a gestator for the weird things we were interested in." Future Constellation artists Sam Shalabi, Frankie Sparo and A Silver Mt. Zion were all Musique Fragile performers.

Meanwhile, rock shows continued at the Hotel. "It was mostly people we knew," says Menuck, "but also people around Patti Schmidt's circle, like [Doughboys'] Jon Asencio, who put on some shows. Also some fucking nonsense: a couple of weeks before rent was due, we'd start answering the phone and rent out the space to shitty DJs, then have mild nervous breakdowns. It led to a lot of weird situations."

Constellation wasn't the only weird new label in town in 1996. Alien8, run by Sean O'Hara and Gary Worsley, focused primarily on Japanese noise artists; Montreal electronic artist David Kristian was the only local act on the label for a while. Alien8 also booked shows at the Hotel, including Silver Apples, the pioneering U.S. synth-rock band of the 1960s. "It was [founder] Simeon Coxe with all these kids," remembers Menuck. "One of the kids came up to me and said, 'Simeon needs to be paid before he goes on stage.' I was like, Wow, I'd only heard about these things before."

Though Godspeed had recorded *F# A# ∞* at the Hotel, it was not a functioning studio. Associated acts started working with Howard Bilerman at his Old Montreal studio. Thierry Amar played bass in slowcore band Molasses, and Dave Bryant engineered Aidan Girt's band Exhaust (a trio with bassist Gordon Krieger and sound sculptor Michel Zabitsky); both records were done with Bilerman. Exhaust's debut album was the fourth Constellation release. A community was developing, but it was by no means evident that Godspeed would soon be the centre of it. Perhaps because Constellation released *F# A# ∞* on vinyl only—and had no real desire to interact with the mainstream music press—initial response added up to crickets. Only a fistful of critics took notice. Those who did noted not only the music but the packaging: inside each *F# A# ∞* vinyl sleeve was a manila envelope containing several pieces of artwork and a Canadian penny, flattened on the railroad tracks behind the Hotel 2 Tango: the smallest unit of currency from a colonized land, with a foreign monarch's image engraved on one side, literally crushed by the weight of industrial progress.

Living beside train tracks incites wanderlust, and Godspeed wanted to hit the road. Aidan Girt had friends in Ottawa's thriving punk community, where they played the Saw Gallery. The Torontonians in the band knew of Symptom Hall, a freewheeling artist's space near Trinity-Bellwoods Park, where Godspeed was invited to play with Fell Gang on March 15, 1997. They booked a show at Montreal's Miami Bar the night before, but half the band decided they didn't want to go to Toronto and play for no money, so they quit. "It was attrition," says Menuck. The new nine-piece incarnation of Godspeed—the lineup introduced to the rest of the world—debuted that weekend at Miami and Symptom Hall. And they decided they wanted to go further afield.

Because of Dave Bryant's time in Bliss, the guitarist had enough contacts in the eastern U.S. hardcore scene to book a tour. The band piled into a GMC wagon and a Pontiac, packing camping gear along with instruments. "It was your typical first U.S. tour, playing to nobody or three people," says Pezzente. "The bookers thought they were getting Bliss, which they weren't. We played crappy bars, though there was a show at the Rhinecliff Hotel, which was amazing, but we played to nobody. It's a hotel right on the Hudson River, incredibly beautiful. It's turned into this super rich neighbourhood now, full of people from Manhattan. At the time it was a rundown upstate New York town. We'd driven all night, got there, and we were falling asleep on their balcony, thinking we could stay there. Typical young kid things."

In Chicago, they were billed at the Empty Bottle with Silkworm. At the show was Joel Leoschke, co-owner of Kranky, a relatively new Chicago record label devoted to ambient post-rock like Low and Labradford, as well as an early '90s Ottawa band, the Spiny Anteaters. Impressed, he offered to put out *F# A# ∞* on CD in the spring of 1998. Godspeed saw this as a good excuse to add some new material and rerecord other tracks, now that they were a better live band. They could also afford to book studio time at Toronto's Chemical Sound, run by Daryl Smith of the band Slow Loris—another weirdo post-rock Canadian band that managed to get some international notice, or at least reviewed. *F# A# ∞*'s track order was shuffled, and some field recordings added. Why? "We were just excited that we could," says Menuck, "and that we could now do longer stuff."

After its rerelease in the spring of 1998, Menuck and Bryant took a job tree planting in northwest Ontario. "Dave had a Hotmail account; I didn't even know what that meant," says Menuck. "There was an internet café attached to the laundromat in Thunder Bay, so on our day off he'd look online, and we could see the record was being reviewed. That's when things got real."

GODSPEED'S SUCCESS STORY owes much to Britain. It wasn't by design. Far from it.

Constellation had been cold-called by someone at Southern Records, a U.K. distributor that also handled Europe and had an American division; Kranky was one of many U.S. labels distributed by Southern, as were Touch and Go and others. Not only did Southern have clout, it was a perfect ideological fit: founder John Loder got his start in the business working with anarchist punk collective Crass and had helped Fugazi's Dischord Records establish a beachhead in Europe.

Southern gave Godspeed a contact for Dirk Hugsam, a German booker who brought over acts like Vancouver's Mecca Normal, New Zealand's Dead C and Chicago's Smog—in other words, someone predisposed to fall in love with Godspeed You! Black Emperor. "He brought them to Europe on a wing and a prayer, this unwieldy nine-piece with four 16-millimetre projectors," says Ilavsky. "He was an indie booker, not an agency, just a one-man show. [Show promoters] just trusted him to be this guy who discovered things." Godspeed flew to Hamburg in November 1998 for their first European tour. They headlined every gig.

"Dirk took it upon himself to ring the bell and took a huge risk," says Menuck. "We met him for the first time in the airport. He had a circuit. In France, they have what are called 'culture bunkers,' these places that used to be squats, which were funded a bit by the government. We played weird places"— the band's Manchester debut was at Amigos Tex-Mex Restaurant, shortly before recording a John Peel BBC session—"and we always broke even on six-and-a-half-week tours. Getting paid in pounds and deutschmarks and other currencies, which were stronger than the Canadian dollar, also made a big difference." So did some tour support from Canadian funding body FACTOR, which was then available even to non-commercial acts like Godspeed, as long as an artist could provide a concrete business plan.

"The first show we played in London was at the Garage, and that was in front of 400 people," says Pezzente. "For us, at the time, that was mind-blowing." The promoter for that show was Barry Hogan, who became another key European ally when he booked them to play the Bowlie Weekender, a small festival in April 1999 largely curated by reluctant live act Belle and Sebastian; the Bowlie Weekender evolved into the All Tomorrow's Parties festival. Godspeed tacked on some other U.K. and European dates that month before returning for a full six weeks in the summer, their third overseas jaunt in six months.

A new EP, *Slow Riot for New Zero Kanada*, had been released in March 1999 on Kranky. As with *F# A# ∞*, Constellation handled only the vinyl edition, as per the band's arrangement with both labels. Constellation did, however, continue to place pennies on the train tracks behind the Hotel to put in each vinyl copy of *F# A# ∞*.

Still not confident about their home recordings, Godspeed had travelled to Toronto to work at the Gas Station studio with Dale Morningstar of improv punk band the Dinner Is Ruined—a frequent guest at the Hotel 2 Tango. However, *Slow Riot*'s liner notes rail against a "botched mastering job" at another Toronto studio, Triumph's Metalworks; the tapes were apparently retrieved during a nonstop drive from Montreal, through a blizzard, and remastered by the band to meet a production deadline.

In two epic tracks, *Slow Riot* distilled all the strengths of both *F# A# ∞* and the double album for which Godspeed was amassing material. The second song, "Blaise Bailey Finnegan III," features an extended field recording of a man at a gas station in Providence, Rhode Island. He rails against the U.S. government ("America is a Third World country!"), tells a story about fighting a speeding ticket, lists his gun inventory and proceeds to recite what he claims is his original poetry. Long after the EP was released, someone told the band that the name the stranger gave to the band was actually that of Iron Maiden's vocalist during Bruce Dickinson's hiatus, and that his "poem" was actually the lyrics to the 1996

Maiden song "Virus." "We didn't know any of that," says Menuck. "Some people thought we'd made it up."

"Some people" thought a lot of things about Godspeed. A lot of rumours were fabricated in the absence of many facts withheld by the band. Outside of liner notes, one of the only public statements from the band at the time was: "No singer no leader no interviews no press photos." Rare exceptions were made for zines so small that few journalists could cite them in the early days of internet media.

That's why it was shocking that the first real feature on the band ran not in the *Montreal Mirror* or *Exclaim!* or *Magnet* but in U.K. music tabloid the *New Musical Express* in July 1999. What made it even weirder: it was the cover story, with a picture of thunderclouds and hydro poles instead of the band, and the opening lines of "Dead Flag Blues" printed in large faded Courier font. The headline in a heavy-metal font read "Godspeed You Black Emperor! Apocalypse Now: The Only Interview." The slugs at the top of the page were for stories about Spice Girl Mel C and an apparent feud between Blur and Mogwai. Inside, the only press photo to ever exist of Godspeed was too blurry to make out much of anything, other than eight nondescript people standing on railroad tracks.

Explains Menuck, "For me and Dave and Mike and Mauro, as kids who grew up in Toronto where people would buy the *NME*, that [magazine] was the first place I'd ever heard of the Jesus and Mary Chain. For us, it was just funny, so we said yes." The headline inside declared them "the last great band of the century" (backhanded praise: the year was 1999, after all). The subhead? Only the Brits can come up with copy like this: "The band who ride with the Four Horsemen at the end of the world, the noise Nostradamus warned us about . . . let's get ready to rubble." An avalanche of further hyperbole from the writer followed. Though some of it is undeniably purple prose, it's hard to read the article without wanting to hear this band immediately.

There were two parts to the piece: one was a conventional profile with an interview conducted backstage in Glasgow featuring a lot of Menuck and a bit of Bryant and Girt chiming in. Menuck talked explicitly about building a mystery. "I remember being really happy trying to decode records when I was a teenager," he said. "There wasn't this wealth of information, just a photo of the band on the back maybe, a lyric sheet insert, whatever was on the cover, and bing-bang-boom-go, you're there yourself."

The second part was a collectively penned missive responding to follow-up questions attempting to chart the band's history and philosophy:

> we sell out in tiny ways every single day, in our own small mis-
> guided ways we contribute to the continuation of a state of affairs

that we find abhorrent . . . some decisions are easier to make than others; recently we were offered an obscene amount of money by an international banking conglomerate in exchange for the use of one of our songs in a television commercial . . . it's easy to say no to the devil's money when he makes blatant offers, it's harder coming to terms w/ the smaller ways we suck corporate cock everyday . . .

we know we're just the tiniest purple feather in a really obscene dogfuck burlesque show—WE KNOW THIS WE KNOW THIS WE KNOW THIS; we just wanna talk a little bit about architecture while the fat male stripper shoots pepsi bottles out of his asshole . . . is that so wrong?

And it all ends up like this, the sound of nine people confused and overwhelmed by the task at hand . . .

but there's gotta be happiness in confronting sadness and confusion . . . to us, the music we make isn't just about sadness, it's also about hope and endurance in the face of real economic and emotional adversity . . . we don't want to make music for people to wallow in . . . alls we can do is try hard to link our own struggle as a band w/ the music we play . . . they're inseparable, these two things . . . lately it's all we know . . .

Godspeed did not want to merge onto the expressway to success. That's not even a metaphor: in North America, the band invested in a blue mini school bus that maxed out at 90 kilometres per hour. "It was a nightmare," says Menuck. "It was always breaking down. We had a tour where we were endlessly being towed to the shows—which was kinda cool as an entrance, I gotta say. Half an hour after doors opened, people were lining up outside and this fucked-up school bus gets towed in, and all these Canadian weirdos pour out of it, hauling amps." It's not exactly Leonard Cohen entering a French festival on a white horse, but close. "Yeah!" he laughs. "I'd argue it's cooler."

En route to a big Chicago show with Kranky Records' other most popular artist, Low, the Godspeed bus broke down on the interstate, an hour out of town. The band arrived at the venue, Schubas, three hours late. "Of course, Low was outside," remembers Pezzente, "looking all disgruntled, thinking, This is the band we agreed to have open for us? It wasn't a good vibe." Venues on that tour ranged from regular clubs to the basement of a Chinese restaurant in Charlottesville, Virginia. Low themselves recall the tour, and Godspeed, more fondly. "They would destroy every venue, every night," the band tweeted in 2021. "Humiliating to have to follow, but what a great band and inspiring group of people to get to know."

The tour with Low was one of the only times Godspeed was an opening act. For a band with only one album and one EP, they were regularly playing three-hour shows. "We did that in France all the time, doing four encores of 15-minutes each," says Pezzente. "It's not like it was part of our contract. That's just how long we would play, playing in places where they'd pack people in like animals, and of course it would be overheating and after three hours of not moving and not drinking anything, they'd collapse."

Plans were made to record the new material in February 2000. In the meantime, the band was splintering. Not surprisingly, a nine-piece band that employs collective decision-making wasn't always the most satisfying creative outlet.

Drummer Aidan Girt already had Exhaust and 1-Speed Bike, his drum'n'bass-influenced solo project. Dave Bryant had started performing experimental tape pieces under the name Hiss Tracts, and he'd assembled a group of players from Godspeed's and Constellation's extended family to create Set Fire to Flames, which drew from the quieter improv passages of Bryant's primary band. Thierry Amar, Norsola Johnson and Mike Moya played in Scott Chernoff's slowcore band Molasses; Amar soon formed the avant-klezmer band Black Ox Orkestar with Sackville's Gabe Levine. And Mike Moya left the band to focus exclusively on his new solo project, Hrsta. He was replaced in Godspeed by Roger Tellier-Craig of Fly Pan Am, a pre-existing band that unfairly got tagged as a Godspeed "side project" for the rest of its career.

Most of those acts were primarily Montreal-only concerns. The most low-key of them all turned out to be the most prolific: A Silver Mt. Zion, which began as Menuck's chamber music project. "It was to do something quieter that I had a little more control over," he says. "My dog had died. I was trying to process that. I didn't want to do that by consensus. Me, Thierry and Sophie would get together, hungover, at the Hotel on Sunday afternoons and record on an eight-track. It was very social. I was craving that, where the process was a bit more domestic rather than antagonistic."

The only member of Godspeed who didn't have any extracurricular musical activities was Mauro Pezzente. He had something else on his mind entirely.

MONTREAL HAS LONG BEEN BLESSED with a plethora of stunning venues, many built early in the 20th century or earlier, many with two levels for balcony views. But they're all for 500 people or more. In the late '90s, those venues were the domain of the city's well-entrenched promoters, like Spectra, Gillett and original Montreal punks Greenland, the latter well positioned to serve the Lollapalooza generation. But many indie rock acts left Montreal off their tour routes entirely. There were few bookings in small to mid-sized venues for locals or new indie acts on tour; most bars were pay-to-play. Hence the need for ad hoc loft parties like those at the Hotel 2 Tango.

Mauro Pezzente and his partner, Kiva Stimac, had a long-term dream of moving out of the city and starting a restaurant: she was a cook and he loved to garden. "In this dream, music wasn't necessarily a part of it," he says. "But the more I toured, I liked the idea of having a place with a European vibe, where bands could stay and enjoy a meal, as opposed to this American vibe where they want you the heck out of there as quickly as possible."

A gallery and venue called Artishow, located on St. Laurent just south of St. Joseph, had been booking the kinds of shows Pezzente wanted to see. When he heard it was closing because the owner had racked up too much debt, he and Stimac jumped in. "We were both psyched to do it, but honestly we had no money," he says. Godspeed was doing somewhat well financially by this point; Menuck could finally afford to extract two teeth that had been rotting since he was 16.[1] But it's not like anyone in the band was building capital. Pezzente did have *access* to capital, however, from a Loblaws credit card he got as a 16-year-old grocer; that funded $10,000 of renovations on the space he reopened as Casa del Popolo (translation: house of the people).

Pezzente and Stimac signed Casa del Popolo's lease on May 1, 2000. There was a soft launch before getting their liquor licence in the summer, hosting shows already booked by Artishow. It was a bar and vegetarian café; the plan was to only have live music on weekends. Demand swelled immediately and it became seven days a week. Capacity was officially 150, but many more were often shoehorned into the room that steamed up pretty quickly during frigid Montreal winters. In March 2000, a new promotion company, Blue Skies Turn Black (which launched with a screening of a Fugazi documentary), focused on indie rock acts who usually bypassed Montreal and started booking lots of them into Casa (notably Spoon in 2002).

"The Casa opening felt very inauspicious," says Ian Ilavsky. "The city still felt like it was nowhereland—in a great way." Within six months, Pezzente started renting a 300-capacity hall across the street, La Sala Rossa. It was the second floor of the Spanish Cultural Centre, which housed a tapas restaurant downstairs and a room for tango dancers upstairs. (It was briefly home to the National Ballet School in the late '60s.) By the fall of 2001, he signed a long-term lease there, and the neighbourhood was now a live music destination. The combined effect was immediate. "Bands from outside Montreal could play at 'Godspeed's club,' which meant that people started routing their tours here," says Howard Bilerman, citing

---

1   Note to non-Canadians: our much-idealized health care system does not include dentistry.

the misconception that it was the band who owned the venue. "There were so many more shows to see when Sala Rossa opened. By extension, there were so many more opening slots to fill." A boon for local acts.

At the same time, Menuck and Amar had plans to turn the Hotel 2 Tango into a functioning commercial studio. They approached Bilerman, who had been operating in a building where his neighbours were subject to burglaries at gunpoint. Still, he was loath to leave the loft space he describes as "2,000 square feet, 20-foot ceilings, wood everywhere, in Old Montreal." When that building was condemned and he was evicted, Bilerman temporarily set up shop above Bagel Etc. on St. Laurent, the favourite haunt of nearby resident Leonard Cohen (on whose final recordings Bilerman worked, 15 years later). "I now had all this equipment but no real space," he says. "Thierry and Efrim had a real space, a 1,000-square-foot loft they could make noise in. We pooled what we had, soundproofed the walls and reinvested any money we made into new equipment. That's how I became part of the Hotel."

Constellation was also ramping up. Though they weren't making money off Godspeed CDs—which came out on Kranky—there was a not insignificant amount of vinyl being shipped. Ilavsky puts the CD to vinyl sales ratio at four to one, which for an international buzz act like Godspeed could add up. In February 2000, A Silver Mt. Zion put out their debut record, followed by Do Make Say Think's *Goodbye Enemy Airship the Landlord Is Dead* the next month. Southern Distribution asked Constellation for 5,000 CDs of each—a fivefold increase in what the label normally printed for a first run of decidedly non-commercial music. "That five-K number was the year the dial shifted," says Ilavsky. "Don and I also realized that year that we could afford to do this full-time and not do other things for money."

The flowchart of relations between Constellation acts created the type of media angle that music nerds everywhere love; Ilavsky himself admits to buying any record associated with Tortoise in the '90s. But he disputes the idea that Constellation was merely a clearing house for Godspeed projects. "It's true that actual members of Godspeed and their offshoots were always part of our story," he says. "But Hangedup, Fly Pan Am, Frankie Sparo—those were all distinct people. Roger [Tellier-Craig] played in Fly Pan Am and then got drafted into Godspeed; we started working with them before that happened. Eric [Craven] of Hangedup did time in A Silver Mt. Zion years later. But Hangedup weren't part of the Godspeed orbit back then. There was a feeling that we didn't want to do everything someone from Godspeed did." Bryant's Set Fire to Flames and drummer Bruce Cawdron's Esmerine are two examples. "We did have to have some strange conversations about managing the identity of the label at a certain point."

In the concentric circles around Godspeed, there was now a label, a venue and a studio—which had been part of the plan for Ian Ilavsky and Don Wilkie from the beginning. "Mauro grabbing the Casa felt awesome, that someone nabbed that space," says Ilavsky. "The gradual transition from the Hotel to a studio felt very organic; it was still Godspeed's rehearsal space as well. The whole thing was about seizing the means of production into our own hands. There was no part of Don or me that wanted to build an empire. We loved that a bunch of like-minded people were connected. It was not even clear at that point that Godspeed would be a juggernaut, but there was some momentum. People were making a bit of money from the band, and in Montreal at the time you didn't need much. And to the credit of all those people, they didn't think twice about taking that money and putting it back into infrastructure. That was an ethos, and many people deserve credit for sticking to that."

"Godspeed created an infrastructure that benefited themselves first and foremost," says Bilerman, "but secondarily all other acts associated with that band, and that record label, and their friends." But Bilerman says it's really easy to retroactively apply motive. "If things were different in Montreal and there were already clubs and artist-run recording studios, I don't know that any of that would necessarily have proliferated from Godspeed," he says. "It was equal amounts necessity and business acumen."

2000: THE YEAR GODSPEED BROKE. Their second album, a double record called *Lift Your Skinny Fists Like Antennas to Heaven*, didn't come out until November. But they toured extensively: twice through the U.S. (a West Coast swing brought them to Vancouver and Victoria for the first time), twice through the U.K., once through Europe and once to Japan, where they had dinner with Mitsuo Yanagimachi, the director of the band's namesake, the 1976 film *God Speed You! Black Emperor*. "We'd asked the promoter if they could get in touch with him," says Pezzente. "He'd never heard of us. He was an older guy. Very nice, traditional Japanese, very respectful. He was happy we used the name from the movie, but it was not a movie he was very fond of."

Audiences everywhere were rapturous—to the point of passing out. "They were such an overwhelming attack on all your senses and emotions," says Broken Social Scene's Kevin Drew, who saw Godspeed's first Toronto show at Symptom Hall in 1998. "They annihilated. It was so fucking loud. If you took acid or got high, people were just dropping like flies. I'd tell people, 'Watch how people just drop. That person there has five minutes.' There was a [2000] show at the Palais Royale, that was like, 'Oh! That person's down. Oh! There's another one. Get this guy some water! Get his grandmother on the phone, he wants to say sorry!' It was so intense but astonishingly beautiful."

On April 3, 2000, Godspeed played their biggest show ever, at London's Royal Festival Hall in front of 2,500 people. As with all shows on that tour, it opened with a recorded spoken-word monologue "dedicating the performance to quiet refusals" and to "every prisoner in the world," while noting that "Miss Céline Dion sings love songs while our cities burn . . . in these times, when everything is denied us, anything is possible."

They were touring Europe with Fly Pan Am. Sigur Rós had been added to a few dates. That Icelandic band—formed the same year as Godspeed and sharing a love for long loping epics with bowed guitars—was just starting to gain traction outside their native Iceland.

The night before the Festival Hall gig, all three bands played in Dublin—but only Godspeed had their van broken into. "A bunch of our bags were stolen, including passports," says Pezzente. "Then ferries were being cancelled because of a bad storm coming in. We stayed up all night trying to find our bags in a pouring rainstorm, walking up and down alleyways. We didn't find them. We went to the terminal at five a.m., got on the earliest ferry and showed up at the Royal Festival Hall three or four hours late, when doors had already opened." Sigur Rós, meanwhile, was flown to London by their record label. By the time the Canadians showed up, there was no time for all three bands to play. Sigur Rós's label pulled weight and Fly Pan Am got the shaft. "[Sigur Rós] were already going to be big, you could tell," says Pezzente. "Jónsi was already a rock star. To us, Fly Pan Am were a more important band than Sigur Rós was at the time. To this day, I'm pissed they didn't play." Sigur Rós, for what it's worth, publicly kvetched for years about Godspeed's three-hour soundchecks on that tour.

A similar dynamic took place at the All Tomorrow's Parties festival in the U.K. in 2002, when Godspeed were touring with Do Make Say Think. Every year ATP asked a high-profile musician to pick the majority of the bands; promoter Barry Hogan picked the rest. In 2002, the curator was Steve Albini, the renowned sound engineer, irascible gadfly and guitarist in Shellac. "There was always a weird dynamic at ATP, where the band would be the curator but Barry had veto power," says Menuck. "Barry was the one who invited us, and Albini wasn't happy about it. Do Make Say Think were on tour with us, and they couldn't just take three days off. So we gave them one hour of our [three-hour] set." In the weekend's program booklet, in the section with normally dry descriptions of each performer, Albini made it very clear that he wanted nothing to do with the Toronto band; he did, however, later work with the Montrealers. Curiously, despite Albini's grumbling, Do Make Say Think were included on the CD compilation commemorating that year's festival; Godspeed were not.

That same weekend, there was another dispute, this one about money. ATP ran the same lineup for two consecutive weekends and covered everyone's backline and flights to get there; in between the two weekends, artists would book other dates in the U.K. and Europe. Because of the way Godspeed's European tour was routed, they only played one of the weekends but were paid the same as everyone else, which did not go over well. An angry American bass player confronted them about it, which put a damper on the whole weekend. "I didn't really understand it," says Menuck. "Like, 'Why are these American bands who license their songs to car commercials busting our balls about what we're getting paid?' My reaction was that we should just give the money back. So we had this five-hour band meeting that was like *12 Angry Men*. When we finally came to a consensus, we gave the money back. It was the proudest I've ever felt in this band."

As Godspeed became popular, so did Sigur Rós and Explosions in the Sky, other largely instrumental bands making "orgasm rock"; one signed to a major label, and the other was happy to soundtrack *Friday Night Lights*, a film about American football. (Godspeed had turned down a similar request from director Oliver Stone, who wanted their music for his football film *Any Given Sunday*.) Godspeed's music did, however, appear in Danny Boyle's zombie film *28 Days Later*—but not on the official soundtrack. The band made it known that they'd only agreed because Boyle pitched it to them as an indie film; it was later bought by Universal. At one point, U.K. electronic label Warp Records offered them a lot of money to sign. Godspeed's dedication to its principles—at a time when "selling out" was no longer an insult—got them tagged with the most vacant slur in music criticism: pretentious.

"I hate it when I get pedantic," laughs a self-aware Menuck, "but at the time I was like, 'Dude! To be pretentious means to have a *pretense*! We don't have any pretense!' It drove me crazy, you know?! 'You're just saying you don't like it because the song titles are long!' It drove us all up the wall. In the community we were a part of, we were [considered] a pop band. And it still is that way. We're sort of stuck in the middle. We've never put anything in the world that we thought would alienate anyone.

"As far as we were concerned, the avant-garde had already happened," he continues. "The great frontier had been breached. Anyone who wants to make music can do whatever the fuck they want, and it's not going to be a formal experiment—people already got their asses kicked establishing those things. We always looked at it like, 'This is liberating. You can do whatever you want in the service of whatever it is you're trying to do.' That's why we were never concerned with song lengths. That was never a statement; it was more like, 'Well, we don't have to do any of that stuff. *Nobody* has to.'"

Godspeed had a prickly reputation that often overshadowed the music—at least in the media, who took it as a personal insult that the band refused to engage in traditional games. Godspeed's success proved that a powerful live show and mystique could sell the product without having to explain or justify any decisions, musical or otherwise, to inquiring journalists who assumed the band was populated by one-dimensional, misanthropic Marxists.

"There's a lot of negative baggage around us that we're always having to work through," says Menuck, in an extreme understatement. "We're conscious of it. But this is a group of very funny people; half the time we spend together is just being jackasses and laughing. We didn't feel any confusion that you could be a goof and also an anticapitalist. From the community we were a part of, that was the most natural thing in the world. We also made the choice to speak by committee, and that type of approach leads to a certain type of language—I get that. That was funny to us, too, to be making these statements as if we were the subcommittee for agrarian reform for the 45th meeting of the politburo, right?"

It was easier to just say no—to almost everything. Things were working well with the professional relationships they already had. Nothing the straight world had to offer seemed remotely appealing, especially media coverage. That was the Constellation ethos as well. "In the early years we would literally hang up the phone if *Rolling Stone* magazine called," says Ilavsky. "I'm not proud to say that we may even have laughed out loud. We were clearly not frontline activists, but we were very much in the antiglobalization movement in Montreal at that time, since the early '90s. Things were principled and combative. There was an arch exchange with *Exclaim!* at a certain point."

The "exchange" involved an *Exclaim!* writer assigned to write about Godspeed in advance of their highly anticipated third record, 2002's *Yanqui U.X.O.* The writer contacted the label several times to receive an advance copy and tried to set up an interview in Montreal. Seems innocent. Constellation politely stonewalled, forwarded the request to the band, who put it off, and six weeks later the writer still hadn't heard a yes or a no. He went to Montreal anyway and attempted to talk to people in Godspeed circles. Left with little information, he penned what journalists call a "write-around," which ended up describing what he called his Kafkaesque experience. Not surprisingly, he got some facts wrong—because no one in the band would talk to him or respond to multiple emails.

A week after the article was published, Constellation posted a 5,500-word response to the 750-word article, reprinting the writer's emails and lampooning him mercilessly for the audacity to request a promo copy and an interview. "You are filled to the ears with shit," it railed. "Guess you should just climb to the top of the mountain and have a brooding existential picture taken of yourself . . . We make no apologies for the hurt feelings of spoiled media brats and their arch sense of entitlement." It got much worse from there. The response ran on the front page of Constellation's website for about a year; if someone wanted to learn anything about the music on the label, they had to click past it.

Menuck, while frustrated by the *Exclaim!* piece, clarifies that the band did not write the response; Constellation did. "Jesus Christ," laughs Ilavsky, when reminded of this. "I'll own all of that, needless to say. I cringe a bit looking back at it. I remember [the response] being humorous, taking the piss out of ourselves and the way the industry works. It was definitely no-holds-barred. We were shooting ourselves in the foot. We didn't ingratiate ourselves very much. Look," he sighs, "at the time, we were obnoxious. Our ethos was: there's no need for all these middle people. Of course, that's stupidly disrespectful to a lot of genuine people, from tour bookers to publicists to managers.

"For the first five, six years, we just wanted to put our heads down and not say anything about what we do or how we do it," Ilavsky continues. "We were just going to let our actions speak for themselves to the people that mattered to us, which was the artists we worked with and anyone else we came into contact with. There were unsympathetic politics around not journalists per se but corporate media. *Exclaim!* probably didn't deserve that—but it is a bit of a rag, let's face it, and it needs to butter its bread by taking advertising from who it can. We've advertised [with them] since. We've made nice."

With those kind of relationships, reviews of *Yanqui U.X.O.* were mixed. Part of that was likely media fatigue with a band who perceived them as the enemy. Part of it was high expectations. Part of it was inevitable when a band has musical formulas they either fall into or try to resist. And with the Iraq War coinciding with the album's release, the anarchists in Godspeed were touring America at one of the most politically volatile times in its history.

While on tour in Oklahoma, the members of Godspeed looked fishy enough—scraggly hippies, foreign accent, not Anglo-Saxon, possibly Middle Eastern—that a woman at a gas station called the FBI to report them as suspected terrorists. The local cops showed up first, pointed guns at the band and told them not to move until the feds arrived. After being held for questioning and background checks, they were free to go. That night on stage in Columbia, Missouri, Menuck told the story, and it made its way to the press, including *Pitchfork*. Michael Moore even mentioned the incident in one of his bestselling anti-Bush books. It wasn't the only troubling incident on the tour.

"We were playing First Avenue in Minneapolis the night that bombs started dropping in Iraq," says Menuck. "We had a little portable radio in the tiny backstage room. We were anxious about this happening. We played the show, came out for an encore and Aidan took the mic. He was gentle and nice to this American audience. But I was pissed off, because this whole tour, after the shows, people would say [about Bush], 'Yeah, well, you know, he's not my president.' That was driving me crazy. [That night in Minneapolis] I stood up and said, 'It doesn't matter whether or not you think that's your president; those are your bullets and your bombs.' Then this entire room full of people started booing. For years after, any time A Silver Mt. Zion rolled through Minneapolis, someone would come up to me after the show and be like, 'That's so fucked up that you did that.' We never figured out how to speak to people in the Godspeed context, and that was frustrating."

After a year and a half touring *Yanqui*, the band held a meeting at drummer Bruce Cawdron's apartment in the fall of 2004. "For me and a couple of others," says Pezzente, "we thought the meeting was going to be about how we would move forward. It turned out most of the people in the band didn't want to be in the band anymore. I was like, 'Okay, I didn't know it was that bad! But if it *is* that bad, we'll see you later and we'll talk then.' Roger [Tellier-Craig] had already mentioned to us that he was out because he was tired. He had joined the band later on, and was definitely a full band member, but what we were doing wasn't fully in his heart. He didn't want to play guitar-based music anymore.

"The way our band works," he continues, "we always have to have this dialogue and discuss what we're doing. It's tiring. It's energy-consuming. Even now, after having a three-hour argument about something, I question, 'Why are we doing this?! It'd be so much easier as a trio.' So after years of playing too many long tours, seven of the other nine people thought it was time to take a break. Which was great. At the time, we didn't have any new songs, and there weren't any ideas about what we were going to do. So if anyone had ideas, great, let's do it, but if we don't, let's just take a break."

Everyone turned to their side projects—except Pezzente. "My heart's always been in Godspeed, and Godspeed has always been in my heart," he says. "I honestly never had any desire to play music outside of the band. When we stopped playing, I just didn't feel like it and I was so busy with Casa and Sala. I had been playing music with those people for my entire adult life, which wasn't that long, but the idea of getting into a room and jamming with someone else was scary to me."

Meanwhile, A Silver Mt. Zion became a busy touring act, promoting four records between 2000 and '05 and another three in the next decade. Menuck was emerging into more of a frontman and vocalist interested in communicating directly with the audience. Initially, A Silver Mt. Zion was booked into soft-seat venues, suiting the chamber-music vibe of the first record. "It was a lot of pressure for what we were doing, which is—we didn't even know what we were doing, really," he says. "We did one tour that was terrible, then we had this revelation that we should just be a fucking bar band. Let's play loud and be happy in a shitty room with a low ceiling. For me, that's when the band started to become good."

Joining A Silver Mt. Zion from 2003 to '08 was Ian Ilavsky on bass and guitar, who finally got to realize his rock'n'roll dreams of touring the world with friends.

Back in the office, Constellation finally hired a part-time bookkeeper, as well as local character Fluffy Erskine as full-time warehouse manager. The loss of Godspeed as an active financial anchor didn't faze Ilavsky. "I don't remember us really worrying or having strategic conversations about what we'd do without this juggernaut," he says. "For sure, Godspeed sold piles of records, but even with *Skinny Fists* we didn't have [rights to] the CD. While we were keeping those records in print as fast as we could make them, the margins were tiny. And the money-makers for us were quite diverse, spread across Do Makes and Mt. Zion. But even Frankie Sparo on CD sold 5,000. Sandro Perri sold thousands. Everything was still selling."

Menuck and Amar also turned their attention to the Hotel, which was being evicted from the auto shop loft. Pooling resources with Bilerman and Constellation, as well as mastering engineer Harris Newman, they bought a building across the street on Van Horne in 2005. Now maîtres chez nous, they truly answered to no one. They still went to the nearby tracks to flatten pennies to insert into every vinyl copy of *F# A# ∞*.

AFTER FIVE YEARS OF SILENCE, there was some mumbling and talk of a reunion. Godspeed slowly reconvened around 2009—around the same time Menuck and A Silver Mt. Zion violinist Jessica Moss had a child—and decided to see what happened after a few practices. Cellist Norsola Johnson opted out; original guitarist Mike Moya opted back in. They gave their European agent, Dirk Hugsam, a heads-up. Soon afterwards, they got an offer from Barry Hogan and All Tomorrow's Parties to curate the December 2010 festival in the U.K. "That was the impetus," says Pezzente. "We wanted to do this, and now we had an offer and something to work toward, an end goal."

They assembled a festival lineup, which included original inspirations such as the Dead C, the Ex and Mike Watt; Canadians NoMeansNo, the Sadies and Tim Hecker; Constellation artists Hangedup, Sam Shalabi's Land of Kush. Oh—and "Weird Al" Yankovic. People assumed the latter was some kind of ironic joke, but it wasn't. "The reason we asked him is complicated and personal," Menuck told *Exclaim!* (yes, that *Exclaim!*). "It was the request of one person in the band for a really beautiful and private reason." Yankovic told the magazine that the ATP date enabled him to book his first-ever European tour.

Godspeed continued playing short runs of shows in the next two years, while secretly recording an album that dropped in 2012: *'Allelujah! Don't Bend! Ascend!* The response was overwhelming. "It exceeded our expectations on sales immediately," says Ilavsky. It reached six figures within six months. "Massive amounts of vinyl—vinyl that we completely underpriced. I'm proud we did that. The band knew that record sales were not going to butter their bread. Playing live was where they'd make their money, and they were doing the festival circuit for the first time, deciding on the lesser of various evils. They weren't sweating small stuff." They played Coachella. They toured with Nine Inch Nails in corporate venues. They printed T-shirts for the first time.

'*Allelujah* was shortlisted for the Polaris prize the next year; the band sent Chicago journalist Jessica Hopper to the gala as a proxy. Her speech, in its entirety, went like this: "Godspeed You! Black Emperor have chosen not to be here tonight. They wouldn't be Godspeed if they had. They've spent the last 20 years defying convention as well as our expectations of what it means to be in a band. In the process, they've shown us exactly what kind of career you can have when you decide to say no." Mic drop, exit stage.

When the album won later that night, a shocked Ilavsky accepted graciously on the band's behalf, thanked those who champion independent music and said the band would donate the $30,000 in prize money to music programs for prisoners in Quebec (which proved harder to do than they'd thought). The next day, Godspeed released a statement. They didn't refuse the prize—which people assumed they would and which revisionist history seems to have forgotten. They did, however, call into question the nature of the award itself, while being careful to praise the underpaid freelance journalists who comprise the majority of the Polaris jury. Unlike past Godspeed rants, this one managed to be gracious more than grating—though few in the media saw it that way. Journalists largely reacted like Godspeed took a shit on the table at Christmas dinner. The music industry's crybaby complaints about Godspeed only proved the band's points.

That day, Vancouver singer-songwriter Geoff Berner, who has no direct connection to the band, posted online: "It seems like any time any lefty makes any statement in the public square, it's always accused of 'hypocrisy.' Environmentalists who ride cars to demonstrations are hypocrites. Musicians who participate in a flawed music biz are hypocrites when they point out flaws. Basically, it seems, the choice is either go along with everything, or stay out of the public square completely. Otherwise, you're a hypocrite. Either be a cheerleader, or be silent. Great."

The website Weird Canada tweeted: "It takes a lot of conviction to do the things that Godspeed does. It's easy to write it off, or trivialize what they do. [So] don't."

CHAPTER 4
DON'T BE CRUSHED

THE CAUTIONARY BALLAD OF
HAWKSLEY WORKMAN

Many of the stories in this book are about artists who arrived with no expectations. Who made records in unconventional ways, found success through word of mouth. Who leapfrogged past local success to an international audience. Corporate machinations may or may not have been involved. For most, that trajectory worked out well—especially if they operated outside mainstream channels to begin with. But Hawksley Workman went from being an indie sensation to diving into the belly of the beast, did it all first, did it to the extreme, and then crashed back to Earth.

━━━━━━━

MYSTERY WAS THE appeal of Hawksley Workman by design, starting with the name: it was constructed from his maternal grandparents' surnames. He didn't tell anyone in Toronto he came from Huntsville, Ontario, a town of 20,000 near southwestern Algonquin Park. In the lead-up to the release of his 1999 album, *For Him and the Girls*, he placed classified ads in the personals section of Toronto weekly *Now* and queer weekly *Xtra*, poetically detailing his love for a lovely mermaid named Isadora. The ads were then adapted into cheap posters he put on telephone poles downtown—with no mention of a gig, the album or a hint that it had anything to do with a musician. Just random bursts of hopelessly romantic poetry illuminating a cold urban existence.

"When I moved to Toronto in 1994," he says, "I couldn't believe that anyone would give a shit about what I was doing if it didn't come from something that looked like it had fallen to Earth from space. 'Here comes a guy from Huntsville, Ontario!' It's like, Womp-womp, who cares? If something is not fascinating, it's not interesting to me. I just wanted to be fascinating."

His early life in Huntsville *was* fascinating, however—if only to the people of Huntsville. His young parents attended a United Church where their son sat in on piano when the organist was sick. His mother, a painter, and his father, an amateur drummer, encouraged his artistic pursuits. By 14 he was a public-speaking champion and taught piano and drums to the children of his schoolteachers. He quit high school to tour with a United Church musical for six months, while his parents were getting divorced. He was overweight, nerdy and obsessed with David Bowie, Chick Corea and Bauhaus. "I always dreamed of being skinny enough to be a true goth," he says. "I went to school with kids who were really cool. I wasn't cool. I went deep into my own thing and then built a persona to reflect that. I was a phenom in my town. 'Can you believe he's this good? He's only 14.' But I could smell it coming: nobody will ever say, 'Can you believe he's this good? He's only 24.' Coming from a small town, I wasn't wired for success. All I wanted was to be weird."

Toronto is a magnet for weirdos like Spookey Ruben, an oddball pop artist often pegged as a next big thing in the mid-'90s, after signing with the label that broke Nine Inch Nails. Workman loved Ruben's debut, *Modes of Transportation Vol. 1.* "I just couldn't believe the inventiveness; it was like Jane Siberry's *Bound by the Beauty*," he says. "When he was putting his second record together, he hired me and Jason Beck [later known as Chilly Gonzales] to be his rhythm section, at his studio at Carlaw and Dundas. He had somehow found hundreds of Max Headroom pillowcases, and the whole studio was soundproofed with these things. We had long days there. We'd run a tune and get a song sounding good, and then Spookey would say, 'Okay, let's make the bridge the chorus and vice versa.' I'm 19 years old and my mind is blowing up. I'd already given up on songwriting because I wasn't as good as Bruce Cockburn. I figured that out when I was 17."

Ruben's career soon hit some bumps, with his follow-up album released only in Japan. Workman then drummed for Jason Collett's band Bird, as well as for John Southworth, another exceptionally talented freak ill-suited for the Canadian pop landscape. "Just by accident, I started drumming with some of Toronto's greatest songwriters right out of the gate," he says. "I could sit back and watch them make mistakes—business mistakes. I never invited friends to my shows in the early days, because I knew you couldn't tell if your career was growing or not if the same 14 people keep coming. You couldn't tell if it was reaching ears past your friends and family." He was also gigging with the hip-hop/rock act BTK as a drummer, "but I ended up playing everything on their record, including horns," he says.

Workman eventually felt ready to write his own songs. Many were written on any piano he could find: at universities, in empty hotel ballrooms or in the basements of churches he'd join just long enough to be trusted to be left alone there. He found an apartment on Hillsdale Avenue, near Yonge and Eglinton, owned by a friend's grandmother who taught ballet in Austria most of the year. He was paying $200 a month and turned the basement into a studio where he made his first album, *Before We Were Security Guards*. That album started circulating through his Southworth and Collett connections, and he soon had work recording Skydiggers, Kevin Drew, Brendan Canning, the Cash Brothers and Paul MacLeod. At a time when studios were charging $3,000 a day, Workman charged "$100 a song: produced, recorded, mixed and out the door. The typical record I would make would cost $1,000. I'd play any instruments that weren't already covered. I was really trying to over-compress drums and doing things quickly—and no one could argue with the price tag. You'd leave with a fascinating-sounding record in a day. The idea of recording in a basement was starting to catch on.

"It exposed me to a lot of people," he continues. "Andrew Cash would come by my studio and that was a big deal to me. He'd come in once a week. He told me, 'Your problem is that you do too many things. You need to figure out the best thing you can do, otherwise you'll end up like [Rheostatics'] Martin Tielli.' I think Martin's a phenom, so even if I ended up a little bit like that guy it wouldn't be too bad." Andrew Cash's manager (and then wife) Sandy Pandya—who made her name with the Waltons, the Lowest of the Low and Hayden—signed Workman as a client in 1997.

Before We Were Security Guards is very much the sound of a young songwriter, albeit one steeped in the Bacharach style of John Southworth and the classic Canadian folk sound of Jason Collett as well as Workman's childhood influences, like Bowie. He barely pressed any copies, and everything about the record was merely a warm-up for his formal introduction to the world: *For Him and the Girls*.

"Singing is about sexual confidence," he sings on "Paper Shoes," and much of *Girls* is about the shy kid maturing into a sexual adult. Much of it was fantasy; the carnal "Tarantulove" was written about a neighbour's loud sex life, not his own. "I wrote about places I'd never been and sexual experiences I'd never had," he says. "I was such a good boy who was raised to do well. When I quit high school, all my teachers were on board with it. I wasn't rebellious, I was just a high-achieving kid who wore out. I didn't party. I didn't have sexual adventures. All I had was this fantasy that I made in order to get a foothold into something that felt interesting to me."

The first track, "Maniacs," opens with the absurd sound of Workman yodelling over a busy drum beat and a droning, distorted organ, before he breaks into an operatic howl. It's the kind of track likely to make programmers and reviewers turn it off immediately. Their loss: there awaits killer pop songs like "No Sissies" and "Bullets," gorgeous ballads like "Don't Be Crushed" and "Baby This Night," and the swoony road-trip country song "Safe and Sound." For much of the album, he sounds like a horny, unhinged Rufus Wainwright, or Martin Tielli dropped into a modern-day Weimar cabaret. Whatever it was, it was an astounding and unique debut.

With Pandya as his manager, Workman's marketing ideas came to fruition. "I had no game for the business at all," he says. "She put those ideas into overdrive. The classifieds were my idea, but Sandy made all this stuff happen." There were weekly residencies at Graffiti's in Kensington Market, the Jane Bond in Waterloo and the Black Mustard in Guelph. Workman looked sharp in a dishevelled suit and ascot with wild curly hair, playing up his flamboyant stage personality. He concocted fictions, such as claiming he studied tap dancing in England, stories that journalists printed verbatim.

Rob Zifarelli, a young agent at the Paquin Agency, landed him a slot opening a Canadian tour for Violent Femmes in the spring of 2000. It was not a high point in that band's career—their last hit had been eight years prior. "This was kind of a failed comeback, but there were still 2,000 people a night coming to see them play 'Blister in the Sun,'" says Workman. "Those guys hated being on stage together. They were funny-looking and old. I was cute, young, energetic and glad to be there. I was selling hundreds of records a night on that tour. I went west with them and then back east on my own. By that point there were already a couple hundred people coming out to my shows, just from that Femmes thing."

At SXSW in 1999, a U.K. Americana label called Loose signed him to a deal, which led to a two-page spread in *Mojo* magazine—something unheard of for a new Canadian artist of any stripe, other than maybe Rufus Wainwright. In France, *For Him and the Girls* came out on Recall, which had distribution through Universal France. "The French make their own cultural decisions," he says. "If you get a great review in *Mojo*, you'll be able to sell a couple hundred tickets in Paris, for sure. But the French had a way of playing by their own rulebook when it came to what they were going to champion."

Back home, Workman recorded *(Last Night We Were) The Delicious Wolves* in his basement studio. It doesn't sound like it: lead single "Striptease" was monstrous, fuzzy glam-rock leaping out of speakers. "That record was largely done on eight-track and then mixed on something I'd never heard of at the time, called Pro Tools," he says. "Being on the radio was absurd, because it wasn't a goal of mine. It was a miracle."

Pandya had secured distribution through Universal Music Canada, which was by no means a guarantee that the major label would invest in promotion; it usually means little more than making it easier for stores to order an album. But as is often the case, it only takes one person in the right department at the right time. "Meghan Symsyk was a young, energetic woman working at Universal in the promo dept who flipped out on 'Striptease' and took it upon herself to make it a hit," Workman says. "She went way beyond what was required. She forced that into being, and it happened."

Because of that single, Hawksley Workman arrived on mainstream Canada's musical radar in the spring of 2001 like an alien being: a snarling sexual creature clad in feather boas, eyeliner and tight suits who played all the instruments on his album and sang like Freddie Mercury. Workman quickly gained a lot of young female fans—not that common in indie rock. "Because of 'Tarantulove' off the first record, there was a lot of spider imagery," he says. "A lot of lush, red, feathery, felt sex-den kind of stuff to prop up that character. I had people building sets for me back then, as one-offs for single Toronto shows. We'd get the club the day before so we could build these sets, like a wall of big spiders made out of papier mâché, and it would be a big deal."

In conservative Toronto, this was just not done. *Now* music critic Kim Hughes sought to expose the man behind the mask. "She put an ad in the Huntsville paper that basically said, 'I need people to call me and tell me who this kid actually is.' She was treating it as an exposé," says Workman. "Then my real name came out. My cover was blown. It's Canada, and someone is going to reveal how I'm doing the trick. It's hard to not be Robert Zimmerman in Canada. We don't buy that shit. I knew I was up against a lot by trying to create that thing out of thin air, and that it would be debunked from the get-go."

No matter. France was calling. "There were gigs there, and the French label was fucking energized," he says. "I played almost exclusively in Roman coliseums the summer I was getting famous in France, in Arles, all that. I played the Nîmes coliseum with David Bowie. The lady at the little local paper thought that *I* was David Bowie, so she wrote this review of me. I was built to win in those contexts back then. It was easy for me to walk on stage in front of 10,000 to 15,000 people, and I had an agent with the power to put me in those contexts. I would get off an airplane, hear my song; get in a cab, hear my song; go to a restaurant, hear my song. That happened for a year and a half in that country. It was nuts. I was too young to know it was extraordinary, what was going on."

The second single was the lyrically unsubtle "Jealous of Your Cigarette," accompanied by a video by Sean Michael Turrell that cost $10,000 for a one-shot romp featuring Workman and three male backing dancers strolling through an alley in Kitchener, Ontario. "I did not want it to be a one-shot video," says Workman. "I thought that would make it [look] low-budget. Sean convinced me that it would really, really work. I didn't believe it." It took off all over Europe. "Russia, Poland, Turkey—all the places that my record company liked to remind me didn't report sales, and not to expect any money."

America was a different story. *For Him and the Girls* had come out on hip New York label Ba Da Bing!, later known for launching the band Beirut. "My big New York showcase was to be September 11, 2001. That night I was going to play in front of all the Universal affiliates. My band was in NYC that morning already." Workman was stuck on a tarmac when the World Trade Center fell. "That rattled me from ever returning to the U.S." Instead, he made plans to move to Paris a few weeks later. It put him in a reflective mood.

"I was confounded by [9/11] being sold to us as a religious war," says the performer who had once been deeply involved in the United Church. "I was looking at my devout stance and feeling embarrassed about it." He was in Paris as his career was taking off, as the days were getting colder. "I was thinking about my grandma, and everything she gave to me in terms of storytelling and kookiness and wildness, while trying to reckon with the fact she always tried to make Christmas so special. I was trying to divorce anything Christian from Christmas and be comfortable with anything that was secular, lovely, warm and familial, that I could celebrate with my grandma in mind."

He quickly wrote and recorded eight new songs in seven days. *Almost a Full Moon* was manufactured and released a month later. The album struck an immediate chord—not just in 2001. For years afterwards, Workman performed it on seasonal tours; there was also both a children's book and a musical developed from it. *Almost a Full Moon* guaranteed him generations of CBC Radio listeners—at the very least, *The Vinyl Café* listeners, who are even more loyal. "That record has an astonishing life of its own," he says. "I wasn't thinking back then, 'Ho ho ho, I'm going to be making one of the few valuable Christmas records out there.' I understand 20 years on that that's kind of what it became. It's only because it was authentic. It wasn't 'Santa, Come Spank Me!' or whatever. It wasn't derivative, because it didn't come from any commercial impetus. It was an honest, starving 23-year-old kid who wanted to make sure his grandma was properly celebrated before she died."

Speaking of starving: "I was starving myself a lot back then to be as skinny as I possibly could, knowing full well that the brand archetype of a rock star is that tragically thin, tragically hairy and dirty thing," he admits. "I wanted so badly to live out that confidence narrative. I went from chubby kid to zitty teenager to a guy who's losing his hair at 22. I could not fucking win! But I was pretty for about a year and a half—and I milked it."

He's hesitant to call what he had anorexia, but admits that he "would fast for weeks leading up to photo shoots. Even when I wrote the Christmas record, I just needed to keep myself busy, so I got a piano in my apartment and didn't eat. It was crazy, really, the pressure I put on myself back then because of what I thought was needed. Beauty still sells rock'n'roll. Rock'n'roll is a hairstyle before it's music. Back then, I thought my career would be made or broken on my skinniness and my ability to sell myself as beautiful. In France I won 'sexiest man of the year' in some magazine, alongside Monica Bellucci as sexiest woman. That was an amazing moment. I see now how much of the artifice was the fantasy of being admired physically."

The momentum in France finally convinced Universal Canada to sign Workman directly, instead of just distributing him. The label's Allan Reid claims they'd been interested in making a deal for a while, but Workman says, "Universal had passed on me three times at that point. It was only because Universal was owned by Vivendi, which was a French company, and I was hanging out with movie stars in France. The head of Vivendi was a flamboyant guy who literally called [Universal Canada president] Randy Lennox up in the middle of the night and said, 'This Workman character, we've got a lock on him, right?' Suddenly I had a deal within a week. There was a big team assembled around me. None of this was in my plan—I just wanted to do my own thing. It was a co-release with Island Records U.K." Universal Canada had had recent U.K., U.S. and Australian success with the pop band soulDecision; they were hoping Workman would be next, with the help of international partners.

Workman's fourth album, *Lover/Fighter*, was considerably more conventional than anything he'd done. Most of his rough edges were smoothed off. Lead single "We Will Still Need a Song" sounded a lot like U2's records at the time. Before the Killers came along a year later, that was still verboten. "There's definitely a U2 guitar part in that song, and I have that big voice; they were a big band for me," he says. "The problem is that U2 is so unloved by British critics to begin with that anything that sounds like them opens you up to problems. I have that same off-putting, Bono-type earnestness—'love me, love me'—that people from a punk aesthetic absolutely hate. I like pop music. I like big things. I like people showing off. That was what I was raised on."

He insists there was no external pressure to mould himself into something more palatable; that was all self-imposed. "Universal didn't tell me to do anything. I had a big studio with a big mixing console and a huge budget, and I made a record that had a lot of U2-type sounds involved. I look back and think, Why didn't I just stick with the eight-track? My U.K. A&R guy was dating a girl in Quebec, and he was flying in quite frequently and kept telling me to check out Beck's *Sea*

Change. That's all he would ever say. He only did that to use his travel allowance to see his girlfriend and then have a one-day meeting with me. He wasn't really invested. Meanwhile, my agent said, 'You do the love song thing so good, why not just do a James Blunt thing?' For fuck's sake! That wasn't who I was.

"A lot of bands do this thing: they know they've been given keys to the machine that will give them access to the world. I was drinking enough wine at the time to not feel the true weight of that. There was an enormous amount of pressure on me to deliver something that people could sell. I had the kind of career where I was a phenom on stage: 'Look at that guy! Look at him go!' But my career was a litany of people around me saying, 'But if you just did *this*, if you just adjusted *this*, if you were less like *this* and more like *that*.' I listened to that for 10 or 12 years. Everyone wanted me to win, but they wanted me to change. That was the narrative of my career.

"Even Universal Canada, their head of radio insisted, against everybody in that building who thought we should lead with 'Smoke Baby,' said, 'No, we're going with "Anger as Beauty."' The week that went to radio was the same week that Billy Talent's 'Try Honesty' went to radio. I called Universal and said, 'We are fucked. Have you heard this? That's real rock music. My thing is pretending to be rock music.' I mean, 'Try Honesty' is one of the greatest rock songs to ever come out of Canada. I was fucked and I knew it. But [the radio head] was a young guy and his dad worked in the industry and there was a lot of bravado: 'You sit back and watch, Hawk, I'm gonna make this thing work.' It was a fucking flop. The label's narrative was, 'Well, once you come from indie rock, you can never cross back over.' It was really rudimentary thinking."

Lover/Fighter, released in October 2003, came close to going gold in Canada; it was actually certified as such years later, in 2020. "I wasn't a natural fit [at Universal], and they were goaded into [the deal]," says Workman. "They put a huge amount of money into Quebec, believing, like silly Anglos, that massive success in France will translate in Quebec—which it didn't in any way. The only time I've ever played for one person was that year in Sherbrooke, Quebec. It was also the only time I've ever played high—I figured that was the night to do it."

The album fell short of French expectations as well, and by 2004 the writing was on the wall—and there was a new Canadian phenom in Paris. "Universal had a big industry showcase at the Olympia, which is like the Massey Hall of Paris. I had played there three times. Leslie Feist was playing this [label] showcase, with Jason Beck [Chilly Gonzales]. I remember hearing that me and the other person performing were going to be flushed down the toilet, and that they were going to put all their money on Leslie Feist. I remember that gut punch, like, 'Yeah, it's over now. You're out.' *Lover/Fighter* was a disappointment for people over and over, because they put so much into it."

That same spring, Workman woke up deaf after a show in Paris. "One ear was very quiet, and the other frighteningly quiet. I went to the hospital in Dijon. It was messed up. This was back when I was drinking fairly heavily. The tour was costing me $50,000 a week to be on the road. I knew that blowing out shows would be very expensive. All the touring team was uncomfortable around me. We sat in Dijon for days while I tried to figure out what was going to happen. There was so much pressure because this thing was really happening. I pulled the plug, one week away from the tour being done. A lot of bridges were burned.

"I was supposed to go on tour with Bowie through northern Europe that summer. He had a heart attack and never toured again. This is how music careers are made and broken: timing. It's one of the biggest things you can't control in this business. You only get momentum once. My relationship with Sandy started to splinter, Universal was losing faith. That 'show must go on' thing will destroy you. I got home, Bowie had his heart attack and that's it. It was a shit sandwich that all happened at once."

His next record was a retreat: the stripped-down, largely acoustic piano album *Treeful of Starling*, released in 2006. "The company hated that record and didn't want to release it," says Workman. "Allan Reid went to bat for me. He was a true-to-life, artist-friendly A&R guy, probably to his detriment. The whole company had a collective sigh of dismay. Now it's probably my biggest record for people who've continued to follow me all these years—that's their go-to record. It's a special record." In 2008, he released two full-lengths on Universal, *Between the Beautifuls* and *Los Manlicious*, before being dropped. He continued to be distributed by them for two more albums released in 2010, *Meat* and *Milk*. He's been an indie artist ever since.

"I considered not being in the world," he admits. "Because all I have is what I do. It's terrifying for me to consider it not being around. That's when I started making two records a year, I doubled down on my touring, and the more the label wanted to forget about me, the more I wanted to stay active. I can't be angry or mad about how things did or didn't work out with Universal. It was an incredible honeymoon but a dreadful marriage. I never should have been on a major label. I'm not built for that kind of thing. But to everybody around me, I was the next big thing and was such a convincing player within that. It all felt like mania.

"I built a thing honestly and worked through a lot of uphill struggles. I had money thrown at me, I was on TV, I won a Juno, I had videos that were absolutely everywhere. What 'Striptease' and 'Jealous' did for my career is immeasurable. [But with] *Lover/Fighter* I went from hero to zero in the course of 14 months. I struggle with understanding the coulda/wouldas around that.

"People only see the final result of someone whose timing was impeccable, who didn't get sick when it was time for the big show or whatever. The other parts of the career—the devastation and humiliation with only occasional glimpses of wins, it's such a bizarre thing to commit to. When people ask me for advice, for their nephew or whatever, I sound old and grumpy. It's like the Jay-Z lyric: 'This is the life I chose, or, rather, the life that chose me.' If that's not true for you, you don't belong here. It's an ugly place. Whatever you think that dream is, it isn't. You have to want this thing in your kidneys. It's not like, 'I gotta get famous,' it's 'I gotta do this.' If you don't have that, you won't survive it."

CHAPTER 5

SECOND ACTS AND '90S SURVIVORS

THE WEAKERTHANS, SARAH HARMER, JOEL PLASKETT, DANKO JONES

"There were no second acts in American lives." That line from F. Scott Fitzgerald's "My Lost City" is oft misunderstood to mean that there are no comebacks, that one's fate is sealed, with no second chance. Instead Fitzgerald was referring to the narrative arc of a three-act play: the beginning, the plateau and the climax—be it celebratory or tragic. American life moves too fast, he was saying; the gap between original promise and ultimate fate is narrow at best.

"If anything," wrote critic Jillian Goodman, "both Fitzgerald's writing and his life show us that there are infinite chances, endless do-overs, that the American mind has no choice but to forge ahead, trying, trying again . . . Fitzgerald's idea was that there are no true endings—but rather that what's wrapped up with a bow is only waiting to come undone; our stories are constantly unfolding, scene after scene."

In the early 2000s, critic Carl Wilson took this trope to a different level, invoking the false starts of many a Canadian career, when reviewing Joel Plaskett's third solo record for the *Globe and Mail*: "It may be just as useful a fiction to propose that in Canadian lives, there are no first acts."

Either way, there definitely *are* second acts in Canadian music. Artists whose initial bands flamed out, solo artists who found their voice and commercial success after they'd been through the machinery once already.

Plaskett was one of four key Canadian artists for whom the '90s didn't exactly go as planned, whereas the 2000s blew away all expectations—which, helpfully, were pretty low to begin with. Other than wielding guitars, Plaskett doesn't have much in common with Sarah Harmer, the Weakerthans or Danko Jones . . . although Sarah Harmer sang on a Weakerthans record and joined Plaskett on stage; she also shared drummers with Danko Jones and Big Sugar, whose Gordie Johnson helped land Plaskett his first radio hit. It's Canada: there are always connections.

All succeeded in the new decade with methods honed from years of jamming econo in the '90s. And rather than burning out, they hit their stride in 2000. Of the '90s, Plaskett says, "We were part of something, being swept up in the zeitgeist, getting opportunity and taking it. By the 2000s it was more like, Do I want to do this? I had an audience, but it was kind of like starting again. I knew I had more to say. The '90s was a leaping-off point."

WHEN PEOPLE TALK ABOUT Canadian rock music in the early 2000s, they talk about Montreal, Toronto or Vancouver. But the first truly great Canadian record of 2000, released in July of that year, didn't come from any of those cities. It came from smack dab in the middle of the country, where the music industry dared not tread, where the hipsters dared not look: Winnipeg. The record is the Weakerthans' *Left and Leaving*.

"The Weakerthans"—not a terribly inspiring name. But rarely had the broken sounded so bold. Sure, the characters who populate *Left and Leaving* are, in their own words, defeated, exiled, heartbroken, poor and lonely. In the hands of a lesser writer, they might be either obviously autobiographical or empty abstracts: anonymous huddled masses. From the pen of singer-songwriter John K. Samson, though, those lives are rich and full, brought to life with Dostoevskian detail, their circumstances universal. That portraiture extends to the music behind him as well: rousing punk anthems with chunky guitars countered by tender ballads that made the band folk festival favourites, all coloured by unusually interesting percussive patterns that contributed to the sonic palette more than simple backing rhythms.

This was not another shitty emo band. These were not mall punks on the Warped Tour. This album wasn't screaming for your attention. This wasn't even Fugazi or Bad Religion. This was something that could only have come from Winnipeg, Manitoba.

THE K STANDS FOR KRISTJAN: there are two other John Samsons in his family, and in the Winnipeg music scene of the early '90s there were too many Johns and John

Ss to not use his middle initial. Samson and his friend Stephen Carroll went to Kelvin High School, across a bend in the Assiniboine River from the Manitoba legislature; the high school's alumni include leaders of business and politics, as well as Marshall McLuhan and Neil Young. There, Samson and Carroll formed a band that only teenagers could have named: Toothpick Hercules.

It wasn't punk exactly. Saskatoon's Northern Pikes were a big influence on Samson, as he says they were for a lot of Prairie kids. He also liked R.E.M. and the Tragically Hip's first EP. He got more adventurous when he heard NoMeansNo on CBC's *Brave New Waves* and started watching *The NewMusic* on TV. (There was no audible campus radio in Winnipeg until 1999; the signals were confined to campuses.) But punk was all around: Samson's first live-music experience was at the West End Cultural Centre seeing local punk bands Red Fisher and Gorilla Gorilla. The latter featured vocalist Bif Naked, who would have rock radio hits as a solo artist within a decade. Red Fisher was a NoMeansNo-ish power trio with metal overtones, occasionally joined by a funk-loving, long-maned guest frontman in a Pantera shirt, singing about Jabba the Hutt (it was the '90s). The drummer was Jason Tait, who later joined Samson in the Weakerthans.

Tait is three years older than Samson. His first show, as a teen in 1984, had been the final show for Winnipeg hardcore punk legends Personality Crisis, on a bill that also featured SNFU, the Edmonton band with godlike status in Western Canada and beyond. Red Fisher hung out at Sk8 Skates, a skateboard shop on Corydon Avenue near Kelvin High that also sold fanzines, records and local cassettes. Red Fisher formed in 1989 and lasted seven years, usually touring for three months straight in the summer with a copy of the punk booking bible *Book Your Own Fuckin' Life*. They'd hit the road with 15 shows booked and wing the rest, sometimes crashing some schmuck's birthday party in a random town. "We'd sleep in the van or in a park," says Tait. "We were all young and reading Kerouac and Bukowski and Jim Carroll. Whenever we played a show [at a venue] with monitors, it was like hitting the big time. 'This place has a stage! Ho-lee shit!' We were super grateful to get opportunities."

"Red Fisher went all over," says Samson, "and had a real fan base in places like Yorkton, Saskatchewan. They could go into the Yorkton arena, there would be 500 kids there—and all of them would buy a hoodie."

The local Winnipeg scene was largely focused around Thursday nights at the Royal Albert Arms Hotel bar, where the booking policy was wide open. Different crowds mingled—for better and worse. "It was rife with conflict," says Stephen Carroll. "A lot of racist skinheads around, also antiracist skinheads. They'd all show up at your show and get into fights. Every Thursday, bands would play, students would drink beer and some warring party would start trouble. But it was the clubhouse we went to every Thursday, between the ages of 18 to 21, to see bands. And lots of big bands went through there."

Toothpick Hercules "played all the venues in Winnipeg, from seedy to a little less seedy," says Carroll. "We were 17 years old. We played the Pyramid, the Albert pretty much weekly, random clubs in the North End and a club called Stripes because it was a mix of Jamaican and Anglo-Saxon food. They'd serve Caribbean food, the punk rock band would play and then they'd blast dancehall really loud, two huge Jamaican guys would get up and dance, then the bands would go back on and the dance floor would clear."

Meanwhile, Red Fisher hosted basement shows, as did their neighbours on McMillan Avenue: some teenagers from Portage la Prairie who had a new band called Propagandhi. In 1991, Samson went to Sk8 to buy the second Propagandhi cassette, *Fuck the Scene* (the follow-up to 1990's *We Don't Get Paid, We Don't Get Laid, and Boy Are We Lazy*). There, he saw a flyer the band had posted, looking to replace their bassist. Figuring he could probably do at least as good a job as the guy known only as Stinky Mike, Samson auditioned and got the gig. Propagandhi's Chris Hannah later admitted Samson was the only person who even answered the ad. A year later, the band shared a bill at the Royal Albert with California band NOFX, who were the second most successful band signed to Epitaph Records, after founders Bad Religion.[1] An impressed Fat Mike from NOFX told them he was starting a new label, Fat Wreck Chords, and offered to sign them. Propagandhi was the second band on the label, after NOFX.

Fat Mike flew Propagandhi down to California to record. "It was their first time in an airport so they were pretty freaked out," he told *Vice*. "We put them in the studio and I think Guns N' Roses were also in the studio that day and they just tripped out. I remember they saw Wayne Gretzky at the airport, they were losing it." The album, *How to Clean Everything*, boasted feel-good favourites like "Stick the Fucking Flag Up Your Goddam Ass, You Sonofabitch." The pop-punk scene that worshipped NOFX were not Fugazi disciples; Bad Religion notwithstanding, most SoCal punks weren't ready for Canadian vegans preaching about homophobia, misogyny and militarism. Nonetheless, *How to Clean Everything* was a massive hit for the label, and the band toured the U.S. and Europe extensively. Canada, not so much. Samson doesn't recall ever playing Toronto with Propagandhi; he was in the band for five years.

Back home in Winnipeg, Samson finished recording an acoustic cassette of his own songs, *Slips and Tangles*, a five-year project he started in 1989; he considered it done when he finally had enough to fill a cassette. Shortly after, he put some of

---

[1]   An Epitaph band called the Offspring soon went multiplatinum.

those songs and others on a split CD with Winnipeg band Painted Thin, which featured his high school friend Stephen Carroll on guitar. Jason Tait was hired as a session drummer. "Someone screwed up the mastering, and it's just one solid track," laughs Tait. "You can't skip from song to song, which is kind of brilliant but not intentional." Tait was mostly impressed by Samson's solo songs. "It was super cool compared to what else was happening in the scene," says Tait. "I was a huge folk music fan growing up. I loved Simon and Garfunkel—even when I was in the depths of punk rock, I hung onto that stuff because they're great songs."

Meanwhile, Propagandhi wanted Samson to learn a song by '80s Satanic metal band Venom. Samson was mystified and frustrated: it was a difficult song, and he didn't understand why they were even bothering. He was more excited when Propagandhi covered one of his favourite songwriters, Ron Hawkins, with the Lowest of the Low's "Gamble." "I remember learning that song," he says, "and thinking, Oh yeah, this is the kind of music I want to write."

The second Propagandhi record, *Less Talk More Rock*, was a game-changer for the '90s generation of punks. The album featured two Samson songs: "Gifts" and "Anchorless." The latter was mere small-town malaise next to the rest of the material, written by a band that quoted Noam Chomsky and called out the meat-eating, macho culture of punk.

That made playing in Propagandhi a harrowing experience. "There were some really serious, strangely frightening shows," Samson told Greg Pratt of *Exclaim!* "In Bakersfield, [California,] the people who brought us there had tire irons out by the stage because the white power people were going to come by. I remember being in Chico, California, and members of the audience throwing raw meat at us because we were vegans. I didn't thrive on the challenge of an antagonistic relationship with certain parts of the audience."

Less Talk More Rock came out in April 1996. Samson was at the end of his rope. "There was a show in Denver, in a legion hall," he told Pratt. "It was like 400 degrees in there and there were way too many kids. They had oversold it. There was a full-on riot going on at the show: 50 police officers with mace just beating the crap out of kids. Helicopters and news crews. I just had no idea what to do. We were in the United States illegally; we basically caused this crazy violent event—it wasn't our fault, but, you know. That whole tour I had just been struggling, I just felt really anxious. It got more and more uncomfortable for me." Samson toured until August and played his last Propagandhi show in San Francisco—a benefit for AK Press, an anarchist publisher.

In 1997, Red Fisher called it quits. Jason Tait had no idea what he was going to do with his life. Three weeks later, Samson called and asked if he could hire him for a session, to play on an album that would be called *Fallow*. He dropped off some demos with Tait, songs that Samson had tried to introduce to Propagandhi but had been met with blank stares. "The demos were in sequence of the album he envisioned," says Tait. "I finally got to the last song, the title track, and I was totally blown away. It's still one of my favourite songs of his, so beautiful. A few days later we started working. It sounded good, and we figured we needed a bass player. John Sutton had been in Red Fisher the last two years, so he came on board and after a month we booked some studio time and made the album in a week."

The band was now called the Weakerthans, the name arguably the Canadian insecurity complex incarnate. It's a name chosen by a band in a Prairie province far removed from the corridors of power, in a country that plays inevitable second fiddle to the superpower to the south. Samson has given various explanations for the name: that it came from the film adaptation of the Marguerite Duras novel *The Lover*, in which a character challenged to a fight responds, "Go ahead, I'm weaker than you can possibly imagine." Observers familiar with Samson's politics noticed that there's also a line in the century-old union hymn "Solidarity Forever": "What force on Earth is weaker than the feeble strength of one." Samson claims he just liked the sound of it, but it also had a practical value for a guy who had left Propagandhi. "The name was going to alert people to the fact that it's not going to be loud and fast, particularly," he says. "There were a lot of reasons for the name, but that was definitely one of them."

One song on *Fallow*, the aching ballad "None of the Above," was an obvious standout: an articulation of the inarticulate, encapsulating emotional ennui and communication standoffs, set in a humdrum diner on the edge of town where strip malls meet farmland. It featured the album's producer, Lloyd Peterson, who'd produced early Crash Test Dummies recordings, on slide guitar. For the release show at the West End Cultural Centre, Samson hired his old friend Stephen Carroll to play Peterson's part. Painted Thin had just broken up after a three-month tour of Germany, Austria and Switzerland. "My band's done," Carroll told Samson. "I'm ready to join yours."

Fallow came out on a new label started by Propagandhi—with $50,000 of investment capital from Fat Mike (which he quickly recouped)—called G7 Welcoming Committee, the name a nod to the antiglobalization movement that was the subject of Naomi Klein's *No Logo* two years later. Its headquarters was located in what was colloquially known as the Emma Goldman Autonomous Zone in downtown Winnipeg, home to a vegan café and a new publishing house, Arbeiter Ring, devoted to poetry and politics. Modelled on AK Press, it was co-founded by Samson. None of this seemed unusual in the city: its socialist tradition is taught in classrooms across the country in the story of the 1919 Winnipeg General Strike.

The album's title refers to unfertile ground, and the lyrics are suitably wintry, rich with themes of languishing in bleak surroundings, with nods to Dostoevsky's *Notes from Underground*. The narrator in "Confessions of a Futon-Revolutionist" wants to enlist his cat in a class war and ponders planting bombs at city hall to kill provincial legislators—out of boredom more than anything. Other characters sing Boney M. songs to themselves to stave off the black dogs of depression. "Wellington's Wednesdays" is named after a '90s Winnipeg club night hosted by Duotang's Rod Slaughter, which usually concluded with New Order's "Temptation." The song's outro directly quotes from the new wave classic; thankfully the British band never sued.

Fallow is a confident and assured debut, but it didn't exist in a vacuum. Winnipeg was teeming with bands at the time, as vibrant as Halifax had been five years earlier. Crash Test Dummies had had a No. 1 U.S. hit in 1993, while the Watchmen were conquering Canadian rock radio. But the new crop was much more exciting. Local label Endearing was a focal point. The scrappy sounds of Transistor Sound & Lighting Co., featuring future Broken Social Scene member Marty Kinack, had somehow scored a major label deal with Sony-BMG, making them one of the last bands to ride the indie wave of the early '90s. The metal scene had Malefaction, Swallowing Shit, and Kittens, who put out the highly underrated 1997 classic *Bazooka and the Hustler* on Sonic Unyon. The smart mod songcraft of Duotang, led by Rod Slaughter of earlier indie fave Zen Bungalow, garnered national attention when they became one of only two non-Vancouver bands on Mint Records (Calgary's Huevos Rancheros being the other). Future CBC Music host Odario Williams fronted the group Mood Ruff, who were on the prolific local hip-hop label Peanuts & Corn. JFK & the Conspirators were a ska band signed to Montreal's Stomp Records. Songwriter Greg MacPherson, who shared influences with Samson and later recorded with Tait and released through G7 Welcoming Committee, released his debut cassette the same year *Fallow* came out. Samson's future partner Christine Fellows was on the scene, playing in Special Fancy.

Samson's personal favourites at the time were the Bonaduces, who spawned from Banned from Atlantis; singer-songwriter Doug McLean wrote pop-punk songs with lyrics laid out like poetry in the liner notes, much like Samson did in all Weakerthans' artwork. The Bonaduces and Painted Thin, much like Propagandhi, toured Europe and the U.S. frequently—certainly much more than most other Canadian bands at any level of popularity. Hustling was essential. When you live in the geographical centre of an enormous continent, you have to go far afield to get anywhere.

The Weakerthans' first trip to Europe got off to a bad start: their flight out of Winnipeg was cancelled because of a Red River flood, so they drove to Minneapolis to fly to a festival in Holland—which was also cancelled, having gone bankrupt right before it started. All was not lost. Germany took to the Weakerthans right away, thanks in part to connections in Hamburg that Samson had made through Propagandhi. "The German constellation of youth clubs was an amazing network of music venues," says Samson. "They were publicly funded, and people could do their voluntary military or government service by working in these places. They'd put on shows, do outreach to the community, youth would play foosball, and in the evening there would be tons of shows. There was also a developed political squat scene. That's how we established ourselves as a band."

The ghost of Propagandhi was both a bane and a boon. For years, on gig posters in the U.S., the phrase "ex-Propagandhi" would be as big as the Weakerthans' name. "That gave us a foothold," says Samson, "but also led to people expecting something they didn't get when they arrived at the show."

"There weren't too many pop-punk bands at the time putting straight-up bummers on the record," says Tait. "It was a weird way for us to gain an audience—by alienating half of them."

"People were upset and would heckle; occasionally there were threats," says Samson. "I always had Jason behind me, so I wasn't that concerned. He was not shy about standing up and confronting people. People would push the mic into my face." But he adds that "any of the challenges that we faced because of being ex-Propagandhi pale in comparison to the assistance it provided." Samson's royalties from the first two Propagandhi records subsidized the Weakerthans' first two tours, as well as the rent at their rehearsal space.

Chris Hannah of Propagandhi took the liberty of sending a copy of *Fallow* to Ron Hawkins of Lowest of the Low, knowing that Samson was a big fan. Word made it back to Samson that Hawkins had started covering *Fallow* material in his live set, and that he'd offered to do distribution for G7 in Toronto, restocking local stores—including anarchist bookshop Who's Emma—with copies of *Fallow*. When Lowest of the Low reunited in 2000, they brought the Weakerthans on a national tour.

Similar Toronto support came from the Rheostatics. The Weakerthans had given a tape to Rheos bassist Tim Vesely at the 1999 World Next Door Festival in Winnipeg; a year later, guitarist Dave Bidini called Samson to invite the band to Toronto for a week's worth of shows in February 15, 2000, an annual tradition they called the Green Sprouts Music Week. That had a profound effect on Samson. "It was the example set by the Rheos," he says. "They were joyous. It didn't have to be perfect. It's music. It's supposed to be fun. That was a big click for me. After that, I tried to figure out ways to actually enjoy performing. I've never entirely felt comfortable on stage, but after that I was able to find something in it that was probably eluding me."

The Rheos then took the Weakerthans on tour in the spring of 2000. "The Rheos tour was hilarious," says Tait, "because they used our backline and flew show to show while we drove all the gear early in the morning to be on time for soundcheck, and then we opened for them. It was kind of a raw deal, but we got to play some nice venues and we brought in 75% of the crowd. But I'm such a huge fan, and it was great to watch one of my favourite live bands every night."

Pretty soon, the Weakerthans weren't taking a backseat to anyone.

———

AT THE AGE OF 27 IN 1998, Sarah Harmer thought she might be relegated to a backseat—and she was okay with that. A year earlier, her band, Weeping Tile, had had loads of critical acclaim, a modest national audience, an American record deal—and sales that didn't exceed a meagre 5,000 copies. Within six months of the release of their second album, 1997's *Valentino*, there were rumours they'd be dropped. The record company asked her if she had any demos of new songs. She didn't. The rumours came true. The label bid them goodbye.

Indie icon Ani DiFranco then came calling, offering the band an opening slot on a short tour—but only if they played acoustically. Weeping Tile recorded an EP on Harmer's porch, *This Great Black Night*, with five songs: "I'm a Mountain," "Coffee Stain," "Weakened State," "Odessa Nights" and "Lodestar." They pressed it on cassette and sold it at the merch table that summer. That fall, they split. No regrets. "We were never a super ambitious commercial band," Harmer says. "We just did our thing and we were lucky to be able to get people to hear our music. When we got dropped, it was freeing, it was good."

Harmer accepted an invitation from younger singer-songwriter Sarah Slean to do a New England tour playing shows held in fans' homes, then a new trend. Joining them was an unknown Leslie Feist, who had yet to finish her first record. The three women traded songs in a format like a folk festival workshop. When Harmer returned, she enlisted her friend Jason Euringer to help her record a Christmas present for her father, an acoustic collection of old-timey family favourites. She also made a few copies for friends, who convinced her to formally release it in April 1999. There were no originals. Nothing about it was hip: "Tennessee Waltz," "Sentimental Journey," hell even "Just a Closer Walk with Thee." The most contemporary song was Nanci Griffith's "Trouble in the Fields."

"It was a good clean break," she says. "'You know me for [one thing], and now here's something completely different.' It wasn't an artistic decision, because it wasn't like I thought I was going to redo 'Your Cheatin' Heart' and it would be my next big thing." She played a solo set at the Black Sheep Inn in Wakefield,

Quebec, which was recorded by the CBC Radio show *Bandwidth*. "I'd barely ever played a solo set before," she says. "My brother heard it in Vancouver and said, 'That's the best you've ever sounded. You should make a solo album.' He's my one and only brother; what he says holds weight with me. But I didn't want to be a solo artist. I always liked the idea of bands rather than individual performers. I like to be in a club."

SARAH HARMER GREW UP on a farm on the north side of Burlington, Ontario, near Hamilton, with five sisters and a brother. Her mother, an organist and palliative care counsellor, enlisted the four younger girls to sing "The Candy Man" at the old folks' home up the road. "My mom worked in hospitals and did a lot of work for the [Southeast Asian] boat people, and they fostered some kids as well," she says. "There were lots of politics." The Harmers canvassed for local Liberal candidates, one of whom was a cousin, a renewable energy activist.

As a teen, Harmer's first concert without her parents was Bruce Springsteen. The first band she ever saw in a bar, when she was 16, was the Tragically Hip; her older sisters knew them from Queen's University in Kingston. "We'd go to Brampton, to Kincardine, Wasaga Beach, when they were playing little shitty bars to nobody," says Harmer. "I was forever changed after that. I vividly remember going into the graffitied band room and being really shy, after watching these guys sweating it up on stage. They would just go song to song to song with such momentum. The segues and the energy they created on stage, with their own songs and covers I didn't know but at the time I probably thought they had written. I just thought they were gods." A year later, she took to the stage herself.

Harmer was friendly with Andrew Lindsay, a record clerk at the Sunrise Records in Burlington, where she hung out in high school. After she returned from a four-month trip to New Zealand in grade 13, Lindsay asked her, "I hear that you sing. Do you want to join our band?" The Saddletramps had already been featured on Toronto radio station CFNY with a minor local hit, "Boomerang." She was 17; they were all 23. She turned 18 on stage with them at the Rivoli. Harmer joined and stayed in the band for more than three years; for a while she commuted from her first-year studies at Queen's, and then lived in Toronto for a year, playing with them full-time. Before one gig at Ultrasound on Queen Street West, Gord Downie told her to stay in school, where she was taking women's studies. After the gig, impressed by the band, he was less certain about his advice.

Also impressed was Patrick Sambrook, a Montreal manager who worked with Newfoundland funk band Thomas Trio and the Red Albino. Sambrook saw

Saddletramps open for Toronto roots act Bag of Hammers (another Sambrook client); Harmer's voice and presence blew him away. But the feeling was hardly mutual. "It was the first time I'd ever seen a band with a manager," she says. "He was really pushy, like, 'Where's our dressing room?' I thought, Who's *this* guy? *Manager*? Who has a *manager*? It was a totally foreign concept to me." The Saddletramps mostly played around Ontario, though Harmer longed to tour far and wide. The rest of the band had full-time jobs; she didn't. "Then I wrote five or six songs and quit the band and moved back to Kingston." One of those songs was called "Don't Get Your Back Up."

Patrick Sambrook stayed in touch and offered her an opening slot for Thomas Trio at Zaphod Beeblebrox in Ottawa, with four days' notice. Harmer was wary: she only had seven songs at that point, and an essay due that Monday. She enlisted Joe Chithalen—an in-demand Kingston bassist—to learn her songs on upright bass, and they played the Ottawa gig without a band name. Harmer spent half the set trying to tune her guitar. Afterwards, drummer Jon McCann signed on to what became Weeping Tile. Sambrook kept offering her gigs with Change of Heart, Rheostatics and other favourites of Harmer's that she couldn't turn down. In the summer of 1993, Weeping Tile recorded with 13 Engines' Grant Ethier, making the seven-song *Eepee*, including "Basement Apt." with Gord Tough on guitar.

Eepee quickly started getting attention, and within a year of its release they had deals with Warner Canada and American Warner's new alt-rock subsidiary, Seed. Harmer's bandmates came and went; by the time of the 1996 Warner debut, *Cold Snap*, her sister Mary was on bass, Cam Giroux was the drummer and Luther Wright was on guitar. Their first major Canadian tour was with the Bourbon Tabernacle Choir, who were about to break up.

"I've seen every one of these bathrooms a million times," singer Kate Fenner deadpanned to the young Harmer.

"I haven't seen any of them!" exclaimed the young hippie, whose band travelled with a hot plate and a juicer, leaving carrot-juice-stained towels behind in every motel.

Weeping Tile's three albums—*Eepee*, *Cold Snap* and 1997's *Valentino*—were all scrappy, raw rock records that were too normal for the alt crowd and too rugged for mainstream radio. There was a Neil Young dichotomy to the band: folk songs set to rock arrangements alongside loud, crushing guitar anthems. Though Weeping Tile had fervent fans, they didn't have enough of them.

That's why in 1999, when Harmer put out *Songs for Clem*, she was largely starting from scratch. She sold most of her initial pressing through a P.O. box; she taught herself Photoshop so she could design ads she placed in local papers. Stuart McLean of CBC Radio's *The Vinyl Café* was a huge supporter; Harmer did a few live dates with him, joined by the same friends who helped her make the record. At two of those dates, at Kingston's Grand Theatre and at Convocation Hall at the University of Toronto, Clem Harmer joined his daughter and her band. It was the first time the 70-year-old had ever performed in public, outside of church musicals. Because McLean was such a CBC mainstay for so long with an intensely loyal audience, Harmer continued to receive "nice handwritten letters from older people from all around Canada" in her P.O. box for years afterwards.

But no one was stepping forth to offer Harmer a record deal, or even a studio to record in. One late night at Ted's Wrecking Yard on College Street in Toronto, Harmer met Pete Prilesnik, who'd had hits with Big Sugar and Ashley MacIsaac, but whose work on *Other People's Heavens*—the debut duo record by Bourbon Tabernacle Choir's Chris Brown and Kate Fenner—Harmer was particularly enamoured with. Prilesnik invited her to his studio on West Lodge Avenue in Parkdale. "It's a low-level, one-storey warehouse in the alley, just north of Queen, full of mice and shit," she recalls. The producer called in drummers he knew from Big Sugar: Gavin Brown and Al Cross. Harmer called drummers Giroux and Damon Richardson (Change of Heart). Gord Tough returned to play electric guitar, reprising his part on "Basement Apt."

"Initially I thought I would do a really intimate recording, and then I got into the studio and it soon became a very produced record," says Harmer, who feels that way about all her albums, with only one exception. "Even though I set out to do a 'This is me' kind of recording, it turned into 'This is what I like,' and I like playing with other people. But the songs are focused more around the voice." As the project gathered steam, Harmer's mother loaned her $30,000 to complete the album, *You Were Here*.

Six new Harmer songs appeared on the 12-song album. Three songs were carried over from the acoustic Weeping Tile EP made before the breakup; one ("Everytime") was a cover of Kingston friend Dave Hodge of the Hellbillys; two were from the first Weeping Tile EP, including the very first song Harmer ever wrote, at age 18: "Don't Get Your Back Up."

One of the late-period Weeping Tile retreads—which was essentially new, as very few heard that EP—was "Lodestar," an achingly beautiful song that begins with intimate acoustic guitar, slowly revealing delicate electric guitar and cello until, in the second half, a muted trumpet heralds the arrival of drums and a chugging cello, which open up into a glorious, anthemic climax—in which a pencil sketch flowers into a lush Group of Seven painting. It became a beloved fan favourite and a staple of every set Sarah Harmer has ever played.

With its imagery of boating at night under a canopy of stars and oil-like water, many fans imagined that it must have been written by an Algonquin Park campfire on a hot summer night. Instead, she wrote it while sitting on a cold Quebec toilet in the late winter of 1998, when Weeping Tile was on their final (electric) tour, opening for Holly McNarland, making a pit stop in Matane. It was not romantic. "I was sitting in the bathroom, getting my own space in a little motel and imagining being anywhere but frozen Gaspé," says Harmer. She wasn't even thinking of Canada at the time. "I was picturing a Mexican night or something tropical and southern. There's a couple of lines from a D.H. Lawrence poem that was literally sitting on my back table. I picked it up and cracked it open and used it in the second half of the song."

Another song was a commission. "Open Window" was written for the wedding of a high school friend. "Writing that one was really easy because it was so unabashedly gushy," she says. "I honestly didn't think it would be on my record; same with 'Around This Corner.' It's hard to get perspective on some of the songs, and so I'd play them for other people, and they'd say, 'Oh, that's great!' And I'm like, 'Really? You don't think it's weird or dorky?'"

You Were Here's strength—other than the songwriting and Harmer's vocals—is its stylistic breadth: jaunty jazzy numbers, folk-rock ballads, alt-rock pop songs, bluegrass numbers. That was partially by accident: producer Prilesnik started going AWOL, leaving Harmer scrambling to finish the record herself throughout the fall of 1999. *You Were Here* was finally mastered and ready by January 2000. Harmer printed a bunch of CD-Rs with a hand-drawn cover. At a Horseshoe show just before she left to play SXSW, she sold one to Allan Reid, A&R rep at Universal Canada. He bought the copy numbered 002. A few weeks later, she agreed to meet him for a drink.

"How many records do you want to sell?" he asked.

"About 100,000," she deadpanned, playing a confidence game.

"Oooh, that's a lot."

"Yeah, well, have you heard the record?"

Meanwhile, two of the drummers who had played on it—Gavin Brown of Phleg Camp and Damon Richardson of Change of Heart—were trading places in a very different Toronto act that was about to blow up: Danko Jones.

———

DANKO JONES HAS a few things to get off his chest. That's what he does.

When he's not playing music, he's an opinionated columnist and podcaster proselytizing about the minutiae of metal, wrestling or *Three's Company*. When he is playing music, on stage in front of thousands of Europeans, his between-song banter is as entertaining, if not more so, than his powerhouse riff-rock. He once released a seven-inch single of just his stage banter. But when asked to talk about the Canadian scene that birthed him, Danko Jones is very clear: "I have to keep my bitterness at bay."

When he arrived in the mid-'90s, Danko Jones became a cause celebre in the media for providing a staid Canadian rock'n'roll scene with sexually charged swagger, driven by post-hardcore garage rock. He eventually scored a hit single with 1999's "Bounce" and got some more rock radio play with 2002's *Born a Lion*, which was distributed by Universal. As a so-called rock revival boomed in the U.S., Danko Jones hit a glass ceiling at home pretty quickly, though his career took off in Europe. To this day, he's better known in Sweden and Germany—where he's a regular at the major festivals—than on the streets of Toronto, where his friends who have sold fewer records than he has are hailed as heroes.

"Our timing was off," he says of his native prospects. "We were perceived as a rock radio band because that's where we serviced our releases and where we were being added—even though we didn't change our sound. That threw me for a spin. I realized people in the industry don't actually listen to music, they just *look* at music. I got really bitter really fast. Fuck all you guys!"

His bitterness is not extended to his peers—for them, he couldn't be happier. "Brendan Canning and I lived together for four years," he says. "I love what Broken Social Scene has accomplished—for Brendan. I met Peaches before she was Peaches, through Justin Small of Do Make Say Think—both artists who went to Europe early. Feist came to see us in Berlin before she had anything going on. I'm a huge Dears fan; Murray [Lightburn] and I are good friends.

"I don't talk shit about my friends, I talk shit about people's reaction to them, because we get forgotten. Our sound doesn't fit the format of New Pornographers, the Dears, Feist, Arcade Fire. I was a huge Broken Social Scene booster, but would come back home and feel the vibe of 'This is now the cool band. We don't want to have anything to do with your band. We're not going to cover you other than making fun of you online.' I look to people like NoMeansNo and [prog-metal wizard] Devin Townsend to soothe me. That's a club I would love to be a part of: the forgotten club! I'm okay with that."

THE '90S ROCK scene in Toronto can be characterized as somewhat dour; with some exceptions, it was a lot of earnest grunge, glum shoegaze—altogether bland. Pearl Jam and My Bloody Valentine were oft-imitated but unfortunate influences. Metal was niche. Garage rock, which was just as "back to basics" as grunge but with a lot more potential sex appeal (but by no means guaranteed), began to bubble up.

A young Danko Jones—not his real name—was, like any music geek of the era, drawn to his local campus radio station: York University's CHRY, where young journalist Matt Galloway was the program director. Danko's local faves included metal acts Malhavoc and Sacrifice but also the post-hardcore art-rock of Phleg Camp, who were revered locally before breaking up in 1993. Danko played in a noise-rock band called Horshack, modelled after abrasive Chicagoans Jesus Lizard. When one member admitted to liking the Rolling Stones, Danko suggested they channel that into a duo modelled on North Carolina's Flat Duo Jets—an influence on the White Stripes as well.[2] The new duo was called the Violent Brothers.

More important, though, was Toronto band the Leather Uppers, led by DJ, writer and overall garage-rock enthusiast "Classy" Craig Daniels. Long before the Deadly Snakes and the Sadies, Daniels was making key American connections; a Leather Uppers album came out on Detroit label Sympathy for the Record Industry, which also launched—yes, them again—the White Stripes. "The Leather Uppers were the one band in Toronto we held in high esteem," says Danko. "They brought performance back. First time I saw them was opening for Blue Rodeo, and 'Classy' Craig smashed what looked like a vintage guitar on stage. And they wore matching outfits, outfits you'd be hard pressed to find one of anywhere. They set a template we always kept in the back of our heads."

Danko had a local reputation for making prank phone calls, akin to contemporaries the Jerky Boys. But his comic side didn't emerge on stage until he was heckled one night at the Cameron House by a member of Satanatras, a band that featured future Sadie Dallas Good. "Bernie Pleskach was in the crowd, drunk, and kept goading us, yelling at us. We were quietly playing our Stones thing like a couple of indie rock kids, and then I started firing back. He got it out of me. I was pissed off, and I had this persona I wanted to come out. It was such a moment for me. I was on such a high. I thanked him the next time I saw him." The Violent Brothers soon split, and in January 1996 Danko Jones became the performer's onstage alias as well as the name of his band. Bassist John Calabrese was enlisted after Danko saw him open for Palace Brothers with his band Kat Rocket, led by Stella Panacci and featuring future Broken Social Scene drummer Justin Peroff. Nothing about that sentence suggests the music Danko Jones was about to make.

The new Danko Jones persona was a mix of James Brown, Hulk Hogan and blaxploitation filmmaker Rudy Ray Moore, with a lot of lewd tongue gestures lifted from Gene Simmons. Danko dressed like a '70s Harlem pimp, in a sharp tapered suit complete with feathered fedora tilted to the side, and the occasional

---

2   Neko Case is also a huge fan of Flat Duo Jets.

white fur coat with a feather boa. This made an immediate impression on a city that hadn't seen this level of commitment to performance since the demise of hair metal—and Danko Jones was way cooler. The music was primitive riff-rock directly descended from Thin Lizzy, AC/DC and Motörhead—music designed to terrorize the Tortoise crowd. "Was it a reaction to shoegazers? Maybe it was," he says, "but it wasn't conscious. It was, 'This is different. I'll get people's attention this way.'"

At early practices, there was no small talk—or much talk at all. They'd show up, write songs and jam for two straight hours, then go home. That code of silence extended to media as well: they didn't hustle for reviews and didn't respond to interview requests, which was anathema in the era of the post-alternative explosion. In that—and only that—aspect, Danko Jones was for a while as obtuse as Godspeed You! Black Emperor. There was no manager, no label, no publicist.

Buzz built before Danko Jones even played their first Toronto show, opening for the New Bomb Turks at Lee's Palace in April 1996. Earlier that year they accepted an invite from Montreal garage-rock band the Spaceshits—which also featured an outrageous frontman, King Khan—to play in Quebec and Ottawa first. "I love that band," raves Danko. "They were five guys who were like a gang. They will fight you if you say the wrong thing or look at them the wrong way. I was scared of them. But they liked our band. They were these tough punk rock kids, in the *Quadrophenia* sense, and we were the mods, in a way."

Montreal had a thriving garage-rock scene, with the most notable exports being Tricky Woo, "a great lost band who don't get their just due," says Danko, who toured with them several times. "We started off as rivals: 'We're the only indie band doing rock, fuck you, who are you?' We hadn't met the guys face to face. Once we did, [guitarist/singer] Andrew Dickson was such a nice dude and he totally gets it. I still tell people to play [1999 single] 'Fly the Orient.' It should be the 'Seven Nation Army' of that generation." It wasn't. And Danko Jones imagined a similar fate for his band if he limited his vision to Canada, where there was "an audience that didn't know how to behave, because they were bludgeoned by indie rock and shoegaze and the kind of folk music that tramples all over Canada, and I hate it." He immediately set his sights on scenes in Detroit, Chicago and Washington, D.C., while bassist Calabrese worked on bringing U.S. acts (the.Make-Up, Trans Am, the Dirtbombs) to Toronto, dealing with all finances and immigration issues.

In Toronto, Danko Jones's only real competition was the Deadly Snakes, a group of teenagers who had been fans of Danko's first band, Horshack, and attempted to sneak into Lee's Palace to see them play. "I knew them when they were little twerps," he says. "They were so into it, they were so invested and it was endearing. It was cute. Then I heard them play, and the first couple of times I thought they were years ahead of where I was."

One legendary show took place in the summer of 1996 in a Kensington Market venue called Laundry Mat. "That Laundry Mat gig was a watershed show, representing the new wave of Toronto bands coming up," Craig Daniels told Danko biographer Stuart Berman. "It was a heat wavey, sweaty summer night, the kind that made it hard to even get your drink on—you just sweated out the booze as fast as it came in. The show was phenomenal, and Danko came out swinging hard. The night was a study in two takes on blues-punk rock'n'roll: Danko with his hard, stadium-rockin'-fuzz-bass-bravado sound and the Snakes with their loose Stones-on-a-bender thing. It was the kind of show that set the pace for a while and let people know there was a new breed coming up, for sure."

The honeymoon between the two bands soon ended, however; Danko Jones claims that someone in the Snakes was shit-talking him to various American contacts. "We were more than willing to be brothers in this thing," he says. "Then when Deadly Snakes got a name for themselves, we got all this shit talk. With every band, you get a window of acting like an asshole when your band gets a bit of notoriety. Then that window should close really quick, or you're just a dick. I did that a bit, and they did that, too—though they did that in my general direction. It wasn't cool. I wish we could all be friends."

Journalists were soon clamouring to write about Danko Jones, who didn't yet have a record out, but the band turned them down unless they could get the cover. "Isn't that the biggest punk-rock fuck-you?" he laughs now. "It was insane to do." Larissa Gulka of *The NewMusic* aired a segment in which she interviewed fans and other musicians—including members of Sloan and Trans Am—about Danko Jones, with no word from the band. In one scene, Danko slams a door in Gulka's face. "People thought I was a dick, but we rehearsed that," he laughs. "I had an idea, and to Larissa's credit she ran with it." Danko Jones was already on MuchMusic, though not with his own band; he co-stars with Floria Sigismondi in Bruce LaBruce's video for the Rusty hit "Empty Cell," which was in regular rotation on the station.

Mainstream bands like Sloan and Big Sugar gave Danko Jones opening slots. He was an early inspiration for Merrill Nisker as she was transforming into Peaches; the respect was mutual, and the two sexual outlaws wrote a song together shortly before she moved to Berlin. "I got obsessed with Danko Jones really quickly—I just kept going to see them," she told Stuart Berman. "That was because it just seemed really raw and real. And the way he relentlessly hit himself in the head throughout his shows just told me that he's in it for life." Other bands tried to be cool by knocking back shots of Jack Daniel's, or lighting a joint on stage, or even, in one case, a crack pipe. Danko Jones chugged milk on stage and licked anything that wasn't already spilling down his chest. The milk shtick became a problem when they opened for Sloan, whose techs were not amused to find sticky milk all over the gear.

Danko's mainstream flirtations were about to get more explicit. His long-made attempts to sign with Touch and Go, home of Danko's beloved Jesus Lizard, ultimately failed—allegedly because someone at the label thought his male-gaze music was sexist rather than sex-positive. Danko was disgusted with these shades of Spinal Tap. He was through with indie rock, a fickle club he didn't want to be a part of. Instead he looked to acts like Motörhead, whom fans would boast about seeing 75 times or more. He knew hard-rock fan bases were among the most loyal in music. Danko headed in that direction.

Danko Jones also didn't look like other Canadian rock acts. "I identify privately and publicly as a mixed kid," he says. "Nothing more and nothing less." But Brown men in popular bands? You could count them on one hand: Safwan Javed was the drummer in Saskatoon's Wide Mouth Mason; Ashwin Sood was Sarah McLachlan's drummer (and husband). Guitarists Dave "Brownsound" Baksh of Sum 41 and Ian D'Sa of Billy Talent were a few years away from breaking into the mainstream. Rishi Dhir of the High Dials had just introduced his sitar into his psych-pop band. Other than King Khan of Montreal's little-known Spaceshits, there were no other South Asian men on lead vocals. Danko Jones would taunt his crowds, "I feel so good, I'm in the mood for a little race mixing tonight!"

In 1998, Danko Jones put out an EP with Hamilton's Sonic Unyon label on the condition that it be limited edition and not be reprinted after the initial run of 2,000. It sold out quickly. Sonic Unyon defied the artist's orders and reprinted it; Danko showed up at their offices demanding that they stop. A 1999 EP, *My Love Is Bold*, came out on Sound King, a label started by Richard Switzer, who was room-mates with Danko and Brendan Canning. Featuring new drummer Gavin Brown of Phleg Camp, the single "Bounce" became a local radio hit on Q107 and CFNY, thanks to enterprising indie publicist Yvette Ray. The rest of the country soon followed: a rare grassroots indie hit on commercial radio.

Creative clashes with Gavin Brown led to him being fired in December 1999; two months later, with a temporary fill-in, they opened for Beck at Maple Leaf Gardens, after an overnight drive from Ottawa during which their van broke down, jeopardizing their soundcheck at noon. New drummer Damon Richardson, recently of Change of Heart, joined in time for a national tour with Sloan in February 2000. *My Love Is Bold* ended up selling 10,000 copies on a bedroom label. It seemed like Danko Jones was finally going to be the Next Big Thing.

Major label A&R reps came calling—the first one, Steve Jordan of Warner, was only authorized by his bosses to offer a demo deal. "We were getting played on the radio, for fuck's sake!" Danko laughs. "What did we have to demonstrate?" Universal Records was more welcoming, though concerned that the band didn't have a manager; bassist John Calabrese had been taking care of business. The label set Calabrese up with someone they thought would work well; the bassist showed up on time for the nine a.m. meeting, the manager was 15 minutes late. Calabrese presented a spreadsheet outlining how the band could make $1 million in the next 12 months. The manager threw up his hands: "Get out of here! You don't need me." He then called Universal and told them to do whatever Calabrese said to do.

———

JOEL PLASKETT WAS AT A CROSSROADS in 2000. He was 25 years old and had been a professional musician since he finished high school. His band, Thrush Hermit, formed when he was 15. A year later, he saw Sloan's first show and the effect was seismic. The two bands were so similar that the teenagers were soon tagged with the unfortunate nickname "Clone." By 1994, Sloan's Murderecords put out the debut Thrush Hermit EP, *Smart Bomb*; that led to Sire Records' Seymour Stein coming to see the band at the Five Fishermen Restaurant in Halifax and signing them. Their major label album, *Sweet Homewrecker*, was produced by Doug Easley (Pavement, the Grifters) and put them on the road across North America in 1996 and '97. The timing was terrible: the bottom had fallen out of so-called indie rock, and within a year the label bought the band out of their contract.

Yet Thrush Hermit was finally hitting their stride as songwriters and as a live band. They went into Toronto's Gas Station studios, in the spring of 1998, with engineer Dale Morningstar, to make *Clayton Park*, an album named after their Halifax suburb. They funded it themselves, and in 1999 secured a deal with Hamilton's Sonic Unyon Records. Released in the spring of 1999, *Clayton Park* was hailed as an instant classic at a time when '70s-inspired rock'n'roll was not in vogue.

On tour, Plaskett was becoming more of a frontman, while the band's other guitarist and songwriter, Rob Benvie, felt he was getting squeezed out. Crowds were not growing. By September, Benvie quit and the band packed it in. The silver lining was that they felt they were going out on a high point, having made their best album. They announced a farewell tour across Canada for later in the fall, with Local Rabbits and the Flashing Lights. Their peers in the so-called Halifax Pop Explosion were also retiring: Jale, the Hardship Post, Eric's Trip and Cool Blue Halo all split. Sloan had moved to Toronto. The scene was in disarray.

For years Plaskett had been working on solo recordings with a more country feel, influenced by Vic Chesnutt and by the death of his beloved grandfather. He had no plans for them until the fall of 1999, when he released *In Need of Medical Attention* on a Minneapolis label. Plaskett put together a five-piece band, including drummer Dave Marsh and bassist Charles Austin, to play a small series of shows, including one at Arlene's Grocery in New York City for the CMJ festival. He had enlisted Marsh during a street hockey game held in a liquor store parking lot.

"I need a band," Plaskett reportedly told Marsh. "It's a bit of an emergency."

"That's your band name right there," replied Marsh. "The Joel Plaskett Emergency."

After the New York show, he was feeling low and went to his doctor. Tests showed Plaskett had a very low white-blood-cell count; his doctor commanded him to stay home, to rest and to get a bone-marrow test. The Thrush Hermit tour had to be postponed. They ended up playing only a handful of dates in Toronto and the East Coast in December. Thrush Hermit played their final show on December 11, 1999, in Halifax. Twenty days later, on New Year's Eve, Plaskett ditched a house party at Dave Marsh's house—whom he'd already convinced to join his new band—to try to enlist bassist Tim Brennan, who had played with Marsh years ago in Blackpool, a linchpin band of the Halifax scene.

Both men were at least a decade older than Plaskett. Brennan had been living in New York and Toronto and was rumoured to be moving back home. Plaskett headed up to the Brennan family homestead in Cape Breton, in a car with song-writer Al Tuck and Plumtree's Catriona Sturton, arriving at the party uninvited. It being the East Coast, plenty of music was made and whisky flowed. After midnight, when most everyone had collapsed, Plaskett popped the question. Brennan accepted. Plaskett now had a power trio.

In early 2000, Plaskett rented a room in the Khyber, a three-floor arts mecca by the harbour, around the corner from the Nova Scotia College of Art and Design. Plaskett was on the "third and a half floor," he says, which sounds like something from the 1999 film *Being John Malkovich*. "There was a rep cinema in the building in the '90s, and above that there was a little staircase to the half level, half the height of the ballroom. There was a bar on the ground floor. The second floor had a large gallery space and a number of art studios. There was a record store in there for a while. A couple of rooms were offices or art studios. The top floor had the turret room. That was where Ultramagnetic Studios was, a two-room studio space with a third room for storage that we took over and tried to insulate against the rest of the building—pretty unsuccessfully. It was just another level of drywall so we could jam in there at full volume."

That attic racket paid dividends pretty quickly.

LEFT AND LEAVING CAME OUT JULY 25, 2000. The Weakerthans were on the cover of *Exclaim!*; in the piece, John K. Samson admitted that both his landline and cell-phone had just been disconnected and that he was rolling pennies and eating peanut butter to survive. Few other outlets were initially paying close attention to the band, other than CBC's nascent and niche Radio 3 service (to this day, host Grant Lawrence cites the Weakerthans as his favourite Canadian band ever). Within a year, mainstream artists like Gord Downie and Sarah Harmer were champions. A young Ontarian band, called the Constantines, was taking careful notes as they prepared to record their own debut album. *Left and Leaving* eventually landed on the radar of Stuart McLean's *The Vinyl Café* and was nominated for a Juno award. The Weakerthans were no longer the cherished secret of punks, poets and people likely to buy anarchist books—people like Samson himself. Their popularity spread through word of mouth: this was an independent band raised on DIY methods and ethics, existing outside corporate culture. If you heard the Weakerthans on CBC, campus or community radio and wanted to buy *Left and Leaving*, you had to find a physical copy (or, uh, on file-sharing). Once found, it was often cherished forever.

The album was produced by Ian Blurton of Change of Heart, a Toronto band beloved by Samson. The feeling was mutual; Blurton was into Propagandhi, having even written them fan letters (which they though were a hoax). After Change of Heart ended, Blurton had moved into production, notably on 1999's *Sometimes I Cry* by Tricky Woo—one of the greatest-sounding Canadian guitar records ever made.

The Weakerthans cold-called him and flew him to Winnipeg. "He worked so hard on our record," says Samson. "There was a lot of silence, of him thinking, and then everything would suddenly and magically sound amazing."

Blurton loved the whole experience. "I was coming out of a big relationship, and the songs on that record are very emotional," he says. "For me personally, I just thought, Don't fuck this up, because this is a really good record. It was the first time I'd ever been given a lyric sheet with notes about what each song was about. The best productions are generally when the band is on fire and you just have to stand back and watch it burn." Blurton wanted to mix the album at Chemical Sound in Toronto, so the Weakerthans booked a tour on the way there. "We were obsessed with keeping the two-inch tapes safe," says Samson. "We'd take them into basement shows we were playing and keep them on stage with us." Once in Toronto, engineer Daryl Smith wisely advised them to ditch the extremely dated drum'n'bass double-time drums they'd placed over the intro to "Everything Must Go!"

Samson had done most of his writing while working at Heaven Art and Book Café, on Corydon Avenue in Winnipeg's Little Italy. "It was a very quiet place— maybe to the detriment of the business," says Samson. "There was a monthly art show, a lot of readings and films. I got a ton of writing done there. We put cinnamon in our coffee. It was nice."

It was there he wrote "My Favourite Chords," a song that includes a line about how "the mayor is out killing kids." It was not about leftist mayor Glen Murray, who served from 1998 to 2004, but about his predecessor, Susan Thompson. But Samson says his strong language could be about any Winnipeg mayor in his lifetime and "the age-old—and still relevant—refusal of Winnipeg mayors to raise property taxes. They're unable or unwilling or there's some force field that goes down on their brains as soon as they take office, and it literally kills people: [defunding] social services, libraries, swimming pools—things that actually make people's lives livable. That lyric unfortunately has not really changed as long as I've been an adult in Winnipeg. I started that one at the bookstore and performed it for the first time there when I opened for bill bissett, the sound poet."

Left and Leaving's title track is a beloved song about longing, about loneliness, about watching people and buildings disappear until your hometown is unrecognizable. It's about a transitory time in one's mid-20s when friends are leaving: to other towns, to other lives. Set to a descending chord pattern and a percussive brush pattern with a triplet skip at the end of each bar, it registers deeply with any Canadian who doesn't live in Montreal, Toronto or Vancouver. "My city's still breathing, but barely, it's true / through buildings gone missing like teeth," sings Samson. Writer Sheldon Birnie later borrowed the phrase *Missing Like Teeth* to title his book about '90s Winnipeg music. It's a phrase that could apply to economic depression, to 9/11, to gentrification.

"It's been an interesting song to play at different historical times," says Samson, who wrote it after returning home from a tour in January 1999. "I was living in a loft, a big room with a shared bathroom down the hall, in downtown Winnipeg. I got home, went out for a walk, and the [century-old] Leland Hotel was in flames, burning to the ground. I stood there and watched it. We'd just got off tour with Plumtree, and I was really affected and interested and inspired by the songs of [guitarist/singer] Carla Gillis. There was some responding to her work in that song. And that sense of dislocation, arriving back home and having this literally missing building and not being able to remember what it looked like."

While in many ways a textbook folk-punk record descended from Billy Bragg and the Clash, drummer Tait provided textures unusual to the genre. "There are not a lot of sizzle cymbals in punk rock—or brushes, for that matter," Tait says. "I had bought Miles Davis's *'Four' & More* record, live at Carnegie Hall, which is all the material from *Kind of Blue* but played three times as fast. I still don't understand Tony Williams's drumming at all; his feel and phrasing is bananas. Ian

[Blurton] was really accommodating with my annoying ideas that most people would shut down right away."

Samson welcomed all of Tait's ideas: "I think that album is Jason-led, musically, in a lot of ways. In the beginning it was just the songs and Jason. Then he started with different percussion sounds, tempos and dynamics—it was outside. He's an original musical mind. Jason does what he wants—and he's almost always right."

Stephen Carroll also brought some surprises. His nimble guitar work injected countermelodies and flourishes when not doubling up Samson's rhythm guitar and John Sutton's bass for extra chunk. Though not a piano player, Carroll plays the barroom piano on "Slips and Tangles."

From Tait's bag of tricks Carroll pulled out a whirly tube—a corrugated piece of bendable plastic that changes pitch depending on velocity—for the solo on "Elegy for Elsabet." "I just grabbed it at one point, and it became part of the song," he says. "I believe the Dirty Three used it on a recording, I'm not sure about live. It's a silly thing. It would break and was impossible to play. It was a bit humiliating."

Opening ballad "Everything Must Go!" begins with a minor-key fanfare of sorts on electric guitar, four bars that give way to unaccompanied bass chords. Those underpin Samson's voice singing about a garage sale to "pay my heart's outstanding bills," eventually offering a "complicated dream of dignity" in return. Jason Tait enters with a syncopated boom-bap beat on the brushes, with a sprinkling of sizzle cymbals, and later plays a vibraphone solo. The chorus boasts a soaring melody, in which Samson sings of a place "where awkward belongs" and how "recovery comes to the broken ones." It ends with a shower of cymbals and Tait's snare run through distortion, then gives way to a four count on an open hi-hat announcing the punk flurry of "Aside," with its fire-alarm guitar riff. That song's bristling musical confidence contrasts with lyrics about agoraphobia and "leaning on a broken fence / between past and present tense" (a line Gord Downie quoted on stage during the Tragically Hip's induction into the Canadian Music Hall of Fame in 2004).

Third track "Watermark" keeps up the furious punk assault. "A lot of it was super easy to record: one or two takes to get the drums," says Tait. But a microphone issue meant that Tait had to redo what he thought was a perfect take on "Watermark." "It took forever," he recalls. "I got really mad, throwing drumsticks across the studio, being a total fucking baby about it. It was a hard time for me. I'd just ended a 14-year relationship, and we were playing all these sad songs. In the end, I think all that frustration and anger is shown. Especially at the end, I'm so pissed off in the last eight bars of the song, shooting up the tempo."

Throughout, Blurton's production gives the guitars the glory they deserve, with clarity that never sacrifices the sense of volume. The entire record rings with the immediacy of a live performance and with the attention to minute detail required of any great recording, like the way the bell of Tait's ride cymbal is amplified as it anticipates the bridge in "Aside," before shifting to a triangle playing eighth notes at a key moment of transition. Julie Penner provides weeping violin on "Slips and Tangles." The beat poetry of "Without Mythologies" is set to malleted toms. Tait plays musical saw on "My Favourite Chords." Each member of the band sees Samson's lyrics and melodies as a black and white picture with which to imbue colour, no matter the tempo or style.

The biggest draw, though, is Samson's songs. In the years following *Left and Leaving*, his writing became more adult, less understood to be autobiographical; he became more of a short story writer, always with an abundance of empathy. His writing changed and evolved, but it didn't get better—because it didn't have to. He was fully formed at 27 years old, with an album that perhaps he could only have written at that age—the same age Joni Mitchell was when she wrote *Blue*. There are lyrical elements that speak to the melancholy of youth but are hardly exclusive to that time in one's life. In "This Is a Fire Door Never Leave Open," Samson sings about one emotionally stunted character's "forty years of failing to describe a feeling." Decades after *Left and Leaving*, the strength of the Weakerthans is that they never failed at anything, least of all the ability to describe a feeling.

Released on a tiny, politically oriented record label with modest distribution and no marketing, *Left and Leaving* could easily have remained a cult record. "I remember G7 took out an ad in *Exclaim!*," says Tait, "and I thought, Oh, Jesus, these guys are trying to get us to go big time! That's fucking crazy. But we weren't discovered by one person who helped things along; there was nothing specific, no hinge. [The record's success] was very much word of mouth."

The Weakerthans flirted with a couple of managers before Stephen Carroll assumed those duties. "One manager gave us a bunch of good ideas; we took them and then let them go after six months," says Carroll. "We were hard to manage. Someone like me is impossible to manage. And I always joked that John's favourite word was *no*. Everything we did involved negotiation. He didn't use that word when it came to creation, but when it came to trying to operate in the world of normal music-business practices, it was tricky. He had a vision of how he wanted us to engage with the public. John's motivation for his voice in the band was never financial. It always had to have a practical and artistic motivation, or to promote the work."

Left and Leaving came out in the U.S. on Hopeless Records, a label closely associated with the SoCal pop-punk scene that also embraced Propagandhi. They felt pigeonholed. "We had a U.S. booking agent with punk-rock roots, that was her niche, and she'd always book us with punk bands that a couple

of us just loathed," says Carroll. "That was wearying. We wanted to participate in the wider community of artists we liked: Vic Chesnutt, Calexico, people
doing interesting things outside our genre." They switched agents, and things
improved. They were offered an opening slot for Wilco, a big favourite of Tait's
in particular—though he was dismayed the offer was for only $300 a night on a
Canadian tour, at a time when the Weakerthans didn't have any trouble drawing on their own. "We told them, 'We love you guys, but we don't love you that
much,'" says Tait.

They did love the idea of signing to California's Epitaph Records, founded
by Bad Religion. Epitaph had started a sister label, Anti-, to put out a Tom Waits
record and then signed acts like Merle Haggard, Solomon Burke and Nick Cave.
That had a lot of appeal for the Weakerthans. "They're former musicians who
now run a label," says Tait, "whereas G7 were active musicians doing their best to
run a label. *Left and Leaving* came out on Hopeless in the U.S., Bad Taste in Sweden
and another label in Hamburg. We wanted to consolidate all areas of the world
with one label. We gave Epitaph our terms, which were a lot of career suicide
moves, and without blinking they just said, 'Great. Let's make a record.'"

"They puzzled over what to do with us," says Carroll. "We were technically
signed to both sides of their label: Epitaph and Anti-. We walked in both worlds
for them, which was nice for us. If we were on Epitaph alone, it might not have
been the best course of action." The label marketed them to both punk and public
radio audiences.

Their Epitaph debut, 2003's *Reconstruction Site*, is a favourite of fans—but not
of John K. Samson. "I like some of the songs," he says, "but there's a lot more ges-
tural stuff. *Left and Leaving* was very deliberate: every song was pored over. A lot
of *Reconstruction Site* was written really quickly." In 2001, Samson had moved in
with his partner, fellow songwriter Christine Fellows. At one point that year they
challenged each other to write a song a day; it was a particular challenge for the
slow-moving Samson. "At least six songs on the record came from that," he says.
"But there was also a great splintering then. The whole rhythm section moved
to Toronto. It was sort of the end of the band, when we no longer got together
once a week to practise. Everything after that was an echo. Obviously people were
much happier moving. But to me that record is a bit more ad hoc than the other
ones, in a way."

One of those song-a-day experiments worked out exceptionally well, however.
The title of "One Great City!" is borrowed from Winnipeg's civic motto, seen on
signs as one enters town. The song was written as a short sketch, almost as a joke.
In the first two verses, a retail worker and a bus driver lament the monotony of
their day before concluding in the chorus, "I hate Winnipeg." In the final verse,

Samson animates the statue of a boy on top of the Manitoban legislature, imagining him to be a developer swinging a wrecking ball toward the city's neglected North End, singing, as he does so, "I hate Winnipeg."

"The song is about the pitfalls of boosterism, and trying to be honest with who we are, where we're from, and also the kind of right and duty to critique the place you're from," he told the *Winnipeg Free Press*, which in 2020 picked "One Great City!" as the greatest song every written by a Manitoban, tied with the Guess Who's "American Woman." "Also I think of it as a song about cherishing the things that are good about the place and not knocking them down. When I sing, 'The Guess Who suck, the Jets were lousy anyway,' what I'm trying to say is that the Guess Who are kind of amazing, and uniquely Winnipeg, and something we should actually cherish. And that the Jets, the original Jets, being lousy was actually kind of beautiful."

"John was nervous about playing it in Winnipeg for the first time—obviously," says Jason Tait. "But everybody got it right away. There was a huge laugh when he hit the chorus, which was a huge relief. And it's our crowd—if we played that song at a suburban picnic where no one knew our band, they'd be like, 'What the fuck are you talking about?!' There are certain people, like [*Exclaim!* writer] Chuck Molgat, who strongly suggested that we leave it off the record, out of fear people wouldn't understand it. But people around the world love it. We play that song in New York City, and people say, 'That song could be about my city.' People in Stockholm, same thing. Who'd have thought that ragging on your city would be such a universal theme? But I guess it is."

The artwork for the 2003 album was done by Marcel Dzama of Winnipeg collective the Royal Art Lodge; he soon became an internationally acclaimed visual artist. Harmony vocals on the song "Benediction" were performed by one of the Weakerthans' biggest fans: Sarah Harmer.

HAVING BEEN CHURNED through a major label deal once already, Sarah Harmer was tempted to go it alone, looking to Ani DiFranco for inspiration. "I did start Cold Snap [Records] and drew my own logo, just to have my own P.O. box and corporation," she says. "But the lure of an easier ride [with] a larger infrastructure in place was appealing. It was an important crossroads for me. I hadn't hitched my pony to any post yet. The decisions I was making would influence the direction the next records would go." She knew *You Were Here* was a pop record, destined for big things. A deal with Allan Reid at Universal gave her everything she wanted: "I had complete control over what I was doing and when it was being done." In the U.S., she signed with Rounder Records, a long-respected independent folk label that had recently branched into pop music (and soon began signing many Canadians, including Gord Downie, Cowboy Junkies and even Rush). Harmer was Rounder's first pop artist who didn't hail from its Boston home.

You Were Here was rereleased in August 2000—with a professional headshot replacing her hand-drawn sketch on the original cover. Rounder provided marketing muscle, racking up lots of rave reviews in the U.S.; it eventually landed in *Time*'s top 10 of the year. She wasn't drawing many more than 300 people per gig there, but that was a lot better than Weeping Tile ever did. Over the course of the next year, she opened U.S. tours for Cowboy Junkies and Barenaked Ladies, at a time when the latter were playing in front of 20,000 people a night.

But she wasn't cut out for the kind of nonstop U.S. touring that BNL and Sarah McLachlan had endured in order to break big. "I suffered from exhaustion," she admits. "At the end of one leg of the tour, I did a show at State College, Pennsylvania, and when I got home I couldn't move any part of my body, even my eyeballs, without it hurting. I was in bed for a number of days. My friend took me to the hospital, because he was so worried. They said, 'Yeah, you have exhaustion.' I just had to rest for a few weeks. It can be intense. Especially when you're getting all these opportunities that you want to say yes to. You can only go so long." She toured *You Were Here* until November 2002, which included three trips to the U.K.

In Canada, things were going very well. "I remember Sarah calling me from a truck stop on the way back to Kingston," says Universal's Allan Reid, "and she heard her song come over the loudspeaker in the parking lot. That's when she knew she was on the radio in a big way. This was the same time Nelly Furtado was the It Girl. The industry put them in competition: they were nominated in the same Juno categories, which fuelled this thing where Nelly was signed to Dreamworks"—the label co-founded by Steven Spielberg and David Geffen—"and Sarah was an independent artist signed to a label here and Rounder in America. Sarah was the Little Engine That Could. They weren't played off each other deliberately, it just became a thing people talked about and helped her get on the radio in a bigger way and fuelled the success of that record. MuchMusic was also a big help."

In September 2001, shortly after 9/11, Harmer appeared on David Letterman's show, where a seemingly minor event turned into a moment. Stage manager Biff Henderson, a sidekick of Letterman's known for his man-in-the-street interviews, was celebrating a birthday, and Letterman called him to come in front of the camera just before Harmer's set. She recalls, "Dave said, 'Hey, why don't you stay out here and sing with the band?' I couldn't see it, but apparently he was making a beeline for my mic." Her bassist pulled Henderson back to his own mic, where

Henderson attempted to sing along. "In the control room, both my sound tech and my manager were asked, 'Do you want to keep this going?' 'Yeah, it's good television.' I didn't see it until we pulled the bus over hours later on the drive home, and I thought, Oh, he totally cut my grass there. The next night I watched the show, and Letterman mentioned it again. That was almost more exciting to me: being at my friend's apartment in downtown Kingston watching David Letterman talking about our performance, saying, 'Last night something happened that's never happened before!' That was more thrilling." Mainstream press turned it into a story, because it was a rare moment of spontaneity on network television. For a veteran of folk festival workshops, it was just another day at work.

At a time when women-led rock bands were in scarce supply in the mainstream, it was somewhat disheartening to see the kinder, gentler solo performer succeed commercially in ways that her rock band never had. But mainstream female-fronted rock bands evaporated in Canada after Crash Vegas; in the U.S., Hole and Veruca Salt were outliers. In 2004, Harmer revisited Weeping Tile albums for the first time in years when the band reunited for a Christmas hometown show. "It was really hard for me to listen to," she said then. "I didn't hate it, but my voice is so different and I'm really belting it out. I was really into the Breeders and I can hear that in there. It was scrappier. On *You Were Here* I did a couple of radio mixes, so I did compromise a little bit more." Weeping Tile had resisted its label's advice on song choices and remixes. "We were harder to please back then," she continued. "It's not surprising to me that *You Were Here* had more doors open to it. Different setup. Different labels, publicists, focus. Weeping Tile was a collective. But I think [*You Were Here*] is different enough that they're completely different situations. As much as I don't see it myself, people see me now on an industry level as soft rock. I go to [those radio stations] and I think, Really? Is this the kind of music I do? But I don't care about label stuff. There are pigeonholes and formats, for sure."

Though she was a solo performer who longed to be in a gang, Harmer had no shortage of invitations. Bruce Cockburn personally asked her to help induct him into the Canadian Music Hall of Fame at the 2001 Junos, where she gave a speech and covered "Waiting for a Miracle." She also got a call out of the blue from a young guy named Kevin Drew, with whom she had mutual friends. She went to see him play at Jeff Healey's bar. "I remember thinking, Holy shit, this guy has some serious charisma. But it just seemed like something they were doing in their living room. At the time I was doing my stuff full-time, and I didn't want to do something where I just sing a couple of songs. I was in my own world. Years later, [manager] Patrick [Sambrook] said, 'That's when he was putting Broken Social Scene together. And you blew him off!' I don't know if that's what happened, but

I like to think I got the invitation."[3] She was also a huge fan of Drew's friends in Metric, from whom she and Prilesnik borrowed gear while making *You Were Here*.

Harmer took most of 2003 off, working slowly on a new record. Both Universal and Rounder were pressuring her to work with a major producer. CBC Radio host Nora Young commissioned Harmer to write a song for a series about the seven deadly sins. She recorded it with Marty Kinack, the sound tech she shared with Broken Social Scene, in his basement on Toronto's Dovercourt Avenue. They finished the task in 24 hours, which inspired them to build a studio at Harmer's house just north of Kingston, dubbed the Slanty Shanty—"which should give you an indication of the tilt my brain is on when I'm here," she says.

The album, 2004's *All of Our Names*, was decidedly more downcast than *You Were Here*, having more in common with Cat Power or Hayden. In retrospect, it's an archetypical follow-up to a smash: interior, withdrawn. Its best moments are the quietest and eeriest: "Greeting Card Aisle," "Things to Forget," "Dandelions in Bullet Holes," "Tether." "I thought it was a bit more upbeat than anyone I played it for," she shrugs.

At the label's request, she rerecorded singles "Pendulum" and "Almost" in a "northern Toronto strip mall studio" with producer Gavin Brown, her former drummer who was now making multimillion-selling albums for Three Days Grace and Billy Talent. The singles didn't really take, though the album did well enough, going gold in Canada. By that point in time, legions of Harmer acolytes were on the ascent, not the least of whom were former Sambrook client Amy Millan of Stars and then current Sambrook client Kathleen Edwards, who had also scored a Rounder deal and made a big impression on David Letterman.

ONE NIGHT IN MALMÖ, SWEDEN, in 2001 changed Danko Jones's life. The show itself was a bit of a bust, because of a broken guitar and other tech issues, but he met his future wife that night. And the band's set caught the attention of a Swedish guitarist who soon booked Danko Jones an opening slot on a five-week tour of 1,000-seat venues.

Meanwhile, Danko's booking agent got the band on the waiting list for the Roskilde Festival in Denmark, the largest festival in northern Europe. The night before it opened, there was a cancellation and Danko Jones got the nod. They were in southern Germany at the time: they could only make it to Roskilde if they turned around immediately and drove straight there, above the speed limit.

---

3   Drew doesn't recall this specifically but says, "Of course I would have wanted Harmer." Years later she signed to his Arts & Crafts label.

They didn't make it in time, but they did get slotted in the next day, on the same stage as PJ Harvey, and slayed in front of 18,000 people. At a smaller festival in Sweden, they played for a crowd that included Jello Biafra and some of the most influential music writers in Europe.

How did Danko Jones become a Swedish success story? Chalk it all up to Bad Taste.

Bad Taste is a Swedish punk label who worked with many North American acts (including the Weakerthans). The first Canadian album the label put out was in 1997: the Almighty Trigger Happy's *I'll Shut Up When You Fuck Off*. Trigger Happy's Al Nolan was a big Danko Jones fan. At the Toronto sex shop where Danko had a day job in 1999, Nolan had asked him for a copy of *My Love Is Bold* to bring on tour to Sweden, where he promised to give it to Bad Taste. The label loved it and in 2001 put out a Danko Jones compilation called *I'm Alive and on Fire*.

Danko Jones had long suspected that Europe was a better fit for his band than Canada. Peaches pointed the way. Danko first saw her at an *Exclaim!* party in 2000[4] and was blown away: here was an outrageous performer, sexually provocative, with back-to-basics music that pushed back against staid Canadiana—the two performers might as well be siblings.

"I told our booking agent we had to get her to play with us somewhere," he says. "That double bill would be amazing. She called me and said, 'Thanks for the offer, but I'm moving to Berlin. I can't do those shows.' I thought, Why are you going there? I had no concept of Berlin or anything. All I knew was New York and Detroit and every hot spot of punk rock. Then I saw some article in the *NME* about her, then *Spin*, and I realized there was more shit happening. By the time we got to Berlin in 2001 on our first European tour, she was living there and was a name there. We played Wild at Heart, a legendary Berlin punk rock bar, and Leslie [Feist] and Peaches and [Toronto visual artist] Shary Boyle came and that was great, they were all in the front row. Later on, [Peaches] wanted to write songs with us. We met once [in Toronto]. Her dad drove her over because she was just visiting. We were just sitting on our amps. Here we were, two 'sex people.' She took a riff we came up with that day, but I don't think she ever released it."

As European prospects proved positive, Danko Jones made their first proper full-length, *Born a Lion*, in early 2002. Like Sarah Harmer's deal, it was licensed to Universal with the band retaining control. It spawned the rock radio hit "Lovercall" and sold 18,000 copies—good numbers for an indie record at the time but a failure by major label standards, especially after the marketing money Universal had spent. Bands like Danko Jones and Tricky Woo were yesterday's news once the

---

4   The Weakerthans were also on the bill.

Strokes and the White Stripes started captivating the press. Within a year, by 2003's *We Sweat Blood*, Danko felt that Universal was throwing all their weight behind Sam Roberts as the next great rock hope—and meanwhile Nickelback was the biggest new rock band in the world. Danko Jones barely toured Canada to promote *We Sweat Blood*. It only sold 8,000 copies domestically. But by then, they had Swedish fish to fry. Canada didn't even matter anymore.

JOEL PLASKETT WAS IN HELL, singing "Maybe We Should Just Go Home."

Hell was a venue underneath Halifax's Marquee Club, where in 2000 the Emergency got a weekly Monday gig, workshopping Thrush Hermit leftovers and new songs. "What I wanted to do was play music," he says. "I had no university education. No backup plan. I just dove into it and continued from where we'd left off and started building it again." His mother found him a job digitizing tapes at the local CBC affiliate, a gig where the 25-year-old could set his own hours.

He saved enough money to buy a Chevy Suburban, so the band could tour. The trio did a short jaunt in Ontario, including a stop at Toronto's Horseshoe Tavern, where the fact that he could draw people on his own was a shot in the arm. In the fall of 2000, he started recording with Charles Austin—who also worked at the CBC archives and in whose band, Neuseiland, Plaskett played drums—in the attic of the Khyber to capture the Emergency. Austin ran his Ultramagnetic recording studio in the building. Thrush Hermit's Ian McGettigan co-produced the *Down at the Khyber* sessions, which, as on *Clayton Park*, had a large classic rock tinge hanging over them—now even more ramped up.

"That album has a particular sound: not hi-fi but mid-fi, very limited in a good way. It had character," says Plaskett. "We had a shitty Yamaha board and a one-inch tape machine I bought after doing *Clayton Park*. We just had a handful of microphones, none of which were very good. We had really deep bass because we were running the bass into this Avalon DI, so it has this big thumpy sound—it's swimming in low end. And I was so into treble on guitars, I'd wind an amp as trebly as I could make it."

Zeppelin was one reference point. "It's often best to mic a drummer like Dave Marsh at a distance," says Plaskett. The same was true for Zeppelin's John Bonham. "Dave responds to dynamics. If you mic him close, it's more challenging because he's the kind of guy who puts a big rim shot in there and his snare goes from quiet to loud. If you mic him from a distance, it sounds more like jazz records or early rock'n'roll records. Any kind of drum reverberance is us dropping mics outside the room the drums were in. A lot of drum stuff was done at night when the bar was running downstairs. A lot was done post–bar hours, so we could open up the fire escape stairway and record [the ballad] 'Light of the Moon' at three in the morning and get a good vocal sound. They were such boxy little drywall rooms; they didn't sound that great. But the rest of the building—the fire escape and the hallway—you could get a lot of reflection. Then Charles had a big plate reverb for the vocals."

The new material was not only classic rock. Tim Brennan loved both country and reggae; the Congos' *Heart of the Congo* became a touchstone for Plaskett. "I loved the reverb on that record," says Plaskett, who may or may not have sampled it on the title track, which has a bovine moan particular to the work of Congos producer Lee "Scratch" Perry. "The breakdown on 'Clueless Wonder' was referencing what I heard on those Congos records, when it sounds like the band is underwater. And the Congos were hugely influenced by Curtis Mayfield and the Impressions, which was another big reference for us. We were covering Mayfield's 'I Loved and I Lost.' I was really into soul music and the way it influenced reggae music." Marsh had lived in Britain in the early '80s, and there was also an element of Elvis Costello–style new wave and Clash energy in the mix. "Our idea was to cross-pollinate all that with the Halifax vibe," says Plaskett.

The sonics of *Down at the Khyber*, of course, are just one part of the overall picture. The band is whip-tight, with Marsh in particular displaying all the tasty bits that had made him one of the city's most in-demand drummers for decades. Plaskett, handling rhythm and lead parts, proves to be a subtle shredder throughout, with some dual-lead harmony parts indebted to childhood influence April Wine. The opening track features a monstrous glam-rock riff over a reggae bassline, and Plaskett sings with clarity and vigour, ready to shake off his teenage years and stake new claims: "I've been away and I've been travelling / I've been lost, I've fucked around . . . I got sick / and I got sicker / then I spent a month in bed . . . Am I still alive? Where did I collapse? Was it Edmonton, Alberta? / or home in Halifax? / Float me down the river / to the Musquodoboit Harbour / Because I'm getting nowhere."

Though it's likely the first rock'n'roll reference to central Nova Scotia's Musquodoboit Valley, it isn't the only time on *Down at the Khyber* that Plaskett takes the Canadiana trophy away from Gord Downie: there are also references to Sault Ste. Marie, he rhymes "Saskatchewan" with "it's catching on," and more. "Hearing reference points that speak to me is important, and I've always liked regional voices in music," Plaskett says. "I want music from Montreal to sound like Montreal. Music from New Orleans talks about those streets. And why are those songs still talked about now? Because of their insular specificity. Everything was always about the personal."

Musically, *Khyber* might have sounded retro but is anything but myopic. More multidimensional than most rock or roots music at the time, it features a cover of Jamaican rocksteady singer Alton Ellis's "Cry Together," redone as a Beatles' *Let It Be* era blues in 6/8. Songs like "Clueless Wonder" and "Unconditional Love" are more soulful takes on the alt-country trend. "Blinding Light" is a duet with the Guthries' Ruth Minnikin. "Maybe We Should Just Go Home" and "This Is a Message" sounds like less angsty Constantines. Closing track "Light of the Moon" evolves from a lonesome campfire acoustic song into a Allman Brothers–esque electric guitar epic before dissolving into a mandolin and banjo duet played by Plaskett and his father, Bill.

With the record in hand, Joel Plaskett had no idea what to do next. The idea of a major label deal didn't seem feasible. The tiny Minneapolis label that had put out *In Need of Medical Attention* had shut down. Other indies weren't in great shape. He took a gamble on a new Halifax label with a mouthful of a moniker taken from *Gulliver's Travels*: Brobdingnagian, run by Dennis Stewart. "I didn't know what to do with it, and Dennis was psyched about it," says Plaskett. "I was self-managed. I just wanted someone to do that work for me; I didn't want to self-release. Dennis was a bit of a mysterious guy. He showed up in Halifax and started putting out records by [local bands] the Guthries and the Heavy Blinkers that got British press."

Down at the Khyber came out in the U.K. on a different label, however: the short-lived Multiball, run by former Murderecords employee Mark Brown, whose day job was working for Creation Records founder Alan McGee. Brown had enough clout to get Plaskett's record reviewed in most of the big British magazines, which were beginning to wake up to raw rock'n'roll again in 2001. *Q* magazine called the album a "need-to-know guitar-rock triumph." *Down at the Khyber* was every bit as exhilarating, if not more, as albums by the Strokes and White Stripes, and it was less one-dimensional. The Joel Plaskett Emergency certainly rocked harder than any British—or American—bands at the time. They opened for Interpol on the latter's first trip to London, and it's not hard to imagine who commanded the stage.

Considering the strength of *Down at the Khyber*—and the decrepit state of commercial Canadian rock music at the time—it was shocking that it didn't get more mainstream traction. It's certainly conventional and catchy enough for anyone raised on classic rock, and it's full of the kinds of songs the Tragically Hip wished they were still writing at that point in their career. Plaskett's melodies often push the upper part of his natural register. The guitars sound like they are in the listeners' living room. But for whatever reason, it remained a word-of-mouth sensation, with the explosive live band making an impact one fan at a time in small clubs across the country. "I've kicked around this city for too long / waiting for someone to hear my song," Plaskett sings. "Uncharted and untraced / waiting to be discovered."

CBC Radio 3 was a big champion, particularly of the track "True Patriot Love"—a Nick Lowe–ish song that was hardly full of nationalist slogans; it's about losing a love, coming home from the bar, and falling asleep with the television on in pre-cable times, when local stations played the national anthem before signing off. But, like Plaskett himself, CBC Radio 3 was a largely unknown entity based in a coastal city far away from Montreal and Toronto, struggling to make an impression on the country's music fans, with a small but dedicated audience.

In Toronto, Plaskett had a huge fan in CFNY DJ Dave Bookman, who told Plaskett biographer Josh O'Kane, "Not wanting [Joel] to be forgotten was really important to me. I began a decade-long crusade of getting Joel into the mainstream." Bookman easily brought on board his friends Jeff Cohen and Craig Laskey, bookers for Toronto's Horseshoe Tavern, who were happy to host the Emergency for multiple-night runs.

Plaskett was still self-managed in 2001. Mike Campbell—a long-time MuchMusic VJ who hosted *Much East* and was a champion of East Coast music of all stripes—thought that was ridiculous. *Down at the Khyber* blew him away the first time he heard it. With each successive track, he was more and more convinced he was listening to the greatest rock record to ever come out of Halifax. He became evangelical, playing it for everyone he knew. In particular he nagged at Sheri Jones, who had managed the uneasy career of Ashley MacIsaac. Jones came from different musical spheres and didn't know the history of Thrush Hermit. Campbell begged her to listen to *Down at the Khyber*; she kept putting it off. On one bone-chilling winter night when taxis were scarce, Campbell offered her a ride home from downtown—which came with a price. He put on the album and forced her to listen to it. She was intrigued, and they went back to his place and listened three more times. She agreed to pitch Plaskett on a co-management arrangement with Campbell and to try to get him a record deal. In February, they set up a showcase at the East Coast Music Awards—which Jones had co-founded in 1991. There Plaskett impressed Kim Cooke of the MapleMusic label, who signed him.

Now with an eye on a prize, Plaskett's next record, *Truthfully Truthfully*, was a slightly slicker affair. It was once again recorded with Charles Austin and Ian McGettigan in Halifax, though mixed in Toronto. The country, reggae and folk influences were muted: this was a commercial rock record. The regionalism was dialled down, although Plaskett does deliver a line that resonates with anyone east of Winnipeg: "All my friends, where did they go? / Montreal! To-ron-to!"

Like its predecessor, *Truthfully Truthfully* features what should have been slam-dunk singles like "Work Out Fine," "Extraordinary" and "Mystery and Crime," yet any commercial gains in Plaskett's career were incremental. The venues were slightly bigger, now about 500 capacity in the major centres (except Montreal, where he was a mere Anglo curiosity). "No commercial airplay for that record," says Kim Cooke. "I would not have expected rock radio or even Top 40 to play Joel, knowing what they were playing at the time. But alternative radio should have."

Plaskett was destined to be a word-of-mouth artist, unlike his labelmate Sam Roberts, whose career skyrocketed. "Sam's stuff, to be honest, slams on radio," says Plaskett. "Some people would view me as a new artist then, but I felt like an old artist. My expectations weren't that big—maybe I naturally send out some of that energy. Sam was so right-place-right-time but also had great songs. *Khyber* was a bit garage-y for the radio. *Truthfully*, that one I thought would have had more legs."

"What do you want me to do / to make it happen now?" went one of his new songs. Though Plaskett's career was in motion, there were no formulas in place that couldn't easily be broken. Bassist Tim Brennan amicably left the band to join his wife in Ireland and was replaced by McGettigan. Plaskett had been amassing acoustic songs, such as "Love This Town," that he'd started playing solo in Emergency sets.

He also had an offer from Bob Hoag, a fan in Mesa, Arizona—who was introduced to Thrush Hermit through a Canadian roommate—to make a record there in a new home studio for free. It was a hard offer to refuse. On somewhat of a whim, Plaskett packed up his Chevy Suburban in May 2004 and headed south. He played a couple of gigs on the way and stopped in to visit Doug Easley in Memphis. He wrote a few songs about his travels, including "Natural Disaster" and "Nina and Albert." Because he barely knew Hoag, he asked McGettigan to fly down and meet him there as a safeguard.

Through all of June, they recorded at night, because the recording booth didn't have air conditioning. When it was done, the trio played a one-off show with Hoag on drums; he knew all of Plaskett's songs, solo and with Thrush Hermit, inside out. No one knew what would become of the sessions. Maybe it was a real album, maybe it would only be sold at merch tables. Plaskett hadn't even told his management or his band where he'd gone. Dave Marsh later claimed he found out from a random taxi driver. Plaskett disputes this. "Whether it's true or not, it's true to the emotion he felt," he says generously. "There were times when I just had to do something on my own after a while. I found that the nature of our collaboration, the intensity [Marsh] can bring to the situation, sometimes made me want to just retreat with an acoustic guitar. Yet I didn't want to work with other drummers, other than myself. People knew I was going to make a solo record, but nobody heard it until it was done and mastered."

That summer, the Joel Plaskett Emergency were invited to open a few dates for the Tragically Hip, followed by a national tour in the fall that put them in front of more than 10,000 people a night. That was not a high point in the Hip's career; they were touring their least successful record. It wasn't hard for an opener to make new fans in that context, especially fans predisposed to perking up their ears when they hear Canadian geography set to music.

MapleMusic was excited about the momentum from the Hip tour. So when Plaskett showed up at their office with a completed solo album that they weren't even aware he'd been working on, they were baffled. "They viewed it as, 'What if this doesn't count, contractually?' They didn't know what to do with it," he says. It wasn't an acoustic record, but it was certainly subdued compared to the Emergency.

To promote it, he went on a solo acoustic tour with his friend Peter Elkas of Local Rabbits, who was launching his own solo career with Maple. It was low budget, to say the least; they flew to B.C. and bought a 1989 Camry to drive east. "Me and Pete with our guitars in the back, a trunk full of merch and no sound tech," says Plaskett of the six-week cross-Canadian jaunt. "It was relaxed in a way that an Emergency tour could never be. That was a learning curve. I realized I liked the variety and quieter venues. We played a café in Lindsay, Ontario, followed by three nights at [intimate folk club] Hugh's Room in Toronto. But then there were two nights at the Big White Ski Resort outside Kelowna. We cancelled the second night, because, on the first night, the drunk snowboarders started slam-dancing to 'Enter Sandman' the second we finished our set. And we had to rent all the cables and microphones from Long and McQuade, because there was no sound tech there. The only person who came to see us play was Kevin Kane from the Grapes of Wrath."

La De Da did even better than *Truthfully*—but with no help from commercial radio. Its success was part natural momentum, part the Hip exposure and part relentless touring. Plaskett was also exposed to new audiences when he started getting folk festival gigs. He also did a tour with his father accompanying him, on a string of dates opening for Kathleen Edwards. "At the time, I probably could have outdrawn Kathleen," he says. "It was a trade: she brought me to the United States, and we opened for her band in Canada. I was really happy to do that. Then I went to the States on my own when she was touring as a duo with Jim Bryson.

"I was still dipping my toes in the States then, and at the time I wanted to try anything. I was learning how to put on different kinds of shows: solo, as a duo, with a band. In some ways that doesn't do a lot for band camaraderie, that sense of all being in it together. But the nature of the music business—which was changing at that time, if not crumbling—is that you have to be a jack of all trades. It was a survival instinct. Now I could play in rural Nova Scotia in a tiny little room. Juggling that is not my strongest suit; I don't always make everybody feel included."

DANKO JONES PISSED OFF his record company during a 2003 CBC Radio panel hosted by Evan Solomon. The topic was illegal downloading, which Danko favoured—and major labels most definitely did not. "My big mouth fucked everything up," he says. "It was me and Bruce [Gordon] from I Mother Earth and the president of the CMRRA [Canadian Musical Reproduction Rights Agency], who was soon replaced. Backstage, he came in like a total arrogant prick. The first thing he said to me and Bruce was, 'I've got the answers, boys!' I'm like, 'Oh, fuck you.'" That was off-air, but Danko wasn't much more polite on-air. By then, he figures, the writing was already on the wall. His days at Universal were numbered. "Garage rock, rock'n'roll, punk, indie rock—it was all there for the taking, but the [major labels] didn't know how to deal with it," he says. "I still don't know if they do."

North American prospects continued to be dire, especially on a gruelling 2005 tour of the U.S. One show in the northeast still stands out; they played with Wolf Parade side project Sunset Rubdown. "We played a show in the same club that had two [live] rooms; they were in the smaller room," he recalls. "There was a communal office with a computer, where you could check your email. One of the guys from Sunset Rubdown was on it, and before he left he wrote on the screen, 'Danko Jones is corporate rock.' We were using the room as a dressing room; he knew we would see it. When we confronted him, he literally hid, he walked behind their tour manager or whoever she was. She was defending him. We were on a shitty tour of America, starving, sleeping in crap motels, and we were ready to kill someone. If you know anything about our band, we licensed our two albums to Universal and got thrown off like a bunch of punk rockers. So fuck you! And *you hid behind your manager.* I didn't know who they were, and I was like, 'Where are you guys from?' 'We're from Montreal.' I just looked at [bassist Calabrese] and said, '*Ohhhhh.* Of course.' We were doing a lot of American touring and also had inner-band upheaval. We were stressed. I'm not making excuses for our behaviour, but thank god he hid behind her. I don't see red to the point of no return. But in that moment, I wanted to take out everything we were going through on that twerp. That whole moment crystallized everything for us, everything we were thinking people were thinking of us. It confirmed everything."

Drummer Damon Richardson left the band shortly afterwards. A new album, *Sleep Is the Enemy*, came out on veteran indie Aquarius Records in Canada in 2006. The single, "First Date," was an early YouTube hit, racking up two million views shortly after its release. More important for Danko, however, was being invited to sing "Killed by Death" with Motörhead at several festival dates, or having Metallica's Kirk Hammett ask him backstage at the Rock am Ring festival how to play Danko's "Soul on Ice" correctly. As for their non-festival shows, Danko Jones were now headlining 2,500-capacity venues in Germany.

Danko Jones put out a new record roughly every two years, along with two live records and a compilation of very early tracks. He became a prolific podcaster in 2011. He continued to connect with his metal heroes, old and new, touring often with Motörhead as well as 21st-century Danish band Volbeat, who regularly go multiplatinum in Europe. In 2010, Danko Jones opened for Guns N' Roses on an arena tour of Canada and also at Dublin's O2 Arena, where he paid tribute to Thin Lizzy's Phil Lynott and visited with the late guitarist's mother. Scheduled to play a 35-minute set, it was extended an extra 40 minutes because Axl Rose had not yet arrived from Belfast. Danko Jones was still on stage half an hour into the headliner's set time. When Rose and company finally took the stage at 11 p.m., someone pegged Rose in the head with a water bottle after two songs, and he left the stage; 14,000 people rioted.

Danko Jones largely built his reputation from his live show. He claims not to even know his record sales numbers. "I judge stuff by ticket sales and people showing up," he says. "I don't want to know unless it went gold. I know we're not that band. We're on small labels. But now with streaming: different game. I compare our numbers with bands who are gods here in Canada, and we obliterate them. I know that there are exactly 20 of our songs on Spotify that have more than one million listens." One song, "Had Enough," from 2010's Below the Belt, has more than 20 million streams 10 years after it came out.

"But, you know, whatever," he shrugs. As much as those numbers boost his already healthy ego, "you quickly get put in your place. I hope I don't sound bitter. I truly love the Canadian music scene I'm from. I'm genuinely happy [for my peers]. I'm on their cheerleading squad."

WITH HEALTHY SALES but no radio attention, Plaskett's label made a push for him to be playlisted, suggesting producer Gordie Johnson of Big Sugar might be the man for the job. "I always thought Big Sugar records sounded great, but I didn't know the music outside of the radio," says Plaskett. Gordie Johnson "loved Khyber and Clayton Park, which was flattering." Johnson was hired for a three-song EP, Make a Little Noise. The Celtic-tinged "Nowhere with You," with a beat Plaskett says he borrowed from Buddy Holly's "Peggy Sue," was chosen as a single. The song wasn't doing much of anything until it appeared in an ad for the department store Zellers—not the hippest association—but the ad's popularity gave radio a reason to finally play Joel Plaskett.

"I'm not criticizing radio, but I don't deliver things that fit that format," he says. "Gordie, to his credit, helped craft something that did. Being an East Coast artist and not part of the industry on a daily basis has its challenges. I'd get love on radio stations out here [on the East Coast]. But in Ontario it took more work. I didn't fit formats, and the fact I was independent might have affected things."

Some of Plaskett's fans from the '90s may have made claims of lost "indie cred" by "selling out" in a major ad campaign. But as drummer Dave Marsh joked to Plaskett biographer Josh O'Kane, "'You sold out to Zellers'—as if that isn't the funniest Canadian sentence of all time." But even on a purely musical basis, the song became a dividing line for any indie rock snobs left over from the Thrush Hermit days. "Maybe they carried over for a record or two," says Plaskett, "but as soon as they heard a tin whistle, they were like, 'Fuck this, I'm outta here!'"

Mike Campbell commissioned a live DVD recorded at the Marquee Club, figuring that if Plaskett's studio recordings weren't enough to convince foreign bookers and press, then capturing his charisma and explosive live show surely would. It led to Plaskett's first tour of Australia, where he continued to return for a couple of years—before he realized he was mostly playing to expats. The DVD sold the equivalent of gold status (5,000 copies) and, like the reissue of *La De Da*, included the *Make a Little Noise* EP, with which it shared a title.

With momentum building, Plaskett's label and management were looking forward to a proper full Emergency album in 2007, with Gordie Johnson again at the helm. But the Maritime contrarian threw them another curveball: *Ashtray Rock*, a rock opera about his high school days, rich with hyper-specific regional references. By then, Plaskett had proven that his instincts were usually right. The album sold well and got him rave reviews. The venues got bigger and so did the band: Peter Elkas was added on guitar and keyboards. New bassist Chris Pennell had joined after McGettigan left to focus on his own music.

The Emergency closed out 2007 by playing six consecutive nights at Toronto's Horseshoe, performing one of Plaskett's albums in its entirety each night (*Ashtray Rock* was performed twice), with guests including members of Sloan, Eric's Trip, Gord Downie and Sarah Harmer.

SARAH HARMER HAD largely stepped away from music to be a full-time activist by 2005, fighting for concerns close to her heart—and her family home.

Mount Nemo, part of the Niagara Escarpment near Burlington, was set to be mined for a gravel quarry in 2005. Inspired in part by her friend Gord Downie's newfound environmental activism, she set out to put her full weight behind the fight by co-founding PERL (Protecting Escarpment Rural Land). She vowed not to be another know-nothing musician.

"This was a full-time thing," she says. "I was in Burlington three days every week. I was passionate. There was so much to learn and so much at risk to learn about—biology, ecology—it was really fascinating. A new part of my brain opened up. But I understand when musicians are wary of putting their name or voice to some cause, because you want to know what you're talking about. You don't want to look stupid; your ego is involved. And it often requires a ton of study and relationship-building. Meeting the planners in Burlington and setting up tons of meetings and volunteer stuff with community members. Our farm was adjacent to this site. I spent my childhood getting to know this land, and I had access to it in a way no one else does, and I had to use that. It's also nice to not always be hanging out with musicians. You learn a lot about different parts of society and career paths and how decisions are made."

In June 2005, she organized a two-week tour of Escarpment community townhalls, with an acoustic band, and talked up a new song she'd written for the occasion, "Escarpment Blues." The tour was filmed for a documentary of the same name. PERL eventually won the case, although they were forced to fight the same battle again 15 years later. The experience wasn't only spiritually and politically fulfilling; Harmer was clicking with her all-acoustic band. Sambrook suggested they capture the moment and head into a studio, which they did in August 2005. *I'm a Mountain* came out in October. "The record label didn't expect it," says Harmer. "They were like, 'Wait, you take four years between records.' 'No, I got this one!' We recorded it in two days and mixed in two days, and I did a couple at home that I tagged on."

There wasn't a lot of new material written specifically for *I'm a Mountain*. There were three covers: of Dolly Parton and of friends Luther Wright, Chris Brown and Kate Fenner. She also resurrected "Goin' Out," originally written for an AIDS vigil, from 1997's *Valentino*. "I definitely had difficulty with free-flowing thoughts," she says of the transition from songwriter to activist. "I went hyper Ms. Credible. I'm sure I was annoying. I got very keyed up on accuracy and science. We were writing so many letters and submissions."

Much like *You Were Here*, it didn't matter whether the material was new or not. *I'm a Mountain* was everything *All of Our Names* wasn't: joyous, unburdened of expectation, spontaneous and a natural display of Harmer's raw talent. Many of the songs had been kicking around for years, including the title track, "Oleander" and "The Ring," the latter written for Marty Kinack. They were originally intended for a follow-up to *Songs for Clem*, titled *Songs with Clem*. But Harmer's prolific days were over; fans didn't hear a new album after *I'm a Mountain* for five years, and the next came a full decade after that.

THE U.S. DIDN'T SEEM INTERESTED in Joel Plaskett as a rock artist, so his management made a bid for the Americana crowd. They booked him as a solo artist into the 2008 Folk Alliance conference, held in Memphis. He could visit his friend Doug Easley and schedule a day in the studio there. Also at the conference that year was his Halifax peer Rose Cousins and Brooklyn songwriter Ana Egge, with whom Plaskett had several mutual Canadian friends, including Peter Elkas. Plaskett impressed Egge by breaking into one of her songs during a hotel jam, and she accepted his invitation to join him and Cousins at Easley's studio. There, they laid down a rambling, half-improvised song over a Bontempi beat, "Wishful Thinking." No one thought much of it, but Plaskett joked with manager Sheri Jones about making a triple album. By that point, Jones should have known to take him seriously.

Back in Halifax, he rented a space downtown and started building his own studio, Scotland Yard. "I knew what I wanted out of a space and wanted to track things on my own," he says. He had a series of songs he wanted to try with Cousins and Egge, as well as with his father, a guitarist who had opened a folk club and helped found the folk festival in Lunenburg, where Plaskett grew up until the family moved to Halifax when he was 12. The Emergency was brought in for one track, but they weren't told what it was for. He soon had 33 songs, which he grouped roughly into songs about home, about leaving and about being alone. It was the year he turned 33. He decided to give many of the songs thrice-repeating titles: "Through & Through & Through," "Precious, Precious, Precious," "Gone, Gone, Gone," etc., etc., etc. The album's title? Pretty obvious choice: *Three*. Again, his management and band were not aware of what he was doing until he presented them with a fait accompli (accomp-three?).

Before 2009, the list of triple albums of original material was slim: the Clash's *Sandinista!*, George Harrison's *All Things Must Pass*, Prince's *Emancipation*, Magnetic Fields' *69 Love Songs*. For an independent Canadian artist to do the same was audacious, to say the least. And yet Plaskett pulled it off. *Three* became not only his bestselling record to date, but it went gold in six months. He embarked on a national theatre tour with his father, Cousins and Egge, culminating in a night at Toronto's historic Massey Hall. As he had for any other gig in the previous eight years, Plaskett drove his Chevy Suburban to load in through the venue's front door. He made sure to bring the Emergency to share the moment that also marked the 10th anniversary of Thrush Hermit's breakup.

"I structured the set so that the first set was me, Dad, Anna and Rose. Then the band came out [to join them], then I stripped it down to just the band, then back to everyone," he says. "It was amazing. At the time, I was so overwhelmed with the work in front of me that I didn't recognize it for what it was, which was a culmination of all those approaches. We didn't get [to Massey Hall] as a three-piece: it was a group effort, all the work that had gone into all those things. The Emergency cut our teeth so hard in the clubs. Sweaty, loading out at two in the morning from Amigos in Saskatoon. Massey Hall was a different tempo. That pushes you into when your audience gets older, and now people my parents' age are coming to the shows, as well as young kids. You realize your act is maturing. Then you recognize where Blue Rodeo's fan base lies, this large version of a family show—and what's wrong with that?"

Speaking of mature artists with a fan base that spans generations, Paul McCartney personally selected the Joel Plaskett Emergency, along with Wintersleep, to open a show in front of 60,000 people at the Halifax Commons two months after the Massey Hall show.

Ten years after Thrush Hermit broke up, Joel Plaskett had built himself into a Canadian institution. (And Thrush Hermit reunited for tours in 2010 and 2019.) He became an acclaimed producer, helming excellent records by Maritimers Two Hours Traffic, Mo Kenney and Dennis Ellsworth. He released four records of his own in the next decade: two with the Emergency, a record with his father and a whopping four-disc, 44-song opus made when he turned 44 (called, yes, 44).

Nothing has yet topped the triumphs of 2009. "My shows are still the same size they are when we did the *Three* tour," says the modest Maritimer. "And I like that. It's comfortable. I've always made better connections in smaller rooms, and my desire to be an arena artist is not there. If the energy you're sending out is that you don't want to be a rock star, there's a self-fulfilling prophecy there. Back then I was working with my head down but also thinking, This is cool. I can control this. I know what this is. Maybe that can be frustrating for people in the industry—or even for my band—who always want to push me up to a next level."

International ambitions are pretty much over. The man whose first Emergency album featured a song called "Maybe We Should Just Go Home" says, "As stuff started picking up in Canada, I just realized [the more] I could get gigs closer to my back door, the more it will be able to sustain itself and the more music I'll be able to make. I like playing in Canada, being Canadian and playing for people who understand what I'm singing about. Not that I don't want to take that elsewhere— I do—but I don't rely on it for my sense of accomplishment. The reason I want to go to other places is to spark up new ideas and get a sense of what's going on in other countries so I can take it back home."

THE WEAKERTHANS COULD DRAW up to 2,000 people a night in Germany. They were slotted at huge festivals like Rock am Ring on the same stage as antitheses like Limp Bizkit. The comparatively esoteric Weakerthans would seem to be a harder sell than German success stories like the more visceral Billy Talent and Danko Jones. But non-English speakers were intrigued by Samson's lyrics. "I feel like there is a more immediate engagement with the lyrics," he says. "They've had to struggle to learn the language, so there's something earned there. There's something really lovely about that." And, of course, the band was always amused when the crowd sang "I hate Winnipeg" in a German accent.

The most rewarding touring experience they had, however, was with Toronto band the Constantines. Tait first fell in love with the Constantines at the Hillside Festival in their hometown of Guelph in 2001, and he played their first album in the Weakerthans' van. Samson wasn't sure. "Like so many things in my life that I love, at first I didn't understand what was going on underneath the noise," he says. "Our first show together was in Austin, Texas, at Emo's. I remember watching them play and suddenly being overwhelmed by how beautiful it was. It was a profound moment. We caravanned around the South for a couple of weeks, and each show I was more excited about the songs and the sounds. We were in three vans. One didn't have AC. It was summer in the desert. Once [Steve] Lambke and Bry [Webb] were in the non-AC van, and they stepped out in their underwear and boots—that's all they were wearing, just looking around. It was such a beautiful image. Then we played bocce ball in the desert. But the Constantines are a thread that run through the rest of my life as a songwriter, as something I'm always alert to and inspired by. Something shifted in me when I started to understand the structure of their songs. I don't think it's audible in what I do, but it's always there somehow."

Based on their mutual affection, in early 2005 the two bands booked a cross-country jaunt dubbed Rolling Tundra Revue—a nod to Bob Dylan and the Band's Rolling Thunder Revue of 1975—which brought them to every major city in Canada for multiple nights, excluding only the North. "I would get up and play with them on 'Draw Us Lines,'" says Samson. "I just had to stand there and play a G chord. It's still the most profound live experience I've ever had, just playing that one chord over and over again. I think about it a lot.

"The last show of that trip was in Vancouver. We played Richard's on Richards, and the venue had that policy of kicking bands out at 11 so they could have a dance night. We played, then came backstage and the Constantines had somehow acquired a paper bag full of mushrooms. Everyone took some; I didn't do that often, but it was a celebratory evening. We went to Bosman's, this bar near there, where they would lock you in after last call and you could buy a bunch of drinks and stay there until four a.m. I remember standing in the middle of that room with my last beer in my hand; it was full, and it slipped out of my hand and smashed on the ground. The whole room went silent. Then Bry and Steve both rushed over to me and gave me these giant hugs, and we were all laughing. That's one of the best moments of my time on Earth, for some reason."

The two bands shared billing on the tour; the Weakerthans always played last. The Constantines were a hard act to follow, but they were still relatively a cult act; the Weakerthans' fan base was larger. There was one show the Winnipeg band played in Portland, Oregon, where they were eager to switch billing with their opening band: Arcade Fire.

"It was just as *Funeral* came out," says Samson. "Before we left on tour, no one knew who Arcade Fire was. By the time we got to Portland, it was insane." The Weakerthans offered to surrender their headlining status; Arcade Fire refused. Drummer Jeremy Gara was an old friend through Ottawa punk circles. "It was amazing and joyful to see him," says Samson, "and to see him in this amazing band. Arcade Fire played an incredible show and then, to the credit of the audience, there was not a mass exodus—though there was an exodus, for sure, which is totally fair. We had experiences like that before. We did a tour with Dashboard Confessional, two weeks where he opened for us from California to Las Vegas. The same thing happened. The week before the tour, his record came out, and there were throngs of 15-year-olds who had no patience for us. They were like, 'What is this?!' and three-quarters of them would leave. So at least with Arcade Fire it wasn't as bad."

Between tours, Tait took on extracurricular work in Toronto. He and partner Julie Penner often played with Fembots, a duo that joined the Weakerthans as auxiliary players for one tour. Tait and Penner also got roped into Broken Social Scene: Penner stayed for years and also joined Do Make Say Think; Tait dropped into BSS whenever he had time. "There were tours in Germany where I would literally get out of the Weakerthans' van at a festival, the last show of our tour, and load my stuff into [the BSS] bus and continue touring," says Tait. "The stars aligned and it all worked out with schedules. And my part was not integral, so the show would go on without me. Later it became like Fleetwood Mac, with weird vibe tension shit. And that's fine, but I bailed. There were conflicts that didn't have anything to do with me. If it was my main source of income, I might have been stressed, but I wasn't. I was happy to float in and out of that situation."

Three-quarters of the Weakerthans were happy to let bassist John Sutton float out of their situation, for reasons never discussed publicly. He left at the end of the tour cycle for *Reconstruction Site*—which had lasted two years. New bassist Greg Smith came from Toronto band Wayne Omaha; he'd once played in a pickup band for Christine Fellows. Tait recalls, "She came back and said, 'I played with this crazy bass player who says "beauty" a lot. He's really good. You should audition him.' We went and played with him, and he had really broad tastes. He could reference Black Flag and Motown and had more psychedelic records than I do. He wrote melodic bass lines like on 'Night Windows,' where the bass line carries the song."

"Night Windows" appears on *Reunion Tour*, the Weakerthans' 2007 album. Four years is an unusual wait between albums for most artists; it was a sign that Samson was a writer who could not be rushed. Doing press for the album, Samson said he admired peers like John Darnielle of the Mountain Goats and Craig Finn of the Hold Steady. "I got to know both in the last couple of years, and they just spew out this really wonderful and impressive poetry, constantly. They are two people who both complained to my face about how slow I was, and how long I was taking with this record. Craig Finn came up to me [in 2006] in New York and said, 'Since you put out your last record, I've put out three.' And what do you say to that? They're all really good records. That was a nice impetus. You don't often get people coming up to you and telling you, 'Get to it.'"

While waiting for Samson to write, the other three members were hired by Greg Graffin of Bad Religion to make his 2006 solo record and to tour. In 2009, they backed up Jim Bryson, a friend and auxiliary Weakerthan, on his album *The Falcon Lake Incident*, recorded north of Winnipeg in the middle of the winter. Also in early 2009, the whole band accepted an invitation from Barenaked Ladies to play their curated cruise ship festival, Ships and Dip. The band accepted mainly to take a free vacation with their spouses, and because the Mountain Goats had also been invited, alongside Sloan, Sarah McLachlan and others.

"We fell from being leftist punk rockers to playing on a cruise ship with a bunch of naked Barenaked Ladies fans," laughs Carroll. "We were pretty leery, but BNL were so genuine in their enthusiasm for us. They were fans. And they picked other good artists. But it was super weird. Like being permanently trapped in a nightmare you can't get out of. 'I woke up on this boat, and every time I turn on the TV they're playing Barenaked Ladies videos on every channel. I turn on the radio, and it's all Barenaked Ladies music. Everyone around me is wearing Barenaked Ladies T-shirts. *And I can't get off this boat.*' It was really rocky seas, too. The entire audience was rocking side to side, in unison, unbeknownst to them. I was able to steady myself while playing, but my wife got seasick and broke her shoulder. It was a nightmare in a lot of ways. But the Kids in the Hall were on it, and Seán Cullen, and they were hilarious."

At the end of 2010, the Weakerthans decided to play each of their albums top to bottom, four albums in four different hometown clubs: *Fallow* at the Royal Albert, *Left and Leaving* at the West End Cultural Centre, *Reconstruction Site* at the

Pyramid and *Reunion Tour* at the Burton Cummings Theatre. "And then another show at the Burton Cummings where we did every album beginning to end in one show," says Tait. "I remember walking off stage, turning to John, and we both at the exact same time said, 'I'm never doing that again.' It was a really bad idea. The last thing we did was another show series where we did all our records each night. We did four nights in New York City at the Bowery, four nights at the Independent in San Francisco. That was it."

The Weakerthans never officially broke up, but there was radio silence for the next five years, until one day Jason Tait tweeted a link to John Coltrane and Thelonious Monk's rendition of "Abide with Me," writing, "Word is getting out that the Weakerthans are done. Here's the song we used to take the stage to for years. Bye bye."

In 2012, Samson released his first solo album, *Provincial*. He followed it up four years later with *Winter Wheat*. By that point, his fans knew that it would always be a long wait between flares. "There is a certain spontaneity and thrill to those artists who can write more productively than I can," he says. "There is an excitement to it. I just don't know how to write that way. I like to carry the songs around with me for a long time, because they are good company. I become attached to them. Especially in my winters, I'm focused on thinking about them. If I put out a record every year or every two years, I'd be kind of lonely."

No matter: he'd already left behind a body of work that inspired a new generation and has endured ever since. As did Sarah Harmer, who watched old friends take her torch and run with it. "Around the time of Feist's *Reminder* and Broken Social Scene, there was that feeling of, okay, Canada has arrived and this has matured to the point where we have our own musical society," she says. "This culture has been nurtured enough and has been influenced enough by its close surroundings, musical and otherwise, where it's tall enough to be seen from a distance. I remember saying that to Leslie. I was in a tough spot in 2007 when her record came out. I said, 'Thank you for contributing to the cultural world here. You're contributing a lot.' I do feel like that's a tangible thing and that it was coming from a lot of Canadians at that time."

What she doesn't say—but Leslie Feist would—is that Harmer herself, and her '90s peers, had a lot to do with making it happen.

CHAPTER 6
FROM BLOWN
SPEAKERS

THE NEW PORNOGRAPHERS,
DESTROYER, TEGAN AND SARA,
THE ORGAN

Vancouver has always been full of "fuck bands"—what other places call "side projects of no consequence." The regional term dates back to the late '70s, when the city had one of the best punk scenes in the world after New York and London (sorry, Toronto and L.A.). Pre-D.O.A. band the Skulls claim to have coined it during a time when there weren't enough local punk bands to fill a bill, so everyone would just trade instruments and write new material.

Vancouver is Canada's third largest city, though it's long been dubbed "no fun city," for its high turnover of live music venues. Despite launching superstars like Bryan Adams, Loverboy and other clients of Bruce Allen's management, Vancouver has often fostered a more defeatist musical attitude than even the rest of Canada—which is saying something. But that can also be freeing. Hence the "fuck band."

In mid- to late '90s Vancouver, Sarah McLachlan was a global superstar, after a decade of dogged determination. Matthew Good conquered Canadian mainstream rock radio. The Rascalz became the first West Coast hip-hop act to achieve any kind of Canadian success. Hippie jam bands are always plentiful in B.C., though they were then ceding ground to trance DJs and other trends in rave culture. Swollen Members, not yet mainstream stars, were connecting with the Californian rap scene.

The city's indie rock community—loosely splintered into competing camps revolving around the Mint label and Scratch Records, a store and distributor—was making few waves outside city limits, with the exception of road warriors the Smugglers. Instead, they gathered at a few key spots. One was Ms. T's

Cabaret, a queer basement bar known for its drag shows, adjoining a bathhouse on Pender Street.

Another was a vintage clothing store, the Good Jacket, run by former CiTR DJ Sean Raggett, that opened in 1997 and started hosting gigs in nearby galleries, metal bars and in the store itself, capacity 200. The Good Jacket expanded into a bigger location at 225 East Broadway; at its one-year anniversary show in April 1998, one of the bands on the bill was Thee Goblins, an Evaporators fuck band with just Nardwuar the Human Serviette and drummer Scott Livingstone, in which they dressed up as sweater-clad ghosts. The headliner that night was making its debut after a year of gestation, with perhaps the best name ever for a fuck band: the New Pornographers.

Two years later, the Good Jacket assembled a compilation of acts who'd played the store. Named after a unique local housing design, *Vancouver Special* came out in April 2000 on Mint Records. It seems strange now, but in 2000 a local compilation album could make a national impact via campus radio. *Vancouver Special* was a window into the city. Early versions of the Organ (Full Sketch) and Black Mountain (Jerk with a Bomb) were on it. Veterans Nardwuar (Thee Goblins) and Slow's Stephen Hamm (Canned Hamm) were on it. Pepper Sands picked up a major label deal because of their song "So Fine" from the comp. And a schlumpy slacker named Dan Bejar is the MVP, appearing as guitarist in Vancouver Nights, keyboardist in the Battles, guitarist in the New Pornographers and with his own band, Destroyer, as remixed by his drummer Scott "Loscil" Morgan. *Vancouver Special* is a near-perfect time capsule of Vancouver indie rock at the turn of the century.

The New Pornographers were only notable at the time as the new project from Carl Newman. He fronted both the '90s nine-guitar grunge excess of Superconductor and that band's polar opposite, the Burt Bacharach–influenced band Zumpano, who put out two albums on Sub Pop. It sounds impressive, but they sold nothing. The New Pornographers' prospects didn't look any better. The fuck band was a priority for no one in the group; they were all occupied with other projects, not only musical: keyboardist Blaine Thurier's film *Low Self-Esteem Girl* had just been accepted into the Toronto International Film Festival. "Letter from an Occupant," their song on *Vancouver Special*, was centred on a vocal performance by American Neko Case, who had already split back across the border and whose solo career was starting to take flight. She soon had reason to return.

Not to slight the other *Vancouver Special*ists, but the appearance of "Letter from an Occupant" was as if "Anarchy in the U.K." first surfaced on, let's say, a compilation assembled by a King's Road clothing shop along with random punk bands. "Letter from an Occupant" was being blasted from the top of Crown Mountain while all the other bands were struggling up the Grouse Grind trail.

"Should be the new national anthem," wrote Rob Bolton in *Exclaim!*'s year-end lists, where other writers said things like "immediate bubble-gum classic," "song of the century, let alone the year." Though it wouldn't officially be released in the U.S. until 2001, the *New York Times* declared it "some of the best pop of [2000]." In 2002, the *Globe and Mail* put it at No. 10 on a list of the top 25 Canadian singles of all time (after "Ahead by a Century," before "Harvest Moon"), claiming it achieves "a kind of pop perfection Canadians seldom even attempt."

Canadian bands weren't accustomed to this kind of hyperbole. In the next five years, thanks to the New Pornographers, they'd have to get used to it. And though the New Pornographers were all heterosexual, they also helped in small ways two of the key queer acts of the day, both based in Vancouver as well—one of whom, Tegan and Sara, became one of the biggest Canadian artists of the next 20 years.

———

CARL NEWMAN DIDN'T pick up a guitar until he was 18. Though a huge music fan, he was intimidated. His snobbery got the better of him while watching ska and reggae bands in White Rock, B.C. "I could do better than this in a fucking second," he said to himself. Newman enlisted as many friends as he could to play guitar and formed Superconductor. No one wanted to be the singer, so Newman volunteered. It was all a lark, until Scratch Records invited them to put out a single in 1991. They then toured down the West Coast, and the California label Boner wanted to put out a full-length. Superconductor were now labelmates with Nirvana's heroes the Melvins. The 1993 album *Hit Songs for Girls* found them a few fans outside Vancouver, including Robert Pollard of Guided by Voices, who took the unwieldy band on tour.

Then Dionne Warwick changed Newman's life. He bought a copy of the '60s singer's greatest hits, loved it and then took deep dives into Burt Bacharach and the Zombies. He wanted to craft pop songs. He formed Zumpano (named after drummer Jason Zumpano) and made a record produced by Kevin Kane of the Grapes of Wrath. Sub Pop put it out in 1995. They were its first Vancouver signing at a time when the Seattle label was showing an unusual interest in Canada's East Coast; Zumpano fit in easily with that scene, sounding like a lighter Super Friendz. At the time, the label was still grunge-heavy; its only act then that remotely resembled Zumpano was the lounge revivalists Combustible Edison. That might be one reason why the record did so poorly. It didn't help that one of the only contemporary reference points in the press release was Barenaked Ladies, who were persona non grata in "cool" indie rock.

Though Superconductor was effectively over, they made one more album, the excessive prog-grunge epic *Bastardsong* in 1996. Newman, who had his melodic attention focused on Zumpano, was happy to indulge himself and make Superconductor completely over the top, with sci-fi synth blurps competing for space with the guitars. They once again joined Guided by Voices for a two-week tour.

"It didn't sound the same if it wasn't eight people at once," says Evaporators bassist John Collins, who was recruited for that Superconductor tour. "They were sensational, one of the most amazing bands ever. I've never known a drummer more amazing than Keith Parry [who also ran Scratch Records] when he was really going. Carl: good singer and good guitar player, too. And a bunch of guys who ranged in musicianship, from acceptable to total novice, and it worked." A review in Vancouver magazine *Drop D* read, "Superconductor may never sell as many records as the Tea Party, but at least they'll end up with their integrity intact by bypassing Canada's corpse-eating music industry schlock-fest altogether."

That same year, 1996, Collins and his fellow Evaporator David Carswell (also of the Smugglers) were embarking on their first recording project together: Maow, a rockabilly-punk band signed to Mint Records, who happened to be hanging out at Carswell's house while the two men were plugging in the last of their new equipment. Newman was a Maow fan; he first saw them play a backyard party, where all three members were decked out in fur bikinis and cat ears. Everyone at the gig couldn't help but focus on the charisma magnet behind the drum kit. Her name was Neko Case.

Neko Case grew up in Tacoma, Washington, and played drums in a band called the Propanes. Her go-go dancing at local shows inspired Tacoma band Girl Trouble to write a song about her in 1990: "Neko Loves Rock'n'Roll." They even brought her to dance with them at a Vancouver gig, which is where she met the Smugglers, who were shocked to discover she was a real person and not just a character in a song. She booked the Smugglers a Tacoma gig and eventually started dating Carswell. That relationship was a factor in her moving to Vancouver in 1993 to attend Emily Carr Institute of Art + Design, after touring as Cub's drummer for several months. She joined Maow, which happened to be the first band Collins and Carswell had ever recorded, under the name JC/DC, in Carswell's parents' basement.

In 1996, Zumpano went to JC/DC to record demos for a new album, where Collins indulged Newman's love of stacked vocal harmonies. When the band flew to Chicago to make the actual record, they were burdened by a tight budget, so Newman didn't get a chance to recreate what he'd captured on the JC/DC demos. It didn't help matters when the record flopped and the subsequent tour was a money pit. That same year, Newman heard Belle and Sebastian. "They've done it," he told himself. "They're doing what I've been shooting for these past few years." With Superconductor gone and Zumpano's future in question, Newman was itching for something different.

So was Neko Case. After the Maow tracks on which she sang lead got the most attention, she sheepishly approached Mint with the idea of doing a solo country record. They immediately said yes. Despite her extroversion, the drummer was not yet a natural in the spotlight. Her friend Carolyn Mark recalls that the first time Case sang for her, in Mark's bedroom, she had to face a wall. But anyone who heard her sing wanted to work with her. Her first solo record, *The Virginian*, made up half of covers and half original songs, featured indie rock all-stars: produced by Brian Connelly (Shadowy Men on a Shadowy Planet) and Darryl Neudorf (54·40, Sarah McLachlan), with contributions from Matt Murphy (Super Friendz), Carolyn Mark, Pete Bourne (Copyright), Ford Pier and Smugglers Carswell and Kevin "Beez" Beesley. Newman co-wrote two songs and sang duet harmony on a cover of the Everly Brothers' "Bowling Green." He also played a handful of live gigs in Case's band.

While Case was getting ready to release *The Virginian*, Zumpano officially called it quits and Newman was half-heartedly working on a solo record at JC/DC. Hanging out in the studio was Dan Bejar, who had hired JC/DC to make the second Destroyer record. Newman was a big fan. "I have a clear memory of seeing him at [Ms. T's Cabaret]," says Newman, "and he did 'Breaking the Law,' and it just jumped out at me. It was one of the first times I'd seen a friend perform, and I thought, This is absolutely world-class, so good."

Newman joked about starting a new band with Bejar, Collins and Case. He invited his old friend Blaine Thurier to play keyboards. Collins invited drummer Fisher Rose of Tremolo Falls. Newman had always wanted to be in a group called "the new somethings," like the New Christy Minstrels or the New Seekers. Shortly before the Good Jacket gig in April 1998, they went with New Pornographers; there is a brief track on Bejar's debut called "The Pornographers," and it's also the title of a darkly comic 1966 Japanese film.

One day he invited Neko Case over to his apartment to sing a song he'd written that was way out of his range. "Letter from an Occupant" turned out to be at the very top of hers.

"The first time I played it for Neko, it was just me and her," he says. "I remember feeling very uneasy, the same way anyone feels when they present something they made. I thought, Will she think this sucks? It seems funny, now that *Rolling Stone* called it the 97th best debut single of all time. Which seems—arbitrary. But at the time I thought she might laugh in my face and tell me I'm a hack and the song is not very good."

In the studio, he asked her to de-twang her country-inflected voice and sing more like a robot. Mariska Veres of '60s Dutch pop band Shocking Blue ("Venus") was a reference point.[1] Case didn't know the song well when she was recording it; on the final version, Collins can be heard giving her a cue for the final chorus. Case, a known control freak when it comes to all aspects of her solo work, was happy to take a backseat for Newman's project. "I just went into it very open-mindedly," she says. "I was really excited to do it that way. Just to have somebody be my Svengali and go, 'All right, young lady: sing like a Germanic space babe from 1981.'"

Case's association with the New Pornographers was likely to be short. After blabbing to an *Edmonton Journal* reporter that her student visa had run out, immigration officials showed up at her solo show there and refused to let the U.S. citizen perform; backing band the Sadies played without her. Case soon moved to Seattle, then Chicago. Though she recorded her next album in Toronto and Vancouver and continued to tour Canada, she made sure she always had work permits.

Newman wasn't fazed. "From the beginning, it wasn't like, okay, there are four people in the band and this is what we do," he says. "It didn't matter to us, because the stakes were so low." He just wanted to finish the record; he never imagined he'd ever tour it. Before October 2000, Newman used to sing "Letter from an Occupant" live himself, in falsetto. Neko sang it during a four-song recording session, which also yielded Newman's "Mystery Hours" and Bejar's "Execution Day" and "Breakin' the Law." No one was waiting to hear it. They spent seven days mixing "Letter from an Occupant" alone.

Newman sent the demo to Sub Pop, who passed, and to Matador, home of Guided by Voices. The A&R rep there, Nils Bernstein, was a big fan but unable to convince anyone else at the label. And so it sat on a DAT tape in the back of a drawer in Newman's apartment, until Sean Raggett at the Good Jacket asked him if he had anything to contribute to a compilation.

THE ONE-NOTE OPENING guitar riff of "Letter from an Occupant" is deceptive. The next three and a half minutes are a guitar-pop baklava: dense, layered and overflowing with honey and butter. When Case starts singing, the drums drop out to a four-on-the-floor bass drum and fills. The chord progression follows a classic '50s "Heart and Soul" pop pattern of I-VI-IV (the same pattern as Arcade Fire's "Wake Up," incidentally, although totally different rhythm and feel). Case's delivery is instantly compelling. Then the pre-chorus hits (hanging on just the IV and V), Case holds longer notes, and the song opens up wide. The chorus itself is

---

1   The New Pornographers later covered that band's "Send Me a Postcard" live.

wordless, impossibly high ooos sung by Newman, an insanely catchy hook in a song already full of them.

But wait! There's more. In an era still marred by beige post-grunge rock, the punchy first bridge finds Case hollering, "Where have all sensations gone?" followed by what sounds like Beach Boys in a blender, unintelligible male vocals muttering about something or another, like Disney dwarves cowering in the presence of a powerful princess. Then another chorus and a monstrous second bridge, a cacophony of collapsing drums, pounding guitar chords and what sounds like an insect crawling over the strings of the lead guitar part, while Case repeats "the song, the song, the song has shaken me" like a mantra. Consider yourself shaken.

But what the hell is this song about? What is a "letter from an occupant"? Why will "the eventual downfall" be "a bill from a restaurant"? Turns out some of the actual lyrics are "The tune you'll be humming forever / All the words are replaced and wrong." Hundreds of critics, and Newman himself, claimed the song was gibberish. "I used to have an old landlord named Michael," says Newman, "and he always used to say, 'What am I, a letter from an occupant?' And then he would sigh heavily. It seemed like a good idea for a song."

There is definitely a power dynamic at play, the lyrics a litany of disappointments, written by someone raised on idealistic hippie teachers: "What the hell have the '70s brought me?" "Where have all sensations gone?" "I've cried five rivers on the way here / which one will you skate away on?" That last one is a twist on a lyric from Joni Mitchell's *Blue*. Maybe the whole song is a jaded GenXer's complaint to a bewildered boomer landlord who fails to grasp the reality of economic anxiety. Or something.

The lyrics were beside the point, though. With a melody like that, with a vocal performance like that, with a band like that, with production like that—does it matter what the song is about? Countless examples from pop music history would suggest it doesn't. It didn't for the New Pornographers. When people went apeshit for the song in the summer of 2000, Mint Records immediately asked Newman if there was more water in that well.

He called Case to come back to Vancouver and record some lead vocals and harmonies throughout. Drummer Fisher Rose dropped out and was replaced by Kurt Dahle. While driving around Vancouver one day listening to the four-song demo, Dahle got T-boned on Robson Avenue. Other people were hurt; Dahle staggered into the intersection to hear the coda of "Execution Day" blaring out of his destroyed car. He wasn't sure whether that was a good or bad omen.

Newman was feeling pressure. Destroyer's *Thief* came out in January 2000. Neko Case's second album, *Furnace Room Lullaby*, came out a month later on Bloodshot Records, the home of U.S. alt-country, and was getting rave reviews. He knew the

New Pornographers record had to be at least as good as both of those. On top of that, Dahle's Limblifter had a new album, *Bellaclava*, out just before *Vancouver Special*, with top 20 rock radio singles. Someone might call them a supergroup instead of just a fuck band. Time to stop fucking around.

Newman had some songs ready. Others came together in the studio, including the title track, "Mass Romantic." Its signature keyboard riff came about when Thurier couldn't play something Newman wanted; the simpler riff won out. A lot of *Mass Romantic* was recorded at the studio of renowned conceptual photographer Rodney Graham, using his keyboards—although the piano heard on the album was recorded in the living room of Collins's parents. All of Dahle's drums were recorded in one night at the band's practice space. "[Carl] would boss people around with really vague ideas," Collins told *Exclaim!*'s James Keast. "In the nicest possible way, people would indulge him. I would think, I'm really glad this guy is putting these songs together, but it's kind of a miracle that no one is saying, 'Stop telling me what to do,' or, 'I like what I'm doing so butt out.' Sometimes I couldn't tell if he was writing the song or if the band was and he was just saying what he didn't like. It was a long process, with him as the chairman."

Newman was also eager to pillage Bejar's growing catalogue. "The idea that I could go to this guy for songs was mind-blowing," he says. "He played an acoustic set at Ms. T's in 1999, and he did early versions of 'Jackie' and 'Testament to Youth in Verse.' I was super high—because it's Vancouver—and it was a great feeling to be incredibly stoned and think, I want those songs. I went to Bejar after the show and said, 'What's the "visualize success" song and the one with the "no no nos"? We gotta have those for the Pornographers.' He was like, 'Okay.' It was that simple."

Reference points in the studio included Belle and Sebastian and Neutral Milk Hotel mixed with the power and energy of a decidedly non–indie rock influence. "The bottom line was that we wanted to sound like some kind of ABBA-style situation," says Collins, "really studio-sounding, and also edgy. We didn't want it to be overly honed, but like an onslaught. Like the best parts of Superconductor and the best parts of ABBA. We put lots of ideas into the songs, [so that] you couldn't really hear a distinct edge to who's doing what. We wanted it to be jam-packed and surprising, the opposite of an intimate, careful, clever, genteel record." Oddly enough, most critics who thought that having three distinct lead singers was highly unusual never compared the New Pornographers to ABBA or Belle and Sebastian (or the Beatles, or the Band, or . . .). Then again, most critics younger than the 32-year-old Newman probably didn't grow up watching the made-in-Canada Bill Murray film *Meatballs*, and so they thought the Camp Northstar Kids Chorus credited at the end of "Breaking the Law" was an actual children's choir. (North Star is the fictional camp in the movie.)

So much of *Mass Romantic* sounds like pent-up teenage energy, of people who've been waiting in the wings for too long and finally get a chance to shine. It demands to be played loud, full of dense guitars, layered harmonies, piano parts that never miss a chance to glissando, ugly synths that sound like creaking doors, galloping drums, saxophones (anathema in the zeitgeist at the time) and choruses revolving around phrases like "salvation holdout central." Then there's "Mystery Hours," a song of constant bluster, where the verse chord progression sounds like trying to maintain balance during a log-rolling competition. The chorus repeatedly pummels you over the head while Newman threatens to sing way out of his range and gets there every time.

The day after Collins dropped off the final master to Mint, he left the label's office and spotted one of his childhood heroes, Rick Nielsen of Cheap Trick, standing at the side of the road. He took that as a good omen.

———

WHO IS DAN BEJAR?

He may not look the part, but Bejar is the bad-boy tempter in the archetypal teen romance: the aloof guy with undeniable allure who couldn't care less whether or not the protagonist is pining for him. She thinks he's fascinating and mysterious and talented. He says so many seemingly brilliant things she doesn't understand. When she tells him all this, he shrugs and says, "Whatever."

Bejar's whole career is based on refusal. His earliest recordings were deliberately obscurist: his voice inaudible, the audio quality so beyond terrible that it had to be intentional, daring the listener to pay attention. The lyrics on 2000's *Thief* and 2001's *Streethawk: A Seduction* used the music industry as a metaphor for living in a compromised, corporate world. When the New Pornographers became a commercial success, Bejar declined to tour with them; when he eventually did, five years later, he'd wander on stage for the handful of their songs he wrote, offer a perfunctory performance with a beer in one hand and exit as soon as he was done.

Destroyer shows were not much different: for much of the 2000s, he employed a guitar-heavy band that was louder than his vocals, an act of self-negation that defeated the purpose of him even being there. There was never any banter, never any indication that he considered a rock show anything more than a chore to be endured.

Dan Bejar is also the first person to call his own bluff, referring to his lyrical subject matter as "typical Destroyer bullshit." Writing a narrative is totally alien to him. "I can't string a four-minute country song together about what happens to Poncho," he says. Bejar's serpentine delivery possessed the kind of distanced vitriol that one would expect from a more abrasive music maker, not one so well steeped in the elements that make a great rock record. He managed to combine the wordplay of '6os Dylan, the folkie / glam affectations of early '70s Bowie, the wit of '8os Morrissey and the free-association word salad of '90s Malkmus.

Though he's not reclusive enough to be the J.D. Salinger of indie rock, he did turn down the cover of *Exclaim!* magazine at least once before accepting in 2006. In 2000, when the New Pornographers were on the cover, Bejar wanted the band to all have their backs to the camera; he was overruled. In 2001, when Destroyer was offered the cover, he wanted a headless photo of him wearing a sweatshirt with a drawing of himself on it. In 2004, he insisted that if he was going to be on the cover, he had to share it with Carey Mercer of Frog Eyes and Stephen McBean of Pink Mountaintops, with the headline "Hordes from the West." *Exclaim!* didn't bite on any of those occasions.

As he slowly gained an audience, no one seemed more incredulous than Bejar himself. "I wasn't born to this," he says. "No one believes me, but I get moments of shock that happen every few months when I'm just like, 'Is it possible that I'm in show business, that this is my profession? How did that happen?'"

———

DAN BEJAR WAS born in Vancouver, though he didn't stay long. It took him a long time to get back there; he's had a complicated relationship with the city ever since. Born to a Spanish Catholic father and an American Jewish mother, he and his family lived in Spain for a year, in southern California for a few more, then some time in Calgary and Fort McMurray before the Bejars returned to the Vancouver area when Dan was 15. He and his older sister went to 10 different schools before they turned 18. Bejar's father died at age 46, when Dan was 13. "It happened right at a time when you're about to bust loose into whatever direction you're gonna go in," he says. "Mine was to become super pretentious."

Dan Bejar was the kind of kid who walked around with a dog-eared copy of *Moby Dick* and listened to the Jesus and Mary Chain; he became obsessed with the latter through a legendary *New Music* segment, in which the Scottish band gave deliberately obtuse answers in an interview. Though he played his mom's Spanish guitar, music was never an ambition; he thought show business was ridiculous. "When I was growing up, there wasn't much rock music in our house," he says. "My dad's tastes were folk music of the Andes, Gregorian chants, medieval music, but my mom had a show-tunes background and my grandfather was an amazing piano player in a very schmaltzy, sweeping style." Bejar's ambition was to be an academic. He took English and philosophy at the University of British Columbia. The only two courses in which he got good marks were creative writing and existentialism. Bejar dropped out after three years, in 1993, when he discovered local indie rock. Local legends Mecca Normal were impressive and intimidating. He saw Blaise Pascal, featuring guitarist Nicolas Bragg, open for Pavement. In 1992 he saw Superconductor and loved them; a year later he saw Zumpano and heard their four-song tape, which blew his mind. It was weirder and out of step with the zeitgeist.

"1992 was pretty noisy, pretty grungy still," says Bejar. "Vancouver was a mix of people who had pretty advanced tastes. I can't speak to the rest of Canada, but in my mind Vancouver's underground left the rest of the country in the dust." That said, his love of Vancouver lies in its people, not its geography, meteorology, architecture or politics. "For me, the most impossible thing to do in the world is to romanticize Vancouver," he says. "If that comes through in Destroyer, then that's good, and I don't mind complaining about this city for 30 years straight."

Bejar formed his first band, True Love Forever. Carl Newman saw one of the band's few shows. "It was very of its time, and having no reference point for Bejar, I heard a Pavement thing," he recalls. "I was struck by his songs. There was one called 'Crimes Against the State of Our Love,' which I thought was such a great title, but he never actually said that line in the song. I told him that. To appease me, he wrote a song where he actually used that line: 'No Cease Fires!' from *City of Daughters*." Bejar later admitted that song, which Neko Case covered live, was his first deliberate attempt to write in a pop format.

For the 1996 Zumpano video "Behind the Beehive," Bejar was enlisted to play the Grim Reaper. He was unrecognizable even to those at the shoot; he didn't take the mask off all day. Future Pornographers Neko Case and John Collins are also in the video, as a go-go dancer and a vampire respectively.

Bejar took over Newman's room in a house on East 18th Street, shared with guitarist Stephen Wood and ambient artist Scott "Loscil" Morgan; future Wolf Parade founder Spencer Krug lived in the basement. Bejar recorded four-track demos in his room, inspired by Smog and Silver Jews, as well as early '70s British records he'd scoured: Bowie, Eno, Roxy Music, John Cale, the Kinks and especially Mott the Hoople. He called his project Destroyer, oblivious to the fact that it was the title of Kiss's 1976 breakthrough album (and also the name of several Kiss cover bands). "I kind of wanted to go for a rock'n'roll name," he says. "In our own special way we're tearing shit apart, you just have to listen very carefully. Musically I knew it was never going to be a metal band, but I thought lyrically there were fangs to the music."

The first Destroyer album, *We'll Build Them a Golden Bridge*, is all but unlistenable. It's lo-fi warbling at its worst, the sound of someone who doesn't want anyone to pay attention. It's somewhat amazing that Bejar didn't bury the album completely later in his career. The album did, however, feature two songs ("Breakin' the Law," "Streets of Fire") that Newman later recorded with the New Pornographers. Bejar was on a songwriting tear, releasing a cassette called *Ideas for Songs* and reserving many for his next few records. He chose one set of songs to comprise his second album, *City of Daughters*, which he hired JC/DC to engineer. Collins also played bass, while Bejar's roommate Scott Morgan played drums. "It's my real Vancouver record," he says. "I'd wander around a lot, hungover, and was still discovering things about Vancouver and finding my 'place' in it, and that record's got a real cast-adrift feel but in a pleasant way. I always said that I was trying to romanticize Vancouver, 'cause it was such a Herculean and ridiculous task."

It was exponentially better than *Golden Bridge*; still, only a handful of songs gave a glimpse at the brilliance yet to come. The full-band treatment brought out the best in Bejar, though at shows he'd perform half the set acoustically. "The band was so good," says Newman. "I told him, 'You gotta drop this acoustic thing. This band is so killer.'" When the album was finished, Bejar's roommate Stephen Wood of the Battles (not the Brooklyn band of the same name) was added on guitar, as was Jason Zumpano on keyboards. "I saw them at the Whip, with that lineup, just off Main Street at Fifth," says Newman, who lived above the club with Thurier. "I couldn't believe that Vancouver had such a good band. It was a place where people just went to hang out. Not enough people were paying attention. I was like, 'Don't you know? Can't you see? Even if you don't know Destroyer, doesn't this make you turn your head?'"

That version of Destroyer went back into the JC/DC studio to make *Thief*. It says a lot about Bejar's output at the time, and the quality of it, that he let Newman have some of the best Destroyer songs and still had plenty left over to fill *Thief* and its immediate successor, *Streethawk: A Seduction*. "There is joy in being barred from the temple," goes the chorus of *Thief*'s opening song. It's a line that summed up the underdog status of Bejar himself, his friends in the New Pornographers, Vancouver's role in Canada and Canada's role on the world stage. Don't worry about not being invited to the party, Bejar seemed to be saying (because—who knows?), but instead celebrate where you are and the freedom that gives you.

Specific interpretations can be tricky; Bejar is nothing if not an unreliable narrator by design. "I see [my songs] as short films with large ensemble casts," he says. "Each character gets a couple of lines and a few seconds of screen time, and once in a while I do a voiceover describing the scenery in some kind of watered-down accent." Throughout *Thief*, Bejar plays a crusty contrarian drunk on verse: "We hung from a thread just to prove poetry undead / We rendered ourselves perfectly suitable to public consumption."

Occasionally, he set his sights on the industry in which he hoped to at least modestly succeed: "What is it about music that lends itself so well / To business-as-fucking-usual?" "I look back at it now and it seems like a very self-righteous record about me being judge-jury-executioner about what is good and bad in music," he said only a few years later. "It's about the decision to express yourself as a moral act—which, to take that position, is insanity. There's no way you're not going to be defeated by looking at the world like that."

THE NEW PORNOGRAPHERS' *Mass Romantic* came out in Canada on Mint Records in November 2000. Two months before, the band travelled to the Toronto International Film Festival to play an afterparty for Blaine Thurier's film *Low Self-Esteem Girl*. While there, he was a guest on Ian Danzig's CKLN show; Danzig, the publisher of *Exclaim!* magazine, was predisposed to love the New Pornographers. He'd already put four associated acts on the cover: the Evaporators, Maow, Zumpano and Superconductor, and Newman's new group would soon follow suit. "It was this weird retrospective looking back on my career," he says. "To me it felt like, 'Yeah, yeah, I used to make music.' I just didn't expect anything to happen with the New Pornographers." But that week, *Now* magazine decided to review the record two months before its release. "It was the first rave review I've ever received in my life—from anywhere," he says. "They called it a 'once-in-a-career lightning strike' or something. I was in Toronto, sleeping on someone's couch, and I didn't want to be there. I was feeling really shitty. Then I read that. It was a nice feeling. But I really had to be convinced that things were happening for us."

Back home in Vancouver, Newman was interviewed by a local weekly.

"I think this record is going to get you a tonne of attention," the writer told him. "Do you know that?"

"Fuck off," laughed Newman. "It's very nice of you to say that, but—no."

One person who dreaded that attention was Dan Bejar. For him, *Mass Romantic* was a source of pride but also bemusement. When it came out, he told *Exclaim!*, "I know you're not supposed to say things like this, but I think it's an insanely catchy record. When I listen to it, I'm fairly wowed. It's such a visceral record, and the momentum is relentlessly upbeat. It's kinda gross, how good it is."

So gross, he had to split. Immediately before it came out, Bejar told the band he was moving to Spain—indefinitely. He played *Mass Romantic* release shows in Vancouver, Victoria, Edmonton and Calgary; by Christmas he was gone. "It was pretty heartbreaking for everybody," says Collins, "because at that point it seemed like we'd already overcome all odds to actually having a record come out."

"I thought that was the end of the band," says Newman. "But then we went on the road, and nobody realized that Dan wasn't there. Nobody even knew what he looked like." Kurt Dahle sang Bejar's songs live from behind the drum kit. Dahle also brought Todd Fancey of Limblifter to play lead guitar, and he's been in the band since.

Being a fuck band helped the Pornographers prepare for polyamory. "There was no question that Evaporators were my main band," says Collins. "For [the New Pornographers'] second-ever gig [in 1998], I was double-booked with the Evaporators, who were playing in Edmonton. So we got a fellow I only know as Dingo to replace me [in the Pornographers] for a show at the Starfish Room, and I don't know that I've ever heard that name since. That was the vibe at that point. We were going to be everyone's second band—everyone always had two or three bands, so to be the *second* band made it pretty serious. I never knew anyone who was only in one band."

One of the Bejar songs sung by Dahle was "Jackie," featuring these opening lines: "Jackie, you yourself said it best when you said / 'There's been a break in the continuum / the United States used to be lots of fun.'" To hear that in a pop song in November 2000, when a contested presidential election was galvanizing America, was a weird, seemingly prescient thrill, especially coupled with songs titled "Fake Headlines" and "Centre for Holy Wars."

Outside of Canada, the New Pornographers did well right away in San Francisco, the one town other than Vancouver where the name Superconductor once meant something. Aquarius Records—which ran one of the first online outlets for mail-order music—sold 500 copies of *Mass Romantic* in a couple of months. (It helped that Robynn Iwata, formerly of Cub, worked there.) The store's newsletter was influential, and word of mouth spread quickly. During the band's first-ever tour, a quick jaunt down the West Coast, they sold out a midsized San Francisco venue. The crowd was so hyped for the New Pornographers that the band was being flashed by women in the front row. Something was in the air.

Just before the new year, Newman was in Vancouver, working at Larrivée Guitars. Kurt Dahle drove by and yelled out the window, "Hey, Carl! The *New York Times* called us one of the 10 best records of the year! See you later!"

"I don't even know if he stopped moving," says Newman. "I left work, took a long lunch and walked to the nearest newsstand that sold the paper. There we were on the list of 'top 10 records you didn't hear this year.' This wasn't just a rave review, this was the *New York Times*." Within a year, the album was also on best-of lists in *Pitchfork*, *Magnet*, the *Village Voice*, and it made the top 20 of the annual critics' poll Pazz and Jop, along with winning a Juno for Best Alternative Album. (Dahle repurposed his Juno as a toilet-paper holder.)

A week after the 2001 Junos, the New Pornographers were in Austin, Texas, for South by Southwest. Ray Davies of the Kinks was a keynote speaker. Someone at the festival suggested he perform with a hot young band, and the New Pornographers' name came up. "I guess he heard our record, thought it was good and that he wouldn't embarrass himself being on stage with us," says Newman. The band got the call a few hours after arriving in Austin the night before the gig. That was all they could think about for the next 24 hours. They bought two Kinks CDs, *Something Else* and *Village Green Preservation Society*, and decided on "Starstruck."

Backstage, Davies confessed that he didn't know the words; the Kinks had never performed the song live. But Newman had them written out, Davies agreed, and he joined them at the end of their set for what became one of the buzziest moments of the entire week, mentioned in coverage around the world. The band of Vancouver underdogs was, well, starstruck. "Maybe," Newman says, Davies "walked off stage and went, 'I'm never fucking doing anything like that again. I can't believe I agreed to that bullshit.' Who knows? But for us, it was a huge moment. Through the whole song, I was looking back at the band, making eye contact, going, Holy shit, can you believe this?" That first tour had no shortage of strange moments for a bunch of Canadians in the U.S., especially when they sold out the Great American Music Hall in San Francisco, where the crowd showered them in panties. Matador Records, which had passed on the 1998 demo, picked up *Mass Romantic* for international distribution.

But a month after the triumphant SXSW show, Newman was in a rut. "Even though I was in this hot new band, I still hadn't made any money from it," he says. "I still had my [guitar store] job, I didn't have a car, there was a transit strike, and for whatever reason I had to walk home five miles in the rain. I felt so sad. My band was getting noticed and everyone seemed to like us, but the juxtaposition was that I was still stuck in this shitty life." That changed in September 2001, when director Kevin Smith licensed "Letter from an Occupant" for his film *Jay and Silent Bob Strike Back*. "I think I made $5,000 from that," says Newman. "This was all new to me. When you never make any money from music, you realize that you don't know anything about the business. All of the sudden, people are explaining that I wrote the song, so I own the publishing. I thought this could be a cushion. I quit my job with $8,000 in the bank and hoped that I could survive a year. And that was the last job I had."

THE WORLD WOKE UP ONE DAY TO PROCLAIM
"Thou shalt not take part in, or make, bad art"
In these tough, tough times
Friends like mine would rather dash than dine

On the bones of what's thrown to them
When a wave of her wand has us back at the pond
Taking notes for a crooked underground

That whopper of a verse appeared on Destroyer's fourth album, *Streethawk: A Seduction*, recorded in the fall of 2000 and released six months later, in April 2001. It was as good or better a record than *Mass Romantic* and just as electrifying. While *Thief* was largely acoustic, *Streethawk* sounded like a lost rock opera from the early '70s, with crunchy T. Rex guitars, piano voicings from the Patti Smith Group and the theatrical flair of Ziggy Stardust.

"The more I wrote songs, the more I delved into the tradition of songwriting," said Bejar at the time. "The more you do it, and the more confident [you become], the more you feel you can pick up old forms, and kind of throw yourself into them without losing yourself. [These] songs now have a lot more structure and muscle to them. But I think at the same time, it's still pretty screwy."

Streethawk proved he'd learned his lessons well. In a year of a supposed rock'n'roll revival, nothing else sounded like this—and nobody else was writing like this. On the heels of the New Pornographers' buzz, it should have been one of the biggest records of the year, even though it came out on a tiny New York City label, Misra. "I was like, 'We are going to be rich!'" says John Collins. "I thought that a lot back then, but when we did *Streethawk*, I thought, I might not be joking right now. This is potentially a successful album."

But the contrarian Bejar left the continent and split to Spain. "I wanted to make a drastic change, and I thought the best thing for me to do would be to dissolve the version of Destroyer that existed, bail on the New Pornographers and leave Vancouver forever," he says. He lasted only three months in the fatherland, then rented a Montreal apartment and couch-surfed in New York City before landing back in Vancouver at the end of the calendar year. By not touring *Streethawk*, which to this day remains his greatest rock'n'roll record, he made it crystal clear that he wasn't playing the industry game he spent the last two albums mocking. *Mass Romantic* had done well enough that its royalties floated him for a while.

For the few paying attention, *Streethawk*'s lyrics seemed to be some kind of indictment of his ex-bandmates. *Now*'s Tim Perlich claimed the album was "a song cycle concerning the rock-star myth . . . cleverly coded in rock-opera language" and that the song "The Sublimation Hour"—with the lyric "so you had the best legs / in a business built for kicks"—was a jab at Newman and company. "But in trying to bury the Pornographers," wrote Perlich, "he's made them a focal point." Bejar laughed this off in other interviews, saying that both *Thief* and *Streethawk* used imagery of the music industry as tools, as background scenery, that the lyrics weren't meant to be taken literally, but as metaphors for other relationships and philosophical quandaries.

"Whenever I use the word *you* in a song or a piece of writing," says Bejar, "I'm talking to myself. Not to get all Joker on it, but it means, 'Oh, this is a song where the narrator is somehow split in an unhealthy, weird way and is possibly demented.' When you're conscious of making something, you can't help but assume some kind of voice that's not your own. Even if someone's writing just the most pure, confessional music, you have to believe that that's not actually them talking. No part of me really thinks that I know someone through what they've sung."

Back in Vancouver, Bejar debuted an all-new Destroyer at the Blinding Light!! Cinema in early 2002, featuring guitarist Nicolas Bragg and original New Pornographers drummer Fisher Rose. A review in *Discorder Magazine* compared the show to Bob Dylan's set at the Newport Folk Festival 40 years earlier, drawing a distinct line between those in the audience who thought it was brilliant and those who thought it was meandering crap. Many of the new songs had been written in Spain, while Bejar wandered the streets of Madrid and got lost. He wanted to call the album *Night Moves* and had to be talked out of it, for the obvious reason that it's also the title of Bob Seger's blockbuster album of 1976 (the same year as the Kiss album *Destroyer*—coincidence?). He settled on *This Night* instead.

Destroyer became the first Canadian act ever signed to Merge Records, the North Carolina label run by Superchunk and best known for releasing Neutral Milk Hotel and the Magnetic Fields. Because Destroyer's first four records were exceedingly difficult to find, Merge's support meant that *This Night* was Bejar's official coming-out party—and, in the words of one ardent fan,[2] he "shit the bed." Bejar's sardonic vocals had dissolved into whiny caterwauling; the tight band arrangements of *Streethawk* were nowhere to be found, and instead it delved into jam-band territory. The album was 68 minutes long and felt like it, seemingly designed to alienate fans of the economical New Pornographers.

None of this was an accident; it was by design, by the man who calls himself Destroyer. He enjoyed sitting back and watching the guys in his band "not give a shit about anyone's precious Destroyer songs," he told the *Globe and Mail*. "I didn't want to make any assurances to the listener that they would make it to the end, or that what they were listening to was even a finished record. And if they did manage to wade through the first 64 minutes, there was a drunken pirate

---

2   The author.

song at the end, saying, 'I don't really care if you made it or not, and there's an Interpol or Hot Hot Heat record out there executed by expert hands for a desired listening reaction if that's more your cup of tea. Now pass me the strawberry wine.' I just think it needed to be established that I have no interest in being this Canadian band writing smart pop songs. That's not what any of this has ever been about. I think that's clearer now."

John Collins and Dave Carswell didn't record *This Night*, though they did mix it. Meanwhile, for the first time, JC/DC were working with someone outside their social circle: twin sisters from Calgary who were too young to be jaded, too earnest to be cynical.

TEGAN AND SARA QUIN had zero qualms about reaching the biggest audience possible. Like on, say, the Oscars.

Many artists in this book have played major international festivals, including Glastonbury and Coachella, in front of tens of thousands of people. Several were nominated for a Juno or a Polaris; some performed at those ceremonies. Two have played the Grammys. But only one has played the Oscars before an international television audience of more than 60 million people.

Tegan and Sara are the vocalists on "Everything Is Awesome" written by Andy Samberg's Lonely Island project for *The Lego Movie*, nominated for Best Original Song at the 2015 Academy Awards. On the Oscar stage, Tegan and Sara were one small ring in a circus that featured breakdancing construction workers, astronauts, cowboys, Questlove of the Roots and Mark Mothersbaugh of Devo, as well as the Lonely Island. It was undoubtedly the most surreal moment of their career (or anyone's, really).

Fifteen years prior, they were teenagers who had fired their manager and were sleeping in Greyhound bus stations between gigs. Having been introduced to the public as "teenage twin lesbians," they struggled for years to be taken seriously, to be viewed as musicians who couldn't be dismissed by any combination of those three words.

They also struggled to simply stay together: by the mid-2000s, sibling fistfights were not uncommon. It was only in their second decade that critical consensus started to turn, and when they had their biggest pop hits, from 2013's *Heartthrob*. But "as that indie rock Canadian movement exploded, we were not part of that," says Tegan. "The Dears, Broken Social Scene, Feist, Metric: that was such an Eastern Canadian thing, and we were playing with American bands. Especially as we got deeper into 2007, '08, '09, we were living in America, signed to an American label, predominantly touring outside Canada. We became very disconnected with what was happening in Canada."

Not unlike the man who had signed them to his record label: Neil Young.

TEGAN AND SARA QUIN grew up in suburbs of Calgary, where they dropped acid, went to raves, grew up as grunge kids, and discovered their sexual orientation by the end of high school.[3] Once they picked up guitars, their immersion into music was almost immediate. "There was a store in Calgary called the Attic that sold band merch, but also bootlegs and posters," says Tegan. "I had a bootleg collection of tapes I bought there by Nirvana, Hole, 7 Year Bitch, Babes in Toyland. We were so obsessed with female-fronted Pacific Northwest music." A clerk there asked Tegan if she'd ever heard of the local band Placebo, which featured three women in it; the singer's name was Leslie Feist. The sisters went to see that band and other local acts: the Smalls, the Primrods, and "we were obsessed with Red Autumn Fall," says Tegan.

"To be honest, it wasn't about the bands, it was just about being there," says Sara. "We'd buy local demo tapes and it was cool to have them, but mostly I just wanted to listen to Smashing Pumpkins."

They recorded demos at their high school, dubbed cassettes that they sold to their friends, and in 1998 entered a competition called Garage Warz at the University of Calgary. They were 17 years old and only allowed to be in the bar while on stage. It was the '90s: the competition included a besuited Beatles-y band, something called Fistfulloftoes and a guy who took the stage and proclaimed, "I am the king of conspiracy!" Tegan and Sara won. The prize was studio time and a headlining set at the campus pub, which none of their underage friends could attend. The Garage Warz promoter, Greg Curtis, offered them a weekly slot hosting an open mic, as well as an all-ages gig opening for Hayden.

It's hard to understate Hayden's influence on late '90s Canadian teens; he's second only to Sloan in terms of the country's kids seeing rock music as something accessible and aspirational. Hayden's video for "Bad as They Seem," in which he holds an all-ages show in his bedroom, is a particular landmark. His fans were intense and loyal—and young. "We were huge fans," says Tegan. "It was our first time meeting a famous person. It was very thrilling." They made enough of an impression on Hayden that they were invited to open for him again that fall when he played a licensed venue. In between, Calgary media had a field day touting the

---

3   Their many teenage misadventures are captured in their 2019 memoir, *High School*.

hot new twin act. Mike Bell of the *Calgary Sun* helped the Quins get a slot at the Music West conference in Vancouver in May 1998.

Their showcase didn't go all that well: the duo were forced to play earlier than their already early timeslot, to a sparse audience. They did, though, impress Bryan Potvin, the former Northern Pikes guitarist who was working A&R for Polygram Canada. He was ready to offer them a demo deal shortly afterwards, but the twins were not allowed to sign anything until they turned 18. The same week they played Music West, they were selected to be a special guest at the hometown stop of the Scrappy Bitch tour, featuring Veda Hille, Kinnie Starr and Oh Susanna. The Calgarians were only slotted to play one song in the middle of the show, but the crowd went nuts. The three headliners immediately granted them another song. Tegan and Sara had no idea what they were walking into, but they walked out changed.

"I was not hip at all to what was going on with any of the Scrappy Bitches," says Sara. "We found them absolutely astonishing. We bought their CDs and became obsessed. Pre-internet, this was like bringing home a treasure: 'Omigod, there are these artists you won't believe, they sound amazing.' I don't think we understood the grey area between the local punk band and Smashing Pumpkins. We weren't clear on what a career could look like in the middle. You could actually tour and play shows and not necessarily be the biggest band in the world or on radio. I was looking for the answer: how can we do what they're doing?"

Tegan and Sara graduated high school in 1998 and decided to take a year to pursue a music career. They got part-time jobs and lived at home, where their mom charged them rent. After their second opening slot with Hayden, in the fall of 1998, Calgary promoter Greg Curtis sent Tegan and Sara's cassette to Hayden's managers, Sandy Pandya and William "Skinny" Tenn. One of their assistants, Amanda Davis, heard the tape and loved it. Bryan Potvin flew to Calgary, introduced the pair to engineers at local studios and signed them to a demo deal. They recorded two three-song demos in Calgary with engineer Jared Kuemper. Polygram did not pick up the option after the demo deal.

Tegan and Sara played three shows in the Toronto area and one in Hamilton, at which Davis and Pandya were the only audience members. One of Pandya and Tenn's other clients, Hawksley Workman, recalls seeing Tegan and Sara at the Free Times Café on College Street. "Their whole gag was bickering on stage," he says. "These girls were money, everyone could see that. It was obvious. They came at an age where they were blissfully unaware that [their success] would be anything but a done deal. They had 100% full belief." Several supportive A&R people at Canadian major labels told them, "You guys need time to develop. You're not commercial, and that's good. Don't sign to a Canadian major."

"They were honest," says Tegan. "It took the wind out of our sails a bit. After Bryan Potvin left Polygram and no one offered us a deal, we were just like, 'Oh well,' and hired Jared Kuemper to make our record."

Kuemper recorded the debut album, *Under Feet Like Ours*, at the Quin household during an ant infestation in April 1999. They made a business pitch to their grandfather, a self-made farmer, who agreed to loan them $10,000 to record and press it. While mastering the record in Toronto, Tegan met with Skinny Tenn and started talking about working together; though Sandy Pandya might have been a better fit, Tenn and Pandya's business partnership had ended, and they split their client roster between them. "We were 19 and working with this older man, and generationally it was so strange," says Tegan. "But Skinny made the suggestion—at our first meeting—that we send our record to a label run by an artist. We sent the record to the Beastie Boys' label, Madonna's label, Dreamworks. None of them responded."

They did, however, send it to Elliot Roberts, Neil Young's manager, who had started Vapor Records to release special Neil Young products (box sets, vinyl releases, soundtracks). It was a boutique label: there were very few other acts, other than Jonathan Richman and, for one album, Spoon. Hayden had seriously considered signing to Vapor for his major label release, and therefore Tenn had a business relationship with Roberts. The American came to Vancouver to see the release show for *Under Feet Like Ours* at the Starfish Room on November 9, 1999. He pitched them on a deal, touting Vapor as the ideal label that would allow them to develop. Back in Calgary, they got a one-page memo from Vapor. Tenn and Roberts made plans to fly to Alberta and talk to the twins about it.

The twins faxed it to a lawyer, who advised them not to sign it as is, that it was essentially a one-page demo deal. When Roberts and Tenn showed up at the Quin family's house, the music industry veterans were shocked that the twins had pages of notes they wanted to discuss. Roberts and Tenn "also got stoned the second they got to our mom's house, which we found hilarious—if not a bit strange—because our mom was there," says Tegan. She and Sara may have been teenagers, but they weren't about to accept the first deal that came their way, even if it was from the guy who'd made the American careers of Joni Mitchell and Buffy Sainte-Marie. "We had a nice afternoon and went for dinner as a family with them," says Tegan. "Our mom was very hardline and protective of us and took both men to task for trying to get us to agree to sign something without a lawyer."

Tegan and Sara then opened for Hawksley Workman on a tour of Ontario universities. He was already making a name for himself as a producer as well as a performer, and he was convinced he could capture the twins' live essence. "[*Under Feet Like Ours*] doesn't sound anything like you," he told them. "Let me make your record. You guys will eventually sign with Vapor, you'll get an advance, I have a studio in my basement." They took him up on his offer and made *This Business of Art* in February 2000 in Toronto.

"It was our first experience of a man coming in and telling us what we were," says Tegan. "I don't think he meant it to be mean or unfair to us. We were really scrappy. *Under Feet Like Ours* had been smoothed out. Jared [Kuemper] is a wonderful, intelligent engineer. But Hawksley was watching us playing in bars and screaming through our set and he said, 'Your record should have more energy. It should sound like *you*.' We hadn't [yet] signed the deal, but we decided to make a record with him anyway." As per Workman's usual style, the 11-song album was made quickly, each track recorded and mixed in one day each, with the producer playing every instrument the twins didn't. He charged them $100 a day, his usual rate. The record took 10 days.

"It wasn't often they made it into the studio together at the same time," Workman recalls. "One would go deep with drugs and alcohol the one night, so I'd see the other one at the studio the next day, and vice versa. They were in Toronto and being 18 and partying like kids from Calgary who were given the keys to the city. They were interested in the record being made, but they were more interested in becoming people. And back then I almost preferred it when the artist didn't show up. Then I could just do my own thing."

That March, Elliot Roberts invited them to a screening of Young's concert film *Silver and Gold*, after their own showcase at SXSW with Hawksley Workman. "We all had dinner together," remembers Workman. "Elliot Roberts, me, Sandy Pandya and Skinny, Tegan and Sara, Neil and [his wife] Pegi Young. I couldn't even believe I was there, because I wasn't yet used to this kind of celebrity encounter. But Tegan and Sara couldn't have been less interested. I was like, 'Holy shit! These kids, they don't pray to the same gods I do. Who the fuck are they?' They were like, 'Well, we're here. Where's the record deal? Let's do this.' I'd never seen anything like it. It was that kind of confidence."

"Thinking about that dinner, of course we were fazed and 'holy shit,'" says Sara. "I didn't grow up listening to Neil Young, so maybe we wouldn't be able to hide how overcome we were if [it was] Madonna or Billy Corgan. When you're a young person, having your first experience with a truly famous person is just odd. It was my first time stepping into the force field of fame, where everyone in the room is looking at the person who is famous. Neil and Elliot and Neil's wife, Pegi—everyone was extremely warm toward us.

"I mean, we were *children*," Sara says. "We probably came off as precocious. We were used to entertaining people, being the youngest people in the room. We spent most of our childhood with adults. My mom and dad were working, we were with our grandparents, who were very cool, and they'd take us to their friends' houses on Friday nights. We'd have one glass of pop and one bowl of peanuts and then be told to skedaddle and not be seen for the rest of the night. We learned to say funny things to the adults, and we also knew when to get out of the room."

Tegan and Sara soon got out of their eight-month relationship with Pandya and Tenn. "We hadn't signed a contract with them," says Tegan. "We were negotiating, and Hawksley was our friend, and we'd just made this record and it was our first grown-up experience in the industry: 'Holy shit, we need to stop the machine and take a second.' Sara and I were very at odds with each other: unhappy as siblings and in a band. But we both 100% were like, 'This all feels wrong.' The only thing that kept us going was playing live. We were like, 'Let's put out the record. Let's just focus on that part of our career.'" They didn't feel like their music fit in the same management stable as Hayden, the Cash Brothers "and even Hawksley, to a degree," says Sara. "We were hungry to be around female artists."

"We realized that the kind of people we needed to work with needed to understand our culture and our world and that we were gay," says Tegan. "We were so uncomfortable with everything those first few years. We were moving out of our hometown and to Vancouver and having girlfriends and being adults, and we were so cut off from any community or friendship with all our friends who had gone away to school. We were going and playing shows opening for people and being ignored, or playing to five people, sleeping on fans' floors. We were just miserable."

"I give Tegan credit for a lot of this," says Sara of her sister's chutzpah. "Tegan always had this vision. She was so matter-of-fact. I was more like, 'Are we allowed? Are we going to get in trouble? Will [Skinny] be mad at us?' Tegan was like, 'He doesn't have the vision. We have the vision. We need people to help us reach the goals we set for ourselves.' I found it really incredible. She flew to Toronto alone to fire our manager in person. I cowered. I was hiding under my blanket with my girlfriend crying like a teenager: 'I'm so scared!'"

"We went almost three years without a manager," says Tegan. "Now, in hindsight, I believe that what truly helped us was a desire to prove that we were smart and running a business. For us, a manager seemed redundant: this was *our* business. This was on our shoulders. These are our decisions. We should be responsible. We should learn how to run a business, how to run a website, how to make money. Vapor was not really a record label; it was Neil's managers. Everything was about the live show. No one could tell us what to do and how to build a show. We wanted to learn and mature and prove ourselves and do it without older, wiser men telling us what to do."

When Tenn had been shopping around for a record deal, one A&R rep told him, "This is dyke music." "I remember crying and feeling sick," says Sara. "That was the first time I started to grapple with the reality that there's going to be a lot of people who are not into this because we look a certain way, or because we're gay." Not that it deterred them at all. "We were building our career and our early adult identity as queer people, and I didn't delineate between the two," Sara continues. "There was no part of me that was like, 'I'm not going to talk about this.' I was already doing the uncomfortable work, coming out, and I didn't see my musical life and my personal life as being different at that point."

That wasn't a concern for Roberts and Vapor Records, who became one of the few North American labels to ever sign an openly queer artist.[4] "We were basically looking for permission: 'Is it okay to talk to these publications about the fact we are gay?'" says Sara. "[Vapor] was like, 'You're gay. You should talk about it.' They were not hesitant at all. No one in our career made us feel that by talking about who we are that we would lose something being offered to us."

"Which is incredible to look back on, but at the time it didn't feel supportive, it felt flippant," says Tegan. "Not in a mean way, but Elliot was just like, 'Whatever.' He wasn't being a dad, holding us and telling us it will be okay no matter what. He was literally like, 'Just go out into the world and do your fucking job then! You're gay? Just go!' It was good. We had a lot of tough love in our lives. When we graduated high school, we had to pay rent [to our parents] and start a business. My parents had a very blue-collar mentality: 'This is a job and you are the boss. You are the company and you need to be responsible for everything.'"

This Business of Art was released in July 2000. Tegan and Sara moved out of their mom's house and to Vancouver. On their first high-profile tour that August, they were the third act on a bill with Neil Young and the Pretenders. Before the Toronto show, they rode a roller coaster at the CNE with Chrissie Hynde and Eddie Vedder. The press started paying attention. Tegan sported a Tim Hortons T-shirt during their performance of "My Number" on *Late Night with David Letterman*. They toured opening for Rufus Wainwright. They also realized that signing to a boutique label with major label distribution didn't include

---

4   Glam rocker Jobriath (Elektra Records) was the first, in 1973; disco singer Sylvester (Blue Thumb/ Fantasy) was next. Folk singers Michael Cohen (Folkways Records) and Steve Grossman (Mercury Records) also put out openly queer records in the early '70s. The Village People (Casablanca) were marketed to a queer audience but weren't all queer themselves. The '80s were rich with closeted winks and nods, though "all-American Jewish lesbian folk singer" Phranc signed to British label Island in 1989. Icons the Indigo Girls came out around the same time, shortly *after* signing to Epic in 1988. Melissa Ferrick signed to Atlantic Records in 1993, after established artists k.d. lang (Sire) and Melissa Etheridge (Island) both came out. Atlantic encouraged Ferrick to be open about her sexuality, but she wasn't ready yet. She did come out when her second record was released in 1995. Groundbreaking B.C. lesbian folk singer Ferron signed to Warner in 1996, almost 20 years after her debut album. Rufus Wainwright signed to Dreamworks in 1997. In 2000, Tegan and Sara were still very much outliers—especially for their generation.

tour support. Their request for the label to pay for a backing band was laughed out of the room; they were told they were signed as songwriters, not as a band. Their 2001 Canadian tour was far from glamorous and became their first real test.

"We'd play at bars at 11 at night and then sleep for a couple of hours at an Econo Lodge before catching a six a.m. bus to the next city in the dead of winter," says Sara. "It was scary. It wasn't fun. We were probably in danger, we didn't make any money, the shows probably weren't very good. But the only thing we had to compare it to was our high school years, where you had to be uncomfortable and in a little bit of danger to be doing anything you wanted to do.

"That cliché story of a guy and his buddies who start a band and get a 15-passenger van and drive it around—I'm like, 'Fuck you, that sounds amazing!' I was on a Greyhound," says Sara. "I remember thinking, Wow, we're definitely doing this the hard way—and we didn't know any other way to do it." Both twins lost a bunch of weight, and their parents worried. The tour had been underwritten by another loan from their grandfather, this time for $20,000, to print merchandise. Such was their frugality and business acumen that they returned from the road able to pay him back in full and pay themselves $6,000 each.

Musically, the acoustic guitars were becoming an albatross. Tegan and Sara were tired of being lumped into the alt-folk scene, billed with and compared to artists with whom they felt little in common. Ani DiFranco was the most obvious comparison point, one beaten to death in every review and article about the duo. For their next record, they wanted to do something more true to themselves. But they weren't yet sure how, or with whom.

Their American publicist Brendan Bourke came to Vancouver to visit them, largely as a social call to escape post-9/11 NYC. Staying with Sara, he noticed she had an unopened copy of the New Pornographers' *Mass Romantic*. "These guys are in Vancouver, maybe you should consider working with them," he said. Sara brought it with her on their German tour opening for Bryan Adams. She and Tegan fell in love with the record and reached out to its engineers, John Collins and Dave Carswell, who were confused by the cold call. Tegan and Sara were the first people outside their social circle to approach them for work.

"When we first met with them, they were skeptical," says Tegan. "Not in a mean way, but a funny West Coast way. They were like, 'You guys are great, we listened to your first two records, but that's not really the kind of music we work on.' We were like, 'No, no, listen to these demos.' We sat in my living room in the west end and played them 'Time Running,' 'Not Tonight' and a few others." The men were won over by the twins a decade younger than them. "Time Running" could have been a deep cut on *Mass Romantic*.

"We chose them because we loved the New Pornographers," says Tegan. "They were bearded men, and we were 22 but we might as well have been 16; we were so baby-faced. They were like, 'You want to pay us *how* much money?' I think the budget was $35,000 or $40,000. It was a lot to them."

"They had no idea they were cool," says Sara. "John and Dave were more like father figures—or older, heavy-drinking brothers. We were showing up with our packed lunches and they were drinking Johnnie Walker."

If It Was You marks the beginning of the Tegan and Sara the world soon came to know. Shedding their folk image, the twins returned to their '90s alt-rock roots. They'd been playing electric guitars since they got a pair for their 16th birthday; Ani DiFranco's *Living in Clip* live album in 1997 had inspired them to pick up acoustics again. That's what they'd played at Garage Warz and the sound had defined them for the next five years. "When we started opening for other acts," says Tegan, "people would actually say—and I have no idea if this happens to men—'No electrified instruments.' I'm assuming it's easier, setting up a stage, and they don't want you to be louder than the headliner. Those first couple of years felt like we were in the wrong skin, very uncomfortable. There were casualties of that. In 2000, we got a live review that said we were 'the punk rock version of the Mini Pops.' That is to this day the best description I can think of about our early days. We were child-like figures singing punk songs, but slowed down because we were acoustic. We felt out of place. Genre-less. We were lost. John and Dave helped us craft a sound that was the beginning of us doing a new genre: indie rock but kind of pop. That's when we aimed the camera in the right direction."

The electric sound meant a change in their live show as well. For the first time, Tegan and Sara toured regularly with a full band, although some jaunts or opening slots were still more economical as a duo. "Those first couple of years, from 1999 to 2002," says Tegan, "that's when we learned how to win an audience over—which is talking to them, make your story personal, banter, make people laugh. That was good for a much older demographic when we were opening for Joan Osborne, Ben Folds, Jonathan Richman. Then we started working with this agent, Bruce Solar, in the U.S., and that's when we got the Killers, Cake, more rock bands. Immediately we started selling fucktons of records. It was weird. We did a tour opening for Melissa Ferrick, who's a large artist in the queer community—and we never sold anything! The audience talked through our set the entire time. People just wanted to socialize; it was a social event. Then we went out with the Killers, and we'd barely have time to get to the merch table before there would be a lineup, and we'd sell 200 CDs." That's per night, kids, not the whole tour.

"That's when we realized we also had been consuming misinformation about our band from the media," Tegan continues, "which is [the idea] that we were only for women, we were only for queer people, only for college-age people. No. We were for anybody who liked rock music. We opened the floodgates. Then we did another tour with the Killers, then the Black Keys and Paramore. We started to see ourselves as a band with a more mixed audience in rock and alternative. It took a long time."

MASS ROMANTIC SOLD more than 100,000 copies in North America. But it became obvious there was a glass ceiling for a band called the New Pornographers in a way that there wasn't for equally stupid band names like, say, Cowboy Junkies and Barenaked Ladies. "The person who ran Starbucks Music was a big fan," says Carl Newman, "but they said, 'No, we can't put your CDs on the counter. Feist can go there, but the New Pornographers can't.' But it's possible the name brought us as much as it took away. The name to me was never a political statement. I wasn't like, 'I love pornography so I'm going to name my band for it.' It just seemed like an odd word. And why not? It's just a name."

Shortly before *Mass Romantic* came out, Newman discovered that televangelist Jimmy Swaggart had written a book called *Music: The New Pornography*. "Ever since," Newman told *Exclaim!* in 2000, "I tell people, 'Jimmy Swaggart said music was the new pornography. The New Pornographers are merely musicians.' It's completely innocent and poo-poos people who say, 'What an offensive name you have.'" It did, over the years, lead to gig cancellations at Christian colleges and municipal stages—and even, after one U.S. public radio gig in 2017, incurred the Twitter wrath of Raffi. Most amusing, however, was when a writer from *Magnet* magazine flew to Vancouver to interview the band and got detained at customs when he said the purpose of his visit was to write about the New Pornographers. The customs officer found actual pornography on his laptop and confiscated it for 30 days.

While preparing their second album, the New Pornographers covered "Your Daddy Don't Know," a single by '80s band Toronto, for the soundtrack of *FUBAR*, a low-budget, surprise hit comedy directed by Newman's former roommate Michael Dowse, who had helmed the videos for "Letter from an Occupant" and "The Slow Descent into Alcoholism." The song was a perfect match for the band, delivered faithfully with Case handling lead vocals in the role of Toronto's Holly Woods.

Neko Case's solo career was getting busier. Her 2002 album *Blacklisted* was another critical hit, and her first with a full U.S. launch via Bloodshot Records. Between that and her work with the New Pornographers, she started getting attention from actual pornographers. *Playboy* ran a 2003 online poll asking readers to vote for the "sexiest babe in indie rock"; Case won with 32% of the vote, coming out on top of Cat Power, a "victory" that came with an offer to pose for the magazine. While initially flattered, she soon became loath to talk about it—because it came up in every single interview, and she hated the idea of someone asking the Pornographer to sign a copy of *Playboy* instead of one of her records.

While she was still game to play with Pornographers of her choosing, Dan Bejar was happy to be mostly a voyeur. Newman told him they were going to do "Testament to Youth in Verse," whether or not he would sing it. Newman extracted another one from Bejar, "Chump Change," which turned out to be the poppiest song on the next record, and then one more, "Ballad of a Comeback Kid." Bejar thought "Painter in Your Pocket" would be perfect for the New Pornographers; Newman disagreed, arguing that only Destroyer could do that song. (It surfaced on 2006 album *Destroyer's Rubies*.)

"His songs are so separate from mine, I think they're easier to work on," Newman said at the time. "I don't second-guess them. My own songs, I listen to them and sometimes think, This is just some stupid thing I made up in my head. It doesn't sound complete to me, because I know the genesis of it. When I hear Dan songs, because they're someone else's, they already seem fully formed. With Dan songs, I always do vocal stuff with four or five people singing, maybe because that's something Dan would never do."

When it was released in May 2003, *Electric Version* did well, at the very least proving that *Mass Romantic* was not a fluke. Case joined them on tour; Bejar, as always, had his own plans. Newman put out a solo record in 2004, in part because he knew Case's touring plans would keep the Pornographers off the road. The next year, the band got an invitation to play a Canada Day show with Stars at Brooklyn's Prospect Park. Newman initially turned it down, knowing Case was in the studio making a new solo record. The organizers insisted.

An obvious solution was right in front of Newman: his newfound 23-year-old niece. He had recently connected with an older sibling, who had been given up for adoption at birth and whose own child was Kathryn Calder. Calder was based in Victoria and played in Immaculate Machine, a band also signed to Mint Records. The New Pornographers invited her to play piano and contribute some vocals to their third record, *Twin Cinema*; there were plans for the two bands to tour together in the fall. For the Brooklyn gig, Newman decided to see what it would be like with Calder handling Case's parts.[5]

The gamble, which played out in front of 8,000 Brooklynites, worked. A review in *Spin* praised Calder for filling Case's shoes vocally, if not in star

---

5   At that same gig, he also met his future wife.

wattage—although the writer argued that worked in the band's favour: "The end result was a better performance than Pornographers shows with Neko, which are usually plagued by a collective audience restlessness during the songs on which she doesn't sing lead vocals. A Neko-free Porno pushes the focus back to the songs, which are solid enough to hold up to the scrutiny." The tour that fall proved to be the band's best yet: not only were there now two powerful female voices on stage, but Bejar decided to tag along. He would stumble on stage during the headlining set, pint glass in hand, to sing five or six songs with killer five-part harmony behind him—and then leave. And he brought a version of Destroyer, with Collins on bass, to open every show with a *Streethawk*-heavy set, eschewing his latest release entirely. It was an oddly conservative move for the most unpredictable artist in the indie rock underground—and that only made him even more unpredictable.

WHEN DAN BEJAR finally agreed to tour with the New Pornographers in 2005, it was after two years of left turns, which Destroyer fans were coming to expect. After *This Night*'s release in October 2002, live shows to promote the album were rare; there was a one-month tour to show off his new band, three weeks of which were opening for Calexico. The next time he went into the studio, he ditched the band entirely.

Working with JC/DC, Bejar wanted orchestrations this time out, though he knew he didn't have the budget. MIDI technology would have to suffice, and so 2004's *Your Blues* was made entirely on MIDI synths, with only a bit of guitars. That meant not only canned strings and horns but even percussion, flute and Uilleann pipes, all rendered digitally. Working within such constraints meant no sprawling jams as on *This Night*. But the synthetic approach baffled the indie rock crowd, who were not terribly well versed in the oeuvre of Scott Walker and John Cale, two key influences on *Your Blues*.

"I wanted it to be along the lines of a weird, crooning record," says Bejar. "I was questioning from beginning to end whether the whole thing was completely misguided. Like, was there some sort of strange death wish I had in making the record? I still listen to it with a certain amount of trepidation. I think it came out way more palatable than I first thought it would be."

Co-producer John Collins says Bejar's direction for the album was to "sound like the movie music to *Blue Thunder*—a heavy Jerry Goldsmith influence. Which was true: that's what he wanted and that's what we tried to give him. We had this one synth module that belongs to [renowned visual artist] Rodney Graham, who has also underwritten just about every record I've done. Dave [Carswell] played some MIDI guitar, but it went straight into the Roland module."

"John edited it to make it sound . . . not completely embarrassing," says Bejar. "Once in a while he'd have to say, 'You know, maybe MIDI congas aren't a good idea.' *Your Blues* was all about obstructions, like there was definitely a 'no rhythm section' rule in a desperate attempt to make it sound classical. Because my ears are so bad, when I first heard that '101 Violins' sample on the MIDI box that we were using, I was like, 'Holy shit, that's it, we nailed it!' Then a few months later when a review would come out, it would just talk about how it sounds like Sega Genesis. *Your Blues* is a really good example of me thinking I'm doing one thing when I'm actually doing something quite different."

As if *Your Blues* itself wasn't its own kind of fuckery, Bejar decided to tour it with an abrasive rock band. He was a big fan of Frog Eyes, the Victoria band led by Carey Mercer, who had followed in the Captain Beefheartian steps of their mutual friends in Daddy's Hands. Frog Eyes had managed to get some American campus radio buzz when their albums were released on San Francisco label Absolutely Kosher. Though Bejar and Mercer were friends, fellow contrarians and kindred spirits, they were like oil and water on stage. Frog Eyes ran ramshackle over the *Your Blues* material, and Bejar revelled in it. Audiences, not so much.

"There were some mad, literary Destroyer fans," says Stephen McBean, whose Pink Mountaintops project opened the Canadian dates on the tour. "Dan's got a certain set of fans who are very into the lyrics, but when you add the frantic cat-erwauling of Frog Eyes behind him, you can't hear those lyrics." And if you could hear them, they could easily be misinterpreted. At the Montreal stop, Bejar pains-takingly drew out the first three syllables of "Don't Become the Thing You Hated" in a way that caused one woman in the audience to audibly wonder, "What did he just say? 'Don't be a cunt?'"

"People just hated it—it was awesome," says Wolf Parade's Spencer Krug, who played keyboards on the European leg of the tour. "We were clearing rooms. One of the mistakes we made was that Frog Eyes opened, then there'd be a five-minute break, then Dan would join us. Nothing would change, just this other guy started singing. People who really liked the original *Your Blues*, with all its digital textures, were getting their ears screeched off by Carey's guitar and some Wurlitzer [electric piano] that I was running through distortion. It was brutal and sounded nothing like the record. There must have been some good shows, but I remember a pretty empty big room in Berlin. It might have been sobering for Dan, but he took every-thing in stride pretty well. He's a pretty chill guy." Undeterred, Destroyer went into the studio with Frog Eyes, sans Krug, to record new arrangements of six of *Your Blues'* 12 songs, released in 2005 as the *Notorious Lightning and Other Works* EP.

So the trajectory of Destroyer's first decade goes like this: unlistenable debut, two albums that are each exponentially better than their predecessor, one rock'n'roll masterpiece, one wet fart, one ingenious left turn, one baffling tour decision cemented with an EP. "It wasn't like, 'I have to reinvent myself to stay fresh for the market.' I couldn't care less about that," he told writer James Keast in 2006. "I'm not changing for the sake of change—that has a whiff of desperation about it. There are just a handful of styles of records that I wanted to try my hand at, and did. I don't know if I hit the mark, but I tried anyway."

SARA QUIN WAS ready for a change. In January 2003, she did what she'd needed to do for a long time: she took a break from her more alpha twin, who was dividing her time between L.A. and Vancouver. On a whim, Sara moved from Vancouver to Montreal, becoming her own person in a new town.

She arrived just as the city's music scene was coming to fruition and quickly became immersed. "I was seeing shows and going to queer nights and dating and going to parks and riding my bike, in ways that I don't feel I've done in any other city I've ever lived in," she says. "It was also the perfect time. I was 23 and had a little bit of disposable income, which goes a really long way in Montreal. I had a ridiculously inexpensive lifestyle. For a broke musician making $20,000 a year, I felt like I was a king. For most of my time I lived just east of Parc La Fontaine, outside the cool neighbourhood. I'd snowshoe in the park in the winter, and ride my bike at all hours of the day and night the rest of the year. I was at Sala Rossa or Casa del Popolo every night. I remember seeing the Constantines and the National and all these bands play to 300 people or less, and knowing that something exciting was happening. But I didn't feel part of a scene, or that it was connected to struggles I was feeling as an artist. I was there purely as a fan and loving music.

"I saw the Rapture, which was off the hook. The Gossip, which was fucking amazing. I used to go to [lesbian club night] the Meow Mixes. Everything felt easy. If the show was sold out, someone would let you in. Everyone would sing and dance and drink. It was the most ecstatic, joyful period of music as a fan. I also remember [Tegan and Sara] not having much of a fan base in Quebec or Montreal, so I had an anonymity. There was a relief that we weren't part of that scene and people didn't know us. Then the business/art/competitive side of me would wonder, Why don't we fit here? There was this duality of loving being just a person in this room, while wondering if *I'll* ever hold space in this room."

Tegan and Sara were not cool—yet. Despite headway made with their JC/ DC record, they were still perceived as a novelty. They weren't part of any scene. They wanted to change that with their next record, *So Jealous*. The opening track, "You Wouldn't Like Me," features the chorus lyric, "I feel like I wouldn't like me if I met me." It was time to bury the Ani DiFranco comparisons once and for all. "With Ani, our first couple of years, I was like, sure," says Sara. "When we put out *So Jealous*, I thought, We're squashing that whole Ani thing now, right? This is a cool record we made with the guys from New Pornographers, right? But [the Ani tag] was still there—what the fuck. Obviously, we got the last laugh in a weird way, because we persevered. And as adults we've reconciled: whereas once we were like, 'Stop comparing us to Ani DiFranco!' Now we're like, 'We should be so lucky! She's a goddamn hero!' I think back then we wanted to be compared to the Stills, who were a great band who made a great record. But Ani DiFranco is a fucking legend."

Sara brought the Stills' 2003 album *Logic Will Break Your Heart* into the studio while recording *So Jealous* to play for returning producers John Collins and Dave Carswell. "What about this sound?" asked Sara. Collins snapped back, "You don't want to sound like them! You want to sound like *you*! Just stop! You don't want to be doing what other people are doing. You want to be ahead of it."

"John was holding me to truth," Sara says. "That made an impression on me. John is a snob. I thought he was the most knowledgeable person I'd ever met in music. It mattered to me that he liked us. He said, 'I like your songs. I like what you do. I like that they don't follow this pattern, this sound that everyone else is doing.' That was the first time we'd heard that."

Fourteen months after the release of *So Jealous*, the ultra-cool White Stripes covered Sara's song "Walking with a Ghost" and titled an EP after it, giving the Calgarians a major shot of so-called credibility. (The first time the sisters heard it, Meg White showed up to a Tegan and Sara show in Detroit to play it for them on a boom box, and they all went bowling after.) The not so cool, but extremely popular, TV show *Grey's Anatomy* placed a handful of the songs from *So Jealous* in various episodes of its first season.

And the definitely not cool yet still influential *Rolling Stone* picked *So Jealous* as one of the top 50 records of 2004; the only other Canadian on that list was Arcade Fire. "That was one of the biggest things that had ever happened to us," says Sara. "It confirmed something amongst the adults in our life. My grandma had a big black fridge in her kitchen, her beloved appliance, and there wasn't a single magnet on it. But that Christmas, she had cut out the *Rolling Stone* review and put it on the fridge. It was so awesome. She was quite aloof; I don't know that she would ever say, 'I'm proud of you.' But I knew she was proud. Though even that Christmas, she said, 'You can't do this for the rest of your life. You must have another plan.' I was like, 'Really?'"

"*So Jealous* might be the only record I've ever made to go gold," says John Collins. "It's the only gold record I own, that's for sure. That's the other thing about Tegan and Sara: everybody I've ever worked with might have gone gold and I wouldn't know it, but Tegan and Sara called me and said, 'Hey, would you like a gold record?' And it came. They don't miss a trick. They're very thoughtful."

Since the release of *If It Was You* in July 2002, Tegan and Sara had been working with managers Nick Blasko and Piers Henwood. The skeptical twins had put them on a reduced salary (7.5% of earnings, as opposed to industry standard 15%) for the first six months as a trial. They remain partners to this day. With their management's help, much of Tegan and Sara's success in 2004–05 was the result of years of hard work. But some of it was due to pure circumstance or in spite of the industry. Ryan Adams, then at the height of his popularity, loved their record and took them on tour. The Killers' drummer, Ronnie Vannucci Jr., picked out their CD from a pile of potential opening acts and insisted the duo join them on tour. The Killers were 2004's breakthrough mainstream rock act; their debut album went multiplatinum around the world. "Our agent at the time said, 'You are so lucky that those guys like you and selected you, because I can't get you those kinds of tours,'" says Sara. "We weren't the band that everyone was falling all over themselves to put everywhere. There were specific moments where some straight white guy said, 'I really love your music!' So it's hard for me to complain about old straight white guys, because that's literally why we have a career."

Straight white guys still wrote most of the record reviews, however, which were seething with misogyny and homophobia. *Exclaim!* writer Andrea Warner took stock of some of the worst in a June 2016 *Exclaim!* piece: "The critical reviews of *So Jealous* range from overwhelmingly positive to misogynistic garbage, sometimes within the same piece," she wrote. "*Spin* says that although they were once a 'Wicca-folk nightmare,' *So Jealous* is 'indie pop bliss' and 'a self-defence guide for smart girls in an emo boys' world.' . . . *Pitchfork* gives it a 3.4/10. Among the choice lines is this summary of 'Walking with a Ghost': 'I suppose it's almost as catchy as the latest McDonald's jingle, but it's also utterly boring.' *NME* wrote 'they're quite lovely, even if they do hate cock.'" Somehow, that last one was deemed acceptable for a mainstream music publication to print in 2004.

Women in the industry put up some of the biggest obstacles. One female radio host in San Diego asked the twins on the air if they had sex with each other. "I didn't know whether to cry or to bludgeon her," says Tegan. But it wasn't just the press. "We'd be looking at festivals where the Killers were playing and would wonder why we weren't on the bill," says Sara. "We'd be told, 'Well, the woman who books it hates you guys.' Or, 'You're never going to do that TV show because the booker, she really doesn't like you.' Or, '*Pitchfork* hates you and you're never going to get anything there.' We literally had to wait for a new generation to come in before we started to see what I think are fair critiques of our work, when young writers came up and didn't have the same biases. They didn't know us as precocious, annoying 18-year-old kids."

———

KATIE SKETCH WAS 20 years old when she worked for Bryan Adams, and a few years later her career was launched in part by Nickelback. The music she made with her band, the Organ, sounded nothing like either—in many ways, it was the total antithesis. Like Tegan and Sara, the Organ had some early help from a New Pornographer, mostly managed to dodge sexism and became one of the biggest buzz bands of the decade on the strength of one perfect album under 30 minutes long.

The five women in the Organ could barely play when they began; by the end of their career, they were playing festivals in France in front of tens of thousands. They landed a TV spot that proved to be a transformative moment in North American queer culture. A novel yet ultimately destructive record deal stymied their future, and as a tragic result, it seemed unlikely Katie Sketch would ever make music again.

THE PERFORMER WHO became known as Katie Sketch had played violin as a teen and fooled around on the drums but didn't have her own musical aspirations. Through a family friend, Vancouver punk staple Ron Obvious, the 18-year-old got a job installing wiring at Bryan Adams's new Warehouse Studio, and then stayed on as a general assistant when it opened. The job was exciting but also frustrating: underpaid, overworked and "really dude-ish," she says, "but nerdy dude-ish. Misogynistic but laughable. Not directed at me. It would be people talking about their wives. They didn't see me as a female amongst them. Most of them had been living this life since they were teenagers, and they just hadn't been around females. The few times they'd bring in women to listen to their new mix, the nerdy, show-offish side was so unattractive. They didn't know how to socialize with women at all. It was weird." That was the staff. The clients were "any Canadian band that had money and one iota of recognition": the Tragically Hip, 54·40, Amanda Marshall, Wide Mouth Mason. When Adams himself came in to make his own record, he was so impressed by the young intern that he gave her a guitar.

She didn't play guitar, though; she played drums in an instrumental band called Full Sketch. Late-night CiTR DJ Sarah Efron played bass, Barb Choit on guitar, and later Jenny Smyth was recruited to play her Ace Tone organ after dancing on the Starfish Room stage at a Full Sketch gig. À la Ramones, they all took the surname Sketch. Smyth made a fanzine with the Riff Randells' Mar Sellars, devoted largely to Mint Records acts; through that connection, in 2000 Full Sketch landed on Mint's *Vancouver Special* compilation where the New Pornographers also made their debut. Full Sketch soon splintered when Choit went away for university and Efron became too busy to commit to Sketch's intense four-nights-a-week practice schedule. Sketch and Smyth decided to start over, and Katie Sketch wanted to sing.

It wasn't their intention to start an all-female band. But after one too many wanky bass solos during the audition process, they decided to recruit their friends with whom they attended local live shows. Ashley Webber had never played bass before. (Her twin sister, Amber, soon joined Jerk with a Bomb as it transformed into Black Mountain.) Guitarist Debora Cohen only knew four chords and had to sit on the floor at the first practice because she couldn't play standing up. Sketch shared drum tips with Shelby Stocks, who was new to the instrument. "Everyone was very green," says Sketch. "But we did a lot of practising and we all became best friends. Everyone learned to play together. I also wrote a lot of the music parts. I'd write the left hand of the organ while Jenny would write the right hand. We'd complement each other that way. We kept it simple. No one felt a need to jazz it up a bit."

Their inexperience was not evident on their recordings, the 2002 debut EP *Sinking Hearts* or the 2004's full-length *Grab that Gun*. Maybe they were newbies, maybe they might not have fit into just any band, but they were the perfect players for each other. There was an undeniable chemistry in which every component was essential. Groups of better musicians did not play together as well as the Organ. They were certainly more accomplished than local antecedent Cub, who became wildly popular in the mid-'90s with very little experience. Cub, certainly on their first record, sounded like a green band. The Organ did not. "Obviously I heard a lot about Cub," says Sketch, "but I never listened to them."

Sinking Hearts was recorded at the Warehouse, which by then had an international reputation as a top-notch facility. Because Sketch still worked there, and because a friend was engineering, she got the studio for free; the EP cost the band only $100 for mastering. Smyth played it for Mint Records' Randy Iwata while driving with Mint act Operation Makeout. One of them teased Iwata about when he was going to sign the Organ. "Do you want me to?" he asked Smyth, who grew up idolizing Mint artists. "Yes!" she responded. "Sure!" he replied, although he later said he thought the Organ was out of Mint's league. Instead, the *Sinking Hearts* EP came out on the much smaller upstart Victoria label Global Symphonic, home to Atlas Strategic, Frog Eyes and other art-damaged B.C. rock bands.

It was Hot Hot Heat, however, that they studied closest. "We played a few shows with them, and we were friends," says Sketch. "I saw them in a bar with 100 people, and they blew everybody away. It was one of those bands that you knew were going to be big, but nobody knew them yet, and a year later they were huge. Them and Metric were the two bands we looked at as being where we wanted to be in a year. We'd watch to see how they were navigating. Not musically; they weren't similar to us. But in the way they would play *this* size of show, and four months later they'd be playing *that* kind of show. Who were they opening for? Who was their lawyer? Who was their tour manager? We bought our van off Hot Hot Heat. They were a barometer of where we should aim to be. They had some missteps that were similar to our missteps—which means maybe we should have been studying them even closer."

Sinking Hearts did well on national campus charts, riding the wave of a Joy Division revival along with New York City's Interpol, who released their debut album the same month, September 2002. Touring was limited to B.C., some opening slots for the New Pornographers and a NXNE showcase in Toronto followed by a few southern Ontario dates and one in '80s-Britpop-obsessed Montreal. "Everything we did felt over the top," says Sketch. "Our set was about 14 minutes long. At the very end [of our career], I think our set was 38 minutes long. It never really got much longer." During their six years together, the Organ only wrote and recorded 18 songs in total, six of which appeared on a posthumous EP. They never played covers.

As soon as the Organ started gaining steam, Sketch started getting daily phone calls from Jonathan Simkin, a local entertainment lawyer who had represented plaintiff Darryl Neudorf in a songwriting lawsuit against Sarah McLachlan and Nettwerk Records. He'd seen the Organ play at the Piccadilly Pub and fell in love. "I saw these five girls sounding like the Smiths and it blew my mind," he told writer Kaitlin Fontana. "Falling in love with a band is sort of like falling in love with a woman. It's all you can think about. You find yourself thinking the stupidest, goofiest stuff, like, 'What do they think of me? Do they like me?' I'd have a meeting with them, then analyze it, like, 'Did I say something stupid?'"

"The calls weren't necessarily long, but they were persistent," says Sketch. "It became like a regular phone call from an uncle who just wanted to check in. 'Got any shows coming up? Love the new song.' It was mostly him just talking." Simkin had recently helped Nickelback's Chad Kroeger launch a new label, 604 Records, which did very well in September 2002 with their debut signing, Theory of a Deadman, a band not dissimilar to Nickelback. The Organ sounded nothing like either. But Simkin was a new wave fan who didn't want everything on 604 to sound the same. "My history is as much rooted in alternative music as it is in mainstream rock, but I've become Mr. Nickelback," he told Fontana. He didn't want to lose the Organ to his nemeses at Nettwerk, though he didn't have to worry.

A Nettwerk staffer loved the Organ and set up a showcase for the execs. The band had a headlining gig at the Piccadilly Pub three days earlier, so they didn't advertise the Nettwerk gig, which was an opening slot for a random band. "There was absolutely nobody there, just three guys sitting in the front," says Sketch. "It felt like an audition." The Nettwerk guys left after the set without speaking to the band. Which was fine—musically and socially, the Organ had their eyes on Mint Records.

Simkin wanted the Organ to sign to 604. He offered them a deal, citing the label's money and clout, but the band had qualms, worried mostly about the association with Nickelback. Mint had contemplated offering a deal, but knew they couldn't compete with Chad Kroeger's bank account or Simkin himself—who was also Mint's lawyer—and so they didn't bother. When the Organ turned 604 down, Simkin panicked. "'No' was not an option," he later told *Exclaim!* He knew they loved Mint, so he approached Iwata and offered a joint record deal for Canada: signing the Organ to 604 *and* Mint. Iwata agreed. So did the band.

This kind of joint deal was unheard of in the music business—with good reason. Sketch thought it was an ideal compromise at the time, but later came to regret it. "I got help from a lawyer when we signed the agreement, but I didn't have anyone advising me before that," she says. "I had a lot of dudes from other bands giving me advice that I hadn't asked for. Everybody had something to say, and it's all conflicting hearsay information—and mostly shitty information, seven beers in, at somebody's house party: 'Don't go corporate!' Or, 'Take the money, you should go corporate!' It was not well informed. I wish I had someone I trusted ask me questions and walk me through potential options and what they'd look like. Alas."

Work began on the debut album, with New Pornographers drummer Kurt Dahle producing; the two bands had done some brief touring together. It was a professional affair—too professional. "But Kurt was only trying to do what he thought was best for us," drummer Shelby Stocks told *Exclaim!* "He wanted to take us in a bigger direction than we were willing to put ourselves out for, 'cause we're not those kind of girls."

After recording and mixing the album, the Organ decided to scrap it right before the mastering date, throwing the entire release schedule off. The Dahle recordings "didn't sound anything like our band, and not a band I would want to listen to," says Sketch. "It was highly polished but not well done, which is the worst sound. If something is highly polished, it had better be goddamn good, because I can hear and see everything. Everyone [in the studio] was playing on different instruments and amps other than their own, and it didn't sound like what it was supposed to. I was horrified, but it wasn't just me. We were all horrified. There wasn't one person in the band who said, 'I actually like it!' That makes it a lot easier. That speaks to how bad it was. Typically, there would be one or two of us who would be the devil's advocate. But not in this case. We just flat-out said that we weren't releasing it, that we'd rather break up."

They decided to keep the drum tracks and redo everything else in the back office of 604 Records, with Sketch's friend Paul Forgues engineering, who "was paid very poorly for the amount of work he did," she says. The band had already blown through their budget on the scrapped recording. This time, Sketch was in charge and the band used all their own equipment. "I was very, very, very, very involved," she told *Exclaim!* "We couldn't afford, mentally, physically or financially, to have any more mistakes."

Released in June 2004, *Grab That Gun* was greeted with ecstatic reviews. *Exclaim!*'s Lorraine Carpenter wrote, "Eloquently illustrating cold, pain, darkness, despair, loneliness, longing, self-mutilation and suicide, Sketch's lyrics also reflect her musical influences, as well as the band's collective history of clinical depression and severe social alienation." Though the sound was undeniably retro, the songs were extremely catchy, the aesthetic was impeccable, the players all gelled and Sketch was a commanding vocal presence. It had a beat and you could dance to it. But it was also bleak as fuck. "New wave is a haircut. We're too dark and moody for that," Sketch told Carpenter.

WITH THE SUCCESS of Tegan and Sara's *So Jealous* came the pitfalls of arrested adolescence. The twins were grappling with a lot of unresolved issues in their relationship, with occasionally violent results. On the rare times when they toured as a duo, things were relatively calm. But touring with a band seemed to bring out the worst in both of them. "When we were alone, we were probably better behaved because there wasn't pressure to act like normal adults who like each other," says Sara.

The twins went into therapy while making *So Jealous*. "I didn't think of it as therapy," says Sara. "I thought of it as crisis management. It wasn't a fun spirit walk to find my inner child; it was like going to the ER. It was about not fucking up our entire lives because we couldn't deal with the smallest conflicts. At 23, I was like, 'I'm going to murder her.'"

On top of this internal turmoil, Tegan broke up with her long-time partner, and the twins' beloved grandmother passed away. For their new album, they wanted to work with Chris Walla of Death Cab for Cutie (who had produced Hot Hot Heat and the Decemberists), but he wasn't available for their original time-frame. So they continued to write, burning their demos onto CDs and mailing them back and forth to each other from Vancouver and Montreal. It was the longest time they'd spent writing. When Walla was finally ready, it was clear that the material was different from anything they'd recorded before. For a duo poised for greater pop success and now signed directly to Warner rather than Vapor, it was a left turn. The album was called *The Con*.

"I think any other sane band would've tried to make a slick record and try to capitalize on what we'd accomplished with *So Jealous*," says Tegan. "Instead we made an antiestablishment, messy, unconventional, dramatic, long, complicated, anxious, depressing record." Yet *The Con* proved to be even more successful than *So Jealous*, selling more than 300,000 copies in the U.S. during its initial cycle (and half as much more in ensuing years); it's still the fan favourite of their earlier records. On its 10th anniversary, Tegan and Sara enlisted an all-star cast of peers to cover it, including Cyndi Lauper, Ryan Adams, City and Colour and Grimes. All proceeds went to their new eponymous foundation promoting LGBTQ+ rights, health care and youth programs. Reviewing *The Con*'s tribute companion, Laura Snapes wrote in *Pitchfork*, "It's become a touchstone for a wealth of diverse young artists who grew up with a healthy disregard for genre . . . Thank god artists like Paramore, Against Me! [with whom Tegan sang a duet in 2007] and AFI could see in them what critics couldn't, taking them on the road and noisily singing their praises while the indie press were too cool to take the twins seriously."

Pitchfork's original review of *The Con* in 2007, by Jessica Suarez, opened with this beyond-backhanded line: "Tegan and Sara should no longer be mistaken for tampon rock, a comparison only fair because of the company they kept." It also referred to producer Chris Walla as being in "fellow lesbian band Death Cab for Cutie."

"We wrote them and said, 'Do you understand how toxic this is on so many levels? What, because [Death Cab] are not Tool, they're girly? Why are you writing like this?' We were pissed with the whole review," says Sara, "which had misquoted lyrics, lots of lame stuff. They left everything as it was, but they did take out the 'lesbian band' reference. I remember saying, 'Well, we know now who has a tougher publicist.' Because [Death Cab] were able to get it changed but we weren't."

The opening track on *The Con* is "I Was Married," about Sara's marriage to American graphic designer Emy Storey, so that Storey could become a Canadian citizen. Canada legalized gay marriage on July 20, 2005; it took nine years before the U.K. followed suit, 10 for the U.S. The novelty of a young lesbian singing "I Was Married," at a time of volatile debate over the basic humanity of queer people, was significant and inspiring: "I look into the mirror for evil that just does not exist / I don't see what they see."

In 2008, they joined Cyndi Lauper's queer-positive True Colors tour, alongside the B-52s, Indigo Girls, Joan Jett and fellow Canadians the Cliks and Deborah

Cox. And yet, back in Canada, Sara still felt "there was a small sliver of people who I thought represented 'cool gay,'" she says, citing the Hidden Cameras, the Organ and Gentleman Reg. "I couldn't figure out whether we weren't androgynous enough or too androgynous. Maybe we were too outspoken or sounded too much like guys. I couldn't figure out what specifically we were doing wrong. I thought, Why are the Organ so cool but we're not? I couldn't figure it out."

"COOL" WOULD BE a polite way to describe the Organ's relations with 604 Records' Jonathan Simkin shortly after the release of *Grab That Gun*. He and Katie Sketch were no longer on speaking terms. Manager Linda Noelle Bush was hired not solely because the band's popularity brought new demands, but to mediate that particular relationship. The discord began when the Organ attracted American interest but Simkin wouldn't let them sign a U.S. deal for anything less than "an obscene amount of money," says Sketch.

The Organ toured the U.S. five times in 18 months. "It also felt like a lot because we would be in a van with no windows, and the drives aren't short," she says. "It was freezing cold and we were usually staying at some fan's house on his couch. There was no glamour whatsoever." They turned their attention to Europe instead, where they were sure it would be easier for them to find an audience. They toured the U.K., signed to a French label and released a single on a London label. That got the attention of Too Pure (PJ Harvey, Stereolab), who signed the band, necessitating more trips to Europe.

The real breakthrough came in early 2005, when they were invited to perform their song "Brother" on *The L Word*, a groundbreaking lesbian TV drama that was essential viewing for queer audiences in the 2000s. Though the androgynous band seemed like a perfect fit for the show, the Organ was not the producers' first choice. "The song had been used in the background of another episode at first," says Sketch. "But they originally wanted the New Pornographers, who were out of town. Mint said, 'We do all have this all-female band who are queer-ish.' They were like, 'Oh, okay, perfect!' Total happenstance."

It wasn't just any episode of *The L Word*: it was the pivotal moment when a long-simmering flirtation is consummated in the back hallway of a club where the Organ are playing, a hotly anticipated narrative moment juxtaposed with the Vancouver band's performance. "There were very, very few queer shows on the air, so every lesbian in the whole world was watching this show," says Sketch. The episode aired in late February 2005. "We'd been to Europe a couple of times, and it was grim—like literally playing for 10 people, or opening a show at a 500-person venue but only 75 people there when we're on. Then we went back to play small rooms, but they were packed with lesbians. Which is strange because no women came to our shows before then. It was a huge shift in our fan base."

Wait, seriously? No women? "I honestly don't remember any," she continues. "It was mostly gothy indie guys. There were a few women, but not many. [After *The L Word*] it became barely any guys. It was a huge shift."

The L Word scene in question is deadly serious and erotic. The actual shoot—not so much. "They were blowing this dry ice in our faces, and it was making me hysterically high," says Sketch. "I had the giggles and couldn't stop, so they had to redo the scene a number of times. What I thought was particularly funny was our drummer was fake drumming, but she would accidentally hit a cymbal occasionally. I'm lip synching, the playback music is so quiet—not like a music video where they blast it to make you feel something. You could barely hear it, the dry ice machines were blowing and there's all this wind, and then I'd hear this ping-pong of the cymbal. Every time I would lose my mind, I just thought it was so hilarious."

Everyone assumed the Organ were queer—androgyny! Angst!—though the band never identified as such publicly. "I was very closeted," says Sketch, who was already worried about the stigma of being an all-female band. "I wouldn't say everyone in the band considers themselves queer. Somebody in the band was closeted to their parents, so that was a stress, and they didn't want to be represented that way in an article. And I was freaked out, too, that we would be pigeonholed immediately and our fan base would disappear. It felt like it would have been a death sentence to ever have mentioned it at all."

That came to a head when Sketch was approached to be on the cover of *Xtra*, a queer magazine in Toronto. She turned it down. "I said, 'Will I have to talk about sexuality?' They said, 'Of course.' 'Then I can't.' Which felt terrible. But I didn't have a choice. I didn't want to get into it politically. It was a can of worms I was not comfortable with. What made it even more complicated for me was that the person [in the band] who wasn't out to her family was my girlfriend. So if I were to be talking about how I'm gay, that would have implicated her because we lived together."

That might all seem strange for a band best known for being on *The L Word*. "I may have had qualms about *The L Word*, but we also needed money really badly," says Sketch. "We were paid decently enough. But people forget how the early 2000s was not queer-friendly. I don't know if we would have been signed to Too Pure if we'd presented ourselves that way. People might say, 'Well, who cares? Maybe you shouldn't be on that label then.' But then, okay, we can't do music because our lifestyle won't be sustainable. It was complicated. People do forget that even though it wasn't that long ago, there has been so much change for queer people over the last 20 years that it's hard to believe it's even true. Gay marriage wasn't even legal, and it was a big debatable issue and people said horrible things on the news all the time. That was the climate."

The constant touring took its toll. Ashley Webber left the band at the end of 2005 and was replaced by Sketch's sister, known only as Shmoo. Shelby Stocks left in early 2006, replaced by future Austra drummer Maya Postepski for a European tour. The social bonds had frayed. When the band started, says Sketch, they were all very good friends. "We would practise and then all go to a show together. We did that for a year. Every band says this, but it's like you're married to four people in the same house and you travel to work together in the same car. It's not sustainable. At the end of the day, it boils down to money. Once you have money, you have more space, and you can put up with people's -isms, and everyone has -isms."

The Organ never made a lot of money, but there were always new carrots dangled in front of them: an Australian tour, a key festival in Europe, opening for the Cure in front of a French castle. "The first time you do a new region is exciting," she says. "Driving around North America is exciting. Flying to Australia is exciting. Europe was definitely exciting. Opening for a big band is exciting." That kept things going—until it didn't.

They turned down offers to play lucrative U.K. festivals Reading and Leeds in the summer of 2006, for the sake of Sketch's mental health. The final crack was when the band had an U.S. offer from Beggars Banquet, the venerable label that had launched the careers of Gary Numan, Bauhaus and more recently the National. "A woman from the label flew to Toronto, gave me her pitch, offered the most money she'd offered any band," says Sketch. "I said, 'You're going to have to ask Jonathan Simkin and he's probably going to say no.' She said, 'I will try.' She flew to Vancouver and had a meeting with him. He told her to 'fuck off.' She wrote me and told me that. At this point everyone's mental health was really bad. If that deal had happened, it would have given us a bit of life to carry on, but that was it."

The Organ had been asked to play Coachella in April 2007, and a prime spot at that. They turned it down and formally broke up in December 2006. Sketch was concerned that 604 might release some demos of new songs, so she reconvened the band a few months later to record a six-song EP, *Thieves*. "In the final rift of the band, two of the people couldn't be in the same room at the same time," says Sketch, clarifying that it wasn't her and her ex. The EP was recorded on Galiano Island in a room with a large window view of whales, eagles and towering cedars. It was a placid conclusion to a turbulent career. "It felt good," says Sketch. "I would've been really upset if we hadn't recorded those songs. It was 100% worth it. It was sad to me that not many people heard it or noticed it. I've had people confess to me that they're the biggest fan in the history of the band.

Then the EP will come up and they're like, 'You have an EP?' I don't think it even got sent out for review."

Sketch was surprised to learn that if she were to embark on any new musical project, she was still contractually bound to 604 after the Organ's demise. "This is what's upsetting about the timing of the band," she says. "In 2003, when we were signing a contract, the idea was that you needed a record label to do anything. Then Arcade Fire blew up on this small label, and the internet got bigger. We signed an old-school record deal and we're one of the last bands that did. And it's really unfortunate."

She and Jenny Smyth moved to Toronto to join their partners, and opened a bar together, the Henhouse. Sketch formed a new band, Mermaids, that performed just once in 2007, and she sang a gorgeous duet with Gentleman Reg on his 2009 album *Jet Black*. "I had a bunch of people ask me to sing," she says. "I didn't really enjoy doing it, so I didn't. I felt like when I was not able to do music, that I needed to get on with my life and focus on other things. Anything around music always felt very negative. Which is a shame." She and her wife started a popular '80s hair-metal cover band, Vag Halen, in 2017. In 2019, she surfaced with new music, working with Owen Pallett and opening for Broken Social Scene. That same year, Jonathan Simkin agreed to end his contractual relationship with Sketch—11 years after the Organ's final EP.

In the meantime, since 2010, Simkin had been running a 604 subsidiary label for non-mainstream acts. He called it Light Organ Records. When asked to comment on the name, Sketch simply sighs and says, "Yep. Uh-huh. Yes."

TEGAN AND SARA had three bus accidents on tour in 2008. Sara broke up with her wife, while singing "I Was Married" every night. "It was a tough record cycle," says Tegan. "I was similarly ending a relationship and was displaced and anxious. But I got a lot back from the audience. I enjoyed seeing their misery and their connections to the songs. It really bolstered me and made me feel better. For Sara it was worse. It was weird, because for the first time in our career we were selling out big rooms, playing to thousands and thousands of people, and for her it was just misery. It made me feel very detached from her and angry at her."

On February 29, 2008, the twins had their worst fight yet, while on tour in Glasgow. "I told Sara she was being impossible and she just broke," says Tegan. "She just walked across the room and attacked me in front of everybody. It took two grown men to get her off me. We played the show, which is crazy, but we got on the tour bus that night and I told her I was going to quit. We wrote letters to our management saying we were quitting." Their front-of-house engineer, Chris

Hibbins, wrote them a 5,000-word letter on his BlackBerry urging them not to quit, after all they'd been through, and that the crew had a responsibility to take better care of the duo. Tegan credits him with saving their career.

It was time for a break, something they'd never done. They finished their winter European dates but cancelled summer festival appearances. "We had been in bad or worse places in our relationships," says Sara, "but in those earlier days there was a sense that we couldn't stop. We were on the edge of a cliff and if we stopped moving, we'd fall off. There was no option. But around 2008, we had infrastructure: management, agents, institutional support. Our crew wasn't a ragtag group of people; we had history. Our tour manager was 25 years older than us. These were people who had seen bands deteriorate and implode because of alcohol or drugs or affairs or people hating each other. We realized there would still be a career on the other side.

"Not to throw people under the bus," Sara continues, "but there were a lot of people in our lives who said, 'You should absolutely not [stop].' Not just in our professional life but in our family. There was a lot of 'Can't you two figure this out? Can't you two just get along? Really? You're 28-year-old women punching each other backstage and fighting like you're five years old over a toy?' A lot of people didn't understand the profound, entwined conflict.

"We had been offered all these big summer festivals we'd never been offered before, like Glastonbury and Leeds, and that was a big point of contention with our managers; they didn't want us to cancel those festivals. They felt a real sense of disappointment. But Neil [Young] and Elliot [Roberts] were like, 'Fuck the festivals. If you're unhappy, it's the relationship that is important. No show or opportunity is more important than what you have between the two of you. If you're miserable and beating the shit out of each other, just stop.' Our managers are older than us, they're men, they're straight, they don't necessarily understand us on an intrinsic level, and they took Neil and Elliot's word: 'Yeah, maybe they should take some time off.' We're like, 'Yeah, no shit.'

"As ambitious as Tegan and I have always been, there was also an arrested development. While the rest of our lives was shuttling ahead so fast, there was this central part of the equation—our relationship—that had been frozen in time. We hadn't really done the natural thing, which is break away from your primary relationships with your parents and your siblings. You have to go out into the world and sever those ties in order to stand on your own two feet. Tegan and I, because of being twins but also starting a band at such a young age, everything just froze. We had to do the full clean break and then start as adult people on equal footing. What do we really want this relationship and this band and this life to look like, now that we're not 17?"

As part of their rebuilding process, they decided to write together for the first time. They went to New Orleans, sat face to face and wrote six songs. It didn't yield anything usable. Back home in Vancouver and Montreal, however, they wrote "Feel It in My Bones" together for a DJ Tiësto single, a sign that they were willing to move beyond their indie rock roots. For the next record, they returned to Chris Walla, who wanted to record the material live, running 50 or more takes to work them in—with Death Cab drummer Jason McGerr and Walla himself on bass, leaving the duo's touring band at home.

Released in October 2009, *Sainthood* marked the first time a Tegan and Sara album got universally positive reviews. It was shortlisted for the notoriously snobby Polaris Music Prize, up against the cool crowd: Broken Social Scene, Caribou, Owen Pallett, Shad. They were even invited to participate in Fucked Up's charity Christmas single, alongside Vampire Weekend, Yo La Tengo, Bob Mould and TV on the Radio. Offstage, things were also going well: their 2011 tour marked the first time they didn't fight.

Tegan, however, wanted to be even bigger, and Sara felt she'd outgrown the duo's sound. They both lamented the paucity of queer voices at the top of the charts and wanted to climb that mountain and sit beside Katy Perry and Taylor Swift. For their next album, 2013's *Heartthrob*, they went all in on big pop production, hiring Greg Kurstin (Lily Allen, Sia, Kelly Clarkson, Pink) and delivering their first bonafide pop smash, "Closer." Taylor Swift invited them on stage to sing it with her. Yet all the success was hardly seen as a sell-out, because a) that wasn't a thing anymore, b) a new generation of poptimist listeners saw no distinction between genres and c) Tegan and Sara hadn't changed who they were, how they ran their business or how they wrote songs, other than adding a few more synths and drum machines and slightly slicker production. They were still dorky, still transparent, still earnest—and all that authenticity, plus their perseverance, now made them cool.

"I don't know if we thought we would be as big as the bands we grew up listening to," says Sara. "I always thought of us in a very middle-class way, with the hustle and the hunger that my mom had. That was our influence growing up: watching our mom be an outstanding parent, but also be hip to what was happening in social justice movements, and she was a feminist and cool and interested in clothes. She was probably living week to week. But she was holding space and saying, 'I deserve to be here.'

"We emulated that. We had our dukes up. We knew we were going to have to fight for whatever space we were going to hold. The easiest way to do that was to tell people, 'Yes, of course we deserve to be here.' Show no weakness! If you tell people that you're unsure whether you're supposed to be there, they will tell you that you don't."

TEGAN AND SARA, a duo, had trouble staying together. The Organ, five women, did not stay together. How did the New Pornographers, with seven members and three—at times four—lead singers, manage to last so long?

For starters, they didn't become a real band until 2005, when they added Kathryn Calder and could tour without the constraints of Neko Case's schedule. It was only in 2006 that Newman decided to hire a manager, which he'd been reluctant to do since the outset. "There were too many crazy moving pieces, and at some point, I decided that I couldn't deal with it anymore," he says. "We needed help. I needed to show banks how I make money. There was a point early on, during *Electric Version*, where we got an advance from the label. All that money got split up evenly, and then I was in the studio with John and Dave, and I realized some of that money was supposed to be used to make the record."

The band then did more touring than ever, including a 2006 jaunt with original inspirations Belle and Sebastian. Newman moved to New York City, his wife's hometown; his wedding reception, at which he sang Phil Collins's "Against All Odds," made the *New York Times* society pages. Neko Case continued to be more famous than her old friends, but she appeared on every New Pornographers record and at least one tour a year. Even Dan Bejar seemed to enjoy the occasional New Pornographers tour.

"I don't think it's a coincidence that it was around the time [Bejar] bought a house," says Newman. "He was at a point in time where he had to make money. He looked at playing with the Pornographers as a job, though obviously we were friends. There was one tour where he said, 'You know I just did the math, about putting together a Destroyer band versus going out with you, and it seems so much easier just to show up and sing five or six songs.' I said, 'That works out for everyone then. You've got an easy job, and everyone's happy you're there.' The downside of having Bejar with us is that for years, no one had ever said, 'Where's Dan?' Then he tours with us for a month [in 2005], and ever since then all we hear is 'Where's Dan?' It's like from 2000 to 2004, no one once ever fucking yelled, 'Where's Dan?' Now they do. Fairweather fans."

Bejar has never appeared to enjoy performing—because he doesn't. "I don't go to rock bars at home, so I don't know why I should have to spend a month constantly in one," he told James Keast in 2006. Many years later, he didn't like it any better. "It used to feel more like a cool drunken frolic, and it's become more anxiety ridden or confusing to me, or just more obviously self-conscious," he says. "The thing that most people dig when they're younger is just to get up on stage and go for it. I used to have to drink for two days just to get on stage, and then drink for another two days after I got off to be able to deal with how shitty I thought it was. I don't advise that as a coping mechanism. I think I'm just a slow learner. I needed to get literally 1,000 shows under my belt before I started to relax and feel good and confident on a stage."

Destroyer finally appeared on the cover of *Exclaim!*, solo, for the 2006 album *Destroyer's Rubies* and toured regularly for 2008's *Trouble in Dreams*, when his band became more interesting than most of Bejar's newer songs. In 2010, he took a leap by changing his singing style completely: he no longer tripped over his own words, packing stanzas with syllables that made melodies near impossible. The new Bejar was smooth like butter, with a backup band to match, including avant-garde trumpeter JP Carter and saxophonist Joseph Shabason. Bejar described the initial concept behind the album *Kaputt* thusly: "Let's make a record that sounds like you put it on at the salon or a dinner party, something that people wouldn't instantly request to be taken off." It was wildly successful, a commercial break-through that he toured for two years, finding himself on bigger and bigger stages. The guy who early on wrote a song called "War on Jazz" was playing jazz festivals.

"*Kaputt* just happened to line up with a certain zeitgeist or vibe that seemed to click with 2011, but that's something that will only happen to me once," he told *Pitchfork*. "There were a few situations I ended up in after *Kaputt* came out that just seemed wrong. I remember being at Coachella and thinking, What the fuck am I doing here? That's just one obvious one. But I didn't have to play Coachella. No one forced me. That was a choice and that's me just dabbling in this certain careerist version of myself. It fucking exists! I don't regret it, though, and I'm really proud of *Kaputt*. But it became clear to me very quickly that there are a few places where I have no business being—and that I wasn't going to be returning to those places again, whether out of my own volition or because I would not be invited back. Maybe I'm totally wrong. But I feel like I'm right."

When your success has seemed improbable from the beginning, expectations are easy to keep in check.

CHAPTER 7
FIRST WE TAKE
BERLIN

FEIST, PEACHES, GONZALES

"**W**HO'S THAT GIRL?"

Leslie Feist was hard to miss in early 2000s Toronto. She'd been on MuchMusic and toured with the Tragically Hip as a member of By Divine Right. She played the role of hypeman for her roommate, Peaches. She briefly played guitar in Royal City. She was often on stage with Broken Social Scene. She also performed her own songs, but nobody outside her peers and a few critics cared about that yet.

"I was always supporting other people—kind of like *20 Feet from Stardom* but in a small Canadian sense," she says. "Being in By Divine Right was just a chance to play songs from [their 1997 album] *All Hail Discordia*. For Peaches, it was the same. She was my roommate and my awesome close friend. Playing with her was an inside joke, because it's what we'd do in our apartment anyway."

"Every musician I knew had had some kind of [musical encounter] with her," says her closest collaborator, Jason "Chilly Gonzales" Beck. "She was playing drums with this band or guitar with another, or setting up an evening of music somewhere. She was really in a rush to get in as much experience as she could. She had a burning ambition to master her craft—and also insisted on goofing around at every turn. I remember thinking, Wow, if this girl ever gets her focus together, she'll be unstoppable." It was Gonzales who helped give her that focus and engineered her European success—which, in typical Canadian fashion, then made the hometown industry very curious.

But if Feist was focused on success, she was never going to adhere to standard formulas. "I don't like being spoon-fed anything," she says. "I like the shadows being left in there so you fill in the blanks yourself. It's like holding a lantern up to the possibilities, squinting. You know, it's like when you look in the back of a cave and there's a glint of something and you're like, 'Is it a kitten or a sabre-tooth tiger?' It's whatever draws you in there."

Feist's MO was to explore every possibility she could until she found her path. The girl who grew up in Regina and Calgary—a punk kid with 20-hole cherry-red Doc Martens, five layers of ripped fishnets, a *Phantom of the Opera* poster on her wall—had no idea that path would one day have her headlining the Olympia in Paris. Or tap dancing in Berlin. Or performing with Muppets on *Sesame Street*. Or singing a Leonard Cohen tribute at the Junos after his death. Or selling more than a million records.

Before becoming the It Girl of early 2000s indie rock Toronto, she first had to follow her friends to Europe to find herself. It was Peaches who brought her there.

———

PEACHES IS A gender-bending performance artist, internationally known musician, sexual pioneer and activist, based in Berlin since 2000 and most associated with that city's cultural scene.

But Merrill Nisker, the woman behind Peaches, is as Canadian as it gets: her high school was named after a member of the Group of Seven (near, uh, Cummer Park) and she worshipped Rough Trade's Carole Pope. She got her musical start as a folkie in a band named after a Joni Mitchell lyric, who had a weekly gig in the same club that birthed the Rheostatics. She later played in an art-rock band with the son of renowned CBC personality Peter Gzowski, and is indirectly responsible for the international success of Feist. She's also the proud inheritor of an avant-garde Toronto tradition that stretches from the filmmaker Michael Snow to the art collective General Idea to *SCTV* to proto–riot grrrls Fifth Column to porn provocateur Bruce LaBruce. The friend who brought her to Berlin comes from a family who built the CN Tower.

Peaches is as Canadian as maple syrup.

To top it off, she grew up around the corner from Rush. "They scared the shit out of me when I was little," she told *Exclaim!* in 2003. "I used to play British Bulldog and Red Rover with Geddy Lee's brother while Rush were practising in [Lee's] garage. They all looked like weird wizards."

Nisker grew up the youngest of three in a household where artistic pursuits were little more than a curiosity. She credits Citytv's *The NewMusic* with saving her life by exposing her to the likes of the Ramones and Nina Hagen. At Jewish summer camp when she was seven years old, her best friend came out to her as trans. She attended Hebrew day school and earned a rep as a class clown. "I would jump out the window in class and the teacher would lock it," she told the *Guardian* in 2003. "I'd be left outside in the winter. I wasn't particularly smart." She battled with teachers, even those in her favourite subject, drama.

At North York's A.Y. Jackson Secondary School, at a time when Rough Trade's "High School Confidential" was on the radio, Nisker was intrigued by her biology teacher, a leather-clad woman who rode her motorbike to school. Suddenly, Nisker became very interested in biology and won the award for "most improved science student." In 1985, when Nisker was 17, she and 9,000 other Torontonians went to High Park to see a free Rough Trade show. In August 1987, when David Bowie came through town on his Glass Spider tour, Nisker was just as excited to see Rough Trade open as she was to see the headliner. "Carole Pope is my No. 1," says Peaches. "She's my girl. I'm always advocating for people to understand Rough Trade and her lyrics and what she represented and how important she was."[1]

Future sexual provocateur Nisker identified as bisexual in high school, and left home after arguing with her parents about her first girlfriend. She enrolled at York University to study drama, with dreams of creating psychedelic musicals like *Jesus Christ Superstar* or *Phantom of the Paradise*. But an academic approach to drama didn't sit well with her; she dropped out after a particularly revelatory acid trip.

She channelled her frustrations into entrepreneurship, developing a drama program for children between the ages of four and six. She delivered it first at the local YMCA and then expanded to daycare centres and private homes. After the first class at the Y, the staff wanted to know if she was drugging the children, because why else would they be listening to her so attentively? They then asked her to teach the other teachers. Children would ask her, "Are you an *adult*? Or a *kid*?" She soon started her own business giving private classes, and that gig lasted 10 years. "I wanted [the kids] to remember the creativity in music," she says, "not how their drama teacher dressed them up in a little sailor costume and their parents clapped at what good little adults they were."

In 1989, she and her girlfriend, known publicly only as Andi D., formed a folk trio called Mermaid Café with guitarist Joe Moon. Though Nisker was listening to Bongwater and the Pixies at the time, this project was decidedly influenced by Indigo Girls. They got a weekly Wednesday gig at the Cabana Room at Spadina

---

1   In 2015, Peaches appeared on Carole Pope's song "Lesbians in the Forest," used in an episode of *Transparent* at Peaches' urging.

and King, a favourite haunt of the Rheostatics and Skydiggers, and started packing the place; the residency lasted 18 months.

A CBC TV news clip likened them to Yorkville hippies and featured them singing a song about homeless people. In the clip, Nisker says, "If you think of pizza, there are so many different toppings people like, and we take a little bit of each and put them on to create our own homemade acoustic pizza . . . If you think of roots music and folk music, it's not a fad kind of music." One song was a tragic tale of a queer teenage romance that ends in a fatal car crash; it would leave the audience in tears—not only at the Cabana Room but at Jewish teen summer camps where the band was a big hit. But Nisker soon got bored and the band split by 1991.

She started gigging occasionally at the El Seven Nightclub, a cabaret series at the Rivoli featuring Gordie Johnson's Big Sugar backing up guest singers, such as Lee Aaron, Molly Johnson, Barenaked Ladies' Tyler Stewart and many others. Nisker would do a slow, loungey version of Led Zeppelin's "Black Dog," in which the guitar solo was played on flute. She'd also do a slinky "High School Confidential." Though Gordie Johnson was a bona fide guitar god versed in blues, jazz and rock, Nisker's mind was blown by someone else. "Dale Morningstar [from the Dinner Is Ruined] is my guitar god," she told *Exclaim!* "He was the coolest. Like, what the hell did I know about Sonic Youth and give a fuck? I saw Dale Morningstar play and that really made me wanna play electric guitar."

In turn, she made a high-profile fan early on, when Mary Margaret O'Hara saw Nisker perform "Black Dog." "She asked for my phone number and sent me the most incredible message about how much she loved my singing and my style," says Nisker. "That was the first time ever, *ever*, that I got any real compliment from Toronto. That's important to me. Then I went on to do those nights at the Gypsy Co-op where there was a theme, and Mary Margaret was always running them. Mary would always ask to sing with me, and I couldn't believe it. Carole Pope was there one night. I went to try and talk to her and she kept running away from me. She thought I was trying to pick her up." With musicians she met on Queen Street, including guitarist John Gzowski, she joined another band, Fancypants Hoodlum. This was something else entirely: avant-garde players twisting rock music upside down, not unlike Mike Patton's Mr. Bungle. Nisker promptly lost her entire fan base of earnest folkies.

Meanwhile, her drama program was going gangbusters by 1998. Her roommate Leslie Feist recalls, "She had a discipline I'd never seen before. She was getting up at six a.m. to drive up to the suburbs where she taught little kids in affluent Jewish households. She told me how much she made per kid, and she did three or four basements filled with kids for an hour each, and by noon she'd have made $1,000. I was in awe."

"I learned a lot from working with kids," says Nisker, "because if you don't give it [your all], they just jump all over you. Adult audiences want to jump all over you if you don't give it, but they're more polite. I really learned to keep it going because of kids."

That sense of joy came into play on one fateful night in 1996. Nisker had asked her friend Rebecca Gould—who played bass in Sarah Harmer's Weeping Tile—about forming an all-female band. Gould had other plans; her neighbour had a jam space in his basement, and she had a crush on one of his friends. Nisker didn't like this idea at all but showed up, didn't say hello, grabbed a mic and started free-styling. The neighbour, Dominic Salole, played drums. Gould played bass. Her crush played a synth. Soon everyone was freestyling and trading instruments they may or may not have known how to play. Nisker, who was normally allergic to keyboards in rock bands, tackled a synthesizer for the first time.

What no one in the room knew at the time was that they were all frustrated with their regular musical outlets, and there was also clear sexual tension in the air. Catharsis drove creativity. One jam consisted of them all singing, "I wanna fuck you!" Gould's crush told Nisker that she played guitar like Joey Santiago of the Pixies. It was the first time anyone had complimented her guitar playing, and he had compared her to one of her musical heroes.

They decided their new band should be called the Shit, so that they could introduce themselves on stage by saying, "We are the Shit!" Everyone took new names that night: Nisker became Peaches, Gould became Sticky, Dominic Salole became Mocky, and the man with the compliments, Jason Beck, renamed himself Chilly Gonzales—"Gonzo" to his closest friends.

———

JASON BECK GREW up in a rags-to-riches house of Euro snobs. His Ashkenazi Jewish grandparents fled Hungary for Montreal during World War II. In 1957, Beck's grandfather founded a concrete construction company that was eventually taken over by his father and renamed Aecon. Aecon built, among other things, the CN Tower, the St. Lawrence Seaway and Vancouver's SkyTrain. The family moved to Toronto when Beck was 12, right around the time the young piano player unsuccessfully tried to convince his grandfather that Lionel Richie was a music genius on par with the great European composers.

Beck went to the private Crescent School, in the shadow of Toronto's ritzy Bridle Path. The school's motto is "Men of character from boys of promise." He studied jazz piano with men who gigged at George's Spaghetti House, the venue booked by Moe Koffman. Beck went back to Montreal to study classical music at

McGill but soon switched to jazz. He sparred frequently with his instructors. Most of them were musical purists who challenged him in ways he appreciated; Beck figured he had to learn the rules in order to break them. While in school, he wrote musicals with his brother, Christophe, and recorded a demo of his own songs.

Returning to Toronto after McGill, he took random piano gigs, including one at a Yorkville lingerie store. (The owner told him, "Hey, I know it's not Carnegie Hall in here." "Believe me, *I know*," Beck responded.) He formed a pop band called Son, an odd combination of Elvis Costello and that particular early '90s meld of hard rock and funk, with a bit of Ween in the mix. He was nothing if not audacious: the album was called *Thriller*. Word reached Warner A&R rep Steve Jordan, who bought the album off the indie rack at Sam the Record Man and soon offered Son a three-album deal. To celebrate, Son played a show at the Rivoli ignoring their own material completely and instead performing Prince's *Purple Rain* in its entirety.

Thriller was rereleased in 1996, making minor waves with the single "Pick Up the Phone," and they opened for Barenaked Ladies in Western Canada. Things weren't moving fast enough for one half of the quartet, who quit, leaving just Beck and Dave Szigeti. Beck was finally getting the validation he'd always craved, and yet something was amiss. "When I signed a record deal in Canada," he says, "I thought my problems were over. But that was just the beginning of my hell ride through the music business. I was grossly underprepared for being on stage, being in interviews, knowing how to act in meetings, so I made a bunch of mistakes and it was a disaster. I felt like a zero, I was going nowhere."

That's when the Shit hit the man.

The Shit only lasted a year before "it turned into diarrhea," in the words of Mocky. When a relationship between Gonzales and Sticky fizzled, he and Peaches regrouped as Feedom with Son's Dave Szigeti, playing driving, one-riff hard-rock music. "It was a lot of very repetitive drone music, everything from the Melvins to no wave, the Boredoms and John Zorn, up to and including Trans Am, and the translation of electronic aesthetics played in a rock manner," says Beck, intellectualizing what was very visceral, simple music. "[It was] an aesthetic of techno music, in that we only played one riff per song, arranged in peaks and valleys intricately and intuitively." Feedom's recordings with Shadowy Men on a Shadowy Planet's Don Pyle were never released—though one track resurfaced years later on an Iggy Pop album.

Around this time, Beck and Szigeti went to L.A. with Beck's brother, Christophe, to make the second Son album, *Wolfstein*. The press release tried to sell the album as being about a musician turning into a wolf after a roadkill incident on a Manitoba highway. It was decidedly uncommercial; the only viable single was a song called

"Making a Jew Cry." Oddly enough, Warner hated it. They asked him to go back to the drawing board. Beck stubbornly stood his ground and insisted it come out as is. "The letter of the contract said they had to [release it]," he says. "They were like, 'You're knowingly forcing us to do something we don't want to do. Why would you do that?' I said, 'Well, this is what I need to do.' The other choice would have been to make a different record, to be their bitch."

And so Warner called his bluff, put it out with no promotion, and it was effectively stillborn. No radio, no video, no press, no sales, no shows. Beck was devastated. In retrospect, he says, "It was a choice I made to handle the disappointment of being on a major label. The way I dealt with it was to court a certain kind of failure." It worked. In 1998, Warner rejected the demos for a third Son album, and he was dropped from his deal. To rub some competitive sibling salt in his wounds, Christophe landed his first major gig as a film composer when he got a job on the *Buffy the Vampire Slayer* series (which lasted its duration; Christophe's credits now include Disney's blockbuster *Frozen*).

A lawyer extracted the money from Warner promised to Beck for a *Wolfstein* video. He nursed his wounds in Peaches' apartment, above the sex shop Come as You Are at 701 Queen Street West. The two of them, with Mocky, Dave Szigeti and others, would stay up deep into the night improvising rhymes over beats. Most were composed on Peaches' new hardware, the Roland MC-505 Groovebox, a 1998 device that combined a drum machine, a sequencer and a synth with controls that emulated vintage sounds heard in early electro. Well before every musician had recording software on their laptop, a tool like this was ideal. The 701 crew self-identified as jackass pranksters, taking the piss out of anything and everything. Beck had only recently got into rap music. The genre's outsized characters, role play and braggadocio were perfectly suited to his own pettiness, cockiness and sense of competitiveness.

Occasionally they'd be joined by Peaches' roommate, Leslie Feist. Feist had first taken a room in the apartment when Dave Szigeti lived there; when he moved out, Peaches moved in. She was 10 years older than Feist and recently divorced. Feist was working as a waitress at the cocktail bar Lava Lounge, and would arrive home at three in the morning to find her living room buzzing with creative energy. "They'd be making beats in the living room and freestyle rapping and there was a trunk full of costumes," says Feist. "I'm notoriously terrible at any kind of freestyling, so I'd instinctively launch into some melodic hook. I'd come home from the bar really late with pockets filled with loonies from tips, and everyone was still going deep into the night in this low-grade party, this kind of study they were all undergoing—though I'm sure they didn't think of it that way. There was a formalist repetition."

Though Feist had little in common with them musically, the group of misfits became her closest musical family. It was this group, not Broken Social Scene, that led directly to her multimillion-selling commercial success in the next decade.

LESLIE FEIST WAS born in Amherst, Nova Scotia, in the hospital closest to where her parents lived in Sackville, New Brunswick. Her American father was a professor at Mount Allison University, routinely rated the best small postsecondary institution in Canada. He was also an abstract expressionist painter; her mother, a ceramicist. They split when Feist was nine months old. She moved with her mother and siblings to live with her grandparents in Regina until she was seven, then moved to Calgary—a city preparing for the 1988 Winter Olympics. Feist joined a team of 1,000 dancers who rehearsed for two years in advance of the opening ceremonies, held on her 12th birthday. They performed to a truly wretched David Foster song—not, sadly, to k.d. lang's barn-burning show at the closing ceremonies. Feist's first-ever concert, a Tina Turner show, was in the same stadium, the Saddledome.

Feist left home at 16 and transferred to an arts school. That might have seemed inevitable for the daughter of artists, but her father had tried to steer her away. "There was something very pragmatic about the way he approached it," she says, "an absolute void of romanticism, like, 'Don't become an artist, you won't survive. I barely am, and I'm the exception to the rule.' Not discouraging exactly, but reeling off statistics about how of the hundred kids that graduated every year that he'd taught, only one would ever sell a painting." Nonetheless, she swapped her Doc Martens for a bass guitar and her life path was set.

In high school, she fronted a band called Placebo (unaware of the soon-to-be-chart-topping British band who began around the same time). She had never heard of Bikini Kill, but the two bands shared a genetic makeup: three women on voice, drums and bass, and a guy on guitar. "I was in no way politicized," she says. "The songs were about dreams I had, just nonsensical noise-making. If a zine had reached us, or if I had any knowledge of riot grrrls, I'd have said, 'Hey, we're a chapter!' and put some intentionality behind it." She befriended staff at campus station CJSW, which was a vector to the outside world; Placebo's EP *Don't Drink the Bathwater* went to No. 2 on the station's chart in June 1995, behind local heroes Huevos Rancheros. Years later, U.S. presidential candidate Beto O'Rourke got in touch with Feist; they had met when his punk band passed through Calgary in the mid-'90s. The highlight of Placebo's career in Calgary clubs was when they opened for Chicago's Jesus Lizard; lead howler David Yow complimented the teenager's voice from the stage.

Leslie Feist's life changed the day Placebo played Infest, a big rock festival just south of town in High River; they were the token local act on a bill that included the Ramones, Violent Femmes, Bad Brains and Toronto grunge band hHead, with guitarist Noah Mintz and bassist Brendan Canning. hHead were the first act of the day, even before the teenage band, which reveals their status in the industry at the time.

"I don't remember much" about the teenage Feist, says Canning, "other than the nose ring and the bare feet and green streaks in the hair—or maybe that was my goatee. She was a cute little hippie, and they rocked pretty good for 16-year-olds." When Placebo made their one and only jaunt east in 1995, both Mintz and Canning showed up to their show at the Horseshoe, at one of Dave Bookman's Nu Music Nites. Bookman was also impressed; he asked them back the next week. Mintz invited Feist to his first-ever solo show the next week and to accompany him at a songwriters' circle hosted by Hayden, called Hardwood Wednesdays. The 19-year-old Calgarian punk had never sung quietly before. "I was backstage with the lyrics, the paper shaking in my hand," she says. "I wasn't going to be able to hide behind the noise. I sang this weird song about abortion and bleeding [called 'Inbortion']. The chorus was 'I bleed, I bleed.'"

A year later in 1996, Feist lost her voice and went to Toronto for treatment, staying at her father's house on Delaware Avenue, learning guitar and how to work a four-track recorder. She was there for nine months and didn't know anyone in the city. One day Mintz called 411 in Calgary looking for her, because he was about to record the song they did together at the Rivoli. He found her mother and she gave him Feist's number. When they connected, both were shocked to discover that they lived only a block apart in Toronto.

She recorded Mintz's song and joined his band, playing bass; everyone in the band was instructd to play an instrument new to them. Synth player Dan Kurtz[2] was normally a bassist in Andrew Whiteman's Que Vida; he introduced that guitarist to Feist. It was the beginning of a lifelong bond, though sometimes frayed.

Intrigued by the new kid in town, Whiteman and By Divine Right's José Contreras went to see her play one night at We'ave, a basement bar across the street from the Art Gallery of Ontario. "Going down the stairs," says Whiteman, "we could hear her already on stage, solo with her 'Lady Lado' guitar, singing 'Sirena,' and it was instant: 'Oh, shit. This. Is. It.'" Soon afterwards, Feist went to see a show by Que Vida, where Whiteman played the sexually boastful song "A Hundred Heads." That week she invited him over to her basement apartment to hear something. "She was like, 'Check this out,' and played me a song called 'Cherry Tree' on her four-track

---

2   Kurtz later joined the live electro jam band the New Deal, and his pop band Dragonette had an international No. 1 single, "Hello," in 2010.

that she'd written in response to 'A Hundred Heads.' I said, 'You're fast, eh?' It was Feist as PJ Harvey."

Though they all ran in the same circles, Leslie Feist met Jason Beck and Dave Szigeti completely randomly: they approached her while she was hanging out with jazz singer Coco Love Alcorn at a solar-powered music festival in Withrow Park, where intermittent clouds resulted in comically fluctuating volume levels. The two men soon became key collaborators on Feist's first solo album, *Monarch (Lay Your Jewelled Head Down)*, for which Szigeti was the string arranger. Joining them were Kurtz, Contreras and Whiteman, as well as Jamie Shields, of Kurtz's band the New Deal, and Rheostatics' Martin Tielli. Some tracks were recorded in Feist's apartment, while Peaches was out at work.

Monarch is the mystery of Feist's discography; she's been more than hesitant to make it publicly available. Which is a shame: it shows how Feist was instantly a stellar songwriter, both melodically and lyrically. Her eye for careful detail and melancholy is apparent in every one of the album's 10 tracks. Szigeti's tasteful string arrangements are an indie rock analogue of Björk's *Homogenic*. Feist funded the album through her waitressing tips and a $200 loan from her mother, who sent her daughter an invoice. (Feist says that when she paid her mom back, the cheque was never cashed.) But she had no idea how she was going to put it out, or when.

The We'ave club offered her a regular cabaret night to curate, which she dubbed Ramrod Hurrah. "I felt like, 'Well, this is a racket.' In Calgary, you'd have to rent the halls to do all-ages shows and go out-of-pocket," she says. "I'm like, 'Wait, I can do a show here and they won't charge me? They'll pay me 50 bucks?!' Somehow Emily Haines found out about it and walked in one day to give me a cassette of early songs. We became fast friends. She played some of her first solo shows at Ramrod Hurrah." Feist also booked Jason Beck, Peaches and José Contreras, because she was a huge fan of By Divine Right's *All Hail Discordia* album. She played some live gigs with Bodega, a band signed to Universal Records' subsidy London that featured future Broken Social Scene auxiliary guitarist Sam Goldberg Jr.

In early 1999, Feist accepted an offer from By Divine Right to join them on a tour of Canadian arenas opening for the Tragically Hip that spring, followed by a full Ameican tour of various-sized venues. Brendan Canning was also in the band at the time. Though she was far from a slouch as a guitarist, Feist had never played lead before. Contreras taught her all the solos he'd just recorded on the *Bless This Mess* album. "I thought it would be cool for all the girls at the show to see another girl playing lead guitar in a rock band in a hockey arena," he says.

The six-month-long Hip tour was a trial by fire, playing in front of thousands of people who don't care who's on stage before their heroes. It wasn't just arenas; the tour took them into the U.S. to play for considerably smaller audiences. "There were five tour buses and two trucks parked down a residential street in Eugene, Oregon, to play a community hall," she says. "This was two days after playing two sold-out dates at GM Place in Vancouver. That whole thing of how even the most monolithic gods of music in Canada were not able to make it elsewhere—I was seeing that." Feist was making $250 a week on the tour, with catering provided by the Hip. Her rent in Toronto was $400 a month. "By all appearances, it was a big deal," she says, "but I could not let it be a big deal. It couldn't be some kind of capital-m moment that I spend the rest of my life living up to."

Feist first saw physical copies of *Monarch* when a box arrived from the manufacturer at a Hip tour stop in Kamloops, B.C. "I was so excited and running around telling everyone," she says. The 35-year-old Downie was intrigued. "I don't understand," says Feist, "why he—as a guy carrying a show like that—asked this girl in the opening band, with genuine curiosity, about her record. He came to hear it in the front lounge of the bus and listened to the entire thing beginning to end. He asked me questions, made notes and comments. Only encouragement, nothing critical. He gave me the time of day."

The gruelling three-month Tragically Hip tour of 1999 took its toll, ending with a straight-shot drive to Toronto from Boulder, Colorado, during which no one was speaking, including Canning and Feist, who had been romantically involved on the tour. That lineup of By Divine Right played their last show on the CBC TV afternoon teen show *Jonovision*. "I remember walking up to Queen Street from the CBC building with my guitar on my back," says Feist, "hearing the whomp from the big metal door close behind me and this feeling of joy filling the essence of my being—knowing that that was it, that I wasn't playing with those guys anymore. I felt this rising autonomy and self-worth."

When she returned to her Queen Street West apartment, it was empty. Nisker and Beck—now known as Peaches and Chilly Gonzales—were busking around Europe, turning heads in small clubs and getting record deals. That seemed not only more viable but a lot more fun than waiting around in Canada to ascend to the level of the Tragically Hip. "The idea of DIYing yourself out of Canada was pretty attractive," says Feist. But she'd spend a couple of years DIYing in Canada first, before joining her friends in Berlin.

"I WENT TO EUROPE with a sense of vengeance." Chilly Gonzales stormed the Continent in the summer of 1998, with Peaches and no particular plan other than to fully embrace the spirit of the Shit. They'd often been told that they'd do better in Europe than they would in the staid Canadian scene. Gonzales was free from his record deal and had money from his Warner buyout. "We just felt like that was a moment that was a fermata in our lives that allowed us to go on a long trip and explore," he says. "So we did it. We stayed wherever we could, whether it was family friends, friends we knew or just pressing our luck."

It did help that Gonzales's father, the construction magnate, had an apartment in Paris they could use as a home base. Peaches considered the experience a summer vacation. She suggested they go to Berlin, which makes perfect sense with what became the Peaches aesthetic: it's the home of Nina Hagen, the locale for Bowie and Iggy Pop in the '70s, the epicentre of Weimar Republic burlesque and decadence as portrayed in *Cabaret*, the home of '90s digital hardcore. But Peaches claims that Berlin was no particular mecca for her; she just wanted to do more than slum around in Paris and get high in Amsterdam—which was Gonzales's plan. She had her MC-505, and he had two CDJs—a dual CD player that functioned like a turntable—and they improvised in any bar or makeshift art space that would have them, plugging directly into the house PA system.

On the night that changed their lives, they were staying in West Berlin with a friend of a friend of a friend in an uncool neighbourhood nowhere near the artists' enclave in East Berlin. They wanted to find "the scene." They checked in their mainstream guidebook and ended up at a bar where they spotted two girls dressed like what the Canadians perceived to be the "Berlin underground" of recent yore. The locals directed them to Galerie Berlintokyo. The Canadians walked into the club, unknown and uninvited, and asked the scheduled DJ if they could play there that night. They were given a half-hour set, after which Gonzales approached the DJ to say they were done. "No, this kicks ass!" he said. "Keep playing!" Which they did—for another four hours. The people who ran the post-rock label Kitty-Yo were there and invited the duo back for a festival in December.

That wasn't the only fluke connection made that night. "The huge majority of what the Berlin universe became to me and Peaches was incarnated in that night," says Gonzales. "Personal relationships, friendships, romantic relationships, business relationships. I met the woman who, to this day, does all my album covers, many of my videos. It's all Nina Rhode, a.k.a. Ninja Pleasure."

Decades later, Gonzales is still incredulous at the series of circumstances that led to that night. "What's amazing is that no one hangs out in West Berlin," he says. "In the next six years, I never would have gone back to that area, much less that specific bar where we met those girls. One of them was a Polish girl named Magda. I would see her around the east for a really long time after we moved there. As we got more and more well known, I kept on running into her and saying, 'Can you believe that?! Thank you! In the timeline where we don't meet you, because we show up an hour later, we might have just left Berlin and gone to

Amsterdam or something.' In this version of *Sliding Doors*, there's a version with and without Magda, and I doubt Peaches and Gonzales would be able to do what we did without that very chance meeting."

Gonzales decided to stay on in Berlin, signing to Kitty-Yo and paying his bills by playing piano in a restaurant near his apartment; that gig lasted two years. "It's a great job to have when you don't speak the language in the country you've moved to," he says.

PEACHES WENT HOME to Toronto and her drama-teaching business, figuring she'd do one more year before returning to Berlin. Almost immediately she regretted coming back to Canada. "I'd learned that there was a bigger world out there," she says. "I had to reinvent my whole life. I was very focused." Having recently gone through chemo to treat thyroid cancer, as well as heartbreak from divorce, the 30-year-old was reassessing her entire life path.

She started recording an EP's worth of material with her MC-505, what she referred to as her "Japanese boyfriend"—one of several beaus, including her Italian boyfriend (her espresso machine) and her American boyfriend (her bong). One hot summer night, she ran into her friend, MuchMusic VJ Sook-Yin Lee, and exclaimed, "ARGH! I just feel so fucking HORNY!" It wasn't easy to make the avant-garde artist Lee blush, but Peaches did exactly that. The material Peaches was writing "became about more than sex," she later told Lee. "It was about people feeling empowered—not just about sex but about being comfortable in your own body. That's all I want people to feel."

Returning to Berlin in December 1998, she signed a deal with Kitty-Yo and started plotting a permanent move for the following spring, using her savings from 10 years of teaching drama—and a $7,000 (Canadian) advance from Kitty-Yo. "I'd never moved anywhere," the Torontonian says. "It just seemed like the right thing to do: a place for my creativity and the kind of music I was interested in." Berlin—specifically East Berlin—was a bohemian playground of cheap rent, still largely undeveloped 10 years after the fall of the Berlin Wall, with plenty of space that could be repurposed for artistic pursuits, ephemeral or otherwise. Rent in East Berlin was about the same she was paying in Toronto: $400 for her own apartment, as opposed to the $800 she split with Feist on Queen Street. It was an ideal place to incubate artistic experimentation—not unlike post-referendum Montreal in the mid-'90s, but with all the advantages of being a major European city.

Peaches also cites the waning digital hardcore movement, spawned by Berlin's Atari Teenage Riot. Two women from that band formed Cobra Killer, with whom Peaches played upon arrival. "They did really raw performances, electronic music that was just screaming," she says. "They were loud, messy, throwing red wine everywhere. I felt I'd found my inspiration." American and Australian expat duo Chicks on Speed were also in Berlin, using glitchy digital electronics to update late '70s post-punk new wave. "It was exciting that women were at the forefront," says Peaches. "It was electronic, very artistic and based in performance."

In the spring of 1999, *The Teaches of Peaches* began to take shape in her Toronto bedroom. A studious music fan, Peaches had some very specific reference points, while other seemingly obvious ones escaped her. She didn't know proto-punk synth duo Suicide, post-punk all-woman band ESG or contemporaries Le Tigre. She was a big fan of harsh Finnish electronic act Pan Sonic and wanted some of that digital abrasion. She loved Iggy Pop and "Push It" by Salt-N-Pepa. She was disappointed that riot grrrl had fizzled by the late '90s and wanted to channel some of that energy.

Peaches was steeped in the history of the male gaze that permeates blues, rock and hip-hop—all full of sexual innuendo that was largely unimaginative when it came to female pleasure. "Like [Led Zeppelin's] 'Squeeze my lemon till the juice runs down my leg,'" she told journalist Nick Dwyer. "I don't have a lemon, I have Peaches, so I thought, If I just twist this stiff a little bit around, it would relate to me. And that should be normal. So I just spun it around a bit and came up with new sort of clichés, saying things like, 'Diddle my skittle,' or, 'Suckin' on my titties.' I had this idea that everybody, guys and girls, straight, gay, would want to sing, 'Suckin' on my titties!' But I never really thought that anybody would really hear it."

"Suckin' on my titties like you wanted me" is the first line on "Fuck the Pain Away," the opening track on Peaches' self-titled debut. The song featured the refrain "I.U.D., S.I.S. / stay in school coz it's the best," which, together with the empowering chorus, made the song more than a one-dimensional come-on, by coupling a nerdy slogan your parents might tout with an acronym for a contraceptive method. Then, of course, there is the closing refrain—the title lyric doesn't appear until more than halfway through the song, after the first verse is repeated twice. Even if it wasn't sung by a 31-year-old divorcée who'd recently gone through chemo, "fuck the pain away" could mean all kinds of things, particularly to abuse survivors. Despite the way the song was often received, this was not cheap smut. It became one of the most iconic songs of the coming decade. It had incredibly humble beginnings.

Shortly after writing it, Peaches had a gig at the Rivoli, opening for her friend Howie Beck, a soft-spoken singer-songwriter—an incongruous bill, to say the least. At the end of her set, she accepted an offer from the sound tech to buy the board recording for the price of a five-dollar cassette. Listening at home, she thought the vocals were too loud and the beat was off, but with some friends' encouragement she put it on her first EP anyway. The same version, untouched—hence the audible tape hiss—later appeared on *The Teaches of Peaches*. The rest of both the EP and the album was recorded to eight tracks on an ADAT machine, through a 16-channel mixer, all perched on a precarious keyboard stand next to her bed. When writing her vocal parts, the accomplished singer purposely chose to focus on chants and raps to make the lyrical message more direct.

Her roommate, Leslie Feist, had no problem with the noise, but the neighbours on the other side of the apartment's thin walls were not happy. "Anytime I would try and make beats," she says, "the neighbour would call or ring the doorbell and say, 'Please—the bass, stop the bass!'" The recordings were primitive but incredibly effective; using the MC-505 as a rock'n'roll instrument with punk attitude, with expediency and efficiency, was the primary goal. The bass lines are dirty and gritty, the drum sounds murky; the rhythm on "Diddle My Skittle"—a song with a clitoral metaphor used by Beyoncé in 2013—is largely two alternating tones of white noise.

Years later, Peaches still got compliments on the production, even in Germany, a country full of perfectionist technophiles. She thought that was hilarious, because she'd set all the EQ levels to zero. Its amateurism made it unique and helped it stand apart from accepted norms. "Nothing on *The Teaches of Peaches* starts on the one [the first beat of every musical bar] because I just didn't really get where the one was, actually," she told Dwyer. "It's funny because I've met so many producers who are like, 'Oh, it's so cool that you didn't start on the one!' I remember that 2 Many DJs were really upset because they really wanted to put 'Lovertits' in their set but they were like, 'We love that, but we can't mix it in. The timing's wrong.' It's really cool though, because all those mistakes have really made a mark."

Music wasn't Peaches' only outlet at the time. With artist Kika Thorne and others, she was part of a collective called 246, part of the burgeoning trend to revisit 8-mm film technology, largely associated with the first home movies. Between 1997 and 2006, Toronto was home to the Splice This! Super 8 Film Festival. She and friends made Super 8 films like a collaborative exquisite corpse game, which were projected behind her during her live shows. One became the "Lovertits" video, which features Feist and a friend in some chaste bicycle porn. It was total happenstance: Peaches and Malcolm "World Provider" Fraser had simply run into three friends that day who didn't know each other; one of them had cool bikes. "I was like, 'Bikes! Friends! Let's do this!'" says Peaches. Another film featured Feist "walking around as a Lydia Lunch–style tough girl with a knife," she says. "She's trying to start a knife fight with everyone and nobody will knife fight with her, so she just knife fights with herself." Much like the

MC-505, what appealed to Peaches about Super 8 was its limitations: one roll of film is only three minutes long.

A landmark moment for Peaches took place at Vazaleen, the queer electro-rock bacchanal club night run by DJ Will Munro. Vazaleen launched in January 2000 at the El Mocambo, while Peaches was recording her album, and she was inspired by the amalgam of raunchy rock, glam and electro with nary a trace of the disco and house that dominated Toronto's Gay Village on Church Street. "The DJ would always play hair metal or Iggy Pop or the Runaways, that kind of rock, and then there was the electro and the loving of the '80s underground, Suicide, and stuff like that," she told Munro biographer Sarah Liss. The first time Peaches played at Vazaleen, it went a little something like this:

"It was kind of an improv night, and I was sort of a conduit for everybody to be as shameful as they could," she told Liss. "Will came up in diapers and high heels and undid his diapers and then all these baked beans that were supposed to be diarrhea or whatever came out. Then he pulled out a little rainbow flag from his ass and wiped it off and started waving it—the ultimate shame moment. I was playing some of my songs, but I was also just rapping about whatever was going on around me at the time. [Visual artist] Shary Boyle came on stage without pants on—just underwear, and she actually had her period—and just started pissing all over the stage and dancing. Then [artist and curator] Andrew Harwood and his boyfriend were dressed as metal dudes, and they'd drilled a hole in a big watermelon and fucked it together." Naturally, this night became legendary. There were no cellphone cameras present.

Harwood described the Vazaleen scene as "un-Toronto." He told Liss, "It was super friendly, cruisey and so fabulously mixed. There were dykes, fags, straights, bis, drag kings and queens, genderfucked folks and people of colour from almost every community in the city who all came together to party and flirt and dress up." Says Peaches, "It was queer, it was BDSM, very arty, very rock'n'roll, very electronic, very retro and yet future-forward. There was a shift from 'You can't do this' to 'Please, can you do this.'" She'd found her people.

Peaches' debut self-titled EP came out on Toronto label Teenage USA, and its release party was held at Anoush Gallery on Nassau Street in Kensington Market, in March 2000. Feist was part of the act, in character as hypeman "Bitch Lap Lap"—with no particular musical role on stage, more of a sidekick situation. Peaches didn't want a traditional venue, because she wanted to include a Super 8 element and local artists. "That was a big shift," she says. "We could invite whoever we wanted to play, without a club saying, 'Well, it won't be a draw.' It was packed. The different scenes of people who were there, in such a rock-dominated scene, to have them come over to this show and also to get the cover of *Eye Weekly*, that was exciting. I was saying, 'Fuck venues, you can do it yourself.' Another level of DIY."

Outside that scene, however, Toronto was not ready for Peaches. "I thought it was so good," says Teenage USA co-founder Phil Klygo, who tried in vain to get her some press outside Toronto. "I don't think we even got much love from college radio. It was too out there for people. It was aggressive, it was racy. Some people actively hated it." After the release of the EP, she played a songwriters night alongside performers with acoustic guitars and pianos. One reviewer later wrote, "Peaches made her one-woman, hair-raising throwdown, and then we got back to what music is." "That," says Peaches," proved to me that I was doing something right." She started using the phrase "one-woman, hair-raising throwdown" in her press material as a compliment.

She made better connections at *Exclaim!* magazine's annual party in April 2000, where members of an Ottawa hockey team were more eager than she expected when she asked for volunteers to get an onstage spanking from her and Bitch Lap Lap. She also met people like Bruce LaBruce and Danko Jones, one of the only other Toronto musicians who boasted a bold sexuality. "That was exciting for me, to see the local stars," she says. "I'd never really been able to connect with them before." Photos taken at that show, by Three Gut Records' Tyler Clark Burke, were used for the cover and inside artwork of *The Teaches of Peaches*.

Around the same time, she claims she was scheduled to open for Welsh band Super Furry Animals at the Horseshoe, "but the club cancelled me because I'm too dirty," she told *Now* magazine. "The only time they paid any attention to me was when they threw me out for smoking a joint." (The Horseshoe's Craig Laskey denied both stories in the same article.)

No matter. Berlin was waiting.

GONZALES DIDN'T WASTE any time in Berlin. In 1999, he released the *O.P. Original Prankster* EP, followed by 2000's full-length *Gonzales Uber Alles*. The latter was surprising: rather than the raunchy electro funk he'd been performing on stage with Peaches, the music on *Uber Alles* is largely downtempo instrumental beats, with some genuinely beautiful torch ballads sung by Sticky ("You Are," "Why Don't We Disappear?") and three electric piano instrumentals. Feist can be heard cooing in the background, and one song features two clarinets taking the melody. (It's called, uh, "Clarinets.") At times it sounds like Gonzales is aiming to be a 21st-century Esquivel.

That changed on his second release of 2000, *The Entertainist*, in which Gonzales became an embittered, petty rapper out to settle scores. It was deliberately ridiculous—"I'm like a combination Joe Stalin / Woody Allen"—and, well, entertaining.

But a white Canadian Jewish rapper working a shtick could only ever work in a culture without an actual thriving hip-hop scene—i.e., Europe. There were plenty of white nerd rappers in North America at the time (MC Paul Barman, Buck 65, Princess Superstar), but Gonzales would likely have been laughed off his home continent, and not because of his punchlines.

Chilly Gonzales was a deliberately absurd alias, spawned from the Shit. "I just picked a name that was a bit far away from me," he says. "A Hungarian Jew with a Cuban name is impossible in a way, but I like the impossibility of it. There are a lot of musical geniuses called Gonzales, too, so it seemed like a good pedigree. Another thing was that people warned me about being too all over the place musically and that it could work against me. I was really not intent on repeating the same thing over and over, so I decided to make the personality so intense that it could link it all together."

Chilly Gonzales was also an attention-craving "supervillain" character in which Jason Beck's ego and embitterment could run wild. "When I left Canada," he told *Exclaim!* in 2000, "I had all these emotions that aren't necessarily bad, but that if channelled in the wrong way can turn out bad: competitiveness, jealousy, superiority, megalomania—things that are definitely in me. I just created this Chilly Gonzales idea as a receptacle for all that shit. It gives my real life maybe one percent more peace because I have [an outlet] for that."

Berlin also gave him permission to do things he never could in his hometown, in which familiarity most definitely bred contempt. "When I got to a place where I didn't speak the language and I wasn't aware of what was happening, it liberated me to try things that I maybe would have loved to have tried in Canada," he says. "Seeing what I brought to the table was exciting for the Berliners. Then I grew a pair of balls." Gonzales got cojones.

That involved declaring himself a "musical genius," an act of arrogance that was much more honest about the artist's ego than the insincerity of "authenticity." "In some ways, [the declaration of genius] was done to shock, but it was coming from a very sincere place," he says. "I do view music as something to be mastered, as something that has science and mathematical secrets to be learned that create emotions. I find it awful when I'm watching a performance and someone is pretending to be such a humble guy, when you can tell that this guy is a shark. I'd rather say that first: I'm full of myself; I'm frustrated; I'm incapable of just living in a world where the music should do all the work for me. That way, no one can say that about me first. It's pre-emptive. In that superficial forum, you reveal so much more about yourself than when you're supposedly being authentic."

As Gonzales's German profile grew, he decided to go all out and stage a press conference in city hall, where the government held media briefings. Journalists actually showed up. He declared himself president of the "Berlin underground" and challenged Alec Empire of Atari Teenage Riot for the title. Of course, the title didn't exist; no one who actually lived in the city ever identified the scene as the "Berlin underground" and Empire was a perfect, po-faced, black-clad foil to Gonzales's prankster character.

In the fall of 2000, Gonzales and Peaches released the joint *Red Leather* EP; her *Teaches of Peaches* was about to come out. They were invited by '90s Britpop band Elastica to be the opening act on a comeback tour, which included a stop at Toronto's 2,500-capacity Kool Haus. Feist joined them, as Bitch Lap Lap. It was not a triumphant homecoming. The repatriated duo was met with hostile indifference at the show and scathing reviews in the coming days. It didn't help that the two Torontonians played a longer set than the headliners, to the crowd's chagrin.

"It did go quite poorly," says Gonzales. "There was a lot of pressure on us, coming back to Toronto. We had left in a huff. My parents were there, seeing me for the first time since I left. And obviously we had the opening act disadvantage anyway, it being a crowd of Elastica fans. I reproduced a defensive illusion of the craziness we'd been able to channel successfully in Europe. I had to leave [Toronto] because I conformed and was overthinking and couldn't be myself. A year and a half later, and I realized I was still overthinking and not being able to be myself."

The next night, however, became legendary. Peaches and Gonzales took the stage at College Street bar Ted's Wrecking Yard, joining old friends the World Provider, Dave "Taylor Savvy" Szigeti, Mocky and others. Elastica and their entourage came along for the ride. Their young videographer, Maya Arulpragasam, was offered a microphone by Peaches and freestyle rapped for the first time in her life. Five years later, she was the international pop star M.I.A.

Back in Berlin, Gonzales and Mocky joined another jackass crew, Puppetmastaz, which, as one might guess, was a joke rap band involving puppets. Gonzales also embraced the idea of being a Jewish MC in Berlin. He figured it made him that much more of a supervillain in a city still struggling with its Nazi past.

Peaches took a similar tack: "People would come up to me and say, 'You're Jewish. What are you doing? Why are you going [to Berlin]?' I said, 'I'm taking it back. Let's go. Bring it on.'"

PEACHES' FIRST HEADLINING gig in Berlin was packed, thanks entirely to word of mouth: no radio play, no video, no internet hype. The album's reach continued in the same vein around the world. Kitty-Yo got calls from record labels owned by Madonna and the Beastie Boys, both interested in licensing the record. Renowned '80s remixer Arthur Baker wanted to work with her.

The Teaches of Peaches found a surprising home on fashion runways. "Prada and Givenchy were using it on the catwalk," she says. "'Fuck the Pain Away' and 'Lovertits' were voted the number-one fashion catwalk songs for the spring 2001 collections, and it was like, 'What?' It wasn't really like I had a team of media people going, 'We think we can get you in the fashion world,' or 'We think you could be a poster girl for this.' It just kind of happened."

On February 3, 2001, she found herself in London opening for all-boy bands Rocket from the Crypt and Trail of Dead, with another added to the bill at the last minute—the Strokes, playing their first-ever U.K. show. The British press had been tipped off to the hyped New York City kids and showed up to see what the fuss was about. Before the Strokes took the stage, the crowd was confronted by a 33-year-old woman with a much bolder vision of sexuality than they might be expecting. In the pedophilic era of Britney Spears, apparently any woman over 25 was not allowed to be a sexual being; one blogger called Peaches "some wailing, PVC-clad ropey old slapper from Canada 'playing' the most god-awful Sigue Sigue Sputnik–esque stilted electronics from her beatbox."

In the Strokes' hometown, *Village Voice* critic Robert Christgau didn't learn anything from *The Teaches*. "Not cock-rock, [it's] bukkake-rock," he wrote. "And though you may be lucky enough not to know what that means, Peaches had better. Doesn't matter whether she's a performance artist, a concept rocker, a bored schoolteacher or an expat with a gimmick. 'Come on, hot rod / Give me your wad' etc. is pro-sex post-feminism for the age of internet porn, in which thousands of women a day prove how cool they are by smiling through their semen facials. It's wish fulfillment for boys who make passes at girls who wear glasses. And given a beat by Chilly Gonzales's low-techno bump and grind, it's perfect for a fashion industry finally past the embarrassment of junkie chic."

Never mind the sexist assumption that Gonzales made her beats—he appears nowhere on the album—the accusation that Peaches' music is somehow about debasement says more about the reviewer than the artist. To be certain, it was the era when porn became widely available for free online, when a term like "bukkake" might unfortunately bubble up into mainstream consciousness, an era when a popular porn site called Suicide Girls would be a much better target for Christgau's oddly specific assumptions about Peaches.

At the Siren Music Festival on Coney Island in July 2001, Peaches' 30-minute set got cut short. "A stagehand was holding a sign that read *Say goodbye!*" she says. "I said, 'I know what a half hour is; forget it.' I jumped up on the speaker, and I started singing 'Fuck the Pain Away.' So they cut my microphone. I picked up another mic and said, 'They're censoring me! They're making me get off the stage!' Some mothers were complaining. They were like, 'Look, that girl's got her hands down her pants. Make her stop! She's masturbating!'" Meanwhile, Peaches got word that she was unusually popular in Louisville, Kentucky, where her music was the soundtrack of choice for middle-aged swingers. "The [audience] doesn't want to have sex with me, necessarily—they just want to have sex," she says. "I see myself more as a conduit for sex. In the middle of one show, my sound guy grabbed his girlfriend and went to the bathroom to fuck."

Sony Music soon came calling. Kitty-Yo had commissioned remixes of "Set It Off," and one by German DJ Tobi Neumann had commercial potential in the eyes of the major label—despite the fact the opening line is, "Motherfuckers wanna get with me." Peaches picked a director and pitched the concept for her video. She'd always thought it was hilarious how shocked audiences were at the sight of pubic hair peeking out from her short shorts. "So then I started thinking about hair and how if it's on your eyelashes or long on your head as a woman, then it's beautiful, but if it's under your arms or on your legs, then it's ugly," she told Nick Dwyer. "I wanted to make this video of me dancing and growing hair and with eyelashes so that everybody would be like, 'Oh, she's getting prettier.' And then, all of a sudden, there would be hair growing everywhere, and then it gets really, like, ill." Descriptions of the now-unseen video used the word "lycanthropic," and apparently her pubic hair grew to "Rapunzel proportions."

Peaches was excited about using high-end equipment and a commercial director, but when it came time to shoot, she was alarmed to find that a bunch of models had been hired in lieu of her friends. The label representative wanted a lesbian kissing scene, and so Peaches insisted on two men kissing as well, only to be refused by the gay director. Six months later Christina Aguilera broke barriers by having two men kissing in her video for "Beautiful." It wouldn't be the first time Peaches was ahead of a curve. It was, however, the one and only time she didn't control one of her videos. Shortly after, Sony got her booked on the BBC's *Top of the Pops*, but her performance was deemed unsuitable to community standards.

She was dropped by Sony, and the "Set It Off" video was buried—as was *The Teaches of Peaches* for eight months, until she signed a new contract with XL Recordings in 2002 and rereleased it that October (with the remix as a bonus track). That deal, with an artist-friendly label, happened after a tour of Australia on the Big Day Out festival; XL artists Basement Jaxx and Prodigy gave glowing reviews of Peaches to their label. XL's A&R rep came to a Peaches gig at a Parisian restaurant, where the tables had been cleared out for the show. Peaches thought the sound mix was so terrible that she crowd-surfed back to the sound booth, where she promptly instructed the tech, on the mic, how to do his job. XL offered her a contract at the end of the set.

Concurrent with the rise of Peaches was electroclash, a trend which largely meant using '80s electronics combined with digital deconstruction, performance art—and lots of cocaine. Peaches was one of the few artists to survive the fad, though its influence led directly to LCD Soundsystem and Lady Gaga. The trend sparked an immediate backlash, in part because a rockist press still yearned for guitar music, but also because much-hyped New York City duo Fischerspooner signed a $2-million record deal based largely on their visual spectacle.

Nonetheless, Peaches accepted an invitation from Fischerspooner's manager, DJ Larry Tee, to go on an all-woman package tour dubbed Electroclash 2002, with somewhat dour video art project Tracy + the Plastics, models-turned-musicians W.I.T. and Berlin's more reputable Chicks on Speed. Every night, Peaches blew them all away: conceptually, musically and in pure raw performance.

That same year, Leslie Feist was sitting in with a new Toronto band, alongside Andrew Whiteman, Brendan Canning and others, called Broken Social Scene. She only sang lead on a couple of songs but was the focal point whenever she took the stage. She'd spent the last three years slowly coming out of her shell, learning from Peaches and Gonzales along the way.

FEIST'S *MONARCH* WAS officially released on August 24, 1999, with a joint CD release party for Jim Guthrie's debut *A Thousand Songs*, which was the first recording from Three Gut Records. Feist became close with Three Gut co-founder Tyler Clark Burke. Among other commonalities, they were both Western Canadians with fathers who were American arts professors. "Someone sent me to her to make the gig poster," Feist recalls. "We were set up on a blind date. It was kind of romantic. She was waiting for me on a tire swing outside a loft building where she lived. She had platinum blonde hair, rose-tinted half-sunglasses and was truly so cool and so talented and so nice. She had skill sets I didn't know anything about."

To further promote the show at key spots in the city, Burke enlisted Feist to help her hang string with clothespins clasping sealed envelopes that advertised the show. This was also a technique Burke used to promote her boyfriend's band, Royal City. In the summer of 2000, Feist joined that band as third guitarist, beside Jim Guthrie and singer Aaron Riches.

"Aaron and I were going to do a living-room tour, starting in Rochester and going down the New England coast," says Feist. "He had five places and I had five places. We were going to split the expenses and the money. Two days before we left, he had kept adding people until there were now six of them, until it was all of Royal City plus Tyler. I was struggling to understand the math. 'Now we have to divide this eight ways—but how do you divide three dollars eight ways?' We played New York, too. Tyler found the office of *Rolling Stone*, and we pulled up in this jalopy van with Ontario plates and hung up this string and covered it in envelopes. She had been melting wax in the van and monogram-stamping each one as we drove south." Feist also shot the video for the *Monarch* song "Family" in Three Gut's old stomping grounds of Guelph, Ontario, directed by Black Cabbage's Nick Craine and featuring Burke, Guthrie and others associated with the label (as well as future Broken Social Scene violinist Julie Penner).

In the summer of 2000, Feist set out on her first tour as a solo artist, to Western Canada and back. In her band was Royal City's Nathan Lawr on drums, the World Provider on keyboards and Dave Szigeti on bass. Szigeti played his own set at every stop, using the same band.

"I booked the tour myself," says Feist, with a list of venues and press contacts from Shauna de Cartier of Edmonton/Toronto label Six Shooter Records. "I pretended to be a girl named Jenny, because Jenny could advocate for me and describe me. I thought it was poor taste to do that on my own behalf. I played the Sugar Refinery in Vancouver for maybe 40 people. There was a show at a community centre in Medicine Hat with people sitting cross-legged on the floor. We'd show up somewhere and hope that someone would show up to unlock the bar."

In early 2001, Feist toured as a solo act, travelling on two jaunts with Sarah Harmer, one with Sarah Slean, one with Veda Hille. "They were living-room shows," says Feist. "I was first of three and really uncomfortable. Just like the early Emily Haines shows, when she'd sit petrified behind her electric MIDI keyboard. Similarly, I didn't know what to do. I was doing something quiet and stripped back, and I was coming from these big rock bands. It was a transition period. Whereas Harmer had real roots in entertaining and telling stories and making everyone in the room at ease. I admired that and looked up to her. She was definitely an institution by then.

"When I think about who I'd been looking up to all along, it's Harmer," Feist continues. "I remember walking down the street with Pete Prilesnik, who produced *You Were Here*." She asked him how many copies it had sold. "He threw out a number that had three extra zeroes in my mind, like maybe he said 30,000 but it sounded like three million. Meanwhile, I'd sold 30, and most of those were consigned at Rotate This."

Feist only made one pressing of the *Monarch* CD, in a run of 1,000. She was approached by a small Toronto label, Bobby Dazzler, to reprint another 1,000. "I was like, 'Why? No one wants it.' I was taking three copies at a time to sell on consignment at Rotate This. But anyway, they printed more, and I came into possession of probably 1,800 of those," she says. "I had a P.O. box on Queen Street. Maybe half a dozen times I got letters ordering CDs. The very first one was a woman I'm still in touch with whenever I play in Vancouver, because it was so thrilling that someone ordered a record." Feist refused to repress it until 2012, when a vinyl version was sold only at her merch table and from her website, with proceeds going to charity. "It's an awkward yearbook photo," she says. "I don't even catch a whiff or a strand of somewhere I would end up. I hear it as full growing pains."

Those growing pains were impressive. Every writer and musician who saw her play was bowled over. Stars' Torquil Campbell was one of those who heard it and fell in love with it. "When I was in Toronto, people asked if I knew her; I didn't," he says. "I went to see her at the Gladstone. She was sitting and playing solo and fucking up every song. She was so nervous and couldn't look at the audience, just paralyzed. Everyone coalesced around believing that Leslie was amazing."

Feist recorded four new songs in 2001, with some help from new boyfriend Chris Murphy of Sloan, who took her four-track recordings and showed her how to use the Logic software—"which I promptly forgot," she laughs. "But for that one summer I felt like this master engineer, because I could bounce four-tracks onto a computer and back again. We took my four-track to the Sloan space. [Chris] played on it. I think [Local Rabbits'] Pete Elkas did too. This was all in one afternoon. Maybe [Sloan's] Andrew Scott on guitar for a second." These became known as "the Red Demos," never officially released but available for a brief while at Feist's shows.

She then started making plans to move. Not to Berlin or Paris but to New York. Her friends in Metric, who had renovated a loft in Williamsburg, were heading out on tour and needed someone to be the superintendent. "I would live in their loft and collect rent—basically live for free in New York in exchange for helping them with this side hustle," says Feist. Her plan was to work with Tony Scherr, a jazz guitarist she'd met through Chris Brown and Kate Fenner, and get a bar gig somewhere. She was still dating Chris Murphy, "but we'd only been together a few months, and then I was going to move to New York in October. But 9/11 happened and New York shut down. Emily and James didn't leave, the world ground to a halt and I ended up living with Chris as a kind of 'Oops, now I live with my boyfriend.' That was the first time I'd ever [done that]." Staying in Toronto meant that she continued to play in Broken Social Scene, who were getting ready to record *You Forgot It in People*.

That's also when she got a call from Peaches, telling her to come to Europe and tour with her as Bitch Lap Lap. Peaches' invitation was more of a demand, and it came with a free plane ticket—an offer Feist could not refuse. She might also have wanted to be outside of Canada while an unusually juicy Sloan single was all over Canadian radio: "The Other Man" is a Chris Murphy song about the transition period between Feist's relationship with Andrew Whiteman and Murphy himself. Good time to disappear.

"It was my first trip in my life to Europe," she says. "I was meeting her in Vienna—a word I had heard before, but I didn't know anything about it. I transferred through Amsterdam and had a 12-hour layover, as you do on extra-cheap flights. I arrived at dawn and took the train into the city. I still remember that first step into Europe, before anyone was on the street, the glowing orange light outside the train station and smelling fresh bread baking and being in awe of the canals.

"At the end of the day I went back to the airport and was crying in panic because I couldn't find any flight to Vienna—because I didn't understand that [the German word for] Vienna was *Wien* and I didn't know how to get there. On that tour, I stayed with Gonz when the Peaches part of the tour ended. Gonz had all these songs that Sticky from Weeping Tile had sung on his record. He asked me to stay and be his Vanna White and light his cigar. We toured as a duo, with me singing these torch ballads, almost karaoke showmanship with tracks."

As wild and ridiculous as the European shows were, they were also ephemeral. Cellphone recordings were still a few years away; online video was barely a thing yet. Peaches and Gonzales shows were playgrounds where anything could happen, devoid of expectation. "Our life was a rolling circus of Berlin vaudeville," says Feist. "Things could be done in obscurity and with real commitment, like the walls were closed in on that experience. Everyone was there at this squat at three in the morning, off the clock, far from home, and there's a safety and an anonymity in it because you know you'll be in the next town the next day and nothing of that night was going to follow you—except maybe an STD."

There's video footage of Peaches, Gonzales and Feist performing in Glasgow for a BBC program called *BeatRoom* that fall. The host exclaims, "They're dirty, they're sleazy, they're disgusting—but best of all, they're here, in the BeatRoom!" Parading around in their underwear, it's outrageously raunchy and raw—and hot—as they exhort the crowd to ecstatic release. The act was refined over the years; by 2003, Feist tap danced to a Gonzales squiggly synth solo, while dressed in a pink-and-orange-striped leotard with gold lamé frills hanging off her left sleeve. Everything about it was a rejection of the po-faced indie scene in Toronto. And Europe ate it up.

In 2002, she bounced back and forth between that and Broken Social Scene. In Berlin, she slept in a makeshift storage space above the kitchen in Gonzales's apartment: a ladder leading up to a plywood plank with a mattress on it. Glamorous, it was not. "I was being asked to be in both [continents], and they were equally interesting," she says. "If [Gonzales] was going to pay me to cross the ocean, there was no way I wasn't going. My own thing was becoming something that I could hold in my hand and understand that it could be a thing, parallel to the Gonzo and Broken stuff." She missed Broken Social Scene's release party for *You Forgot It in People* in November, but a month later she was at the Montreal show where they were sandwiched between Feist's old bandmates in Royal City and a brand new band called Arcade Fire.

PEACHES' LIFE CONTINUED to get more surreal. One day she checked her messages to hear a deep, velvety voice say, "Heyyyyy, it's Iggy. I want to cover your song 'Rock Show.'" She called Iggy Pop back and made a deal: he had to appear on her new album. At her next gig in Miami, where the punk legend lived, Peaches' guest list only had one line: Iggy Pop plus one. No one at the venue believed her—until he showed up. The next day, she went to his studio and recorded the song she'd written for them, "Kick It," with lyrics poking fun at both their public personas. The proto-punk icon humbly asked Peaches for tips on his vocal delivery. The result was arguably the greatest Iggy Pop song in 25 years.

Peaches appealed to macho male musicians. They invited her on tour as a way of challenging their audiences. She relished the role. When opening for Queens of the Stone Age, in front of a predominantly male audience, some of the crowd would literally turn their backs on her, prompting her to leap into the crowd and start shouting in the mic, *"I'm over here!"*

She toured with Marilyn Manson, an ultimately monstrous artist peddling the most punishing definition of hedonism, the antithesis of Peaches' positivity. She taunted 10,000 Parisian Manson fans by telling them, "You're not black sheep; you're sheep in black!" She was then met with a tidal wave of spit. At a London stop on the same tour, she could sense the tension, so she threw a plastic bottle into the crowd and received hundreds back. She returned the volleys, telling the crowd, "You throw like girls!" She concluded the set by grabbing an empty water-cooler container—the biggest water bottle in the venue—and swung it over her head before lobbing it into the audience. "I had no problem injuring people," she told Nick Dwyer. "I'm sure if I was more famous, I would have [had] a lot of lawsuits. I would go into the audience and you'd just hear 'bmph, bmph,' the sound of me hitting people with my microphone over the head, like, 'Fuck off!' And then [later] Manson would say, 'Good job,' and pat me on the head."

A much more suitable touring partner was film director John Waters, known for pushing every boundary of bad taste before he broke into the mainstream with *Hairspray*. Peaches opened a 2002 speaking tour of his. Madonna was a huge fan of hers, playing tracks from *The Teaches of Peaches* at her live shows. After hearing about this, Peaches sent the star and her husband, film director Guy Ritchie, a pair of signed underwear that read, "Dear Guy, fuck ya later, love, Peaches," and, "Dear Madonna, fuck ya now, love, Peaches." When playing the Reading Festival in the U.K., she ran into Boy George backstage. She greeted him with a simple hello, and he responded drily, "Fuck the pain away." So she promptly removed her underwear—her own merchandise emblazoned with the title of that song—and gave them to the Culture Club singer, who sniffed them and then shoved them down his own pants.

Toronto still didn't know what to make of her. In May 2003, she was invited to play the Power Ball, a major high-society gallery fundraiser at the Power Plant. "I decided I was going to put some white pants on and pose with a microphone and just bleed out of my white pants in a pose," she says. "It really scared people. They were tearaway pants. People were fascinated but horrified. It was really raw. I remember chasing one woman around the whole room, just because I could; she was so afraid. Eventually I just went back on stage—which was the bar—and continued. Also, at these art events you don't really set up a stage, so the idea of respect or performance is quite different for the audience, the patrons who pay a lot of money to be there."

The Teaches of Peaches had sold 50,000 copies worldwide by August 2003, but its cultural reach was larger. "It was funny because major record labels would not touch me," Peaches told Nick Dwyer, "but [artists] would go in for meetings, and [execs would] be like, 'Be more like this girl Peaches.' Then they'd play my tracks: 'But not too much, just be a little bit like that.' There are major stars who came to my shows, and before they were who they were, would say, 'Oh yeah, I'm really into what you're doing, and you're really influential.' A lot of the time it was the pop stars, like Avril Lavigne and Christina Aguilera and Britney Spears and Kelis, like, when they were going from their girl pop to sexual power, they always cite Peaches as an influence and it always amazes me." This was the era when Spears covered Joan Jett on the same album she did "I'm a Slave 4 U," while Aguilera went "Dirrty."

There is a world of difference, however, between Peaches' version of sexuality and that of mainstream pop stars: in one, the performer holds power; in the other, the performer is passive to the male gaze. "You look at Britney Spears's video for 'Slave 4 U' and it's, like, gang rape," Peaches told Lorraine Carpenter of *Exclaim!* in 2003. "And she's not singing about that shit. Same with Jennifer Lopez, she's always getting wet and you see her nipples and ass, but it's just totally manipulative sensationalism. If you're gonna give out images like that, you'd better have the lyrics to back it up. I give it directly, but for some reason it's acceptable to do it visually, but not lyrically.

"Would anybody ever ask 50 Cent why he's into having sex and not making love?" she continued. "Would anyone wonder why Biggie Smalls said, in his song [with the chorus] 'dreams of fucking an R&B bitch' that he wants to remind Tina Turner of Ike by slapping her? Nobody questions them and, in a way, that's another example of ghettoising, like, 'He's a dirty Black rapper, he can say that, not a white Jewish girl.'" In Peaches' music, there's never any hint of violence or lack of consent.

Peaches had a licence to confuse. In the same Lorraine Carpenter interview, she said, "I did Brazilian interviews and they were like, 'Is it true that you are an ex-prostitute?' Then I'd do a French interview and they'd be like, 'Is it true you're a lesbian icon?' And then I'd talk to Americans, back to back, and one would say, 'You're an angry woman,' and the next one would tell me, 'You're so funny!' Some people react like I'm completely politically incorrect, the furthest thing from cool, but all I'm talking about is equality. If we're saying motherfucker, let's say fatherfucker; if we're saying shake your tits and shake your asses, let's say shake your dicks."

She refused to water down her act for her second album, which came out in September 2003. It was called *Fatherfucker*.

BY THE TIME PEACHES WAS PEAKING—NOT that her career was over, far from it—Gonzales was finding his true calling. His third Kitty-Yo album, 2001's *Presidential Suite*, moved away from the abstractions of *Uber Alles* and the pranksterism of *The Entertainist* by featuring more pop songs and wittier rap songs than his earlier efforts. One song sung by Feist, "Shameless Eyes," was key to everything that has happened since.

Gonzales wanted to rerecord the song in French with a French singer. Guesch Patti was an '80s star akin to Mitsou or Debbie Gibson. "I thought, well, she has a great voice," he says, "and she had a very sexy video in the '80s to which many people my age in France would've had their sexual awakening. I thought, This fits!" The song, retitled "Dans tes yeux," became a hit. Gonzales sold out the Élysée Montmartre shortly afterwards.

The engineer on the Guesch Patti session was Renaud Letang. "I heard from a couple of people, 'He's good with someone like you,'" says Gonzales—meaning someone who can do everything but is a bit disorganized. Letang had shepherded the work of Spanish-French artist Manu Chao into fruition, starting with his 1998 breakthrough *Clandestino*, which mixed traditional acoustic folk music with found sound, electronics and the anything-goes spirit of Chao's '80s punk band, Mano Negra. "The day they recorded the Guesch Patti song, Gonzo played every instrument," says Feist. "Renaud told me he'd never worked with someone that unaffected, so quick and capable: turn on an amp, adjust knobs for 30 seconds, plug something in and nail it in one take. Renaud thought, I want to work with that guy again. I want to do anything and everything with that guy."

After the Guesch Patti single was released in October 2002, Letang asked Gonzales if he wanted to work on his own material. The Canadian demurred; he wanted to shift from performing to producing. And he had a perfect test subject right in front of him.

"IT WAS A THOUGHT EXPERIMENT," says Gonzales of the album he started making with Feist. It wasn't meant to be anything official. Gonzales wanted to record Feist's songs from her Red Demos. She refused. "I'd never worked in a studio before," she says. "I said, 'We can [work together], if you want to, but not with my songs. I'm not going to throw them on some sacrificial fire.' So we started with covers."

She was still struggling with songwriting, and what the difference is between the performer and the writer. One of the first covers they tried was Ron Sexsmith's "Secret Heart," which Feist says she "loves as much as one of my own." Gonzales wanted to do Dusty Springfield's "The Look of Love" and Stevie Wonder's "All in Love Is Fair," but Feist "barely knew who those people were," she admits of her 26-year-old self. "I knew Tool and Jawbox and Sinéad O'Connor. We also did a Bee Gees song ["Inside and Out"], which I figured must be kind of cool because they were on the *Grease* soundtrack. That was my innocent thinking." There were also two songs ("Tout doucement," "Now at Last") popularized by Blossom Dearie, an American singer of the 1950s who first found success in Paris. "I'd been listening to those songs on my Walkman constantly," says Feist, "and for different reasons both those songs were killing me."

The covers "gave us a way in," says Gonzales. "She heard more of herself in them than she thought, and then it was possible to go back to her own songs, and possible for me to find a way to produce them in a way she liked at the moment. Something in the attitude and the way I allowed her to approach working was liberating for her."

On expanding the "thought experiment" to include her original songs, Feist says, "I literally had the conscious thought: Well, I'm so far from home, it's not like anyone is going to hear it, so no harm done. I knew no one in my crew would approve of this synth-y, light pop stuff." But she set some conditions. "I pointed at [Gonzales] and said, 'Okay, if we're going to experiment this way, you got this Berlin thing you've been doing for years, so now you can't use any electronic instruments and you can't program beats or use any synths from the '90s.' Then he pointed at me and said, 'Oh yeah? All right, girl from the rock'n'roll past, no Fender amps and cool guitars.' Most of the guitar on the record is a nylon-string classical guitar. That's why it sounds so different than everything else I've done."

The album is infused with a Parisian spirit and whimsy: the nylon-string guitar, the soft-pop disco, the glockenspiels. It also helps that Feist covers '60s yé-yé icon Françoise Hardy ("L'amour ne dure pas toujours")—despite not speaking French at all. The songs are largely about melancholy and longing ("Lonely Lonely"); one is about a one-night stand ("One Evening"), and other than the Bee Gees song, only one of Feist's originals is actually seductive: "Leisure Suite," which she wrote in Toronto and appears on the Red Demos. Yet *Let It Die* sounded familiar to the French and seductively exotic to North American ears, the audio equivalent of a scintillating nouvelle vague film starring an alluring yet unattainable heroine. "A guaranteed jean creamer," raved a rather crude *Exclaim!* review, "where every note is sensual bliss."

"It certainly wasn't sexy when we were making the record," she told that reviewer.[3] "We were staying at the cheapest hotel in the whole city. We could only afford one tiny room, so we pushed the two single beds as far apart as we could. It was winter and there was no heat, with a draft coming through the windows, and we were shivering. It could be that amidst all that we were dreaming of a warm, fuzzy paradise, but no, it was entirely unsexy."

It was also immediately apparent—in ways that are not at all obvious in her roles with Broken Social Scene, Peaches or Gonzales—that Feist is an exceptional vocalist, pitch-perfect and able to project strength and confidence even at the lowest volume. Though stylistically on a different planet than k.d. lang, Feist's vocal skills may well have made her the greatest white Canadian female singer since her fellow Albertan. She humbly pleads ignorance. "Your voice is a part of you like your arms or your ankles: it's a tool you're able to use," she says. "I end up with nothing to say about compliments on my voice, although I appreciate them, of course. I have no perspective on it."

She and Gonzales did, however, consciously choose to centre *Let It Die* on her voice and surround it with different musical styles. "I'm always the friend who's borrowing albums because I don't really have the encyclopedic knowledge of music that came before," she says. "But I do know about how Patsy Cline, Peggy Lee and singers of that era were naturally shifting from style to style: one song would be bossa, the next would be country, and it would sound like the most natural thing on Earth. It wasn't about defining themselves through a genre; it was just singing a song. It's like formalism in art, where it's defined by the elements

---

3   The author.

shifting around it. The voice and the intention inside it isn't shifting. Those singers had to define themselves very clearly, like Dusty Springfield, and it wasn't one-dimensional. Chilly said that he wanted his arrangements to 'stay out of the way'"—an unusual act of humility for the man whose ego at the time was too big to fit inside Canada.

In between sessions throughout 2003, she returned to Canada to play with Broken Social Scene, including a June gig at Lee's Palace (with Stars, Jason Collett, Apostle of Hustle and solo sets by Feist and Amy Millan) where the band covered Sloan's "The Other Man" with Andrew Whiteman on stage and Chris Murphy in the audience. Feist sublet an apartment above the Soundscapes record store on College Street. "I wrote 'Let It Die' while walking from Kensington Market to Soundscapes," she says. "My goal was to not stop at a payphone and call my answering machine to leave the song on there. If the song was still in my head by the time I got home, it was worth remembering. If I can't remember it after five blocks, then screw it. At that point, I felt more comfortable that this album had something to do with me and it wasn't just covers. I trusted these guys."

Others didn't. Her Norwegian friends Kings of Convenience, whose 2004 album she'd worked on, thought it was daft. At a Broken Social Scene gathering at Kevin Drew's house, Feist hesitantly debuted some mixes for her friends. There was an uncomfortable silence until "Leisure Suite" came on. "Evan Cranley [of Stars] was the only one who stood up and shouted, 'YEAH, SUMMER JAM!'" she laughs. "The rest of them were shell-shocked and not sure what to say, because maybe they were worried for me."

At the same time, Gonzales was working on Z, for which he recorded slicker versions of material from his first three albums, as a way of introducing himself to the pop audience that made "Dans tes yeux" a hit. When Z came out in May 2003, he was playing bigger venues on what he called his "pre-tirement" tour, suggesting that he was ready to abandon performing to focus on production. He was joined by Peaches, Feist and Mocky; they'd perform collaboratively and roast Gonzales.

"We'd have a piano on the rider," says Feist, "and we'd cover it with cloth for the first half of the show, the amped-up, fake hip-hop dancing, theatrical thing. Then halfway through, we'd dramatically rip the cloth off the piano and he'd sit down and play. I'd watch people's faces, and they couldn't believe that he could do that. It wasn't just 'Hey, look at what a virtuoso I am.' He played with it and he doubled the impact by surprising people. He was saying, 'Hey, it's not me that's oversimplifying myself. Everyone else wants to oversimplify what they're seeing. It's one-dimensional and easier to digest. But no one is as one-dimensional as they appear in the magazines or even on stage, and you can play with that.' He had fun flattening himself out for that and then puffing himself up like a blowfish."

"You have to keep people in a sense of being shocked once in a while," he says. "It's one of the many tricks of being an entertainer. As much as you have to please people, once in a while you have to make them hate you and then earn back their respect. It's something politicians do all the time. They calibrate according to the overstepping and then ask for forgiveness, and it works to their advantage. It's an old trick for any kind of mass communication. That's just there to have those layers and be able to transgress and be redeemed."

Perhaps the strangest gig was opening for Mary J. Blige at Scala in London. Reviewing the show, the *Independent* called Gonzales a "cartoon Canadian gigolo . . . he's a spellbinding rhyme spinner, and his beats are the work of, if not quite a Dr. Dre, then at least a junior nurse."

Gonzales's new notoriety helped get Feist a record deal. "Word [was] out to labels that he and Renaud were working on some Canadian anglophone's record," says the anglophone in question. "Before anyone heard a note, I had four or five offers—not offers, but interest in hearing it. Gonzo was very selective in who got to hear it first, so that word would spread that *this* guy had heard it so now *that* guy would want to come. Meanwhile, I was sitting in a stinky van in Northampton [with Broken Social Scene] beside Kevin [Drew], who's grumpy because he wants a granola bar."

What Feist didn't know at the time was that Gonzales had paid for the sessions out of his own pocket. "I was so punk, in the sense that you don't spend a dollar you don't have," she recalls. "I had no conception of budgets. I was so dime to dime. By the time we finished the record, I said, 'How did that even happen? Who paid for it?' It was the kindest thing anyone had ever done for me at that point, and not making me feel any stress about it. Without me being aware, he conjured an album for me. He said, 'Well, I knew if you got a deal I'd be paid back.' That's crazy." Which is a real investment, not just of time and money but of trust. "Yeah! But once someone has a minute with money, then you're not afraid of it or in awe of it," she says. "He was just deeper into his career. He'd come and gone from Warner, now he was on Kitty-Yo in Berlin. Money was always coming and going for him, so it wasn't unthinkable."

Feist then decided to move to Paris; prior to that, she'd been bumming around Berlin, "and it wasn't apparent that it was going to be my new home or anything. But the few times I'd been to Paris, I was a complete sucker for it. You can walk one block in two weeks, because there's so much detail. If you have an imagination, it's unbelievable there."

Let It Die came out in the spring of 2004 on Polydor in France and on Arts & Crafts in Canada, the label run by Kevin Drew and Jeffrey Remedios, initially designed for Broken Social Scene's extended family. Polydor let them have it because they didn't consider Canada lucrative; it ended up selling more copies there than in any other territory—not per capita, but overall. In the U.S. and U.K., it came out in 2005 on Cherrytree, a new division of Interscope—itself under the Universal umbrella, like Polydor—designed primarily to release non-U.S. artists. Feist was the third artist signed to Cherrytree and the most significant until Robyn and Lady Gaga. Gonzales's manager, an American in Paris named Melinda Cody, put the deals together.

"I'm so grateful that Melinda came along and drew various deal structures on a napkin one day over coffee," says Feist. "They have very different ideas about how to fairly pay workers there—including artists. Record deals are structured very differently: they don't recoup. Everywhere else in the world, the artist pays for everything: videos, promo, tour support. The musician will make a puny percentage of the sales—and there is expense in the recording and distributing. But when you're expected to pay for that out of the 8% of revenue, the deck is stacked in the label's favour. But in the French case, it's not. There are all kinds of non-recoupable elements. By complete luck, I got into a deal in 2003 that I'm still in now. I'm a product of so many lucky little turns in the road."

One of the strangest of Feist's lucky turns was that a month before *Let It Die* came out in France, she was featured on a Jane Birkin album, singing a duet with the British singer and actress who is an icon in Europe, largely because of her work with ex-husband Serge Gainsbourg—and Gainsbourg is a god in France. In the wake of the Guesch Patti single, Letang and Gonzales were approached to work with another French legend, Charles Aznavour, who fired them just before recording his vocals. They were then hired by Birkin, who wanted to make a comeback record of duets, *Rendez-vous*, with the likes of Françoise Hardy, Caetano Veloso, Bryan Ferry and Portishead's Beth Gibbons. Somehow Feist snuck in there, co-writing a song with Gonzales for Birkin, "The Simple Story."

"The fact that I'm from Canada and I'm oblivious to the hierarchy of French culture has served me really well," says Feist, who coincidentally became a style icon for a hairstyle similar to Birkin's at the height of her fame in the '60s. "I've been in situations with people where months later I realize who they are. I don't know who Jane Birkin's Canadian counterpart would be; maybe Anne Murray if she remained a sex symbol? She's this totally kooky, cool woman. I have no perspective of her as an icon. They suggested I write a song for her, and she loved it, and before you know it, we were singing it together on Belgian TV." Not a bad introduction to la francophonie.

At home, *Let It Die* was far and away the most commercial-sounding record to have yet come out on Arts & Crafts, putting some financial wind in the sails of her friends' new venture. Kevin Drew recused himself from all label decisions pertaining to Feist. "This is great!" she told him. "I get to be on your label, but we don't have to ever talk about it." Released in the spring of 2004, the record did well in Canada, slowly but surely: it took one year to go gold, another year to go platinum in 2006.

Let It Die didn't immediately catch fire in the U.S., but it did get attention. Feist opened for Stars on a 2004 tour there. Torquil Campbell recalls telling a San Francisco crowd, "The young woman you just saw play—you will be begging someone for a ticket six months from now." Of course, he was right. "Finally, I was right about something," he laughs now. Because Stars got their first break thanks to L.A. radio station KCRW, he took Feist's cause up the chain of command there. By the end of 2005, André 3000 of Outkast was telling several outlets that "Mushaboom" was his favourite song of the year. The album sold more than 400,000 copies worldwide.

Feist toured *Let It Die* for 33 months. When she was done, she celebrated by buying a property two hours north of Toronto, tucked in the woods and out of sight. There, she'd talk to the neighbours and tip her cap, on a little road barely on the map.

AT THE SAME time as making *Let It Die*, Gonzales was recording himself playing piano, performing original miniatures modelled on Satie—an artist who, it should be noted, like fellow Gonzales influence Debussy, got his start playing in the 19th-century Parisian cabaret Le Chat Noir, a bawdy, avant-garde venue considered at the time to be just as déclassé as the Berlin demimonde of the 21st century would become a century later.

After Feist's deal, Gonzales signed to No Format, a new label focused primarily on African expats in Paris. They put out his *Solo Piano* album in 2004. It went platinum in France, finally making Gonzales the household name he longed to be. Ironic, that the showboating supervillain achieved his greatest success by telling himself to "shut up and play the piano"—a phrase that became the title of a 2018 biographical documentary.

Solo Piano took off for a few reasons. One was a key appearance on a French talk show, where Gonzales gave the host a quick music lesson before playing 45 seconds of the lead track, "Gogol." Though the pianist loathed the experience, the effect was immediate: the next day he was being recognized by strangers on the street. The songs on *Solo Piano* became licensing favourites; one was featured in a bank's ad campaign that lasted for years. It also did well on radio across Europe.

But mostly it was Gonzales's live show that made *Solo Piano* more than a brief coffeehouse trend. On stage, the affable performer was able to engage pop audiences who would likely never pay money to see a solo classical pianist. Tapping into his insecurities, he transposed his rap songs to the solo piano format, told tall tales, read fake reviews that he'd written filled with anti-Jewish slurs and generally delivered his serious compositions with a wink and a nod. He became a 21st-century Liberace, though aimed at twentysomethings rather than grandparents.

"I write piano songs that are constructed like simple pop songs: they're two minutes long with clear verses and choruses," he says. "Because my ego is so linked with what the public thinks of me, I cut out the part that only pleases myself. Other jazz and classical musicians rarely do that; they're so concerned with proving their musicianship to themselves [that] they take long solos or develop a melody over a 10-minute improvisation piece, and it's too challenging. Most people can't witness that kind of masturbation and enjoy it. The idea that I just want to please the audience means that I write these simple songs, but it also means that I have to serve it with a side dish of entertainment."

That often meant illustrating basic theory by playing "Happy Birthday" in a minor key or, without introduction, playing well-known polished pop songs as sombre piano songs. "For me, Erik Satie is the same as Billy Joel," he says. "I have sincere musical respect for both. Just like when I would play 'Maniac' [from *Flashdance*] in my *Solo Piano* show, for the first minute people wouldn't know what song it was. They knew that they knew it and that it was a beautiful song, but all of the sudden they realized it was 'Maniac' and they start to laugh. 'Oh, now I understand—this is a joke!' But for that minute, they didn't know it was a joke because they were just hearing what a great song it was. At that moment, I manage to equate Maurice Ravel and Michael Sembello."

The only problem was that audiences would often also snicker at his straight-up compositions, as if technical proficiency was somehow funny, as if laughter was the only way to make actual sincerity less uncomfortable. Gonzales relished walking those thin lines, which he considered his provenance of sorts. "Jewish humour—as opposed to parody, which is just 'Ha-ha, look at that idiot'—to me, Jewish humour is about look at *this* idiot," he says, pointing to himself. "*I'm* the idiot. I'm the one who needs to protect myself also from being considered just a straight-ahead musician. Maybe that's my flaw, that I need to create this distance by putting in a joke where it doesn't need to be."

No matter: it worked. Among other things, it led to the return of the prodigal son to Canada for a 2005 show at Pop Montreal, alongside fellow cross-genre Jewish pianists Socalled and nonagenarian Irving "Bagels and Bongos" Fields. There was a 2006 Toronto show at Harbourfront, and he opened for Feist at Massey Hall in

2007. He put out a smooth pop record in 2008, *Soft Power*, which fizzled. Touring it, he had a triumphant homecoming show in Montreal in front of 800 people, while in Toronto the next night he climbed over the empty seats in the half-full small theatre while he half-jokingly berated the audience for not knowing his "hit" song, "Take Me to Broadway." The U.S. continued to elude him entirely.

"The lesson of *Solo Piano* isn't that I've found my formula," he said in 2008. "The lesson is that I should keep taking risks." He then wrote and starred in a campy 2010 feature-length film, *Ivory Tower*, about two brothers who play competitive chess. Berlin-via-Montreal DJ Tiga played the brother, and Peaches played the love interest; Feist and Gonzales's parents had cameos.

That same year he discovered that Drake had sampled a *Solo Piano* song on the "Outro" track on his debut mixtape, *So Far Gone*; it wasn't a clever use, just a straight-up lift with the sound of champagne popping over it. The two met at the Junos the next year, doing a shtick on-air with Drake as a lounge singer and Gonzales his pianist. They hit it off, and Gonzales was invited over to Drake's studio; he'd just finished the track "Marvin's Room" and asked if Gonzales could play some kind of outro. Without thinking, Gonzales started improvising on a piano, exploring ideas, figuring he could shape it into something. Drake stopped him, told him that was great and put it on the track, which became one of the best-known songs from his blockbuster 2011 album *Take Care*.

Also in 2010, Daft Punk—whose Thomas Bangalter used *Solo Piano* to soothe his infant—invited Gonzales to work on what became their 2013 album *Random Access Memories*, which won the Grammy for Album of the Year. The egomaniac finally had a Grammy on his shelf, and he'd collaborated with the biggest rapper in the world.

In 2018, he recalled a career highlight that illustrated his evolving relationship with his own fame. "I had this great moment with my song 'Smothered Mate,' which was written for the climactic chess battle at the end of the *Ivory Tower* movie," he says. "It was supposed to be the triumphant-sounding stuff that I call 'sports music.' Then at the [2018] World Cup final, it was time to present the trophy. [French president] Emmanuel Macron gets onto the platform. It's pouring rain, he's embracing all the players, Vladimir Putin is shaking their hands. And what had FIFA chosen to play in the fucking stadium? 'Smothered Mate.' *My* song. My phone blew up with people going, 'Oh my god, your song is playing in the stadium!' It's quite surreal to think maybe a *billion fucking people* heard it simultaneously.

"If something like that happened 15 years ago, I would have been happy but also frustrated because no one would know it was [mine]. But here I just thought, This is where I want to be. I had finally made that shift. I want my music to be recognized, to be well known; I want people to have an emotional relationship with it; I want it to mean something to them. But I care less and less if they project onto the person who made it."

His 2014 book of sheet music aimed at lapsed pianists, *Re-introduction Etudes*, sold tens of thousands of copies, a complete anomaly in the 21st century. And while he continued to release original music—including three more *Solo Piano* records, an orchestral record, a collaboration with Jarvis Cocker and more—he focused on "pop music masterclasses" and setting up the "Gonzervatory," an annual week-long, all-expenses paid, residential music and performance school in Paris open to international students.

The supervillain now used his powers for good.

"I'D RATHER FUCK WHO I WANT than kill who I am told to," goes a line in the title track from Peaches' 2006 album *Impeach My Bush*, one of the precious few political songs of the hyper-politicized time. She worked in L.A. with pop producers Mickey Petralia (Beck's *Midnite Vultures*) and Greg Kurstin, soon to be a huge pop producer for Sia, Kylie Minogue and others, including Tegan and Sara. The leap to L.A.-level pop production went seamlessly, rocking as hard as a classic Joan Jett record (Jett herself even showed up) and with slick pop as good or better than the superstars who were constantly ripping her off. While the album didn't put Peaches on any pop charts, it marked an ongoing evolution in her songwriting and her rhyme skills. She was no longer afraid to use her singing voice, now employed on pop hooks rather than just shouted choruses. One song, "Boys Wanna Be Her," was later used as the theme song for fellow Torontonian Samantha Bee's *Full Frontal* TV series.[4]

Between 2009's *I Feel Cream* and 2015's *Rub*—both of which had videos made for each song, cementing her rep as a multimedia artist—Peaches designed her own jukebox musical, *Peaches Does Herself*, performed in Berlin and captured on film. (It debuted at TIFF.) But perhaps the most audacious thing Peaches did in the latter half of her career was her one-woman show *Peaches Christ Superstar*, where she earnestly performed Andrew Lloyd Webber and Tim Rice's musical in its entirety, accompanied only by Gonzales on piano. There was no irony, no in-joke: she'd sincerely loved the musical since she was a teenager. She toured it around Europe and performed it in Toronto on December 21, 2010, getting a near-perfect rating from the *Globe and Mail* the next day.

---

4   Peaches performed it at the 2017 Bee-hosted counter-event to the cancelled White House Correspondents Dinner.

The York University dropout and the McGill grad who once thought they were the Shit were now international stars who could fill the Queen Elizabeth Theatre in their hometown with something earnest and dorky, the type of thing they might have done in the wee hours above a sex shop on Queen Street West in 1998, while a young Feist gaped in awe.

But it was their former sidekick, Feist, a.k.a. Bitch Lap Lap, who continued to lap both of them several times over.

WITH COMMERCIAL SUCCESS came control. If everything about Let It Die was a thought experiment, in Gonzales's words, its successor, The Reminder, was 100% Feist.

In the spring of 2006, in a manor house outside Paris, she assembled her live band: bassist Julian Brown (from Andrew Whiteman's Apostle of Hustle) and brothers Bryden and Jesse Baird on trumpet and drums respectively. Dominic "Mocky" Salole, an old friend from 701 Queen West days, joined Gonzales as producer. British singer Jamie Lidell is credited with "energy arrangement." The entire experience was meant to be the antithesis of Let It Die, which was Gonzales and Feist alone in a hermetically sealed studio, playing all the instruments themselves.

This time, they were in an idyllic location, a country house with large windows, filled with birdsong and canine company. Headphones were referred to as "musical condoms" and to be avoided at all costs in favour of experiencing the live chemistry in the room. They moved out of the proper studio in the house's basement and set up nests of microphones on the top two floors and outside the house. Feist's vocal microphone was sent to an amp in one corner, with her guitar amp in another corner. Two drum kits were set up; Brown played upright bass in the hallway, where there was more natural resonance.

The only cover this time was "Sealion," an interpretation of the African-American folk song "See-Line Woman," popularized by Nina Simone (who also did the best-known version of "When I Was a Young Girl," a cover on Let It Die). Feist first heard it on a Library of Congress field recording; she had no idea that one of her favourite bands, the Constantines, had also performed it live. Five songs were solo compositions; seven were co-writes with either Mocky, Gonzales, Andrew Whiteman or Brendan Canning. Feist knew what she wanted. On the song "Honey Honey," she booked a session harpist and gave her these instructions: "You're the mermaid 40 feet down under the raft, you're in the doldrums, there's complete silence, but the guy on the raft hasn't had anything to drink or eat for two weeks, and he doesn't know if he's hearing things or if it's real. And that's you."

"Brandy Alexander" was written in fragments with Ron Sexsmith, whose "Secret Heart" she had covered on Let It Die. After that album came out, the two finally met at an Ottawa party, where he told her he was drinking the cocktail that had been the imbibement of choice for John Lennon and Harry Nilsson the night they got kicked out of the Troubadour during their "lost weekend" of March 1974. Feist sent him lyrics, and the next time they met, he sang her the melody. Uncharacteristic of a woman who usually travelled with a Dictaphone for brainstorming, she didn't have a recording of the moment, "but it's a Ron Sexsmith melody, so my mind recorded it," she says. Two months later in the studio, she sang it for Gonzales, who voiced the chords underneath. When Sexsmith heard the final product, he told them, "Yeah, that's pretty much it."

"I Feel It All" and "Past Is Present" are both similar to a Kevin Drew song called "Safety Bricks"; in the 2010 concert film *This Film Is Broken*, the two perform a medley of all three songs. Some of the quietest songs were recorded live: "So Sorry," "The Water" and "Intuition," the latter song dating back to the Red Demos. But the song that was to alter the course of Feist's life was abandoned during the French sessions, and almost didn't happen at all. It started with a fan who lived a world away.

Sally Seltmann was an Australian singer-songwriter who performed as New Buffalo. She fell in love with *Let It Die* and wrote a song that she shelved because she thought it sounded too Feist-y. A year later, Arts & Crafts made New Buffalo the label's first international signing, putting out her 2005 album *The Last Beautiful Day*. On tour with Broken Social Scene and Feist that year, Seltmann built up the nerve to play the Feist-inspired song on the tour bus in front of her contemporary. Feist loved it and started performing it live at a brisker tempo, adding a melodic outro that became the primary hook. She eventually changed some of the lyrics, with Seltmann's approval. They shared a credit on the song Feist recorded as "1234."

"It felt revolutionarily melodic and simple in kind of a punk way to me," she says. "It felt like this laser-beam lasso, like a weird weapon on a set list. It was so alien to where I came from previously. I was looking for the long way around. I don't want there to be simplicity."

The song had a circuitous terrain of its own. Gonzales hated it. "He thought it was dumb," says Feist. "He was pulling a producer power move and didn't want to finish it. I was sure it had qualities yet to be found." She recalled meeting Ben Mink at the 2005 Winnipeg Folk Festival, where the veteran gave her some sound career advice. Mink's own career dated back to the '70s, when he replaced Nash the Slash in the prog-rock band FM; he's best known for playing violin with k.d. lang and producing her blockbuster album *Ingenue*. In Mink, Feist saw a solution to her problem. In the spring of 2006, she flew to his studio in Vancouver with a hard drive that contained the "1234" bed tracks; he added strings and banjo. The album was mixed at Blue Rodeo's Woodshed studio in Toronto shortly afterwards. "I sprang it on Gonzo that I'd finished '1234'—he was very, very angry with me," she laughs. They did, however, agree to finish another song dropped in France. Feist wanted to record "The Park" outdoors, but in France the takes were usually hijacked by animal noises in the nearby woods. In Toronto, she rerecorded it in a parkette off Danforth Avenue, around the corner from the studio.

There was nothing straightforward about *The Reminder*'s success. Its first single, the jaunty four-on-the-floor piano romp "My Moon My Man" did merely okay, despite the fantastic video choreographed on a moving sidewalk at Toronto's Pearson airport. That clip was directed by American Patrick Daughters, who had also done the second "Mushaboom" clip—in which Feist literally jumped out a window of an apartment in Prague (not Paris, contrary to popular belief), floating down to the street on a wire and then led a parade (including Peaches) on horseback. For the album's second single, "1234," Daughters and Feist decided on even more elaborate choreography, this time filmed in an airplane hangar in one continuous shot. Feist is dressed in a sparkly purple jumpsuit, surrounded by dozens of dancers weaving in and out of the frame and holding her aloft.

Just a year earlier, American band OK Go helped launch the YouTube era—the platform debuted in 2005—with the first video to go viral in the post-MTV age. Like "1234," it featured elaborate choreography, though just with four people on treadmills. "1234" was more old-school Hollywood, a deliberate Busby Berkeley throwback, much like Björk's then-decade-old "It's All So Quiet." *Pitchfork* later placed it at No. 5 on its list of the top 50 videos of the 2000s.

The tour for *The Reminder* was visually elaborate. Artist Shary Boyle had worked with Feist on a couple of shows in Toronto and Paris, creating live animation using an overhead projector, something Feist had first seen her do with Winnipeg songwriter Christine Fellows. This time out, Feist at times performed in silhouette behind a scrim, toying with her exaggerated shadow. Puppeteer Clea Minaker provided elaborate shadow projections and other unique lighting design elements; very few artists not named David Byrne or Björk toured with such theatrical detail. Feist didn't need the bells and whistles, but now that she wasn't a rag-tag, one-woman operation, she wanted to give the audience more than they were expecting—when she was headlining, that is.

She was still performing solo as an opening act, mainly in the U.S.; she already knew she was capable of captivating an audience, not only with her raw talent but by looping and layering her vocals while performing "Sealion," or leading earnest singalongs like she was Pete Seeger incarnate, cajoling cynical crowds into being her backup singers. By the end of a set, wrote the *Guardian* in 2008, the cross-armed, jaded crowd that came to see her was "virtually rolling on their backs and asking her to tickle their bellies: clapping along and happily acceding when she asked them to hum a note to which she could tune her guitar."

Then Apple came calling. They wanted to use the "1234" video to sell a new iPod model; apparently k-os had been approached first and turned it down. Feist agreed, and the effect was instant. Before the ad aired, *The Reminder* was selling a respectable 2,000 copies (including downloads) a week; that quickly shifted to 70,000 a week. To date, *The Reminder* has sold 1.5 million copies worldwide. She performed on the Grammys, where she was nominated in four categories, including Best New Artist; both she and Taylor Swift lost to Amy Winehouse. *The Reminder* won a Juno for Album of the Year and won the Shortlist Music Prize, a short-lived U.S. prize—similar to Canada's Polaris Music Prize—where she beat out LCD Soundsystem, Wilco, Arcade Fire, Spoon and Stars. It's not an exaggeration to say the Apple ad was a huge part of all that.

Feist had mixed feelings. "What happened to '1234' was not the way I ever saw it playing out," she says. "I'm grateful in a practical I-am-my-grandmother's-granddaughter 'just don't be ungrateful' sense, but on the other hand, it oversimplified what I had been doing all those years."

The song had a whole other life when *Sesame Street* asked her to sing it on the show, the lyrics rewritten to be about counting monsters. By that point, she was not at all precious about the song. Plus, she loves Muppets—who doesn't? Fifteen years earlier, R.E.M. had agreed to adapt their most ridiculous song as "Shiny Happy Monsters" for the show. The Feist clip became a viral sensation, with a shelf life longer than even the iPod ad. "I was so glad" to be asked, she says. "In a way, I was so sick to death of '1234' at that point. It was such an amazing cathartic release to have the song turned into a song for kids, which is what, in essence, it turned out to be in reality, too. So many people came up to me and said, 'My three-year-old can't stop singing it!' And the puppets—are you kidding me? I learned to count watching *Sesame Street*. To actually be there—well, it was one of the best days." She also made a cameo at the end of the 2011 *Muppets* movie, singing with an 89-year-old Mickey Rooney.

One of the weirdest consequences of success was when *Stereogum* placed her at the top of an "indie rock hottie list," where she beat out Jenny Lewis, Joanna Newsom and M.I.A. But there was no question she was a style icon; hairdressers in the Western world were besieged by women wanting "Feist bangs."

The Reminder's worldwide tour cycle wound down in November 2008 with a Canadian victory lap that ended in Charlottetown, shortly after a two-night Toronto stand: one at the cavernous Air Canada Centre; one at her preferred venue, Massey Hall. She gave up her Paris apartment, moved back to Toronto and took 18 months off, after almost five years of constant work. She wrote nothing.

She then went back to the French house where she'd made the record, expecting that might trigger some creative juices, but no.

She wasn't surprised. In July 2008, she said, "I need to allow myself to believe I may never write another song before I write another few dozen. You've got to trick the muse into showing itself by pretending you don't care. Sort of like the ghost in the room, and there's a flicker in the corner, and as soon as you look, you can't see it anymore. You can't see it if you stare right at it."

When the songs did come, they resulted in the artistic triumph of 2012's *Metals*, which beat Drake's *Take Care* for the Polaris that year. It took her another five years before 2017's *Pleasure*, a stripped-down record that harkened back to the Red Demos. Other than a trio called Hydra—which she formed with Ariel Engle (La Force) and Daniela Gesundheit (Snowblink) to tour Canadian festivals in 2014—there were no other musical projects to keep her busy. There was just life—outside the public eye.

"Leslie is a lot like Gord Downie in many ways," says Torquil Campbell of Stars. "You can bring her into a room where people have never heard of her; she'll sit with people for three hours and talk to them about themselves and never really mention herself or drop into the conversation that she's a massive rock star. She's a genuine citizen, engaged with the idea of what it means to be a person and is singularly focused on being a good one. That's why her music sounds the way it does."

While promoting *Pleasure*, she talked about hanging out with Peaches and Gonzales and Mocky in Berlin shortly before the album came out. "We're rarely all in the same city at the same time anymore, but we were all at Peaches' house, ordering in Thai food and commiserating," she says. "We are as much in the here and now as we are able to tell versions of the story we had from 20 years ago. We're not stuck reminiscing, or overvaluing that time as 'good old days.' These are good 'now' days, too. But there's something to be said [about] being able to fold 20 years forward with people with whom you experienced it all together. That helps me stand here now and fold forward 20 years from now."

CHAPTER 8
DON'T MESS WITH OUR LOVE

THE DEARS, SAM ROBERTS

There's a bar called Bifteck (translation: steak) near the corner of St. Laurent and Pins in Montreal's McGill student ghetto. In the '90s, it was where the local Anglo rock scene kvetched about who was doing what—and why the rest of the world seemed to hate Montreal bands.

Every so often, something truly weird sprouted, like when extremely loose ensemble Bran Van 3000—a proto–Broken Social Scene—scored a Top 40 U.S. single with "Drinking in L.A." and then signed to the Beastie Boys' label and landed another hit featuring Curtis Mayfield's final vocal performance (accompanied by one of the most Montreal videos ever). Or how Lhasa de Sela, the Mexican-American singer who later joined a circus in France, went from the tiny Café Sarajevo to become Canada's first allophone to go platinum. Or how fellow Café Sarajevo alumnus Rufus Wainwright signed to Dreamworks and spent almost $1 million on his debut album. Local scenester Melissa Auf der Maur got drafted into Hole and then Smashing Pumpkins, and her friend Jordon "Blinker the Star" Zadorozny tagged along and got a Dreamworks deal of his own.

But for most of the Bifteck crowd, that seemed like a whole other world.

Sam Roberts was a Bifteck regular. So was his friend Murray Lightburn of the Dears. "You had to scrap your way to at least earn the respect of your peers," says Roberts. "Anytime anybody from Montreal was able to go off the island, literally, and do anything of note, everybody paid attention. Then we'd all go back to the Bifteck and talk about it. The tall poppy syndrome was very much alive and well, to the point that I was very afraid when we got any inkling of success—I was like,

213

'Oh my god, they're going to tear us apart.' Murray punched someone out at the Bifteck once, right into the popcorn machine, just laid him out flat.

"Everybody can move to Montreal now and start a band and 'be' a Montreal band and the postal code offers you a chance at getting [noticed]," Roberts continues. "It's hard to explain how it was so much the opposite in the '90s. You felt like you were living on this island that nobody wanted to pay the slightest bit of attention to. It was an insular place. We had to fight for every inch. When Blinker the Star or Godspeed or Bran Van 3000 or Melissa or whoever managed to get a foothold in somewhere that wasn't [local weeklies] the *Hour* or the *Mirror*, it was highly motivating for the rest of us. There'd also always be talk of shitty music or how some record exec was conned into signing so-and-so. 'Oh, it must be. Who else would sign that shit band?'"

In 2000, the Dears released *End of a Hollywood Bedtime Story* and quickly gained a reputation as one of the most ferocious new live bands in Canada—and beyond. In 2002, the Sam Roberts Band became the first of the next wave of Montreal bands to score a national pop hit. Hopefully down at the Bifteck, there were more pints raised than punches thrown.

WIN BUTLER WANTED to open for the Dears. According to Dears biographer Lorraine Carpenter, the newly arrived Texan was intent on getting his demo tape to the Dears, hoping to score an opening slot for Arcade Fire, which at that point was more of an idea than a band. They didn't end up sharing a bill until late 2003, a fleeting moment of contact for two bands on very different paths. A year later, in 2004, Arcade Fire had the world talking about Montreal. But Godspeed and the Dears did that first.

As Carpenter points out in the intro to her 2011 book, *Lost in the Plot*, the direct line from one band to the next couldn't be clearer:

"There was one Montreal band, with a husband and wife at its core, with too many people on stage, playing guitars, drums, strings, brass, synths, organs and pianos, their music and lyrics sometimes steeped in malaise and melancholia, sometimes buoyed by anthemic power, evoking the apocalypse, invoking Christianity, losing their sweat and lifting your spirits on stages across the city, around the world, sometimes even at your local church. Ladies and gentlemen: the Dears."

End of a Hollywood Bedtime Story marked the beginning of a Montreal love story. Prior to that, the Dears—which was mostly just Murray Lightburn—had spent five years in drunken obscurity, burning through band members. The latter part never changed. But in 1998, the man who wrote "There Is No Such Thing as Love" met Natalia Yanchak, who lit up Lightburn's life with a new sense of purpose and creative spark. Like their Mile End neighbours in Godspeed You! Black Emperor, the Dears were mysterious, cocky, grandiose, po-faced and had an identity undeniably intertwined with Montreal.

Quebec is a province where prog-rock love runs deep. The most beloved homegrown bands of the '70s were Harmonium and Beau Dommage. Montreal is where a riotous Pink Floyd concert scared Roger Waters into writing *The Wall*. It's the birthplace of a highly successful tribute act devoted to Peter Gabriel–era Genesis, complete with original costumes. It's where Supertramp likely sold the most records per capita: 400,000 copies of *Breakfast in America* sold to the population of 6.5 million in 1979. The most successful metal band to ever come out of Quebec is the decidedly prog Voivod.

Those influences, direct or otherwise, are clear in some of the more ambitious arrangements and certainly the Dears' rhythm section during the band's most popular period (2001–07). Lightburn was drawn to British music of a different generation: the Smiths, Blur, Spiritualized. When Yanchak joined the band, she brought her vintage Farfisa organ with her, which—combined with Lightburn's "Heartless Romantic" crooner's voice—brought a Euro elegance to the Dears that no other English Canadian rock band had at that time.

At the very least, no one else in Canada dared to write an instrumental track as cinematic and lovely as "Where the World Begins and Ends," where the Farfisa sounds like falling snow on Parc Avenue, as violins surge along with the electric guitar in what could be a '60s nouvelle vague soundtrack, only to conclude with ominous suspended strings of Godspeedian grandeur.

As Lightburn told Carpenter for a 2003 article, of the band's classic lineup, "[Drummer] George [Donoso] moved here from Chile when he was nine, [bassist] Martin [Pelland] is as Quebec as it gets, au boutte, Natalia is a Pollack-Ukranian from a Pollack area of Toronto, [keyboardist] Valerie [Jodoin-Keaton] is half-American, [guitarist Rob] Benvie is a straight-up Canadian white guy and I'm the son of immigrants from Central America." Carpenter added that Benvie's replacement, Patrick Krief, is a Moroccan Jew. Lightburn later joked that his band's mixed makeup was like *Degrassi Junior High*; it certainly had its share of teen angst.

Lightburn was one of the few racialized singers to ever front a popular Canadian rock band, alongside generational contemporaries Danko Jones and Julian Taylor of Staggered Crossing (all three playing drastically different variations of rock music). "Murray is a fighter," says Torquil Campbell of Stars. "He's an NDG tough. He's a Black guy playing indie rock, so he's seen his share of people hoping the worst for him. He always thinks the world is against him—and he's right about 80% of the time."

Though the Dears made friends in different scenes, they were riding their own train for much of their career, despite their loose association with Toronto indie rock superstars. "The Dears didn't really buy the whole Broken Social Scene thing," says Campbell. "They thought it was all airy-fairy hippie bullshit. The Dears were about leather jackets and black jeans. They were Quebec rock'n'roll. They weren't into bringing your babies on stage to play tambourine. The Dears were like, 'What are these amateurs doing?' They wanted to come out and destroy every night."

"In the whole Broken Social Scene and Arcade Fire name-dropping parade of bands, they get left out a lot," says Danko Jones. "When people ask me about Canadian music in the early 2000s, I always lead with the Dears."

MURRAY LIGHTBURN GREW up in the Brossard neighbourhood of Longueuil, a Montreal suburb on the South Shore, to parents who were both born in Belize and arrived in Montreal via New York and London. His mother was a nurse working overnight shifts and his father was a jazz saxophonist—until he gave it up to become a Pentecostal minister. As a toddler, Lightburn accompanied his dad to gigs, sleeping in dressing rooms. After the family found religion, it was not a rock'n'roll house; the four sons were forbidden to watch any non-Christian television.

Nonetheless, young Murray fell in love with the Smiths after a school bully recommended them. His first band, Wren, morphed into the Dears by 1995. They were part of a tight-knit group of anglophile musicians in Montreal, including Sam Roberts, who recalls "sitting in Murray's apartment building above the Oxford Café in NDG, listening to the new James album. We'd sit there and close our eyes and listen and, obviously, completely overintellectualize everything."

Sam Roberts, who was born in South Africa, wanted nothing more than to be British—though he was a big fan of Montreal garage band the Gruesomes and proudly wore their pin on his jean jacket. His first band was called Northstar. "We gravitated toward the Charlatans, Stone Roses, Spiritualized, those bands in the early '90s who were doing something completely different than grunge," he says. "We were basically a bad Ride cover band. We were a pale Primal Scream. The Canadian band we all put on a pedestal was Sloan." Lightburn's own anglophilia was such that he brought some demos with him to London in 1995 and hung out at a café Graham Coxon of Blur was known to frequent. Nothing came of it, which is for the best; the Dears were nowhere near ready for prime time.

Also in Montreal's anglophile posse was Marlowe, with future Dears guitarist Joseph Donovan, and Moebius Strip. These bands played primarily to friends and family and not many others. "If by 'many' you mean 'any,' then yes, you're right," laughs Roberts. "The exact number would be zero people outside that crowd." They did once manage to book the larger rock club Foufounes Électriques and pack it. "In all our minds it was the greatest thing we ever accomplished, either individually or as a collective," says Roberts. "We were literally swinging from the rafters that night."

Otherwise, they shared bills at Terminal, Station 10 or Stornoway—places where bands had to supply the booze themselves. "Murray was the godfather of our whole unit," says Roberts. "He was more experienced than we were, and making more interesting music. He was always very brave in his creativity." He was also confrontational. "Murray was the first guy I ever knew to use a megaphone on stage," Roberts continues. "He could be lippy up there, but that was the time: you were expected to throw attitude everywhere. Back then it was part of your onstage persona to give the audience a shot here and there."

The Dears' first gig outside of Montreal was at El Mocambo in Toronto, where heightened tension caused one band member to be fired and another to quit. Bad omen. "You can't just randomly start a band with people—especially if you want it to go anywhere," reflects Lightburn. "But I didn't know if I *wanted* it to go anywhere. I was in my mid-20s, with zero understanding of anything. All the band meant to me was drinking Colt 45s and jamming in a grubby basement with garbage equipment." Drinking and recording seemed to go together; during one mixing session, the notorious control freak Lightburn blacked out and his guitarist had to finish the job.

Meanwhile, Sam Roberts was studying English lit at McGill. He and his friends hung out at a bar at St. Laurent and Prince Arthur called Angel's; it had a Britpop night and cheap pitchers every Wednesday. "We all lived nearby," he says. "I did my laundry next door to Angel's and ate 90% of my meals at the 99-cent pizza joint across the street."

It was there that Roberts met his future manager, Dave Spencer. "He had one table of beer guzzlers and we had another and there were only 15 of us in the bar on any given Wednesday, so we put our two tables together."

"You got a band?" asked Spencer.

"Yeah!"

"You got a manager?"

"No. You ever managed a band before?

"No. But I get free long distance at my job at Legal Aid Ontario when I get back to Toronto."

"All right, you got the job."

Roberts gave him a cassette. Spencer told him it sounded like the Boo Radleys. "Okay, cool, great reference," said Roberts. "You're in." Spencer has been his manager and one of his closest friends ever since.

MURRAY LIGHTBURN WAS working a crappy telemarketing job. He was in a relationship that was falling apart. His band didn't seem to be going anywhere. He was drinking heavily and depressed. One night at Bifteck, he noticed an attractive DJ. He was further intrigued after discovering she also played keyboards and hosted a campus radio show dedicated to Canadian indie rock, *Underground Sounds* on CKUT. This was Natalia Yanchak.

Yanchak was a Toronto transplant, who wrote CD reviews for the nascent *Vice Magazine*; she'd met the founders at a zine fair while still in high school. She'd moved to Montreal in 1995 with her then-boyfriend and played in a '60s bubblegum pop band, Smile Factory. At Bifteck in 1998, Lightburn invited her to the next Dears gig, held up the street at the tiny Barfly, capacity about 50. "It's a venue with zero spectacle," she says. "There's no stage, there's barely a PA. There's a piece of burlap behind you and some crates. It was a scrappy show, but Murray was a charismatic performer. There was something there." She signed on to play keyboards.

She also loaned him a four-track, one of many he'd borrow from friends while recording demos for what became *End of a Hollywood Bedtime Story*. "When Natalia joined the band, things really fell into place," says Lightburn. "More structure. Goals. She was like, 'We gotta have a photograph, a press kit, a CD.'" The two soon became a romantic couple. Recording engineer Howard Bilerman, who first recorded the Dears in 1995, says, "People often get skeptical when a girlfriend joins a band, but she really was the missing piece and subverted the overt guitarness and maleness of the band."

Lightburn had big sonic ambitions. He wanted what he later called "orchestral pop noir romantique" and envisioned strings and a horn section. He cobbled together an album in bits and pieces on borrowed time. "I was frustrated by my lack of resources, but my brain was exploding," he says. "I would go to one house and lay down a piano track, then go to some jazz space and lay down a drum track. Then I'd bounce it all [to a master tape]. It would take me forever to get these ideas down. I'd do all the orchestral ideas with synths. I was also dead broke, and I don't come from rich parents." The album was mixed in Yanchak's Parc Avenue apartment on borrowed equipment.

When *Bedtime Story* was done, the band quit. They'd grown tired of Lightburn's drinking, drugs and depression. He now had the album he'd always wanted to make and, other than Yanchak on keys, no band to play it live. He pinched two former members of Sam Roberts's Northstar: bassist Martin Pelland and guitarist George Donoso, who had shifted to drums in a couple of bands before joining the Dears. "When [Donoso] started drumming for the Dears, that was a huge part of the switch," says Roberts. "A light went on. The band became a really special thing."

Word had made its way to Toronto. Phil Klygo, who ran the Teenage USA label, invited the Dears to open for Mean Red Spiders at Lee's Palace in May 2000. There were only two dozen people in the 500-capacity club when the Dears went on. But in attendance were the Toronto rock cognoscenti: Stuart Berman from *Eye Weekly*, Matt Galloway from *Now*, Kieran Grant from the *Toronto Sun*, Ben Rayner from the *Toronto Star*, among others. They were all instantly smitten.

But the gig Lightburn had been dreaming about was the Montreal release party on June 3, 2000, at Café Campus. He enlisted various local players to comprise string and horn sections. The Dears' rehearsal room was across the hall from one rented to Pest 5000, featuring former Doughboys bassist Jon Asencio. "I remember being frustrated about trying to pull together strings and brass, trying to get rehearsals together, and what I wanted to come out of the speakers was not happening anywhere," says Lightburn. "I couldn't even describe what I was trying to do. We'd show up at gigs with this giant organ and this Farfisa and the Korg Polysix—all these analog keyboards—and then cramming six horn players and a string quartet on stage. I was super frustrated by the whole thing. Jon Asencio said to me, 'Whaddya expect, man? It's indie rock.'

"I was so offended!" says Lightburn, still offended talking about it 20 years later. "First of all, I had no idea what indie rock was. That was the first time I heard the phrase. It was like finding out you're a replicant [in *Blade Runner*]. 'What?! *I'm not indie rock!* What the fuck is he talking about?' I don't even think he meant offence, which made me even more angry."

Things didn't go terribly well at the album release show, with an expanded 18-piece lineup dubbed the Cosmopolitan City Orchestra. Lightburn recalls it being "disastrous." Yanchak recalls someone describing it as "a train without brakes." Howard Bilerman says, "Murray fancied himself a young Quincy Jones, and the stage was way too small for a string section. Chairs would be cascading off the stage while Murray was conducting. He would be prone to 'woe is me' Charlie Brown outbursts."

In the fall of 2000, the Dears made their first forays outside Montreal and Toronto. In London, Ontario, they were on an incongruous bill with Danko Jones, who straddled the worlds of garage rock and metal. "I saw the name and thought they'd be a generic rock'n'roll band," says Danko. "Then Murray started singing, and I went straight to the front. His voice betrayed what I thought was going to come out. They sounded a bit like the Smiths, and I don't even like the Smiths, but their songs were so good and dramatic and epic and I wasn't used to that. I went to see them the very next night [in Toronto] at the El Mo, and all the right people were there. I knew it wasn't just my little secret."

ONE YEAR AFTER BRAN VAN 3000 scored a surprise North American pop hit with "Drinking in L.A.," Sam Roberts decided he should take that advice. In 1998, he and manager Dave Spencer invited themselves down to California to visit Blinker the Star's Jordon Zadorozny and shop the Northstar EP. "Jordon was living with his girlfriend in this pool house of some dude up in the Hollywood Hills," says Roberts. "We had a pager to alert us if any music biz who's whos were trying to track down the masterminds behind the now-circulating Northstar demo. It didn't ring much." Northstar imploded within a year.

Roberts decided to go the eponymous route, but he feared his friends' opinions. "We played one of our first gigs as the Sam Roberts Band, and Murray came in. He had his shades on in the club and a hoodie and I'm like, 'Shit, Murray's here. We better make this a good one.' I was wearing a mesh camo tank top at the time, flirting with a glam chapter I wasn't entirely sure about. When I saw Murray sit down, I regretted my fashion choice instantly. Those are the people to whom we looked for affirmation."

Roberts was on a writing spree and recorded 20 songs in the bedroom of keyboardist Eric Fares. George Donoso played drums. Zadorozny brought it to the attention of Melissa Auf der Maur, who was back in Montreal working on an Angelina Jolie film, *Beyond Borders*. She was tasked with finding a Clash cover band for a wedding reception scene; Roberts got the gig. Auf der Maur also passed on his demo to someone at V2 Records, then riding high on the success of Moby and the White Stripes. "This guy from V2 flew up to Montreal to meet me and took us for dinner and put us up in a hotel where I could literally throw a tennis ball from the window to my apartment," laughs Roberts. "We were like, 'This. Is. The. Best.' This is what we all waited for: to be wined and dined and told how great we were. At the end, we'd have a record deal and could indulge in whatever Oasis and Blur had been up to. That was still resonating at that time."

Harsh reality soon sunk in. The Sam Roberts Band, now with Jordon's brother Corey Zadorozny on drums, went to SXSW in March 2002 to play four showcases. "We'd been playing around Toronto and Montreal for a number of years, but we'd never played side by side with bands who were tour-hardened veterans—even young veterans. We show up to the Chuck Taylor–wearing masses with more denim than you've seen in your life, and we watch these bands play and we were so out of our depth. We hadn't put in the time on stage. The Dears were the only band who went down there that year, 2002, and really turned heads.

"The guy who'd been scouting us for V2 came to one of our showcases, in a place where all the walls were glass, basically the worst-sounding room you could ever play. Everything was glass and metal. The house sound tech was playing pool instead of mixing the show. The bass drum was feeding back, just insane cacophony coming off the stage. The guy from V2 sees this, and that was it. Our sure-bet ticket to whatever had just walked out the door. I was crushed. I knew that across the street the Dears were killing it. We'd gone to Texas thinking we'd dot our i's and cross our t's on a new contract, and it couldn't have been further from the truth."

That night did mark a turning point, however. At the show was Linda Noelle Bush, who worked for the publishing wing of Universal Records; k-os had been her first signing. She knew Dave Spencer through Toronto Britpop circles—she DJed at popular club night Blow Up—and had once been dragged to see Northstar, leaving unimpressed. Two years later at Canadian Music Week—immediately prior to SXSW 2002—she ended up at a Sam Roberts show at Rancho Relaxo. "I couldn't believe it was the same person," she says. "He had an everyman-ness about him, whereas at that other show he seemed to be pretending. I didn't even initially realize it was the same guy. I turned to Dave and said, 'What the hell?!' There were maybe 16 people there. He played like he was Springsteen in a stadium."

At SXSW, Bush brought influential Toronto booker Jack Ross along. He was hooked, promptly signed Roberts as a client and booked the band into a residency at the Rivoli. Between that and a Maritime swing opening for By Divine Right, the Sam Roberts Band was quickly whipped into shape—while sleeping on floors and driving in a van with broken windows in a Canadian winter. Bush managed to get Roberts a Universal publishing deal, but the label didn't think he was ready for a recording contract. They shifted him onto a new subsidiary, Maple Music.

Within three months of that SXSW gig, Sam Roberts was introduced to the world through an EP called *The Inhuman Condition*, featuring rerecorded tracks from his demos. It was Maple Music's first release. It wasn't a band record: Roberts and Jordon Zadorozny played all the instruments.

The first single, "Brother Down," released before the EP, made an immediate impression and became a radio hit—and not thanks to Universal marketing muscle or Maple's startup energy. It was because of Matt LeMay (not the *Pitchfork* writer with the same name), a random friend of Roberts from Pembroke with no music industry experience, who took it upon himself to promote the single to radio. "He started working Ottawa really hard and got some adds there, and then started working Montreal," says Bush. "This was as soon as the record was released. He beat these doors down and got adds. It was a good song, an undeniable song."

"Brother Down" opens with a simple minor-key electric guitar riff and a percussion instrument rarely heard in pop music since the 1970s: bongos. The arrangement is minimal: acoustic guitar, handclaps, big harmonies. The guitar solo has long, sustained notes played with an EBow. The lyrics tap into an anxiety both timeless and very much of the post-9/11 moment: "The only sound you hear is a closing door / been looking for peace but they're bringing you war." Then there's the refrain in the chorus, articulating an everlasting ennui: "I feel my life is passing me by." Roberts wrote it about his own diminishing chances at a career in music; ironically, it became the lyric that launched his career.

Once Montreal and Ottawa were on board, Universal pushed it to the rest of the country. "I was in Vancouver on vacation," says Allan Reid, head of Universal A&R at the time, "when 'Brother Down' had just been released to radio. I was driving down Granville, listening to CFOX, and the DJ goes, 'Every single time we play this song, the phones light up! This is Sam Roberts!' I called Linda and said, 'Everyone is talking about "Brother Down" out here.' She's like, 'Allan, it's happening *everywhere*.'"

It was soon obvious that Roberts was not a one-hit wonder: that six-song EP spawned two more radio hits, "Don't Walk Away Eileen" and "Where Have All the Good People Gone." The EP went on to sell 60,000 copies—unusual not only for a debut artist but for an EP, an uncommon marketing strategy at the time. "It was such a dry, boring time for Canadian music; it was still Céline and Shania," says Bush. "Sam was a breath of fresh air. I was surprised that everybody got it, but they did. And I feel like Sam started 20 years of beards. As soon as Sam had a beard, everyone did. Every commercial, every jean ad, everyone in Canada looked like Sam Roberts for at least six months. It was really a phenomenon. I honestly blame him!"

THE DEARS BROKE THE NO. 1 RULE of radio with "Heartless Romantic"—it fades *in*. The song is little more than a crushing dream beat, droning organ and Lightburn's massively distorted vocals; though there is bass, the song has a stark simplicity akin to Prince's "When Doves Cry." But most critics did little more than compare Lightburn to Morrissey.

For all of the Smiths' enduring cultural impact, there were very few singers who crooned in a similar style. But the Dears were not the Smiths. If anything, they were a unique Montreal take on the expansive, swirling space rock of Spiritualized or the Verve. And thankfully there was a lot more in the mix. Lightburn and Yanchak were weekly regulars at a francophone DJ night, C'est Extra, at the Cabaret Just for Laughs, where they'd hear plenty of Serge Gainsbourg, yé-yé and Stereolab. "We'd watch these young French kids partying their brains out to ['60s pop star] France Gall," says Lightburn. That wasn't happening in Halifax, Toronto, Calgary or Vancouver. It was, of course, happening in Quebec, and one of the Dears' first labelmates was Montreal garage-rock yé-yé band Les Séquelles.

In the summer of 2000, Stars' Torquil Campbell was splitting his time between New York City and Toronto, with no money, and was contemplating a move to Montreal. "I listened to *End of a Hollywood Bedtime Story* and it was life-changing," he recalls. "Suddenly there was someone in Canada who was versed in Serge Gainsbourg and Spiritualized and all this shit that was huge for me that no one else was really listening to at all. My parents were living in Montreal, so I moved in with them. I went to see the Dears at Cabaret. I went backstage and lay on the floor and prostrated myself in front of Murray Lightburn. I said, 'You're a fucking genius. You're incredible.' Which he is. And he [chuckled], 'I know, I know, I know.' He has never let me forget that."

End of a Hollywood Bedtime Story was only the third release from tiny Montreal label Grenadine. The first had been a national compilation of indie rock, *Syrup & Gasoline, Vol. 1*, which aimed to be a successor to the seminal *It Came from Canada* compilations put out by Montreal label Og Music in the '80s. This helped get the Dears national attention at campus. But promotional plans were stymied when the Dears played their first U.S. gig, at the invitation of Stars, for a showcase at the CMJ Music Marathon in New York City. Grenadine was supposed to ship a box of CDs, which never showed up. The Grenadine deal gave the label global rights to *Bedtime Story* and its follow-up. The Dears didn't want to trust their potential international career to two guys running a label out of a shared apartment.

Counterintuitively, the Dears then put their trust in *another* two guys in a tiny apartment, who ran the new Shipbuilding Records. That label released a four-song EP, *Orchestral Pop Noir Romantique*, recorded by Howard Bilerman. The EP almost sold out its entire run at a single Lee's Palace show in Toronto. The Dears were now being courted by major labels, but liked the idea of not being locked into anything. "Having that experience of not even being able to get out of an indie deal, we thought, How are we going to get out of a major deal?" says Yanchak. "That was the biggest level of foresight we ever had, that sense of not wanting to be trapped somewhere."

To get out of their Grenadine contract, the Dears agreed to let the label put out a compilation of the band's '90s cassette releases and demos, *Nor the Dahlias: The Dears 1995–1998*, which Lightburn disavowed in the album's own liner notes, somewhat embarrassed that his growing pains were now on display at a time when he was hitting his creative stride. The band was now managed by Jeff Rogers, who had guided the Pursuit of Happiness and Crash Test Dummies to international success.

Stuart Berman of *Eye Weekly* proclaimed the Dears "officially the best band in Canada" in advance of a sold-out Horseshoe gig in 2001. That October, they opened for Jane's Addiction at the Air Canada Centre, Toronto's hockey arena. Then Sloan brought them out across Ontario and Quebec as an opening act, and the Dears went west and back from there. Now audiences could see what the fuss was about, and the band delivered. Cellist Brigitte Mayes and guitarist Jonathan Cohen were added. "We quickly realized we had to bring our own sound person," says Yanchak, "because nobody knows what to do with keyboards. Or cellos. Or female vocals."

On the first night of the tour in Kingston, Ontario, a drunk Lightburn got into a playful backstage fight with Sloan's straight-edge bassist, Chris Murphy, and ended up tackling him into a pile of garbage and kissing him on the lips. "It was traumatizing for both of us," laughs Lightburn. "I was, and am still, a huge Sloan fan. When Chris first called my landline to offer us the tour, I couldn't believe I was talking to him. [Sloan's 1996 album] *One Chord to Another* was such a big deal. There must have been 15 guys in my apartment the day it came out, and we all worshipped that record." Later in the tour, after Lightburn's fandom became a bit more diplomatic, Murphy sat him down and gave him a history lesson about Sloan's ups and downs and running their own record label. "They went through a lot of shit, and it was all valuable information," says Lightburn. "He was a fountain of knowledge. Having that conversation with him at that time was crucial."

The Dears were getting ready to record new material that was even bigger in scope. Lightburn now had a seasoned band with him, including a rhythm section that was the envy of any musician who saw the live show. The album was going to be called *No Cities Left*, or "no shitties left," as he joked to friends.

SAM ROBERTS GOT a game-changing phone call in 2002 while in the middle of Lake Ontario shooting the video for "Brother Down." "We were on a boat and trying to make it look like the South Pacific," he says. "I was incredibly seasick that day. Only one person on our team had a cellphone, and they got a call from our manager saying the Tragically Hip had asked us to go on tour. I barfed right away." It wasn't just a few dates; it was a full national tour that fall to launch the new Hip album, *In Violet Light*. But the spring was a roller coaster of emotions: the night after a triumphant EP release show at Ted's Wrecking Yard, the Sam Roberts Band played Sin City in Peterborough to a total of one patron. (His name was Kevin; Roberts never forgot him.)

By the summer of 2002, the American press had rediscovered rock'n'roll that wasn't metal or grunge. More than most of his contemporaries, Roberts was a rock'n'roll believer testifying on stage every night, evangelizing, eager to please, and shouting, "I bleed rock'n'roll!" Audiences were hungry to hear it—and more so, Roberts figures, than they would have been if "Brother Down" had come out a year before.

"It was post-9/11," he says. "It's hard to overstate how profound that moment was on everything, how we all had this feeling that the way we lived before was not going to be a possibility anymore. It felt like the world had changed. I do feel that there are times where rock'n'roll music specifically can give you answers that other kinds of music can't. Or even just a feeling. It can either speak to your frustration or your optimism. We didn't consciously tap into that, but people were unconsciously looking for it. We weren't mystified about how the music was connecting."

Based on the buzz in Canada—both the *Inhuman Condition* EP and the CD single of "Brother Down" went gold in Canada, highly unusual for both formats— Roberts was soon signed to Universal in the States by exec Avery Lipman, who had signed Bloodhound Gang, 3 Doors Down and anarchist pop band Chumbawamba, who sold three million copies of their album in the U.S. "Sam will be the biggest male artist in the world," Lipman boasted to *Maclean's*. Looking back at that quote now, Roberts says, "The discrepancy between the more conservative opinions and hyperbole was quite wide at that point."

In some rare downtime, Roberts was in Montreal and dropped by a Dears recording session to play violin on *No Cities Left*.

THE DEARS FELT that signing to a Canadian major would be a kiss of death, that they should seek out a smaller or more flexible deal at home while pursuing international partnerships. That's why the Dears signed only a distribution deal with Universal for the *Orchestral Pop Noir Romantique* EP. "We didn't want to only break out in Canada," says Lightburn. "We wanted to go everywhere." That said, Lightburn's catastrophist streak was always looming over future plans in the wake of 9/11, least of all long-term record contracts. "I mean, there might not even be a world two years from now," Lightburn told the *Montreal Mirror*'s Lorraine Carpenter in 2003. "At least then we'd be released from the contract," added Yanchak.

They started recording *No Cities Left* with Sloan sound tech Brenndan McGuire, shortly after the Dears opened for Spiritualized in Toronto. But in the first week, guitarist Jonathan Cohen announced he was leaving, the very day he was supposed to lay down his parts. Lightburn quickly assumed sole guitar duties, creating multiple layers, playing until his fingers were swollen and McGuire insisted he stop.

The record ended up taking more than a year to finish, partly because of Lightburn's increasing perfectionism but also because McGuire was touring with Sloan while making Sam Roberts's debut album. "We knew it was big," says Lightburn. "We knew it was super ambitious and going to take a long time." They called in a horn section, featuring Stars' Evan Cranley, Chris Seligman and the mutual friend who'd introduced the two bands, trumpet player Matt Watkins. The Kingpins' Josh Fuhrman played sax. The 12 songs on *No Cities Left* were the 12 songs they demoed, in the same running order. "It has a very Kubrick-y approach to detail," says Lightburn. "I worked 18 hours a day, no problem."

Manager Jeff Rogers booked the band into Bryan Adams's Warehouse Studio in Vancouver to mix the record. The band foolishly didn't inquire about cost and got a bill for $8,000 after they left Rogers a few months later. "We were so green," says Lightburn. "It was weird being at the Warehouse and thinking that's just how things are supposed to sound. Then you come home and put it on your system, and it's like, 'Nope, not like that.' The whole band and some friends gathered in our living room, to listen to our masterpiece for the first time. I was in another room, listening from a distance, just thinking, 'Oh my god, what the fuck are we going to do.' This was the 'final' mix. When we finished listening, it was quiet. I think George was the first one to say, 'I don't know, man.' I was waiting for someone else to say that; I didn't want to be the super picky one."

Lightburn decided he had to start the mix from scratch. He took the tapes to Godspeed's studio, Hotel 2 Tango, which was co-run by his old friend Howard Bilerman and Godspeed's Efrim Menuck. The studio was booked fairly solid, but Bilerman gave Lightburn the same overnight session deal he gave Arcade Fire later that year. "I'd have to wait for Godspeed to finish their rehearsal at 11 p.m. so that I could do a graveyard shift mixing this record until three p.m. the next day. I'm crazy allergic to cats and there were three cats in there. I had to take wheeze breaks outside: just go outside and breathe for 20 minutes at a time."

It wasn't just Lightburn's allergies the cats messed with. "One was always hiding in the fucking piano," he says. "Every night around three a.m., I'd leave the control room to go make myself a coffee. The cats would run into the control room and get up to some bullshit, every time. This one time, I left the door open and I heard a crash. I started freaking out. I called Howard, left a message: 'The cats got in here and knocked over a vase with potpourri in it or something.' He's like, 'Those are the ashes of Efrim's dog!' Efrim showed up later that day, and I was convinced he hated my guts. We never talk about that now, even though I see him all the time, dropping our kids off at the bus stop. People were in and out of that studio constantly, but of course it only happens to me at three in the morning. It just added to the bullshit we went through making that record."

Eventually the band had a record but no deal and no guitarist. They held a meeting at St. Laurent watering hole La Cabane to discuss options. Outside the large bay windows, they saw Rob Benvie walk by. The former Thrush Hermit guitarist had just moved to Montreal to attend Concordia, after the dissolution of his band in 2000 and a brief solo career that didn't develop as well as that of his old bandmate, Joel Plaskett. The Dears rapped on the bar's large bay window and beckoned him in.

"Are you a good guitar player?" Lightburn challenged him.

"I'm the best," replied Benvie. He got the gig.

The guitarist moved into an apartment on Parc Avenue, north of Mont Royal, across the street from the Dears' central couple. "I was really into Benvie," says Lightburn. "I was into his playing, into him as a dude and a brain. He made me laugh. We hung out a lot, drank so much. He was at our house four or five days a week for dinner." His first gig with the Dears was in front of thousands at Quebec City's Festival d'été. His second and third were in front of thousands more, opening for the Tragically Hip at Toronto's Molson Amphitheatre.

Knowing that they wanted to find the right home for *No Cities Left*, the Dears headed back into the studio, with Benvie, to record a three-song EP, 2002's *Protest*, centred on the droning, ominous anthem "Summer of Protest," the most stirring piece of music they'd made up to that point, informed by the build-up to the Iraq War. Initially a tour-only item, it was packaged in 500 individually numbered, hand-cut aluminum sleeves made by Yanchak's father.

Universal A&R rep Dave Porter secretly pressed the CDs for them at his workplace, though the label had nothing to do with the recording or distribution. "He was very sweet to us," says Lightburn. "He was really trying to make something happen. I think there were a lot of [other] people [at Universal] who weren't convinced. Ultimately a deal did wind up in front of us, and we turned it down. Which sounds crazy, right? To dozens of bands at that time, it sounded like we lost our mind. But we didn't. Universal flew the whole band [to Toronto], put us up in a hotel, drove us to the Victoria Park office, met all these people, sat in [CEO] Randy Lennox's office—God bless them all. But there was something that was a little bit off about the whole thing. Whenever we started doing any kind of deals, we introduced term limits, never anything in perpetuity." Owning one's master recordings is now the norm for acts like the Dears. "But back then it was, 'Whoa, who do you think you are?' We started introducing performance-based options [into the contracts] that put pressure on [the label] to perform. I guess that's where we got the reputation of being 'hard to work with.'"

The band finally settled on a compromise: Universal-funded MapleMusic, who'd already scored with Sam Roberts. After the deal was signed, they started working with Nadine Gelineau, a manager who'd come up in Ottawa and Montreal campus radio in the '90s before working for major labels in the U.S. The Maple deal gave her freedom to, within the next year, sign deals for the Dears with U.K. label Bella Union (founded by the Cocteau Twins) and U.S. label SpinArt (home to Frank Black, the Apples in Stereo and the reformed Echo and the Bunnymen), as well as labels in Japan and Australia.

The hype and hyperbole around the Dears led to expectations of world domination, which was not anything anyone had expected from a Montreal band for a very long time. Gelineau was determined to make it happen. "She was super ambitious on our behalf," says Lightburn. "She really put a lot of chess pieces on the board for us. She'd always tell us, 'This is the most important gig of your life—again.'"

SAM ROBERTS WAS a proven pop entity with a major label deal, after Universal signed him directly from Maple. He hired his dream producer: Brenndan McGuire, who'd made Sloan's *One Chord to Another*. They rented an apartment together in Vancouver and made *We Were Born in a Flame* over three months. The Dears' Donoso played some drums, but as with *The Inhuman Condition*, Roberts and his producer played most of the instruments; the band played auxiliary roles on later overdubs. "I was just used to making music that way," says Roberts, "and I didn't want to tamper with whatever worked to get those songs out in the first place. The band was still finding its legs."

We Were Born in a Flame featured rerecordings of Roberts's three radio singles, as well as a curious song called "The Canadian Dream," with a bass line that nods to Pink Floyd's "One of These Days" and the chorus "S.O.C.I.A.L.I.S.M. is here to stay / S.O.C.I.A.L.I.S.M. is the only way." "It was definitely not a favourite song at our New York–based record label," laughs Roberts. Travelling to the States in general was fraught at the time, especially after Canada refused to join in the Iraq War. "We were crossing into New York when the war had just started; there was heightened security all over the place," he recalls. "We got stopped by a cop, and he was like, 'Where you guys from? Canada? You guys don't like freedom up there, huh?' We'd get that shit all the time. They were embarking on a new war, and now I had this song with a socialism chant in the middle of it."

Socialism aside, the American label was also unclear who they had signed exactly. They thought, based largely on "Brother Down," that Roberts was a laid-back surfer dude, like the hot new artist Jack Johnson. "Instead we were playing nine-minute-long, Spiritualized-inspired psychedelic jams at the end of every song," says Roberts. "There was now a possibility of being dropped before our record came out. There was already talk of a 'problem' brewing. Part of that was the record itself, maybe references to socialism." That would be a weird objection for the exec who signed Chumbawamba, but it seems the Americans were not prepared for a bunch of beardos playing jam rock.

Within two weeks of the album's U.S. release date, it was clear things were over. Universal Canada head Randy Lennox, "to whom I owe an enormous debt of gratitude," says Roberts, "stepped in and took our contract back from the U.S. in some master stroke of diplomacy. He moved very swiftly and saved the contract, and probably our careers."

Less than two months after the album came out, Sam Roberts stood on stage in Toronto in front of 500,000 people as the first act at SARSfest, headlined by the Rolling Stones, AC/DC and other mostly classic rock acts. "We were put on as the expression of the youth movement—when I was 30 years old," he laughs. They were given a 15-minute set, which they burned through with four minutes to spare. "That was my 11 minutes of fame, 11 minutes of the most mouth-drying, fear-inducing, fast-playing rock'n'roll we've ever done. Sheer adrenaline. But man, it was one thing after another then, all these things happening. You don't expect them to happen, but you get used to the pace of it. 'What momentous event is about to take place today?' Thankfully that doesn't last very long."

We Were Born in a Flame went platinum by the end of 2003. The songs were on the radio. By many accounts, the Sam Roberts Band upstaged the Tragically Hip on their tour together that fall, though the headliners didn't take it personally; Roberts and crew were often invited back over the next 15 years. In April 2004, Roberts scooped up Junos for Rock Album of the Year, Artist of the Year and Album of the Year. Not bad for a newbie at a ceremony notorious for being at least one generation away from relevancy.

That's a hard act to follow. And it wasn't easy.

THE DEARS FASCINATED their Toronto peers for being otherworldly: the intense and brooding Black rocker in a leather jacket, the muscular rhythm section, the francophones and, most of all, the air of defiance that naturally comes to Montreal musicians eternally suspicious of the Toronto elite. In an industry town where deals were made, the Dears showed up to the game but were not playing ball. Not unlike another beloved Montreal groundbreaker at the time. "There was this weird struggle of trying to keep it real and keep it pure," says Lightburn. "We joked about how we were Godspeed, but with singing. I absolutely admire their whole thing, how they've gotten away with that. Any time you're faced with any philosophical thing about your band, you just have to say, 'What would Godspeed do?'"

Like Godspeed, the Dears' ascent was very much due to their live show, word of mouth and ecstatic press. Also similar to Godspeed, Lightburn's relationship to the media was frayed from the outset. He gained a reputation for being painfully honest, both self-deprecating and outwardly critical. It started early on.

Before a Canadian Music Week show, MuchMusic sent a reporter backstage to interview the band. "Apparently I was in a mood," Lightburn recalls. "The host was saying, 'Do you guys hope to get signed?' I was like, 'Signed to what? *To WHAT?!*' I was super fucking pissed off that she even asked me that question. K-os saw that and told me later that he just loved it. 'Who is this guy? I have to know this guy!' At that point, every interview I was doing was terrible. I told someone, 'Michelangelo didn't have to do interviews.' They were like, 'Oh, you're comparing yourself to Michelangelo?' '*No, I'm not comparing myself to Michelangelo!!* The point is, Why should I be doing interviews?' I still have that feeling now." And yet he never wasted an opportunity to project his insecurities in the press. One particularly deep dive into his psyche, in a later article for the U.K.'s *Independent* newspaper, found a self-deprecating Lightburn repeatedly chugging cans of beer and then smashing them into his head. The article was titled "Big Mouth Strikes Again."

Speaking of big mouths with a prickly reputation in the press: Matthew Good. The month before *No Cities Left*'s release in April 2003, the Dears accepted an opening slot on a national tour with Good, who had just put out his first record after the bitter dissolution of his chart-topping, eponymous '90s band. "Kevin Drew called me and begged me to not do the tour," says Lightburn. In those days, his generation of bands was attempting to distinguish themselves from '90s CanRock. "We were trying to keep each other in check: 'Don't do that commercial!' Now, of course, we're all sucking dicks for everything. I told him, 'It's just people. It's just music.'"

Maybe so, but the dramatic art-rock of the Dears didn't always fly with Good's more mainstream audience, the "beer-soaked fans with backward baseball caps," as Lightburn described them to the *Montreal Gazette*. In the article, he compared the tour to a five-and-a-half-week one-night stand, with all the regret that entails. It was not a good time.

"God bless Matthew Good, but that tour was a spiritual beatdown, every day," Lightburn recalled years later. "Natalia threw a glass at me in the dressing room in

Winnipeg. It was awful. One day we pulled up to the venue in Ottawa, and [Good] was yelling at the drummer during soundcheck, saying, 'Do you even listen to music?' Which is the harshest thing you can say to a bandmate. Years went by and I spoke to Matt about it, and there was all kinds of weird stuff going on for him at that time. It was fucked up. We were just seeing the outside of it."

Near the end of the tour, in Toronto, Lightburn was booked to do a live interview on MuchMusic, mere weeks before *No Cities Left* came out. "Everyone at the label is super excited that we got this interview, because for our weird-ass band with our weird-ass album to get this was a big deal," he says. "They put me on TV with this person asking me questions like, 'Why is the album divided into part A and part B?' Which to me was the dumbest thing you could possibly ask me. That compounded with being in the green room beforehand and someone handing me a [review that] took a shit on *No Cities Left*, particularly the production. I took it very personally.

"I got hit with this two minutes before I went on TV to talk about the album. The whole time I'm having an existential crisis about what the fuck I'm even doing here on this tour that makes me want to blow my brains out daily, and now I'm talking to someone asking me about part A and part B and some guy just took a shit on a production job that I fucking busted my ass on. I get on the set, and I'm borderline catatonic with all the worst thoughts in my head. I'm surprised I didn't walk off. Instead I had this Velcro wallet, and I just kept ripping it open all through the interview. People in the industry were watching this happen, and they all thought it was terrible."

Lightburn was also in a bad mood at MuchMusic because Benvie had tendered his resignation the night before in Ottawa. "I was fucking devastated," says Lightburn on the death of all the bromance. "I cried. I couldn't handle it." Joseph Donovan, the band's guitar tech, took over on guitar until the end of the year. Bassist Martin Pelland's girlfriend, Valerie Jodoin-Keaton, joined on keyboards, flute and vocals.

Listening to *No Cities Left*, it's obvious Lightburn is drawn to drama. It opens with an absolutely stunning vocal performance, in which he explores his lower range overtop a Fender Rhodes keyboard and droning strings, before an upside-down beat and West African guitars enter the picture at the two-minute mark. Near the end of the song, a trumpet announces a countermelody, before all instruments except the strings drop out and leave Lightburn intoning, "It won't ever be what we want." Eventually a choir of voices joins and overtakes him. The whole thing sounds like a million bucks. And that's just the first song.

Strings and horns add foreboding heft throughout. The keyboards and sonics draw heavily from '70s Pink Floyd and sound just as big. The electric guitars swirl and dance and rage, while the acoustic guitars offer a warm counterpoint. Lightburn alternates between dramatic crooner and wild howler. At times it sounds like Scott Walker singing *OK Computer*—an album (far too) many post-Radiohead bands tried to emulate; the Dears are one of the few who came close. A track called "Who Are You, Defenders of the Universe?" is the rare rock song that works in 6/8 time. Melodicas that sound like Parisian violins hover over-top a dub reggae beat on "Postcard from Purgatory," before erupting into a *Led Zeppelin II*–style rave-up, while a flute weaves a countermelody underneath the crashing guitars. The epic "Never Destroy Us" concludes with a 30-second hard-core punk outburst of "Destroy! Destroy! Destroy! Destroy!" Amid all this, there are two bona fide pop singles: the string-drenched duet "22: The Death of All the Romance" and the anthemic "Lost in the Plot," with a bridge even better than its chorus, a lyric of love as defiance in a paranoid age: "Our love / don't mess with our love / our love is so much stronger."

The *Montreal Gazette* gave it a five-star rating and predicted world domination. Stuart Berman in *Eye Weekly* wrote, "While the album boasts some of the band's signature suicide symphonies, it's more about raising fists than slitting wrists . . . Those of you who've been waiting three years for the Dears to drop the bomb may now assume the air-raid position." It caused the Dears' peers to up their game. "I remember hearing *No Cities Left*," says Broken Social Scene's Brendan Canning, "and thinking, Ah man, we gotta make a record at least as good as this one."

In the year of the album's release, the Dears focused on Canada: two national headlining tours, plus the opening slot on the Matthew Good tour. There were only a fistful of U.S. shows, including one in Central Park opening for Rufus Wainwright and Daniel Lanois. It was a scramble to get to: 12 hours before that gig, they were in Vancouver hoping to fly out of Seattle at six a.m., but an immigration snafu with their booking agent meant they had to eat the cost of the flight, buy new flights to Montreal and then rent a van and drive to NYC for the after-noon gig. Miraculously they made it.

Twelve days later, the highest-profile press they got in the U.S. was a dismissive *Pitchfork* review that belittled the Britpop references, as the writer displayed an unusual familiarity with the work of C-list Britpop band Gene. In Canada, press was great but radio refused to bite, and the album peaked at 18,000 copies sold.

In 2004, however, the international assault began with a U.S. West Coast tour with Stars. Guitarist Patrick Krief joined the week before they left, after only two rehearsals. *No Cities Left* came out in the U.K. in October 2004; there, the Dears were much more easily understood and appreciated. Reviewing the album in advance of two showcase gigs in May, the *NME* called them "probably the best new band in the world right now." Had that ever been said in the British press about a Canadian band? It was enough to convince Alex James of Blur to show up at the Dears' London gig. (Not Graham Coxon, but that's fine.)

The band parlayed that good press into a full British tour that September and a European tour in November. They also opened for Morrissey at Toronto's Hummingbird Centre and in L.A. in front of 30,000 people. Despite bristling at being constantly referred to as "Black Morrissey" in the press, Lightburn was beyond thrilled to meet his teenage hero. By the time they returned to the U.K. in early 2005, most shows were sold out, including one at Manchester Academy. "I was almost in tears when I found out we sold it out," says Lightburn. "When I was a teenager, and poring over the Smiths records, I never dreamed in a million years that I, from my shitty little house in Brossard, Quebec, would ever, ever even wind up in Manchester, let alone play a sold-out gig there. That blew my mind." *No Cities Left* sold more than 50,000 copies in the U.K.—which is more per capita than it did in Canada—and another 40,000 in the U.S.

SAM ROBERTS LOVED TO SURF, and he wanted to make his next record somewhere he could do that.

On tour with the Tragically Hip in L.A., Roberts met producer Mark Howard, who had made the Hip's 1994 classic *Day for Night*, as well as many records with Daniel Lanois. They started talking about surfing and recording. Howard suggested Australia and mentioned that he could ask world champion surfer Kelly Slater for recommendations. Roberts was starstruck and invited Howard to Montreal to hear some demos. Howard wasn't impressed by the three songs, or by Roberts's drummer, but told Roberts that Slater had recommended Byron Bay, the easternmost tip of Australia, with seven surf breaks. He'd also found an abandoned church there that was available to rent; part of Howard's job for Lanois had been setting up studios in unusual pockets of North America, including a Mexican cave.

Roberts was in. He told Universal he was going to visit extended family in South Africa and would write the rest of the record there. The label was nervous. A&R rep Allan Reid was worried that going to Australia was going to be the most expensive surf holiday ever. Promises were made—and broken. Reid was right.

Howard arrived in Australia with a bare minimum of gear, getting the rest from his friends in Midnight Oil. Roberts arrived in Australia with a bare minimum of new songs, i.e., none. His friend Matt Mays, a Halifax musician beginning to break through on Canadian rock radio, was also in Australia on a surf vacation. The two of them tackled six-metre waves every morning. Every afternoon, Mays hung around the studio and encouraged the creatively stuck Roberts. A week later, the rest of the band showed up, along with a new drummer. The surrounding environs were full of pythons, deadly spiders, frogs in the toilet and great white sharks close to the beach. Twelve songs were tracked, each one usually written, rehearsed and recorded in the same day.

Allan Reid flew over to hear it. "We took him out to the beach, showed him around," says Roberts. "The place is magical. Macadamia nuts, the bluest water, kookaburras waking you up. We made him a big dinner, drank a lot of wine, got him nice and primed. Then we pulled out these couches and lined them up in this amazing old 19th-century rural church. We thought, If anyone has ever been in the right frame of mind to listen to new music, it's right now. We played the opening song, 'The Gate,' which has this slow, jammy build and breaks into these punches. It's a reveal. Everything is going according to plan. Allan opens his eyes, nods at everyone and says, 'Guys, this rocks. Sounds great.' We're like, 'Yes, we got him!'

"Then as the record goes on, we're into the long jam in song number four"—a turgid eight-minute epic called "Mind Flood"—"and we could tell that he's listening for something that isn't there, namely a single. Meanwhile, in our mind, we're like, 'How's he going to choose a single? There's at least seven or eight.' That, of course, became our sticking point. Not to mention that if you listen to the record at less than 110 decibels, you could tell that there were some holes in the recording. We went back and the label was like, 'It's not ready.'" The album was rerecorded at home in Montreal.

The album, *Chemical City*, went gold by the end of 2006 but was considered a disappointment both in Canada and with his new U.S. label, Lost Highway. Roberts spent less time on the road and nine months in a Montreal studio—with old friend Joseph Donovan of Marlowe producing—on 2008's *Love at the End of the World*. It came out in the States on Rounder Records. "We had this unusually long and loving and trusting relationship with our label, Universal Canada," he says. "Whereas in the U.S., we're playing musical chairs, different labels all the time. To this day, every time we put out a record in the States we're starting some new relationship. It's been one of the more challenging aspects of the business side, to find that consistency. Every time you start with a new label, there is all this optimism and excitement, but it takes half a record cycle to get to know each other—and maybe find out you don't like each other. But some of our most diehard, loyal fans are south of the border."

Roberts was a big fan of the new school of Canadian acts that appeared shortly after he did: Broken Social Scene, Constantines and Arcade Fire were all inspirations. But he didn't hang out with them, unless he saw them at a festival. As for Montreal specifically, "There was a whole new crop sitting in the chairs at the

Bifteck and eating popcorn," he says. "That was the changing of the guard, but I didn't stick around to watch what happened."

BEFORE A GIG IN BRUSSELS IN EARLY 2005, Natalia Yanchak learned she was pregnant. She announced it to the band a few weeks later in Australia. By this point, their touring schedule was relentless; some members were relieved that her pregnancy would necessitate some time off. That didn't happen right away: they did two American tours and another U.K. and European jaunt, as well as a quick detour to Japan and some summer festivals. Her pregnancy didn't change the band's behaviour; Lightburn lamented to the *Globe and Mail* that the band's excess on the road had reached Mötley Crüe levels.

The roller coaster ride had to be shut down; they turned down a tour with Beck, because by then Yanchak was in her third trimester. They closed their own tour with a triumphant hometown show at Montreal's Spectrum in July, and Yanchak gave birth in September—20 days after marrying Lightburn. They bought a house in the Parc Ex neighbourhood, building a studio in a backyard shed where they recorded the next album—because, among other reasons, Lightburn didn't want to be working 16-hour days in a studio with a newborn. When the album was done, the band voted five to one to fire manager Nadine Gelineau; Lightburn was the holdout, and he still considers it "the dumbest thing we ever did." In spring 2006, they were playing Coachella and getting ready to release *Gang of Losers* in the late summer.

"I don't know if you're going to like it," Lightburn told *Montreal Gazette* writer T'Cha Dunlevy, adding that he was telling everyone the same thing. *Gang of Losers* ditches almost all the fine detail of *No Cities Left*, no doubt in part a result of years of touring as a guitar-heavy band, with shredder Patrick Krief taking a central role. "There are certain things we were just not going to do on this album," Lightburn told the *Gazette*. "One was violins. Another was the huge, sweeping orchestral stuff we've done in the past. We wanted to push the band forward. It was six people making as much noise as they can." The only real nod to the past is a French horn part, played by Stars' Chris Seligman, on "Ballad of Humankindness."

Lightburn went to Europe to do press before the album release, 10 hours a day for 10 days. The *New Musical Express*, which had fawned over the Dears two short years ago, tried repeatedly to get Lightburn to shit-talk Arcade Fire, which he refused to do. *NME* ended up not running a piece or even reviewing the album. It did, however, get five stars in the *Guardian* and four in both *Uncut* and *Mojo*. Despite plenty of touring in Europe that year, album sales didn't meet expectations, and they were dropped from Bella Union, who reportedly weren't fond of the guitar-heavy turn the band had taken.

The Dears had become a side note in a story they helped write. International attention heaped down on Montreal in the wake of Arcade Fire's success; most, not all, stories took care to mention the Dears, but the focus was on a new generation. The Dears were never home long enough to know who most of these new bands were. "We missed so much that was happening, because we were out," says Lightburn. "I saw the *Spin* story [on the Montreal scene] when I was at JFK [airport in New York City]. I picked it up and said, 'What the fuck is this?!' When the *New York Times* story came out, we were in England. I had no idea Montreal was blowing up. We'd come home for four or five days and then be gone again for four or five months. When there was a lull between tours, our manager would get us a house by the beach, or shitty hotel rooms by LAX, and we'd be stuck there before a West Coast tour started.

"One time we were home, and [Pop Montreal's] Dan Seligman dragged me out to a show. It was in some weird space that wasn't a venue, very Montreal at the time. We Are Wolves were playing and the place was packed, sweat dripping off the wall, and the band was crushing it. I felt like a caveman waking up in the future."

It wasn't like the Dears weren't doing well. In North America, the gigs kept getting better, and they even played David Letterman's show, a total rarity for Canadian indie bands. *Gang of Losers* was shortlisted for the Polaris Music Prize in June 2007. The band spent 11 months on the road in total.

The band now had two couples—bassist Pelland and keyboardist Jodoin-Keaton tied the knot shortly before the album release—but it was not sunshine and roses. There was tension between the two married couples; Donoso sided with the francophones and Krief was caught in the middle. Communication had hit an all-time low, and there was now a toddler in tow. Money also became an issue when Lightburn, who claimed all songwriting credit, signed a publishing deal. Donoso claimed to be making more money DJing in Montreal than he did touring with the Dears in Europe. Meanwhile, Lightburn and Yanchak turned down lucrative corporate gigs that the rest of the band wanted to do. During a band meeting conference call about whether or not to take a gig in Istanbul, Lightburn hung up in disgust. Some Dears had started a separate project, which Lightburn and Yanchak only learned about by stumbling across its MySpace site. Everything came to a head in July 2007 on the band's first trip to Mexico City, where they played a sold-out venue in front of thousands.

"We hated each other," says Yanchak. "We went to Mexico with no expectations. We got there, and it was the most insane audience ever. They knew all the words and were singing along. We were like, 'What the hell?' It makes me sad that we were so fragmented that we couldn't enjoy it together and see how positive it was. But it was definitely inspiring."

"In my mind, I had quit the band many times," says Lightburn, who suffered from coughing fits and panic attacks that year. "I thought of telling everyone I was done. After the first gig in Mexico, I came to realize that was not going to happen. I think [those shows] had that effect on the whole band, but it was too late by that point. It was too far gone. I felt petered out in terms of how much I'd shared with these people for so long. I had a super selfish view of these people. It makes being in a band really hard, when you're in a group of people who are like children. You're always in the position where you're making a huge sacrifice to make them happy all the time. Natalia and I had done that for years and years: making sure everyone else could pay their rent, and then we couldn't pay our rent."

Some friends felt the seeds of dissolution had been planted years earlier. Said one, "As soon as I read the liner notes for *No Cities Left* and it said, 'Produced, written and directed by Murray Lightburn,' I thought, That's it, he just killed his own band. It's the biggest no-no. It's how to demotivate your entire band in one easy step: by taking all the credit."

There was never any doubt among the core couple that the Dears would continue in some fashion, with or without everyone else. In the fall of 2007, Lightburn announced that he was going to make another Dears record, the much more subdued *Missiles*. Donoso and Krief agreed to stick around for the recording. Rob Benvie also came back, as did *Bedtime Story* bassist Roberto Arquilla. None of them, however, wanted to tour. And so, just as in 2000, Lightburn and Yanchak had a completed Dears album but had no band. They recruited five newbies for the tour, including guitarist Chris McCarron from Land of Talk (and later of Stars). "There's a spirit that inhabits the Dears," Lightburn told Lorraine Carpenter, "and when you become a part of the Dears, you're basically walking into a haunted house and anything can happen."

Things did happen. "It was me and Natalia and a bunch of people who had never been in a co-ed band before," says Lightburn, referring in part to the fact that two new members had played in the all-female Pony Up. "We came home from that tour, and half the band was saying, 'I have feelings for this other person in the band.' I'm like, 'What?! Fuck off! You gotta be kidding me.' So much drama, after just one tour. I had to nip it in the bud immediately. They literally had no friends of the opposite sex, and they were getting these feelings confused with romantic feelings and [were] not mature enough to handle it."

"Touring is quite intimate," says Yanchak, "and you're with these people all the time. The tour was super fun but clouded by this weird, unnecessary high school drama. We tried to keep it from imploding—as Mom and Dad do." The band was "honourably discharged" in 2009.

Again, the Dears showed no signs of quitting. New drummer Jeff Luciani arrived, and Arquilla, Benvie and Krief all contributed to 2011's return to form, *Degeneration Street*, which was recorded in L.A. and produced by Tony Hoffer (Belle and Sebastian, Beck, Phoenix), the one and only time the Dears spent money on a producer. It got them enough buzz to land another Letterman gig but no level of success they didn't already have. The next decade was spent with ever-changing lineups—Luciani and the core couple being the only constants. The records were lower profile, Lightburn released solo albums, and then in 2020 came the album *Lovers Rock*, which was widely hailed as their best record since *No Cities Left*.

Critics revisiting the band's 2003 masterpiece took note that the title track of that record opens with the lines: "Let's just keep fighting the end / We're holding hands / We're making plans / For life."

CHAPTER 9
NOW MORE THAN EVER

ROYAL CITY, THE HIDDEN CAMERAS, CONSTANTINES, JIM GUTHRIE, OWEN PALLETT, THREE GUT RECORDS

Toronto: Canada's music industry town. There are playbooks and accepted rules. One of them is: don't piss off your audience. Give them what they expect. Fit into a mould, whether that's pop music or math rock, singer-songwriter or hip-hop MC—it doesn't matter. Keep it predictable. Show them something they can sell.

Mind you, Toronto has always been weirder than most people thought. Its thriving underground has often been left out of official histories. In 2000, several threads were pulled together from the art scene, the queer scene, the activist scene and by a bunch of small-town folks who treated the Toronto music business like an art project. A sense of possibility and freedom bubbled up, and suddenly the cold corporate heart of Canada felt a lot more welcoming.

"Until the moment I moved to Toronto, I wouldn't have thought that I was headed there," says Constantines' Bry Webb, who grew up in southwestern Ontario farm country. His band signed to Three Gut Records, a new unconventional label, in early 2001. "I never really wanted to live in Toronto. But Three Gut was such a strong community. It seemed like rather than living in a small town to have a sense of community, you could build your own community in any place."

Three Gut had crossover with the Hidden Cameras, who preferred to play in art spaces rather than clubs. Ex–Hidden Cameras in turn spawned the Blocks Recording Club co-operative, who started loosely defining a concept called "Torontopia." Torontopia was easily misunderstood, because it was meaningless—or rather as meaningful as you wanted it to be.

"The way people talked about Torontopia wasn't in purely musical terms," says Jonny Dovercourt, who co-founded the Wavelength Music series—named after a 1967 film by Toronto artist and musician Michael Snow, a key figure in the city's avant-garde history. "We talked about how one lives in the city, your personal relationship to where you're from as an artist and a citizen. It becomes more universal in that sense, and not something that only musicians can take a lesson from."

By 2003, Toronto was finally rid of mayor Mel Lastman (an international laughingstock) and premier Mike Harris (whose policies hobbled Toronto for decades after), and a new generation was determined to remake Toronto in its own image, to ensure that Toronto would never be an embarrassment again. (No one anticipated the Ford family.) Three Gut Records, founded in Guelph, had unintentionally changed conversations about what Toronto could be. Likewise, the Hidden Cameras was a solo project that became a social club, connecting several different scenes. Blocks Recording Club, and the concentric circles surrounding it, aimed to be hyper-local, even as one of its founders became internationally acclaimed.

It was Blocks' Steve Kado who first put the word *Torontopia* on a show poster. It was mostly meant as an ironic joke about the mundanity of the major Canadian city that was not Montreal. But he also saw it as imbuing a sense of permission: to not wait for recognition from the city's cultural institutions, to create new models, to stage shows in parks or under bridges or wherever possible.

Wavelength—a pay-what-you-can weekly night founded in February 2000 by Dovercourt, Derek Westerholm and Duncan MacDonell—was Torontopian before the term existed, aiming to showcase acts not (yet) covered in the media and to cross-pollinate sounds. "Wavelength started with a small group of people taking a good hard look at itself," says Dovercourt, whose series featured most of the Toronto artists mentioned in this book. "In terms of our acceptance and recognition from the rest of the world, all we did was complain about the lack of it. That led to this sentiment of, 'Oh, because we're in Toronto, Toronto sucks.'

"We thought we shouldn't blame Toronto; we should blame ourselves for giving up in advance. Maybe we're not giving the rest of the city enough reason to care. Maybe we need to figure out how to generate more excitement around what we're doing. That was the purpose of Wavelength: let's celebrate our own music, let's celebrate our rich history that goes undocumented, let's celebrate the cool stuff that's going on here under the radar. There wasn't one nexus to the music scene; we realized we had to create it."

Torontopia was soon used loosely to describe everything from DJ Will Munro's queer visions to the mainstream success of civic boosters Broken Social Scene to the surprise 2003 election of leftist mayor David Miller to the December 2004 launch of the urban-affairs magazine *Spacing*. In 2005, Coach

House Books (founded in the idealism of '60s Yorkville) published an essay collection called *uTOpia*.

Little of that had anything directly to do with Wavelength or Three Gut or Blocks. But Blocks' motto was "Don't try, do!" One song by Barcelona Pavilion, sung by Kado and fellow ex–Hidden Camera Maggie MacDonald, was titled "How Are You People Going to Have Fun If None of You People Ever Participate?" "What was exciting about what some people were calling Torontopia at the time was that it had to do with doing things for yourself," says Kado. "That was the only way to participate in that experience. You really couldn't relax about it and think, 'Don't worry, they have it taken care of.' Because then you weren't having any of the fun. Then you weren't invited to the party."

In this environment it didn't seem so strange to discover a solo violinist applying classical technique and modern wizardry to absurdist yet emotionally resonant pop music. Or a guy who looks like Buddy Holly leading 12 people on stage with balaclava-clad topless male dancers. Or the fiercest rock'n'roll band with a poet at the centre. Or a fragile folk singer suddenly barking at the audience. Was this really Toronto? It was now.

<hr>

THE INDIE ROCK singer sits on stage, playing delicate, hushed guitar. The musicians behind him tread lightly; the drummer in particular is deliberately sparse. The lyrics are plain-spoken and earnest, with poetic detail. There are Biblical and Shakespearian references for those paying attention—for those who even *can* pay attention. The Toronto audience is typically talkative, the bar populated by industry types and hipsters who want to be seen more than they want the music to be heard.

Suddenly the singer unleashes a blood-curdling howl; the rest of the band follows suit. The music careens instantly from lullaby to gale-force wind and then back again. The crowd is stunned. Annoyed. Confused. Some are intrigued and lean in to listen closer. Wait, what did that guy just sing? "My beloved, you are a snapping crocodile."

Royal City's bandleader, Aaron Riches, was a teen punk drummer and show promoter before turning to Pete Seeger–esque folk music and then to the fractured folk-rock that became Royal City. The first album, in 2000, was titled *At Rush Hour the Cars*—a sentence fragment, like all the titles on the album, pulled from the first lyric of each song. The artwork featured a simple, child-like pencil drawing. The album opened with a long organ drone, not exactly "focus track" material for radio programmers or critics. Its love songs had choruses like "Sojourn yourself with me." Shows were promoted with wax-sealed envelopes hung from clothes-lines at key spots around the city. Their record label was run by two women, one of whom treated the business as an art project.

Everything about Royal City and Three Gut Records was unusual in the Toronto of 2000. "We didn't have a clue about anything," says Lisa Moran. "It wasn't like we thought we were being big rule-breakers. It was just what we were going to try."

Very early on in the label's history, Moran and founder Tyler Clark Burke went to the NXNE conference, where they heard Peter Jenner give a keynote address. Jenner was a Brit who, among other things, discovered Pink Floyd in 1966, helped launch the Notting Hill Carnival that same year and managed Billy Bragg for 30 years. "You break all the rules in the beginning because you don't know what they are," he told the audience. "Then the more you're in the business, you can't break the rules because people say, 'You know better than that.'"

LIKE ANY OF THE BEST PUNKS OF THE '90S, Aaron Riches grew up worshipping Fugazi. He even booked shows for them in Toronto and in his hometown of Guelph. His own bands, first Burn 51 and later Minnow, were the opening acts. Minnow played Ontario, the northern U.S. and Germany; Riches was a gig hustler who was always open to adventure.

Near the end of high school, he became interested in punk's antifascist pre-decessors in folk music: Woody Guthrie, Pete Seeger—not very popular names in youth culture in 1995 when Riches put out his first solo album, *Over the Lamp Post*. That record came out on local Guelph label DROG, home of the Rheostatics. He formed a small collection of players to bring it to life, including 16-year-old violinist Liz Powell, who formed Land of Talk many years later. Within weeks of releasing his second solo album, *Rain*, in 1998, produced by Black Cabbage's Nick Craine, he was ready to bury it and move in a whole new direction.

Fascinated by the no-fucks-given attitude of Bob Dylan and Will Oldham, Riches started purposely breaking his voice, singing like a pubescent. His music became less authoritative and more vulnerable. His new songs took the directness of his punk days and applied them to romance and longing; his love of T.S. Eliot made Riches's lyrics much more fascinating than the boy next door with a broken heart. "Eliot is such a fragile figure," says Riches. "His later poetry is so serene and understated and mystical, but doesn't mind being quotidian. That helped give me a frame from which to write the songs."

Riches had moved to Toronto for school in 1998, into a house at 9 St. Patricks Square, in the shadow of the MuchMusic building. His roommates were members of King Cobb Steelie, a Guelph band 10 years his senior who'd graduated from being campus radio darlings to being the black sheep of EMI Canada's roster. Riches's new songs ached with the displacement of a small-town boy in the big city, who reads Russian literature while pining for a beloved.

Her name was Tyler Clark Burke, who studied art at the University of Guelph and fashion in Toronto before spending a year in New England coping with chronic fatigue. ("Get well, get well / and rage like a stallion," sang Riches.) Burke's father was an American film scholar who specialized in Fellini; when her dad met the Italian director for an interview, Burke drew hundreds of clowns for him, which he autographed. She sought to bring a bit of Fellini's controlled chaos to everything she did. The next few years of Riches's career would not have happened without her.

He started recording a new album with Jim Guthrie and James Ogilvie, who lived in a Guelph house known as the RokSak. Live shows were held in the basement; it was the site for a variety of home recordings from a young generation of Guelph musicians obsessed with Sebadoh, Eric's Trip and the like. Guthrie was the centre of the scene. His campus radio show was called the *Home Rock Explosion*, the slogan of which was "home is where the rock is"—also the title of Guthrie's debut 1995 cassette release.

That was the year Palace Brothers' Will Oldham reinvented himself as Bonnie Prince Billy and released *I See a Darkness*, in which the oddball American songwriter cleared away some of the sonic cobwebs of his earlier work. Riches's new songs were in a somewhat similar musical vein as Oldham's. Guthrie was intrigued. "It was a total 180 from everything," says Guthrie. "Aaron had figured out exactly what he wanted to do. The songs got really simple and the writing was very clear, almost like a children's book."

Riches didn't know Guthrie well; the latter was a homebody, preferring to record as much music at home as possible rather than play it live. Riches was gigging with electric guitarist Evan Gordon, the 15-year-old son of Guelph folk legend James Gordon. Most of Guelph's indie community contributed to Riches's new record in some small way. Nathan Lawr, frustrated with his role as the latest drummer in King Cobb Steelie, one day got a call to play a simple shuffle, which was eluding both Riches and Guthrie, on a song called "Baby Let Your Heart Out." Everything was going well—until all the sessions, stored on ADAT tapes, got erased by accident. "I don't know if it was inexperience or a total machine fuckup, but it was devastating," says Lawr. "It was a good early lesson in not getting married to things." It also proved to be a good omen, facilitating a complete rebirth.

Meanwhile, Guthrie had assembled material from years of cassettes and released his first CD, *A Thousand Songs*, in the summer of 1999. He wanted to put a label name on it to make it sound official. He asked Tyler Clark Burke to draw him a logo; when she learned that his childhood friends called him "Jimmy Three-Guts" (an inversion of his surname), she told him the label should be called Three Gut.

They mailed *A Thousand Songs* out to campus radio. Guthrie's mind was blown when Patti Schmidt at CBC's *Brave New Waves* became a big supporter. It wasn't unfounded: Guthrie's home recordings displayed an unusual amount of technique for a self-taught musician. His eclectic ear incorporated everything from pots and pans and toy pianos to cut-and-paste sound collage to heartbreaking bedroom ballads. It was part Ween, part Elliott Smith, like Paul McCartney jamming with Can for a Wim Wenders soundtrack, conflating tiny moments of intention and accidents and daring the listener to tell the difference. It was profoundly curious and not at all precious. For every moment of sublime beauty, there's a moment where Guthrie might be heard screaming into a crappy microphone, "Wama-lama-ding-dong-*wooooo-EEEEEE-woooo!*"

Guthrie assembled a band to play a couple of shows around Guelph—Evan Gordon on guitar, Simon Osborne on bass, Nathan Lawr on drums, James Ogilvie on keyboards—known as the Jim Guthrie Quintet. When they all contributed to Riches's new session, they also became known as the Royal City All-Stars. Ogilvie and Gordon eventually dropped out, and the band became known simply as Royal City, a nod to Guelph's official nickname since 1879, and its overall history: the town was named after Saxon ancestors of German and British monarchy.

The name was also a link to Riches's past: Guelph was where everyone in the musical community knew him, where he had strong connections to the campus station and to the folkie Hillside Festival, which Burn 51 had been the first punk band to play. In Toronto, he was a small fish in a big pond. "I remember feeling like I wouldn't trust anyone who wasn't from Guelph," he says. "The Guelphites were our safety blanket. In a big city that is a bit insecure and bureaucratic and full of social climbing, these small-town guys ran together and were friends. We really loved each other." There was also the shared house at 9 St. Patricks Square where, at various times, most of the Three Gut community lived and rehearsed.

Riches learned that playing shows in Toronto as a singer-songwriter was a lot more difficult than booking DIY punk shows across two continents. "One of the first shows Aaron had in Toronto was at the Cameron House," says Burke. "Two people showed up, who came accidentally and left after a couple of songs. It was heartbreaking." She saw Riches's career as a problem that could be solved. When Riches saw her logo for Guthrie's record, he decided that Three Gut should be a real label. The first three acts would be Guthrie, Royal City and their friend

"Gentleman" Reg Vermue, who in 1998 had assembled *The Goods*, a compilation CD that served as a perfect time capsule of the concentric rings around Jim Guthrie's "home rock" explosion. All the affiliated musicians, as well as Burke and Lisa Moran, who was Aaron Riches's manager, met at Guelph's Bookshelf Café and signed a document, agreeing to pony up $50 each in startup capital. Three Gut Records was officially born.

Burke's first order of business was getting attention for Royal City any way possible. She took out Missed Connections ads in *Now* magazine, in which fictional lovers made plans to meet at a Royal City show. Her day job was as a graphic designer at *Eye Weekly*; she'd use their printer to make 500 posters with only an image, no text. She and Gentleman Reg blitzed the town with them, then went back the next week with another 500 that had the same image plus info about a Royal City show.

She also decided to pin envelopes containing show flyers on a clothesline between two trees on Queen Street West. "I'd go hang up the strings, then hide around the corner and watch people open them," she says. "I would see the delight on their faces. We went from having two people at the Cameron to having 50 people at the Cameron. Between that, the posters, the ads in *Now*—if we could get people to hear about the band three different ways in two weeks, that third way might make them go to the show."

There was not yet a Royal City or Gentleman Reg record to promote, but there was Guthrie's *A Thousand Songs*—and an invitation from Leslie Feist. Feist played guitar in By Divine Right, who were all big fans of Guthrie, and had completed her first solo album, *Monarch*. She booked Guthrie to open for her at the Rivoli, a joint CD release party in August 1999. Feist and Burke met to discuss the poster and quickly became best friends. To promote the show, Burke once again used her clothesline method, this time with wax-sealed envelopes. "It was an installation art project," says Burke. "We put 1,000 invitations around town, outside a mix of record stores and key targets: Brendan Canning's house, the Sadies' house, the *Globe and Mail* or a building where all the entertainment lawyers worked." Within weeks, Three Gut had a lawyer and a distributor.

Burke lived in a large warehouse space south of King and Portland that she'd found through friends of Riches in the hardcore scene. "It was me and four vegan guys who listened to death metal and only ate pasta," she says. "All of them were sweethearts." In an adjacent loft was the "activist pod," featuring future Hidden Cameras Maggie MacDonald and Dave "Mez" Meslin. Richard Reed Parry, later of Arcade Fire, spent a lot of time there with mutual friends, silkscreening T-shirts. "There were six people living there, but it was never clear who exactly was paying rent," says MacDonald. "It was super cheap. A rotating cast of characters. No one had a key. People would book our space for an anarchist book club, or puppet making, without us even knowing. When the Battle in Seattle happened, Naomi Klein came to our house to debrief us on what she experienced. All the people in Toronto who went to Seattle came to our house, and Naomi passed the mic."

The two groups of neighbours organized two massive parties in the courtyard between them. The first was a "Heaven and Hell" Halloween party, with large props and decorations, and then on March 4, 2000 ("march4ward" read the invite), a party dubbed "The Aliens Have Landed," which culminated in a papier mâché spaceship descending on the courtyard, filled with Three Gut paraphernalia. The members of Royal City were somewhat begrudgingly enlisted in the arts and crafts of it all. "We had to build spaceships and shit, and then clean up afterwards," says Riches. "I cursed her half the time for it. Everything with Tyler was such a crazy production, because no matter what, you worked like hell until the very last minute. If there was an extra 15 minutes, she'd get an idea for another crazy fucking thing. But those parties were as fun as any of the shows we ever played."

If you were between the ages of 25 and 30 in 1999 and 2000 and/or frequented Toronto rock clubs or art galleries, you were likely at one of these parties. They were bacchanalian, ecstatic affairs, which didn't really line up with the subdued music of Three Gut, but they were very effective at making an impression. "It was about pulling together a community," says Lisa Moran, who had nominally been Riches's manager since his second solo album. "Tyler knew a million different interesting people who were creative, interesting artists and musicians, people who wanted to be involved. It pulled different circles of weird, cool people together. Then maybe people thought, Oh, that party we went to, those people work with that band Royal City."

"Tyler had an art project," says Riches. "Royal City was a part of it. Three Gut was a part of it. Her drawings were a part of it. Her parties were a part of it. Everything she did fit into a unity that was a single art project."

Riches, too, was determined to conquer Toronto with small victories. "I've never played in a city that cares less about live music," he said in a 2000 *Eye Weekly* cover story. "It's all people who are on the guest list, people employed by a record company or publicity company. They come in, and they just talk. It could be Patti Smith up there singing, and they don't even fucking notice." (The punk icon played a surprise set at the Rivoli that year in front of a chatty crowd.) "Our job in that scenario," said Riches, "is to get people to listen. If we have to throw a shit fit on stage, we'll do what we need to. Sometimes we have to be downright alienating to do that. And sometimes we have to be downright engaging."

That sometimes meant playing so quietly that the audience was compelled to lean in and listen. Sometimes it meant encouraging them to sing along, hootenanny style, to painfully plain if lovely platitudes, like the chorus of a song that went, "Your naked body is so beautiful," or "C-I-T-Y Royal City."

Then there was the barking. Riches often howled in the middle of a song, which was jarring to say the least. "I don't think I necessarily understood at the time what Aaron was doing," says Moran, "or what kind of statement he was making to people not paying attention. It was compelling. Sometimes there would be these screaming moments in these weird, quiet sets."

"We had a fearless attitude," says Lawr, "which is a weird attitude to have for real quiet music. My favourite example was playing at the Blue Rodeo picnic at Fort York. We were on the side stage. There was nobody around, nobody paying attention. We just started making noise as loudly as we could, it drew a crowd, and then we started playing our regular set. It felt like we needed to push back a bit and wake people up."

At Rush Hour the Cars came out in the summer of 2000. Riches wanted to hit the road in the U.S.; he knew better than to pin his hopes on Toronto, the industry town. He had plenty of punk rock contacts; Burke tried her hand at publicity and tour booking. "I was emailing famous journalists," she says. "Back then you could easily look up information on who registered websites, and so I would look at code and try and figure out people's contact information. I'd say that Royal City had been mentioned in *Now* magazine and then something like 'Patsy Cline's tear in Will Oldham's beer,' just weird mash-ups that seemed obviously poetic nonsense. But I guess they seemed like the most amazing press quotes. We got into so many good clubs, even in New York City, and I later realized it was because my emails were misleading. Then booking agents started calling me, wondering how I did it."

There were some things she didn't need to invent: Riches had, in fact, kissed actress Neve Campbell when they went to elementary school together in Guelph, and internationally acclaimed children's author Robert Munsch had, coincidentally, just published a book called *Aaron's Hair*, about meeting Riches as a young hippie child during a classroom reading. Canada: it's a small town.

Burke also used the MP3.com website, a precursor to MySpace that allowed independent bands to post files for streaming, to find similar-sounding bands in small towns and ask if they wanted to host a Royal City show. "Every day I'd wake up at nine and stay up until three or four in the morning working on Three Gut," says Burke, who was approaching her post-chronic fatigue period the same way Stuart Murdoch of Belle and Sebastian had dealt with his: with a flurry of productivity. It was clear she needed more help with the label.

Enter Lisa Moran, Riches's manager. The Brockville native had moved to Guelph to work for DROG but was now in Toronto working a corporate bank job.

Among other skills, Moran brought organization and focus to Burke's constant idea generator. Though Moran had been involved since the beginning, she was made a 50/50 partner with Burke in 2000. The musicians quickly realized that they were happy to do what Burke told them to, but that they didn't have the stomach to actually run a business.

"At the beginning I made very little money," says Burke, who was paying less than $300 a month in rent at her warehouse space. "I lived three minutes away from the *Eye* office. I never wanted for anything. I'd go out for lunch all the time. I'd spend $500 on stamps and envelopes. I paid for all the posters. I could never do that if I was paying $1,000 in rent. The difference between $250 and $1,000 all went directly into the record label. That experience launched every part of my life now."

"The first year of Three Gut was a conspiracy," says Riches. "No one gave a shit about any of the bands on the label at that point. It was a conspiracy mainly between me and my punk rock ideas from the past, and it was also that Tyler had this quacky, crazy art thing, and Lisa had a practical mind and this unbelievable fidelity to the people she worked with and to making music happen. Then Jim had his whole 'home is where the rock is' philosophy. It was a combination of all those things that gave it its spirit."

All of that attracted Toronto media that didn't normally pay attention to upstart indie labels. It had the devoted attention of the so-called Gang of Four: *Eye Weekly*'s Stuart Berman, *Now*'s Matt Galloway, *Toronto Star*'s Ben Rayner and *Toronto Sun*'s Kieran Grant, who all bar-hopped together. "You wouldn't just have one article about your show, you'd have four, in the four major publications," says Burke. "Now, I can't get arrested trying to promote things. It came so easily before, and people who worked forever to get press coverage would get mad. I didn't realize then how difficult it was; now I do."

Royal City's first U.S. tour was a brief affair shortly after *At Rush Hour the Cars* came out in the spring of 2000. Joining the band was new guitarist Leslie Feist. "It felt like a big deal to be associated with Royal City and Three Gut," says Feist. "Tyler and I disagree about these memories, but I wanted to be on Three Gut so badly. But she did not like [Feist's debut] *Monarch*, or as a good friend, she thought, No, this is not a good fit. She wasn't wrong! But now she says it's not true and that she totally would have. But I was begging to be on Three Gut. I understood that something valuable and interesting was there. Royal City was a real band; Three Gut was a real community. Tyler had such clear art direction. I envied her mind and creative powers and her fearlessness and deep ambition. She put so much into everything and I wanted to be a part of it—though I hadn't made a record that merited being a part of it."

Feist soon started hanging out at 9 St. Patricks and sitting in on Royal City rehearsals. "She was always really generous and into what we were doing," says Guthrie. He remembers one of his own gigs where she was loudly cheering his band on, "literally vocal support," he says. "She was in Royal City long enough to be on the cover of *Eye Weekly* with us. It never felt like she was a lifer, more like, 'Let's do this while it makes sense.' She obviously had her own thing going on. She could sing and play guitar better than anyone in our band, that's for sure." Feist's time in Royal City was over in mere months; her fidelity was to her solo career, and she was also performing in then-new Broken Social Scene. But she did a brief U.S. tour with Royal City, including a gig in New York City that her friend Gord Downie came to see.

Nothing about Three Gut was conventional. That's why it worked, and what attracted people like Feist. "When I was starting to work on the label, I was a temp at some ad agency," says Burke. "There was a woman there who was a manager, and she was always printing out these 8 x 10 glossies. She had the handbook of how to manage a band. She was always telling me all the mistakes I was making. It wouldn't have mattered if I wanted to follow the rules; I don't have the personality to even read the manual. It's not going to be fun for me if I do it the way you want me to do it."

———

ACCEPTED WISDOM HAS never been part of Joel Gibb's method. He grew up rebelling against music class, against church, against heteronormative society, against punk rock—even against right-handed guitar players. Joel Gibb was always going to do things in a very Joel Gibb way.

Gibb grew up in Mississauga, Ontario, which is normally referred to as a suburb of Toronto, even though it's the sixth largest city in Canada. He does not recall it fondly—as one might infer from his Nina Simone–inspired song called "Mississauga Goddam," in which he wrote the line, "Mississauga people carry the weight of common evil."

His parents took him to Baptist services held in his school gym, where the pastor played acoustic guitar and used overhead projectors for singalongs, even inviting modern dancers to perform—all of which Gibb later did with the Hidden Cameras. If it sounds like a post-hippie congregation of Jesus freaks, Gibb says, "Maybe to a conservative Baptist they appear to be hippies because they have shaggy hair, but it was a pretty traditional Baptist congregation."

Gibb took piano lessons, had a bass guitar and played clarinet in high school band, but he dismissed all of those as alienating and "some sort of power relationship." He cherished the music lessons he had when he was eight, using the Carl Orff method, in which children learn experientially in an informal approach. "For some reason we had to get into these dance slippers, a bunch of kids parading around playing a bunch of xylophones, metallophones, glockenspiels," says Gibb. There was no theory or sight-reading involved, "just playing around with rhythm and we danced a bit, too. That was the only musical thing I excelled in." From his Baptist congregation and the Orff method came the template for the Hidden Cameras.

Gibb didn't come out as queer in high school. "Definitely not," he says. "There's no reason to. People called me a fag before I even knew I was one. That was the big issue for me; the hurdle to get over was accepting what other people already knew."

At 16, Gibb and his friend Paul P. started a zine, *The Bitch*, featuring campy clip art. They'd hand it out wherever they could; one time they tried to pass it to members of Teenage Fanclub before an on-air interview at CFNY, but security tossed them out. Paul P. loaned Gibb a four-track recorder and gave him a 20-minute tutorial, and then Gibb went to work. He wrote snippets of songs and experimented with overdubbing. "I searched for a cheap reverb unit, and once I had that, then I was on my way," he says. "It was really just a guitar pedal with an effect called 'oldies.'"

Gibb studied semiotics (essentially the study of signs and symbols) at the University of Toronto, and his songs were full of double entendres that drew from the rock'n'roll tradition of conflating the sacred and the sexual, though in Gibb's case they were unmistakably queer. There was little precedent for this. Tom Robinson wrote the anthem "Glad to Be Gay" during the punk explosion in the late '70s. Lesbian folk music became a subgenre in the '70s and '80s, through artists such as Ferron and Phranc. In the '90s, San Francisco punk band Pansy Division pioneered what they called "homocore," sexually explicit pop-punk that scandalized the macho mall-punk culture at the time; Green Day took them on tour specifically to challenge their new Top 40 audience. At Bay Area gigs, Pansy Division had go-go dancers, a nod to the dominant disco culture in the gay scene while rejecting its musical stereotypes.

Toronto had its own queer history to celebrate. From Jackie Shane to Rough Trade to General Idea to Craig Russell's *Outrageous!* to Fifth Column to the Parachute Club to Kids in the Hall to Peaches, there had always been a strong queer undercurrent in the city's music and arts scene, even though a series of sparks were treated as isolated incidents, not a through line. In typically amnesiac Canadian fashion, new generations were largely unaware of the city's rich queer history.

In January 2000, one DJ and artist set out to break down more barriers. Will Munro, who went to the same high school as Gibb five years earlier, started club night Vazaleen. It sought to take queer culture away from house music and Toronto's Gay Village and reintroduce the sleaze of glam rock and an anything-goes attitude. There was always a live act in the middle of the dance party; over the years it attracted Peaches, Nina Hagen, the Gossip, Jayne County and others. Gibb figured if he ever got his band off the ground, Vazaleen would be the ideal gig. Fifteen months later, that happened. But at the time all he had were some home demos and no one to play them with. Enter Maggie MacDonald.

MacDonald had been a punk teen from the eastern Ontario town of Cornwall, who had often travelled to Ottawa to see hardcore shows. She was involved in the NDP's youth wing, where her extroversion and public-speaking skills landed her on TV a few times as a "voice of the youth." As a student at the University of Toronto's University College, she'd go for the daily free tea and cookies from two to five p.m. She spotted some familiar faces there that she recognized from Vazaleen, several of whom soon formed the initial core of Hidden Cameras.

"Joel was a very distinctive looking person," she says. "He had these big Buddy Holly glasses. I said, 'Do I know you?' He said, 'You don't know me? I'm the most famous person at U of T.' He started messing with me. I was offended, because I thought *I* was the most famous person at U of T. I was very well known on campus! I was on TV! So we had this ego clash, but he started calling me a lot. That's how we became friends. He was a class clown kind of person, always joking around and doing inventive performance things. When he first told me he was doing music, I thought it would be like 'Weird Al' Yankovic or something."

They often drove together in Gibb's mother's Jeep. He'd play different tracks for MacDonald and see if she could guess who it was. Their tastes were similar; she was rarely stumped. One day he put on something she was pretty sure she'd never heard before.

"Okay, what is this?"

"Hmmm. I don't know."

"Well, what does it sound like?"

"Well, a little bit of Belle and Sebastian, a little bit of Velvet Underground, a little bit of Rolling Stones in their Andrew Loog Oldham period."

"This is my band."

"No, it's not. Get out."

"No, really, it's my band. You should be in it."

"I don't play an instrument!"

"Doesn't matter. You're in my band."

Except that there wasn't a band—yet. He needed one, though, because he had a gig. His friend Paul P., a painter, was involved with the West Wing Art Space in Parkdale, one of the first galleries to make West Queen West a cultural destination. In the summer of 2000, Paul P. convinced the gallery to book a Hidden Cameras gig that December—but didn't bother to tell Gibb, who was backpacking in Europe. When Gibb returned in September, he needed his imaginary band to become a reality. MacDonald was not yet ready to play an instrument, so she agreed to work the overhead projector that illuminated the lyrics. She also became Gibb's roommate on D'Arcy Street, near the Art Gallery of Ontario.

The next recruit was Justin Stayshyn, a close friend of the Three Gut crowd who lived at 9 St. Patricks with most of them. Gibb met Stayshyn at Buddies in Bad Times Theatre, where they discovered shared tastes in music and humour. They also had a mutual friend in Magali Meagher, who was dating Dave Meslin at the time and whom Gibb had also tried to recruit. "I didn't really listen to the CD at first," says Stayshyn, "and then I was talking to Magali about it and saying, 'Wow, this is actually really good. Like, really, really good.' And she said, 'Yeah, but did you listen to the lyrics?' Then I did and I was even more excited." Matias Rozenberg, who played in Meagher's Pine Needle Players, was also recruited for the first show. All four new members traded instruments, depending on the song.

As rehearsals progressed, often held at the Three Gut house, a glib Gibb started calling it "gay church folk music." The label stuck around for years, because, well, it was fairly accurate: explicitly queer lyrics set to songs rooted in acoustic guitar that sounded like hymns over a propulsive beat that could be a distant cousin of disco. "I always knew that I had a church aesthetic that came through without me even trying," he says. "I didn't even think it sounded that churchy, but my friends said it did. And instead of getting indignant and saying, 'No, it doesn't,' I thought maybe it was cool. I mean, it's better than indie rock."

Christianity and queer culture have never been comfortable bedfellows, to say the least, but Gibb insisted the phrase wasn't meant to provoke. "I'm sure it's offensive to some Christians," he said at the time, "but there are tons of Christians who wouldn't find it offensive at all. I have nothing against Christianity. It's a better alternative than what most people believe in now, which is greed."

The debut gig at the West Wing, on December 28, 2000, was an uninhibited, joyous affair on a winter night inside steamed windows. "I had asked certain people to take these papier mâché suns and put them on poles, and they became the dancers," says Gibb, who was wearing a T-shirt that night that read *I found my calling*. "No one was leading the dancing, it just happened."

"This is like a puppet show from the '70s or something," quipped someone in the crowd. Mike E.B., whose boyfriend ran the gallery, was working the bar and was soon recruited to be a dancer.

But the gig wasn't auspicious. It was a random gallery event, at a time when Toronto's art scene was changing and evolving—and moving west, part of what urban geographers call "the shock troops of gentrification."

"That was the peak of the Queen West art moment," says Gibb. "West Wing was past the Dufferin bridge, which was considered really far out. Katharine Mulherin had already started her gallery; Paul Petro wasn't there yet. It was cheap rent. Me, Paul P., Will Munro, [future Camera] Luis Jacob, we were all smashing down walls in Paul Petro's space [to create his gallery]. And people lived in their spaces."

The gig marked not only the debut of the Hidden Cameras but the first time Gibb sang in public. Deadly Snakes bassist Yuri Didrichsons played the second show, at Graffiti's in Kensington Market—which was packed. There was a gig for students of the Ontario College of Art and Design at the Great Hall—also packed. The fourth Hidden Cameras gig was at Vazaleen on March 30, 2001—obviously, that was packed. MacDonald and Mike E.B. did choreographed dance moves. Gibb's teenage zine pal, Paul P., and Will Munro's boyfriend, Alex McClelland, go-go danced in underwear and balaclavas.

At each subsequent show, more and more people joined, many from the tea-and-cookies scene at U of T, including fellow semiotics student Steve Kado. Kado in turn enlisted his friend, Owen Pallett, a violinist and composition student who joined in September 2001. "Owen walked into the room and had long straight hair and a trench coat," recalls MacDonald. "I thought, Either this is a metalhead or a classical musician. Either way, a nerd. He had this intensity. When he joined, we didn't know his deal: straight, gay, bisexual? When you're 20, you want to date everyone new you meet. We soon learned that he was dating a 40-year-old dominatrix." ("She was 36, not 40," Pallett clarifies. "She'd be devastated!")

Pallett brought cellist Mike Olsen into the fold. Recruitment "was always done in a social setting," says Gibb. "'Hey, do you want to play with us? We have this gig.' Or 'This person's boyfriend plays this.' It was also intertwined with Will Munro's world, and we were very close friends at the time." Gibb wasn't looking for professional musicians, or even people who would necessarily stick around. "I was never—ever—into the idea of having a small, set band," he said in 2004. "I was always interested in asking people who weren't musicians to play. I've always found that to be a good thing for a band. Just as I would assume that a lot of visual artists would prefer to have non–visual artists to be their assistants. It's so good to mix minds and mediums."

Meanwhile, Gibb assembled his solo four-track recordings for *Ecce Homo*, a remarkably complete vision that announced a strong melodicist with a rhythmic debt to early Jonathan Richman, accompanied by persistent eighth-note pulses on acoustic guitar, electric guitar countermelodies, drum machines and handclaps.

It opens with "A Miracle," about a sacred visit that could be the tale of immaculate conception or a clandestine lover, with the twist, "He tells me that I'm the only one who can carry his disease."

"In a lot of my lyrics, it's hard to distinguish whether I'm talking about God or talking about a boy," said Gibb in 2002. "I always envisioned [the character in 'A Miracle'] to be some angel, like the visitation. I like the ambiguity. You can read it any way. It could be, 'In my head I'm envisioning you suffering,' or it could be, 'In my head I see you suffering and I don't want that.' It could be really sympathetic."

Knowingly or not, Gibb was dialling into part of rock'n'roll's origin story: R&B evolved from gospel music, and lyrics of devotion once written about God were repurposed to be about lovers. Because the history of rock'n'roll is predominantly heterosexual,[1] it was long overdue to be queered. Gibb, who had never considered veiling his sexuality, simply subscribed to the old axiom of "write what you know." "If you're going to set out to write a love song and it's from a gay perspective, it's going to be sexual," he said in 2002. "It just wouldn't be honest if you didn't. When you come out, you're asserting your sexuality to your parents or to whomever, but a straight person never has to do that. They could be asexual all their life and be straight, but they never have to say to someone, 'I have sexual thoughts.' There's such a long tradition of euphemizing homosexual narratives and language—so that's boring, that's already been done."

Another *Ecce Homo* track tells the story of a "mild-mannered army," positing that "peace can beget from buggery, I'll bet." On "Ode to Self-Publishing, Fear of 'Zine Failure," he boasts, "I've got a whole Bible in me." And on the rousing "I Believe in the Good of Life," an instant live favourite, he "kneel[s] for a taste of man." "High Upon the Church Grounds" documents how "the drugs get dealt and the cocks get felt on the church grounds." The inside artwork featured a crucifix shaped like a penis. The conflation of homoeroticism and Christian imagery could not have been less subtle.

The idea of being out and explicit didn't seem controversial to Gibb, though it was to most everyone else. "Part of the concept [of the band] was normalizing sexuality," he says. "It's weird, because the '80s were so androgynous, and there were so many gay people from that era. It's interesting how all these people were somehow closeted—all of them were! Boy George never said he was gay; he was bi. George Michael was forced out of the closet. Michael Stipe sort of came out later; he said he was bi. [Pet Shop Boys'] Neil [Tennant] did come out, but that took awhile. Chris [Lowe] never came out; to this day, he's private. Then the '90s hit, and the '90s were so straight. I guess some people were coming out then:

1   Little Richard, Lou Reed, Elton John and Freddie Mercury notwithstanding.

movie stars, some rock stars. I had all that in the back of my mind. I'm like, 'Can someone please do this?'" Rufus Wainwright, who was out when he released his debut record in 1998, "was an inspiration," says Gibb. "He was out, proud, normal. And [Magnetic Fields'] Stephin Merritt was out."

The Hidden Cameras were "definitely a queer/straight alliance," says Gibb, "but with really out-there queer songs. The whole point was to have a real mix of people. That's what made the shows really fun, really welcoming and inclusive. It connected the art scene with the music scene. I created a band that I would have liked to have been asked to join, a band that's inclusive of sexuality but also musical proficiency. It's a place where you could learn about playing music. A lot of people learned how to play music in my band and then started their own bands. They weren't interested in being musicians; they were characters and performers."

Ecce Homo was all very raw, but it was powerful. It also foretold the future of the band: the live show required lots of people to make it fun, but the players were interchangeable. The core of the band was and always would be Joel Gibb. This later became an issue.

ROYAL CITY HAD formed to back Aaron Riches, but after a year of touring, it was most definitely a real band of brothers and equal voices.

It was on their second U.S. tour in the spring of 2001 when everything clicked: 18 dates in three weeks down the Eastern Seaboard and through the Midwest. Joining them was friend Vish Khanna, who treated it like a music history trip, making stops at the Band's Big Pink house and the Rock & Roll Hall of Fame. In Nashville, Sarah Harmer came to see them on her night off tour; she was impressed enough to offer them the opening slot on her Western Canadian tour that fall. Also in Nashville, they ended up staying at Ryan Adams's house, jamming with him in the basement and later listening to him argue with his roommates all night. In Brooklyn, they played at the apartment of a random new artist Tyler Burke had contacted: Sufjan Stevens.

"It was so magical," says Riches. "We'd play anywhere people would take us, and pass the hat at the end of the show. There were poor times: in Indianapolis, we had no place to stay and no money and we were eating green beans out of a can. It was a grim moment, materially. But we knew it was infused with something more than us. Who makes music for music's sake? No one. Everybody makes music because it's more than music, something to do with friendship, the quest for life, everything. We knew we were happy. We all had a sense that this was a moment in our lives that would never come back, so we lived it conscious that every step we were living eternity.

"The dirty secret is that we played 30 shows and probably only played to 60 people the whole tour," Riches continues. "We played on porches for five people, we played in cafés, opened up for some bands and had bigger shows. I'd always said, 'People in Canadian music are so fucking stupid that if we just go down to the States, they'll think we're doing something.' And it was true! That got us a certain kind of cred in Toronto. We didn't even bother with Canada [initially]." "There was a fake-it-until-you-make-it [mentality] on our part," says Guthrie.

Riches was privy to some direct inspiration: his day job in Toronto was working in the warehouse of distributor Outside Music, alongside Danko Jones and members of the Sadies and the Deadly Snakes—all of whom had set their sights on the American underground rather than wait for Canadian labels and press to give a shit. What none of those other bands did, however, was get up first thing every morning of a show and hang clothesline around a foreign city— which Royal City did in the U.S. as they attempted to replicate Burke's success in Toronto. "We hung those fucking envelopes [for] every single night of the first American tour," says Riches. "We had four boxes of envelopes, twine and clothespins. Tyler made us promise that we would hang them up before every show. I was dating her, and I couldn't let her down—the one thing I couldn't do is *not* hang these things up. We took photos of them all. She wanted us to show up in every town at around six in the morning and do the whole city, anywhere where people would be."

American connections were key. Steve Earle's guitarist, Roscoe Ambel, took a shine to the band and recorded some demos for them in New York City. The Secretly Canadian label set up bills with some of their acts. Sufjan Stevens became a close friend, eventually altering the lives of Riches and Moran personally and professionally: Moran became Stevens's manager; Riches married Stevens's roommate. Years later, Stevens released a Royal City B-sides compilation on his own label.

And Three Gut managed to get American press—rare for a Canadian label in 2001 and absolutely unheard of for a Toronto indie. A review of *At Rush Hour* in *Magnet* inexplicably lambasted the band for recording in mono, but a year later *Pitchfork* raved that "they prove that the best post-modern, devil-haunted, gothic Americana is currently being made by a pack of Canadians. And if there are any questions about authenticity, I give you four words: *Music from Big Pink*."

Connections made through Royal City were key to launching the next Three Gut act, the one that soon would set Toronto aflame and spread its gospel across North America and Europe.

NO MATTER WHERE they were, no matter what the conditions, the Constantines treated the rock'n'roll stage as an altar, with themselves the conduit between the congregation and a higher power—not that they'd ever be so pretentious themselves to make that suggestion. That's the writers' job, and more than a few came home drooling after a Constantines show.

"We like to play each show like it could be our last," drummer Doug MacGregor said in early 2001. That's hard to maintain for an entire career. But it was certainly still the ethos 18 months later, when the Constantines played the dingy Trasheteria in Peterborough, Ontario, on the Friday of the 2002 Labour Day weekend. After an initially endearing yet ultimately punishing opening set by a teenage amateur punk band who covered Kiss's "Heaven's on Fire," the band squeezed onto the tiny stage. By the end of the first song, guitarists Bry Webb and Steve Lambke had already moved their mic stands off the stage and five feet onto the dance floor, where they remained for the rest of the night, face to face with the small crowd, who didn't take long to dance and clap alongside the band, singing along: "Night time, any time, it's all right—turn it up!"

That night, an excited older man stood right at the front, feeling every beat in his bones, quivering ecstatically and beaming like it was the first music he'd ever heard. At one point, the band passed him a tambourine, which he started waving frantically and passing through Lambke's legs, when he wasn't trying to two-step with bassist Dallas Wehrle's girlfriend and the rest of the audience. He had totally surrendered to the music, pushing the already-intense performance even further. The band ended the set by leaping from various parts of the stage, while Wehrle draped himself backwards over a speaker, scraping his droning bass against the heating duct above. Now *that's* a goddamn rock'n'roll show.

At their best, the Constantines could turn anyone into that man: free of inhibitions, feeling the music like a shot to the heart, feeling like the first time, a willing and equal participant in an artistic exchange that sent audiences home bathed in sweat, with sore legs, a hoarse voice, a satisfied mind and a sense of community.

Should we ever demand less of rock'n'roll?

BRY WEBB AND DOUG MACGREGOR were farm kids who grew up on the northern outskirts of London, Ontario. They were skateboarders taunted by Tragically Hip fans in the schoolyard. By the time they turned 18, they had found the only other kids around into hardcore punk and formed a band, Shoulder. Two weeks after finishing high school, Shoulder toured down to Tampa, Florida, and back. "It was pretty amazing—even if you're only playing for five people in Murfreesboro,

Tennessee," says MacGregor. At home, their biggest thrill was opening for Propagandhi in London, although they were somewhat upset that John K. Samson had left the band; Webb and MacGregor were big fans of a solo cassette Samson had just put out.

Ontario peers included Shotmaker from Belleville and Aaron Riches's Minnow from Guelph; Shoulder was invited to play Minnow's farewell show. One New Year's Eve, they played a 10-band bill at a Kensington Market squat in an abandoned abattoir. Shoulder split in 1997, when one member moved to British Columbia. Webb, suffering from depression, started volunteering at campus station CHRW and soon became music director—an experience he credits with literally saving his life. When he felt the itch to play music again, the remnants of Shoulder poached Dallas Wehrle, the bassist in Captain Co-Pilot, a band from Cambridge, Ontario. In 1999, Wehrle's bandmate, guitarist Steve Lambke, joined them and it was clear that this was an entirely new band.

The new blood gave Webb a sense of purpose at a time when he needed it badly. "In 1999, I had a problem with ecstasy—I didn't want to do it anymore," he says. "For a while, I had been involved in a terribly dark scene in my home-town, which seemed to function on the notion that there was nothing else to do. Ultimately, this was nonsense." The first practice with Lambke was held in the attic above nightclub Call the Office. "It was structurally unsound," says Webb, "and whenever Doug would hit the kick drum, pigeon feathers would rain on him from a hole in the ceiling. The song we wrote that [first] night would eventually become the track on our first record called 'No Ecstasy.'"

The band's first show was on September 2, 1999, at Call the Office, opening for L.A. pop-punk band the Muffs. "We didn't even have a name yet," says MacGregor, "but Bry and I had a good relationship with [booker] Tony Lima. Then we opened for the Gaza Strippers, a lot of retro-rock bands like Murder City Devils. But a lot of shows were in basements or rented halls." MacGregor was studying inorganic chemistry at the University of Waterloo; Lambke lived in Guelph; Wehrle went to York University in Toronto. All three commuted to London for practices above Call the Office. When the Constantines identified as being from southwestern Ontario, they had the Highway 401 mileage to prove it.

Musically, the band was moving beyond their hardcore punk influences. "We got more into songcraft," says MacGregor. "We were leaving behind wil-fully untuneful music and odd time signatures, and we got into Clash and Talking Heads and Patti Smith. Steve and Dallas told us to listen to old Bruce Springsteen. Bry told them they should listen to the Replacements. We wore all that on our sleeves. We were trying to learn how to be a rhythm section like Paul Simonon and Topper Headon. Listening to Motown and Booker T., figuring out how to do all that. We thought we were becoming mature."

By 2000, Werhle transferred to Guelph, and he and Webb moved in with Lambke at 106 Huron Street. It soon became a frequent site of basement shows for local and touring bands, with the hosts also on the bill. The hippie vibe of Guelph suited them more than the frat culture of London. "When I was younger, Guelph was this almost stately scene," says Webb. "London was more beer-fuelled indie rock and punk and it was a lot of fun; the hardcore scene was great. But Guelph seemed to have diversity and was very conscientious. It was what I imagined D.C. to be like in the late '80s and early '90s."

But they returned to London to record their debut album. Andy Magoffin was the house tech at Call the Office; the Constantines noticed that shows he worked sounded better than others. Magoffin, who led the Two-Minute Miracles, had just opened a new studio, House of Miracles. He'd made records for local pop-punks the Weekend (the band who made a future R&B superstar change his name) and math rockers Ivy League. The Constantines liked his work and they liked his price: $200 a day. "We recorded it in a weekend, and then we mixed it on two separate days a month apart," says MacGregor. "Four days total, then a day of mastering."

The result is one of the greatest rock'n'roll records ever made in Canada: not just for the electrifying jolt of the performances, not just for the songs, but for the way it sounded. The listener might as well be sitting between the drum kit and the guitar amps in the band's basement. When they printed CD-R promos to send to labels and booking agents, the working title was *13 Songs*, after Fugazi's 1989 debut.

Fugazi was an enormous influence. Though that's true for an entire generation of political punk bands, the Constantines were one of the few where it was audible. In 1998, Lambke had gone on a road trip with Minnow's Aaron Riches, Captain Co-Pilot's Vish Khanna and sound tech Steve Clarkson to see Fugazi in Chicago and Detroit. "It was with Shellac and Blonde Redhead, in massive theatres," he recalls. "We had tickets to Chicago but not Detroit, and Aaron got us in and we watched from side stage. It was crazy. So amazing. Seeing how they worked as a musical unit was fucking insane and super inspiring." In the Constantines' first-ever live review, Stuart Berman of *Eye Weekly* described them with fan-boy fervour as "children of Fugazi . . . the grandkids of Springsteen and Strummer . . . we have something to believe in again."

That was written after the Constantines' fourth foray into Toronto. The first was at the El Mocambo, opening for Minneapolis hardcore band Killsadie. The next was opening for Jersey at Lee's Palace on the night of the 2000 U.S. election. "We went on stage and Al Gore was president," MacGregor recalls. "We played to two people. We came off stage, and George W. Bush was the president." The third Toronto show was at the Jewish Community Centre with Rockets Red Glare, friends and peers from Mississauga who were a big influence. The fourth Toronto show, the one Berman witnessed, is what made the Constantines' entire career.

It was at Ted's Wrecking Yard on February 4, 2001, part of the Wavelength Music series, which had begun only a year earlier. Two months earlier Kevin Drew had debuted a band he called John Tesh and the Broken Social Scene. But after the Constantines played, they became the act most associated with Wavelength as a source for discovery. Probably because they blew the roof off the building.

It was "a cold, crappy Sunday night," remembered *Toronto Star* critic Ben Rayner in 2009. "The crowd was sparse, although they did have the music writers from two dailies and two weeklies in the room. All of us would soon be tumbling over each other in a rush to heap praise upon the band because, frankly, none of us were expecting to have our minds blown so completely that night. The Cons opened with 'Arizona,' and I remember being immediately struck by the disciplined ferocity of their playing and Bry Webb's old-soul voice. By the time they hit the 'We want the death of rock'n'roll!' chorus and then tore the song apart with that wicked breakdown—where all the sound suddenly drops out and the guitars weave back in, Fugazi-style, before one last crescendo—everyone in the room had looks of genuine awe on their faces. By the end of the set, most of us had a new favourite live band."

Stuart Berman of *Eye Weekly* remembers them opening not with "Arizona" but with "Young Offenders." When the song "reached its mid-song pause," he wrote in a later *Eye* cover story, "a stone-faced Bry Webb muttered, 'We like rock music'—a not entirely popular sentiment in the post-rock/pre-Strokes/Stripes era. And with that, the Cons crashed into the song's monstrous 'Can I get witness' chorus, furiously practising what they preached. [There were] floor divots caused by all the jaws that dropped on that cold February night."

The band themselves were considerably more humble about it. "I have vague memories of it being cool," says Lambke. "I don't think there were all that many people there. We probably just did what we did and then loaded up whatever borrowed minivan we had and drove back to the 519 area code. I don't remember any sense of 'We just made it, boys!'"

"It was weird," says MacGregor. "The band who booked it for us, Full White Drag from Windsor, had to drop out. Someone in that band lost a parent, and we got everyone at the show to sign a flyer for them. We played with another London band called the Ivy League. It was just another show for us."

Show aside, it was a momentous day for another reason. The day before the show, the Constantines had met with Sonic Unyon Records in Hamilton, who were extremely interested in signing them. On the day of the show, they met with Three Gut at 9 St. Patricks Square. In December 2000, Royal City had played a show at 106 Huron Street with Constantines and raved afterwards to Tyler Clark Burke and Lisa Moran. Webb and MacGregor knew Aaron Riches from the days of Minnow and Shoulder. Lambke and Wehrle had recorded at Jim Guthrie's RokSak with their previous band. And they were all huge fans of Royal City's debut album, *At Rush Hour the Cars*.

"That record has such an atmosphere, almost like Godspeed," says Lambke. "It was mysterious and evocative. The songs were beautiful, and it sounded like people playing music together rather than a constructed thing. It's awkward and earnest. Anti-cool and direct. I was still living in Guelph, so hearing someone singing about the streetcars was really romantic. It's hard for me not to picture 9 St. Patricks Square when I hear that record now. That's the world it feels like to me."

The day of the fateful show, Royal City drummer Nathan Lawr cooked a large spaghetti dinner. The entire environment felt like family. The Constantines cast their lot with Three Gut, and their album, now self-titled, was set for a June release. Werhle designed the artwork, inspired by Constellation Records; it involved hand-assembled folded cardboard and an individual match embedded in each insert. The label held a house party to help manufacture the first 250 copies; much of the rest of the first run of 1,000 was done by Lisa Moran's boyfriend, Kevin Fitzpatrick. After that, to appease retailers, Burke reconfigured the album's design into a standard jewel case, where it was nowhere near as effective. The original run became a coveted collector's item.

The album was a critical hit on both sides of the border, and the initial hype ensured solid turnout on the band's first Western Canadian tour. Weakerthans drummer Jason Tait saw them at Guelph's Hillside Festival; soon the rest of his band fell in love, too, beginning a close relationship. An early kinship with Brooklyn band Oneida also proved to be mutually inspiring, though the Constantines were far more conventional than that band's full-freakout jams. In the fall of 2001, new keyboardist Evan Gordon, who played guitar in an early version of Royal City, added an element of chaos into the tightly wound Constantines.

For Three Gut, the Constantines were a much easier sell than Gentleman Reg—whose 2000 debut *The Theoretical Girl* was a tentative step toward the artist he'd become—or even Royal City. "We felt like such underdogs with Royal City," says Moran, "trying to get people to check out their shows. So much work went into that. With the Constantines, people were coming to us before we approached them. It was so weird, such a different situation."

Wherever they went, the Constantines came across as rock'n'roll evangelists. Their live set might include Springsteen's "I'm on Fire," Eddy Grant's "Police on

My Back" via the Clash, the Talking Heads' "Thank You for Sending Me an Angel" and even Nina Simone's "See-Line Woman" (before their mega fan Feist also covered it). The night after Peggy Lee died in 2002, singer Bry Webb led a sold-out Lee's Palace crowd in a singalong to "Fever" tacked onto the end of their own "Hyacinth Blues," while guitarist Steve Lambke and bassist Dallas Wehrle clapped along and drummer Doug MacGregor passed out tambourines to unsuspecting Torontonian percussionists.

"Salvation seems like a big word," Webb said in 2001; the campus radio enthusiast has the Replacements' song title "Left of the Dial" tattooed on his arm. "But when I think about where I would have been or what I would have been doing without music, it doesn't seem that far off. When we first started the band, I was listening to Lou Reed songs like 'Rock and Roll.' We've always been into music that's self-conscious about the medium, and from the beginning we put a lot of thought into what we were trying to do and why we were even in a band."

ROYAL CITY HAD become a rock band. They'd been covering Iggy Pop's "Success" for a while. The earlier fragility had formed a firm backbone. Their next record, *Alone at the Microphone*, was recorded—like the Constantines' debut—with Andy Magoffin in London, Ontario. If *At Rush Hour the Cars* was pencil-drawn, tentative and fragile, this was bold and full-colour evidence of what two years of touring does to a lo-fi bedroom band, though they hadn't lost an ounce of their hushed, sweet charm. They flexed every new muscle in the first 60 seconds of opening track "Bad Luck": stuttering drums, pulsing country bass, rich acoustic guitar, drunken blues, spacey banjo, starlit piano, crackling yet confident deathbed vocals, and a tone of doom and disgust. And it only got better, and scarier, from there. Guitarist Jim Guthrie was a more integral part, co-writing and sharing lead vocal on the album's poppiest song, "Spacy Basement."

Riches's lyrics were preoccupied with death, darkness and the seamy side of life, referencing copious amounts of bodily fluids—hence the feel-good hit "Blood and Faeces." Yet there was hidden hope and beauty behind such desolation: "Dank Is the Air of Death and Loathing" contained the optimistic chorus "Ray of light, a petal in my room, I will not go forth without you." To Riches, there was no cleanliness without filth, no virtue without vice, and the narrator in every song is on a journey somewhere between two extremes. In interviews, Riches explained that the narrative arc of the album is a combination of the Book of Exodus and Dante's *Inferno*, with tangents about Shakespeare's *Timon of Athens* and St. John of the Cross, the Spanish Catholic mystical poet best known for coining the phrase "dark night of the soul." You didn't hear the Strokes doing that.

The release show at Lee's Palace in Toronto on December 14, 2001, was triumphant. Riches was on the cover of *Now*, and one of the openers was the Hidden Cameras, making their debut in front of indie rockers unlikely to hang out at Queen West art galleries or Vazaleen.

But Royal City was falling apart. Drummer Nathan Lawr had fallen in love with a Vancouver woman and quit the band to move there. Burke ended the fabled romance between her and Riches, who was soon engaged to Sufjan Stevens's best friend, Melissa Herwaldt. They were married in early 2002, right after Royal City toured with the Constantines out to Newfoundland and back. Riches and Herwaldt moved to Montreal, where he finished his thesis and hung out with old friend Tim Kingsbury. He was making plans to move to Charlottesville, Virginia, to do a second master's degree.

Riches thought Royal City was finished. Then he got a U.K. record deal, thanks to the Hidden Cameras.

FOR ALL OF 2001, the Hidden Cameras focused on promoting their own shows at unconventional venues. Gibb booked a gig at the Church of the Redeemer, a historic Anglican church across from the Royal Ontario Museum. There was a Pride gig sponsored by the Splice This! Super 8 Film Festival that introduced the band to the wider queer community. In November, at the decrepit Metro porn theatre in Koreatown, the band "had local artists show films and some women did some dances about menstruation," says Maggie MacDonald. "There were all sorts of masks and costumes. It was a real community event, a very different kind of concert." That's an understatement.

There were more conventional gigs at Wavelength and at Dave Bookman's Nu Music Nite at the Horseshoe. Finally, there was the show opening for Royal City at Lee's Palace. "That's when people outside our little scene paid attention," says Gibb.

The Hidden Cameras' mild-mannered army took the stage that night numbering more than half a dozen. Gentleman Reg was enlisted on the spot to sing harmony, because Magali Meagher was stuck on the tarmac at the Toronto airport. Everyone else on the bill that night played music that was either quiet, fractured or weird; the Hidden Cameras were undeniably an onstage party shaking up the asexual indie rock crowd. In the town that still wasn't sure what to make of Peaches' international success, this was a wakeup call. "There are so many asexual indie boys, it's not even funny," said Gibb in 2002. "It's a pretty repressed culture. They don't dance at shows, and they don't really express themselves. They're blinded by cynicism. It's rooted in fear. At indie shows, you usually mumble your lyrics, not look out and just play for yourself, and perhaps really loud. I find a lot of shows like that very alienating. [Our go-go dancers are] almost challenging the crowd to be less uptight."

In April 2002, the Hidden Cameras were hired by *Exclaim!* magazine to co-headline a three-city tour, playing Montreal, Ottawa and Toronto with Brooklyn Afrobeat revivalists Antibalas and DJ Dan Snaith, then known as Manitoba. Montreal proved to be a tough crowd, even more so after Gibb quipped into the microphone, "Wow, and I thought *Toronto* was uptight!" The Toronto show packed Lee's Palace well beyond capacity, with the audience literally climbing the walls to get a better view.

That same spring the Hidden Cameras were invited to one of the most prestigious art galas in town, the Power Ball at Harbourfront. The band showed up with a phalanx of dancers, who were directed by Gibb to interact with the moneyed crowd as much as possible—and pretend to steal their wallets. "It was pretty funny," says Gentleman Reg, "because it was such a chi-chi audience who had never seen or heard us. And they were totally dancing and getting into it with our 20 dancers in their underwear." That's where booking agent Rob Zifarelli saw the band and signed them to his roster—even though they were still trying to avoid the conventional club circuit whenever possible. "The idea of playing southern Ontario is not appealing," said Gibb at the time. "I'm most happy doing Toronto shows, and producing a show instead of just playing songs."

Even weirder than the Power Ball was when one of its attendees booked the band to play a prom for engineering students at Queen's University in Kingston—not traditionally the most progressive faculty. "We were offered good money to play it," recalls Owen Pallett, "and we thought, Sure, we've never played Kingston before. We got there and set up, and we were playing with people doing Spirit of the West covers. There was genuine prom drama going on: beautiful, made-up girls splashing drinks in their dunderheaded boyfriends' faces, and there was one couple dancing and she was crying while he was kissing her and telling her to stop crying. We got up there dressed rather shabbily, and most of us were barefoot. We were playing in front of an ice sculpture. We played and it was out of tune and rushed and we just banged our way through it. At the end we played 'High Upon the Church Grounds' for ten minutes straight. The result was that some girls got up on stage and tried to make out with Reg. Me and Steve Kado were on the dance floor shouting at people and dancing with them."

Justin Stayshyn, who was always up for baiting homophobes, adds, "Mike E.B. and I went through the audience making out, which we thought would be funny, but most of them didn't care at all. They were more like, 'Get a room!' If it was 10 years [prior] at an engineering prom, they would have killed us. [In 2002,] it was ho-hum."

"After that," Pallett continues, "we all got wasted and went into the hot tub at the hotel and stayed up until four a.m. I actually woke up in a bed I didn't recognize, with a boy I didn't recognize, and wearing underwear I didn't recognize. If only there were naked women and coke, we would have been Guns N' Roses." The "boy" in question ended up being Pallett's partner and manager for years, Patrick Borjal.

Bob Wiseman, a singer-songwriter and producer twice as old as anyone in the band, was now a second keyboardist. Gibb didn't know or care that Wiseman had once been in Blue Rodeo—which suited Wiseman just fine. Other than the Vazaleen crowd, Gibb didn't feel he owed Toronto anything. Growing up, his only local favourite were riot grrrl progenitors Fifth Column, whom he discovered through U.K. music mag *Melody Maker* and a few random plays on CFNY and *Brave New Waves*. Though Fifth Column arrived in the mid-'80s, he saw them play a side stage at Lollapalooza in 1993, and interviewed them for his zine. Co-founder G.B. Jones is internationally recognized as a queer zine pioneer. "Their music spoke to me; most other local music did not speak to me at all," says Gibb. "In fact, the Hidden Cameras were a reaction to how uninspired it felt in Toronto, how nobody was doing anything interesting. All my favourite music was from England or the States. Vazaleen and Toronto's visual art world is really what inspired me to do everything the way I did it."

Gibb certainly wasn't on any kind of schedule. There was no rush to herd his band into a studio and capture the live energy, or even to tour. Things were going fine in Toronto. "There was a year of shows before a lot of people knew about the band," says Gentleman Reg. "It was basically just a small scene of friends—and when you have 12 people in the band, that's a lot of friends. People took this band very seriously and became very fanatic—just freaking out at the shows, taking off their clothes and screaming out the names of songs endlessly until we played them. People felt comfortable to be themselves. We weren't a glamorous band."

There was little to no chance of the Canadian music industry getting on board—and Gibb wasn't aiming for that anyway.

THE CONSTANTINES' DEBUT somehow got nominated for a Juno for Best Alternative Album—almost unheard of for a new punk band on a microscopic indie label. (Danko Jones had got a nod in 1999.) The band's next release was an EP with the knockout songs "Dirty Business" and "Blind Luck," released on the Seattle label Suicide Squeeze. After the EP's release show at Lee's Palace in February

2002, keyboardist Evan Gordon quit. "It was a crazy, sold-out show," recalls Steve Lambke, "and that was when he was like, 'Nope, I don't want anything to do with this.' He brought a whole lot to the band, kicked it up a gear. He's an amazing presence and energy, with intuition and freedom. Before Evan we were trying to be tight. We had more abandon because of him."

A few weeks later, the Constantines headed to Austin for the SXSW festival in March 2002, on a bill with the Sadies and Luke Doucet, presented by Toronto counterpart NXNE. Important people from Sub Pop and Touch and Go Records were expected to show up. Bry Webb and Tyler Burke decided to get a drink around the corner from the venue, to take their minds off the pressure. Tequila seemed like the thing to do in Texas. "But what they do in Austin," says Burke, "is not just measuring a shot and pouring it in a shot glass—there it's a free pour, and the glass was half full. Bry and I were not 'shots' people. We had two of those, went back, and I have literally never been so drunk in my life."

It wasn't a good omen. "Within one song, Bry's guitar dropped and he broke a string," says MacGregor. "Two songs in, his amp broke. He was like, 'Screw it.' Behind the stage, a window opened out to the street. He was on the ledge, screaming to the people congregated there, like a cross between Iggy Pop and a televangelist." The venue's bouncers kicked Webb out of his own show in the middle of the set. The sound tech wasn't impressed either. "He accused us of destroying the stage, because we were using their backline, but really it was shitty gear," says MacGregor. "When we got home, we got sued; they claimed we broke all this stuff. But three bands played after us—there's no way we broke it! We ended up paying a couple of hundred bucks for a microphone. They were trying to push around the unknown Canadian band, but one letter from our lawyer and they changed their tune."

Back home, they replaced Gordon with Will Kidman, who grew up with Lambke and Wehrle and who'd moved into 106 Huron when Lambke moved into the Three Gut house. Kidman's first weekend of rehearsals with the band resulted in three new songs; he'd bought a Vox organ only the month before, and barely knew how to play it. That wasn't the only new element in the band: MacGregor had to sit out an East Coast tour with Royal City after slicing his hand open while fence-hopping into a City of Toronto pool late at night. His fill-in was ex–Royal City drummer Nathan Lawr.

Despite the SXSW debacle in March, Sub Pop was more than impressed, and a courtship began. Rather than being starstruck by the label that had launched Nirvana, the Constantines were exceedingly cautious. "We came in as punks who thought anybody who wanted to sign a contract with us was bad," says Lambke. "It was fear manifesting as political righteousness." There were also negotiations happening with Touch and Go. In the end, there was significant appeal in being the first central Canadian band on Sub Pop.

"One of the biggest factors in the deal was that they were cool with us staying with Three Gut in Canada," says Webb. "Three Gut, for us, was like a balloon ride into the hype and the industry. We weren't being represented in any way that we didn't want to be. That was a really great creative motor. It was the community that we still believed in and wanted to be a part of. It would have been impossible for me to say, 'No, we're not going to work with you guys anymore.' It was too much a part of my life."

Listening to the Sub Pop debut, *Shine a Light*, it's hard to imagine that its creation involved any second-guessing or uncertainty. Upon its release in August 2003, it was hailed as an instant modern classic. Along with Broken Social Scene's *You Forgot It in People* and Feist's *The Reminder*, it's one of three Toronto albums of this era that still gets near unanimous praise, 20 years later. But *Shine a Light* did not have an easy birth. "The record everybody knows came after this long process of confusion and rejection," says Lambke. "We wanted to make a weird, noisy, fucked-up record." They succeeded a bit too well on its first pass.

It was tracked at Blue Rodeo's new studio, the Woodshed, with engineer Steve Clarkson, formerly of King Cobb Steelie. "We were all in the same room, with the board in the same room, everything was turned up way too loud," says Lambke. Vocals and overdubs were done at Chemical Sound, which is also where Clarkson did a mix that was submitted to Sub Pop. "I don't want to say they rejected it," says Lambke, "but they did firmly suggest that we revisit some stuff. Honestly, [Clarkson's mix] was probably exactly what we were aiming for, but we didn't realize that what we were aiming for wasn't cool, or wasn't really working. That was hard to hear. 'My gosh, are we terrible? How are we going to do this?' We had no money left [in the budget]. Then we thought Andy [Magoffin] could help us, but he came in and listened to it and said, 'I don't want anything to do with this.' He probably thought it was irreparable, that he couldn't get it to the point where he'd want his name on it."

The house engineers at Chemical, Rudy Rempel and James Heidebrecht, offered to take a stab at it for free: that version—with entirely rerecorded vocals, among other tweaks—is what entered the world. (They did get paid.) The only vocals from the original session that remained were on "National Hum," which Webb recorded using a handheld mic run through a small tube amp. It's the album's noisiest track, its most jarring—and, curiously, the song the Constantines chose to open the album. "It was tough emotionally, that time," says Lambke.

Everything about *Shine a Light* reeks of resilience, of young lions roaming the city streets at night, of clinging to those you love, of eking out an existence in a corporate world. Tambourines hiss like snakes. Guitar amps buzz, anticipating the return of a dead-stop riff. The organ sounds like it was trucked in from a haunted house. The guitars can be both crushing and delicate; the Constantines were one of the few rock bands of their ilk to have true command of dynamics. The entire band is a well-oiled machine, but Doug MacGregor's drumming truly elevates every move his bandmates make.

There's at least three fist-pumping anthems of tightly wound tension: "Nighttime Anytime," "Young Lions" and "Tank Commander," the latter written about the band's first meeting with Three Gut. After a monstrous first half, things come down to whispers on "Goodbye Baby & Amen," then to a breather of a pop song, "On to You." "If sanctuary still exists," sings Webb on closing post-punk country stomp "Sub-Domestic," "it's among the shaking fists."

"National Hum" finds Bry Webb howling, "The state ain't my shepherd!" Canadian state-sponsored radio, however, was in the process of shepherding Hidden Cameras, and by extension Royal City, into international attention via a British record label.

CBC RADIO 3 was a lot of different things, which made it impossible to explain. It was a division of what was then known as CBC Radio 2, in charge of so-called youth music that aired on weekend evenings and overnights. It was a web magazine with original video content. And like MP3.com, it was a proto-MySpace, a music discovery vehicle that enabled indie acts to upload music, bios and contact info. Much like the CBC Radio 2 show *Brave New Waves*—which leaned more toward the experimental fringes than indie rock—it had a small but dedicated niche audience and was invisible to the general public. And much like John Peel on his BBC Radio show, CBC Radio 3 invited young bands into its professional studios to record sessions. One of those bands was the Hidden Cameras.

Twenty-year-old CBC Radio 3 producer Mar Sellars happened to be in Toronto in December 2001 and was blown away by the Hidden Cameras' set opening for Royal City. She bought a copy of *Ecce Homo* and brought it back to host and producer Grant Lawrence, who also fell in love with it and started playing it. They booked the band for a session at the CBC Toronto building. Gibb showed up not just with the band but with go-go dancers, knowing that the session would be filmed; he insisted the dancers be paid alongside the musicians. It was the band's first experience in a professional recording environment, and it was chaotic, to say the least. Gibb had very particular ideas about how the band should be recorded. "We were often apologizing for Joel's behaviour," says Gentleman Reg. "Me and a bunch of people were like, 'Sorry, he's so rude. Sorry that this is happening.' We had to be extra nice because he was so hard to deal with."

Geoff Travis of Rough Trade Records saw the session online and was intrigued. The man most famous for signing the Smiths, one of Gibb's favourite bands, flew to Toronto in October 2002 to see a show at University of Toronto's Victoria College. The show was a bit ramshackle—extension cords had to be run inside from adjacent buildings—but an unflappable Gibb claims he felt no pressure to impress. If Rough Trade didn't bite, he figured he'd just put out his next record on his own again. But Travis made the Hidden Cameras the first Canadian band on his label.

The Rough Trade deal proved to be a turning point—because it was a deal for Joel Gibb, not the Hidden Cameras. The label also insisted he trim the band down to six people for a U.K. tour: Gibb, MacDonald, Stayshyn, Rozenberg and Gentleman Reg; original member Magali Meagher was sidelined. Being a group of socialists, they held a large meeting about it, with Dave Meslin moderating. "That's when we realized that Joel was signing—and we were session musicians," says Gentleman Reg. Several people soon quit, including Meagher, Wiseman and Kado.

"Everybody's replaceable," said Pallett in 2004. "The moment of truth for me was when I saw Joel open for Gentleman Reg's CD release show [for 2002's *Make Me Pretty*]. Joel played by himself, and he was so compelling and had the audience in the palm of his hand, and his songs shone as being wonderful, terrific songs. I—and everyone else present, which was pretty much the entire band—had to acknowledge that the band is Joel. He's what is special about it."

Pallett effectively wrote himself out of his own job with the Hidden Cameras in May 2003, when he took two weeks to transcribe all the string parts "so that now Joel could tour around the world and hire string ensembles in every city and play concerts," said Pallett in 2004.

"I think it's much better, musically and performance wise, when you have a solid group," says MacDonald, the non-musician who was always invited on tours while some of the "real" musicians were not. "But from an ethical standpoint, if you write the music and you're the bandleader, you can do what you want. The question [for side players] is: are you along for that ride or not? It gets more complex, too, because there were difficulties with how the project was managed."

"I don't think anyone could have run that band the way it needed to be run," says Pallett. "Joel did not understand how to wrangle that many people and make them feel appreciated. He didn't know how to run it financially. Everyone seemed upset that it wasn't being run like a collective. Not everyone was getting paid the same amount. I remember having to say to someone in the band, who thought they deserved a songwriting credit because they'd written a drumbeat, I said, 'That's just a Moe Tucker beat. What are you talking about? That's not how song-writing credit goes. Can we be more logical about this?' But then Joel later took credit for my string arrangements, and I took issue with that. He said, 'Sculptors seldom actually sculpt their own work, and they don't have to credit the factory that makes their finished product.' I said, 'That doesn't matter. I'm the one put-ting pen to paper and who wants to work as a string arranger as a career, and it makes no sense for you to take credit for my work.' He refused to back down, so I stopped working for him."

Hidden Cameras' *Ecce Homo* was rereleased in early 2003, while Joel Gibb started working on the follow-up, *The Smell of Our Own*, with producer Andy Magoffin. The album, featuring most but not all of the live Cameras, was a decidedly orches-tral affair: the first sound on the album, after the opening drone of a pipe organ, is a harp. The strings by Owen Pallett and Mike Olsen are as lush as the backing vocals, which on four tracks involved a 25-piece choir that included Gibb's high school hero G.B. Jones of Fifth Column, along with old and new friends from the art and music community. Though *Ecce Homo*'s "A Miracle" was rerecorded—and other than the addition of strings, it's not much different from the original—several live favourites were excluded, including "I Believe in the Good of Life" and "Music Is My Boyfriend." Gibb, who had a large backlog of songs dating back to his four-track days, wanted to make a concise and cohesive album, and not necessarily put all the crowd favourites out at once.

A new song, "Ban Marriage," was recorded while same-sex marriage was before the supreme courts of Ontario and British Columbia, both of which legal-ized it shortly after *The Smell of Our Own* was released. The satirical song captured the suddenly complicated idea that maybe not all queer people *do* want to buy into a straight institution like marriage. "Ban Marriage" was chosen to be the album's first single, and therefore many people's introduction to the band.

The song that got even more attention, however, was "Golden Streams," which—despite Gibb's protestations to the contrary—is about piss sex. The taboo practice was not entirely unheard of in Canadian musical discourse: in 1996, Cape Breton fiddler Ashley MacIsaac blew up his career in a *Maclean's* interview, in which it wasn't his queerness that was controversial as much as his admission that he was a urophile. In 2002, Broken Social Scene's Kevin Drew sang about it in "I'm Still Your Fag" on that band's breakthrough *You Forgot It in People*. Still, it was unlikely lyrical material for a gorgeously melodic song with harps, strings and an angelic choir.

Gibb pointed out that contrary to popular belief—and poorly copy-edited album reviews—the name of the song is not "Golden Showers." "That song is not even about piss sex," he insisted in *Exclaim!* in 2004. "'Golden showers' is a sexual term. 'Golden Streams' can refer to tears, or anything." Either way, the lyrics to the otherwise lovely song are juvenile at best: "My golden bone meets the golden bun / Buns held high in our dreams of men."

Closing track "The Man That I Am with My Man," however, *is* explicitly about gay sex, including water sports. The *Pitchfork* review of the album raved, "Honestly, this pack of queer Canadians make pissing on your loved one a most holy and glorious of act deserving of its own special Hallmark greeting."

"From a conceptual point, I think the Cameras' greatest feat is that it is absolutely not a gay band," said Owen Pallett in 2004. "It's a Joel band, and Joel is gay. The music is about gay sex, community, participation and all the things Joel is into."

"I like the way the music functions on different levels," said Gibb that same year. "That's important to me. I don't mind it being called a gay band; it doesn't bother me. But it's not gay novelty music where only gay people go to the show because there's one element of it that's good—which is that it's gay. The more we play, there are people who found the music through a similar music community, in which case it's just music. Our audience is not a gay audience."

That said, when the Hidden Cameras came to town, there was action to be had. "It was the show to go to and fall in love at," says Pallett. "This was pre-Grindr, obviously; you'd have to go out and meet gay men if you wanted to have sex with them. It was important for that reason alone."

Recalls MacDonald, who is not queer, "One member of the band got to a hotel in New Brunswick, asked to borrow my computer for five minutes and said, 'Okay, there's a pizza on the way, and I just got myself another room and I found a guy to come and hook up with me right now. So, bye, everybody! Enjoy the pizza.' I mean, people in this band knew how to improvise. We knew how to take care of business."

In Ottawa, a promoter had booked the Hidden Cameras at a Baptist church. "That's very different than the Anglican and United churches in Toronto we usually play," said Gibb in 2004. "There was lots of press saying that there were going to be strippers, just a total degradation of information. Some congregation members called and the pastor had to have a sit-down talk with the promoter. But they came to the show, and it was fine. [Most churches] don't function as a church when they book shows, they function professionally: Do you need a stage built? Do you need lights? They don't ask you what your band is or the morality and ethics behind your band."

Prudes aside, many found the band too dorky, too awkward, too amateurish. They certainly weren't slick. The Hidden Cameras were twee, but they were more punk rock than, say, the Polyphonic Spree, a concurrent chamber-pop band from Texas that travelled with a large choir clad in white robes and whose music sounded like Andrew Lloyd Webber's leftovers. The Canadian music industry was generally baffled by the Hidden Cameras' modus operandi, which made Broken Social Scene seem like Rush by comparison.

The Hidden Cameras made their New York City debut in February 2003, at Fez Under Time Café in Greenwich Village, where attendees included Sufjan Stevens, Le Tigre and filmmaker John Cameron Mitchell; the latter followed up *Hedwig and the Angry Inch* with the sexually explicit *Shortbus*, shot in Toronto, starring Sook-Yin Lee and featuring Gentleman Reg.

The Hidden Cameras' first year of touring took them to the U.K., Dublin and select European cities, as well as a pair of Chicago shows with Belle and Sebastian, a tour of Western Canada (in Vancouver, their opening band was called the Gay) and a short eastern U.S. tour that included a stop at the Warhol Museum in Pittsburgh. There, they were opening for Mark Eitzel of American Music Club, one of the few prominent queer figures in North American indie rock. He was performing solo; the Hidden Cameras were travelling with their entire circus, including Will Munro as road manager. "When [Eitzel] saw our soundcheck," says Gibb, "he was like, 'I'm not headlining this. I want to play now and then leave.' A few people came to see him, then left, and we played to three people. It was terrible. Maybe he was intimidated by the energy and the youth, or maybe he just thought we sucked, I don't know. But I thought that was super unfriendly."

Meanwhile, the Hidden Cameras were proving to be an incubator of sorts—even if it was driven by negative energy from disgruntled members. Ex-Camera Steve Kado started Barcelona Pavilion with Maggie MacDonald and put out fiery, funny and political electro-punk that caught the ear of the BBC's John Peel, who invited them to the U.K. for a session. Gentleman Reg and Owen Pallett were both busy solo artists and in-demand collaborators. Dancer John Caffery started his electro project, Kids on TV. In later years, keyboardist Laura Barrett had an acclaimed solo career, and trumpeter Shaun Brodie founded the Queer Songbook Orchestra.

"Reg would probably have been the only person who had stuff going on before the Hidden Cameras," says Gibb—though Magali Meagher was another, and Bob Wiseman had an entire career. "I think it brought people out of their shells. Me pushing people on stage inspired them to do something on their own. There's a DIY ethos to the band. It's a pool of ideas and inspiration for everybody. I was inspired by a lot of my friends, too. It really fostered creativity."

THREE GUT'S LISA MORAN knew Rough Trade Records' Geoff Travis was in Toronto to see the Hidden Cameras, so she made sure she got an introduction—and slipped him a copy of Royal City's *Alone at the Microphone*. He loved it and wanted to release it in the U.K. in 2003—almost two years after it'd come out in Canada—paying the band an 8,000-pound advance. He also asked them to contribute to a compilation of new Rough Trade artists covering other acts on the label; Royal City did the title track of the Strokes' *Is This It?* (Hidden Cameras did a song by New Zealand band the Clean.) Drummer Nathan Lawr did not return to the fold; he had joined a new Three Gut band, Sea Snakes, and was recording his own debut as a singer-songwriter. Drummer Lonnie James (Super Friendz) was recruited, and the reformed Royal City hit the ground running on an East Coast tour with the Constantines (this was the tour with Lawr on drums, sitting in for an injured Doug MacGregor). Royal City played the U.K. for the first time in the summer of 2003; *Alone at the Microphone* got positive press there, thanks to the British fascination with warped takes on Americana—especially by exotic Canadians (see also: the Be Good Tanyas).

Three Gut remained busy with the Constantines as well as Jim Guthrie's second album, *Morning Noon Night*, and Gentleman Reg's *Make Me Pretty*, which featured the Constantines' Bry Webb. Kevin Drew was a huge fan of Reg, often inviting him on stage with Broken Social Scene in several different cities to sing his song "Give Me the Chance to Fall"; he also performed it with Feist in Paris. Three Gut signed its first artist outside its social circle: a young band from Oshawa called Cuff the Duke, whose stunning 2003 debut, *Life Stories for Minimum Wage*, was an odd combination of alt-country, art-rock and Godspeed. While Cuff the Duke easily fit on bills with the Sadies and Blue Rodeo, they were equally at home with the Weakerthans or Constantines.

A lot of the work fell to Lisa Moran. After the Constantines' Sub Pop deal in 2002, Tyler Burke retreated to work on her own art projects and promote a transient club night called Santa Cruz; the label formally announced her departure in 2003.

"When I turned 28," says Burke, "I realized that not everyone is walking around thinking this is just a fun party we're having. I'm sort of a big idea person but not always good at maintaining the details and minutiae. Lisa and I were a dynamic duo. We both had different superpowers. Lisa is very good at everything to do with being a manager. I was able to work on art if I hid behind the record label, and that worked really well for me because I was shy. I needed to learn how to be an artist on my own and have my own show.

"The bigger reasons," she continues, "were that I felt let down by how people were treating us, by how sleazy parts of the so-called friendly indie industry was. People were constantly handing me records—sometimes when I thought I was on a date. One time [at a club] a guy danced up to me, pretended he had bone cancer and then asked me to sign his band. Another guy sent me a 4,000-word email with insane ideas. I was stalked by a guy in another band, who had attempted to kill his father, and he was leaving wet red-painted objects for me at 9 St. Patricks. And on and on and on and on and on. I didn't care about celebrity culture or making anyone famous. I wanted real, meaningful connections with people, and I was finding I couldn't trust people's intentions anymore."

As the Constantines kept Lisa Moran more than busy, Three Gut's records became comparatively lower profile. There was one exception: label founder Jim Guthrie's late 2003 album *Now, More Than Ever*. Recorded with Andy Magoffin, it was the first time Guthrie had recorded his own material anywhere but in his bedroom. His band featured Royal City's Simon Osborne, Evan Clarke of Rockets Red Glare and the Hidden Cameras' string section of Owen Pallett and Mike Olsen. The Unicorns' Jamie Thompson and Constantines' Bry Webb also appear. A far cry from 2000's *A Thousand Songs* or 2002's *Morning Noon Night*, it is autumnal in tone, rich with melody and melancholy: a peculiar yet welcoming cross between Nick Drake and '80s TV-theme composer Mike Post. Guthrie admitted he'd aimed for a *Hill Street Blues* vibe.

Though Guthrie's songwriting was exceptional, much of the album's success was attributed to the string arrangements—most done by Pallett in the studio, without rehearsal. "That was the first time I'd scored a record," says Pallett. "I would never write something now as weirdly baroque as [Guthrie's] 'The Evangelist.' I couldn't; it's been sanded off me. We didn't know if it was good or bad, because the string arrangements don't sound the way strings normally do. It got five stars in *Eye Weekly*, and we were like, Really? *Pitchfork* gave it [an 8.3 rating], and we thought, Really? We knew the songs were good, but we weren't sure about the gilded presentation. That record had some very loud naysayers on the message boards: 'Owen ruined this record!' You know, the same way [Wilco's] *Summerteeth* is 'ruined' by Jay Bennett. I didn't know what I was doing."

Now, More Than Ever became one of the most acclaimed Toronto albums of the year, even nominated for a Juno. For a tiny label that only ever put out 16 releases, four of Three Gut's records ended up with a Juno nomination—not a bad batting average.

Royal City reconvened in 2004 to make their third, and last, record, *Little Heart's Ease*. Rough Trade brought them over to Europe for a month-long tour, sharing a van with French band Herman Dune. But it felt like a last gasp. The album had a lukewarm reception across the board. Riches's lyrics and interviews—in which he talked about his theology studies—prompted confusion about whether or not Royal City had become a Christian band. (It hadn't.) No matter: Riches was focused on his academic career and planning to do his PhD in Britain. Royal City quietly packed it in at the end of the 2004 tour, after a show in London, England.

"It's so funny because by the end of it all of our friends were way bigger than us," said Riches in 2005, "whether it was the Constantines, or the Hidden Cameras, or Sufjan, the Arcade Fire—they all opened for us. Leslie Feist was in our band at one point. If we played shows with any of them now, we'd be on the bill at, like, three o'clock in the afternoon!"

———

OWEN PALLETT SEEMED to be in an enviable position. In August 2004, the 24-year-old violinist was one of the busiest musicians in Toronto. He'd just left the Hidden Cameras, and played his last gig with them at Toronto's Harbourfront. His work on Jim Guthrie's *Now, More Than Ever* helped that album get a Juno nomination. He also led his own band, the avant-garde folk-rock band Les Mouches, and was part of the Blocks Recording Club, the most promising new label in town. Oh, and he'd recently recorded string parts for the debut album by Montreal band Arcade Fire, which was due out in a month.

But acclaim and respect didn't pay the bills—yet. "I had literally zero dollars," he recalls.

Les Mouches was the sideman's first experience as bandleader, in which he alternately whispered and screamed sexually perverse lyrics over gentle acoustic guitar and free-jazz drumming. Formed just over a year earlier in the spring of 2003, it already seemed poised to splinter. He was focusing on a solo violin project he called Final Fantasy, its moniker shamelessly taunting the copyright holders behind his favourite video game of the same name.

Things changed one night when Final Fantasy played CineCycle, a sweaty 100-capacity bike shop and cinema off a Spadina Avenue alleyway. The audience included the host of CBC Radio's most popular program, *The Vinyl Café*. Stuart McLean, the family-friendly storyteller and bestselling author, approached Pallett after the show and casually asked him about his non-musical pursuits. The musician became quite emotional, detailing how tough things had been financially, since quitting his job at folk club the Free Times Café in March in order to tour Europe with the Hidden Cameras. McLean invited him to audition for a job at *The Vinyl Café* as a music programmer. Pallett got the gig.

That fall, as Arcade Fire began conquering the U.S., Pallett turned down a chance to open for them because of his new job. Instead, he performed as Final Fantasy at *The Vinyl Café*'s live show in Western Canada. Enraptured audiences demanded a CD. Between Christmas and New Year's, he made *Has a Good Home*.

In January and February 2005, he opened for Arcade Fire on the West Coast of the U.S. and started selling hundreds of CDs a night.

OWEN PALLETT ARRIVED at the University of Toronto from nearby Milton, Ontario, in 1998 to study composition. He'd been playing violin since the age of three, and at 13 wrote music for a video game by one of his older brothers. In high school, he started gigging at Renaissance fairs and country bars for cash. At U of T, which he attended on a scholarship, he wrote operas for his assignments, while moonlighting with a Milton friend in a Celtic band called Enter the Haggis. That helped pay the rent, along with busking.

None of it was the music he wanted to make. "He had pretty typical closet-case-dude taste in music," says his friend Steve Kado. "Björk, Tori Amos, Kate Bush. We both liked [British band] James; we thought it was hilarious. They're kind of the worst band ever, yet amazingly good. I got him into Gastr del Sol." Kado and Pallett were a combustible pair: highly opinionated, philosophical, curious social connectors and motivated to create. It was Kado who, in September 2001, enlisted Pallett into the Hidden Cameras. A whole new world opened up.

There's little question that Pallett was the most professional musician in a circle of punks, indie rock amateurs and folk musicians. Few of his friends shared his enthusiasm for Béla Bartók or Charles Ives. But he learned plenty from his peers: improvisation, for starters. "Gentleman Reg asked me to play viola at his [in-store] Soundscapes performance," says Pallett, "and Jim Guthrie was playing guitar. That was my first exposure to being part of someone's creative project from an indie background." Guthrie became the first in Toronto's indie scene to tap Pallett for a string arrangement, which appeared on his 2002 album *Morning Noon Night*.

Guthrie, like many of Pallett's friends in the scene, was entirely self-taught. Pallett came from an extensive academic background. He didn't see a discrepancy there. "I have a deep love for music made by non-musicians," he said in 2006. "Nine times out of ten it's better than music made by musicians. It takes a bunch of art students to come along and say, 'We don't like your music with no ideas. Let's have music with ideas!' And now students have risen up and said, 'Well, we have ideas, too, and we can play our instruments!' All it takes is an encounter with a guy like Steve Kado to take someone out of their funk band and into some band that involves wall-painting as a live performance practice, and then you have the best band in the world." Soon enough he was performing with the entire Three Gut roster, as well as Liz Hysen's Picastro.

Pallett started writing his own songs, made brass arrangements for them and took them to Andy Magoffin's studio to record *The Polite Album*. "Nobody heard it; I think I burned five copies," he says. "But Steve Kado had one and came into the Free Times Café where I was working and said, 'Dude, your album is awesome!' I was playing some solo shows, but it wasn't doing anything for me. I wanted to start a band." He had seen guitarist Matt Smith play improv at the Free Times; he knew drummer and DJ Rob Gordon through mutual school friends. Together they became Les Mouches.

Pallett says he wanted it to sound like "U.S. Maple meets the Carpenters," referring to an abrasive and difficult math rock band of the '90s, and his unironic love for soft-pop '70s stylings. He was also heavily influenced by a new American band, Xiu Xiu, which featured emotionally unhinged vocals over unconventional folk songs that often erupted into distorted explosions. "I don't think I ever really understood music-making until I heard Xiu Xiu in early 2002," he says. "Les Mouches were trying to have that aesthetic married to not necessarily conventional songwriting, but really pretty songs."

Pallett played acoustic guitar; Smith played electric; Gordon threw all kinds of things all over his drum kit and played as if Keith Moon solos were condensed into 10-second bursts scattered throughout any given song. The lyrics were perverse, provocative, occasionally juvenile, never boring. "After *Blood Orgy!!!* came out, Rob's dad used to make fun of him by quoting Les Mouches lyrics at the dinner table," says Pallett. "He'd say, 'Well, Robbie, you know, I never had a woman inside my dick.' My stepfather had a very negative reaction to it. He went to my mom and said, 'I think Owen may be seriously disturbed.' Then she listened to the record and said, 'Nick, he's joking! These are jokes!' Which was true. 'Daddy Needs a Daddy' is making fun of tropes of gay male desire, while at the same time being very emotional. 'I want to hold him in my arms and cradle him until his hair turns grey': that was pretty much how I felt about who I was falling in love with. 'Carload of Whatever' was satirizing bugchasers, which I didn't know was a thing until I met one. It's so fun to sing shit like 'My dream has a title: cunt marries asshole.' I don't know—maybe they're just bad jokes. But I have a lot of affection for it."

Les Mouches' first gig was in April 2003 in Guelph. A recording session that summer captured material for the debut EP, *Blood Orgy!!!*, released that December, as well as the April 2004 release of *You're Worth More to Me Than 10,000 Christians*. That gig, a beyond-packed show at the Music Gallery, was opened by Arcade Fire precursor Bell Orchestre and Woolly Leaves, the solo project for Constantines' Will Kidman. "We asked everyone to wear white clothing to the show—and they did," says Pallett, still somewhat incredulous. "Matt Smith said, 'Thank you all for wearing white. Congratulations—you're all racist!'"

Richard Reed Parry of Bell Orchestre says, "That was one of my favourite shows I'd ever seen—ever, of any band."

Critic Carl Wilson says, "One of the first things that made me sit up and take notice was when Les Mouches were covering 'Close to You' by the Carpenters. Not that it was a unique indie rock move at the time, but there was an earnestness to their delivery, very tender but with an edge to it. [Pallett's] sensibility has always embraced vulnerability and truthfulness and professionalism—all of these things that were in some ways uncool."

Les Mouches was not remotely an accessible band. But through his work with others, Pallett's stock had risen considerably in the year between Les Mouches' first show and the CD release. Pallett was considered so ubiquitous on the Toronto scene that punk band Fucked Up pranked him by crediting him with string arrangements on a single called "Ban Violins"; the media believed it, and both parties found it hilarious. *Now, More Than Ever* also caught the ear of Arcade Fire, who had opened for Guthrie in early 2003. When they wanted strings on their debut album, they summoned Pallett and Olsen to Montreal in early 2004. Les Mouches opened a show for them the same week.

Pallett, who could often be seen on stage with Arcade Fire in the coming years, is often incorrectly credited with string arrangements for *Funeral*. "I always get far more credit than I deserve with Arcade Fire," he says. "It's a product of the fact that they're always bigging me up, and also just confusion. I had nothing to do with the strings on 'Wake Up,' for example. I don't even know who played on that." (That song was recorded six months before the rest of the album.) Pallett and Olsen joined Arcade Fire's Sarah Neufeld and Richard Reed Parry to arrange parts. "It was very much a collective effort," says Pallett. "Pretty much all the frilly shit is me: the bridge on 'Backseat,' for example; the ascensions on 'Laïka.' 'Tunnels,' I had nothing to do with that. 'Rebellion,' there's nothing there I wrote. That's all stuff that Régine [Chassagne] dictated."

Shortly afterwards, Pallett accepted an invitation to play a highly niche event: a local tribute night to Bobby Birdman, a musician from Portland, Oregon, who had only two albums and an EP to his name, none of which were widely heard. Pallett performed four songs that night at Sneaky Dee's: two originals, Birdman's "Better Than Worse" and local legend Mary Margaret O'Hara's "When You Know Why You're Happy." He did so using only his voice, his violin and a Boss RC-20 looping pedal.

Like the Roland Line 6 DL4, which had been on the market for five years by that point, the RC-20 allows a musician to loop their parts while playing. Toronto singer-songwriter Tamara Williamson had been using something similar on her voice for years, as had Kitchener-Waterloo guitarist Danny Michel.

Kid Koala at Montreal's St. Viateur Bagel, 2000.

Régine Chassagne at Lollapalooza, 2005.

PAUL MACEWAN

Win Butler at Lollapalooza, 2005.

PAUL MACEWAN

JULIE PENNER

The Constantines at the Hillside Festival in Guelph, 2006.

JULIE PENNER

The Weakerthans' Jason Tait, Do Make Say Think's Justin Small, Broken Social Scene's Charles Spearin and the Constantines' Steve Lambke partying at La Sala Rossa in Montreal.

Godspeed's one and only press shot. This 2010 photo is an updated version of a 1997 original, scanned to the highest resolution provided.

Godspeed You! Black Emperor live. Efrim Menuck and Mauro Pezzente with back to camera.

Peaches, 2001.

*The unlikeliest cover of
Britain's NME, July 1999.*

Gonzales in Berlin.

*Peaches promotional
photo, 2000.*

Leslie Feist, Julie Penner (Broken Social Scene, Do Make Say Think, Fembots) and Louise Upperton (Arts & Crafts designer) at the 2006 Junos.

Give the drummers some. From left to right: the Constantines' Doug MacGregor, Arcade Fire's Jeremy Gara and the Weakerthans' Jason Tait.

LUTHER WRIGHT

Sarah Harmer, 2000.

DAVID WALDMAN

PHOTO BY JOHN MILLAR, COURTESY OF ISADORA RECORDS

Joel Plaskett at the 2010 Polaris Music Prize gala.

Hawksley Workman, 1999.

RICHARD SWITZER

Danko Jones, 1999. From left to right: Danko Jones, Gavin Brown and John "JC" Calabrese.

DAVID WALDMAN

The Weakerthans at the Phoenix in Toronto, 2003. From left to right: Stephen Carroll,
John K. Samson and Jason Tait.

The Weakerthans, 2000. From left to right: Jason Tait, John K. Samson, Stephen Carroll and John Sutton.

New Pornographers. From left to right: Blaine Thurier, Carl Newman, Neko Case, John Collins and Kurt Dahle.

Tegan and Sara,
2000.

Destroyer, 2001.
From left to right:
John Collins, Scott
"Loscil" Morgan,
Jason Zumpano,
Dan Bejar and
Stephen Wood.

Superconductor, featuring Carl Newman (right).

The Organ. Clockwise from left: Katie Sketch, Ashley Webber, Jenny Smyth, Shelby Stocks and Debora Cohen.

Dan Bejar of Destroyer, 2006.

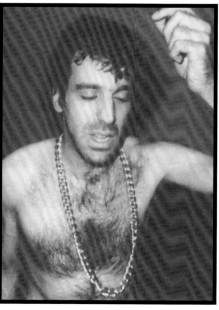

A young Jason Beck, pre-Gonzales, signed to Warner under the name Son.

Gonzales, shortly after arriving in Berlin.

Leslie Feist and Andrew Whiteman, 2008.

Peaches at the Drake Underground, 2012.

Noah's Arkweld, 1998: Noah Mintz and Leslie Feist.

Below: Feist at the Phoenix in Toronto, 2004.

By Divine Right, cover shoot for Exclaim! *magazine in 1999. From left to right: Leslie Feist, José Contreras, Brendan Canning and Mark Goldstein.*

The Dears, 2003. From left to right: Murray Lightburn, Valérie Jodoin-Keaton, Rob Benvie, George Donoso III, Natalia Yanchak and Martin Pelland.

The Sam Roberts Band, 2003. From left to right: James Hall, Dave Nugent, Corey Zadorozny, Sam Roberts and Eric Fares.

Murray Lightburn and Martin Pelland of the Dears at Lee's Palace in Toronto, 2006.

Three Gut Records at SXSW 2003, with Royal City, Constantines, the Jim Guthrie band and Cuff the Duke. Top row, from left to right: Jeff Peer, Will Kidman, Owen Pallett, Paul Lowman, Brad Fudge, Bry Webb and Tyler Clark Burke. Middle row, from left to right: Dallas Wehrle, Jim Guthrie, Lisa Moran, Steve Lambke, Doug MacGregor, Mike Olsen, Aaron Riches and Wayne Petti. Kneeling in front, from left to right: Simon Osbourne and Lonnie James.

*Lisa Moran and Tyler Clark Burke of
Three Gut Records.*

*Joel Gibb trying
new things.*

*Aaron Riches of
Royal City at the
Jane Bond Café in Waterloo.*

Aaron Riches of Royal City and Three Gut Records'
Lisa Moran.

A Hidden Cameras dancer.

Jim Guthrie and band, 2003. From left to right:
Simon Osbourne, Mike Olsen, Jim Guthrie, Evan Clarke
and Owen Pallett.

Jim Guthrie at the Three Gut house, 9 St. Patricks Square in Toronto.

Owen Pallett at the Danforth Music Hall in Toronto, 2008.

The Constantines outside Emo's in Austin, 2008. From left to right: Doug MacGregor, Bry Webb, Will Kidman, Dallas Wehrle and Steve Lambke.

Be Good Tanyas, 2000. From left to right: Trish Klein, Frazey Ford and Samantha Parton.

Corb Lund, 2001.

Ian Tyson and Corb Lund at Tyson's ranch in Longview, Alberta.

The Sadies, 2001. From left to right: Dallas Good, Mike Belitsky, Travis Good and Sean Dean.

AMANDA SCHENK

FRANK YANG

Neko Case and Dallas Good at Lee's Palace in Toronto, for the show captured on In Concert Volume One.

FRANK YANG

CATHERINE STOCKHAUSEN

Jim Bryson, 2003.

Kathleen Edwards at the Dakota Tavern in Toronto, 2008.

ROBERT KARPA

Be Good Tanyas, 2003. From left to right: Samantha Parton, Trish Klein and Frazey Ford.

Stars at Toronto's Olympic Island, 2008. From left to right: Torquil Campbell, Pat McGee, Amy Millan and Evan Cranley.

Metric at the MuchMusic Video Awards, 2005. From left to right: Josh Winstead, Emily Haines, James Shaw and Joules Scott-Key.

Family portrait, 2006. Top row (from left to right): Ohad Benchetrit, producer Dave Newfeld and Evan Cranley. Middle row (from left to right): Charles Spearin, Lisa Lobsinger, tour manager Adam Marvy, Jo-Ann Goldsmith, sound tech Marty Kinack, Jason Collett, Julie Penner and Amy Millan. Bottom row (from left to right): John Crossingham, Justin Peroff, Kevin Drew, Brendan Canning, Leslie Feist and Andrew Whiteman.

In Chicago, violinist Andrew Bird was beginning to experiment with a DL4, as was St. Vincent's Annie Clark, but no one in Toronto had heard that yet. French musician Colleen also used an RC-20, as did Tune-Yards' Merrill Garbus several years later. Pallett admired Craig Dunsmuir, a clerk at Soundscapes who used a DL4 in his Guitarkestra. "I admired his technical wizardry," says Pallett, "and wanted to have the same effect, to have each song feel like it was a thrill to see executed. I only used an RC-20 because that's what Matt Smith had, and he lent me his." Even after Pallett became better known, the complex harmonies and rhythms he conjured with the loop station set him far apart from his peers. Looping could be a lazy tool, and in many others' hands it often was.[2] Pallett laid out small building blocks of complex rhythm and melody, often in unusual time signatures, one by one, in real time, as he built his ornate creations. Blocks upon blocks upon blocks.

ON THE STRENGTH of *Shine a Light*, Toronto rock fans expected the Constantines to conquer the world—as if that was an easy thing to do based on talent alone. But the band's first trip to Europe was kiboshed completely. "The *NME* was on board, we had agents over there, stuff was rolling out the way it's supposed to," says Lambke. "We were supposed to open for the reformed Mission of Burma. This was a good exposure gig, because they'd just got back together and there was excitement and they're another 'intelligent rock band' or whatever. We were opening, so it's minuscule money, but Sub Pop was supporting the tour. Then Sub Pop's distributor went bankrupt. They called us up and said the record was not coming out when it was supposed to, and that it would all get sorted out, but it would take a few months. So we cancelled the tour."

While in California in the spring of 2004, the band's lone cellphone rang. It was Canada's federal NDP, asking the Constantines to play an event at Toronto's Palais Royale. "It was something like 'NDP Supports the Arts,' with the Sadies," says MacGregor. "We hung up, called the Sadies, and they said they'd do it if we did it. So we called back and said, 'Yeah, we'll do it, but only if [party leader] Jack Layton and [his wife, city councillor] Olivia Chow do 'Rockin' in the Free World' with us.'

"While we were still in the U.S., the [Liberal minority] government fell and an election was called. We had no idea; we didn't have smartphones. Now this gig became the de facto campaign kickoff for Jack Layton. We got a phone call the night before that Jack and Olivia agreed to do the song. Now we had to learn it. I was approached after soundcheck by some NDPer who said, 'Do you mind if

---

2   Ed Sheeran, who somehow wowed mainstream audiences with his RC-20 loop pedal in 2011, was 13 years old in 2004.

Steven Page joins you on stage?' I thought I recognized the name; I thought it was an MP from B.C. or something. Then we're on stage in this surreal moment with Jack Layton, Olivia Chow and two Barenaked Ladies.

"The next day there was an article in the *National Post*," he continues. "Jack Layton was not yet an MP, and he was challenging the Liberal who set up SARStock. There was a quote: 'Dennis Mills has the Rolling Stones in his corner. Jack Layton has the Constantines. They don't have much in common, but they both have voracious appetites for drugs and you should probably keep your daughters away from them.' My mother read that and was not too happy. She said, 'I'm going to write them a letter!' I said, 'Don't, because this is hilarious. If I knew I was going to get press like this from a right-wing newspaper, I'd have played for the NDP years ago.' Later we did an interview with them, and they cut out anything I said about NDP policy but somehow mentioned the Sadies were potheads. They deliberately tried to make us look stupid."

After casting their lot with Canada's social democratic party, a new highlight of their live set was "Working Full-Time," with its chorus "We will not be undersold." It was their most obvious ode to the classic rock they loved, at a time when they could also be heard covering AC/DC's "Thunderstruck" unironically. "We'd also done 'Ride On,' AC/DC songs no one else did," says MacGregor. Of "Working Full-Time," he says, "The drum fills are from 'Won't Get Fooled Again.' The drum beat is lifted directly from an AC/DC song on *Stiff Upper Lip*. The bass line for one part is inverted from 'Living on a Prayer.' The keyboard line is the same notes as the guitar line in 'Sweet Child O' Mine.' We figured it was all analog sampling."

New material was workshopped in spring 2005 on a 32-date tour with the Weakerthans across Canada, from Sydney to Victoria, on the Rolling Tundra Revue. "It was amazing but crazy, just so long," says Lambke. "We were doing multiple nights in almost all the towns. Being somewhere for two or three nights and not having to drive or load in and soundcheck—that was amazing. Great audiences, great performances. I don't think anyone felt competitive. There were obvious similarities between the two bands but huge differences, too. It was presented as a co-headliner, but the Weakerthans played last. There was always an opener, too, different in every place." Later that year, both the Tragically Hip and Foo Fighters tapped the Constantines to open arena shows.

Either because of or despite the relentless touring, the material on *Tournament of Hearts*, released in September 2005, found the Constantines softening some of their edges to no less powerful effect. A slight Neil Young influence was surfacing, which came to a head in 2006 when the band recorded four Young songs for a split EP with the Unintended—a band featuring Blue Rodeo's Greg Keelor, Elevator's

Rick White and some Sadies—and when most of the band formed a Young cover band, Horsey Craze, as a lark.

American music media were a bit mystified by the thoughtful Canadian hippies behind such a monstrous sound. Wrote one *Pitchfork* writer in 2005, "Given the tenacity of their music, both live and on record, I figured this band worked menial labor jobs from ages five to 22, stole their instruments, ate glass and shit earnestness. One interview with singer Bryan Webb, and all those notions were dispelled. I couldn't believe what I was hearing: Eco-spirituality? Houses by the lake? Gordon Fucking Lightfoot?"

The launch of *Tournament of Hearts* got off to a weird start in New York City, when the Constantines played a Sub Pop showcase at the Bowery Ballroom with new signees Wolf Parade and Chad VanGaalen (with four non-Canadian acts further down the bill). "Everyone was so excited to see Wolf Parade: they were the buzz band, *Queen Mary* had just come out," says Lambke. "We played directly after them, and we played to a bunch of backs. That was a harsh night for us. Nothing against those guys, but wow, that's how this biz works. [Wolf Parade's] Dan [Boeckner] was clearly into our band; he and Chad VanGaalen were on stage with us. I think we're all around the same age, but at that show we felt like the old guys there. They became way bigger than us, and that's how we learned those ropes."

After CMJ, the band embarked on a five-week North American tour with the Hold Steady, on whom they made more than a strong impression. "I loved watching them every night," singer Craig Finn told *Eye Weekly*. "They had everything I wanted in a rock'n'roll band. By the end of every set they played, I felt bulletproof and amazing. They made me believe in rock'n'roll and fall in love with it again and again."

There were then dates booked opening for Sub Pop labelmates Sleater-Kinney in Europe, which was hopefully going to finally be the band's entry there. "I loved Sleater-Kinney so much growing up and I was so excited," says Lambke. The band was driving across Kansas when they got news that the tour was cancelled. "Carrie [Brownstein] was sick and there was a bunch of stuff, and within a year they'd broken up. But we suffered the effects of that. The flights were booked, the gear was booked, we had a whole tour after that we still had to do. But now we had an eight-day hole in the middle of our tour, in a very expensive place to be. We ended up with a few shows, and the craziest, most back-breaking U.K. tour, just zig-zagging all over the place with no rhyme or reason—wherever we could get gigs with two weeks' notice."

"We then did 15 more countries, from Glasgow to the boot of Italy," says MacGregor. "We entered and left Germany five separate times during that tour. Like America, there were pockets where people knew who we were, and places where there were only 10 to 30 people. The small towns in eastern Europe got weird. In Leipzig it was a dirt floor in a basement squat. We were freezing and had to throw lumps of coal into this little oven, sitting around it for warmth." Chad VanGaalen's "Clinicly Dead" played over the German club's PA, haunting them.

In Italy, a border guard accused them of bootlegging their own albums and claimed they owed duty on 500,000 euros worth of merchandise; the charges were later dropped. "Gradually, as we went south in Italy, things got better and better," says Webb. "We ended up in a town called Lecce and we played a show at this abandoned old sportsplex country club. There were dogs running around. The show was great, and then after the show they took us to our accommodations and it was this beautiful villa in an olive grove in the country. The weather was beautiful because we were in the south and they made us this glorious meal. We sat on the rooftop underneath the stars drinking wine and that was one of the most unifying moments in the Constantines' career."

"We ended the tour with a chaotic cover of [Lou Reed's] 'Temporary Thing' in Diksmuide, Belgium," says MacGregor. "Then we lit broken drumsticks and tambourines on fire and ceremoniously tossed them over a wall into what was thought to be one of the many canals slithering throughout the city. Turns out it was just a parking lot. After 51 shows in 65 days, we departed Brussels for YYZ the next morning. That tour made us brothers."

But it also drew a line in the sand in their career. "It was tough," says Lambke. "That was the end of us doing everything we could. That was when we started placing limits on our band." Both Webb and Lambke moved to Montreal; Lambke soon moved to Sackville, New Brunswick. "There was an increasing dysfunction in the band," he says. "The internal vibes shifted. It was a natural course rather than a conscious decision."

WHEN *TOURNAMENT OF HEARTS* was released in 2005, so was the news that Three Gut was packing it in. Lisa Moran moved to New York to work for Sufjan Stevens; she's done so ever since. Royal City was done. The Constantines were on Sub Pop. Cuff the Duke moved to Hayden's label. Jim Guthrie stumbled into a job as a jingle writer and scored an incredibly popular credit card commercial with his song "Hand in My Pocket." Gentleman Reg briefly landed on Arts & Crafts.

Three Gut's influence had been felt all over, in the birth of labels like Arts & Crafts and Paper Bag and contemporaries like Six Shooter, all of whom acknowledge the debt. The combination of label and management, which Nettwerk had pioneered in Canada 15 years earlier, was still controversial at the time, seen as a conflict of interest; now, for better or worse, it's entirely normal for artists' business interests to be consolidated. Three Gut never qualified for any grants. There was no capital and no investors. They had a distributor and a booking agent, but everything else they achieved was because of the quality of the music and the dogged determination of Tyler Clark Burke and Lisa Moran, with help from the community of friends.

A DIFFERENT COMMUNITY of friends, including Owen Pallett and Steve Kado, had formed Blocks Recording Club in 2001, which, like Three Gut, was more of an art project than a business venture. Several of its first releases were on three-inch CDs, unplayable in many drives; everything involved hand-assembled packaging. The idea was not to be a record label but a worker's co-operative, which it legally became years later.

Five of the first seven releases on Blocks were by soon-to-be-ex–Hidden Cameras: the Barcelona Pavilion, with Steve Kado and Maggie MacDonald; Magali Meagher's the Phonemes; Matias Rozenberg; Kado's solo project the Blankket; former Warner Records recording artist Bob Wiseman; and Les Mouches. There was also a scene-defining, time-capsule compilation titled to troll the rest of Canada: *Toronto Is the Best!!! Toronto Is Great!!!*—released on February 29, 2004, at a seven-hour show at CineCycle—features the Hank Collective, Picastro, Kids on TV, the Creeping Nobodies, the Singing Saw Shadow Show and other acts. What made the "scene" interesting is that it wasn't just punk or electro or folk or arty experimentation or pop or noise—it was all of those things. Part of that was the post-Napster generation's interest in all kinds of genres and eras. Part of it was being adjacent to the eclecticism of Will Munro's Vazaleen parties.

Les Mouches drummer Rob Gordon and Luca Lucarini (Pallett's roommate) DJed a night typical of the era, at Club 56 in Kensington Market, called Expensive Shit, after the Fela Kuti song. As journalist Denise Benson wrote, "Expensive Shit became known for well-programmed sounds that ranged from riot grrrl to Krautrock, DAT Politics to dancehall, DFA [Records] to Dizzee Rascal, and other grime, soul, mash-ups and indie rock, often recorded by their many friends." Those friends, of course, included Blocks artists. Kado, who lived a two-minute jog away, debuted his cover of Outkast's "Hey Ya"—recorded the week the original song was released—live in front of the DJ booth there. And Kado recalls Pallett barging into his bedroom in the middle of the night before the *Toronto Is Great* release party, desperate to find a copy of the Hank Collective CD so that Lucarini could play it at Expensive Shit.

Gordon told Benson that the scene at Club 56 "was a temple of tolerance that allowed young creative energy to explode with reckless abandon. I remember it being so unbearably sweaty that everybody started stripping. I remember every-body making out, people hooking up right on the couches, fuelled by a creatively hyper, totally ambiguous sense of sexuality. The energy of every party was so high that it was too much for the little club."

This wasn't the Arts & Crafts crowd. This was younger, wilder, sexier. "There aren't that many non-participants and spectators," said Kado. "If anything, that's what my problem with a lot of the commercial-type stuff is, is that it doesn't encourage any behaviour at all. It encourages you to buy your ticket to the giant show on the [Toronto] Islands; it encourages you to get sunstroke with a bazillion other people."

Blocks never put on an outdoor festival, though many of the acts participated in one called Track and Field, held outside of Guelph. Held on the family farm of Ryan Carley from We're Marching On, the event featured acts like the queer electro Kids on TV, Jennifer Castle's early no-wave band Fox the Boombox, early performances by Timber Timbre and Bruce Peninsula, as well as the compara-tively mainstream Great Lake Swimmers (with Serena Ryder on backing vocals). Some performances took place in an orchard, some around a large campfire, most on a back porch. A droning metal band played in the woods after dark. A midnight cornfield performance of the Singing Saw Shadow Show was later described in a story on *The Vinyl Café*, written by Fembots violinist Julie Penner.

Shortly after Track and Field 2004, Les Mouches was scheduled to go on a short tour with U.S. dates—the first time Pallett had booked his own music any-where other than Toronto, Montreal or Guelph. Beforehand, Les Mouches went to Carley's farm to record new material. While there, Pallett lost a fanny pack containing his birth certificate and passport. "I had no ID and no way of getting anywhere, so we scuttled the tour," he says. "I was pretty depressed." On top of that, the session didn't produce anything usable.

Stuck in Toronto, Pallett tried to figure out the best way to record Final Fantasy. His friend Justin Small of Do Make Say Think invited him over to his house to set up a bunch of amplifiers to which he could split the signal from the loop pedal. That didn't work out, but a simpler setup at the home studio of friend Leon Taheny did. That autumn, they recorded "Peach Plum Pear," a cover of Californian harpist Joanna Newsom, another classically trained performer reimagining her instrument; Newsom's song was only a few months old at that point. Taheny and Pallett made a plan to record a full-length between Christmas and New Year's. In the meantime, as a musical guest on short stints with Stuart McLean's live show, Pallett developed his act on stage in front of 500 to 2,000 people a night. It was a far cry from CineCycle.

"His singing became stronger, and his sense of comfort to put himself out there certainly grew," recalled McLean in 2006. "Sometimes when you hear a performer, there are moments of transcendence, when the music fills up the space and we're all whisked away to somewhere else. It becomes a moment out of time. Some nights you could just feel the audience erupting with joy. They had never seen anything like that, and it was one big collective wow. It's a confirmation: 'You're on the right track. We want more of this.' Which can be both a liberating and limiting thing at the same time. I think Owen is a musical genius—and I use that word advisedly when I'm talking to someone who's going to write it down."

Buoyed by the *Vinyl Café* response, Pallett was determined to finish Final Fantasy's debut sooner than later—because audiences far beyond "Torontopia" were demanding it. He also had a clear deadline: Arcade Fire, now the biggest buzz band in North America, had once again invited Pallett on tour, this time across the U.S. in January and February of 2005.

They'd actually invited Les Mouches, but drummer Rob Gordon was busy with his prog-punk band From Fiction, who had been signed to Last Gang Records. Gordon and Pallett were also at odds, and besides, Pallett knew that Les Mouches were unlikely to convert many Arcade Fire fans. Les Mouches' show at Casa del Popolo for the Pop Montreal festival turned out to be the band's last. Pallett sold Win Butler on the idea of Final Fantasy, even though Arcade Fire had yet to hear a note of his new material, or even the format. Stuart McLean gave him time off work.

Right before Christmas 2004, Pallett went to see Montreal no-wave band AIDS Wolf at Sneaky Dee's. He got really drunk, got hoisted and spun around the room by a friend, and landed badly on his ankle: "I was too drunk to realize I'd broken it, hobbled home to 19 Major, went to the hospital the next morning and got a cast put on." A few days later, on Boxing Day, hobbling down frozen sidewalks on crutches, he started recording *Has a Good Home* with Taheny. He had five songs down pat, rough sketches for three more. One was his Bobby Birdman cover. Seven more songs were written during the session. "Furniture" was spawned from Arcade Fire's cover of Talking Heads' "This Must Be the Place (Naive Melody)," which Pallett introduced to the band and arranged for them with Sarah Neufeld.

Four songs that were a regular part of his live set were avoided for lyrical reasons; he wanted an album to sell to the *Vinyl Café* crowd. "I envisioned it as [Guided by Voices'] *Alien Lanes* for the blue-haired set: a long album, as many songs as possible, written and recorded really quickly and bucolic enough to not scare anybody." Having said that, "Please Please Please" has the line in its chorus "Don't let your cock do all the work!"

"It was definitely made with the idea of it being popular," says Kado. "He left a bunch of awesome gems off it, a lot of his live 'hits.' He made up all this other stuff and put those on instead."

The recording was finished on New Year's Eve. Pallett and Taheny had been working around the clock, oblivious to the outside world; they hadn't even heard the news of the Indian Ocean tsunami. The album was mastered on January 3 and Pallett flew to San Francisco to meet Arcade Fire 11 days later. "I had a walking cast at this point, but hadn't told Arcade Fire about the broken ankle," he says. "I got off the plane, met them, and they were kinda annoyed that I hadn't mentioned anything. I didn't want them to get cold feet about asking me. For the first few shows, I was literally hobbling onstage with a cane, playing while seated on a stool, but Arcade Fire and the audience were immediately so, so enthusiastic."

"Owen was the perfect [opening act] and amazing to watch for so many reasons," says Arcade Fire's Richard Reed Parry. "So full, dramatic and beautiful with really interesting and unique songs. Watching someone alone up there and getting the audience spellbound when nobody knew who he was, just him and his little violin, shrieking. I watched his whole set every single night of the tour. He could go out on stage in Dallas in front of a bunch of drunken Texans, and skinny, faggoty Owen, doing his weird songs, would have them eating out of the palm of his hand. People who don't even listen to lyrics loved the beauty and virtuosity of it. Then he would come and play in Arcade Fire, and the whole thing developed that much further, another thinking head in the band."

One song in particular got a big crowd response, and Win Butler was a big fan of it, too.

"That one song is awesome, what's it called?" he asked after one show.

Pallett smirked and said, "It's called 'This Is the Dream of Win and Régine.' It's about you guys."

"Huh," responded a smiling Butler. And they never spoke of it again.

The song title interpolates "This Is the Dream of Evan and Chan" by Dntel, a pre–Postal Service project. It's about a "prince of buzz" and an accordion player who worry that success will ruin them. The chorus is, "Montreal might eat its young / but Montreal won't bring us down." It's one of the more obvious pop songs on Has a Good Home, of which Pallett was selling anywhere from 50 to 100 CDs a night.

Because the album was completed right before the tour, Kado didn't ship the first boxes until the third night of the tour. More shipments arrived as Pallett sold them out. "There was a fiasco in New Orleans," says Parry, "where there was a lot of Owen and Leon driving around in a minivan trying to find these CDs that hadn't shown up. It was a bit of a nightmare." Because the packaging required hand assembly, it was done in short runs, with or without a booklet, until eventually Kado surrendered to a standard cardboard-and-plastic digipak later in 2005.

Within a year of its release, *Has a Good Home* had sold close to 10,000 copies. Carl Wilson profiled Pallett in the *New York Times*—a coup unheard of for a Torontonian indie artist. Blocks Recording Club—initially envisioned as a small, sustainable community project—now had a star artist whose popularity stretched limited resources even thinner. Says Pallett, "There were times when I would come over to Steve's place with a cheque, and he'd say, 'Oh, man, you're totally killing me.' I'd say, 'What are you talking about? I'm giving you money here!' He'd say, 'You're ruining my life!'"

THE CONSTANTINES WERE almost killed on stage in a hailstorm in the middle of Washington State. It was the 2006 Sasquatch! Music Festival. Before their set at the Gorge Amphitheatre, funnel clouds started approaching in the distance while Band of Horses played. "I was getting pelted with hailstones," says Doug MacGregor. "The roof was tin, and it was hard to hear on stage because [the hail] was hitting the roof so hard. Water was piling up. We were covering guitars with spare towels. I thought I could hear our sound guy, Cam [Loeppky], telling us we had to stop. It was hard to hear him over the hail. We got four or five songs in, and then the PA blew. Dallas said, 'I thought I might die up there. What a way to go.'" By the time the band stopped, there was an inch of slush covering everything on the stage. "It was one of the greatest shows I've ever seen in my life," says Sam Roberts, who was scheduled to follow them. "We were standing behind the stage watching. We ended up not playing, because by then the hail had ripped through the tarp covering the soundboard."

"But as soon as we were done, it kind of went away," says MacGregor. "I think 30% of people at that festival come from Vancouver and Calgary. They were flipping picnic tables over to shelter themselves from the hail, which was coming down at a 45-degree angle. Once it went away, all these hosers reluctantly emerged from behind their picnic tables and crowded the stage to sing the [Canadian] national anthem while we were taking our gear down. The Sub Pop guys were all there laughing. They thought it was hilarious, this national pride at being pelted by hail in a sub-desert in the middle of July."

Another album, *Kensington Heights*, came out in 2008, this time on Arts & Crafts in Canada. Reviews were mixed, and despite some highlights it sounded like the once-mighty band was running on fumes. Will Kidman quit in early 2010. That February, the Constantines played two very different gigs: the Vancouver

Winter Olympics and the 10th anniversary of Wavelength, the music series that had launched their entire career. Without Kidman, they decided to play the debut album front to back at the latter.

A few weeks later, Webb had a reckoning. "On a cold night walking down Mont-Royal," Webb wrote on the band's website years later, "I called Doug, who I'd been playing in bands with since early high school, and said, 'I can't do this anymore.' Doug was kind and understanding, and we spoke as brothers do. That was a basic fact with the Cons: we were as real with each other as people could be. The band played a few shows that year, fulfilled what responsibilities we could, and then we went our separate ways." The final show was at the Dawson City Music Festival that summer.

"I thought we should cut the crap before we made [the equivalent of the Clash's] *Cut the Crap*," says MacGregor. "We were tired. We each had a different vision for what the band should be, and I thought we'd make some bad compromises. It wasn't going to be as good, and it wasn't going to be fun, so it wasn't going to be worth it. It wasn't something I was vocal about, but I think we could all tell. A friend rode with us to a gig in Sudbury, and he said it was the quietest van ride he'd ever been in. We'd been together so long and ran out of things to say to each other."

THE HIDDEN CAMERAS, a band who started out never playing in clubs, became a touring machine. In 2004, the Hidden Cameras did three European tours in one year, on top of dates in Ontario, Quebec and the eastern U.S., all supporting that year's *Mississauga Goddam*. On a November jaunt to Boston and New York City, they were forced to forfeit their headlining status to their opening act: Arcade Fire.

The two bands had shared several bills before. "Win [Butler] emailed me many times to open up for us," says Gibb. "They saw our second gig in Montreal [at Le Swimming in December 2003]. Win and Richard [Reed Parry] came to the gig and stood right at the front. The next time we played Montreal [in February 2004], they opened for us in an art gallery, and that's where they debuted 'Rebellion.' I liked that they had a similar vibe to us. Same tricks: running around with one tom, switching up instruments, those sorts of things." Butler has often acknowledged his debt to the Hidden Cameras in interviews and acceptance speeches over the years.

It's somewhat surprising the Hidden Cameras made it back into the U.S. at all, after a thwarted attempt to play SXSW in March 2004. A manager that Rough Trade assigned the band had forgotten to renew work visas, which expired 11 days before the gig. Everyone but Gibb made it through U.S. customs at the Toronto airport. (Most major Canadian airports have U.S. preclearance on the premises.) "There's lots of things you can say to a customs agent," says Maggie MacDonald, "because you don't get paid for playing SXSW. You can say 'industry showcase' or 'vacation weekend,' whatever—many legit things. Joel showed up with a guitar and a bunch of T-shirts and said, 'I'm going to play a gig.' They're like, 'Who is this guy?'"

The rest of the band was waiting to board. They were told that if they waited for Gibb their tickets would be forfeited and they'd need to buy new ones, so they flew to Texas without him. Gibb tried two more times in the next 24 hours to get on a plane, to no avail. "We all had this luxurious weekend at a hotel paid for by Rough Trade," says MacDonald. "Joel was dating this really sexy bisexual Swedish guy at the time, who came to [Austin] to meet up with Joel, but he and I just hung out instead and I met all the Swedish guys at the festival. We had a blast. We had no gigs. It was amazing. Joel never arrived. Joel has this attitude about the world, where, 'It's my world, and I'm Joel.' I was in England with him once and saw him try to get on a plane without a ticket, like it was just some club guest list, like, 'I'm just gonna walk on a plane in a post-9/11 world.' That's Joel."

He didn't bring his whole band with him to Europe, instead relying increasingly on local players. "I'd swell up a nice string section in London, and a Swedish tour with a Swedish string player," he says. "Word got out in Europe that it was this kind of band. In Austria, they even did a competition where an FM station asked local Viennese musicians to apply, and they supplied a whole other group for us. We had a huge band in Vienna."

Much of the next two years was spent on the road. To promote the August 2006 release of the album *Awoo*, six weeks in Europe were followed immediately by a month-long North American sweep, which included a gig at the inaugural Osheaga festival in Montreal. The North American tour did not go well. Drives were long, crowds were sparse, money was tight and inter-band communication was poor. Things got off to a weird start as soon as they tried to cross the U.S. border. They were touring with a prog-pop band of Toronto high school students, children of prominent Ontario folk musicians. It being the youngsters' first time on tour, the kids brought drugs. As MacDonald recalls, the border agent searched the keyboardist's purse, and the conversation went a little something like this:

"So you're musicians?"

"Yep."

"Do you have marijuana with you?"

"No, no, no drugs."

"Listen, it's better for you to be honest with me right now than to lie about this, because we might know something."

"Okay, maybe I have a joint in my purse."

"Good. I know that. What you need to know is that you're musicians, you care about your art. You have to look at what happened to all the great musicians like Janis Joplin and Jimi Hendrix—these people were great, cared about their art, got into drugs and died. You're in the music industry, kids: stay off drugs. Now go into the U.S. and play your gig."

"*Meanwhile*," says MacDonald, still incredulous years later, "we had Americans in our band, dual citizens who can do whatever they want in America, but we had T-shirts where some were made in the NAFTA zone and some weren't. We were stuck at the border for two days, trying to get rid of our non-NAFTA T-shirts. We'd been touring for months and months at that point and everything was mixed together. We missed a gig—and then these kids went across with drugs! That tells you what kind of foot we started out on."

Upon returning to Toronto, several members quit, and Gibb cancelled Australian dates, "because the band were so tired and angry at our then manager for the border debacle," he says. Which wasn't entirely heartbreaking for Gibb, who that June had already decided to move to Berlin. He and MacDonald had hung out there for three weeks between a one-off gig in Austria and another one-off in Sweden. "It was three hours before our flight, and Joel was nowhere to be found," says MacDonald. "Half an hour later he came blazing in and started throwing stuff in his bag: 'I want to stay!' He's lived in Berlin ever since."

BLOCKS RECORDING CLUB was big in Cologne, Germany. That's where the Tomlab label, who'd put out acclaimed records by the Books and Xiu Xiu, took a liking to Toronto by putting out Blocks acts Final Fantasy and Ninja High School, as well as Mantler and Montreal art-punks Les Georges Leningrad. For Owen Pallett, his European label as well as an Arcade Fire connection helped build anticipation for his next record.

Pallett wasn't happy with *Has a Good Home*: he knew it had been rushed, he knew he could do better and he wanted to arrange for an actual string sextet. He also wanted to make a concept record about Dungeons & Dragons. And for reasons known only to him, he wanted to call the album *He Poos Clouds*.

Eight of the nine songs are based on the schools of magic: abjuration (protective spells), illusion, conjuration, necromancy (power over death), enchantment, evocation (manipulated energy), divination (knowledge) and transmutation. "It actually is about the schools of magic, but it's also about normal people," says Steve Kado. "His analogy for divination is the Freedom 55 ads: he thinks divination is meeting yourself in the future, and what yourself in the future says is 'Invest!'

But because it's such lush music and has all the signifiers of being emotional, people assume it's about him or real human feelings, when actually it's about perceiving normal things in funny ways."

Though Pallett is a devoted sci-fi and fantasy fan, he was more of a passive observer when it came to Dungeons & Dragons. "I've only played two or three games of it in my life," he said in 2006. "But I have the second-edition books and I read them a lot. I find them really interesting from an anthropological perspective. It's a new system of belief that's entirely fictional and yet so resolute in its ability to explain everything and simplify the entire workings of the universe with use of statistics and rolling of dice. At the same time, it's created strictly for entertainment purposes." Just like pop music.

Promoting the D&D angle also helped deflect any assumptions listeners might make about Pallett himself, a young queer man at a time when there were still not many voices singing out of the closet. "When you do something that is somewhat confessional," he says, "it creates this assumption by predominantly male music writers that what is happening is automatic rather than intentional. It always frustrates me reading the idea that Tori Amos's records are direct products of her faerie-worshipping, or whatever."

The album was written for a string sextet, which featured players from the Toronto Symphony Orchestra and Canadian Opera Company Orchestra, with Pallett playing only some viola alongside keyboards and bass. Backing vocals were done by jazz singer Lori Cullen with Casey and Jenny Mecija, two sisters who debuted their band Ohbijou opening for an early Final Fantasy show at C'est What. "The Arctic Circle" and "Song Song Song" have enough syncopation to sound like the Meters adapted by a string quartet. "Many Lives —> 49 MP" rides a discombobulating yet driving 5/4 rhythm.

"This Lamb Sells Condos" caused a minor kerfuffle in Toronto media, because its title was lifted from high-profile condo developer Brad J. Lamb; it was the slogan of his ad campaign, seen on billboards across the city. Comedian and drummer Lex Vaughn played the role of Lamb in a song about impotence, the lyrics of which Pallett claimed were verbatim conversations heard through the walls of a building he and his boyfriend shared with the developer. The song boasts a jaunty harpsichord lick, though Pallett says, "It's just Scott Joplin ragtime, really, but there's nothing more ragtime than *Super Mario Brothers*."

He Poos Clouds arrived when classically trained indie rock musicians were less of an anomaly. Joanna Newsom was the first harpist since Loreena McKennitt to make an impact outside of classical or jazz. Sufjan Stevens was making ornately arranged folk-pop in his bedroom. Dirty Projectors' Dave Longstreth was making glitchy avant-pop music with classical and choral overtones. In the eyes of some, including Arcade Fire's Richard Reed Parry, Pallett was doing it better than anyone. "*He Poos Clouds* is the most impressive amalgamation of the modern classical world and art-pop music that actually reaches far on both sides of the equation," he said at the time. "It's not just a pop record that borrows technique and aesthetics from the classical world. It's as much a modern classical record as it is a pop record. I don't know anything else like that."

Critic Carl Wilson said of Pallett, in 2014, "He's a [type] of certain independent musician who once would have been more stubbornly avant-garde and now has a more eclectic approach. He's a particular subset, bringing his classical training to that music. You see in indie music of the last 10 years the emergence of strings and of horns, often just for colouration, but in Owen's case it's really integral. That also informs his skepticism about indie orthodoxies. He's already been through one set of ideologies that he has to resist in order to do what he does. So he's unlikely to be swayed by a new set of ideologies."

Wilson was on the jury for the inaugural Polaris Music Prize in September 2006. Most pundits predicted a heavyweight like Broken Social Scene, Metric, the New Pornographers or Sarah Harmer would win. To the shock of the music industry in general, *He Poos Clouds* won. Pallett was completely unknown outside the indie community in Toronto and a subset of CBC listeners. *He Poos Clouds* was one of three records on the list from tiny labels with very few resources (the others were from Cadence Weapon and Malajube). There wasn't even a genre into which Pallett's record could be easily slotted. If the Polaris wanted a win that proved it was not the Junos, there was no better choice. Its opening track concludes with the repeated mantra, "Your rock'n'roll has gone away." Pallett's win began a long tradition of Polaris upsetting all oddsmakers.

Two months after the Polaris win, Joanna Newsom released her album *Ys*, which was showered with adoration for its ambition and for employing Van Dyke Parks (Beach Boys, Randy Newman) as orchestral arranger. It topped many year-end lists; Pallett's album did not. In early 2007, he had his first real bout of depression. "Admitting this will make me sound self-obsessed," he says, "but I was dismayed that after a year's worth of work and winning the Polaris prize and getting an eight on *Pitchfork*, the end of the year came and I felt forgotten. For many people, Joanna Newsom's *Ys* is a remarkable achievement. I think it is, too, but I also think it's a shitty album, largely because the string arrangements do not work. I say this as a huge Joanna Newsom fan, who thinks [her] *Milk-Eyed Mender* and *Divers* are two of the best albums ever. But *Ys* came out and it left me so frustrated. It's got Steve Albini and Jim O'Rourke and Van Dyke Parks on it. Whereas *He Poos Clouds*, I fucking made that myself, arranged it myself. I still think it's a better record. I'm not saying this because I think I'm better than her,

I don't. She's light years ahead of me. I'm just saying that professional jealousy is real and can be fucking devastating. It happens across the board, and everyone I know feels it."

Pallett spent three months living with his parents while trying to work on new music; he got nothing done. The band Spoon commissioned him for a remix; he procrastinated so long that they fired him. British band Bloc Party took him on tour, which brought him out of his shell. He performed with orchestras in Vienna and Halifax. There was a commission from New York avant-garde institution Bang on a Can. He worked with the band Beirut and sang a song on their second record, made at Arcade Fire's studio. He helped Arcade Fire finish a score for *The Box*, a movie by Richard Kelly, the director of *Donnie Darko*. He recorded two EPs: one, *Spectrum 14th Century*, was a conceptual narrative that set up his 2010 album *Heartland*; the other, *Plays to Please*, was Nelson Riddle–ish orchestral arrangements of songs by his friend Alex Lukashevsky of Deep Dark United.

"Alex and I have a tendency to shoot ourselves in the foot, and with Alex it's kind of legendary," says Pallett. "So this project was like me sabotaging his self-sabotage, by taking his songs and doing my best attempt at defending them in an AM radio format." *Plays to Please* was virtually ignored everywhere but by Toronto's two weeklies. "I was so proud of it," he says, "and for people to see it as some kind of wet fart really upset me."

Then came a gig that changed his career. Through his friend Nico Muhly—another young, queer, classically trained composer, who worked with Philip Glass and Grizzly Bear, among others—Pallett was recommended to Alex Turner of hot U.K. band Arctic Monkeys. Turner had a new project, the Last Shadow Puppets. Their debut, *The Age of the Understatement*, was a rock record, influenced by Scott Walker and Serge Gainsbourg, that featured full orchestration on every track—arranged and conducted by Pallett, performed by the London Metropolitan Orchestra.

It entered the U.K. charts at No. 1. A-listers started calling Pallett for arrangements. Brian Eno sang the praises of Pallett's next record, *Heartland*, and sang on the one after that. In 2010, the *Guardian* wrote that *Heartland* was "perhaps the grandest orchestral pop record since Joanna Newsom's *Ys*."

THE HIDDEN CAMERAS played their biggest gig yet in 2007: a stadium gig in Munich in front of 70,000 people. They'd been personally invited by soccer star Mehmet Scholl to play his retirement party at the stadium and to the subsequent reception. The band had custom lederhosen made for the occasion. The gig featured the German players Gibb used for European tours, the only Canadians being the then-core band of keyboardist Laura Barrett, drummer John Power and bassist Paul Mathew.

By the time of 2009's *Origin:Orphan*, there was a sense that the band had plateaued. For the first three Hidden Cameras albums, Gibb had drawn from a stockpile of songs he'd written before the band formed. Now he was beginning to run dry. "There was a major change in Joel's songwriting," says Owen Pallett. "I was so moved by his early songs, the way he was writing about that stuff in such explicit detail and capturing moments. Then it turned and became very abstract, with songs like 'Doot Doot Plot.' Even 'Bboy'—it didn't make sense. Whereas 'A Miracle' changed my life. So did 'Smells Like Happiness.' I remember joking with [drummer] Lex [Vaughn] that Joel's songwriting was descending so far into an examination of phonemes as opposed to actual topics. I said, 'One of these days you're going to go to rehearsal and he's going to say, "This next song is called 'Sneh.' Or 'Wah.'"' She called me a few days later. 'I just came back from rehearsal and you were right! He just came in with a song called 'In the NA'!"

That said, in 2006 Gibb had started writing songs for a country record that he finally released in 2016, *Home on Native Land*, widely hailed as his best work in years. "There are songs on *Home on Native Land* that are so great," says Pallett. "He is writing songs now that I can't even work on because they're so emotional. His lyrics are so good. People just change and evolve. When I speak critically of anyone, it's because I'm really engaged with the music. I've thought a lot about this music because I love the people involved, and certain songs have meant a lot to me."

Home on Native Land was one of only two records Gibb released after 2009, the other being 2014's *Age*. The Hidden Cameras rarely toured North America anymore—not even for *Home on Native Land*, for which there were only four Ontario dates. It's often a wild guess as to who will be in the band, though at the final night of the 2010 Wavelength festival, several original members reunited to play "I Believe in the Good of Life." A 2020 Wavelength show featured a stripped-down band of Pallett, Dave Meslin and Mike Olsen, with Dorian Wolf of Austra on bass.

"I played my last gig in 2014," says Maggie MacDonald. "I didn't have a dramatic departure. A lot of people got to the point where they couldn't stand it anymore. I was someone who wasn't trained in music and that wasn't my ambition. I slowly drifted into a situation where I worked standard jobs for money, and it left less room for my creative practice. Whereas someone like Owen, who is brilliant and has always trained for that, it's harder [for someone like him] to deal with someone who needs control over a project. Joel has burned a lot of bridges."

Twenty years after the band began, the revolving door had left Gibb at a bit of a loss. But maybe the band was always about more than him. He says now, "I meet people who say, 'I've been in your band. I danced in your band. I've been in your choir.' And I literally have no idea who they are. I don't know half the stories of the Hidden Cameras."

ONLY ONE EX–HIDDEN CAMERA has so far been nominated for an Oscar. Owen Pallett helped Arcade Fire score the Spike Jonze movie *Her*; though the whole band participated, he shared the credit with Will Butler. By the time they got an Oscar nod, the success of the Last Shadow Puppets earned Pallett arranging gigs with Taylor Swift, Pet Shop Boys and R.E.M., among others. He continued to work with the people from the scene that spawned him: the same year he was up for an Oscar, he worked on Jennifer Castle's *Pink City*, Caribou's *Our Love*, Gentleman Reg's Light Fires project and Arcade Fire's *Reflektor*.

His fee never went up: from the beginning, his policy has been pay what you can. And he was never short of work.

THE CONSTANTINES REUNITED in 2014 for Field Trip, a Toronto summer festival staged by Arts & Crafts. In the intervening years, several musicians had admitted their inspiration to start a band was a Constantines show in the early 2000s, including future arena rockers Arkells from Hamilton and internationally renowned power duo Japandroids from Vancouver. They had more famous fans, too, of course—including Arcade Fire, who covered "Young Lions" at the Air Canada Centre in 2014.

"The Constantines are a world-class, unimpeachable, incredible rock band," Leslie Feist said in 2014 on the occasion of the reunion. "They're an institution that I've always observed with a kind of fear and intimidation from a distance. For years, during my solo section in 'Sealion,' I put the riff for 'Nighttime/Anytime' in there because I felt the six people in the audience at the Air Canada Centre who got it would think, Why the fuck is she playing a Cons riff in the middle of her show? 'Young Lions' is another of my favourites. The first time I spent a long time with [*Shine a Light*], I was in the Canary Islands over Christmas, and I rented a car and I went and found a volcano to go climb, and I remember having the headphones on and it being this hazy day, and I was a climbing a fucking volcano, and there's no vegetation around, there's just this porous, sharp rock and this incline . . . and I'm listening to 'Young Lions' full blast on my headphones, climbing a volcano off the shores of Africa, and thinking, *I am* the video for this song!'" That's the way most people felt listening to Constantines, no matter where they were.

Back when *Shine a Light* came out, Bry Webb said, "The closest thing to a deity that I believe in is the bond that exists among a community of people. The most inspiring thing about human nature is that it will find a reason to exist in the midst of a lot of reasons to not exist. I don't know if it's just this weird, paranoid climate that we've been living in, but it seems like it's given licence to people to live for the now, and just celebrate life."

CHAPTER 10

COUNTRY IN THE CITY

CORB LUND, THE BE GOOD TANYAS, KATHLEEN EDWARDS, THE SADIES

"Country in the city / high and lonesome every night
Locals think we're crazy and we don't put up a fight"
—Carolyn Mark, "Country in the City," 2002

Canadians are very good at Americana. That's been true before there was even a term for it.

In his book *Whispering Pines*, Jason Schneider makes the argument that it was a group of Canadians who had the greatest impact on redefining North American roots music in the rock'n'roll age: Joni Mitchell, Neil Young, Leonard Cohen, Gordon Lightfoot, the Band. Few North Americans who've ever picked up an acoustic guitar are immune from their influence. Only Bob Dylan was more important, and he grew up a short drive from the northern shores of Lake Superior. Generations later, k.d. lang, Jr. Gone Wild and others moulded country music in their own image, predating the late '90s trend of Americana, or alt-country—itself a rebellion against superstars like Shania Twain of Timmins, Ontario, who shattered every possible preconception of how popular country music could be worldwide.

Ottawa's Kathleen Edwards, who spent her youth in Seoul and Switzerland as the daughter of a diplomat, found comfort in the sounds of home and followed directly in the footsteps of homegrown heroes Blue Rodeo and Sarah Harmer, though with much greater international success. The Be Good Tanyas were three tree planters who met in the Kootenay Mountains, singing barely above a whisper, and defied all expectations to become one of the first genuine independent sensations of the early 2000s, echoing the Cowboy Junkies' early success: weird, unexpected and playing by their own rules. The Sadies were the hardest-working band not just in Toronto but the whole country, in time becoming the backing band of choice for many ex-punks exploring roots music, with direct connections and collaborations with several characters from the *Whispering Pines* era.

Of them all, however, there was only one real cowboy in the musical lineage dating back to Wilf Carter, a.k.a. Montana Slim, a Nova Scotian who helped popularize western music in American popular culture in the 1930s. All but forgotten today, Wilf Carter hosted a national CBS Radio show out of New York City, and in 1950, he set an attendance record at Toronto's Canadian National Exhibition by attracting 50,000 people to his show.

But even Carter didn't grow up on a ranch. Corb Lund did.

——————

THE ALT-COUNTRY MOVEMENT of the '90s and 2000s was littered with ex-punks who suddenly discovered acoustic guitar and liked to play downmarket dress-up. So maybe it's not that strange that Corb Lund, one of the greatest Canadian country singer-songwriters of the 2000s, was a bass player from a '90s Edmonton prog-metal band heavily influenced by SNFU and Voivod.

What's stranger is that he became "the poet laureate of the Albertan people, basically," says his friend Vancouver songwriter Geoff Berner. "People of the left and the right love Corb Lund and the way he depicts their lives. More so even than Ian Tyson, because Corb goes into far more detail. [Unlike Tyson,] Corb didn't decide to become a cowboy; he was raised on a ranch. He's a fascinating split: he's a big, tough guy with powers of empathy we assign to femininity. His dad was a rancher and an agricultural veterinarian and would take Corb around on his rounds, talking with the ranchers about what the issues were. At the same time his dad could ride and rope everything. Corb can actually do all that shit, too. None of those other fuckers wearing a cowboy hat on TV can do that. But he really listens to people telling their stories about what's going on in their lives. He cares about them. His art comes from a pure place. Then, when it's time to market it and do the business, he's good at it. That's a rare combination."

The five albums Lund released between 2002 and 2012 should all be regarded as modern Canadian classics regardless of genre—if western music (as distinct from country music) was taken seriously in the 21st century, but it's not. His story starts 10 years before that, with a band called the Smalls. It's a story rarely heard outside of Alberta, because while the Smalls were a huge deal in their home province—and only slightly less so in Saskatchewan and the B.C. Interior—they were completely ignored east of Winnipeg. The Smalls should have had their own chapter in *Have Not Been the Same*—and I'm an ignorant eastern shithead for not making that happen. At least they became the subject of an excellent documentary, 2015's *Forever Is a Long Time*. For all those not big on the Smalls, a brief history is required.

CORB LUND GREW UP IN TABER, a 30-minute drive east of Lethbridge in southern Alberta. He and his high school friend Mike Caldwell got into punk music in the most Canadian way possible: through their obsession with *SCTV* and the Sex Pistols parody sketch about "the Queen Haters." Reruns of *SCTV*—its third season was shot in Edmonton—aired every night on their local station at 11 p.m., followed by episodes of the proto-MuchMusic show *The NewMusic*. "I think they only had six or eight episodes that they played over and over," says Lund. "There was a punk one. And one about the Winnipeg speed metal scene. *The NewMusic* was our only little window to non-mainstream music—that, and going to the weird rock shop in Calgary every six months. I could sense there was another world out there. Keep in mind: I'm from three hours south of Calgary and my family are all cowboys, so I had no exposure to this stuff. I found it all exotic."

After high school, Lund and Caldwell went to Edmonton to attend Grant MacEwan College's jazz program. "We didn't like jazz at all—but they didn't have an Iron Maiden school, so there we were," he says. While in town for the audition, they saw a poster for a SNFU gig in a local hall. The Taber boys had been to arena shows to see Judas Priest and Honeymoon Suite and had seen cover bands who'd play a local bar for a week at a time, but never a DIY punk show. "It was intimidating," says Lund. "It changed our lives. It's one of the best shows I've ever seen to this day, just bananas: mosh pit, controlled chaos. The light bulb went off. You could just do this: rent a hall, rent a PA and just do it."

Within a year, the two formed the Smalls with guitarist Dug Bevans, from Leduc outside of Edmonton, and drummer Terry Johnson, from La Glace, a farming hamlet outside of Grande Prairie. This was literally a band of outsiders, and they attracted other outsiders who didn't fit into urban punk scenes. A self-titled cassette came out almost immediately; it was recorded at MacEwan over two nights. They booked the studio until 10 p.m. each day, then shut off the lights, waited for everyone to go home, then fired up all the gear again and recorded all night long. In 1991, SNFU took them on the road. "They were gods in Edmonton," says Lund. "That was a big shot in the arm."

The Smalls soon found their own crowd, especially in small Prairie towns where other bands dared not tread. The Smalls were all small-town guys; they knew the terrain. Guitarist Bevans always wore a John Deere cap. Their music, however, sounded like nothing else. It was prog-rock and speed metal and '90s grunge, as played by guys with jazz chops, a bassist steeped in country music and an enigmatic singer who could sing like Chris Cornell and whose choice in covers involved gender-benders like Aretha Franklin's "Natural Woman." That adds up to a marketing nightmare. One member had rage issues. Another slept through a New Music West showcase, blowing what might have been a big break. One was an alcoholic who shot his friend by accident and spent three years in prison. And one became an internationally acclaimed country singer. No wonder the documentary about their 2014 reunion is like *Hard Core Logo* but with a happy ending.

The Smalls made national headlines with reports that a 1996 gig in Kamloops was a riot dispersed by the RCMP. Lund recalls it differently. "It was an all-ages show in a hall and it was oversold," he says. "There was only one door to the place, so the cops came and told us to shut it down. They got on stage and—I'm not sure whose decision this was—they started pepper-spraying everyone in the front row. Considering their supposed concern was people being trampled in the case of fire, that just created a stampede. People got run over and 15-year-old girls got maced. It was harsh. We had only played two or three songs."

"The Smalls had this reputation for having a lot of artistic integrity—and for being scary," says Geoff Berner, who met them on a tour of Norway. "Except for the drummer, they were all big men: large Alberta ranching boys. They could fight. Nobody fucked with the Smalls—as far as I knew. I certainly wouldn't try and short them on a guarantee. They had this integrity and commitment to art. They weren't just big lunks from Alberta. They were artists. They were ambitious. But they didn't talk much. Except for the drummer, who was a bit of a loudmouth sometimes. They had seen my act, and the singer, Mike, who rarely spoke, we were backstage, and he looked at me deadpan and said, 'You're a funny guy. *You say funny things.*' It was chilling, the way he said it. I decided to take it at face value and said, 'Thanks! Trying my best. You guys are great.'"

DIY was built into the bones of the Smalls—out of necessity. Helping hands were few. Quebecois band GrimSkunk—another hyper-regional success story— took the Smalls on an extensive tour of their home province, including small towns like Matane on the Gaspé Peninsula. In a rare Alberta-Quebec crossover, the Smalls fit in more comfortably in la belle province than they ever did in Ontario. Part of it was their love of some native sons. "I fucking love Voivod," says Lund. "Especially *Dimension Hatröss* and *Nothingface*. Another unappreciated band that we loved was [Vancouver's] Sons of Freedom. Love that band. I never felt they got their due. I think I saw them either just before or after their first record. There's this old prairie hotel called the Grand Hotel in Edmonton, classic hotel with an old-man bar and shitty rooms upstairs. Every Tuesday was alternative night, and it was a blend of Smiths-and-Cure-type people mixed with people who loved the Cult record and speed metal guys. The community wasn't big enough to have sub-genres; all the weirdos gathered in one place. Sons of Freedom played there, and they were fucking great. They were all dressed in lab coats."

A young band on the Alberta scene at the time made a big impression on Lund, particularly the singer: a teenage Leslie Feist. "Her old band, Placebo, used to play with the Smalls all the time," he says. "They were remarkably good, really heavy, with a great singer. A lot of times in that scene, the music was really good but the singer would not be so good. I'm happy for her success and I love the music she makes now, but her voice was really great in a heavy rock format. She was a big supporter of my country material. She'd always come out when I played Calgary. She's one of those people who is absolutely a free spirit, and it's awesome."

Like many Canadian musicians who don't live in Montreal or Toronto, Lund chalks up the Smalls' commercial limitations to geography. "Fans of the Smalls will say we were undiscovered or ahead of our time or whatever, but I don't think that's true," he says. "The baked-in issue is that we were from Edmonton. Which is a cool artistic scene, but it's tough to go national or international from there. We tried living in Vancouver for a while, and it was okay, but we just didn't fit. So we focused on what was working, which was all these mid-sized [or] small cities through the West. Which doesn't necessarily lend itself to commercial success.

"I've witnessed this in other genres: in metal, in Americana, it's universal. There are always the bands who get fortunate with media coverage, and I think, They're kinda good, but why these guys? I know five other acts in this genre who are stronger. That comes from playing the game, being in the cultural centres and spending more time schmoozing than playing. We always took the opposite route. We just wanted to get good at what we do and let the chips fall where they may. It may not have been the best career move, but it was good in terms of making real music and connecting with people in a real way."

One of the last big things the Smalls did was a tour of the Balkans in 1999. They were the first Western act to tour there just as it was emerging from years of civil wars. It was organized by Cam Noyes, a notorious figure in Western Canadian music who knew how to hustle the Canadian grant system to get fringe artists touring overseas, including Tanya Tagaq.[1] "He pulled off some crazy shit," laughs Lund. "And he also *failed* to pull off some crazy shit, for us and a lot of other

---

1   Noyes is the thinly veiled inspiration for Geoff Berner's 2013 satirical novel *Festival Man*, which should be essential reading for any Canadian music fan. Lund is also fictionalized in the book.

bands." As exciting as that tour was—and it could have been a launching pad into a continent more predisposed to idiosyncratic prog-metal bands—the Smalls were near the end of their collective rope. After another Noyes-booked tour of Norway in 2001, they decided on a final gamble: move to Austin, Texas, or break up.

"The Smalls were around for 11 years," says Lund. "I could see that it wasn't going to work in Canada any further than it was: on a modest cult-following level. If there was any chance of us getting onto a bigger platform, we'd have to move. At the time Austin was a hip rock'n'roll city. At the last minute, not everyone wanted to go. I just said fuck it, I'm going anyway."

THE SMALLS' MUSIC didn't fit into easy boxes, nor did Lund's solo material. By the time he landed in Austin, he had already put out two albums of solo material that tapped into his country and folk roots—albeit with his own twist. "My loose intentions were to make the most of the Smalls and see how far we could take it," he says, "but I was never into playing speed metal into my 50s. That's young people's music. I don't begrudge people doing it at an older age; if it works for them, great. I always assumed I'd move into some kind of roots music when I was older. I figured the sooner I could get good at it, the better."

His debut, 1995's *Modern Pain*, "was a lark," says Lund. "I didn't know what the fuck I was doing." Nonetheless, three of its songs later reappeared on some of his strongest albums. There's also a song in French, an instrumental waltz and a live Stompin' Tom Connors cover. The follow-up, 1999's *Unforgiving Mistress*, features an uncommonly large dose of Spanish guitar. "I was experimenting," he says. "I also deliberately didn't want to blend a bunch of rocky Smalls stuff with it. I wanted it to be a departure. Two distinct sounds." Both records were barely heard outside of Edmonton, though they suggested that Lund would be right at home in Austin, the spiritual home of the storyteller songwriters he admired most.

It was there that he wrote his third album, *Five Dollar Bill*. Though he was inspired musically by his Texan surroundings, the lyrics were the most distinctly Albertan he'd written to date. "There Are No Roads Here" is about his Danish ancestors migrating across the continent from Texas. "Short Native Grasses" follows an Albertan to the streets of Montreal, where "you can do what you want / on Boulevard St. Laurent." The title track is about Albertans running booze over the border during Prohibition. "Roughest Neck Around" is about the oil riggers of Fort McMurray "pulling dragons from the ground." "Buckin' Horse Rider" is an ode to Lund's beloved rodeo culture.

The common thread is the level of detail and local vernacular that place Lund in the tradition of cowboy poetry; he's a frequent performer at the annual

National Cowboy Poetry Gathering in Elko, Nevada. Lund is also careful to separate country music from western music; he plays the latter, which was a more regional genre until Nashville DJs started conflating the two in the 1950s.

Most important: even without the lessons in history, geography and musicology, the dozen songs on *Five Dollar Bill* are a master class in songwriting in terms of melody and the use of jazz chords in folk songs, delivered via meticulous, muscular band arrangements with swing and a punch. Lund staked his claim as one of the great Canadian songwriters—precious few of whom have ever delivered a single album as strong as *Five Dollar Bill*. He felt liberated, and not just musically. "The Smalls were very democratic," he says, "which made it problematic." There are traces of his speed metal past: the nimble finger-picking, rapid-fire lyrics and rhythm section shots on "Expectation and the Blues" and "Daughter Don't You Marry No Guitar Picker."

Five Dollar Bill was produced by Harry Stinson, best known for recording '80s classics like Steve Earle's *Guitar Town* and Lyle Lovett's *Pontiac*, as well as for writing No. 1 hits for Trisha Yearwood and Martina McBride. Nothing about *Five Dollar Bill* sounds like a slick Nashville recording, however. "I didn't want any reverb on anything, and I didn't want electric guitars," says Lund. "It's dry as a bone, and very sparse."

Half the album features drummer Ryan Vikedal, who'd played in Lund's solo band since 1995. He hailed from Brooks, Alberta—halfway between Calgary and Medicine Hat—and in 1998 started playing with the increasingly popular band from up the road in Hanna: Nickelback. "I was in no position to tell him not to," says Lund. "But he double-booked himself once when I had a big show in Edmonton, so I got the Smalls drummer, Terry [Johnson], to fill in. But there was a period of time where me and Chad [Kroeger] had scheduling meetings to prevent that kind of thing." Nickelback's blockbuster breakthrough happened in the fall of 2001, and it was more than obvious that Vikedal couldn't remain loyal to Lund. "There was no ill will," he says. "I was happy for him. It got to the point where it was obvious he had bigger fish to fry."

Smalls fans other than Chad Kroeger proved to be very supportive in Lund's early solo days. "I was surprised how many carried over," he says. "Now my audience is mixed: half urban indie people and half legit cowboys and ranchers. The blend depends on where the venue is. But at the beginning, it was very much an extension of the Smalls. And in Edmonton at the time, there was a big so-called alt-country scene." As former *Edmonton Sun* critic Mike Ross wrote, "All the Edmonton punk rockers from the early '90s seemed to unplug their guitars and 'go country' at the same time. By the end of the decade, you could barely find an alternative rock band playing in an alternative rock bar. They were all playing country."

It's part of the long legacy of '80s and '90s band Jr. Gone Wild, whom Lund covered on the 2001 *Have Not Been the Same* compilation. One group of peers was Old Reliable, who put out several brooding, crunchy country-rock records that remain highly underrated outside of Alberta.

Unlike most everyone else on the scene, whether or not they grew up on a farm, Lund sang about the life he knew as a child. "There are very few bands who write about rural stuff or western stuff or ag-based stuff," he says. "It's got that aroma to it, but there's not a lot of meat in terms of lyrical content specific to agricultural life. And mine does." Lund's father was a horse veterinarian and a Canadian Pro Rodeo Hall of Famer; his mother was the Calgary Stampede's first barrel racing champion, in 1959. Both sides of his family migrated west through Utah and Nevada and up into Alberta around the turn of the 20th century.

Most non-Albertans are unfamiliar with the reasons why there is a cowboy culture there, why it's the "Texas of Canada." Lund is happy to explain. "The history of the North American cowboy started after the Civil War, when there were all these cheap longhorn cattle running around in Texas, to the point where they were almost a nuisance," he says. "As people started to move west, above Texas, there was a market for beef. They'd have all these trail drives, where they'd put a cattle herd together and move them up north to the railheads, where they could sell them to the people in the West. That moved up the Rockies all the way to B.C. and Alberta, and my people are part of that migration. It's not a coincidence that I play a lot in the west of Canada and the U.S. We play out east and people like it, but it's akin to me going to see someone like [Maritime icon] Stan Rogers in Edmonton. I'd love the music and find it interesting and think he's great, but it's not my culture. When we play in Wyoming or Colorado, people really connect to what we're singing about."

Lund can walk the walk—and steer the steer. "I did junior bull riding, or steer riding, until I was 15," he says. "I did a bit of steer wrestling in high school, which is where you jump off the galloping horse onto the steer. That's right about the time I got into Black Sabbath, so I retired and got into music. But a lot of my cousins and uncles and grandpas, they're all cowboys. The first songs I ever sang I learned from my grandfathers, who were ranchers, and would sing these ancient cowboy tragic story ballads that had been passed down thru oral tradition in the West, before recorded music. 'Strawberry Roan,' 'When the Work's All Done This Fall,' 'Little Joe the Wrangler.' Those are my bedrock, sort of touchstone songs."

Classic album though it is, *Five Dollar Bill* didn't immediately change Lund's fortunes. Certainly not in Ontario, where he was playing tiny cafés on tour with Geoff Berner. His 2003 NXNE showcase in Toronto took place in a sparsely attended Tranzac Club, where Lund passed out his custom merch: *Five Dollar Bill* playing cards. (Berner later wrote a song called "Don't Play Cards for Money with Corby Lund.")

Word spread slowly: through Smalls fans dispersed across Canada, through Albertans who listened to province-wide public radio CKUA and through fans of serious songwriters of any genre. As authentic as Lund's approach was to his music, the lyrics alone drew in new listeners, not unlike some of his heroes. "My heroes are the guys who transcend style, whether it's Neil Young or Bob Dylan," he says. "Most people who go see Willie Nelson aren't country fans: they're Willie Nelson fans. Steve Earle and Lyle Lovett are others like that; they start out in whatever scene suits them best, and they grow to a point where it's not necessarily a country fan that goes to see them. Hopefully, well-written honest music can transcend those boundaries."

Five Dollar Bill was intentionally far removed from corporate country music, but it did get commercial radio play—starting in Red Deer, which latched onto first the title track and then "Roughest Neck Around," the song about oil rig workers that struck an obvious local chord.[2] Other stations followed suit, and Country Music Television (CMT) played the video for "Shine Up My Boots."

Even more love came for his 2005 follow-up album, *Hair in My Eyes Like a Highland Steer*, again produced by Harry Stinson. CMT put the video for "The Truck Got Stuck"—a lark of a local tale about Alberta neighbours—into high rotation. In 2006, *Highland Steer* won the Canadian Country Music Association's Album of the Year, "which is crazy," says Lund, who now sees that two-year period as "a torrid affair. It's awesome, and I give them credit for having an open mind, but it faded after that. I don't begrudge them. I thought the whole thing was an anomaly from the beginning. In some towns, radio people have told me that they were inundated with requests to the point where they couldn't ignore it. Which is kind of how things are supposed to work, but strangely it doesn't." Both *Five Dollar Bill* and *Highland Steer* went gold in 2006.

It wasn't only Lund's melodies and lyrics that roped listeners in: it was his band, the Hurtin' Albertans. Bassist Kurt Ciesla, for whom Lund wrote the crowd favourite "Big Butch Bass Bull Fiddle," was there on day one, back in 1995; drummer Brady Valgardson joined right after *Five Dollar Bill*; guitarist Grant Siemens joined for *Highland Steer*. All three have been with him ever since, with a Lightfootish loyalty. "I know a lot of guys in Texas and up here who are roots songwriters, and they go in to make a record and just hire guys to play on it," he says. "As far as I'm concerned, there is no substitute for a good band of unique players and taking

---

2   Lund later recorded a version with entirely new lyrics about Edmonton's hockey team, "The Oil's Back in Town."

them on the road. That brings a whole new dimension to it. I could take my songs and play them with studio guys and it would be okay. The lyrics would be there and the melody would be the same. But it wouldn't have the same personality. My experience in the Smalls made me aware of that."

Lund's career in the U.S. has been a long, slow burn. He didn't play the commercial country game: though he has heartthrob good looks, his music was too acoustic and had too many words. He was more likely to appeal to NPR listeners and folk festival attendees. That meant touring econo south of the border. "When we tour Canada, we can afford to hire professionals," he says. "In the States, for years it was a bit of a grind. The road managers we had would be complete fucks, because if they had their shit together at all, they'd be in a bus with a bigger band. Almost necessarily, they were complete idiots. We had at least a dozen, and each one is worth a chapter in a book.

"For a while, in Texas, we had a whole second van and second set of equipment. We played down there so much, do a month of touring and then park at this guy's place and then come back a few months later. Through sleuthing and weird clues, we discovered that he'd been renting out not only the van but all the gear, including the guitars, like a turnkey service." The a-ha moment came when they found other band's set lists in their road cases.

"Then there was this guy Wayne, from Kentucky, who was really into pistols, and he'd always want to talk to the cops about their guns and it would get really tense. Another guy was an idiot from Texas who didn't know Texas was once part of Mexico, which is unbelievable. He came up here to tour with us, and we played a club in Jasper run by this Greek guy who had a strong accent. The [road manager] was way too high-strung and aggressive, and started telling the Greek guy to speak English and 'Get the fuck out of my country.' We had to gently remind him that he wasn't actually in his country."

In the U.K. and Ireland, Lund was doing well enough that he played to hundreds of people a night and landed a plum slot at the Glastonbury Festival in 2007, opening for the Waterboys on the main stage. Early on, Australia took to him, thanks to a promoter who saw Lund in Canada and promptly booked the band into all the Australian festivals and TV shows. Major airplay on Australia's CMT equivalent followed suit. "For a time there, we were arguably bigger and more well known to the mainstream in Australia than we were in Canada," says Lund. Australia, of course, has its own ranching culture, so Lund's music was right at home. But part of his appeal is that you don't need to ride a horse to get his music.

"If you write honestly and authentically about your own culture, no matter what it is, people will pick up on the realness and the universality of it," he says.

"Regionalism is missing in commercial music. Everybody's going for generalities, when sometimes the interest is found in the quirky details. As a young guy having grown up on the Prairies, hearing Springsteen songs about New Jersey was the most alien thing ever, very much outside of my life experience. But I got it because he wrote it so well and with so much humanity. That's the writer's job. If the specifics ring true, interest is held, and universality is achieved. I had the same insecurities about whether people outside of my culture and geographical area, the Western Canadian Prairies and foothills, would be interested, but they have been— in Europe, the U.K., Australia. Hell, even Toronto."

Regional peculiarities were key for many of Lund's friends. Geoff Berner shifted from Billy Bragg–influenced folk songs to the klezmer music of his Ashkenazi ancestors. Carolyn Mark wrote country music rich with regional references and clever wordplay. Tanya Tagaq turned heads on the Western Canadian folk festival circuit more than a decade before her Polaris-winning 2013 album *Animism*, by reinventing Inuit throat singing as modern avant-garde music. "We all draw on our regional, cultural roots," says Lund of that particular group of peers.

Though Lund recorded in Nashville and toured extensively in Texas, his records didn't have strong distribution or promotion in the U.S. until he signed with New West Records in 2009, a label that straddled college radio and country music, building its reputation with bands like Drive-By Truckers and eventually attracting Steve Earle, Dwight Yoakam and John Hiatt. Lund's New West debut, *Losin' Lately Gambler*, didn't make an immediate splash; he was still a Canadian interloper in Americana, writing songs like "Alberta Says Hello" and "Long Gone to Saskatchewan."

"The label didn't tell me to tamp [my regionalism] down, but they did tell me after the fact that it might be a reason it didn't do too well," he says. "That might not have been the smartest thing for my debut American release."

Lund did much better by 2012's *Cabin Fever*, one of his strongest records: it debuted in Canada at No. 1, making him the first Edmonton artist to do so. (He also bumped Justin Bieber off the top spot.) The U.S. couldn't help but take notice. Years of work finally started paying off. By 2020, his album *Agricultural Tragic* was in the top 10 of a year-end list from roots music bible *No Depression*, alongside Jason Isbell, Lucinda Williams and other leading lights. Perseverance developed in his punk days had paid long-term dividends.

"I feel the DIY culture was a perfect learning ground for survival now," he says. "I've heard it said that the new model is to do things yourself. I'm like, Oh really? I know people from the commercial country world, and it's a drag because if they don't get on the radio, they're hooped. I'm told that we sell more hard ticket sales across Canada than a lot of the big country acts here; they just can't sell tickets.

Not all of them, but a lot of them. There's a lot of smoke and mirrors in the Canadian music industry, all this machinery to make you a star.

"All the decisions I've ever made have been for longevity. I've never been in this to make a zillion dollars. I truly do just want to make music and play it for people. Everything from artwork to writing to working with my band to touring strategy, it's all about thinking long-term and finding people who will be loyal supporters. A lot of the approach in the commercial side doesn't do that. If you zoom out, you see a million commercial artists come and go, but who's still there? The labels and the agents. The business is still there. The acts are sometimes interchangeable. My whole career—like Geoff [Berner]'s, like Carolyn [Mark]'s, like Tanya [Tagaq]'s, like the Sadies', like all my friends'—it's been based on honest expression and making art for people who want to hear it, regardless of what's on the radio."

Three women from the other side of the Rockies, contemporaries of Corb Lund, could not have agreed more.

JULY 8, 1999: Outside the lineup to get into Lilith Fair in Vancouver, the opening date of Sarah McLachlan's third annual, all-female touring festival, are four buskers who couldn't afford a ticket. They thought they might sneak onto the Jericho Beach site, or just hang out and listen from outside. They were too new a band to have been considered for even a secondary stage; they'd only formed a few months ago, performing at cannabis cafés and vintage clothing shops.

They weren't even sure they'd all be together that day; one of them, Frazey Ford, had just returned from several months in Guatemala and hadn't told anyone she was back in town. She wasn't officially in the band and wasn't sure if she wanted to be. But from the band's van, Trish Klein spotted her wayward friend walking down Commercial Drive at Broadway.

"Get in the van!" Klein shouted. That van ride lasted 10 years.

The busking gig went predictably well: if there was ever a crowd predisposed to enjoy four hippie chicks playing acoustic instruments, it was the Lilith Fair crowd. The band made $60 in change, along with some pot brownies that some kind Vancouver soul tossed in Sam Parton's mandolin case. They used the money to buy some snacks at a Safeway in Kitsilano, headed to the beach, downed the brownies and Ford started playing "Oh Susanna" on guitar. The American among them, Jolie Holland, knew verses that the Canadians didn't. Klein worked out a banjo part. The four-part harmonies clicked. The women knew then that their casual porch project could become a real band. They all joined hands and spat on it. The Be Good Tanyas were born.

Two years later, minus Holland, the Be Good Tanyas were signed to Nettwerk, the label that had launched Sarah McLachlan. They were a smash hit in the U.K., were doing well in the U.S., and even Canada seemed to care. Lilith Fair wasn't around to help, but another cultural wave was. Entirely coincidentally, the Be Good Tanyas' debut album came out a month before the soundtrack to *O Brother, Where Art Thou?* Many acts rode the wave of that unexpected, platinum-studded revival of acoustic Americana, but the Be Good Tanyas were different than most.

They weren't careerists. They weren't opportunists. They weren't lightning-fast finger-pickers. They weren't American (after Holland left). They were three women who'd met in a B.C. tree-planting town. They barely survived their first tour, and by the time their wild ride was done after a decade, the three women were barely speaking to each other.

In between, however, they created uncompromised magic on stage and in the studio. It had to be magic. Because the story of the Be Good Tanyas' success is entirely improbable.

"WELL, I FEEL LIKE AN OLD HOBO."

That's the first lyric one hears on their 2000 debut *Blue Horse.* Sam Parton wrote that line when she was splitting her time between Vancouver and New Orleans in 1999, along with stints tree planting in the Kootenays. The three women with whom she'd soon form a band were also wandering souls. Jolie Holland was a Texan living in Vancouver with a San Francisco boyfriend. Trish Klein grew up in Regina, Minnesota and Winnipeg before bouncing between Vancouver and Nelson, B.C. Frazey Ford was born in Toronto to two American draft-dodgers who moved to Ootischenia, a tiny Doukhobor town in the Kootenays outside Castlegar. Her parents took their four children backpacking across Asia, including a hike through the Himalayas, when Ford was 10 years old. There were no normies in this band.

Sometime in the summer of 1994, in the Kootenay Mountains, Parton was singing Joni Mitchell songs to herself while tree planting, when she heard an otherworldly sound in the near distance. It was the sound of Ford, singing Aretha Franklin. The two connected immediately and started playing guitar around the campfire at night. Playing music was something Parton loved to do. But it was something Ford needed to do.

When Ford had finished high school, her mom bought her a ticket to Guatemala to go and study Spanish. It was a chance for her to escape a turbulent family life, to get as far away as possible from what she describes as a traumatic situation. It worked, for a while. She loved the country and the people. It was there that a boyfriend persuaded her to sing in public for the first time. But the trip went sour after she saw someone killed in the street. A decades-long civil war had ended only recently; the country still suffered immense political tension. An English teacher she met tried to recruit Ford into a rebel militia. She saw mass graves. It was all too much. After seven months there, Ford had a nervous breakdown and came back to Canada. She moved in with a friend in a cabin in the Kootenays. She was 19.

"My mind just shattered," says Ford. "But Guatemala is an incredible place and I do love it there. It was an important part of my development, to be forced to go through a spiritual death of my sense of self." Back in B.C., she worked on "piecing myself back together, though I'd never be the person I was before. I didn't sing for about six months, but when I did, I'd do it while running in the woods. It became a lifeline. My brothers ended up being addicts and alcoholics. I was really forced to either face my past or be suicidal. That decision was forced on me at a young age, which I appreciate now. It really drove me toward music: not necessarily as a career, but a source of such meaning and strength.

"That was my approach when I started performing at open mics [in Nelson, B.C.]. Having that basis of spiritually knowing why I was doing something, that protected me eventually when I [later] found myself unexpectedly in the industry— it allowed me to pay attention to an internal voice."

Ford enrolled in Selkirk College in Nelson, near her family home, to study vocal music. There she met Trish Klein, who'd dropped out of a general arts degree at UBC to study jazz guitar. The two became friends, bonding over music and poverty; they'd take discarded loaves of bread from local bakeries and lived on grilled cheese and PB&Js. A weekly gig at the Heritage Inn paid them in meals; they played Al Green and Ben Harper songs in the posh restaurant attached to the century-old hotel.

"Because Nelson is so landlocked and far away from any city, nobody is expecting that they will necessarily make money off their art," says Ford. "There was something beautiful about these open mics, where people would drive for two hours in from the mountains to play a little flute solo or read their poem. It was very meaningful for people to have creativity and fulfill the cycle of it by sharing it."

One of Ford's open mic friends was Pauline Lamb, who was almost 10 years Ford's senior. "Her husband was a musician who passed away," says Ford, "and there were these wakes where we stayed up all night and made music and there was this spiritual reverence. She had a new baby and was widowed, but I'd drag her out to these open mics. We had an intense connection and we sang together.

She was a huge influence and an amazing guide, because I was younger. She was like, 'Do what you want to do. Don't let these bands tell you to sing louder.'"

A more casual connection was made with Sam Parton, who would drive three hours through the mountains from Edgewood to try to meet musicians. When Sylvia Tyson came to play Nelson's Capitol Theatre, Parton tried to sneak a cassette backstage with some of her originals on it, including "Don't You Fall," which eventually appeared on *Blue Horse*. Music was also an escape for Parton. Living with her boyfriend in a farmhouse, she learned he was cheating on her. Devastated, she decided to go to Mexico in early 1996. Ford and Klein didn't see the mysterious traveller again for two years.

One night Parton was wandering down a Mexican beach, playing her mandolin, when she passed an American man coming the other direction—also playing a mandolin. They struck up a conversation, obviously. Then another American strolled by—not playing a mandolin but wearing a T-shirt from the Kerrville Folk Festival. A curious Parton asked about it and was enchanted by the idea of a weeks-long festival in Texan hill country, full of songwriters. The mandolin player suggested to Parton that they go to Kerrville together. But first, he said, he could get them a gig in the children's tent at the Telluride Bluegrass Festival in Colorado. Parton had no other plans, so she wrote a bunch of children's songs and played the festival. For the first time in her life, she made money playing music. At Kerrville, she was in heaven, in a world of possibility surrounded by great songwriters and professional musicians. One of them, Chris Chandler, invited her to be in his band. She moved to his hometown of New Orleans and toured with them for the next 18 months, working tree-planting gigs back in B.C. during downtime.

Most tree-planting contracts are for three or four months at a time, but Parton cut a sweet deal with her boss. "I was planting away one day," she recalls, "and I found a perfect, brand-new chainsaw that had been dropped and snowed on and survived the winter. I was like, 'Look at this!' My boss was like, 'Oh wow, that must be worth two grand.' 'Okay, let's make a deal. I'll give you this chainsaw if you let me come and go as I want, because I need to be on tour.' So that was the deal for the next three years."

Frazey Ford was still in Nelson, where "there were three career options: growing weed, tree planting and being on welfare." Some fellow tree planters told her she would really love Montreal, so she took the plunge. "I moved when I was 24 and focused on writing songs. I moved there right before the 1998 ice storm. I was looking for a job when the storm hit, and I remember thinking, That ice is getting thicker and thicker. This is a real tough town!

"I loved Montreal, but I was literally starving," she says. "I had a great life, great apartment, but I had a boyfriend back in Vancouver. I went planting again that summer and I didn't know if I could face another [Montreal] winter. The place I was working was closing. Poverty drove me away." She landed in East Vancouver, where she reconnected with Trish Klein.

Klein was a square peg in a crowd enamoured by electronic dance music; the room she moved into had recently been occupied by electronic musician Tim Hecker. "Literally everyone else I knew at that time was super into the rave scene," she says, "wearing giant pants, talking about their evenings out, and I didn't understand what language they were speaking. 'Yeah, it's goa trance with a mix of jungle and house with DJ So-and-so.' I was really into playing the banjo and studying old songbooks. I didn't grow up in a folk music environment. I didn't have anyone to learn from. At music school I was in a jazz program. On my own time, I'd go to the library to find old songbooks and photocopy them and try to figure out how to play country blues from the sheet music, because it wasn't even that easy to find recordings. If someone did have a recording, you'd dub it. You had to work hard to find the music."

Without other folk musicians in their social circle, Klein and Ford started a Portishead-inspired six-piece all-female band called Saltwater June. They gigged all around town and landed a main-stage slot at the Under the Volcano festival. Some of Ford's Montreal-penned originals were in the mix ("Broken Telephone," "Only in the Past").

Sam Parton had also landed in East Van by 1998. One day on Commercial Drive she was standing outside a coffee shop, wearing handmade cowboy boots she'd bought in Texas. The barista stepped out to compliment the boots, asking where Parton got them. The barista was Jolie Holland, who was born in Houston and had lived in New Orleans and San Francisco before landing in Vancouver. The women discovered they both played red Stella guitars. They knew many of the same people in New Orleans. In the strangest twist of all, Holland said, "I just started playing with this banjo player named Trish Klein," a name Parton recognized from Nelson.

Parton, Klein and Holland started playing together. Holland had heard a new song by her friend Obo Martin titled "Be Good, Tanya" and joked to Klein that it would be a good band name. That week, while the two were jamming on her porch, someone walked by and asked what they were called. "The Be Good Tanyas!" they both exclaimed. Ford, who was studying to be a doula, hung out and occasionally added the sorts of close harmonies she'd grown up singing with her mother. "When I met those three," says Klein, "it was unique that we were all interested in old blues, country blues, old folk, Alan Lomax, old gospel. It was nerdy and not cool. It felt awesome to meet other people I could explore that with."

The three women started busking outside Burcu's Angels, a vintage clothing store then located on Main Street between Broadway and 10th, and got a weekly gig at the New Amsterdam Café, a cannabis shop near Gastown that paid them $100 plus food and tips. Ford occasionally sat in. Songwriter Geoff Berner met them at an open mic around the corner. He'd recently left his punk band, Terror of Tiny Town, and was reinventing himself as a solo accordionist.

"We were pretty much the only people there," he recalls. "It was them, me and maybe some guy playing 'Wish You Were Here.' Frazey hadn't joined yet. I think I knew Sam from before. Maybe I knew Trish from environmental stuff. They were unapologetically sad and gloomy. Not peppy. Look at the bands who came up in Canada after them, who imitated them, where all the darkness is bled out until it's just nice ladies singing nice songs. But the Be Good Tanyas had a bacchanalian darkness that made them good. They were all pretty weird people—and unapologetic about it. They weren't hiding it. There was an emotional authenticity that was immediate."

The respect was mutual. Holland fell in love with Berner's song "Light Enough to Travel" and sang it in the Be Good Tanyas; Ford later took over the song and it became a fan favourite on *Blue Horse*. "He's one of the most brilliant and underrated artists of our time," says Ford. "I was very afraid of him," says Parton of Berner. "My heart and my soul could not handle what I was taking in. I didn't have the intellectual or emotional capacity to understand. I'd come from Neil Young songs and some punk stuff; I was really into the Clash. But I'd never heard anything like Geoff Berner. It was so beautiful and wild. I could not believe this person lived in my town."

An unlikely Tanyas fan was a man known only as Futcher, part of a Skinny Puppy–esque industrial band called Hellenkeller. Though it was not at all Klein's preferred style of music, she went to one of their shows. Futcher mentioned that he taught a college class in recording engineering and was intrigued by the idea of Klein's all-acoustic band. He came to see them at Lug's Café on Main Street and brought his friend Mandy Wheelwright, a music manager who had just shepherded her main client, Kinnie Starr, through a boom of early hype and a subsequently scuttled major label deal in the U.S. Both Futcher and Wheelwright left that night with a new client.

"It was very different from what Kinnie was doing," says Wheelwright, whose connection to folk music didn't extend far past a childhood love of the McGarrigle sisters. "But the voices were so magnificent. It didn't sound like anything else. At that time I was being sent a lot of demos from young women artists who sounded a lot like Ani DiFranco, and I was sick of it. The Tanyas were very real. They just loved playing that music."

Futcher recorded eight songs in two days at Columbia College, mostly covers and mostly with Holland on lead vocals, including the version of "The Lakes of Pontchartrain" that ended up on *Blue Horse*. It was a one-take performance and the first time Parton had ever attempted a mandolin solo. Ford sang on a few tracks, but didn't consider herself part of the band.

Ford was planning a return trip to Guatemala. She put the eight-song session on one side of a cassette and Lhasa de Sela's *La Llorona* on the other, and she wore it out while in Central America. After a couple of months, Klein called Ford and told her that she had to come back because they had a manager and were going to finish the album. Ford was shocked that it was turning out to be more than a few porch jams and café gigs. She came back to Canada in July 1999, just in time for the Lilith Fair busking performance. Shortly after, the other three went to San Francisco for the summer, where Holland's boyfriend lived, and they all got joe jobs.

The Be Good Tanyas were still not anyone's priority—except for Sam Parton. She was trying to set up a six-week tour starting in April 2000 through contacts she made while touring with Chris Chandler, as well as by combing through U.S. phone books and cold-calling venues. She somehow extracted $300 guarantees for a band no one had heard of, with only a cheaply dubbed cassette with a photocopied cover to their name.

In Canada, it was easier to get gigs around the B.C. Interior and the Kootenays. Parton booked a New Year's Eve gig at the town legion hall in Edgewood (population: 1,800), but it wasn't any old New Year's Eve. "It was Y2K, so people were afraid of that, and this place was off the grid so we thought we'd be safe up there if shit went down," says Klein. But the venue was double-booked. In a small town ready to party like it finally was 1999, a local band had laid claim on the date 10 years earlier. They were not going to surrender a decade's worth of practice to four interlopers. So the legion called Parton back with the most British Columbian compromise imaginable: "You can still have the gig, but we can't pay you. All the door money will go to the other band. But we can donate a quarter pound of weed, and you can raffle it and that can be your pay." The Tanyas sold raffle tickets for $5 each to friends and at shows around Vancouver. They made $600.

Parton ended up losing her voice before the gig, so her twin sister, Erin, filled in. "We went up there and stayed in an amazing loft above a barn someone had renovated," says Klein. "Because we were done early, we got hosed while this band did every most overplayed, ridiculous cover imaginable, hit after hit. They weren't very good, but they were playing the gig of their life and they were so into it. And then, of course, nothing happened on Y2K. We had a naked sauna by a riverbank in the snow."

A month later, they were ready to embark on their first proper tour. To raise money, they held a keg party at Parton's house, a six-bedroom at the corner of East Georgia Street and Clark Drive, with a high-ceiling practice space in the basement, where the total rent was $1,200. Parton made 200 CD-Rs of the *Blue Horse* demo; Klein drew the artwork. The goal was to make it to New Orleans in time for the city's jazz festival; they wanted to see cornetist Olu Dara, as they were all obsessed with his 1998 album *In the World*.

The first gig of the tour was in their old stomping grounds of Nelson. "But we couldn't get a venue," says Klein. "We ended up playing someone's dad's birthday party. They had this incredible hippie house on the side of a cliff with an outdoor hot tub and shower. The mom was 50, which at the time I thought was *very old*; she answered the door basically stark naked, wearing a translucent, sheer, skin-tight, floor-length dress—and a silver thong. The place had all this carved cedar and hand-crafted pottery. I'd never seen such opulence in my life."

Things took a quick turn when the band's vehicle caught fire in Crowsnest Pass. "It was this weird, big Dodge camper van that ran on propane and gas, with a giant propane tank on the undercarriage, running along one side of the van," says Parton. The driver's seat had fallen out a few years before, so she'd replaced it with a 1950s living room chair, which rocked back and forth. She figures that probably dislodged a screw that rubbed up against a wire connection to the propane tank and created sparks. "I guess the sparks went straight into the engine, and next thing we knew the engine was on fire," she recalls. "Luckily the propane tank did not blow up, which is what we thought would happen." They managed to evacuate and call the closest fire department, an hour away. The van was towed to Fernie and repaired the next day. The band didn't miss their next show, in Saskatoon.

They didn't have a show in Winnipeg, but they crashed one by Alberta folk-blues veteran Bill Bourne, whom Parton had booked to join them in the U.S. He was travelling in a 1972 Lincoln Continental with "suicide doors" and fishing rods attached to the dash. "He doesn't even fish," says Klein. "He said it always softened up the border people." Bourne is 20 years older than the Be Good Tanyas and is one of Western Canada's most celebrated folk musicians, instantly recognizable on the festival circuit in his top hat. His elderly presence was a welcome, if odd, presence on the tour. "Bill was chill," says Ford, even as they drove through treacherous February ice storms in North Dakota after the Winnipeg gig.

The Tanyas took turns riding with Bourne to keep him company (and awake), as well as to seek respite from tension that was already rising in the band. "Right from the start, pretty much, there was bad blood," laughs Parton. "There were five of us in that van. My dog was with us, too. Our drummer Paul [Clifford] was there, and I was kind of dating him at the time—which was dumb. And I broke up with him on the tour—which was also really dumb. We were all these emotional amoebas, with no real perspective on anything except our own needs and whims. Very intense. They should train bands before they send them out on tour, on interpersonal dynamics."

Between Ford and Holland, there was an unspoken fallout—as in, they weren't speaking. "I had this idea that this would be a really good time for everybody," says Parton, "and I learned really quickly that it wasn't. I learned a bit about how other people have different experiences than I do—and that's okay."

One thing the band did bond over was the soundtrack to their travels. "The whole time we were on tour, the playlist in the van was awesome," says Klein. "It was endless. We compiled all our recordings and CDs and put on Alan Lomax and Smithsonian collections and Sister Rosetta Tharpe and Blind Lemon Jefferson, and then Dylan and Van Morrison." They'd all felt like misfits for so long, and were eager to share their influences and research.

The venues were spotty and weird. "In Dallas, these rich businessmen were offering us a 'private party' at their place," says Ford. "In a lot of places, we were playing for tips. In Wichita, there was some guy with a cigar who put five bucks in the tip jar and was acting like we belonged to him for the evening." Parton decided to liven up the Wichita set by breaking out a hula hoop on stage and passing it to the crowd.

But nothing topped Webb's World of Fun in Ponca City, Oklahoma (population: 25,000). "It was this little juke joint roadhouse outside of town," says Klein. The bartender had a tracheotomy and spoke slowly in a robotic voice with a strong Okie accent: "Welcome . . . to . . . Webb's . . . World . . . of Fun." "He had a thing for Sam," says Klein, "and he was like, 'I . . . love . . . you . . . Sam . . . -an . . . -tha.' It was really cute. He had a history of bank robbery and regaled us with stories. At night, they had this massive BBQ outside. There was basically no food but ribs and two kinds of beer. I was trying to be vegetarian, but I was so hungry; I ate an entire plate of ribs and it was so goddamn delicious. It wasn't raining, just hot and humid and overcast, with big bolts of purple lightning flashing in the sky while we were playing horseshoes next to the BBQ pit. This First Nations dude opened for us, and he was amazing. Big dude, sang incredibly."

"It was one of those evenings that got weirder and weirder," says Ford. "People were more wasted than I've ever seen human beings wasted in my life. There were these twins there, and one of them was trying to high-five Bill Bourne while he was playing. Webb was begging us to take him with us, because it seemed like the owner of the place—who wasn't Webb—was in some kind of horrible abusive situation. He kept trying to give us pecans: *'Take these pecans!'* As we were piling in the van, Trish was like, 'Shut the door, shut the door!' Later we heard that Webb got murdered."

They finally made it to New Orleans, where they saw Olu Dara, the Wailers, Erykah Badu and others. At an on-air performance in the WWOZ radio studio, they met iconic Meters drummer Zigaboo Modeliste, who showered them with praise. The Be Good Tanyas' drummer, Paul Clifford, was ecstatic. It capped off a life-changing adventure for the band, but by the time they got home Ford had serious doubts. "I was honestly on the verge of saying, 'I don't think I can do this.' I loved the music and the people, but the vibe was toxic."

That spring, manager Mandy Wheelwright had got the band a FACTOR grant to finish their album, along with an eight-date Canadian tour booked for the fall of 2000. "They were making the album, but deadlines didn't mean anything to them," she says. "I'm like, 'But we have to have it out by the time of the tour, because otherwise we won't get this FACTOR money and we need it!'" But in July 2000, after starting another session with Futcher, Jolie Holland quit the band and headed back to the States.

Holland's decision wasn't entirely related to the band dynamic. She could no longer legally work in Canada. She'd been couch-surfing with either Parton or Klein for the last year. And she'd been offered a paying gig backing up California singer-songwriter Victoria Williams. "Our band was struggling and not making money, and our relationships were in the toilet," says Klein, "and [Holland] had this stellar boyfriend, an amazing jazz drummer with a beautiful place in San Francisco. It was a better life for her there."

"We thought, Is this over?" says Ford, who was also ready to quit. "The other girls were pretty demoralized, but in my mind this was the only way to go forward. 'Let's just give it a shot; it might be okay.'"

They decided to keep Holland's contributions to date. She plays violin on four songs on *Blue Horse*, shares the lead on "The Littlest Birds" with co-writer Parton, and the band kept her version of "The Lakes of Pontchartrain" from the original demo. The rest of the recording Parton recalls fondly. "It was the most fun record to make," she says. "We were all completely new to this thing. It was spontaneous. Everybody involved brought something so special. We met Mathieu Gagné on the street, and he came in and played a violin part on 'Coo-Coo Bird' that was mind-blowing. I might have met him tree planting somewhere. I was a little bit in love with him, so that was flying around, too. He came in and was probably really stoned—we probably all were. Futcher was like, 'Let's flip that around and run it backwards and see what happens.' 'Yeah, let's do that, it sounds cool!' And all of us had crushes on Futcher by the end. 'Don't kick us out! We want to stay!'"

The beauty of *Blue Horse* is its unadorned simplicity. Much of it sounds like it could have been recorded around a campfire in the Kootenays. The harmonies are spine-tingling. Ford's lead vocals are enigmatic and mysterious, using slippery phonetics to hypnotizing effect. (Ford's father had a lisp; she grew up with him telling her to "enunthiate.") Drums are used sparingly. There's only one truly rousing number amidst otherwise moody tunes: the cover of Geoff Berner's "Light Enough to Travel," in which the narrator smashes the windows of a logging company.

The seven originals more than hold their own against the three traditionals and the Stephen Foster covers, notably the opening track—and the band's best-known song—"The Littlest Birds," which is a deceptive introduction to the minor keys and melancholy that pervade the album. It appeared in commercials and on numerous compilations, including the soundtrack to the TV show *Weeds*, collections from NPR and Putumayo and one comp called *O Sister, Where Art Thou?*

"That song got written right around that time when I was travelling between Vancouver and New Orleans," Parton told *No Depression* magazine. "I didn't want to be a drifter anymore, but I just didn't know how not to be. It was springtime. I was walking by the Union Market in Strathcona, on my way to the Greyhound station to catch my bus heading south. And there was this bush full of birds, all singing, and I stopped. [They] were having such a wonderful time, were all together, knew where their home was, and I didn't know what I was doing. I was having this moment, and then it was like someone just leaned into my ear, like an angel or something, and whispered 'The littlest birds sing the prettiest songs' loud and clear. That line just opened me up. I wasn't high. I was just emotional and open. I started walking to the bus station and the rhythm of my walking became the song as I sang that line over and over again. I got on the bus and wrote 10 verses—most of which I scrapped, but I knew that for me the song was a guide. Then Jolie picked it up and started messing with the lyrics, and eventually it morphed into what's on the record."

Blue Horse was released independently in October 2000, with distribution through Festival, a popular choice for artists on the folk circuit. Stuart Derdeyn of the *Vancouver Province* called it an "instant classic" in a preview he wrote for the CD release show at the Silvertone Tavern; Geoff Berner was the opener and the cover was $4. In a truly tasteless analogy for a band from East Van, an *Exclaim!* reviewer[3] described the group's vocal sound as that of "junkie angels." More accurately, the writer described "spooky, drowsy gothic folk that sounds better after midnight,

---

3   The author.

somewhere where shadows dance with suggestion around the campfire and the dawn seems days away."

The eight tour dates they booked to fulfill their FACTOR grant were a mixed bag. They played to two people in Ottawa, 10 people in Toronto. Opening for Martha Wainwright in Montreal went considerably better, and they were chuffed when Wainwright's mother, Kate McGarrigle, showed up with compliments. In New York City, friends of Parton's hosted them at the Urban Cowgirl Cabaret, held on the back of a pickup truck in front of a pop-up restaurant run by two lesbian chefs under the Brooklyn Bridge. The Tanyas were a huge hit with this crowd. The owner of a popular Manhattan sex shop bought their CD and put it into regular rotation at the store; the next time the band came to town, they received vibrators of appreciation. But by far the biggest breakthrough they made on that first trip was catching the ear of CBC host Shelagh Rogers, who was hosting the flagship national morning show. She interviewed the band and fell in love with the record; the rest of the national broadcaster soon followed suit.

In February 2001, the North American Folk Alliance convention came to Vancouver. This is an annual event in rotating cities where all the folk festival bookers come to watch new acts showcase; a buzz at the Folk Alliance can lead to summers packed with lucrative gigs. The Be Good Tanyas had this in the bag. Their shows at the convention hall were packed. They were featured on the local newscasts. But the coup de grâce was the Little Red Hen showcase, in a hotel room and booked by their friend Jan Bell, who had curated the Urban Cowgirl show in NYC. "They had it done up like a New Orleans bordello," says Geoff Berner. "That became *the* place to party. It was full of pretty girls in thrift-store dresses playing awesome songs, with lots of bourbon and weed. I mean, where else do you want to be?! They were at the top of their game, and there was nothing more transfixing than seeing them right there in front of you in a hotel room. They would just shut the thing down, so mesmerizing."

"Every single person in that whole scene—women from New Mexico, Florida, New York City, California, us, everyone—was so incredible and we jammed for days straight," says Klein. "We slept in that hotel room, 10 of us on the floor. And my friend had a totally finished cedar-style sauna inside the back of a truck; one night he parked it in the hotel loading zone and had the sauna going. We all went down there from the Hyatt and had a naked sauna, it was awesome." American labels came sniffing around, including folk giant Rounder Records and a new Nashville label co-owned by Anne Murray; both wanted the band to rerecord *Blue Horse* and make it shinier.

Expectations were high for their main-stage performance at the Edmonton Folk Festival, the crown jewel gig for any Western Canadian artist. But they bombed—and

319

that's according to their own manager. "They basically soundchecked through their entire set," says Mandy Wheelwright. "They weren't organized. They were green. Not that far from Lug's Café days. It was a daytime slot; they had a 40-minute set and they played for 10. I'm sure [festival programmer] Terry Wickham was like, 'I'm not doing that again!'"

By then they had inked a deal with Nettwerk Records, which in 2000 was putting out a lot of the kind of electronic music Trish Klein rebelled against: BT, DJ Tiësto, Delerium. Nettwerk kingmaker Terry McBride, who also managed Barenaked Ladies and Coldplay to superstardom, was tipped to the Be Good Tanyas after his wife heard the band on CBC while driving and pulled over to write down their name. The Tanyas were far less slick than anything else on the label, but the fact that they'd sold 5,000 copies independently attracted McBride. As a result, they were left entirely to their own devices. Nettwerk rereleased *Blue Horse* internationally in the fall of 2001, which started a whole new touring cycle, including Canadian dates opening for Sarah Harmer. In early 2002, they headed to Britain.

Compelled solely by Klein's album cover drawing, influential BBC roots-music DJ Bob Harris had actually bought the demo version in early 2000, at a Nashville record shop where the band had left copies on their first tour. The more he played it on his show, the more requests he received. That helped Wheelwright secure one of the biggest booking agencies in the U.K., Asgard, who also handled Alison Krauss, Dolly Parton and Emmylou Harris. They played small theatres across the country. "We sold out our first tour, which was unheard of," says Wheelwright. "Sam Parton kept saying, 'I thought we'd be playing to 10 people in a pub somewhere.'" Eight months after the Edmonton fiasco, they went over well at some of the biggest festivals, including the biggest field festival in the world, Glastonbury. At the Cambridge Folk Festival, Joe Strummer gave them effusive praise and asked Parton to sign his copy of *Blue Horse* with "something that will make my wife jealous."

In a country long obsessed with "authentic" North American music, "the Brits just lapped it up," says Wheelwright. "The BBC thought it was the most exotic thing; they didn't know what a tree planter was. And the band was scrappy on-air, which the Brits loved. They weren't twee, and that worked in their favour." *Mojo* magazine picked *Blue Horse* as the country album of the year.

By far the strangest part of their initial foray into the U.K. was an invitation to attend the Brit Awards. "We just got invited because people thought we were cool," says Parton. "It was a big huge thing; Janet Jackson was there, Kylie Minogue. All these limos were pulling up with all these stars. We showed up in our West Coast woollens. We all looked like what we were: tree planters. We walked down the red carpet while all these photographers were going click-click-click, and then everything went quiet."

"WHO ARE THEY?" yelled one paparazzo.

Another responded, "NOBODY!"

"Then we went in and had drinks with Lemmy [from Motörhead] and watched Justin Timberlake," says Parton, "wondering, How did we get here? What the hell is going on?"

Meanwhile, O Brother, Where Art Thou? was a sensation. Released before Christmas 2000, the film didn't go into wide release until February 2001, just as the Tanyas were wowing the Folk Alliance crowd. The soundtrack went gold in the States that month; before the end of the year, it sold eight million copies worldwide and went quadruple platinum in Canada. One of the most memorable moments in the film is when the main characters encounter a trio of sirens, voiced by Emmylou Harris, Gillian Welch and Alison Krauss. For listeners new to the genre, Blue Horse provided a full album of similar siren sounds in three-part harmony.

The O Brother sensation was the best and worst thing to happen to the Tanyas; though they had nothing to do with the phenomenon, it undoubtedly boosted their profile. It also became an albatross in just about every interview and review. The Be Good Tanyas were not bandwagon-jumpers. "We all did music to save our own lives," says Ford. "For me, that singing tradition was a direct family lineage. That was our personal music. There's a difference between that and saying, 'Hey, that's popular, let's emulate that.' With Blue Horse, we'd always get this question from other artists: 'How did you decide to do that song? How did you decide to do that style?' We didn't decide. That's just what we felt."

For Ford in particular, the spiritual aspect of performance took its toll. "When I started performing, I was coming from such a place of pain that I was reckoning with, and there was this response from the audience: if they had that same pain, they were getting what I was getting out of this desire to find some spiritual strength within. Sam came from that, Jolie did, we all did. That human need to reckon with very painful things. People would walk up to me on the street and start crying. The reaction was very deep. I both appreciated it and found it hard."

"The early shows were my favourites," says Geoff Berner. "They were terse in between songs. They would bicker on stage. They would hypnotize people. The room would grow quiet, watching this. They were singing about their East Van lives, living in poverty. There was a defiant adoption of the language of the wandering, Depression-era unemployed person. They were taking ownership of it as women. I remember reading [the Boxcar Bertha autobiography] Sister of the Road around that time, and it's the ur–Be Good Tanya. They met tree planting, which is a hard job and hard on women in particular. There's a lot of bad stuff that goes on. There was a reclaiming of power: 'We're not going to be your happy, fun, pretty singing girls.' That air of defiance was amazing—and pugnacious, despite the fact they played defiantly slow. What they don't do is wank off in ways men feel they need to do. To me, that choice makes them superior. They might not be able to play as many notes per second as Earl Scruggs or whoever, but they have great taste and know when not to play."

They were no longer a secret, playing small stages. They were touring Australia and having streets shut down in Stockholm while they played at a retail outlet that had sold 1,500 copies of their album. This was now a professional band, which caused some natural tension. "We went from 'I'm going to be in New Orleans this year,' or, 'I'm going to be in Montreal this year,' to suddenly being locked into a committed adult situation for the first time in all of our lives," says Ford. "When you're a bohemian and you suddenly have a manager and a record label telling you what to do and when to do it—we didn't know how that would be. We were used to our gypsy whims."

Recording a follow-up to *Blue Horse* should have been relatively easy. They'd been playing new material for the last two years and were eager to capture it. They hired the engineer who'd made the Olu Dara record that had inspired them to go to New Orleans and flew him to Vancouver. They got Olu Dara himself to overdub some cornet in New York City. Jolie Holland, who was now signed to the Anti-label as a solo artist, contributed violin and vocals to three tracks. There were three traditionals, including a barely recognizable "House of the Rising Sun," seven originals and two covers. One was Townes Van Zandt's "Waiting Around to Die," which was almost dropped for being "too depressing," says Parton, who managed to make it even more haunting than the original. "We all thought it sucked. It was a real last-minute addition." Years later, it became one of the band's best-known tracks after it was used in *Breaking Bad*.

Ford became pregnant while making the record, which features the traditional song "I Wish My Baby Was Born" (a song the band performed at a pro-choice rally in Vancouver). She was five months along when *Chinatown* was released in March 2003 and toured for three months afterwards. Her guitar rested high on her belly, and she had to take pee breaks in the middle of the set. She finally cracked during a U.K. tour. "I was sick, pregnant, just fighting for time," she says. "I was coughing up blood. I was seven months pregnant. *Nobody* suggested I slow down or stop. I'd waddle out on stage every night, and I thought, Man, if I just had one day off, I might get better from this flu. I asked our booking agent, 'What do people do when they're very sick and they have to tour?' He said, 'They cancel shows.' 'Okay, can I cancel tonight?' 'Yes, you can.'

"Everyone was mad at me," Ford continues. "I was literally like, 'Fuck you all.' The only one who gives a fuck about your mental health in this industry is yourself. Everyone else is too busy feeding the machine. It really scared me. Even though the Be Good Tanyas had a meteoric rise, I didn't give a shit. I wanted out of the circus. I became agoraphobic and couldn't just walk into a room and be there. Having a kid and taking a big step back allowed me to set boundaries with the industry that probably saved my life. People kept telling us that if we didn't tour, that people would forget about us. It's all bullshit. That album sold way better than *Blue Horse*. And when we finally came back a few years later, the shows were even more full."

Chinatown was a hit right out of the gate; the band recouped their advance in the first week, selling 80,000 copies in the U.S. and 30,000 in Canada. After a show in Nelson, the band went on an unannounced hiatus. Klein dove right into a side project, Po' Girl, with Allison Russell, which put out two albums in two years and toured extensively. Parton went back to New Orleans and to Fayetteville, Arkansas, where she made a short film that won an award at the Vancouver Film Festival. In 2005 they reassembled to do a bit of touring with their old friends in Nashville's Old Crow Medicine Show, whom they'd introduced to Nettwerk with great success.

"A lot of it was really fun but the same issues were there," says Ford, who travelled separately with her child. "Now that I was a mom, I definitely didn't have as much tolerance for being in an uncomfortable environment. Not that it was all negative: we do have a lot of love for each other. Every relationship has its difficult sides. You hope it's going to change, but sometimes that's just the dynamic."

They owed Nettwerk another album in their contract, but were in no hurry to finish it. They were happy in their zones. They struggled to finish what became *Hello Love*, which Parton says she "doesn't have a lot of feeling for. I just remember it was hard to make and we didn't want to be there. I did a lot of my stuff from home. I wasn't even going to the studio." Klein tried to lighten the mood with ecstasy, chocolate, cheese and whisky. A version of Prince's "When Doves Cry" was recorded without Parton. There are 13 songs; two are traditionals and five are covers, including Neil Young's "For the Turnstiles" and two by friends Sean Hayes and Jeremy Lindsay (a.k.a. JT Nero, who later formed Birds of Chicago with Po' Girl's Allison Russell).

The album came out in October 2006. Two months later, they headlined the iconic Royal Albert Hall in front of 5,300 Londoners. Even there, they were still second-guessing themselves and had fickle whims. At soundcheck, Sam Parton asked that the Steinway grand piano be moved off stage and a more humble apartment-size upright be brought instead; she changed her mind again before the show, by which point it was too late to switch. Another year and a half of intermittent touring followed, concluding with a spot at the Calgary Folk Festival in 2008.

Ford started working on her first solo album for Nettwerk, the more soul-inflected *Obadiah* (titled after her middle name), which she produced with Klein's partner, drummer John Raham. It was released in 2010. Klein continued to perform in Po' Girl, went back to school for a history degree and shifted into arts management. Parton moved to New York City. "As soon as I hit the ground there I was in four different bands," she says. "It was all totally under the radar but super beautiful. Within a week I'd been recording with Ferron, played with Levon Helm—it was just nuts. Plus I had this cool job as a folklorist researching the history of jazz and funeral traditions in Brooklyn."

The band reunited briefly in 2011 when they were invited to play a festival celebrating Vancouver's 125th anniversary. *Blue Horse* was reissued on vinyl. A best-of collection was released with some new material. There was a gig at the Winnipeg Folk Festival and some U.S. dates with the Carolina Chocolate Drops. Sam Parton suffered a series of health complications after car accidents in 2012 and 2013 but resurfaced in 2017 in a duo with Jolie Holland. Ford released acclaimed solo albums on her own schedule—rarely. There was little push to reunite.

"Sometimes I wonder how four people who came from such intensity got together," says Ford. "None of us had any kind of normal childhood, which is an advantage and a disadvantage. There's something between women who are all quite alpha. Between men, there's this way of operating in that situation; you're socially allowed to be as dominant as you are, and men find their hierarchy within that. Whereas women, because of patriarchy, we've had to suppress all our directness. Even though each of us sensed we should be the one in charge, there was no way out of it. We had such strong individual views that we couldn't synthesize and have anyone follow anybody. Especially creatively.

"Each of us had a very close competitive sister," Ford continues. "Trish and I, we drove each other crazy, but we're the type who can fight it out and then it's over and get through it. Sam and I had such different communication styles, we never resolved anything. We were both firm in our positions. Ironically, the music was so beautiful. I mean, we had fun and we loved each other and had amazing experiences. When it ended, I thought I could either forever project my frustrations onto the band, or I could look at myself and see what's driving these difficulties. It took years and years of personal therapy.

"We were just who we were. It's such a learning curve about group creativity. At the same time, the fact we were these three strong-willed young women, it also really protected us from any pressure. There were too many layers to get through. We came from our own scene. We weren't going to let anyone dictate to us what our aesthetic should be. We had a strong sense of our culture and what we were doing.

"Absolutely nobody could mess with that."

KATHLEEN EDWARDS HAD no problem with ambition or being on the radio. But it looked like she had created a self-fulfilling prophecy when her debut, *Failer*, came out on September 7, 2002. She was playing a Tuesday night gig, the second of three nights at a campus bar at the University of Guelph. There were three people there. The big launch at Toronto's Rivoli wasn't much better, drawing only 30.

There had been high hopes. Edwards shared a manager and an American label with Sarah Harmer, and the two artists were not dissimilar. In Canada, she was on MapleMusic, which had great success that summer with another nobody, Sam Roberts. But in the first few months of *Failer*'s release, it sold fewer than 1,000 copies in Canada.

Failer was a flop.

The American label had bigger plans. Instead of releasing the album in the middle of the busy autumn season, they put it out in February 2003. And the man in charge of hustling the record to media was not one to take no for an answer. "Rounder Records was on fire, between 2000 and 2004," says Edwards. "They'd signed a ton of new emerging or Americana acts, and Alison Krauss was blowing up, so they had money to spend. Jeff Walker, the head of marketing, came from a very wealthy American Republican family. All his brothers worked on Wall Street, and he acted like that. He got my record in front of the music programmers at *Letterman* and told them they had to hear it."

They did. They loved it. They booked her for a January 17 slot. And in the most typical Canadian turn of events, "As soon as I was booked on *Letterman*, everyone in Canada wanted to talk to me. It changed everything." Letterman invited her back a mere five weeks later, and other TV show bookers followed suit. She spent the bulk of 2003 on the road, mostly in the U.S., racking up rave reviews and breaking sales expectations for an unknown female singer-songwriter from Canada—or anywhere else. The songwriter who had signalled her low expectations in her album title had been proven wrong.

Failer was a success.

KATHLEEN EDWARDS WAS born in Ottawa, though didn't spend much time there as a kid. Her father, Leonard Edwards, was a Canadian diplomat posted to Switzerland and South Korea until Kathleen was 16. She grew up playing classical violin; her parents met in a choral group, and her mother was a pianist. As a teen, she came home for Canadian summer camps, where she had her musical awakening.

"When I was 12, I was this teeny bopper kid who loved New Kids on the Block and everything that was on the radio [in 1990]," she says. "The first girl I met at summer camp said, 'I'm into Jane's Addiction and you're into shit music.' That really burst my bubble; I thought I was cool. At that camp I learned songs I didn't even know were John Prine songs, Joni Mitchell songs, Neil Young songs. My brother and I could both pick up a guitar and learn a few chords for every song. Before long I was bringing my guitar on every canoe trip we took"—including one two-month trip when she was 17, from Yellowknife to the Arctic Circle—"and my counsellor, Nick Purdon, who is now a producer at the CBC, he said, 'You ever think about writing songs for a living?' I was like, 'Who the hell does that?!' Then I moved to Seoul and was really uprooted at a hard time, 13, to be removed from your peer group. Part of living overseas then, my identity was so rooted in the fact that I was from Canada. It's the one thing you have to hold on to, where you're from. Music was my buddy."

Finishing high school back in Ottawa was a struggle; she describes getting mono in her final year as a blessing, because it meant she didn't have to show up for the last four months. After she barely graduated, she moved out to Metcalfe and Gilmour in downtown Ottawa, where she worked at a Starbucks. "It was three blocks away from the Manx Pub. I didn't even know that was where cool people hung out, but it was the epicentre of the legitimate arts scene in Ottawa. Especially for literary people and folk music. The people who owned it took me under their wing." Her first gig was playing violin with Slo' Tom Stewart, a former member of Furnaceface who was moulding himself anew à la Stompin' Tom Connors. Not yet writing her own songs, she was soon playing three sets of covers for $50 at pub gigs.

Carleton campus station CKCU had an audio classified feature called Band Aid, where Edwards put a call out for a bassist. Kevin McCarragher answered; they soon became a couple, and he encouraged her to write original material. Like many aspiring young female songwriters at the time, "I was a huge Ani DiFranco fan," says Edwards. "I learned to play her songs from listening to her records. The turning point was working at Starbucks, at a time when they were really into selling music. You'd get these themed cassette tapes, and every day you'd play Cuban or blues or one that was essentially Americana: Steve Earle, Gillian Welch, Whiskeytown. I didn't have a clue about any of that music. That was the first time I heard Wilco. That's when I realized I loved that type of music." It wasn't completely alien: there had been earlier gateways—Blue Rodeo, Cowboy Junkies and Tom Petty.

After her grandmother passed away, a small inheritance paid for a 1988 Chevy Suburban and a demo recording—the EP *Building 55*. She was eager to hit the road and tour the country. Booking agents didn't return her calls—why would they? She was barely a draw at the Manx. "I didn't know where to play in any of these towns, but I knew that if I walked into Songbird Music in Ottawa and asked two or three guys where I could play, they could name every venue in town based on style or size of crowd, etc. So I started calling music stores in other cities. And people would give me promoters' numbers, and before I knew it I was calling someone at the West End Cultural Centre in Winnipeg, or someone who ran a little café in Edmonton that had folk music. I put one foot in front of the other, sent out a ton of demos. It was a very long tour for a small amount of shows, but I drove to Victoria and back and had gigs in every town." This was in October 1999.

"My first gig was in Thunder Bay. I only had enough money in my pocket to get to Winnipeg. I played Thunder Bay and made maybe $100, filled my gas tank on the way to Winnipeg to open for Jane Siberry at the West End Cultural Centre, where I was paid maybe $250. I think Veda Hille was also on the bill. It was a great audience, and I'd never really played for anyone outside Ottawa. The woman who booked the show also booked me on the way back, into an all-women's club, a.k.a. a lesbian bar. It was a private club so that it could be a safe environment."

Back in Ottawa, local journalist Tralee Pearce helped Edwards get a slot on the side stage at Blue Rodeo's Stardust Picnic. "I was this little shithead kid with a stupid EP. I snuck backstage to try to meet Blue Rodeo. I have a clear recollection of walking up to [drummer] Glenn Milchem and saying, 'Hi, where do I meet the guys in Blue Rodeo?' He turned around and pointed to the dressing room. I thought he was the caterer. I barged in and said, 'Hi, I'm Kathleen and I'm playing one of the side stages and this is my demo and can I play a song for you?' I thought if they heard me play, I'd be set. So I played. They were so gracious about it. They asked me for my demo and ushered me out. I never had a hint of them rolling their eyes, wondering who this annoying girl was."

The promoter of the Stardust Picnic, Patrick Sambrook, was also Sarah Harmer's manager. He and Edwards met briefly that day. They met again at a Harmer show at Barrymore's a few months later. "I was this chubby hippie, unshowered, messy—I swear to God, I looked like Pig-Pen," says Edwards.

Sambrook took the demo and followed up, inviting her to Toronto to play a showcase. They signed a deal and in November 2000 Edwards started work on *Failer*, with Ottawa producer Dave Draves and her friend Jim Bryson on guitar and helping with arrangements. Sambrook started shopping a demo of Edwards's new songs to Canadian and American labels. She had her U.S. hopes on Lost Highway, a new roots label launched to put out records by Lucinda Williams, Whiskeytown and the Jayhawks. They told her they didn't hear any radio singles. She channelled the rejection into a new song, "One More Song the Radio Won't Like."

She was now living in Wakefield, Quebec, just outside of Ottawa. She left the capital city after her low-rise apartment building burned down; she was able to rescue her guitar and violin but nothing else. Wakefield was the home of the Black Sheep Inn, a regional hub for live music.

"One of my first gigs ever was opening for Tom Wilson at the Black Sheep Inn," she says. Though she'd never met the Canadian rocker 20 years her senior, "I'd seen Junkhouse play. In my mind, he was a huge star, he'd been in a huge Canadian rock band. So I opened the show, did my thing, thanks very much. Tom was still in the trenches of drinking and was fucked up all the time. This was a matinee show, and I was leaving to go play the Sunday night show at the Manx. He says, 'Oh, I know the Manx.' So who comes storming through the door— midnight on a Sunday, with only three or four people there—but Tom Wilson. We finished the night together and he ended up staying at my place. I was 19, 20, I was a kid. 'Why does this guy think I'm anything special?' Well, turns out he thinks a lot of women are special. Tom ended up taking a real shine to me, and he and I had a thing going on for a while. But he had a girl in every town, so it wasn't really a big deal."

It was another older man who would remain a constant champion, friend and key presence for the rest of her career.

JIM BRYSON WORKED at Songbird Music, as did Tom Stewart and Dave Dudley of Furnaceface. Thanks to national campus radio play, that Ottawa band sold 15,000 copies of their 1992 album, *Just Buy It*, and were popular enough locally to book Lansdowne Park stadium and headline what they called Furnacefest for several years in the mid-'90s. Bryson was a contemporary, having played in local pop-punk band Punchbuggy, who toured the U.S. extensively and played often on comedian Tom Green's TV show, both its cable access and national versions. Bryson left Punchbuggy in 1996, after realizing that touring triggered his depression.

He re-emerged as a solo singer-songwriter a few years later, around the same time Edwards arrived on the scene. His first gig was at the invitation of popular local band Dog Day Afternoon. "I showed up with a banjo, straight from a cottage, wearing a stupid hat," he says. "I sat down on a chair and the whole room went quiet. That was my first experience playing music where people listened. It blew my mind." It gave him a new sense of purpose, and he was determined to make a solo record, *The Occasionals*. "I'd never really been good at achievement," he says. "I dropped out of school. My solo record was the first thing I didn't quit in my life, the first thing I followed through on."

Local CBC producer Bill Stunt took an interest and offered to produce. Marty Jones, another ex-Furnacefacer, engineered. Bryson enlisted other friends, including Ian LeFeuvre and Peter Von Althen from local buzz band Starling. It was made entirely on borrowed favours from friends. The Manx gave him an interest-free loan so that he could afford to press the CDs. *The Occasionals* got a local release in 1999 and, after some rave reviews beyond city limits, was rereleased nationally by Outside Music in 2000. It's a melancholic gem of Canadian Shield roots rock, the sound of driving highways 416 and 401 on a tank full of regret and longing. Based entirely on word of mouth, critical acclaim and CBC play, the album sold 4,000 copies.

Edwards had been smitten since the first time she saw Bryson play at the Manx. "Huge influence," she says. "I'd go see him play, and I'd be in musical ecstasy, where someone is performing and singing these melodies and I'd have this euphoric feeling. Then we became friends." And collaborators: he plays on her debut EP, and by the time she was recording *Failer*, Bryson was heavily involved in arranging Edwards's songs. *Failer* and *The Occasionals* are very much siblings sonically and in terms of songwriting.

It's a debt Edwards has openly acknowledged—and repaid—throughout her more than 20-year career. She covered his song "Somewhere Else" on her 2005 album, and her 2008 song "I Make the Dough, You Get the Glory" is a semi-satirical comment on their relationship that includes the lines "I'm sure it's been said in the finer print / you make me look legitimate / heavy rotation on the CBC / whatever in hell that really means."

JIM BRYSON BROUGHT Edwards on the road as his opening act, which was the first time many Ontario critics heard her name or her music. In Toronto, Jason Collett hosted a weekly songwriter circle called Radio Mondays. At one legendary evening, Bryson and Edwards were on the bill alongside Carolyn Mark and her guitarist, Tolan McNeil. Mark had a reputation as one of the most biting wits in Canadian music. Upon hearing a surprising guitar solo, the West Coaster was known for saying something like, "That was like a finger up the ass during hot sex!" But that night, Mark was a class act next to Edwards, who drank a bottle of Fireball Cinnamon Whisky before going on stage, unleashing a flurry of awkward barbs with others on stage and continuously threatening to play Bryan Adams's "Summer of '69" for the horrified hipster crowd. At one point, she jokingly called Mark a "cunt." Recalls Bryson, "I remember Carolyn Mark telling me, 'Oh my god, I felt I needed to shower after that show.' And that's coming from Carolyn Mark!"

Edwards's boozing also got her in trouble with Jon Bartlett, Ottawa scenester and founder of Kelp Records (later Kelp Management, representing Andy Shauf and Lido Pimienta). Bartlett's country band, Greenfield Main, was being recorded live for a CBC Radio 3 session; Bryson and Edwards were recruited to play accordion and violin respectively. Edwards kept interrupting Bartlett's banter, which rattled the usually unflappable bandleader.

There was no real pressure to be professional. Ottawa's music scene was full of low expectations. Other than Alanis Morissette, who is a whole other story, the city had had very few successful musical exports since the days of Paul Anka and Bruce Cockburn. Furnaceface plateaued at the campus radio level. Bands like Wooden Stars—Edwards plays violin on their 1999 album *The Moon*—were too odd. Power-pop hopefuls Starling never took flight, after their American label folded right in the middle of their U.S. tour; the band literally turned their van around, cancelled all remaining shows and headed home. The low-key Bryson seemed destined to be little more than a critic's favourite. And the *Ottawa Citizen* had described Edwards's music as "rich-kid-with-a-rusty-truck songs."

Failer was finished in May 2001, but took a year to find a home. Sambrook eventually signed her to MapleMusic, a Universal subsidiary co-founded by former Warner A&R rep Kim Cooke—who'd signed Sarah Harmer's Weeping Tile in 1993—and singer Andy Maize of Skydiggers, another band in Edwards's musical lineage. *Failer* was the label's second release.

Meanwhile, Edwards went to SXSW in Austin to find an American deal. At an inauspicious gig in an Indian food restaurant, she met with a Rounder Records rep. The venerable folk label from Massachusetts had recently branched out into pop music, including Sarah Harmer; it seemed a perfect fit. In April 2002, she made her Maple debut when her song "Hockey Skates" appeared on the *Men with Brooms* soundtrack—not an auspicious introduction necessarily, but in the track listing she was sandwiched between Harmer and the Tragically Hip.

But it's not like *Men with Brooms* made any impact outside of people who wear CBC sweaters as a fashion statement. That spring, Edwards accepted an invitation from former flame Tom Wilson to join him on a Western Canadian tour with fellow geezers Paul Hyde of the Payolas and Dave Rave from Teenage Head. "It was certainly not the winner's circle of people," she says. "We were all nobodies hoping someone would show up. We laughed and it was a fun time. I didn't know Paul Hyde from Adam. He's a spectacular guy, a lot of fun. Tom had by then gone through rehab. This might have been one of the first things he did sober. He was pretty fragile, navigating this whole new chapter of his life, wondering what the fuck planet he'd just landed on."

When *Failer* was finally ready for release, Edwards did a photo shoot for the album art in Wakefield. The photographer set up the shot on a country road. Edwards didn't like it and wanted to go off road—although her car got stuck in the mud and had to be towed out. The photographer was furious; to make him laugh, she wrote the word *failer* with her finger on the vehicle's back window. He took a photo of it. Later that day, she went to see Sarah Harmer play Ottawa's Centrepointe Theatre and took her mom as her date. "I was feeling a bit defeated," she recalls. "Here was this artist doing incredibly well, and I was just ready to take on the world and felt like I was constantly having to manage my expectations. My mom could tell I was feeling discouraged."

They walked out to the parking lot to say goodbye. As Edwards got in her Suburban, she could see her mother vigorously wiping down the back window.

"Mom, what are you doing?"

"Nothing! Nothing!"

"Are you wiping off *failer*?"

"I know you're feeling sensitive and it's so terrible that someone wrote that on your truck."

"Mom, *I* wrote that on the truck."

"Oh, well, I just didn't want someone to see that written on your truck."

As *Failer*'s release date approached in September 2002, Edwards found herself short a guitarist. Bryson was preparing his second solo album and fielding label offers. Her backup guitarist—Sarah Harmer's Gord Tough—was also unavailable. Enter Colin Cripps.

The former Crash Vegas guitarist was managed by Bernie Breen, Sambrook's officemate: Edwards and Cripps had first met in January at a farm benefit head-lined by Jim Cuddy at the Danforth Music Hall; Cripps was now in Cuddy's band. It had been her first time meeting Cuddy since barging into Blue Rodeo's dressing room in 1999. "Cuddy said, 'Kathleen, I love the way you sing the words *hockey skates*. Just so you know: that's why you're here tonight.' I was like, 'Oooh.'"

That fall, at Breen's suggestion to Sambrook, Cripps joined Edwards's band. "He must have really liked me," she says, "because he did all these shitty gigs with me when *Failer* came out." It was more than that: the two soon fell in love and married two years later. "Colin is 17 years older than me," says Edwards. "My mom had kept my Christmas lists from when I was a teenager, and when I was 17 I'd put Crash Vegas on my CD list. After we were married, she sent it to us in a Christmas card that year. It was so horrifying."

When *Failer* entered the world, listeners would be forgiven for thinking Ottawa women have foul mouths. Alanis Morissette became a global pop star in part by talking about blowjobs and dropping an F-bomb in the lead single from her blockbuster 1995 album, *Jagged Little Pill*. Kathleen Edwards introduced herself to the world with a narrator who said things like, "I'm a little bleeder with white pants on." She's a loud-mouthed girl who crashes the boys' shinny game but doesn't own a pair of hockey skates. She sleeps with married men and steals a gold watch from a bedside table after her lover has passed out drinking in their cheap motel room. To him, she sings in a chorus, "If you weren't so old, I would probably keep you / If you weren't so old, I'd tell my friends / But I don't think your wife would like my friends."

In Edwards's first profile in the *Globe and Mail*, Canada's national newspaper, writer Tralee Pearce began a question by saying, "I have a serious question to ask you." Edwards cut her off: "I'm not a virgin." Pearce claims to have been so stunned that she forgot her question. Several critics considered Edwards the anti–Avril Lavigne, a young woman making music for people 10 years older than her, instead of playing up teen angst. (It wasn't a fair comparison: Lavigne was 18 when she became a huge star in 2002; she's six years younger than Edwards.) *Failer* was promoted to DJs and critics in the U.S. with a mini bottle of Maker's Mark attached, playing up Edwards's bad girl image. It was an era when critics, including women, seemed to fetishize female boozers; reviews of Oh Susanna and Amy Millan always made sure to mention the narrators' fondness for whisky.

Once *Failer* was released stateside, support came from all corners: from the press, from late-night TV, from booking agents offering opening slots and from radio. Unlike in Canada, there was a radio format designed for artists of Edwards's ilk: adult album alternative, where Lucinda Williams and Nick Lowe and Wilco thrived. *Rolling Stone* booked a photo session, which turned rocky when Edwards rejected the revealing clothes they wanted her to wear. She insisted on her plaid shirt and jeans.

Edwards toured nonstop, on her own and opening for others, including Blue Rodeo, with several TV appearances along the way. Most of her dates were in the U.S., where she was in demand. Her Canadian gigs were largely at summer festivals, "where I was usually in the third or fourth slot—not that I was expecting to be anywhere else." *Failer* sold four times as many copies in the U.S. as it did in Canada: 80,000 vs. 20,000.

By the summer of 2003, she was looking forward to some time off. "I had been going since the fall of 2002, in a van nonstop," she says. "I toured and toured and did everything I was asked to do. I had booked two weeks at my friend's cottage in Kingston for the middle of the summer." Then Sambrook called her with an offer to play a 15-minute set at SARSfest, the large, free outdoor concert signalling to the world that Toronto was safe after a deadly coronavirus outbreak had made international headlines. It was headlined by the Rolling Stones and AC/DC, whose song "Money Talks" Edwards had been covering live.

"We've got this thing," said Sambrook. "I know it's in the middle of your cottage time, but you'll come to Toronto and do this."

"I'm not doing it."

"I don't think you understand what this is."

"Don't care. Not doing it."

"Let me rephrase this: *you're fucking doing it.*"

She caved—and was glad she did. The July 30 show was a huge success, drawing almost 500,000 people to Downsview Park. "I'd just been in this incredible circus of six months," she recalls, "where I went from living in Wakefield, putting out a record, nobody cares, to being on *Letterman* twice in five weeks, having my face on a full-page ad in *Rolling Stone*—all these weird things. When you don't have time to actually see what's happening, you don't have time to worry about what's happening tomorrow. That's what SARSfest was. I had no idea how huge it was. I had a good team of people behind me. My band was hot. We were in a real zone, so we didn't have to think about it too hard. We just showed up and played."

In a coup for MapleMusic, Sam Roberts opened the day. Edwards was on second. Three acts later was the Flaming Lips. Both Edwards and Roberts danced on stage during the Lips' set in giant furry animal costumes, as was routine at that band's shows of that period. "All the musicians and their spouses did it," she recalls, "because the Flaming Lips needed 20, 30 people in those flea-infested fart baskets [in which] total strangers had been sweating in for months. But we had fun."

AS EDWARDS'S STAR ASCENDED, Jim Bryson stayed in Ottawa and worked on his second album, *The North Side Benches*, with Starling's Ian LeFeuvre producing. Though he had an offer from MapleMusic, he accepted a larger one from Orange, another farm-team affiliate of Universal. They dropped him a year after the record was released. Despite being just as strong as his debut, and featuring solid pop songs like "Sleeping in Toronto," the album failed to meet the label's commercial expectations. Bryson was a hard sell: he was not as young, pretty or ambitious as his friend Kathleen.

He did, however, finally quit his job at Songbird, so that he could open for the Weakerthans across North America. It was financially draining, as a solo performer paying a backing band (which included drummer Jeremy Gara, who, a year later, joined Arcade Fire). But it was a good long-term investment: Bryson joined the Weakerthans as an auxiliary player on their 2007 tour, and in 2010 they backed him up on his album *The Falcon Lake Incident*. His reputation as a sideman led to his enlistment into the Tragically Hip on their 2009 tour, providing a calming presence in an otherwise difficult period in that band's career. "I never meant to be a side person," he says. "It was an occupational hazard. I didn't need to get into any of those bands. I never asked for it."

But he admits that, in 2003, part of him wished he had been at Edwards's side on the road.

JIM BRYSON WAS at Kathleen Edwards's side, in her bridal party, on Friday, August 13, 2004, when she married Colin Cripps. For the last 18 months, reviewers rarely failed to note the sexual chemistry on stage between Edwards and Cripps, which was certainly not an act. He proposed to her in the back of a tour bus in Philadelphia. They were married in her parents' backyard in Ottawa; Cripps's best men included his brother, Jim Cuddy, Tom Wilson and Junkhouse's Dan Achen (who is Leslie Feist's cousin). The couple moved in together in Toronto, while scouting for a new spot in Cripps's native Hamilton. Edwards and Cripps bought a house next door to his ex–Crash Vegas bandmate Jocelyne Lanois.

For their honeymoon, they drove down the coast of California en route to mix her new record in L.A. Edwards had to fight with her record company for Cripps as producer; they had wanted a big-name American. As a compromise, they hired Jim Scott to mix it, a renowned engineer with hundreds of credits— including Tom Petty's *Wildflowers*, one of Edwards's favourite records. *Back to Me* was received warmly, mostly because it was a slicker album than *Failer*. Highlights included the title track, one of the great sexual revenge songs of the decade, co-written with Cripps. Whereas on *Failer*'s "Six O'clock News" the pregnant partner of a felon watches events unfold on television, on "In State" she calls the cops herself and turns him in. "Copied Keys" captures the displacement of moving in with a lover in a different town. One of *Back to Me*'s best songs was "Somewhere Else," written by Jim Bryson, who rejoined her band on keyboards and rhythm guitar.

On *Back to Me*'s cover image, her body is turned away from the camera—a pun on the title, and consistent with her decision to not feature her face in closeup on the cover of *Failer*. During press rounds for that record, she noted how every female singer-songwriter was expected to use their visage as a vending point.

Edwards and her band toured hard for *Back to Me*, including opening slots for My Morning Jacket, Willie Nelson, the Tragically Hip, Aimee Mann and one of her songwriting heroes, John Prine. During this time, Edwards learned some valuable rules of the road—like how it might not be a good idea to drink a bottle of bourbon on stage every night. She credits Cripps with telling her, "It cheapens you and makes you seem like you're acting like your music is not good enough with people watching you drink."

Edwards's third album, 2008's *Asking for Flowers*, was as big a creative leap for her as *Failer* was from the first EP. The growing pains were over: Edwards was now a writer setting fully formed short stories to music. It found her an audience beyond the now-fading Americana crowd and landed on the Polaris prize shortlist. But playing in a band with her husband put a strain on the marriage; they split in 2009. Edwards took a job at a Niagara winery to clear her head of the music biz.

When she returned, her 2012 album *Voyageur* was an even bigger critical hit—deservedly so, as she continued to improve and expand her sound. It even cracked the Billboard Top 40, a first for her. Gossip about her new (and brief) relationship with the album's producer, Justin Vernon of Bon Iver, the indie folk It Boy du jour, over-shadowed much of the album's accomplishments. As Edwards—more than a decade into her career—struggled to fill rooms in the U.S., she felt increasingly removed from the circus. "She's had the fewest challenges to launch a career of anyone I've encountered," says one peer. "But her dues came in the middle of her career, when attendance went down and radio play dropped off." Touring was taking a physical toll, and she was diagnosed with clinical depression. The artist, whose early success was as lightning quick as it was unlikely, slammed on the brakes. For the last several years, Bryson had dared her to walk away and open a coffee shop called Quitters. In 2014, in the Ottawa-area community of Stittsville, she did exactly that.

Edwards didn't return to the public eye until 2020's *Total Freedom*, unanimously praised and that led to large profiles in the U.S., U.K. and Canadian press. After some false starts in Nashville, she finished it with Jim Bryson at the helm, helping his old friend out of a depression and back onto a creative track. "Her work ethic is second to none," says Bryson. "When she wants to do something, she works like nobody I've ever met." On *Total Freedom*'s album cover, for the first time in her career, a radiant Edwards looks directly at the camera.

THERE'S ONLY ONE act in this book related by blood to the initial explosion of Canadian country, rock and folk in the '60s. There's only one artist in this book equally at home with hardcore punks and bluegrass pickers. There's only one artist in this book likely to have played every town in North America that has a stage. There's only one artist in this book to have been the backing band for U.S. and U.K. punk legends, for Canadian rock'n'roll icons and even, once on-air at the CBC, for Margaret Atwood. Ladies and gentlemen and everyone in between, this is the Sadies.

TRAVIS AND DALLAS Good, born in 1968 and 1973 respectively, were raised in a thriving Toronto musical community. Their father, Bruce, and his twin brother, Brian, founded country band the Good Brothers, who were managed by an heir to the Eaton department store dynasty. That connection got the Good Brothers booked on Festival Express, the ill-fated proto-Lollapalooza that travelled Canada by train in 1970, featuring the Band, Janis Joplin and Great Speckled Bird, the latter a country rock band led by Ian and Sylvia Tyson. Also on the bill was the Grateful Dead, who were impressed enough by the Good Brothers to invite them to San Francisco to make a record, released by Columbia Records.

Upon returning to Canada, the Good Brothers became a favourite of Gordon Lightfoot, who often employed them as his opening act. Lightfoot's long-time guitarist, Red Shea, was young Travis Good's first guitar teacher. The Good Brothers put out records on major and indie labels and were successful enough to justify a double live album in 1980, on Solid Gold Records—which, as fate would have it, went gold. By the end of the '80s, Travis joined the family band on bass, though he could play most stringed instruments.

Brother Dallas also toured with the Good Brothers, but only did three jaunts, in Europe and on a cruise, whereas Travis did it for years. "My folks did everything they could to discourage me from becoming a musician," says Dallas. "There was never any sort of false pretense about how easy it would be or anything like that. My dad always made a joke where he said, 'Okay, look at all of these instruments— now don't touch them!' That's what made us musicians. Truth is, I hated piano lessons and had no intentions of doing anything like that until I started hearing my friends butcher songs on guitar. Even then I only really started playing guitar to play in punk bands."

Dallas left home at 17, with his parents' blessing, to move in with Jeff Beardall of Guilt Parade, a hardcore band from Fredericton who'd relocated to Toronto. Dallas had joined that band near the end of its run; he and Beardall then started Satanatras. While attending Parkdale Collegiate Institute, Dallas worked at Songbird Music, the preferred guitar shop of Greg Keelor of Blue Rodeo and Brian Connelly of Shadowy Men on a Shadowy Planet. Both played a huge role in Dallas's life.

"I won the lottery with that job," he says. "Great way to meet the community, to learn your instrument, to have access to great instruments. Shadowy Men promptly took me and the Satanatras under their wing; we did a lot of shows with them. [Bassist] Reid [Diamond] especially was so nurturing to me and was a true mentor. I have so many records that he gave to me because he thought it was important I had them. Being significantly older, he just filled in so many blanks. Those guys were the best. Same with Keelor. Such a lovely, approachable person with no airs. A great customer who was very supportive of all my early projects."

Another Songbird customer was Sean Dean, bassist with local arty hardcore band Phleg Camp. Dean shared Dallas's love of country, rockabilly and psychobilly like the Cramps and Pussy Galore. Phleg Camp were respected by Toronto peers for not only their inventive musicality and unique sound but because they toured the States relentlessly and could somehow draw 500 people in Pensacola, Florida. Guilt Parade's Jeff Beardall had recorded Phleg Camp's first cassette, and Shadowy Men hooked them up with Steve Albini. When Phleg Camp broke up in 1993, Dallas Good and Sean Dean moved in together and started a band with drummer Ted Robinson of Liquid Joy (which featured future Venice Biennale artist Shary Boyle on vocals). The new band was initially called SeDaTe, using the first letters of each of their names. It soon became the Sadies.

The Sadies were slowly becoming a country band—a uncommon trajectory for the hardcore scene. "A lot of punk rock singers ultimately become folk troubadours, and that's great," says Dallas. "It makes the stretch not as contradictory. But the only thing faster than hardcore is bluegrass, if you're a guitar player." Dallas was interested in more than just speed. At Songbird Music, he sold Dean an upright bass, solidifying the new direction. Brother Travis started sitting in as well. "In short time, we would do two sets: the first with Travis and upright bass, the second as a three-piece, loud and electric. We sounded a bit like Phleg Camp but more stoned and sloppy." Ted Robinson left. The new Sadies drummer was Andrew Scott, fresh off the heels of Sloan's breakup, and he gave the new band some serious star power on Queen Street West.

Scott enlisted the Sadies to join his new band, Maker's Mark, with fellow Haligonian Mike Belitsky; the two drummers were the creative engines there, trading off between guitar and drums. "It was very melodic and happy," says Dallas, "in the vein of Haligonian rock at that time." Soon enough, Scott was recruited back into Sloan. Belitsky took his place in the Sadies. But he, too, was in a Halifax band, Jale, who were about to release their second album on Sub Pop.

The Sadies, who put out a self-titled cassette in early 1995, were largely a side project, even as Travis joined permanently on second guitar and fiddle. "That changed everything," says Dallas. "It was so gratifying, because we could change our sound on a dime and it wasn't as weird." From the outset, the Sadies set themselves apart from every other band in Toronto—if only because they were all tall, thin men dressed in suits with dress shirts and skinny ties.

The suits came from the Good family closet, and they made them look like funeral directors. That only underscored the goth underbelly of their music. "We don't jump around on stage, so it's something to look at," says Dallas matter-of-factly. "It's a level of professionalism. These are obvious, stock answers. But the truth of the matter is that I just feel like I'm ready to play when I'm dressed up in a suit. It's more of a uniform than, 'Hey, look at me, I'm super dandy.' It's also easy maintenance. People don't understand that suits are actually really great to wear in a hot venue—way better than jeans and a T-shirt. Suits are baggy and made to breathe! I can't validate the tie or the rhinestones on my jacket that add an extra 30 pounds, but the suit itself is very clever stage equipment."

As cohesive as the Sadies looked and sounded, there were always guests involved—including Travis's Alaskan malamute, who sang backup. The dog "had no fear of crowds or anything, so what may sound like cruelty, I assure you was not," says Dallas. " He'd sing right into his mic. And no, it wasn't a thing where he was so annoyed he howled. He just knew the melody." Human harmony came from Fiona Highet, Andrew Scott's wife, who "was totally integral to the band in the early days," says Dallas. "She'd sit in as a special guest for maybe five songs a night, singing duets with me, old-time country stuff. Reid Diamond would play pedal steel. Danko Jones was on stage with us one night, and accidentally kicked over Reid's pedal steel."

Diamond recruited Dallas for a new project, Phono-Comb, a Shadowy Men project that began when guitarist Brian Connelly opted out of recording an album-length collaboration with American oddball Jad Fair (despite co-writing all the material). A stand-alone Phono-Comb record followed, released on Chicago's Touch and Go Records, recorded with Steve Albini, and Dallas had his first taste of touring the U.S. Back home, the Sadies played the Good twins' 50th birthday party at the Horseshoe with a set primarily of old country covers. Gordon Lightfoot loved it and told them so, adding, "The only advice I'll give you is to do your own songs."[4] Two years later, Neko Case came calling.

Case was just starting her solo career; her first band, Maow, had split, and the New Pornographers were not yet much more than a random recording project. Her first album, 1997's *The Virginian*, featured an all-star cast of Vancouver players. The only Torontonian on it was Shadowy Men's Brian Connelly. Before she went on tour across Canada, Connelly bowed out and Dallas Good took his place. "I was available to do a long tour with no money. Brian was not," he says. Neko wanted Dallas to tour the States as well. The Sadies were scheduled to record in Chicago—just like Phleg Camp and Phono-Comb before them—with Steve Albini. "I told Neko that I loved playing with her, but that I wouldn't be able to divide my time in the future," says Dallas. "I thought the Sadies would be a more

---

4   This is the only paragraph in any book you will ever read to feature both Jad Fair and Gordon Lightfoot.

immediate fit for what she was looking for. That happened really naturally." They joined her tour as both opening act and backing band.

The charismatic Case blew people away everywhere she went—as did the Sadies. Premier alt-country label Bloodshot Records agreed to release Case's records stateside; they soon also signed the Sadies, releasing debut album *Precious Moments* in 1998 and the follow-up, *Pure Diamond Gold*, just over a year later. The first album was half recorded by Albini in Chicago and half by Shadowy Man Don Pyle at Greg Keelor's farm.

The Sadies weren't necessarily trying to break the U.S. first. "I wasn't chasing it down because, 'Ooh, it's America,'" says Dallas. "It was just where people I knew were. The first booking agency I ever worked with was Billions, through default because Shadowy Men had been booked through them." Drummer Mike Belitsky, who has dual citizenship, was living in New York and Chicago until the early 2000s. In 1998, he briefly quit the Sadies to tour with Boston's Pernice Brothers. "Luckily, we suckered him back into rejoining," says Dallas.

Bloodshot hooked them up with Detroit singer Andre Williams, a '50s R&B artist on the comeback trail after years of addiction. *Red Dirt*, credited to both Williams and the Sadies, came out in 1999, featuring eye-raising tracks like "She's a Bag of Potato Chips" and "Pardon Me (I've Got Someone to Kill)."

"We'd never met, but I was a big fan," says Dallas. "I also knew he wanted to make a country record. If he already wanted that, we weren't going to fuck him up. It made sense." Several years before the trend of young white musicians backing up Black elders, the album gave the Sadies stock in U.S. Americana circles. In Canada, Sadies records were only available on import.

"The Sadies, in the '90s, were deemed an American band—which fucking sucked, so bad," says Dallas. "There was a clear-cut border that made it difficult for us to travel, visas included. It forced us to play really long tours and try to develop while still not being a part of any specific touring circuit. We can't appeal to the cowboy hats; we can't appeal to the [punk] kids in Creepers; we can't appeal to the instrumental fans because we're only instrumental half the time. We quickly discovered that there was an audience for us at home in Canada, who were fantastic and completely in line with other bands we wanted to play with. It would have been easier if we had just signed with a Canadian label." On the radio, the Sadies didn't even qualify as Canadian content, which requires a song to have at least two Canadian components in either music, artist, producer or lyrics. Not only were all their covers American, but so was their producer, Steve Albini (despite the fact that Albini never took production credit, only engineering).

Canadian support instead came from one of the biggest bands in the country: Blue Rodeo made the Sadies their preferred opening act. Keelor routinely proclaimed them "the best live rock'n'roll band on the planet," among other hyperboles, to anyone who would listen. He again invited the band, and Albini and Don Pyle, to join them at his farm east of Toronto to make their next record, 2001's *Tremendous Efforts*. In exchange, they let Keelor howl through Elvis Presley's "Loved on Look." The rest of Blue Rodeo also made appearances, as did Dallas's good friend Rick White, of Eric's Trip and Elevator, who painted the album cover and played synth. It's White's influence that's most audible: *Tremendous Efforts* took a decidedly more psychedelic turn than the first two Sadies records. Two of the hazier tracks—covers of the Byrds' "Wasn't Born to Follow" and the Gun Club's "Mother of Earth"—were recorded with White at his Moncton studio.

Dallas Good, Rick White and Greg Keelor were an odd trio of roommates, at 624 Queen Street West. (André Ethier of the Deadly Snakes also lived there briefly.) Keelor had been there since the late '90s, using it as a Toronto crash pad when he wasn't at his Kawartha farm; Rick and Tara White moved in in 2001. Dallas Good was there from 1998 to 2003; during his time, he joined Elevator and toured with them opening a U.S. tour for Built to Spill. Dallas also helped make two of that band's records in the 624 living room. Keelor produced the 2002 Sadies album *Stories Often Told*.

The three men—Good, White and Keelor—soon started writing together, forming a band with the Sadies' rhythm section called the Unintended, who released one original album and split an EP with the Constantines, on which that band did Neil Young songs and the Unintended covered Gordon Lightfoot. "Rick was able to contribute more directly to our psychedelic cloud and vice versa," says Dallas. "With the Unintended and Elevator, I was able to bring out Rick's folkier side, just by playing along with him. Some of those songs were just naturally suited for whatever formula the Sadies had, whether he meant them to or not. It's been a fruitful collaboration." That stretched to Blue Rodeo as well: in 2002, one song written by Keelor and Jim Cuddy appeared, in two slightly different versions, as the title track to both the Sadies' *Stories Often Told* and Blue Rodeo's *Palace of Gold*.

Another resident at 624 Queen West soon talked his way into the Sadies. Paul Aucoin was a Halifax composer and vibraphonist who led orch-pop group the Hylozoists.[5] Vibraphones are not an obvious fit for the Sadies—or any rock band, really. But after contributing to *Tremendous Efforts*, Aucoin convinced them that if they let him apply for grants on their behalf, then they could afford to bring him on the road. For two years, it worked—on paper, on record and socially. On stage was another story.

---

5   His brother, Rich, later became an acclaimed electronic artist.

"Unfortunately for him, we were playing such small venues that it was very, very rare that we could make proper use of the vibraphones," says Dallas. Vibraphones are amplified through overhead mics, "and he was always forced to be behind my amp and beside the drums. At almost every show, people would say, 'What the fuck? I can't hear the vibraphones.' Also, he would bow the vibes a lot, which I thought was a fantastic addition, creating this creepy, ambient, haunted sound. But in a live setting, it just didn't translate. Also, Travis and I play so many notes, there's not a lot of room in the music. Shortly after that, we worked with a pedal steel player who also played trumpet. But we were still on the same small stages and it didn't work. For a band who loves collaborating," Dallas laughs, "we really fucking hate collaborating."

He's joking, of course. "We were always up to a collaboration," he says. "The music lent itself well to it. Having said that, we never set out to have a side hustle." In 2002, Bloodshot again made them a connection, this time with Jon Langford of the Mekons. The co-leader of one of Britain's longest-running punk bands, immortalized in many a Greil Marcus essay, was living in Chicago and reinventing himself as a key figure in that city's alt-country scene. He made a full-length collaboration with the Sadies, *Mayors of the Moon*, released in 2002.

"Our relationship with Langford is another lottery I won," says Dallas, who admits he was merely ambivalent about the Mekons before the relationship. "The sense of community and family he's brought to me, I could never underestimate how important he was to the Sadies. At one point in the early 2000s, the Mekons hired us to open for them on a U.S. tour as a Mekons tribute band. We learned a bunch of songs, a set we were confident with. Then we found out that for certain shows, they would play certain venues depending on which era of the Mekons they wanted to perform. In New York, they did the '70s at CBGB, the '80s at Mercury Lounge and the rest somewhere else. We didn't know that, and they expected us to follow suit. We either did or didn't. Then they'd go on stage and be like, 'Did you see that opening band? That was weird.' It was an amazing joke." Langford also brought the Sadies to the U.K. for the first time, where they've been packing clubs ever since.

The Sadies were renowned work horses, touring more than 100 dates a year on top of their various other projects, which over the years have involved everyone from Gord Downie and John Doe of L.A. punk pioneers X (they made full-length albums with both) to Neil Young and Buffy Sainte-Marie. They took a page from Blue Rodeo—albeit on a much less mainstream scale—by touring almost every corner of Canada, in every kind of venue. One could argue that you haven't truly experienced the Sadies live unless you've seen them on the back of a flatbed truck on a farm in the middle of nowhere on a humid summer night, with a lightning storm approaching in the distance, while they barrel through their set of originals and covers of early Pink Floyd, Teenage Head and Johnny Cash.

In 2004, they once again backed up Neko Case, this time for an excellent live album of new material, *The Tigers Have Spoken*, recorded at Lee's Palace in Toronto; they also toured with her to promote it. Two years later, they were back at Lee's Palace to record their own live album, a *Last Waltz*–like affair featuring almost every high-profile name in their circle: Case, White, Langford, the Good Brothers, Blue Rodeo, Jon Spencer, the Deadly Snakes and newer friend Gary Louris of the Jayhawks, who produced their next two studio records. There was also one guest that linked them directly to *The Last Waltz*: keyboardist Garth Hudson of the Band.

"We'd worked with him in New York, when the Sadies were with Neko at the Bowery Ballroom for a couple of nights," says Dallas. "He made it for the encore of the second night—even though he was expected at soundcheck on the first night." The day of the Sadies' live recording, they found out by chance that Hudson happened to be in Toronto. "We were presented with: 'If he comes, can he use someone's keyboard?' That's how it went down, and it's so good it worked that way," says Dallas of the legendary sideman, who has a reputation for being, um, spontaneous in every aspect of his life, on and off stage. "To be honest, if we had invited him and planned on it . . . Let's just say it was a great surprise.

"We just wanted to celebrate all the people we'd worked with over the years and made us who we were," continues Dallas. "Everyone did whatever they had to do to make that all happen. I can't believe how little we offered in terms of hospitality to everyone involved: 'You're here! Great. There's no guest list and here's a bottle of Jägermeister. I have no idea where you're staying, and I hope you like the mix because you get no say in it. Okay, bye.' The only person I can think of, other than Fiona Highet, who didn't play on it was Andre Williams, and that was for pretty sound reasons: he wasn't doing great at the time. In retrospect, we didn't work much with most of those artists after that live album, so I'm glad we did it when we did."

It was hardly a last waltz, of course. The Sadies soldiered on. Their albums produced by Louris—2007's *New Seasons* and 2010's *Darker Circles*—focused more on songwriting in the Lightfoot and Blue Rodeo tradition than the short, sharp bursts of instrumental energy and psychedelic textures that had become their stock in trade. Sadies albums were no longer just souvenirs of the live show. The band who put out 11 records in their first decade started to slow down their studio output.

There was another record with Andre Williams. There was also the inevitable *Good Family Album*, made with the Good Brothers and their spouses. There has not yet been a sequel to *In Concert: Volume One*, but there will be no shortage of guests clamouring to fly in and participate. Their New Year's gigs at the Horseshoe, starting in 2001, became as much of a reliable Toronto tradition as Gordon Lightfoot at Massey Hall. In 2012, Dallas joined Shadowy Men on a Shadowy Planet for reunion shows, playing the same instrument owned by Reid Diamond, who died in 2001. A circle had been completed; there was no one better suited to pay tribute to Diamond's legacy.

And there was always another Sadies gig, somewhere in Saskatchewan or in Spain or Seattle or a small corner of southwestern Ontario. And they'd always open with "Cheat" from 1998's *Precious Moments*. And Dallas would always announce near the end of the set: "Ladies and gentlemen, we are the Sadies from Toronto, Ontario, and we have eleven more songs we want to play for you tonight."

CHAPTER II

YOUR EX-LOVER
IS IN THE BAND

BROKEN SOCIAL SCENE,
STARS, METRIC

In 2000, two new friends made an ambient record in a Toronto basement, with a loose collection of peers and low expectations. In 2000, an ambitious Toronto couple had already bounced between Brooklyn and London and scrapped a recording with a noted British producer before starting anew in Los Angeles. In 2000, some old Toronto friends living in New York decided to move to Montreal in search of a drummer.

Some of these people grew up together. Some were total strangers. Some were or would soon be lovers and then ex-lovers and still bandmates. Many were the sons and daughters of actors, painters, poets and publishers; many had at least one U.S.- or U.K.-born parent. One would sell millions of records as a solo artist. Together, they rewrote the rules of what a mainstream Canadian rock band could be, and the world paid attention. One of them was called Broken Social Scene, but that name could apply to them all—and they did all end up in Broken Social Scene in one way or another, certainly in the eyes of the media, and sometimes, to their chagrin, at the expense of their own identity.

They all have their own unique stories worth telling, though they'll be forever intertwined. Superconnected.

Stars. Metric. Broken Social Scene. It's no wonder they gravitated toward one another. Though they didn't share a sound, they shared a mission: big sound, big passion, love in the face of evil, hope in a time of war, lean on your peers, ageless beauty. Love would tear them apart, and forgiveness would keep them together.

THERE ARE TWO bookends to the story.

The first is in 1996 at a club called the Mockingbird, where Kevin Drew worked. Drew was a budding impresario at age 20, managing a local band and booking acts into the Mockingbird, like his old high school friend Emily Haines, who had a duo with James Shaw called Mainstream. Shaw had told his childhood friend Torquil Campbell about Drew.

"You gotta meet this fucking kid, he's unbelievable," said Shaw.

"What's so special about him?" asked Campbell.

"You'll see. He's just the King of Kensington."

Campbell went to the Mockingbird and saw a kid in full hustle mode. "He was [barely] even legally working there, and he ran the place," says Campbell. "He was ordering the bartenders around. He was promoting gigs there. He knew everybody's name. Everyone was 'babe.' His charm was electric. His good nature and his playfulness, and his certainty that he was special, was infectious and fun to be around."

Drew had his own band, KC Accidental, which was just him and Charles Spearin of Do Make Say Think. A home recording project, the band had never played a gig before. So they enlisted some friends for a Mockingbird gig: drummer Justin Peroff, who they'd met through mutual friends and had played on the record; James Shaw and Emily Haines; Justin Small of Do Make Say Think and Evan Cranley, who was about to join Campbell's band, Stars. A torrential rainstorm raged outside, while the band recreated hypnotic, ambient jams. Everyone involved felt like something had just happened that was bigger than any individual person, that this was something truly special.

Flash forward to 2005: Broken Social Scene, Stars and Metric are all in Japan with the Dears and Death from Above 1979. A local promoter brought them all there, with the help of the Canadian embassy. It should have been the trip of a lifetime. But, to quote a Dears title, they were pinned together, falling apart.

Broken Social Scene was finishing their self-titled album, the follow-up to their international breakthrough. Pressure was immense. The band whose lineup had always been loose had swelled in numbers—and everyone had to be involved. There were two simultaneous recording sessions going on. Tensions were high, between friends and between lovers, and a band once filled with optimism had taken a darker turn. Metric was also preparing their second album, the first since Haines and Shaw had split as a couple; she was working on a solo album. Stars was perhaps the worst off, with Fleetwood Mac style romantic drama among three of the five members, while singer Torquil Campbell was having a nervous breakdown and thought he had lung cancer.

Adding to the tension, "The Dears were Led Zeppelin–level partying," says Campbell. "A great deal of fun—if you didn't have to be in a band with them. They brought Montreal chaos into this group of people who thought they were pretty badass but were actually from Etobicoke and not that crazy."

Everyone had to meet on a bus at nine a.m. to go to the Osaka train station. "If we missed the bus, the promoter was going to take a bath on $7,000 worth of train tickets," says Broken Social Scene co-founder Brendan Canning. "No refunds, and there were 30 of us. Kevin was the minister of information, giving a speech in the bus: 'Here's the deal!'" But there was no sign of two Dears. They eventually arrived with a half-empty bottle of Jack Daniel's and started pissing out the window of the bus. Meanwhile, says Canning, "Torq thought he was dying, so he was crying. [The Dears'] Natalia [Yanchak] was six months pregnant. I was looking at Murray [Lightburn] like, 'Get your fucking troops in line, buddy.' He said, 'Don't take me back to Bible camp, Canning,' like I was being all high and mighty or something."

Kevin Drew tried to keep it all together and play peacemaker. "Kevin doesn't like that kind of thing, people being debauched—even though *he* is utterly debauched," says Campbell. "He likes cozy, cuddly debauchery, not peeing-out-the-window debauchery. Kevin doesn't like it when people are inconsiderate. 'Don't do that around a pregnant lady—that's not cool.'"

After running through the station, with minutes to spare, the entourage did make it on the Osaka train. But for Stars, the drama continued after the Tokyo gig. "We broke up on the flight home from Japan," says Campbell. At that point, the only person in Stars on speaking terms with everyone in the band was drummer Pat McGee. "That's what our song 'Bitches in Tokyo' is about. It was disastrous, all the time. But when there's also constant success, is it the forgiveness that keeps you around or the success? If there's no love, then you can't forgive. And if you can't forgive, you're doomed. People are going to fuck up and do things that upset you and hurt you and annoy you. If you don't love them, you won't find forgiveness."

"When you start going around the world with your friends, it's an emotional pinball—the only way the shows really work is if you're emotionally raw," says Kevin Drew, whose band burned through 29 different tour managers in the course of its career. "We were impossible. There were so many of us, having the best time, ups and downs. It took a toll, as it does. You spend your whole life not wanting to be a stereotype, and then you get sucked into it and you don't even see it." That said, Drew remembers the Japan trip fondly. "It was wild, and very family-esque and sweet and earnest as well," he says. "I had a great time. Whatever was going on in the background, I didn't see it. We were in Tokyo!"

"Kevin is a catcher in the rye, man, catching all the lemmings from running off a cliff," says Campbell. "That's his life's work."

———

ANY STUDENT ATTENDING the Etobicoke School of the Arts hopes they'll meet people who will shape their future career in creative pursuits. For Kevin Drew, it happened the summer before he even got there. At age 13, at the YMCA Camp Pinecrest in Ontario's Muskoka region, he met Amy Millan, who showed him her ESA yearbook. Then, in frosh week of grade 9, as bullies insisted he push a penny down a hallway with his nose, an older girl walked around the corner, saw what was happening, demanded they stop and delivered a lecture about how degrading it was. Her name was Emily Haines.

Drew didn't pick up a guitar until he was 17. His first musical foray was a four-track album called *Suburban Masturbation*. After high school, he attended Toronto's Harris Institute to study audio engineering. He fell into a downtown scene centring on Blue Dog Pict, an androgynous, acid-drenched prog band featuring former child actors Keram Malicki-Sánchez (*Catwalk*) and Keith White (*Degrassi High*). Also in the scene were Latino punk-funk band Project 9, Dig Circus (featuring future Fembots) and, Drew's favourite, a glam band called Nancy Despot. "It was the most intelligent and glamorous scene," says Drew. "I was mesmerized by them all. They were highly intellectual: in fashion, food, music, writing, literature, they were like nobody I'd spent time with before. They were eccentric. They showed me community, strength in numbers."

One of his Harris Institute assignments was to manage a band. He approached Nancy Despot. When they finished recording their debut album in 1996, Drew set up an interview for them at campus station CIUT. That day, singer Brian Gunstone went AWOL. Just before the interview, Drew learned that Gunstone had died suddenly, at the age of 27. "It was a catastrophe," he says, "and a social one at that, too. It ripped the scene apart. It never really came back." Drew finished his school assignment by stuffing envelopes for Gowan's manager, an instructor at the college.

At school, Drew was intrigued by fellow student Charles Spearin. "You look like the kind of guy who listens to Tortoise," said Drew. "I am!" responded Spearin. The two became fast friends.

Spearin had just formed a band with friends, including Justin Small of venerable industrial metal band Malhavoc. The new band, Do Make Say Think, was instrumental and not at all aggressive; it was instead inspired by Yo La Tengo and Stereolab—bands unafraid of amorphous compositions without choruses, influenced by the repetition of electronic music, the improvisation of jazz and the sound experiments of dub reggae. Some of Do Make Say Think's first shows were at raves, held in warehouses or abandoned slaughterhouses; the band played in chillout rooms where dancers took respite from house music and lay about in beanbag chairs.

Drew became a huge Do Makes fan, going to all their shows. He formed his own band, Djula, in which he played drums and invited Spearin to join. He also corralled Emily Haines's boyfriend, James Shaw. Djula only played three shows before it morphed into a recording project with just Drew and Spearin. "It was easier and more satisfying than putting a band together," says Spearin. "I knew Charlie had so much music in him," says Drew, "so much musicality, that he could be in three or four different bands."

The project was dubbed KC (for Kevin and Charles) Accidental, and its debut album, *Captured Anthems for an Empty Bathtub*, was released in 1998. Limited to 100 copies with a cover made of orange construction paper, it was sold only at Queen Street West record store Rotate This. The shop put it at No. 1 on their sales chart— which was not accurate. It was a total ruse to mess with Drew, who was a regular customer. But it did sell out.

Do Make Say Think also put out their debut album in 1998. Justin Small gave a copy of it to Godspeed You! Black Emperor at that band's first Toronto gig; they in turn brought it back to Constellation Records in Montreal, who offered to give it a proper release in 1999. It was only the fourth catalogue number on the label, and its first non-Montreal signing. With Godspeed, the Do Makes toured the East Coast of Canada, en route to the 1998 Halifax Pop Explosion and back, and to Europe for the first time in November and December 1999.

Justin Small and James Payment of the Do Makes showed up on a second KC Accidental album in 2000, along with Keram Malicki-Sánchez of Blue Dog Pict, singer-songwriter Jason Collett, violinist Jessica Moss from Godspeed, Justin Peroff, Emily Haines and James Shaw. Bill Priddle of Treble Charger, a band transitioning from indie darlings to major label pop-punk, is also on the record, because his wife worked for Drew's father, who ran a book distributor. A star-struck Drew—who loved Treble Charger's power ballad "Red" as much as any '90s Toronto indie kid—pulled Priddle into the fold.

"I didn't really understand, at first, Kevin's obsession with bringing in guests," says Spearin. "He's like, 'Let's bring in Bill Priddle, he plays guitar!' I'm like, 'Uh, I play guitar. We don't need a guitar player.' Then I got the sense that everyone was adding spice. It wasn't about technical ability; it was about choices, and blending those choices to make this accidental soup that was really enjoyable. It was the template for Broken Social Scene, opening the doors and not worrying so much about your identity as a band but adding some ventilation, letting new people come in and open your mind a bit and steer it in a different direction. There was a rudderless quality to it."

Future Stars Amy Millan and Evan Cranley were also involved. A track Millan was asked to sing, "Porno Boy," didn't make the cut. Drew knew Cranley because they'd both dated the same girl when they were 14. Cranley's high school band, Gypsy Soul, got signed out of high school; he was now playing trombone with neo-swing artist Big Rude Jake. "KC Accidental were making this weird instrumental music that, honestly, took me months to wrap my head around," says Cranley. "I thought it was really original and weird and had no real structure to it."

Both KC Accidental records are hard to pin down. The first one opens with fuzzed-out rock guitars and frenetic drumming, but after that the band alternates between three modes: Tortoise-influenced cinematic instrumentals, not too far removed from Do Make Say Think; ambient jams; and what sounds like a rock band who listens to a lot of drum'n'bass and electronic music. They had high hopes that Constellation would put out the album, but the label passed. "It broke my heart," says Drew. Instead, it came out on Noise Factory, who had put out the Nancy Despot record in 1996 and was now dedicated primarily to experimental electronic music. KC Accidental was situated somewhat in between.

The next time the Do Makes left for a European tour, in the fall of 2000, Spearin's eight-track was entrusted to Drew. He was living with Jeffrey Remedios, who worked for Virgin Records Canada, in a house on Gladstone Avenue. Music writer Stuart Berman lived upstairs. It was there that Drew got a cold call from Brendan Canning.

Canning was the former bassist in the early '90s Oshawa grunge band hHead, who were pegged for big things after winning a $100,000 prize in a 1993 CFNY contest. The big things didn't happen, and they split in 1997. Canning then played with Spookey Ruben, who many thought would break out of Toronto. (He did eventually, in Japan.) To pay his bills, Canning became a house music DJ and cashed in when he helped friends in the band Len craft a top 10 U.S. hit, "Steal My Sunshine." He thought he might give up on rock music entirely, but he joined By Divine Right in 1999 for a tour of North America opening for the Tragically Hip. He also tour managed for his roommate, Danko Jones. After six years of playing in several next-big-things in the Canadian music industry, he was left frustrated and nauseous.

Toronto being the small town it is, Canning's best friend and his cousin lived in the same house as Kevin Drew, in a different apartment, as Stuart Berman's roommates. Canning heard about KC Accidental when Drew approached him with a flyer for the Mockingbird gig. He heard the record while high at a mutual friend's place and joked, "Maybe I'll make this kid a star." Canning cold-called

Drew shortly after. Drew didn't call him back for a while; he wasn't a fan of hHead. When they did meet, Drew was immediately smitten with Canning's softness and generosity.

Canning started hanging out at the Gladstone house—which Drew shared with his wife, Jo-Ann Goldsmith—making a record called *Feel Good Lost* with Drew on Spearin's eight-track. They roped in some of the same guests who'd appeared on the last KC Accidental record: Peroff, Cranley, Moss and new addition Leslie Feist.

Feist had played in By Divine Right with Canning. Drew met her one night at a Peaches party, where she thought he was gay. She was shocked to find out he was married to a woman five years his senior. Shortly after the party, Canning invited Feist to sing on a recording project and gave her Drew's address. When she showed up, she connected the dots.

Feist was dating Andrew Whiteman at the time. That guitarist had met Drew through another mutual friend, filmmaker Eric Yealland, who thought the two would hit it off. Whiteman, 10 years older than Drew, had already spent a dozen years playing in a large band with many songwriters: the Bourbon Tabernacle Choir, an R&B group he co-founded in high school that became one of Canada's most popular bar bands in the late '80s and early '90s. He knew Canning from that circuit.

In December 2000, Whiteman went with Feist to see Stars at Ted's Wrecking Yard and met the extended scene. When he heard the recordings, he told Drew it sounded like U2—which was not meant as a compliment but was taken as such. "I could sense the inner Bono in him instantly," says Whiteman. The elder guitarist learned a lot from the young music nerd. After Whiteman lost 5,000 vinyl records in a robbery, he collected insurance money and went record shopping with Drew, who introduced him to '90s post-rock.

When Spearin returned from Europe, Drew greeted him with some news: "I've fallen in love with this guy named Brendan." He played him *Feel Good Lost*, and Spearin agreed to mix it with the Do Makes' Ohad Benchetrit. The social scene was expanding. They didn't yet know how they were going to credit this new project: was it KC Accidental if Spearin didn't play on it? Drew had a gig booked on December 17, 2000, at the weekly Wavelength series, with the Russian Futurists and Raising the Fawn. Drew asked promoter Jonny Dovercourt to be billed as John Tesh Jr. and the Broken Social Scene. It wasn't a band performance, however: it was a Drew solo performance on synth, guitar and improvised melodies.

The first band show was January 26, 2001, also at Ted's Wrecking Yard, featuring Drew, Canning, Peroff, Feist and Whiteman. There was a rehearsal at Feist's apartment. Whiteman remembers, "Kevin came over to my pedals—I only had four pedals—and took my distortion and said, 'You won't be needing this.' But he had a point." This time it was clearly a new band: Broken Social Scene. Even though the show was a release party for the mostly ambient and spacey *Feel Good Lost*, no songs from the record were performed. New material was debuted.

"I didn't think of [*Feel Good Lost*] as pieces to be recreated," says Canning. "I thought of them as blueprints. Then we started jamming and everyone was basically on the same page, in terms of music we could vibe to."

Feel Good Lost was much softer and more consistent than the KC Accidental records. Torquil Campbell, for one, fell in love with it. He was back from New York City, living with his parents and plotting his next moves. *Feel Good Lost* suited his mood perfectly. "I listened to it endlessly on my headphones," he says, "feeling this sense of wonder at finding this other group of people who grew up looking at my city in the same way: the sun going down, the flat grey sky, the emptiness of Toronto back then, the wind coming off the lake and the sense of loneliness. Toronto was a lonely city when I grew up. You could easily walk downtown in the middle of the day and not see another soul for blocks. They turned all that into atmosphere—which is always what was beautiful about growing up in Toronto, the solitariness of it."

TORQUIL CAMPBELL'S CAREER peaked when he was 10 years old. A child actor, he appeared in the 1983 Hollywood film *The Golden Seal* and made more money that year than he has in any 12-month period since. His parents were both actors; his father, Douglas, was a renowned Shakespearean who was in the original company of Ontario's Stratford Festival, and starred in the title role of the CBC kids show *The Great Detective* in the early '80s. The young Campbell's musical pursuits began while he was making a living as an actor in New York City. The woman with whom he would one day co-front Stars, Amy Millan, also studied drama: first at the Etobicoke School of the Arts—where she took a major in drama, a minor in music—and then at Concordia University in Montreal.

Twenty years after Millan joined Campbell in Stars, they staged an autobiographical play about their band—there was no shortage of material. Stars' harsher critics often accused the band's music of being overly dramatic. But it was in their bones. "It turned out drama was major in our lives," says Millan, "just behind the scenes."

CAMPBELL GREW UP IN TORONTO, with childhood friends Chris Seligman and James Shaw. A lot of Canadian kids grew up with anglophile musical taste, but Campbell came by it honestly: he was born in Sheffield, England. "As a young person, anything Canadian I tried very hard not to like it—actively," he says. "I would secretly enjoy the Pursuit of Happiness's 'I'm an Adult Now,' but I wouldn't buy the record—it wasn't cool enough." That said, on his friend Charles Spearin's 12th birthday—and Toronto's sesquicentennial—they were among the 25,000 people outside Toronto City Hall screaming for Platinum Blonde.

Campbell's life-changing concert was the Jesus and Mary Chain's legendary Toronto debut in 1987. "I was 15," says Campbell. "There were 100 people there. It was empty. They didn't come on until two and a half hours late. They were the first band I ever saw play with a drum machine. It broke in the middle of every single song in the set—at which point, [brothers Jim and William Reid] would turn around and poke at it, with their backs to the audience, for 10 minutes at a time. They'd restart songs, and it would break again. It was one of the best-slash-worst gigs I've ever seen in my life. At some point, some geek in the front row yelled something like, 'Get your shit together!' Then Jim Reid picked up his mic stand and clocked the motherfucker in the head. [He was charged with assault and spent the night in a Toronto jail.] I was in heaven. I thought it was the best thing I'd ever experienced in my life."

Thinking of that gig years later, when Stars was beginning, Campbell says, "I thought we could be like that, but sound like Burt Bacharach."

After high school, Campbell and Shaw became as close as two heterosexual men could. "Every single day, I'd go over [to Shaw's house] for 12 hours, smoke weed and listen to Steely Dan and eat macaroni and cheese," says Campbell. Joining them occasionally was 15-year-old Evan Cranley, who'd dropped out of Oakwood Collegiate and was playing trombone in Gypsy Soul. "He'd always come to the door and apologize for coming over: 'I really hope I'm not bothering you guys.' I guess we seemed incredibly cool to him at the time," says Campbell, "though we were such losers."

Shaw had gone to the Curtis Institute of Music in Philadelphia, while still in high school. He dropped out after a year. Campbell convinced him they should both apply to the Juilliard School in New York City, an institution renowned for its drama, dance and music programs. Campbell didn't get in; Shaw did. They moved to the Big Apple together, with Campbell instead enrolling in Circle in the Square, a Broadway acting academy. Shaw quickly tired of the conservatism of classical music. He sold several trumpets he had, investing in an eight-track reel-to-reel recorder and some rock instruments. He and Campbell became prolific writers. Campbell estimates they wrote 200 songs together over the course of the next several years. "We'd go to school until about four p.m.," he says. "Then from six p.m. to three a.m., seven days a week, we'd write songs." Their old friend Chris Seligman was going to university in Boston and came to Manhattan every weekend.

In 1996, Shaw moved back to Toronto for the summer. There, he met Emily Haines. He fell in love and decided to follow her to Montreal, where she was going to school. Campbell was crushed: "It wasn't *like* having your heart broken by a romantic partner—it *was* that. I felt like I had lost my love. Emily Haines stole him from me."

EMILY HAINES WAS ALWAYS A SATELLITE. She was born in New Delhi to American parents—a painter and a poet. They moved to Fenelon Falls, two hours north of Toronto, on the Trent-Severn canal system, where houseboats parade by every summer. Her father, Paul, taught high school French to pay the bills, though he was a renowned poet in the New York City jazz scene of the late 1960s; he wrote liner notes for Albert Ayler and penned an acclaimed jazz opera with Carla Bley, 1971's *Escalator over the Hill*. The Haines house was full of books and records made by his friends around the world, to whom he'd mail out daily mixtapes.

Emily Haines left home at 16 to attend the Etobicoke School of the Arts, staying in the apartment of her eight-years-senior sister Avery (later a prominent newscaster) in Toronto's Cabbagetown and taking the subway an hour west to school. Haines met Amy Millan on the first day of school, while they were both searching for music class. Millan's family lived not far from Haines's sister's apartment. Haines was already writing her own songs, which she worked on in the school's practice rooms. Millan would sit and listen, enraptured. "I was completely blown away," she told writer Helen Spitzer. "Here was this young woman who seemed so formed, writing music that already sounded to me like songs on the radio."

Haines went to the University of British Columbia in 1992 and then Concordia in Montreal for electroacoustic studies. While there, she recorded a solo album of piano music, *Cut in Half and Also Double*, in 1995. Some of the lyrics were written during a routine of nursing a single cocktail at the Jello Martini Lounge on Ontario Street, a haunt of hers. She formed a folk duo with Millan, who was also at Concordia, called Edith's Mission. They played a show at the Horseshoe in Toronto, where Kevin Drew offered to manage them. The band lasted one more gig.

Haines found herself at the Horseshoe beside James Shaw in 1996, both there to see a mutual friend's funk band—which may or may not have been Gypsy Soul, featuring Evan Cranley on trombone. "This is brutal," lamented Haines. Shaw was smitten. While she finished her degree at Concordia, Shaw worked on his own solo project, an album called *Life on the Clock*. It's a smooth, mid-'90s soft pop album, with Haines singing backing vocals on four tracks; one is written by Torquil Campbell. Shaw launched it in 1997 with a release show at the Rivoli in Toronto, with Evan Cranley on bass; Charles Spearin was the sound tech that night. Looking out at the crowd, seeing the familiar faces of Toronto A&R reps, Shaw knew he needed to leave town. Toronto was not the place for him. Nor for Haines. They split for the Big Apple.

TORQUIL CAMPBELL WAS a full-time actor in New York: Shakespeare in the Park, the inevitable *Law & Order* role available to every New York actor, and the acclaimed British play *Shopping and Fucking*, which ran off-Broadway for seven months. After every performance of the latter, co-star Philip Seymour Hoffman would tell Campbell, "Why are you going home to write those shitty pop songs? It's so fucking embarrassing, dude. You sound like the Pet Shop Boys. You have to stop!" Campbell, of course, loved the Pet Shop Boys, which very few people did in the mid-'90s. Chris Seligman moved into Campbell's one-bedroom apartment in the West Village.

Amy Millan was in Toronto performing solo; her first gig was opening for Jason Collett's band, Bird. She soon started a country band, 16 Tons, first as a solo project with help from Skydiggers' Josh Finlayson and then with her boyfriend, Derek Downham, as guitarist and co-songwriter, plus a rhythm section. They rehearsed in Kensington Market. One day leaving the studio, she ran into Emily Haines, who lived next door. They had been estranged since their university days. "That's the band you're in, the one I hear all the time?" asked Haines. The two friends instantly reconnected. Haines became one of Millan's biggest supporters.

Sarah Harmer's manager, Patrick Sambrook, signed 16 Tons. Through his connections, Millan got slots on Blue Rodeo's Stardust Picnic shows in 1998 and '99; they recorded one EP of demos with producer Colin Cripps at the Tragically Hip's studio and another with Change of Heart's Ian Blurton. She was deeply plugged into the last vestiges of Toronto's '90s scene—and she didn't like it. "The Canadian music industry was so formulaic, and that rubbed me the wrong way," she says. "I was this person in a cog. 'We're going to do a demo, then get money, then do a bigger thing, then you'll get a record deal.' It was like being in a factory and it felt gross." Her relationship with Downham also soured. Millan went to L.A. for a change of scenery. She hated that, too. She moved back to Toronto, moving in with Jenny Whiteley and Dan Whiteley, young bluegrass musicians and offspring of Toronto's first family of folk music.

Haines and Shaw had moved to New York City in 1998 into a 4,000-square-foot industrial loft above an auto body shop at 249 Metropolitan Avenue in Williamsburg. Shaw put up drywall to make six bedrooms and charged $500 a room. Chris Seligman moved in. So did a Belgian jazz duo and a young photographer, Nick Zinner—who later formed a band called Yeah Yeah Yeahs. "We always called Zinner 'Two-Dimensional Nick' because if he turned sideways he'd just disappear," says Campbell, who lived not far away in Greenpoint. "So skinny, that guy."

"It was horrible when we first moved in," Shaw told *Exclaim!*'s Joshua Ostroff. "Every penny was going to another quart of blue paint. It was really hard for the first couple of years; we had this insane roommate with dogs that would run around and shit everywhere. It was pretty dark."

Williamsburg was still a no man's land, on the verge of becoming a hipster haven, an incubator for much of the Brooklyn rock explosion of the early 2000s; the band Liars later lived in the same loft. But Campbell had utter contempt for his new neighbours: "We called them 'floaters': trust fund kids floating around and not doing anything, just being cool. I felt like Molly Ringwald in *Pretty in Pink*. All the popular kids started coming to our neighbourhood and I hated them." He didn't like the music scene much better. "With every fibre of my being, I hated everyone and all the music," he says. "I was into Serge Gainsbourg and Dusty Springfield and Aretha Franklin. I wanted to be in the Jam. Everyone in that neighbourhood was making noise. I didn't understand it at all. And they hated us. We were so unfashionable and so not what was going on. So against the tide."

Shaw, Campbell and Seligman had a band called Paris Smith, after a Prefab Sprout song. "We were minor celebrities on the theatre school band scene," laughs Campbell. "We had an Irish pub on 8th Avenue we'd play occasionally, and our friends from school would watch us. When we got a bit more ambitious, we'd play some shows downtown at pay-to-play places: CBGB cost 50 bucks. We played one place with a chain-link fence over the front of the stage so that people wouldn't throw shit at you. We had a drummer we found through an ad in the *Village Voice*, named Fleming Rothaus. Fleming was a big deal, because he was an amazing drummer and he was older than us. He was in his 30s. He came in and was like, 'You guys need to get your shit together. You're not good enough. *This isn't good.*' Jimmy [Shaw] really latched on to Fleming: 'This guy is right. We do suck.' That's when Jimmy started to get super serious about recording equipment and using synthesizers." Once Paris Smith renamed itself Stars, its first gig took place in that Williamsburg loft, where Shaw had built a stage and a bar. Also on the bill was Nick Zinner's Challenge of the Future.

Word trickled back to Canada about Stars. Evan Cranley heard some early mixes and wrote from Toronto to say how much he loved it. They invited him down to New York. He hopped on a bus in December 1999 and ended up staying for five months, crashing in Campbell's Greenpoint apartment. "We had a blast," says Campbell. "We never fought, never stopped laughing."

There was still a missing piece, a feminine presence. Campbell was a huge fan of the Beautiful South, a British band who had hits in the late '80s and early '90s, many of which were written as male-female duets. Campbell loved "this idea that if you have a boy and a girl, you can tell two sides of a story and have much more opportunity to subvert traditional tropes. Suddenly I was not constrained by having to sing about my own feelings. When I listen to what I made with Jimmy, so much of it is cringey because I'm writing about my own life."

The songs on Stars' 2001 debut *Nightsongs* featured five different vocalists, including Emily Haines on the album's highlight ("Going, Going, Gone"). Three of the women had other projects and didn't want to commit to Stars. One potential solution was to combine Metric and Stars, which their friend—and lawyer—Chris Taylor suggested to them. "Emily and I have had a tempestuous relationship over the years, which is much more sanguine now," says Campbell. "Back in the day, she and I used to battle pretty heavily. [The Metric song] 'Combat Baby' is about me. We went out to dinner with Chris Taylor, and literally within 10 minutes, something came up and I was like, 'You know what, Haines? Go fuck yourself.' We both left the restaurant and that was as close as Stars and Metric ever became to being one band. But they were in Stars, playing with us, because we didn't have anyone else."

There was a last-minute addition before *Nightsongs* came out: Amy Millan. Evan Cranley suggested her; he'd gigged with 16 Tons and played on their demo. Campbell had met her through Haines, but only socially.

"I don't know. Is she a good musician?" Campbell asked Shaw.

"Amy? She's the best," Shaw responded.

They went to Toronto to play with her. "Within three seconds of her opening her mouth," says Campbell, "I was like, 'This is it.'" Millan confided in her friend Kevin Drew, who advised her, "Don't join that band, they suck."

Twenty years later, he stands by it. "I did think it was ridiculous," says Drew. "She was a whisky-drinking country singer with her career laid out. She can write country songs as easily as other people breathe. It made no sense to me. The jury's still out whether I was right or wrong—depends on the day!" Millan wrote and sang "Toxic Holiday" on *Nightsongs* and insisted that the band split all songwriting equally moving forward.

They needed a record deal. Warner Canada A&R rep Steve Jordan tried his best, says Campbell. "He was the first person in the industry to say, 'Hey, this band is really cool.' He came to New York to talk to us long before anyone else did. He's been a long-time champion. But [Warner] wouldn't let him sign us. They said, 'There's no way you're signing this bunch of nerds. No one will listen to this.'"

Demos were sent to various record labels; Le Grand Magistery out of Detroit took the bait. They specialized in the kind of wispy pop that Campbell loved, like the prolific Scottish songwriter Momus. Ecstatic at the prospect of a deal, Campbell and Seligman foresaw their single career goal being realized: getting racked at hip Manhattan record store Other Music. Le Grand Magistery, a tiny operation run by graphic designer Matthew Jacobson, offered Stars $1,500 for the international rights to put out three records.

The band showed the offer to their lawyer, Chris Taylor, who frequently crashed at the Williamsburg loft when in New York on business. He looked at the contract and laughed out loud. "This is the worst deal I've ever seen in my life," he said. "Do not sign this deal."

They signed the deal. "Don't worry," Campbell told Chris Seligman, "we'll just sue later."

Deal in hand, and with two more Torontonians now in New York with them, Stars needed to play shows. Evan Cranley was on bass, Amy Millan on guitar and vocals. In lieu of a drummer, there was a drum machine they named Stevie. Millan took to the local scene more than Campbell did. She went to see Nick Zinner's new band, Unitard, a duo with singer Karen Orzolek. "She was dressed in this massive garbage bag and they were sitting on the floor," says Millan. "It was amazing, such beautiful art, and it didn't feel at all like anyone was trying to do it for money." Unitard soon added drummer Brian Chase, Orzolek became Karen O, and they became the Yeah Yeah Yeahs.

Campbell, the obsessed anglophile and U.K. citizen, wanted to take the band to his fatherland. After getting a nice paycheque from acting in a Heineken commercial, he flew the band to Britain on his own dime to play three shows in 10 days. "It bankrupted him, but we had a lot of fun," says Millan.

"Nobody really came to the shows. It solidified the four of us," says Cranley. "It turned us into more of a band."

Stars' first break was a short tour of the northeastern states, opening for Trashcan Sinatras, a Scottish band who had minor U.K. hits in the early '90s. The final date was in the New York area, and so they arrived back in town a day early. Seligman prepared a big dinner for the evening, while everyone else went to Central Park to get high on a beautiful Sunday afternoon. Buzzkill: they got busted for cannabis possession and spent 24 hours in jail. A judge released them with just enough time to jump in a cab and make the gig at Maxwell's in Jersey City, with 20 minutes to spare. Campbell took to the stage and announced to the crowd the most rock'n'roll words he would ever say in his life: "Ladies and gentlemen, we just got out of jail!" The audience roared. A limp drum machine kicked in. Stars began playing their fey pop songs.

"It was so bad," laughs Campbell, of "Stevie's" performance in general. "It would break all the time and sounded like shit. But drummers made life impossible. There was nowhere to jam, and we were playing tiny places, so it didn't make any sense. Stevie lasted a surprising amount of time. We played sold-out shows in L.A. and New York and Toronto with that thing. Musically, Evan was like, 'I can't do this anymore.' For a bass player, it was like having sex with 80 condoms on."

Meanwhile, Emily Haines was waitressing in a 24-hour diner and writing songs with James Shaw. Both contributed in various ways to early Stars, live and on recordings. But they were plotting their own path together.

EMILY HAINES HAD restlessness bred in the bone. "If there's any thread to my life and my work," she told *Exclaim!*'s Joshua Ostroff, "it's that I have gone out in the world searching. It's partly been a romantic vision I heard about my parents scouring places, looking for something intangible. I go out with an open heart, as cheesy as that sounds, and more than often I don't find what I hoped would be there."

It took her a long time to find it at home in Toronto. Or in Vancouver. Or in Montreal. Or in New York, London or L.A. With a writer and performer like Haines at its core, Metric was always going to be searching for something bigger. "I don't want to be the Ramones and have somebody else write a song that sounds like me and still live in an East Village studio," she said in 2009, on the eve of releasing a record that would sell half a million copies. "As long as I can remember, we've had people tell us we should be huge." Many Canadian bands have impostor syndrome; Metric never did. Not for a second.

In their first decade as professional musicians, Haines and Shaw floated in and out of Toronto long enough to make friends and key industry contacts, but with no intention of staying long—until the success of all those friends eventually made Toronto appealing enough for Metric to move back, which they did in 2005. "No one burned more bridges and then built them back again than Metric did," says one peer.

WARNER CANADA A&R rep Steve Jordan had failed to sell his bosses on Stars. He tried again with Metric, sliding them $5,000 to make a demo. His Canadian bosses passed. So did the American reps he invited to a Manhattan showcase. But the Metric demo made its way to the U.K., where one manager loved it and sent them plane tickets to London. With nothing to lose except a grungy apartment, Metric packed up and moved.

They signed a publishing deal with Chrysalis and recorded sessions with producer Stephen Hague (Pet Shop Boys, New Order), but there was no record deal and very few shows. Haines had a unique challenge of her own while she was there: everyone thought she was Winona Ryder. "I'd have arguments with people who'd get really mad when I said I wasn't," she told writer Tab Siddiqui. Everything about the British music industry led Metric to believe that they'd have no agency, no control. "I felt like an idiot waiting for someone to tell me I'm cool," said Haines. "I don't want to be fucking cool. I don't want to impress someone in marketing." After 10 months, Metric returned to Brooklyn.

There they met drummer Joules Scott-Key, a Texan. His girlfriend had their demo and he loved it. He approached them at a Yeah Yeah Yeahs show. Shaw told him, "If you like my band so much, why don't you join?" He brought bassist Josh Winstead, another Texan he knew from university. They formed the Metric live band while the duo finished the debut album, *Grow Up and Blow Away*. It caught the attention of L.A. label Restless Records, whose history included everything from the Dead Milkmen to the Dust Brothers. The album was finished in April 2001 but got shelved while Restless was being taken over by Rykodisc. Five months later, living in New York City in September 2001, Haines found herself thinking of a lyric by a former Restless band while she watched the world change.

"It was like that Flaming Lips song ['Waitin' for a Superman']: 'Is it getting heavy? I thought it was already as heavy as can be,'" she told Ostroff. "The smell of 3,000 [dead] people was too much. And mine was already a very toxic environment. There was this window of time where everyone in the [Williamsburg] loft was suddenly talking to each other politically. All the walls broke down between relationships, it was like, 'What are we going to do? This is going to be a breakthrough for our generation.' Big thoughts. Big ideas. Then the door closed and everybody just started drinking in earnest: 'It's the end of the world, so let's trash it.' But I just couldn't do it. I couldn't get really fucked up forever. I wanted to get out. And that's what we did."

METRIC AND STARS decided they couldn't work together, and went their separate ways. Back home in Toronto, all through 2001, Broken Social Scene was trying to include everyone.

The hub was Kevin Drew and Jo-Ann Goldsmith's house at the dead end of Afton Avenue, near Queen West and Gladstone. It was the location of many spontaneous dinner parties, jam sessions, ecstasy trips, where all were welcome.

Goldsmith, a social worker, was the social convenor of the scene; she also played trumpet. It was a voyage of discovery, of falling in love with a community, with one's own city. It was very different from what scene vet Andrew Whiteman recalls of Queen Street in the late '90s, when everyone was too cool for school and drenched in irony. "The palpable difference between that and Kev and Jo-Ann's place," says Whiteman, "and all the people in that scene, was amazing. Nothing but positivity. [Other scenes] were about being a jackass or a prankster, and I didn't feel welcome, or that what I was doing had any merit in their eyes. But Broken Social Scene was about emotion and community and yearning."

Shows were never the same: not the material, not the vibe, not the lineup. "We just kept inventing tunes," says Whiteman. "The chemistry was right there. I didn't know what would happen, but I knew it was really special. It was constant creation." Leslie Feist, Evan Cranley, Emily Haines, James Shaw, Bill Priddle and new associate John Crossingham of Raising the Fawn may or may not have been present for shows. Those shows might consist of amorphous ambient jams or, in one case, a straight-up Dinosaur Jr. homage at a guitar-heavy gig in August 2001 where they were billed as Do the 95. That gig marked the first time Drew embraced the role of vocalist, which he'd previously been reluctant to do.

As the loud guitars came to the forefront, Feist showed up to one rehearsal and strapped one on. "No, you can't play guitar," said Drew. "Just sing. We have enough guitars." That didn't go over well. Feist was a no-show at the next gig, opting to play with Ron Sexsmith at the Cameron instead. "I heard that message loud and clear," says Drew. "It took me a year to get over that one. I was standing on a corner once and she rode up on her bike. I said, 'I think I owe you an apology. I think I rubbed you the wrong way. I told you to put your guitar down, and I didn't mean that.' Let's just say I was very naive to women in rock, and Leslie certainly wasn't. I stepped right into that stereotypical role, and it was a mistake—a mistake she loves to bring up all the time!" Feist says the incident made her compartmentalize the band: she knew then she would simply show up and sing a few songs every now and then.

There was also tension as the relationship between Feist and Whiteman fizzled, following a Broken Social Scene gig at an *Exclaim!* party in April 2001, after which Whiteman destroyed a Queen Street bus shelter out of frustration. ("It was pretty impressive," recalls Canning.) Whiteman considered moving to Spain. Drew convinced him to stay in Broken Social Scene. "We became this band that jammed all the time on weekday afternoons," Whiteman says. "I was in my early 30s and had just got the only real job in my life, as an ESL teacher. I would get off work and then go down to Kevin's basement on Afton. I was no longer broke. I was jamming with new people and my spirits were high."

By the fall of 2001, after one show at Ted's Wrecking Yard with 12 people on stage, including four horn players, it was time to make a record. They had met producer Dave Newfeld while recording a song for a compilation. He had just finished a record called *Stars and Sons* for local shoegaze group Mean Red Spiders; that album was named after his studio, in turn named after the bookbinding business that used to occupy the space—H. Starr & Sons—located on Cameron Street, between the Cameron House and Kensington Market. Newfeld made an immediate impression, primarily for the way he captured drum sounds. He was also cheap, because he had another job: he made $500 every weekend as a wedding DJ. Broken Social Scene had a $3,000 budget, which they blew. It ended up costing a still-reasonable $8,000. It sounded like a million bucks.

Recording began in January 2002 and finished in summer. It's not like they went into the studio with an exact plan. "Someone would have an idea, and it would be, 'Hey, record this!'" says Charles Spearin. "Preproduction was not a thing. Before we went in to record, we wrote down all the songs we played live and there were 71 songs. Even though each one was written in 10 minutes."

"Shampoo Suicide" had been performed live and was toyed with in the studio. Canning sang lead vocals for the first time in his life, on "Stars and Sons," which was written in the studio, as was "I'm Still Your Fag." On Whiteman's song "Looks Just Like the Sun," his original vocal take has him audibly guiding the band through the track. "Almost Crimes" was birthed from a James Shaw guitar riff (one that Crossingham argued was "too Strokes-y") and arranged by Newfeld in the studio. "Pacific Theme" was the sound of the band warming up one day, while Newfeld rolled tape and cajoled it into a song. "That's what Dave loved," says Drew, "witnessing us figure it out."

"The more that people didn't know what was going on, the more I thought we must be onto something new," says Spearin. "There was a lot of friction between me and Dave Newfeld at first, but I learned a lot from him. He had a sound. I kept going back to his earlier recordings to see if I could trust him or not. I figured I won't push all the time, but I didn't want it to sound compressed and flat and no bass. In order to get the sound we wanted, it involved a lot of arguing."

Drew was also very protective and didn't take kindly to Newfeld working by himself on mixes that Drew would reject. The engineer ignored him and secretly made mixes on his own, that he would reveal months later, when Drew felt things were at a standstill—"Pacific Theme" was one in particular. "It rocked my world, it was amazing," says Drew. "I couldn't see past my own ego [earlier]. That changed the game for me. It made me put more trust in others. This guy was a mad genius, and I had to stop doubting that something great could happen when

I wasn't around." Everyone involved gives Newfeld credit for the album sounding as good as it does.

"I was hanging out with all those guys and hearing about this record they were making that everybody was on," says Torquil Campbell. Stars shared a gig with Broken Social Scene at Lee's Palace on May 26, 2002. "Every time I'd ask someone about it, they'd say, 'It's a *disaster*, a fucking disaster. No one knows what's going on. There are 60 tracks on every song. Newfeld is out of his mind. Kevin's out of his mind. All they do is yell at each other.' The general consensus was that it was a big waste of time."

"Honestly, we didn't know anything," says Drew. "When it was done, I was like, 'Well, we made a mixtape.' We were doing it for friends and peers and the community. We wanted to be part of the scene. The friendships were around for a long time at that point. We had so many people coming in and out. There wasn't one person who took all the songwriting credit. We were trying to divide the songs the best we could. Chris Murphy said the reason Sloan was still together was because they split everything. I knew that would be hard with this many people, but I wanted everybody involved to see something out of this."

Hanging out at record shop Soundscapes, Drew ran into Trevor Larocque, a sales rep for distributor Outside Music. Inspired by Three Gut Records, Larocque had just started his own indie label, Paper Bag, and signed Stars after seeing them at NXNE in June. Drew told him about what Broken Social Scene were recording and made sure he got a copy of the just-mastered album. Listening on a long drive to a sales call, Larocque was blown away. It was like nothing he'd ever heard. He immediately offered to put it out.

You Forgot It in People came out in October 2002. It got five-star reviews in *Now*, the *Toronto Star*, the *Toronto Sun* and *Eye Weekly*—what Paper Bag referred to as "a grand slam." Copies were flying out of not only Soundscapes, but the flagship Sam the Record Man store on Yonge Street, where it was the No. 1 seller—not on the indie chart, but overall. To many ears, the Canadian album's diversity was its strength: ambient jams, rousing anthems, bossa nova detours, emo ballads, rock rave-ups, a bit of New Order here, a bit of Dinosaur Jr. there. It certainly wasn't the Clash's *London Calling*, but it was not dissimilar to Yo La Tengo's *I Can Hear the Heart Beating as One*. Drew envisioned it as a tribute to his town: whereas he'd once wanted to emulate Do Make Say Think, he now wanted a band that simultaneously sounded like the Constantines, the Hidden Cameras, Gentleman Reg and Deep Dark United.

Tickets for the release show at Lula Lounge in December sold out almost immediately. Julie Penner of the Fembots was recruited on violin. Drew called Millan and said, "I need you to be the girl," because both Haines and Feist were out of town. The album was the first release from Paper Bag Records—though it also bore another logo for something called Arts & Crafts.

Drew's former roommate Jeffrey Remedios had been working at Virgin/EMI Records Canada since 1996; by 2002, he was head of national publicity. Dissatisfied with the limitations of Canadian major labels, Remedios was itchy to leave—so itchy that he was getting ready to go to Brazil and learn capoeira. *You Forgot It in People* changed his mind. Remedios started a new management company, Arts & Crafts, with Broken Social Scene as his first client. Arts & Crafts was initially going to be a multidisciplinary umbrella: artists, filmmakers, etc. When the album sold out its initial pressing of 1,000 copies within a month, Drew and Remedios decided to take a risk by leaving Paper Bag and making Arts & Crafts its own label. A Juno nomination for Best Alternative Album made it seem more viable. EMI had not wanted to lose Remedios, so they offered him a raise—which he declined. They then offered him distribution and free office space for his new label—which he accepted.

The momentum and circumstances were too good to pass up. "Now [Remedios] was a hotshot," says Whiteman. "He wasn't just a business guy; he was a business guy who said no to the establishment. He was now more desirable, and he said, 'Here's how I'm going to make my mark.' It's not like he had a musical vision, he just wanted to kick ass—and he did." Remedios later told the *New York Times*, "I wanted to rebel well."

It was considered a conflict of interest at the time for a manager to also run a record label, and with the exception of Sarah McLachlan's relationship with Nettwerk, it was uncommon. "In those cocoon days, it didn't matter," says Whiteman. "We were just trying to make something happen. Who cares? It's the same as putting out your records yourself—with a big chunk from EMI to get started. EMI wanted Jeffrey to still like them, so when he left to start this new label, they gave him a ton of cash. It ain't Three Gut." EMI president Deane Cameron was particularly supportive—and was more than familiar with the business model, having brought Nettwerk into the EMI fold in the mid-'80s.

Arts & Crafts was going to be a home for Broken Social Scene satellite projects like Whiteman's Apostle of Hustle and a record by guitarist Jason Collett. There were plans to bring Metric and Feist into the fold as well. It was a family affair.

Paper Bag was upset with Arts & Crafts' decision but nonetheless agreed. They were about to put out Stars' *Heart*, and Drew urged them to sign one of his favourite local bands, the Fembots. "Kevin obviously felt bad about what was going on," says Larocque, "so he was trying to help us not lose everything. I don't think anyone was spiteful. It was just an unfortunate situation."

One thing Paper Bag did early on was send the Broken Social Scene album to *Pitchfork*. Four months later—in February 2003, before the album was available outside Canada—Larocque got an email from editor Ryan Schreiber: "Hey man, just reviewed your record. —Ryan." Larocque clicked the link. His jaw dropped. *You Forgot It in People* scored a 9.3 rating. Schreiber admitted that he picked the CD randomly out of his slush pile and spent days on end listening to it on repeat, because it was *just that good*. This had never happened before—not on a widely read media outlet, not for an unknown Canadian band without international distribution. Even Godspeed had a U.S. label and European distribution.

Kevin Drew's father, David, got a call from a business associate the day the review went up: "Hey, this website I love just knocked your son's record out of the park."

David Drew called his son. "Apparently you got this great review on *Pitchfork*."

"What the fuck is that? Is it a magazine?" Kevin Drew didn't have a computer in his apartment. He went to his upstairs neighbour's place to look it up.

"You want to talk about overnight fame? It was overnight," says Torquil Campbell. "Literally within two days everything had changed. I remember walking along the street toward Kevin's house with him. It was a really cold day. It had snowed. The snow was crunching and we could see our breath."

Kevin Drew said to him, "Well, this is it, Torqie. We did it! We're going to be rock stars. This is happening."

"Yeah, I guess it kind of is."

"No, it is. It's happening. We're doing it."

L.A. WAS ALREADY FULL OF STARS—who loved Stars. When *Nightsongs* came out in February 2001, it found an immediate champion in DJ Nic Harcourt of L.A. radio station KCRW. Not only was the station influential in the area, but it was one of the first to broadcast online. Harcourt's *Morning Becomes Eclectic* became a vanguard of the so-called adult alternative format; he's credited with breaking Coldplay in the U.S. He took a particular liking to Stars' cover of the Smiths' "This Charming Man" and their original "My Radio" (which borrowed from Shuggie Otis's '70s hit "Strawberry Letter #23").

"Because it was in L.A.," says Campbell, "every music supervisor, every movie star, every director listened to KCRW. Your music was being played not just for a listening public but a listening public that could make you famous." Stars toured the West Coast of the U.S., from L.A. up to Seattle, to full houses. TV shows came calling to license tracks. "That's the only reason we stayed together as a band," says Millan. "Without Nic Harcourt championing us, I think we'd have been too depressed to carry on."

They were, however, done with New York. It was expensive and draining and they didn't fit in musically with their Williamsburg friends. Millan was in Toronto, working at the Jet Fuel coffee shop on Parliament (which was writer Michael Ondaatje's favourite haunt). In September 2001, Stars were on the cover of *Now* magazine. Evan Cranley moved to Montreal; Chris Seligman soon followed, living with his brother, Dan, who became the band's manager (a.k.a. "Danager"). Campbell's parents had moved to Montreal, so he bounced between there and Toronto, taking the most common job for underemployed musicians in the city: in the warehouse at distributor Outside Music. He also handed out flyers for gay clubs on Church Street between midnight and five a.m. three nights a week. Somewhere amidst all the flux, they recorded *The Comeback EP* in the Seligmans' apartment, at 939 Mont Royal Avenue.

Their first Montreal peers were the Dears. Campbell had already professed his love privately to them at one of their shows. But when Murray Lightburn and Natalia Yanchak showed up at a Stars show in a basement bar on Ontario Street, Campbell showered them with compliments from the stage. The feeling was mutual. Lightburn, who often drank to mask his social insecurity, approached Millan after the show and told her, "I want to have sex with your vocal cords."[1]

Stars were still short a drummer. They'd met Pat McGee through a mutual friend. McGee suffered from alopecia, the autoimmune disease that causes hair loss. "He came over and was so weird-looking," says Campbell. "He had chunks of hair dyed all different colours, and he had no eyebrows. But he was such a sweetheart and an amazing drummer. We were like, 'My god, this guy is going to change our lives.' He was like, 'Eh, I'm not sure I really like this band.'"

McGee primarily played jazz and electronic music. He agreed to play with Stars live and on 2001's *Comeback* but didn't want to appear on a full-length album. The Dears' George Donoso was happy to step in, accepting a case of beer in lieu of payment. McGee didn't formally join the band for another two years. "The man does not make decisions lightly," says Campbell of McGee. "Going shoe-shopping with him takes seven trips to the shoe store over six months before he eventually chooses a pair of shoes. I think eventually his EI cheques ran out, things were starting to pop for us, and he figured he'd be a fool not to do it. So he was in."

While McGee sat out and Donoso subbed in, *Heart* was made at 939 Mont Royal Avenue in the apartment now shared by Campbell and the Seligman brothers. There was no timeline. It was made with rented microphones and minimal gear.

---

1   "She lords that over me to this day," says a still-mortified Lightburn. "I never bring it up!" retorts Millan. "He's the one who always brings it up: 'I can't believe I said that to you.' It's okay, it was a compliment."

The only budget went to mixing it in Toronto with Ian Catt, who'd worked with British band Saint Etienne, one of Campbell's faves. Campbell was ecstatic when it was done. "It's everything, aesthetically, I had been dreaming about all of my life," he told *Vice's* Cam Lindsay years later, when he cited it as his favourite Stars album. "To me, it's the sound of us all being in love and believing in this idea completely. And it was made in a bedroom in Montreal—true bedroom pop! You can hear my attempt to do every musical style that I've ever been obsessed with: blue-eyed soul, Steely Dan, shoegaze, synth-pop, New Order, the Smiths, it's all in there. It wasn't pastiche anymore, it was just us. It sounded like a band to me."

Millan was still commuting back and forth from Toronto. She hadn't enjoyed Montreal while there for school, a time that included the tension of the 1995 separatist referendum. In 2002, in the middle of making *Heart*, Millan says that "Torq called me up and berated me, screaming into the phone, 'Are you in or not?! If you're not moving to Montreal, that means you're not in!' I was going to a psychiatrist at the time, who said, 'Just go. What's wrong?' My mom made me sit in two different chairs: a yes chair and a no chair. I sat in the first chair and said, 'No, they're all insane.' Then I'd sit in the yes chair and say, 'But they're my family.'" She went with family, no matter how insane.

Stars' success on the West Coast landed some label offers. They were courted heavily by Palm Pictures, a new—and ultimately short-lived—label run by Island Records founder Chris Blackwell. Not only was it not a great offer, but Le Grand Magistery insisted on being bought out of Stars' contract for exponentially more than they paid two years earlier. Palm Pictures took the band, their partners, Grand Magistery's Matthew Jacobson—13 people in all—out to dinner in L.A., where "the bill was bigger than our advance from Le Grand Magistery," says Campbell. Jacobson wouldn't budge, and the Palm deal fell through.

With Chris Taylor's help, Stars finagled their way out of the Le Grand Magistery deal, which cost the band $30,000 as well as points from their next two albums. It was a lot of money for musicians who were still combing their couches for change so they could afford some dep wine in Montreal. Campbell claims *Nightsongs* sold 60,000 copies, of which Stars never saw a penny. They wouldn't get the rights back for 20 years.

When Stars signed with Paper Bag Records, Campbell told label co-founder Trevor Larocque, "Oh, a guy might call from another label. Don't worry about it." Le Grand Magistery did indeed call Paper Bag as well as distributor Outside Music, threatening legal action if they put out a new Stars record. He was ignored. *Heart* was Paper Bag's second release, coming out in Canada in February 2003. They went out for dinner with the label to celebrate. Evan Cranley held up the CD and made a toast: "This is our Stanley Cup!" Meanwhile, Campbell went to the U.K. to secure a deal in the market that meant the most to him. "I didn't care if people in Canada or the U.S. liked us," he says frankly. He signed Stars to Setanta, who had cult artists the Divine Comedy, Edwyn Collins, and ex-Pulp guitarist Richard Hawley.

After a quick U.S. jaunt with the much-hyped Broken Social Scene, Stars headed to Europe in May 2003 to open for their new U.K. labelmate, the Lemonheads' Evan Dando. He'd just put out his first solo record after famously flaming out on drugs and alcohol years earlier. "He was fucking hilarious," says Campbell. "He introduced himself to us every night of a three-week tour. He had no brain cells left. He was on a sobriety kick so that he wouldn't do heroin and drink himself to death. Back then, finding weed in Europe was no easy task; I'd spend most of my time trying to find marijuana. He would just come and suck it all back and then reintroduce himself to me. It's like, 'Yes, dude, you just smoked all my weed—I know who you are!' It was so annoying."

Evan Cranley in particular thought the Lemonhead's amnesia was ridiculous, considering he and Dando shared a first name. To make matters worse, Dando had added to the tour some friend of his, another recovering junkie, at the last minute, bumping Stars to the first of three acts, going on right after doors opened and playing to virtually nobody.

Relations with Setanta Records also got weird right away. Label head Keith Cullen was intrigued by the White Stripes' PR hoax: the Detroit duo was a former married couple but claimed they were siblings just to mess with the media. "Keith wanted us to pretend that Torq and I were brother and sister," says Millan, "and that I was in love with Torq but he was gay." The band wasn't having it. Besides Millan was now engaged to Chris Seligman; they'd fallen in love while making *Heart*.

Stars had applied for a $40,000 touring grant from FACTOR that manager Dan Seligman was confident they'd get. They found out at the Setanta office that they didn't—and now had a six-week tour in front of them that was guaranteed to be in the red. Cullen hit the roof and told the band to go home. When they said that wasn't going to happen, he ordered them to start packing boxes to help around the office.

The tour with Dando was 10 days in the U.K., Germany and Sweden. The rest of the tour didn't go any better. "It was a litany of catastrophe," says Campbell.

"We were just burning money," says Millan. "Patty threw up blood from his throat. Someone left my luggage behind or it got stolen on the streets of Paris, so I had no clothing. The van we had blew the clutch, and there was a hole in the tank so we were all being poisoned by carbon monoxide; within five minutes of driving, we'd all be asleep. We couldn't stay awake. And we played to nobody. Oh, *and* we missed our flights home."

Heart was doing well enough in Canada, but Stars were taking a backseat to Broken Social Scene's meteoric rise, the Dears' long-awaited masterpiece *No Cities Left* and the pending arrival of Metric's album in September 2003. "I'll be honest with you," says Campbell, "when Stars showed up, nobody liked us. Nobody liked our music. They thought we were total fruits. They found me especially embarrassing. As much as we were friends and they were kind to us and let us play gigs with them, behind our backs I know they were all shuddering. It wasn't artsy enough for them. I think a lot of the people *in* Stars were embarrassed to be in Stars. Evan, definitely. Chris continues to be embarrassed. I'm the only one who really likes Stars—I'm not even joking."

That said, their friends at Arts & Crafts definitely wanted to bring Stars into the fold, releasing *Heart* in the U.S.

RIDING HIGH ON the *Pitchfork* review, Broken Social Scene set out in March 2003 for the SXSW festival in Austin, Texas. Broken Social Scene was the It Band that year. Everything about them was novel: they were a huge co-ed band with a huge sound, brass instruments, multiple singers, and they were Canadian. Everyone there had heard about them through *Pitchfork*.

Charles Spearin sat out, touring with Do Make Say Think instead. Guitarist Jason Collett was a new presence in the band. Collett, like Andrew Whiteman, was 10 years older than Drew; his wife had gone to high school with Whiteman. Kevin Drew babysat their kids. In the '90s, Collett, a rootsy songwriter, had led his own groups, Lazy Grace and Bird, and played in Andrew Cash's late-period band Ursula. Since 2000, Collett had had a weekly gig at various venues called Radio Mondays, which were acoustic songwriter circles, not unlike folk festival workshops, with a broad, ecumenical approach to genre—and generations, mixing '90s stalwarts like Bob Wiseman and Ron Hawkins with upstarts in their early 20s.

Collett was the sort of linchpin to a scene that Drew aspired to be in—so it made sense Drew co-opted him. Though Collett had once been on the cover of *Now*, his two solo records never got much traction. In 2003, a compilation of his best material, *Motor Motel Love Songs*, was Arts & Crafts' second release. On tour with Social Scene, he opened the show with various members backing him up and then played Spearin's parts during the main set. He was tall, handsome and mysterious, a welcome visual as well as musical component.

Of the three women then associated with Broken Social Scene—what writer Sarah Liss called "the Broken babe factor"—only Amy Millan appeared regularly on tour, filling in for the absent Leslie Feist and Emily Haines ever since the release show at Lula Lounge. Though Millan is hardly short of star power herself, she is as different a vocalist and performer from either of them as they are from each other, and it's near impossible for anyone to match Feist for sheer magnetic charisma.

None of that concerned Millan. "Because I'm so neurotic, I'm more comfortable doing something I believe in when it's not my own," she says. "I graduated in theatre performance, so I just had to put on the Leslie and Emily thing. I've known Emily since we were 15. The [vocal] challenge was to do [Feist's part on] 'Almost Crimes,' which was so fun. There was no pressure wondering if people liked the lyrics, because they weren't my lyrics. To be able to go out on the bus with all these hilarious and warm and gentle and fantastic humans—Kev and I have been friends since he was 14—there were lots of laughs."

Stars and Broken Social Scene shared a bill on the West Coast in the spring of 2003, one of only two tours featuring Feist in the band every night. Stars normally headlined in the region, but post-*Pitchfork*, the billing switched. Playing on a TV show in Oakland, California, they met booking agent Frank Riley, who became instrumental in the careers of both Broken Social Scene and Feist.

On March 19, 2003, the night the U.S. invaded Iraq, Broken Social Scene played the Silverlake Lounge in L.A., which was the local haunt of Metric. "It was our first L.A. gig, it was a tiny place, and there was a lineup around the corner," says Drew, who was delighted when Metric showed up. "In January 1991, I was in grade 9 when Emily arranged a protest [against the first Gulf War], for everyone to leave class at whatever time it was they were going to invade. I followed this lovely senior's lead, and a couple hundred of us left class and protested along Royal York Road, stopping traffic, holding up signs. Now I was leaning against the bar with Emily, and she was like, 'All right, here we go. It's happening all over again, Kev.' To be with her, watching the news at Silverlake Lounge, it was wild. We were still together. And now we had to go rock out. People were standing right in front of our face [during the set]. From what I remember, it was phenomenal. The audience was the key member in our band. You hear that a lot, maybe, but for us it really rang true. They played such an integral part of our shows."

The audience was also dedicated. In the U.S., some underage fans travelled from other states just to listen outside the club. At the band's first gig in the U.K., they met two Polish girls who'd travelled 24 hours to be there. The record had not yet been released in Europe, but between the *Pitchfork* review and file-sharing, word of mouth was spreading.

The U.K. press was not as kind; the *NME* review of the "Stars and Sons" single said the band looked like "a bunch of kiddie porn collectors." But at least there was no backlash stateside, when, at one of Broken Social Scene's first SXSW gigs, Drew told the audience, "This next song is for your piece-of-shit president."

This wasn't the Dixie Chicks, the Texan trio blacklisted for saying something much milder on stage in the U.K.

Expectations of rock shows had fallen so low at that point in time that seeing a large band with a rousing sound and obvious affection for each other was overwhelming for many. And few other acts, other than Flaming Lips, were this earnest. As that old Canadian chestnut goes, "The honesty's too much." "A lot of people want to tell [us] how they've wept at [our] shows," Canning told Sarah Liss in the summer of '04. "Of course, people weep at Sting concerts, too, but they're a different crowd. I was going through the motions [on stage] in Athens, Georgia, and I looked down to see this one sorta sporto-looking guy up front. The poor kid's eyes were filled with tears. By the end of the tune, when it'd reached its emotional peak, he was bawling. I reached out and put my hand on his head, and after the big release, the kid was just cold. You could feel the bliss seeping out of him." That energy was translating to larger crowds, too. Broken Social Scene played the fifth Coachella festival in California in the spring of 2004, where the band's John Crossingham proposed to his girlfriend on stage (fortunately, she accepted).

In late August, they had a free gig booked at Toronto's Harbourfront Centre, with Jim Guthrie opening. It was only two weeks after they appeared on Toronto's Olympic Island on a bill headlined by Sloan. Drew told drummer Justin Peroff, the band's graphic designer, to write on the poster for the Harbourfront show: "Last Show Ever."

Many took it seriously—why wouldn't they? Unless they happened to have been at a Pop Montreal show the year before, when Drew made the same claim on stage between swigs from a bottle of red wine. Or several dozen times before that. Or if one knew that there was a full European tour booked two months after the Harbourfront show. The concept of "last show ever" was "nothing new to me," says Spearin. "It came from the first 10 shows we did in Toronto. Back then, Kevin would start each set by saying, 'This is our last show.' It was a thing he did, like you might as well assume this is the only time you'll get to see the band, so enjoy it. It felt like a way of acknowledging the music as being more than the band. That was the essence of those shows. There was an element of living for the moment and not trying to be a normal band."

"Kevin Drew is a bit of a fatalist," Millan told band biographer Stuart Berman. "Try taking a plane with that guy—he's like, 'We'll die legends!'"

Then there's the million-dollar question: how did all those people get paid? There were five core members of Broken Social Scene (Drew, Canning, Spearin, Whiteman, Peroff), which already makes it a large band by rock music standards. Between 2002 and 2004, there were also at least three auxiliary players (Cranley,

Collett, Crossingham), three female singers (Feist, Haines, Millan)—only one of which is likely to be at any given gig—and other random brass players or guests. That can spread gig money pretty thin.

The band was making good guarantees. Festivals were a payday. Touring grants, the boon of a Canadian band's existence, certainly helped later on—but not at the outset. "We started at $500 a week in Social Scene," says Millan. "Then it grew. They've always been extremely generous. If Evan plays a horn line [on a record], he gets [part of the] publishing. If they play some big festival that pays more money, they'll pay us generously. [The core five members] get paid more, because they run the business, and that's totally fair. I've never felt in that band like I'm not being respected [or not] treated very well."

"The generosity on stage is the same behind the scenes," adds Cranley. "If it wasn't, it would be a two-faced, dishonest relationship with the audience."

The one clear downside of having a large band was that it impeded perks that other bands take for granted—like a crew. Sound tech Marty Kinack was so essential he was considered a member of the band, even posing in group press photos. But "we always had only one guitar tech for five guitar players," says Drew. "Justin never really had a drum tech. And if we brought a lighting tech, we had to lose a member." Drew's father, who had retired from the publishing business, ran the band's finances, which could be challenging, given the rotating door on stage. "He would receive invoices from people and he'd be like, 'Who the fuck is this, and what show were they at?!'" laughs Kevin. "He'd tell tour managers, 'Take a photo of everyone on stage *so I can see who's fucking playing!*'"

That unpredictability was a key part of the draw for audiences. "We were instantly a great band to go see," says Whiteman. "We weren't a fly-by-night thing, where it's like, 'Oh, I've seen that band. I don't need to see them again.' It was more like, 'I've seen that band, but what the fuck is it going to be now?' That's why people were drawn to go, and we could pack places, so there were enough points to go around." By the end of the touring cycle, *You Forgot It in People* had sold 150,000 copies around the world. Considering the demographic of the band's audience—curious, eclectic music fans under 35 with iPods—it's a safe bet that 10 times as many people had it on their computer.

With hype and success comes backlash, which could be personal and petty. Naturally, in Toronto there was tall-poppy syndrome among people who felt the band were a faux-indie sensation, a bunch of middle-class kids in fashionable clothes currying favour with the corporate music industry while co-opting the underground movement—or something. There was also resentment that even though Broken Social Scene was a tide that lifted many boats, it wasn't lifting enough boats or the "right" boats.

This coincided with the rise of online vitriol in fan communities. "Arts & Crafts had a message board that was supposed to be this happy community place, but people would say the meanest things, and that's when you saw how terrible the internet could be," says Millan. "The moderator had to post things like, 'Yes, Borg345, you're right. [The thread] 'Lead singer is a whiny ass' has been deleted.' We'd have ex-girlfriends come on and tell private stories about us. Kevin was like, 'You gotta shut this down. It's gross.' We all [read the comments]. You couldn't help yourself. I mean, the comment section of [blog] *Brooklyn Vegan*, too—talk about a pit of despair, a hell of cruelty. But then came Twitter!"

Real life was too much fun to worry too much about online chatter. "It was unbelievably celebratory every night," says Torquil Campbell. Stars did two complete tours with Broken Social scene in 2003. "We played in Edmonton and Calgary at the universities and felt the electricity of being a rock star for the first time. People were screaming our name and wanting our autograph and waiting for us after the show. Walking into the venue and feeling everyone looking at you, the ecstatic egotistical high of all that stuff."

What made it even more thrilling was that Campbell was pushing 30 at the time. "I'd been an actor all my life," he says, "and this was my wildest dream come true. That said, things were starting to be complicated somewhat—egos coming into play, people starting to be competitive with each other a bit. But there were 30 to 35 people who individually fell in love with each other. There were intense relationships between two people on every level. I remember being on that tour and wondering, Will this last forever? Will we be this in love and obsessed with each other forever?"

METRIC CAME BACK to Toronto in 2002 and moved into a loft above a downtown bank. It was a different town than the one they left. There was a different creative energy in the air. Possibilities extended beyond the chance of a middling major label deal from a Canadian branch plant. Broken Social Scene was making *You Forgot It in People*. Haines sang lead on one of the album's most popular songs: "Anthems for a Seventeen-Year-Old Girl."

"When Metric played, not just a few of us would go see them: 30 of us would go see them," says Campbell. "Every time you'd see one of those bands, it would be, holy shit, all the people from Stars are here and all the people from Metric. They really are a scene. That added to the level of excitement around it. It wasn't a put-on. We were each other's biggest fans."

Metric played a Canadian Music Week show at the Reverb in Toronto in March 2002, opening for the Hidden Cameras. *Exclaim!* writer Joshua Ostroff was entranced, forgetting that he'd actually seen the band twice—but not with this rhythm section and not with the kind of performance Emily Haines was now delivering.

They were forgettable before. That night, they were the polar opposite. "In fact," he wrote, "it was pretty fucking epic. The typically blasé Toronto crowd fell dead silent as Metric's ethereal analog keyboards and overwhelmingly atmospheric guitars fell upon them in enveloping layers, propelled by an insistent backbeat. Emily, all angular and lovely, stood there with her mic cord noosed around her neck, her heart bleeding on the floor while a roomful of indie rock fans, boys and girls alike, developed an incurable crush."

Metric focused on the idea that their still-shelved album might actually come out. They decided to meet their American rhythm section in L.A., where the Restless office was located, and make a go of it there. Metric booked a weekly residency at the Silverlake Lounge, which was becoming a hotspot thanks to local acts like Rilo Kiley. It wasn't glamorous: the washrooms were located beside the stage. Metric's L.A. life wasn't glamorous either: all four members were living in a one-bedroom sublet, working ridiculous day jobs. "Joules got a job moving breast implants from one Beverley Hills hospital to another—he was an implant courier," Haines told writer Tab Siddiqui. "People were asking me if I'd done any modelling. I thought maybe I'd be a foot model or a hand model—maintain some integrity. But then it turned out that the guy just wanted to photograph my foot or hand on his dick."

As Restless Records was absorbed by Rykodisc, Metric's album was left in limbo. They printed CD-Rs of it to sell at shows. But now they weren't exactly crushed by the idea that no one would ever hear it. They started recording new material that reflected the live show, songs that felt like a cathartic release after years of false starts. They also weren't spring chickens: like Stars, they were pushing 30. On January 3, 2003, Haines's father died. It was time to seize the day.

They had options: two record deals were on the table. One was a U.S. deal with new L.A. indie Enjoy Records, which had huge success with soft-rock surfer Jack Johnson. The other was Arts & Crafts, which started the same week Metric were looking for a Canadian label. They were tempted by an impressive press kit Remedios had assembled, with stark black-and-white photo portraits of everyone involved. Ultimately they decided not to go into business with their friends; the personal relationships were too important. Musically, Metric didn't feel they shared commonalities with the Arts & Crafts family, despite their collaborative role in Broken Social Scene. That didn't stop Metric from sending a package, including a glossy 8x10 photo of Haines and Shaw in the back of a limo, to Stars' label, Paper Bag Records. The label passed. Metric went with yet another new Toronto indie, Last Gang, started by their lawyer, Chris Taylor. They were the second act on the label, after country singer Lindi Ortega. Metric then hit the road for two years. "Our options were clear," says Haines. "Wait around for something to happen or hop in a van and play. Living on cigarettes and coffee in your 20s and seeing the country is hard, but it's not that hard, you know?"

The first tour—opening for Billy Talent across the country, with Death from Above 1979 first on the bill—started at the Capitol Theatre in Ottawa. The crowd was not receptive, and the feeling was mutual. A full water bottle was thrown at Haines; she opened it and dumped it on a girl in the front row. Recalls Billy Talent bassist Jon Gallant, "Then she yelled at some other kids, stormed off the stage and punched her agent in the stomach, saying, 'We're off this fucking tour!' We're all like, What?! To Metric's credit, they showed up at the next gig. They changed their whole set. She was wearing Chucks and jeans and their set was more rocking and they had a great show."

"We ended up getting along thick as thieves," says Billy Talent's Ben Kowalewicz. "The crowds got better, and they became galvanized. Emily has many a night taken me aside and said that it's because of that tour they realized something within them that they didn't know existed before. They thanked us for that, which is really cool and nice."

In such high-energy boys' club circles, Haines's "sexy robot" dance moves were often the focus for the audience and critics. "Certain audiences get the double meaning and some of the references and ironies," she said in 2004, "but there's definitely been shows where I feel like I'm not doing it well enough for it to come across as anything other than 'oh, she's hot and she's dancing.' One show we played in Seattle, I came off stage and I came into the band room and the first thing that anyone said to me was, 'Oh, thanks Emily, you really made my dick hard.' We'd been touring for eight months at that point and it was like, What am I doing? Ultimately the goal is to have it be a really amazing evening where it does feel like something could happen, and I think a sexual energy is a positive energy. It's not my fault that people are perverts."

None of that deterred Metric from playing anywhere and everywhere to crack the U.S. Haines cites a 2004 gig in Tempe, Arizona, as a career low. The festival came at the end of a five-month run; the band had been told 30,000 people would attend. "There were maybe 50 people," she told Siddiqui. "We were playing beside giant blow-up Budweiser cans, and there were Hooters restaurants on either side. There was this ordinance that we couldn't play louder than the music from both Hooters, which were playing Christina Aguilera. There were probably four kids there who actually knew Metric, and they were mortified. They were just like, 'What are you doing here?' In their minds, they loved our record, we were a huge band, and we completely destroyed their respect for us.

Feist with Broken Social Scene at the Drake Underground in Toronto, 2003.

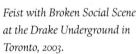

Kevin Drew, 2006.

Leslie Feist and Stars' Torquil Campbell.

Metric at SXSW, 2006.

Stars at University of Toronto's Hart House for a private film festival gig, 2006. From left to right: Torquil Campbell, Amy Millan and Evan Cranley.

*From left to right,
Broken Social Scene's
Andrew Whiteman,
Brendan Canning
and Justin Peroff at
Olympic Island in
Toronto, 2006.*

*T. Dot ambassador,
Canadian hip-hop
pioneer and Raptors
fan Kardinal Offishall.*

Saukrates.

Rascalz. From left to right: MC Misfit, Red 1 and DJ Kemo.

Kardinal Offishall.

Swollen Members at the MuchMusic Video Awards, 2003. From left to right: Moka Only, Prevail, Rob the Viking and Madchild.

K-os, 2005.

*Fucked Up's first
Hallowe'en party
at Sneaky Dee's,
Toronto, 2004.*

DAVID WALDMAN

Alexisonfire's Dallas Green at the Kathedral in Toronto, 2003.

DAVID LEYES

Heavy dudes at an EMI/NXNE party, 2005. From left to right: Scott Middleton of the Cancer Bats, Wade McNeil of Alexisonfire, Ben Kowalewicz of Billy Talent, Dallas Green of Alexisonfire and Jon Gallant of Billy Talent.

Ben Kowalewicz of Billy Talent at Toronto's Bovine Sex Club, 2008.

Billy Talent's Ian D'Sa.

Kid Koala atop Mont Royal, 2000.

Buck 65 at work in Paris, 2003.

Buck 65 at work in Halifax, 1998.

*Dan Snaith,
seconds after
winning the 2008
Polaris Music Prize
for the Caribou
album* Andorra.

Cadence Weapon.

From left to right: Paul Hawley, Dustin Hawthorne, Dante DeCaro and Steve Bays.

Hot Hot Heat at the Troubadour in L.A.

The Unicorns. Clockwise from top: Nick Thorburn, Alden Penner and Jamie Thompson.

Black Mountain at SXSW, 2008. From left to right: Josh Wells, Amber Webber and Stephen McBean.

Wolf Parade at the Wolfe Island Music Festival, 2005. From left to right: Spencer Krug, Dante DeCaro and Dan Boeckner.

Arcade Fire press shot for Funeral. *From left to right: Régine Chassagne, Win Butler, Richard Reed Parry and Tim Kingsbury.*

Signing with Merge Records in April 2004.

Arcade Fire at Toronto's Massey Hall, 2007. From left to right: Richard Reed Parry, Win Butler, Jeremy Gara and Régine Chassagne.

Below: Régine Chassagne conducts the string section for Funeral in her apartment. From left to right: Richard Reed Parry, Mike Olsen, Owen Pallett and Sarah Neufeld.

Above: Jim Guthrie invited Arcade Fire to play their first-ever Toronto show in January 2003.

From left to right: Jeremy Gara, Richard Reed Parry, Régine Chassagne, Win Butler, Sarah Neufeld, Will Butler and Tim Kingsbury.

Will Butler and
Richard Reed Parry.

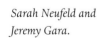

Sarah Neufeld and
Jeremy Gara.

Tim Kingsbury.

Owen Pallett toasting his 2006 Polaris Prize win, with engineer Leon Taheny and Ohbijou's Casey Mejica.

Sarah Harmer, 2006, outside the University of Texas in Austin.

And Joshua lost his girlfriend out of that one, 'cause that show was tacked onto a tour that was supposed to end, and we were told it was really important, and it was all wrong."

Meanwhile, Haines and Shaw had split as a couple. Just like their friends in Broken Social Scene, they didn't let that affect their professional relationship or personal friendship. "It took eight years of being together [as a couple] to realize that music was actually the thing: this musical dynamic and understanding is so much harder to find," Shaw told Helen Spitzer. "And when you find it, it's profound."

STARS WERE NOW A ROCK BAND. They'd spent a year on the road with drummer Pat McGee, sharing stages with Broken Social Scene and watching the Dears become one of the most unstoppable live bands in the country. In the middle of the winter in Quebec's Eastern Townships, they made *Set Yourself on Fire*.

Torquil Campbell's parents had a summer home in North Hatley, just south of Sherbrooke. While the band was in the local pub one night, they met a man who used to be in Robert Altman films and whose band opened for the Rolling Stones in Montreal in the '6os. He was building a home studio and welcomed the band to use it any time. They took him up on the offer and moved in together for five weeks in January and February 2004 to do some writing and preproduction. For the first time in their creative process, they felt like a complete creative unit. It defined them as a five-person band of equals.

It was also a pain in the ass. The cabin comprised cramped quarters with thin walls, and emotions were already running a bit high. Millan and Seligman's relationship was over and the wound was fairly fresh. And now that Millan had had the thrill of singing in Broken Social Scene as well as Stars, she was less willing to concede to Campbell on a variety of issues.

"It's fair to say that everyone had a pretty serious drinking problem," says Campbell. "We all drank—and me and Amy just fought. We were fighting for space, trying to figure out how to be co-lead singers, co-songwriters, how we were going to tell these stories with two sides to them without betraying what was important to us as individuals. I saw myself as the leader of the band, because I'd started it. But by then I should have realized I was not the leader, and that there *was* no leader. Amy thought that was brutal and shitty of me not to realize that and kicked back at my attempts to control things."

Internal battles weren't the only ones on their mind, as they moved to Studio Plateau in Montreal for four weeks to record the album with producer Tom McFall. The band of avowed pacifists—Campbell's father had been a conscientious objector during World War II—were horrified by the so-called War on Terror.

They made their new album three years after 9/11, two years after Guantanamo Bay opened and a few short months before the torturous abuses at Abu Ghraib were revealed in April 2004.

Listening back to radio hits and critical favourites of the early 2000s, and other than Green Day, one would be hard pressed to remember it was the beginning of a never-ending war. Stars didn't feel they had a choice; they had to be true to who they were (and are). But they were well aware of the artistic perils of political songwriting and saved their most explicit statements for the press and the stage. Campbell had once, at a show in the U.S., dedicated a song "to the cancer cell growing in the pancreas of George W. Bush." In song, however, he preferred generalities still relevant to the current situation. The opening lines of "He Lied about Death" are, "What gives you the right / To fuck with our lives?" At the end of the song, guest player Erik Hove's sax solo, interspersed with abrasive electronics, is easily the noisiest musical passage in any pop song of the period not made by Wilco.

At the time, Campbell told an American magazine, "I didn't specifically mention [Bush's] name. It can be about Osama Bin Laden or anyone. They're just not decent people. They don't live like the rest of us. They're perverts and we're going to call them out for what they are . . . Some perverts go to jail, some go to the White House. Osama Bin Laden and George Bush are the same person, fighting their fake war to make money off people's backs. I think fundamentalist Islam and fundamentalist Christianity are best friends, and we suffer under their chaos, while 95% of the rest of the world just wants to find a pretty person to marry and have kids with." Millan was no different. After reading an article about Guantanamo Bay, she wrote the lyrics to "Celebration Guns": "And then the next day, how will you know your enemy? / By their color or your fear? / One by one you can cage them in your freedom / Make them all disappear."

Neither of those songs were singles, though. Instead, opening track "Your Ex-Lover Is Dead" became Stars' best-known, most-loved song, perhaps the biggest of this period by anyone in this book not named Arcade Fire or Feist. It's the story of two ex-lovers, very much alive, introduced as strangers years later, with unspoken silences speaking volumes between them. It opens with strings, brass and piano introducing a lilting waltz, before shifting to melodica, cello, tom drum and electric piano. As the song unfolds and develops, following no standard pop music format, a quiet bridge is the emotional peak of the song—can it be called the chorus if it only happens once?—with the refrain "Live through this / and you won't look back." It says as much in 40 seconds as Gloria Gaynor's "I Will Survive" does in five times the length.

"Your Ex-Lover Is Dead" came to represent something bigger for fans and the band alike. "There was a lot of emotional turmoil in the band at the same time this album was taking off," says touring guitarist Stephen Ramsay, "and this song was the band's emotional flagship moment. I remember playing to a packed Mod Club in Toronto [in December 2004], and Evan Cranley said, 'I'm losing it!' Using my rather large body to shield himself during the climax of the song, he burst into tears as we kept playing. I remember looking around then, and everyone was crying. Audience, band, everyone."

Fifteen years after *Set Yourself on Fire* came out, CBC Music's Melody Lau and Andrea Warner wrote about not the album but that song specifically: "There's a crushing sadness underneath what [the male voice] is saying," writes Lau. "There's awkwardness in the happenstance of running into a former lover. There's a feeling of loss, of losing that familiarity with someone you once knew intimately. And, ultimately, acceptance in knowing 'there's nothing to save.' The multidimensionality of this song is important. Many songs struggle to just get one sentiment right, yet 'Your Ex-Lover Is Dead' encapsulates a lot more than that and nails it in an incredibly satisfying way."

The song was written when Seligman and Campbell still lived at 939 Mont Royal. It was supposed to be an instrumental. "I came upstairs to the apartment," says Millan, "and Torq was singing, and then he said, 'This will be your part.' I thought, Oh, okay. It wasn't remarkable in any way. 'Let's just see how this goes.' That's now arguably the most famous song of our career. It was a beautiful song, but I didn't have that feeling at the time at all. Whereas I thought 'Elevator Love Letter' [from *Heart*] would make us a million dollars. That song gave me shivers when I was writing it. 'This is it! This is our ticket!' And when it didn't, my expectations for anything were gone forever. I'd written the perfect song! What more do you want from me?!"

Likewise, Millan was unsure about the album's other big hit and eternal fan favourite, "Ageless Beauty," a fuzzy guitar song not unlike Sloan's "I Am the Cancer." "I laboured over that song and felt like I didn't know what I was doing," says Millan. "I would make these guys leave, because I didn't want to write in front of them. They had the track and I would try a bunch of vocals, with no lyrics written yet. I call it 'whale music'—not like the Rheostatics, but the Cocteau Twins, just vowels, like a made-up language. The lyrics for that song make no sense. To this day, 'We will always be a light / you can see it for yourself or see it.' See what? What am I talking about? On the internet, all these kids from Singapore would write out words to it and I'm like, 'Oh, *that's* what you think I say? That's good, I should have said that.' Then 'Ageless' became a massive radio success. You don't realize the impact a song will have."

Set Yourself on Fire went gold in Canada, sold at least another 100,000 copies worldwide and became the band's benchmark in the eyes of fans—which Campbell says he resents. "After that, everyone would say to us, 'When are you gonna make another *Set Yourself on Fire?*'" he told writer Cam Lindsay. "It's that child in the family who does everything right and everyone says to the others, 'Why aren't you as good as him?' I guess I feel defensive of [Stars'] other records, in light of how much people praise *Set Yourself on Fire*. For me, everybody else loves it so much so I don't have to."

It wasn't immediately apparent that it would be a breakthrough record. Stars were managed by Jeffrey Remedios of Arts & Crafts, and it made business sense to move to that label. But the band wanted to give Paper Bag a shot: they told Trevor Larocque to ask his distributor, Universal, for a $100,000 advance. He did and was literally laughed out of the room; Allan Reid, head of Universal A&R, told him that there were no radio singles on it. ("I don't remember that at all," says Reid.) Meanwhile, EMI's Deane Cameron was giving Arts & Crafts carte blanche. Larocque was crushed: had Paper Bag not put out *You Forgot It in People*? Did that record not get a Juno? It was hard not to take it personally.

It was also a sign that the game had changed quickly. "We were all indie—until we all wanted to be majors," says Larocque. But he let Stars go without a fight. "In retrospect, it was unbelievably cool and generous of him," says Campbell, still nursing wounds from Le Grand Magistery. "He didn't have to do that. But he wanted what was best for the bands. I gotta lot of love in my heart for that guy."

Paper Bag put out the debut by Campbell's side project, Memphis, and released some of the most widely acclaimed and commercially successful Canadian indie records of the next 20 years.

SET YOURSELF ON FIRE came out on Arts & Crafts on September 14, 2004, the same day as Arcade Fire's *Funeral*. The two bands didn't know each other, although violist Marika Anthony-Shaw played on both records and joined Arcade Fire on tour. Stars had been Arcade Fire fans since seeing them at the Hillside Festival in Guelph that summer, but it was hard not to feel competitive with a band who seemingly emerged from nowhere while Stars had been building slowly for the past four years. And then there was Broken Social Scene, into which Millan and Cranley were constantly recruited. One day, they stepped off a plane from Stockholm, where Stars had played, and went directly to Yonge-Dundas Square in Toronto to play a big free show with Social Scene. In the media, Stars were often referred to as a Broken Social Scene side project. That never changed.

"We were around before that band existed," says Campbell. "The number of people who *still* consider Stars to be a Broken Social Scene side project is somewhat demoralizing. That created a lot of tension between me and Amy. Amy will defend her friends to the death, and she found herself in a position of defending Broken to Stars and defending Stars to Broken, and really torn between the loyalty to two groups of people. But what are you supposed to do when [Broken] says, 'We're going on tour in Europe and playing Shepherd's Bush Empire in London'? You go. I wish I had been more generous and hadn't worried about it so much. In the long run, what did any of it matter?

"Those Broken shows from 2003 to '09 were ecstatically fun to be a part of," he continues. "They were a party that tumbled out onto the stage. You'd look behind you, and some person you hadn't seen in two years was playing tambourine. Stars was like, 'Okay, here's a song about a serial killer who falls in love with someone who works in a bookstore.' It was a lot more high concept and a lot less fun. By the time *Set Yourself on Fire* came out, we learned how to be a proper rock'n'roll band instead of just an idea. Once Evan started playing with Broken, he became a better guitarist and a tougher bass player. Amy learned how to sing louder, because she was with a big band. Everything became more maximalist and expressive."

When Stars went to Japan in May 2005, with Broken Social Scene, Metric and the Dears, it should have been a career highlight. But Millan and Cranley had just announced to the band that they were a couple, which didn't go over well with Millan's ex, Chris Seligman. Relations between everyone else weren't much better. Cooler heads eventually prevailed—mainly Seligman's. "Ultimately what kept us going was Chris's willingness to forgive Amy and Evan," says Campbell. "That act of friendship and maturity and generosity was beyond belief, and we owe everything to him, for seeing past his hurt and embracing the band and his friendships."

KEVIN DREW TOLD Charlie Spearin that Broken Social Scene was going to work with Dave Newfeld again. Spearin burst out laughing. There had been plenty of clashes while working on *You Forgot It in People*, but they both knew that Newfeld brought elements to the project that they could not. It helped that Spearin largely bowed out of the process, and Do Make Say Think was also busy, putting out two records in two years and doing lots of touring. "I would go into the studio, but I wasn't arguing with Newfeld anymore," says Spearin. "I'm generally easy-going, but I have strong artistic views and I defend them with tooth and claw. [On that record,] I'd play my parts and leave. I'm sure if I listen to the record now, I can hear the arguments right away."

The 2005 self-titled record, made over the course of 18 months in between touring jaunts, is intense and dense, even more bombastic than *You Forgot It in People*. It's the sound of saying yes to another excess. The responsibility for that could lay at the hands of Newfeld, though Drew accepts equal blame: "We drowned him in stuff. 'Make sure Charlie's in there. Make sure Andrew's in there. Make sure Evan and Jimmy are heard. Make sure the backing vocals are here.' By the time we would leave on tour, there would be 270 tracks on every song."

Brendan Canning points to the relationship between the two volatile men: "Dave Newfeld didn't do as good a job as producer [on that record] because he was too emotional for the process and couldn't wrangle Kevin—which is part of being a producer." And half the record was made at the home studio of Do Make Say Think's Ohad Benchetrit, because Newfeld only worked overnight shifts at Stars and Sons. This worked out well for Spearin, who'd just had his first child. When the band was away on tour, Newfeld toyed with many of the tracks on his own. "Hotel," for example, started out as a remix of Feist's "One Evening."

Most everyone on the previous record returned this time, as well as rapper k-os, who is only one of too many things wrong with a mess called "Windsurfing Nation." The Dears' Murray Lightburn was asked to come into Newfeld's studio when the band wasn't there. Unsure what he was supposed to do, he followed Newfeld's orders and made screaming sounds on the already thick opening track, "Our Faces Split the Coast in Half." Cranley describes the song as "the sound of anxiety, that's the sound of pressure, that's the sound of things falling apart." Meanwhile, Drew had split with Jo-Ann Goldsmith, a decision that cooled relations in the extended social scene that she had helped to nurture.

Live favourites "It's All Going to Break" and "7/4 (Shoreline)" delivered on expectations, as well as the occasional studio experiment like "Hotel." Fans were a bit confused by a meandering, slow version of "Major Label Debut," another live favourite; some believed it could have been a hit single at its regular tempo. Canning takes the blame for that one. "I could have easily said, with a clearer head, 'Guys, are we fucking idiots? Why are we putting on the weird, non-engaging version of our catchiest song?' But at that point I didn't want the band going in that direction. It turned into a B-side, and the song did get out there and served us well, so maybe I'm just being hard on myself."

"There were various mixes throughout the time we were making it," says Drew. "I remember going to a friend's house in L.A. three months after the record came out. He played me a whole different version of the album, based on rough mixes I'd shared with him. It was this super-coherent, super-laid-back record, not crazy. I was like, Holy shit.

"We came out in the press downplaying it, promoting it wrong," Drew continues. "Newf called me, 'Why are you guys out there saying, "Yeah, we overdid it, we're not sure about this"?' I'm like, 'You're right. I don't know. I should just get behind what we made.' But it was a tough record. I'd be listening to other albums in my car and then put that one on, and it's like, '*Jesus Christ!* What is this?' It was an assault. One review was a guy screaming through his typing, basically saying, 'This is a terrible record! Why are people buying this?!' Yet at the end of the year, we were No. 1 on the Canadian critics poll." It was also shortlisted for the inaugural Polaris Music Prize. When asked by Tab Siddiqui of *Eye Weekly* what the band would do with the $20,000 prize money if they won, Drew said, "We'll use it to pay for therapy." Added Justin Peroff, "We'd be able to give one dollar to each of our members."

On the road, the band added Julie Penner, a recent addition to Do Make Say Think, on violin. Her partner, Jason Tait of the Weakerthans, joined on auxiliary percussion. Millan and Cranley were often on board, as was John Crossingham, making it at least 11 people on stage every night. Feist joined them on a U.S. tour, where she and her band opened the show. That was the last time she did so. Though she'd eclipsed Broken Social Scene in sales and fame in Canada, she had yet to break the States. After she did, in 2007, she only appeared with the band in Toronto or other geographically convenient circumstances.

They added a new female singer to replace the increasingly busy Millan. Without even making a shortlist, Broken Social Scene hired Lisa Lobsinger of Calgary, whose band Reverie Sound Revue had once opened for them. "Brendan got a good vibe from her and called her and invited her to rehearsal," says Spearin. "There was no audition. I can't imagine this band having auditions. It's so much of a family thing. Lisa came in and was excellent and fun to tour with and a great singer. She doesn't really compare to Emily or Leslie, which is the point. She's a different voice."

"She had some very big shoes to fill," says one peer, "and she certainly was not ready for it—she had a music stand on stage. It's like, 'Uh, there's 2,000 people in the audience. You might want to put the music stand away.' She was thrown into the fire. But vocally, she's a great singer: perfect pitch, smart harmony choices."

"We did five years with Lisa," says Drew, of the singer who only ever had one feature track on any Broken Social Scene record (the glimmering "All to All," on 2010's *Forgiveness Rock Record*). "Talk about someone keeping you grounded, she would do that, at least for me. She's soft, and she sang soft. She did it the way she wanted to. She took a lot of shit when we first came out with her. Then she won everyone over."

"I feel the band was at its best, or at the very least great, in 2006," says Spearin. "We did Australia. Julie Penner was in the band. Ohad played a bit then, too. That was a golden year—live, anyway." Broken Social Scene's greatest triumph during this period was at Lollapalooza 2006, when an eight-song set—at a rare gig with Metric, Stars and Feist all in tow—became the talk of the whole weekend. The 20,000-strong crowd screamed for an encore for a full seven minutes, before word came down that headliners Red Hot Chili Peppers refused to delay their set to allow the Toronto band to return. It's still referenced years later as one of the greatest sets in the festival's history. A few months after that, a November show in Ann Arbor, Michigan, was once again billed as the band's last.

Offstage, there was tension between Drew and Whiteman, when Drew and Feist became romantically involved in the summer of 2006; she and Whiteman had been on and off for eight years. There were many gigs where the two guitarists didn't acknowledge each other on stage. Feist joined them during a Broken Social Scene set at a European festival where she was also performing. While singing, she approached Whiteman on stage; in a foul mood, he spat at her feet. When the band resumed touring in late 2007, Whiteman did not come along for the ride, choosing instead to focus on promoting Apostle of Hustle's *National Anthem of Nowhere*, including a U.K. tour opening for Stars. After he rejoined in June 2008 at a Bonnaroo performance, Drew and Whiteman slowly repaired their own relationship by watching movies in the tour bus in silence.

"I had to get Whitey to forgive me," says Drew. "Everyone predicted doomsday when Les and I hooked up. But we did it because we loved each other, and it was the right thing for us to do. I didn't realize that love surpassed actually being in a relationship together." They split in the fall of 2007 but remained close.

Jealousy existed between bands as well.

METRIC, LIKE STARS, were still considered second fiddle to Broken Social Scene. It didn't help when, in September 2005, the self-titled Broken Social Scene album came out a week after Metric's *Live It Out*. The two records were often reviewed together. "Broken were leading the crew," James Shaw told biographer Stuart Berman. "It's like you have the Toronto Maple Leafs and you have the Montreal Canadiens and then you have Team Canada—it makes sense that Team Canada would be better. It felt good because I was a part of it; it also felt frustrating because I wanted the same success to happen to Metric, and it wasn't happening at first. *Old World Underground* never really took off until after almost two years. It wasn't until when we decided to stop touring and make another record that all of a sudden we looked back and went, 'Oh shit, it kind of went well. We sold almost 100,000 records [worldwide].' We didn't really see it happen because we were too busy playing."

Metric booked a show at the Mod Club in Toronto in January 2005. It sold out in minutes. They added three more; those also sold out instantly. "That was definitely a career high because it was such an unexpected and genuine moment of [Toronto] actually claiming us," Haines told Tab Siddiqui. "I've always resisted being from anywhere, or having a hometown, and that outpouring really affected me and made me feel strongly about going forward in my life. Toronto claimed us, and it was a beautiful thing."

It was a change for the woman who once felt that external validation was the primary motivation. "The feeling that no one gives a shit about you is such a wonderful thing about New York, and America in general," Haines said in 2004. "No one's going to pander to you. I think that's a good thing for art. By contrast, in Canada there's an extensive grant system that really allows people to make their work without having to suffer that much, and I'm starting to come around on that—that maybe people don't have to suffer. Maybe you can just not be unhappy and make beautiful music in Canada, maybe that's okay."[2]

With *Live It Out*, Metric firmly established themselves as their own band, with bona fide radio hits like "Monster Hospital" and "Poster of a Girl." Like her peers Feist and Amy Millan, Emily Haines became a pop icon not just for her photogenic looks and style choices but for her lyrical pen, her creativity and critical eye. Whereas many artists get uncomfortable when they're perceived as role models, Haines relished it. This was a band, after all, who were calling themselves Mainstream before they settled on Metric.

"When I was [growing up] in a shitty little town and all we got was Tina Turner and Bryan Adams, my friend introduced me to U2 and Sinéad O'Connor," she says. "Which is hardly the most underground shit in the world, but that was actually the point. I like the idea that [O'Connor] would participate in mainstream culture, especially for young girls and kids who are looking for an alternative. [She] saved my life, and if she had just been an underground phenomenon, it would be something else, but it's the fact that she really came right up next to the prefab shit. I see how 14-year-old girls react to me and I think I'm a good role model. Rock star—maybe not, but I'm willing to play with it for a little while, until my hair gets grey."

After *Live It Out*, Metric spent two years focused on Europe—and booze. "We were raging, raging, raging alcoholics," says Shaw. "By the end, we were all so physically, spiritually and mentally exhausted, the only way to get through a show was [to be] completely piss drunk." In the midst of it, they played France's La Route du Rock festival in 2005. Their set was immediately after Sonic Youth— whose 1990 song "Kool Thing" had been Metric's walk-on music for years. "We were in France, it's just beautiful, we're eating dinner with the Cure—it was just one of those moments where you're happy that you've worked so hard," Haines

---

2   That year, 2004, Metric received more than $100,000 in FACTOR money, one-fifth of what they'd receive over the next decade.

told Siddiqui. "And Sonic Youth played 'Kool Thing' as their last song, and then we went on. That was definitely memorable."

By 2007, Metric thought they had material for their next album ready. On tour, they realized the songs weren't remotely ready, so they scrapped them all. Since they finally retained the rights to *Grow Up and Blow Away*, they released it as a stopgap while they built their own studio in Toronto and started from scratch with producer Gavin Brown (Billy Talent, Three Days Grace). The first two advance singles, "Help I'm Alive" and "Gimme Sympathy," were miles ahead of anything Metric had ever done, as was the rest of the *Fantasies* album when it finally came out in April 2009. It went gold within months, platinum by the end of the year and made the Billboard Top 100 in the U.S.—a rarity for an independent act and a feat that made the band the focus of a *New York Times* article about the modern music industry.

Metric gave a *Fantasies* outtake, "Black Sheep," to *Scott Pilgrim vs. the World*, which was being shot in Toronto in the summer of 2009; the now cult-film favourite is based on a graphic novel by Haines's friend Bryan Lee O'Malley, who modelled the character of Envy Adams after her. Brie Larson, in her breakout role, plays the character in the movie. (Broken Social Scene's "Anthems for a Seventeen-Year-Old Girl," sung by Haines, is also on the soundtrack.)

Metric had started out as two Torontonians trying to make it in New York, London and Hollywood. Now a London director and a Hollywood studio were coming to Toronto to capture the scene that had birthed Metric, with a character explicitly modelled after Haines, for a film that the *New York Times* raved about. Just like Al Pacino's character in *The Godfather: Part III*: they tried to leave, but the city, and their peers, pulled them back in.

"I grew up in a small town in a house that was the world that we lived in," Haines told Stuart Berman. "For whatever reason, my parents—having lived in New York and been a part of the action there—always felt like they were more connected when they removed themselves and then reconnected. I have the same relationship with Toronto as a city as I do with everyone in Broken Social Scene. It's definitely the foundation of my life, but if I'm too close to it, I can't see it.

"I need distance in order to maintain my own character and not become inter-changeable with Amy and Leslie, because we're all very different. I can go as far out as I want, I can go away forever, but I can't escape this band—which is why I can't be too close to it."

THOUGH STARS WERE barely speaking to each other, the success of *Set Yourself on Fire* kept the band going. Arts & Crafts gave the band a $250,000 budget to make the next record. They spent $10,000 of it with Jace Lacek of the Besnard Lakes, at his Breakglass Studio (later released as *The Bedroom Demos*). They then booked five weeks at the Warehouse in Vancouver. "We had a really interesting thing going on at Breakglass, but at the Warehouse we were a bloated mess with no direction," says Cranley.

Nobody in Stars seems to be able to remember the name of the French producer they'd wanted, other than that he may or may not have been involved in Daft Punk, Air and/or Phoenix. Doesn't matter: he bailed on them two weeks before the start date and instead sent his engineer, Bruno Dejarnac (who'd worked with Keren Ann and Eiffel). By then it was too late to hire anyone else. "He had zero personality," says Millan.

The band had a bigger budget than ever before. They were in one of the most high-end studios in Canada. They had aspirations to make a record with Steely Dan–level production. They had tricky interpersonal dynamics that a skilled producer should have been negotiating. Dejarnac "was a brilliant engineer, but he was not a producer," says Campbell. "Every time we asked him if something sounded good, he'd just shrug in the way French people shrug: [in French accent] 'I don't know. Eef yew like it . . .' We needed a leader to keep us in line. We were in this massive studio with shitloads of material and massive pressure on us. And we were drunk."

"I wish we bought three houses in Montreal rather than spend that money on that record," says Millan. "We should have done it at Breakglass. We made the record twice, which is so funny. But, you know, being ballers for five seconds is fun."

None of the band's anxieties can be heard on *In Our Bedroom after the War*, which does sound like a (quarter of a) million bucks and features enduring favourites like "Take Me to the Riot," "The Night Starts Here" and many others. Song for song, it may well be the best Stars record, no matter what bad memories it brings up for the band.[3] Though it didn't sell as well as *Set Yourself on Fire*—physical sales were collapsing for everyone—the band's audience was still growing.

"That was the height of our success," says Campbell. "The record wasn't well reviewed, but it was sold-out tours all the time, thousands of people every night, everywhere. We were playing to a thousand people in Berlin, and 800 people in London, and 3,000 people in Singapore. In the Philippines, it was like being in the Beatles. It was going off. We were making money." That might be the only reason

---

3   It does, however, have the most unfortunate Stars song title in existence: "Life 2: The Unhappy Ending."

the band stayed together. Campbell claims that he and Millan had trouble being alone in a room together for four awkward years, from 2006 to 2010.

Their relationship survived. But it was time to end another one, with Arts & Crafts and manager Jeffrey Remedios. "He was very good at his job," says Millan. "It was the combination of the family dynamic between Broken and Stars, and that A&C started to become bigger than the bands themselves." For a band who often bristled at never getting press that didn't also mention Broken Social Scene, they were now offended by the opposite. "The day that *Bedroom* came out, there was a huge article about A&C where Jeffrey was on the cover of an arts section and there wasn't a single mention of our album. That was the thing that spiralled me into being irritated." It didn't help that Kevin Drew's first solo album came out a week after the Stars record.

Stars took a page from Metric's book and started their own label, Soft Revolution, securing distribution in different territories. They signed with king-pin American manager Danny Goldberg, most famous for shepherding Nirvana. These weren't the only changes in their lives. Campbell and his wife, actress Moya O'Connell, were expecting a child at the same time his beloved father was dying. When their daughter was born, she required intense medical attention. "That's when shit got real," says Campbell. "The people I counted on were the band, and the person who stepped up the most for me in that time was Amy. Everything else between us was erased and all you're left with is the love. When I look back, one of the things I'm most proud of is how hard Amy and I worked, how many times we forgave each other, how deep we had to dig to understand each other's point of view and then share space on stage. It makes me love her so much."

The next record they made, 2010's *The Five Ghosts*, was a retreat from the grand gestures Stars had become known for. It's a more intimate, personal record. "That record tanked," says Campbell. "Nobody liked it. I think it's the best Stars record by a healthy margin. When we still decided to keep going, that's when we became indestructible." Stars put out three more records in the next decade, each of them incredibly strong and incredibly underrated. In 2019 they released a greatest hits collection on Arts & Crafts and starred in a play about their own lives, *Stars: Together*.

They also put out a single in 2018, "Are You with Me?"—produced by Kevin Drew with Murray Lightburn engineering.

ALMOST EVERYONE IN Broken Social Scene's core had another musical project to tend, except for Kevin Drew and Brendan Canning. Around the time they were making the self-titled record in 2005, Canning suggested to Drew that they make solo records. He responded, "Yeah, I don't want to hear your opinions about my songs any more than you want to hear my opinions of your songs."

Because of the wealth of new material for Broken Social Scene's self-titled record, and because there was some concern about trusting everything to Newfeld, Drew worked separately with Ohad Benchetrit on an album released in 2007 credited to Broken Social Scene Presents: Kevin Drew. It was a confusing moniker, and it hurt the brand: Was it a band album? A solo album? The actual complete title of the album was *Spirit If . . .* , which didn't help matters any. It featured all of Social Scene—everyone but Dave Newfeld, who gave the project his blessing—as well as Chilly Gonzales, CanRock icon Tom Cochrane and Drew's teenage idols J Mascis of Dinosaur Jr. and Spiral Stairs of Pavement. What could have been a big mess was actually a better album than *Broken Social Scene*.

By that point some of the shine was coming off as other acts ascended: Stars, Metric and most of all Feist, who released *The Reminder* that year—a multimillion-selling album that is the most commercially successful record made by anyone ever in Broken Social Scene.

Canning's solo record, *Something for All of Us . . .* , released in 2008, sold even worse than Drew's had. Nonetheless, the two founders soldiered on, touring each record with a stripped down, guitar-heavy sausage fest that brought in new players, including Sam Goldberg Jr. of Toronto's Uncut and Andrew Kenny of Austin's American Analog Set. Female singers were recruited by local promoters for each individual gig. Andrew Whiteman released the third and final Apostle of Hustle record, the highly underrated *Eats Darkness*, in 2009. Spearin put out a lovely and odd art record called *The Happiness Project*, in which he recorded his neighbours telling stories and wrote melodies to the pitch of their speaking cadence. It won a Juno for best jazz recording.

During all the drama of the last half of the decade, there was a part of Drew that continued to thrive. Part of the reason he assembled the band that he did, part of the reason he named their breakthrough album what he did, is that he loves people—and their business. "Without getting way too involved with other people's business, Kevin Drew would die. Kevin *is* other people's business," says Torquil Campbell. "That's his specialty. If you want an opinion on something, you'll get it. If you don't want an opinion on something, you'll get it. Kevin will just tell you that you've gained five pounds and you look like shit, or that your shoes don't match your jacket. Or, 'Dude, don't eat garlic before a show.' He has no filter. He just says whatever he thinks you need to hear. And he's right about 70% of the time—you *do* need to hear it. The other 30% you think, Who the fuck do you think you are?! Of course, Kevin would say the exact same thing about me."

At one afternoon gig at a European festival, around the time Drew was going through his divorce, he drank half a bottle of Jack Daniel's before the show. "He got on stage, and 'It's All Gonna Break' turned into a 30-minute song," says one band member. "In the part where we take it down, he wouldn't stop talking. We were in rural Germany, outside, and it's pouring rain. The fans were all wearing plastic coats. Kevin's on stage, with the Jack Daniel's bottle, very Jim Morrison, and he's like, 'I want you to know, that *therapy* is a *German word*.' He went on and on."

"I ruined some gigs, definitely," Drew admits. "In New York I told Canning to fuck off on stage. He was up in my grill and stepping on shit, and I'm like, 'You have to fuck off right now.' Then we went into this hopeful, beautiful song, and I ruined it. I grabbed him after and said, 'Let's never do that again.' There was a point to having Collett and Whitey and Canning [in the band]: they were elders. Once it became clear that I would become the MC [of the band], they would give me notes. You have to push through. Your amp craps out. Your pedals don't work. You're sick. Your ex-lover is on stage. There's tension with the interrelationships. There were a few classic moments that just blow my mind that not only did we get through them, but that we're all still in each other's lives today."

In 2008, Feist told U.K. paper the *Guardian* that her days in Broken Social Scene were likely done. "I don't really know how involved I feel [with Broken Social Scene] anymore," she told writer Sean Michaels. "It's not really as interesting for me as it once was. [It] would be like a reunion to be able to hang out with everyone—but I can do that around a kitchen table, too."

"[That article came out] when we were on the road," says Drew, "and that was not the kind of press we needed. That was hard. It was one of the first times someone had spoken out in the crew. It was hard for her to come on stage with us, because we were so loud, and she was in such a different place in controlling her own ship, and stage sound, and the rest of it. The Toronto shows we did with Les, she was ecstatic and through-the-roof loved it. But that was the thing: if you're going to come and play live, you have to let go or it wasn't going to work for you."

Between Feist, Stars and Metric, the boats of Broken Social Scene were beginning to resist the tide. "The funny part about it is that with Feist, Jimmy and Emily, I always have to remind them," says Drew. "They'll say, 'Well, your band—' 'You mean *our* band.' 'Yeah, but your band—' '*Our* band.' I've been doing that for almost 20 years now. With Stars, I annoyed them. That was the catalyst of them moving on [from Arts & Crafts], and that falls on me and bad decision-making through selfishness. That was a lesson, for sure."

A healing ceremony was required. A July 13, 2009, show was to be held on Toronto Island, but a municipal strike nixed it.[4] Instead, it turned into another free Harbourfront show. This was one for the ages: all three original "Broken babes" were there, as well as pretty much anyone who had ever toured with the band in the last six years. It was filmed by *Hard Core Logo* director Bruce McDonald for 2010's *This Movie Is Broken*. If it had just been a concert document, it would have been thrilling and a valuable time capsule. Unfortunately, it was framed by an extremely clunky (and hastily assembled) script about two new lovers, insufferable hipsters both, trying to sneak backstage to meet the band. "It was all right," shrugs Canning. "It wasn't the worst thing to happen to Canadian cinema." It's almost a crime that a live album didn't come with it.

Alongside its musical highlights, the film does capture a key moment that paved the way for the band's future. In the most Canadian move ever, Drew exhorts the audience, "On the count of three, everyone say, 'I'm sorry!'" as an act of mass absolution—followed by, "I still fucking love you!" Nobody needed to hear it more than everyone on stage. After all the glories and drama of the last 10 years, they needed a psychic boost to bury some hatchets and inject some cosmic juice into their veins if they were going to continue another 10 years, either in a band or even just as friends.

Later that year, they went to Chicago to work with producer John McEntire, a musical hero to many of them for his work with Tortoise and the Sea and Cake, to make *Forgiveness Rock Record*. The album was a welcome return, with rousing anthems, melodic pop songs and no filler. It was the tight, lean rock record no one ever expected Broken Social Scene to make—especially not in 2010. The core band was on fire, and all four female vocalists (the original three plus Lobsinger) were there, as well as Evan Cranley, Julie Penner and Sam Goldberg Jr. The album got rave reviews, a spot on the Polaris shortlist, and audiences returned.

"Everybody wants to be in a gang," says Amy Millan. "Everyone feels alone in the world. Everybody wants to see if it's possible to be in a squad. What we tried to create was making it so that when we're on stage, you're there with us and we are all together. You are Social Scene and I am Social Scene. We are a group of people who came together to make music, but when you come to see our show, you are coming to be a part of Broken Social Scene. In that chaos, everybody felt like they were in the squad with us. That's what made it so powerful. But if you took those narratives away—and just put on the records one by one and didn't know the relations—they'd still stand alone."

---

4   The strike, it could be argued, paved the way to Rob Ford's successful mayoral bid in 2010, marking the end of a certain era of optimism in Toronto.

When asked to remember a key moment during the band's heyday, Millan has an anecdote at the ready. "We were in Germany; we were always in Germany. Leslie was playing solo. This was probably '05 or '06. She was up on stage, this tiny thing with a massive red guitar and a loop station, just owning this crowd. Social Scene had a bus, and [after the show] she said, 'I'm going to Paris, too. Can I get a ride with you guys?' She has this huge guitar case on wheels, and she's lugging it across this garden festival, holding her scarf. She's on her own: no tour manager, nothing, just her. I'm so amazed by her courage and her tenaciousness.

"We get on the tour bus and we're heading through the German hills, all this greenery, so beautiful, windmills. It's me, Charlie, Kevin, Leslie and Evan in the back of the bus. Leslie says, 'It's so beautiful, all these green hills. I feel like any minute a unicorn is going to come over a hill.' Kevin Drew goes, 'I've never seen a unicorn, I don't think. Have I, Chuck?'" The bus went dead silent.

"But for a moment there, unicorns existed—and it was as if Charlie would know about it," Millan laughs. "It was amazing. Just for five minutes there. Then Kevin said, 'Wait, right, they don't exist.' *But they did for a minute there!* Anything felt possible."

CHAPTER 12

AIN'T NOBODY
CAN HANG WITH US

KARDINAL OFFISHALL, K-OS,
SWOLLEN MEMBERS, SAUKRATES

Accorrding to popular wisdom, the pre-Drake history of Canadian hip-hop has only a fistful of names. That's not true at all.

That notion comes from a combination of classic Canadian cultural amnesia as well as institutional erasure. For many Canadians of a certain age, Maestro Fresh Wes was the first homegrown rapper they heard, with "Let Your Backbone Slide." Maybe they know that his records went gold and platinum on native soil. But many people need reminding that Michie Mee was the first to actually *have* a record, or that Dream Warriors were the first Canadian rap act to leave a significant impression outside the country. Few know how that "holy trinity" were first signed to U.S. independent labels of various sizes; in other words, foreigners were invested in Canadian hip-hop before Canadians themselves were.

Only the nerdiest of nerds know that Main Source, who made the 1991 NYC classic *Breaking Atoms*, were two-thirds Torontonian. And very few hip-hop scholars want to talk about Toronto MC Snow, the Irish-Canadian MC rapping in Jamaican patois. But not only was Snow's "Informer" a massive global No. 1 hit in 1993, which helped move millions of copies of the MC Shan–produced *Three Inches of Snow*, but the artist went on to have No. 1 hits in Jamaica and in Asia. Laugh all you want, but Snow wasn't a one-hit wonder. For decades he was the international face of Canadian hip-hop. Before Drake broke out in 2009, Snow was the biggest-selling

Canadian rapper of all time.[1] Then there's the mysterious case of Len, a genre-jumping act who scored a global pop hit in 1999, "Steal My Sunshine," backed with an album of Haligonian hip-hop.

As Canadian hip-hop evolved, it's remarkable how many conundrums it shares with the CanRock canon. In the dawn of the rock era, Canada was still a colonial outpost; many Canadians had direct family relations with Europe, and culture from "the old country" was still a standard to be met. Rock, folk and country acts would feign British accents and sing about anywhere but Canada. Establishing a Canadian voice, one to be taken seriously, was a struggle—both commercially and critically.

Until the days of Drake, Canadian hip-hop had many of the same troubles. Cultural ties to the Caribbean and to the diaspora in the U.S. and U.K. were still crucial; being identifiably Canadian was a curse. On the touring circuit, hip-hop had trouble breaking out of the club level. It was marginalized in the media, with the notable exception of MuchMusic. The American shadow loomed large: if a local track didn't have the same production quality, the same inherent charisma, the same bravado, it was easily dismissed as inferior. Canadians knew what hip-hop was supposed to sound like: records from New York and L.A., mainly. And yet Canadian artists were caught between worlds: if they consciously tried to sound American, they were mocked; if they explored their own voice, they were ignored by all but their closest peers. Yes, Maestro, Michie and Dream Warriors all did their thing—but five years after their respective breakthroughs, each struggled to maintain momentum. Michie Mee reinvented herself with Raggadeath, an unusually good rap-metal crossover, and Maestro staged a successful comeback in 1998. But they still had to hustle. Dream Warriors, who were innovators on several levels, slowly faded from view, though maintained a critical reputation in Britain; Ninja Tune artist the Herbaliser tapped them for a 1999 single.

With the exception of the Rascalz' BMG deal in 1993, Canadian labels didn't sign Canadian rap acts—and those acts weren't going to wait for them. The mid-'90s marked an explosion of independent rap from coast to coast. And yet none of it was on mainstream radio. MuchMusic was a lifesaver, making genuine investments in the scene: several artists won MuchMusic Video Awards (MMVAs)—or Junos, for that matter—before getting a record deal, if they ever did at all. Canadian hip-hop in the '90s was just as DIY as indie rock, if not more so; there was so little infrastructure of any kind outside campus radio. And like the U.K.'s rap scene, the music was different than rap in the U.S.; it had a different flavour. "When the scene was forming within Toronto," says Kardinal Offishall, "we, for the most part, did

---

1   Genre pedants will argue that Snow is not a rapper, but a singing deejay, in the Jamaican
     dancehall sense of the term, a.k.a. a "singjay."

not want to just copy and emulate what was going on in the States. We wanted for the world to know who *we* were."

Saukrates signed to Warner Records in L.A. in 1997, though he himself asked to leave two years later. By then, Choclair had separate major deals in the U.S. and the U.K., and Swollen Members were selling thousands of records up and down the West Coast on their own indie label. Several 1999 articles mused, with good reason, that Canadian hip-hop was finally about to break big.

It didn't. Not yet. For myriad reasons, many beyond the artists' control, that momentum led to stasis between 2000 and '05. Major label deals were offered and then rescinded. At least three records by major artists—Kardinal, Saukrates and R&B singer Jully Black—got buried in corporate-shuffling limbo. The era's biggest Canadian rap star, k-os, went multiplatinum in Canada, yet stalled on the world stage and had struggled personally with the idea of success long before his first album even came out.

It wasn't until 2009 that Kardinal had a top five hit around the world; one year later, K'naan scored even bigger with "Wavin' Flag." And by that time, Drake was off to the races.

———

IS KARDINAL OFFISHALL the new Stompin' Tom Connors?

No, of course not. He is, however, the guy who wrote anthems celebrating his hometown (including, um, "The Anthem"). He's from the T-dot-O; he reps it everywhere he goes. He had a hit song championing the local lingo. He left a Timbaland track off his 2005 album in order to showcase Toronto talent. He made connections across the country, and rapped the hook on the epochal scene-setter "Northern Touch," with Vancouver's Rascalz—who refused a Juno Award (a very Connors move).

"To be honest, it was never about the States for us," says Kardinal. "Our favourite people were from the States, but for the most part we weren't really trying to do what they were doing. I believe you are who you surround yourself with. No matter what field you're getting into, if you surround yourself with people who are not creative and just do whatever the status quo is, that's what you're going to do. In music, it seems like the risk-takers, the ones who are not afraid to create or innovate something, are the ones who got the greater rewards. Those are the ones that managed to stay around longer and have longevity in the business."

To take those risks, there was little choice but to take matters into their own hands. "We realized we didn't have an infrastructure, so we had to create our own," says Kardinal. "We didn't wait for anyone to give it to us."

WHEN JASON HARROW was 11 years old, Michie Mee came to his Toronto neighbour-hood, Flemingdon Park, to shoot a video. She rolled up in a top-down red Porsche, like a baller. Years before Harrow was known as Kardinal Offishall, this was a big moment for the young man. Here was a woman from Toronto making the kind of music he'd hear on family trips to visit relatives in New York City. It was the music they'd record there on "pause tapes" and circulate back in Toronto. It was the music founded in the mid-'70s by Bronx DJ Kool Herc, whose nephew went to Kardinal's Toronto school. Michie Mee was the queen, making "Jamaican Funk, Canadian Style," and the young would-be prince took careful notes.

Harrow's parents both grew up in Jamaica, though they met in Toronto, part of an immigration wave in the '60s and '70s. His mother, Donna, was working at the Bay department store as she put herself through teacher's college. His father was a factory worker who performed as DJ Soul Prince, amassing a large record collection that included all the early rap records. The young Harrow imitated his favourite MCs until his mother, who was also his grade 7 teacher, urged him to write his own bars. At the Eaton Centre downtown, there was a small recording booth in the Mr. Greenjeans restaurant, where anyone could record a song. After cutting a tape there as J-Ski, the 12-year-old Harrow and friends went to amuse-ment park Canada's Wonderland, where you could film yourself lip-synching to a song; Harrow brought his Mr. Greenjeans tape and made his first video. On the strength of that alone, his crew, Young Black Panthers, somehow got themselves booked into community centres and shopping malls across the city. They made $250 a gig, split three ways. Harrow was calling himself Gumby D.

At 14, he entered a contest to write an antidrug rap and won. The prize was meeting Maestro Fresh Wes, who told the young MC to stay in school. (He was likely to do so anyway: his mom was an activist who spearheaded a long fight for an Africentric school at the Toronto school board.) Harrow was interviewed by Barbara Frum on CBC's flagship TV news program, *The Journal*. Young Black Panthers were invited to perform for Nelson Mandela on the South African lead-er's first post-prison trip abroad, in 1990.

In 1993, Harrow enrolled in the new Fresh Arts program, part of the Jobs for Ontario Youth (JOY) project, sponsored by the Toronto Arts Council. After the acquittal of LAPD officers charged with using excessive force on Rodney King spawned a subsequent "riot" on Yonge Street in 1992, a provincial report rec-ommended new arts programs for racialized youth. Fresh Arts paired industry mentors like MuchMusic VJ Master T and CKLN DJ Mastermind with high school kids who were paid minimum wage to get arts experience on their résumés. CIUT DJ and MC Motion was the mentor who meant the most to Harrow. "She taught us everything," Kardinal told writer Karen Bliss. "Motion was our boss, our mentor, our leader, whatever you want to call it. She would bring us to the Toronto Reference Library and we'd be like, 'Aw, what are we doing here?' but then we'd see documentaries on the Black Panthers. She'd teach us about eras of jazz, learning the history of music and where these different things came from—because everything was pretty sample-heavy then." Harrow's class turned out to be exceptional: Saukrates, Baby Blue Soundcrew and filmmaker Little X (Julien Lutz, also known as Director X) were all there at the same time; Jully Black was in the next cohort. The concentric circles around the Fresh Arts crew defined Toronto hip-hop in the '90s.

Harrow went to York University to study mass communications. While there, he rebranded himself as Kardinal Offishall, in part after reading about the ruthless political machinations of 17th-century French politician Cardinal Richelieu—an early sign that this MC was on a different trip than the rest of the English-speaking world. He picked *Offishall* because he loved the Ghetto Concept track "Certified"; he wanted everything he did to be "certified official." With Saukrates and Solitair, they formed Figurez of Speech, soon to be merged with a Scarborough crew called Paranormal, featuring Choclair, into a new unit called the Circle. The concept had shades of the Wu-Tang Clan—or Broken Social Scene.

Circle shows "were remarkable for their military precision," wrote *Exclaim!*'s Del Cowie. "Each one of up to 10 crew members had a specific onstage function; together, they helped raise the performance benchmark within Toronto's moribund live hip-hop scene."

"Kardi was captain," says Saukrates. "He pulled us all together, gathered all the beats and songs we'd been working on and made a choreographed hip-hop show. Everything was calculated; we put a lot of thought into it."

"I was just blessed to be around super creative people," Kardinal told Cowie. "If there was a show, we would practise and practise, so people were just blown away and that's always stayed with me. I don't want anyone to ever come to my show and say, 'That was a garbage show.'"

Toronto had a reputation as the "screwface capital" in the hip-hop scene of the '90s, where unimpressed audiences didn't hide their reactions. It wasn't new: Kardinal had heard stories from his father's DJ days. "If you know anything about how the vibes were in Toronto, they were extremely tough," Kardinal told writer Anupa Mistry. "It's not like [my dad] could go on stage, not be good, and people would just be like, 'He was okay.' You would literally get food, bottles, all kinds of stuff thrown at you. It was not a very receptive environment. You had to be dope. You had to have a certain type of aggression. I think that was within our music, but it was also in the streets. There was a time where me and Drake sat down, before the record deals and all that, and he was explaining to me how much people cared about what people said online. I was like, 'That's fascinating,' because to me, having a gun pointed in my ribs was the way that we knew that people didn't fuck with us."

Kardinal co-produced Saukrates's single "Still Caught Up," which was nominated for Best Rap Recording at the 1996 Junos. Saukrates self-funded a $17,000 video for his own single "Hate Runs Deep," but it was "Father Time" that got radio play across the U.S. and sold 15,000 copies there through distributor Fat Beats. Saukrates's 1997 EP *Brick House* featured guest spots from hot U.S. MCs Common (then known as Common Sense), Masta Ace and O.C. That caught the attention of Warner Brothers in L.A., who made the 19-year-old Saukrates the first Canadian rapper signed directly to a U.S. major label, not a subsidiary. He also signed a publishing deal with the Toronto office of Warner Chappell Music.

Meanwhile, Kardinal Offishall dropped his first 12-inch single, "Naughty Dread" backed with "On wid da Show," on a label run by Choclair's manager, Lee "Day" Fredericks. A video for "On wid da Show" got MuchMusic play, though it was pulled after a complaint—not because of the song or the video itself, but because an extra in it showed up to the shoot directly from work and was wearing his corporate uniform; the company in question was not happy. Unintentional product placement on a nationally aired rap video was not yet coveted—not in Canada, anyway.

"Naughty Dread" landed on a groundbreaking compilation by Dream Warriors manager Ivan Berry, distributed by EMI; the song was one of three tracks from *Rap Essentials Volume One* to get a Juno nom in 1997. After a Toronto show opening for Outkast, backed by the Circle, Kardinal signed a publishing deal with Warner Chappell. For an *unsigned* Canadian rapper to get a publishing deal was unheard of at the time.

The deal put $40,000 in his pocket. "What [they] didn't know at the time was that I sampled Bob Marley, and there was no way [they were] going to get any publishing from that," he told Mistry. "At the time, I was dead-ass broke. I was like, 'Oh, shit. It's about to be on now.' I paid for my university bills, paid my [student loans], gave my mom some money and probably had a few thousand dollars left to buy an Ensoniq ASR-10, the greatest machine ever built. Through that publishing deal, I was able to also go to the studio and create my first independent album."

Eye & I came out in 1997 on Capitol Hill, a label launched by Saukrates— who also appears on the album, alongside fellow Fresh Arts alum Jully Black, Fresh Arts mentor Orin Isaacs, Montreal's Tara Chase and Red 1 of Vancouver's Rascalz. Kardinal hit the road to tour the country, learning about retail distribution along the way: record stores would tell him they had ordered four copies, sold out and didn't restock. The limitations of the indie approach were apparent. But Saukrates's Warner deal aside, it didn't seem like there were any viable options.

"We were just kids from the street," Kardinal told Mistry. "We had blue-collar parents who were doing what they could to provide for us. None of us were well off. But we had this drive, and we had this idea that if we came together, and pulled our money together, that one by one we'd be able to push one guy to that next level. So that's what we did with our independent singles: one side would be Choclair and on the other side it would be Kardinal and Solitair." With acts from Rexdale, Scarborough, East York and North York all uniting, says Kardinal, "what was going on in the city, if all that shit wasn't happening at the time I don't think that the music would have been as urgent."

It was uniting with the West Coast, however, that really set things off.

BY 1997, MAJOR LABELS IN CANADA had started to take hip-hop seriously. The Rascalz signed to BMG Canada in 1993 and had a gold record with 1997's *Cash Crop*. The crew's manager, Sol Guy, was hired by the label. The genre had other A&R champions: Craig Mannix at Sony, Mike Zafiris at Universal. Those three labels worked together on bestselling compilations for MuchMusic, *Big Shiny Tunes* and *Much Dance*. Mannix suggested they do a hip-hop one, with a new posse cut featuring Canadian talent. The Rascalz were an obvious anchor act for a bunch of reasons, one of them being that they were the only rap artist with a record deal. The Rascalz' DJ Kemo had a track he'd made for a Jay Swing mixtape; Swing was a popular CiTR host with Flipside (Madchild's early partner) and Checkmate. When Guy heard it, he knew it could be the posse cut Mannix was looking for.

The Rascalz knew the Circle, with whom they'd shared bills in Toronto. Guy called Choclair at his workplace, a daycare in Scarborough's Malvern neighbour-hood, and said he'd be couriering the two-inch tape of the Kemo track to Toronto. Choclair and Kardinal already had a studio booked for another project, where they laid down Choclair's verse and Kardinal's hook. Thrust, a member of the Circle and one of Kardinal's mentors at Fresh Arts, also laid down a verse.

"Choclair, Thrust, Rascalz and Checkmate on one song doesn't really make sense from an A&R perspective," Kardinal told CBC's Tyrone Callender. "Like Saukrates, who arguably was the biggest artist out of all of us internationally—why wasn't he on the song? Or why wasn't k-os on the song, or whatever. That weird little mix and match of artists and energies at the time for whatever reason just worked in Canadian hip-hop history." K-os was managed by Sol Guy at the time, which makes his absence even more unusual.

What definitely didn't make sense is that whoever was responsible for green-lighting *Big Shiny Tunes* and *Much Dance* didn't think a hip-hop comp was as commercially viable. It was canned. "Northern Touch" was orphaned. Meanwhile, the Rascalz were nominated for a Juno in the spring of 1998 for *Cash Crop*. The awards that year were in their hometown of Vancouver. Guy had lobbied for them to appear on the telecast. No dice. After they won the award, they told the press they were refusing their award, citing the fact that rap had never been performed at the Junos since the category was added in 1991. "We were brash," Guy told Callender, "and thought if we couldn't accomplish anything we wanted to do and if there was no space in the industry, we're going to kick a hole in it and make space for ourselves."

Riding that controversy, the Rascalz reissued *Cash Crop* with "Northern Touch" tacked on the end. Little X made a video. The song was massive on MuchMusic. On Canadian radio, it rose to a mere No. 41. It had been five long years since Snow, the last time a Canadian rap track got played on radio at all; Maestro's come-back single didn't arrive until later that year. "Northern Touch" also got play on BET in the U.S. Kardinal knew it would be a hit the first time he heard it, after a Common show in Toronto when DJ Kemo ran into the club with a test pressing. Choclair quit his job at the daycare after being asked for one too many autographs in between cleaning up kids' vomit.

"Being a part of that whole movement was life changing," Kardinal told Mistry. "Before then, even if you had love for something from your city or from the country, you'd be like, 'It's kind of cool,' but you wouldn't really say that in public. That was the first time across the entire country, every single concert was sold out. The way those shows were, I had never seen that before—ever, ever, ever, ever. It was crazy because it's the first time within hip-hop that there was a national pride. But also it was a wake-up call for us as artists. We were forced to kind of examine who we were as a country. Because to us, the country didn't go far outside of Toronto. All of a sudden now we were really learning about Vancouver, we were really learning about Halifax and everything in between."

"'Northern Touch' was a seminal moment," Guy told Callender, "and you can draw a direct line from that song to the success we're seeing today in Canadian music. Canadian music didn't look like us at that time. We were second-generation immigrant kids who didn't look like the average Canadian. I want to think that 'Northern Touch' was a calling card to all those young people out there who are now the faces and the leaders of the nation in different spaces, not just arts and culture, but across the board."

THE FIRST BENEFICIARY of "Northern Touch" was Choclair, who signed to Virgin Canada that same year and to pioneering U.S. rap label Priority in 1999; both were under the larger EMI umbrella. Choclair's *Ice Cold* arrived in November 1999 with an avalanche of hype; no Canadian rap artist had ever had this level of anticipation for their debut. Virgin spent six figures on the video for "Let's Ride," a song produced by Kardinal. Other production credits stayed in the Circle: Saukrates, Ro Dolla, Solitair. Jully Black and the Rascalz appeared on the album, as did Gang Starr's Guru and Jay-Z hypeman Memphis Bleek. Virgin A&R director Geoff Kulawick told the *National Post* that Choclair was a top priority. "We've invested significantly in this record, because we believe in what he can do," he told the paper. That said, hip-hop was still niche when it came to record sales in 1999: Soundscan reported that so-called urban music accounted for only 10% of the Canadian market, as opposed to 20% in the U.S. (And the Canadian market is 10% the size of that in the U.S.)

Meanwhile, Saukrates asked to be let out of his Warner deal in a situation not at all unusual during the mergers of the late '90s. "Their staff was changing every four months," says Saukrates. "I went through three or four A&R reps. Couldn't get anything done. I couldn't wait anymore. They let me go with all my masters and an apology." Eight months later, in the fall of 1999, he self-released *The Underground Tapes*, featuring his Warner-era material and earlier singles like "Father Time." It was distributed independently in the States and by EMI in Canada; it sold more than 40,000 copies.

Speaking of underground tapes, there was also a strong black-market economy of DJ mixtapes. Since the dawn of hip-hop culture, mixtapes made by club DJs and campus radio hosts were essential disseminators of new tracks, sold out of the backs of cars or at flea markets. They also often featured rappers freestyling over uncleared samples. In the late '90s, CD-burning technology made them easier to produce. The most popular mixtape maker in Toronto was DJ Mastermind, who'd been doing it since the late '80s, when he was a protégé of CKLN's Ron Nelson, the godfather of hip-hop in Toronto. In the U.S., there was a tacit understanding between labels and DJs that mixtapes were a crucial promotional tool; that changed in 2007, when Atlanta's DJ Drama was subject to a helicopter-led police raid.

Canada cracked down much earlier: in 1999, the same year Choclair's record came out, police raided Toronto stores Play De Record and Traxxx, seizing 3,000 mixtapes and arresting five employees. "They even raided the plant in Scarborough that was doing all the duplicating for pretty much all the DJs," Mastermind told *Vice*. "They raided that place and confiscated equipment, tapes, money, and they ticketed people. That ended mixtapes and CDs for quite a while."

That said, there was a silver lining for Mastermind and his prodigies in Baby Blue Soundcrew: they got Canadian major label deals in 2000. After a career of 49 underground mixtapes, Mastermind put out *Volume 50: Street Legal* on Virgin, featuring tracks from American heavyweights alongside Torontonians k-os, BrassMunk, D-Sisive, Citizen Kane and Monolith.

Baby Blue Soundcrew, who became the Toronto Raptors' official DJs, took a similar approach on *Private Party Collectors Edition*; its original songs included collaborations with R&B singer Glenn Lewis, Ghetto Concept and Saukrates. Key track "Money Jane" featured Kardinal Offishall, Jully Black and new Jamaican MC Sean Paul. That song became a big pop hit in Canada, propelling the album to near-platinum status—exactly what Sol Guy and Craig Mannix had in mind to launch "Northern Touch" three years earlier, but that wasn't considered commercial enough at that time. The "Money Jane" video, directed by Little X, won a MuchMusic Video Award in 2001. Baby Blue Soundcrew were also a popular live draw. "They weren't playing bars; they were playing 1,000-capacity venues," says Universal's head of A&R Allan Reid, "and people would show up all across the country."

"Money Jane" was up for a Juno and was considered a shoo-in to win. But a crew from Vancouver had a surprise in store for the Toronto establishment.

MORE THAN 95% of nominees since 1991 for the Juno Award for Rap Recording of the Year are from Toronto. The Rascalz notwithstanding, Vancouver is not considered a hip-hop town.

And yet other than multiplatinum pop crossover k-os, Vancouver's Swollen Members were the biggest rap act of the early 2000s. And they became national stars via the most square route possible: by winning a Juno. And not just winning one, but by winning three in a row (2001–03), then another years later (2007). That first win, in 2001, shocked Toronto rap royalty by coming out of "nowhere"— Vancouver—to beat kingpin Kardinal Offishall, the beloved BrassMunk, the mixtape master DJ Serious and sure bet Baby Blue Sound Crew with "Money Jane." Kardinal, in the audience at Hamilton's Copps Coliseum, was visibly miffed on the telecast; the show's director thought he would win and had already cut to him when the winner was announced. Swollen Members' Madchild, Prevail and Rob the Viking weren't even there; they had just finished an American tour the day before and were chilling in Vancouver.

They didn't *need* a Juno. They'd already toured the U.K., Europe, Australia and the States. Their records had been released in Britain. Swollen Members' 1999 debut, *Balance*, which won the 2001 Juno, was made with leading lights of the California underground rap scene: Del tha Funkee Homosapien, Dilated Peoples, Aceyalone, Divine Styler, Funkdoobiest and the Alchemist. There were also appearances from Beastie Boys' DJ Mix Master Mike and House of Pain's Everlast. In North America, *Balance* came out on Battle Axe Records, the small indie label run by Madchild that was selling thousands of records up and down the West Coast.

"Three things worked in our favour in the early days of Swollen Members," says Prevail. "Breaking out of Canada, breaking out of Canada as a rap group and breaking out of Canada as a rap group from the West Coast. We came out spitting, kicking, pounding booze, thrashing our hair around and making music that we hoped people would appreciate regardless of whether they were a classic hip-hop head or into punk and rock."

Swollen Members already had success that a Juno could never garner. But it sure helped.

MADCHILD WAS BORN Shane Bunting in North Vancouver, raised by a single mother and grandparents. His mom remarried, when he was 12, to a man he described as the "best stepdad in the world." But Madchild was a troublemaker with a skateboard, who was into '80s hardcore before Beastie Boys' *Licensed to Ill* changed his life. "Drinking Coronas and going to the beach in a '63 Mercury, that was the shit," he told writer Alysa Lechner. "Driving in a little ['65] Vespa scooter because I wasn't old enough to have my licence. LL Cool J *Radio*, Ice-T *Rhyme Pays*. That was it. I went from punk rock to hip-hop, and there was no looking back." He was also into ska and local band the Villains. His Vespa earned him the nickname Mod Child. Standing five foot six, he hung out with the tallest guy at school; they once went to a Halloween party dressed as the Jolly Green Giant and Little Green Sprout.

As Madchild got further into hip-hop, he started promoting events called Drunken Monkey. He'd bring up acts from California and put them up at his grandmother's house in North Van, across the street from a police station. Meanwhile, "I was selling more weed than anyone else in North Vancouver," he boasted to Nardwuar. As a rapper he was very briefly part of the Ragamuffin Rascalz, who soon abbreviated their name and became Vancouver's first major hip-hop export; their 1992 album *Really Livin'* was reworked and reissued by BMG in '93. Madchild formed a duo with CiTR DJ Flipout called What the Hell? with the 1993 single "Young Girls" and a full-length album.

In Victoria, 15-year-olds Kiley "Prevwon" Hendriks and Dan "Moka Only" Denton were freestyling outside a McDonald's. They knew there was a club nearby frequented by the U.S. Navy and that when drunken sailors left the bar, they craved fast food. The two teens, known collectively as Split Sphere, were waiting there to challenge them to freestyle battles for five bucks a pop. "I probably made more money battling U.S. sailors than I did at my busboy job," says Hendriks. At a nearby high school, a 12-year-old Nelly Furtado was joining their scene as a dancer and rapper. When Hendriks graduated in 1993, he and Denton went first to Vancouver and then to San Diego on a whim. "We took an Amtrak to L.A., a beautiful trip down the coast, excited about all the hip-hop culture we were going to see," says Hendriks, who by then had changed his moniker from Prevwon to Prevail. "Then in L.A. they kicked us off the nice train and put us on this little commuter train to San Diego for two hours. That's when it sunk in: we don't know anybody!"

Madchild knew everybody. He, too, had split for California, landing in San Francisco. He delivered pizzas for $1 an hour plus tips and slept on the empty boxes at night. When he got a job at the Bomb Hip-Hop Shop, selling records and streetwear, he slept in the back room. Bomb was a hub for the Bay Area scene, particularly the renaissance in turntablism: scratch DJs who battled in displays of dexterity and surprising samples. DJs were no longer solo artists or just backing up MCs; they were starting turntable bands, like Invisibl Skratch Piklz, featuring future Beastie Boy Mix Master Mike.

Bomb Hip-Hop Records, run out of the store, became known for its *Return of the DJ* compilations in the mid- to late '90s. But their first comp, in 1994, featured Blackalicious, Peanut Butter Wolf, and a track by Madchild backed up by the Piklz' DJ Qbert. Madchild followed that with a seven-inch single, "Pressure," made with pro-skateboarder-turned-musician Tommy Guerrero. It caught the ear of Del tha Funkee Homosapien, Ice Cube's cousin who had a big hit with "Mistadobalina." (Years later Del was a part of Gorillaz' biggest hits.) Del sought out Madchild at Bomb to tell him how much he loved "Pressure." The Vancouverite was in the thick of the most influential underground hip-hop scene on the West Coast.

Prevail and Moka Only loved their time in San Diego, where they made connections at the annual B-Boy Summit and hung out at streetwear shop 432F, but they were back in Vancouver after several months. They started a new rap crew, the Q Continuum; it's a *Star Trek* reference; they were nothing if not nerds. On a trip to the Bay Area, they walked into X-Large, a clothing store affiliated with the Beastie Boys, and found Madchild working there (and sleeping on a couch in the back). They'd never met but knew of each other; Prevail had recently battled Madchild's old partner Flipside in Vancouver. They chatted, exchanged respect and parted ways.

"Flash forward six months later," says Prevail. Madchild had moved back to Vancouver. They were all at a mutual friend's birthday party in North Van. The two rappers met again, sat down in two chairs across from each other and started freestyling. At first they were joined by members of their respective crews, "but at one point we realized that no one else was rapping anymore, it was just he and I going back and forth," says Prevail.

"We had 150 drunk kids dead quiet," says Madchild, "listening to us go for like 45 minutes. There was definitely chemistry there." They went into a studio the next week and Swollen Members was born. Moka Only gave them the name.

Madchild had seen the hustle of the indie rap scene in California, and with $20,000 borrowed from his grandmother, he started Battle Axe Records. The first 12-inch single in 1997 featured Swollen Members with assists from Aceyalone and Evidence of Dilated Peoples. The label's second release was a compilation, *Defenders of the Underground*, overflowing with big names in the scene: Kool Keith, Non Phixion and a posse cut with Everlast, Divine Styler and Madchild. Soon enough, Battle Axe was selling thousands of records to hardcore hip-hop heads up and down the West Coast and beyond, even before Swollen Members put out 1999's *Balance*. That debut album caught the attention of DJ Vadim, a popular U.K. DJ signed to Ninja Tune who also ran his own label, Jazz Fudge. Vadim put out *Balance* as well as *Defenders of the Underground* in the U.K., and brought the duo on tour with him in Europe and Japan. Swollen Members had not yet played east of Alberta; Canada was not a concern.

Mainstream radio was also not their goal: in Canada, hip-hop was not on the radio, other than campus stations. And yet Chris "Dunner" Duncombe, program director at Vancouver's 104.9 XFM, put "Lady Venom," a hip-hop song with rock energy and an Ofra Haza sample, into rotation.

"People were calling up, saying, 'I don't tune in to listen to this rap crap.' But that started a buzz," says Prevail, "and that started a fire." Swollen Members got a VideoFACT grant to shoot a video for the song, and for the first time they had a film crew that wasn't just a few friends following them around with video cameras. They delivered a brightly lit, strobe-heavy video featuring a club full of women who turn into vampires and scorpions. It won a MuchMusic Video Award in 2001, shortly after *Balance* won the Juno.

The Canadian music industry scrambled to play catch-up. Nettwerk signed them to a management and distribution deal, making the crew the only hip-hop act on Canada's biggest indie label. "We started touring Canada nonstop," says Prevail. The first full cross-country jaunt, in a motorhome, had them first on a bill with Vancouver skate-punk band Gob and the platinum-selling rock star Bif Naked.

"It worked!" says Prevail of the seemingly incongruous bill. "We had a rowdy, stage-diving, mosh-pit rap show. We didn't craft that, it just came out of the energy Madchild and I had after a couple of years travelling the world. By the time we hit Canada, we were hungry, polished, ready, confident. We knew what our show should look and feel like. And it took hold."

The tour was sponsored by a skateboarding footwear company, one of many lucrative connections to skateboard and snowboard culture the crew cultivated over the years. Shows in Toronto and Montreal were packed. Swollen Members played 250 shows in 2001.

Joining them on turntables was DJ Science, who worked at Vancouver hip-hop shop FWUH (Fuck What U Heard). "It was a real community hub," says Prevail. "They had records, sneakers, graffiti supplies, clothing, but they had a couple of benches outside and you could go there any time of the day—you didn't know who would be there—and have a good conversation, people freestyling, B-boys and B-girls. When that store shut down, things kinda changed. It shifted the focus to nightclubs, lots of independent shows. We brought a lot of people to Vancouver to record and then do a show while they were here: Del, Aceyalone, whoever."

Also on the road was Rob the Viking, working the merch booth and eventually—after Science couldn't do a U.S. tour—behind the decks. Rob grew up on Gabriola Island, where Madchild's father was living at the time. During a visit, Madchild heard about the hot young producer who was also a skateboarder and former metalhead turned hip-hop fan. Rob was about to move to Vancouver to study audio engineering. The Swollen Member offered him a rented room in his house and distracted him from school by putting him to work on other Battle Axe artists, like Code Name: Scorpion (Prevail, Moka Only and Abstract Rude from L.A.).

As Rob became more involved, so did Moka Only—who put out no fewer than 10 albums between 1995 and 2000, followed by five in 2001 alone. The guy had a few things going on. Nonetheless, joining his old friends seemed like a worthy distraction as their star began to rise. In addition to rapping, he provided melodic hooks for new songs like "Fuel Injected."

That song, which samples the same 1972 Giorgio Moroder organ hook used in DJ Shadow's "Organ Donor," was the lead single from *Bad Dreams*, released in November 2001. Thanks in large part to MuchMusic play, it climbed the charts and *Bad Dreams* went platinum, the first Canadian hip-hop record to do so since Snow almost 10 years earlier. Nettwerk's marketing power and Sony's distribution were kicking in. "We went from selling CDs and T-shirts outta the trunk of Madchild's Jetta and a shoebox bank account," says Prevail, "to having cardboard cut-outs in record stores."

"We didn't really tour in the States or internationally once we had big Canadian success," says Rob, although when they did they could fill venues anywhere from 300 to 1,500 capacity. "We opened up shows for Black Eyed Peas in the States and

Australia, which were huge. When we were doing our own shows in Australia, they'd be super packed, 1,000 people. The middle and western states were incredible: Colorado, all over and up and down the coast. Coming off the success in Canada and the connection with snowboarding and skateboarding, all those states ate it up. Prev and I would also pack our snowboards and hit the mountains before we played." They later recorded a live album in Boulder.

Bad Dreams won the band their second Juno, beating Kardinal's *Quest for Fire* and a Ghetto Concept posse cut with heavyweights Maestro, Kardinal, Snow and Rascalz' Red 1—which gave the central Canadian hip-hop legends more reason to be resentful.

While Toronto rap artists were struggling with major label deals, Swollen Members were doing it independently. A platinum record is a huge windfall for a label owned by the artist, even after the major distributor takes its cut. Nettwerk head Terry McBride raved to *Saturday Night* magazine that "Madchild is still learning the rules, but he's already breaking them." It was meant as a compliment at the time; McBride soon changed his tune. Battle Axe was successful enough that they opened an office on Granville Street and hired staff.

B-sides and other tracks were compiled for 2002's *Monsters in the Closet*, which went gold on the strength of the new song "Breath," featuring Prevail's old friend Nelly Furtado—herself riding high off the multimillion-selling success of her 2000 debut, *Whoa, Nelly!* In the video, she plays a vampire who imprisons the band. *Monsters* won the Members their third rap Juno in a row, this time beating k-os's *Exit* and Rascalz' *Reloaded*. The video for "Breath" was directed by Todd McFarlane, the Calgary creator of *Spawn*, one of the bestselling superhero comics of the '90s. McFarlane also did the artwork for the next Swollen Members album, *Heavy*. By that point the group had peaked—though they didn't know it yet.

FOR KARDINAL OFFISHALL, signing with an American label was a no-brainer. He'd had discussions with all the Canadian labels and the highest offer was a $60,000 deal. American labels offered him 10 times that.

A key connection was made while on tour in New York City with Choclair. The two of them appeared on Hot 97's groundbreaking *Stretch Armstrong and Bobbito Show*, which had started at Columbia University and is credited with launching Wu-Tang Clan, Fugees and countless others. On the hosts' recommendation, Kardinal was invited to join a European tour with the Roots and Dilated Peoples. That got the attention of the Roots' label, MCA, who offered to sign him after the release of the *Husslin'* EP on Sol Guy's Figure IV Entertainment. *Husslin'* featured not just the title track, with a video shot in front of the CN Tower, but

"Mic T.H.U.G.S." and "U R Ghetto When," all of which reappeared on Kardinal's MCA debut, 2001's *Quest for Fire: Firestarter Vol. 1* (as did earlier single "On wid da Show"). MCA seemed like a good bet: they had the Roots, Common and Mos Def. At a time when most new rappers needed some kind of co-sign from an established player, Kardinal had a clear agenda.

"I purposely didn't want to put many collaborations on the album," he told *HipHopCanada*'s Jesse Plunkett. Other than Sean Paul, "Every cat is from Toronto. I'm trying to let people hear what's coming from Toronto. I wanted to rep my crew and my city with the album. It really is time for us to rep where we are from. We give ourselves the ability to put our city on the map." That thinking led to the album's key single: the most Toronto song imaginable and the one that made Kardinal Offishall's career. It was called "BaKardi Slang," a play on both his name and a popular Bermudan rum brand—which the rapper claims he doesn't drink because as a Jamaican he prefers overproof.

"You go to New York and they talk about every borough: Brooklyn, Manhattan, blah, blah, blah," Kardinal told Anupa Mistry. "Never did anybody ever, ever say Toronto. For me, at that time, I was arrogant and probably crazy enough to think at some point in time, I'm going to do some shit where people are going to yell out Toronto. When I made 'BaKardi Slang,' every single thing about the intent of that record was to change the way that people thought about the city that I came from, and ultimately my country. That's literally why I wrote the hook, 'Everybody knows it's the T dot,' cause I wanted everybody to yell that out whenever they heard that song." The lyrics are a litany of regional linguistic quirks, defined by Toronto's Caribbean culture, distinct from African-American slang. It's "Northern Touch" on steroids.

"'BaKardi Slang' was one of the first rap records to explicitly sum up a tiny bit of what it meant to be young, Black and Torontonian in the early 2000s," says Toronto radio producer Tyrone Callender. "In the process, it became a bona fide banger in the local clubs. I mean, as a DJ back then, I clearly remember playing 'BaKardi Slang' and it being the first time I found myself having to rewind a Toronto hip-hop record and play it again."

As Torontocentric as it was, "BaKardi Slang" had wide resonance across the diaspora. "I didn't realize how powerful the song was until we went into every city across America," he told Mistry. "All of the Caribbean people would come out of the woodwork saying, 'Yo, I used to get chased and beat up after school for having an accent, and now because of this song people finally know who I am.' It changed a lot of lives. It was really an incredible thing to witness first-hand across America."

The first time Kardinal heard the beat, he was driving with Solitair to Buffalo to do some cross-border shopping. Solitair put on a tape of new beats. When the one that would become "BaKardi Slang" dropped, Kardinal told him to turn around and drive straight to a studio so they could record it. Others had a similar reaction once it was out in the world. While in New York City on tour, Kardinal got a call.

"Yo, Kardi!"

"Who's this?"

"Yo, it's *DJ KHALED*. Yo, I got Bounty Killer on the phone."

The Jamaican dancehall star of the '90s was hot off his top five collaboration with No Doubt, "Hey Baby." He loved "BaKardi Slang" and wanted to "take it to the next level," he told the Toronto MC. They went to a New York studio to do a remix, where Bounty Killer freestyled for an hour. Later that year, the two MCs were performing at a Jamaican festival in front of 30,000 people, where the native star told the crowd, "I want you guys to show love to Kardinal because he is of Jamaican parentage, which means we own a percentage." Back in the U.S., MCA Records just heard the word *Jamaican* and assumed Kardinal should be touring with Shaggy, which, at their behest, he did—opening an arena tour in the U.S. Not the worst gig in the world, but not his ideal audience. Certainly better than in Canada, where he was put on a MuchMusic "Loud" tour featuring rock bands Econoline Crush and headliner Godsmack.

The success of "BaKardi Slang" convinced MCA to give Kardinal a six-figure budget for the next single. "Ol' Time Killin'" featured Jully Black and Scarborough crew Monolith, produced by Mr. Attic of Da Grassroots. (The rest of *Quest for Fire* was produced by Kardinal, Solitair and Tara Chase.) Directed by Little X, the video got all kinds of attention from Timbaland, Missy Elliott and the rest of the who's who of innovative commercial hip-hop in the early 2000s. Busta Rhymes demanded to be on a remix. Pharrell Williams wanted Kardinal on a remix for "Grindin'," the hit single by his hot new act, the Clipse; also on the Clipse remix was Sean Paul, whose career Kardinal had helped launch with "Money Jane" two years earlier. They performed "Grindin'" together at the 2002 Mixshow Power Summit, a CMJ-type event for urban radio in the U.S.

A more unusual nod came from the Scottish pop band Texas, who reached out to Kardinal to rap on their 2003 single "Carnival Girl." He was ready to dismiss the left-field offer until he learned it came with a 15,000 pound sterling paycheque ($37,500 Canadian). "Carnival Girl" was a top 10 U.K. hit, charting also in Denmark and Spain; the album went gold in Britain. He performed with them on *Top of the Pops*.

Kardinal had gone from an underground Toronto crew to enrapturing the U.S. hip-hop elite and capturing international airwaves. And he did it by being true to himself—and his hometown.

K-OS COULD NEVER DO ANYTHING that wasn't true to himself. It's why he has wrestled with being in the music industry ever since his first video hit, back in 1995. It's why he waited seven years after that to put out his debut. It's why he's always dodged left when told to go right. It's why after Lauryn Hill and before the ubiquity of Auto-Tune, k-os was known as one of the only performers equally skilled at rapping and singing—despite the revisionist history of Drake fans. It's why he's a Toronto rapper who got his biggest boost in Vancouver, why he's a huge fan of early '90s Native Tongues rap who also happens to perform with flamenco guitar, tabla and an orchestra. It's why he was just as likely to be seen chumming around with Sam Roberts, Broken Social Scene and Metric as he was the Rascalz, Saukrates or Kardinal.

K-os has a reputation in the industry as a contrarian who constantly shoots himself in the foot. And yet in the pre-Drake landscape, he was the only Canadian rapper to have two platinum albums and several bona fide pop hits that still get played in grocery stores. Not bad for a guy who called his first album *Exit*—and meant it.

KEVIN BRERETON SPENT his childhood moving back and forth between Trinidad and Whitby, Ontario, a city east of Toronto. When he arrived back in Canada for good to attend high school, he was a top 40 kid who missed out on the ascent of hip-hop. Friends got him into rap, inviting him to sing hooks while they freestyled. Eventually he joined their rap ciphers. His parents, Jehovah's Witnesses, were not impressed; his father told him he wasn't welcome at home if he chose a career in music.

"My dad was a minister," he told the *Toronto Star*'s Ben Rayner, "and, until I was 17, my life was me going, 'Okay, Dad, can I go outside now? Genesis, Exodus, Leviticus, Numbers, First King, Second King . . .' My life was highly based on trading off pleasures for my knowledge of the Bible, and so that's what my whole rap career has been. It's been, like, okay, I'll rap and I'll make a dope beat, but the content has gotta say something. I've gotta mean something."

Brereton went to Carleton University in Ottawa, where he recorded a track called "Musical Essence." It was the first beat he'd ever made himself. After transferring to York University in Toronto, he discovered that there were VideoFACT grants to be had; MuchMusic was actively funding new hip-hop artists to play on the station, whether or not there was physical product to push. He applied and got one. The "Musical Essence" video went into rotation—and won the MMVA in 1995 for Best Rap Video.

Presenting the award was John Salley, a championship NBA player who'd just joined the brand-new Toronto Raptors. Salley had a side hustle in artist management and took on k-os as a client. He introduced the rapper to Raphael Saadiq, who was then transitioning from multiplatinum R&B group Tony! Toni! Toné! into production. They started work on an album called *Missing Links*, and had a label deal with BMG before corporate restructuring shelved it in 1996.

K-os was somewhat relieved. He laid low for the next three years, staying away from the industry while studying world religions. "More than anything," he told *Exclaim!*'s Del Cowie, "I started to get in touch with what I really wanted to do, not what I was supposed to do." A show by the Roots at Toronto's Opera House was a life-changing moment: he knew he wanted to only ever play with a live band after that.

Several recording projects went nowhere. "There were several completed records," he told *Now*'s Matt Galloway. "But those records were pretentious and derivative. All I had were my influences—A Tribe Called Quest, the Fugees, the whole Native Tongues vibe—and I was still trying to figure out who I was. Can I sing and rap in hip-hop? Is that allowed? Those were the things I was trying to figure out. People sabotage themselves when they're not ready. I wasn't interested in that. Everything changed in 1996 when I bought an acoustic guitar. I wrote the song 'Heaven Only Knows' and realized that there's a beat inside every instrument."

By 1999, he was up for some guest spots. He appeared with Thrust on "Eternal," a track on Da Grassroots' underground favourite *Passage through Time*. Red 1 of the Rascalz reached out and invited him to Vancouver. Their manager, Sol Guy, soon took him on. He appeared on the crew's 1999 album *Global Warning*, rapping on the single "Top of the World." The track also featured Jamaican reggae legend Barrington Levy; both starred in the video.

But it was another Vancouver group that he fell in love with, a funk band called Namedropper. He wrote and recorded 11 tracks with that group's guitarist, Russ Klyne, and recruited them to back him at a 1999 NXNE showcase, where he proved he could do much more than just rap. The show ended with the band jamming and the rapper head-banging enthusiastically, which caught the eye of the rock-oriented record execs. Linda Noelle Bush at Universal Publishing signed him a deal, which in turn led to an offer from Capitol in the U.S., who saw k-os as a male Lauryn Hill.

"I can't deny who I am," he told Galloway. "I'm from Whitby, Ontario. I was one of three Black people in my high school. My best friend had a U2 jacket. When he used to come to my house to eat roti, I'd play him [early hip-hop hit] 'Jam on It' and he'd play me Echo and the Bunnymen and Siouxsie and the Banshees. It was weird, but as long as there was a melody, I could get on it. Yeah, I'm a dark-skinned Black man whose parents are from Trinidad and Tobago, but I'm also a kid from Whitby who used to listen to CFNY, and to deny that isn't knowledge of self." His stage name, k-os, is an acronym for "knowledge of self."

Exit was released in March 2002. *Exclaim!* put him on the cover—after some negotiation. The rapper wanted to obscure his face with the cover of his favourite philosophical text by Jiddu Krishnamurti, to the point where the photographer didn't have anything usable from the shoot. The magazine went instead with an official press shot, which was blurry at best. k-os was already telling people that his first album would also be his last, that the very idea of being a public figure was nothing more than an ego trip best avoided. Only a Canadian rapper would write in the liner notes of his debut album, "I must take this time to apologize for the 'ego.'"

His American label didn't know what to do with a rapper who also dabbled in Britpop balladry and toured with an acoustic guitarist and a tabla player. Musical choices aside, it didn't really help that, on much of *Exit*, k-os comes off like a crotchety grump, belittling modern-day hip-hop for not being more like his early '90s inspirations. At times, he could be as insufferable as any indie rock snob picking fights about Pavement versus the Smashing Pumpkins. That said, it's more than clear that the many different musical directions in which he was being pulled were one small step away from coalescing. The single "Heaven Only Knows" was one hint: it successfully shifts from jazz guitar to hip-hop to reggae in the space of three minutes.

Within a year, EMI Canada took over his Capitol U.S. contract, signing him with U.S. affiliate Astralwerks for the rest of the world. That label's flagship act was the Chemical Brothers, who had k-os on their 2003 single "Get Yourself High." He changed management, signing on with Nelly Furtado's team. *Exit* was declared Best International Album by hip-hop bible *The Source*. It sold a modest 40,000 copies internationally, 17,000 of those at home. Missy Elliott borrowed from "Superstarr" for an interlude in the video mix of her hit single "I'm Really Hot."

Deciding he didn't want to exit just yet, k-os threw himself into *Joyful Rebellion*. The album's August 2004 release was preceded by "B-Boy Stance," a straight-up hip-hop song based around the "Funky Drummer" beat—which had been a tired cliché for at least 12 years. But knowing that he was about to push harder in a pop direction, k-os wanted to signal his old-school bona fides. The album also featured hip-hop tracks like "Neutroniks," which had more in common with the innovations of Madlib. *Joyful Rebellion* featured an acoustic ballad ("Hallelujah"—no, not that one), a Sam Roberts collaboration ("Dirty Water"), a Michael Jackson homage ("Man I Used to Be") and the song that became his calling card, "Crabbuckit." The latter, with its upright bass played by Maury LaFoy of Starling, as well as a sax solo, was heavily influenced by the Cure's "Lovecats"—something almost every review took pains to point out. Likewise, to the entirely frivolous delight of rock critics unsure how to write about hip-hop, the song also included a shout-out to the Tragically Hip's "Ahead by a Century." Maybe that invocation was a good omen: "Crabbuckit" became a massive hit, fuelling the album to gold status within three months and platinum in six. The song is now considered to be as Canadian as Anne Murray's "Snowbird."

K-os had become a pop star, selling more records than Kardinal and receiving more radio play than Swollen Members. The guy who seemed to want it least ended up on top.

———

SAUKRATES, THE FIRST TORONTO MC from the Circle to get a major label deal, was also the first to get a *second* major label deal: this time with legendary hip-hop label Def Jam, which was entering a second golden age with the monstrous success of Jay-Z.

After the indie success of *The Underground Tapes* in 1999, Saukrates spent more time in New York City, crashing on the couch of Little X. The Toronto director was working with hip-hop's biggest video director, Hype Williams, and directing clips for DMX's "What's My Name" and Mystikal's "Shake Ya Azz." One of X's roommates worked at Def Jam as an A&R assistant and fell in love with *The Underground Tapes*. At the Def Jam office, he'd blast it all day: not trying to impress anyone, just to improve his workday. One day Redman's manager heard through the wall and busted into the assistant's office.

"What the fuck was that?"

"It's this kid from Toronto, Saukrates."

"Is he signed?"

"Nope."

"Let's do it."

"That was a Friday," recalls Saukrates, "and then the album got into [Def Jam president] Kevin Liles's hands the same day. We knew a lady who was an admin assistant there, and she said Kevin blocked his whole day off, cancelled all meetings and was blasting the CD. I was on a plane on Monday. It wasn't whether or not I was *going* to get signed to Def Jam, it was *how*: whether through Red's manager, who found it first, or through Redman, or directly to Def Jam." Saukrates was signed to Gilla House, Redman's imprint inside Def Jam.

The Toronto rapper toured with Redman and Method Man and rapped with them on "Enjoy da Ride," from Redman's 2001 *Malpractice* album. He appeared on the soundtrack to their 2001 film, *How High*. A solo single, "Comin' Up," was meant to promote Saukrates's Def Jam debut, *Bad Addiction*. But it was not to be.

It was a tumultuous time at Def Jam. One of its subsidiaries, Murder Inc., was having assets seized as part of a federal investigation into money laundering. At the same time, Jay-Z's Roc-A-Fella imprint was wildly successful, taking up most of Def Jam's resources. "Even Red and Meth had their own complaints, because they couldn't get anything out; those two subsidiaries ate up all the attention," says Saukrates. "So imagine: if Red and Meth can't get attention, I still have to take a number and wait in line after them. That went on for a few years. It was early 2004 when I asked to be let go. I left with my masters and started over again."

Kardinal Offishall was going through something similar with MCA in L.A., as was Jully Black. Saukrates contributed to her album *I Travelled*, which was ultimately canned and buried by MCA. "Attention goes to the big dogs," says Saukrates, "and when you're trying to break through, the mistake you can make is to assume the label will do things for you. A lot of the people getting attention were hustling at radio and doing it themselves, and then the label turns around and says, 'Why didn't we know about this?' It's knowing how the market works. Coming in as Canadians, we had to learn how they do it there, because we've been used to doing it ourselves for so long. Sometimes it works, sometimes it doesn't."

Back home, Saukrates shifted his attention to a new project. Big Black Lincoln was a funk band he formed with four other producers: Ro Dolla from the Circle, T.R.A.C.K.S. from IRS, Shakari Nyte and BrassMunk's Agile. "I had a whole bunch of music I was working on, honing my craft on the singing side," he says. "I realized I couldn't release it under the Saukrates brand, because people only wanted to hear me rap over street shit. This was about the funk. All five could make beats; me, T.R.A.C.K.S. and Shakari did all the singing. We wrote it all together. It was fun to work with guys with such a high level of talent, and I could just let loose."

Two singles were released on Saukrates's Capitol Hill Music in 2004: the bumping "Pimpin' Life" and the ballad "All of You." "The day 'All of You' came out," says Saukrates, "it got played on Flow [93.5 in Toronto]. Kardi called me and he was like, 'Yo, I didn't know who the hell it was. Is this Luther Vandross?' It was showing Toronto, the country and the world that rappers can do it: we can sing our asses off. Me and k-os bore that torch. It helped propel the next generation to have that conversation. Drake used to hang out in the studio with me and would hear how things were coming together. I introduced him to [producer Noah] '40'

[Shebib]. When [Drake] decided to try singing, he put it on his MySpace space, and we were like, 'That's it! You got it. You can do both.' He was shy at first, just like we all were."

Almost as if Saukrates had a target on his back, Big Black Lincoln was yet another victim of corporate circumstance. "We were signed to Sony [Canada]; Denise Donlon was president at the time," he says. "We had all the backing we needed. All the budgets we submitted were multiplied by three or four times. Everything was perfect. Then in October of that year, 2004, Sony and BMG merged. Denise Donlon was out. We sat for a year, with nothing. Jonathan Ramos, a good friend of ours, was our point person there, but he didn't have any power. All he could say was, 'Let's wait, hold on,' while they were rebuilding the amalgamated label. So we asked to leave and landed [distribution] at Maple, with no marketing or promotional budget. Nothing. Just a press-and-distribute [deal]. Which wasn't enough to carry a five-man group, a full band, to the top."

The album got strong reviews when it came out in 2006. "The album is sonically restless," wrote Del Cowie in *Exclaim!*, "nailing takes on plaintive down-home soul, nocturnal house, sticky funk and esoteric electronica with equally accomplished aplomb, paying homage to past masters yet shrewdly pointing to the future while avoiding comfortable genre tags." Shortly after it came out, Nelly Furtado tapped Saukrates to join her live band, in part as a surrogate for Timbaland, who had produced her smash hit album *Loose*. Agile went back to BrassMunk and started working with hot new Toronto MC King Reign. Ro Dolla continued to work with Kardinal. Big Black Lincoln "fizzled out," says Saukrates. "They told me they couldn't do it without me. It was hard to run the '90s Bulls without Michael Jordan."

SAUKRATES AND JULLY BLACK weren't the only ones with a buried album. Kardinal Offishall was poised to capitalize on the success of "BaKardi Slang" and "Ol' Time Killin'" with *Quest for Fire: Vol. 2*. He had recorded collaborations with the two hottest producers of the day: Timbaland and the Neptunes. There was even a video shot for the Neptunes track, "Belly Dancer."

MCA, which once was nicknamed "Music Cemetery of America," was merged with Geffen under the Universal umbrella in 2003. Most rap acts not associated with 50 Cent or Eminem were dropped. *Quest for Fire: Vol. 2* sat in limbo for a year, before Kardinal asked to be released from his contract. His New York City lawyer, whom he'd had since 1998 and who now represented Eminem and others, got him out of the deal. He quickly put out a mixtape, *Kill Bloodclott Bill: Volume 1*, a riff on the recent Tarantino movies, the metaphor directed at his ex-label.

He wasn't down and out, however. His friend DJ Cipha Sounds, from New York City's Hot 97 who'd recently joined Jay-Z's management team, called Kardinal about a hot new teenage singer the label had found in Bermuda. They were putting together a demo and wanted the Torontonian to rap on the track "Here We Go." The singer was Rihanna. Her song with Kardinal ended up an album cut, not a single, but she did go to Toronto to shoot the video for "Pon de Replay" with Little X, at the restaurant Avocado; Kardinal is prominent in the background. "Nowadays people really understand how Toronto is a big West Indian town, but back then it wasn't so well known," says Little X. "I wanted to put that flavour around her with kids who came from the culture and understood it."

"Pon de Replay" came out in May 2005. By then, Kardinal had signed a deal with EMI Canada to put out *Fire and Glory*, which had some tracks from the aborted MCA album, including songs with Busta Rhymes, dancehall star Vybz Kartel and U.K. singer Estelle. But it didn't include the Neptunes' "Belly Dancer," which Kardinal claims to never have liked, or the Timbaland track.

"The Timbaland and Kardinal song does exist and it did cost a house to produce the song," he told Cowie. "Mind you, it wasn't directly out of my pocket—he got a whole heap of money. But I made a conscious decision not to put that on the album. Not 'cause the song wasn't sick, but I don't believe that the music I create or people that I work with are any less talented than Timbaland. They just haven't had as much opportunity and maybe don't have the light. A lot of these cats have incredible beats, incredible. The only difference between them and other producers is the opportunity."

Three months before the album came out, Kardinal played the Getting Up Festival in Toronto, headlined by Nas, Kanye West, Mos Def and more; he and the Rascalz were the only Canadians on the bill. Midway through his set, he sat down with an acoustic guitar and told the crowd, "They say I have to play an instrument to sell some records." He then proceeded to play it badly, before dramatically smashing the guitar on stage. In a review of the festival, a *Now* writer assumed the stunt was a dig at k-os, who had been performing beside a guitarist for the past three years. It's not an unfair assumption: k-os had become the biggest rap star in the country, while Kardinal had been caught in label limbo and was far down the bill at a festival populated by American acts. But it would also have been odd, seeing as how Kardinal employed Russ Klyne, k-os's guitarist, to play on *Fire and Glory*.

Nonetheless, k-os read the *Now* review and fired back in the letters section the next week. "Children like Kardinal are living in a dream world," he wrote, "because the fact is he is not American and no matter how many cameos he does, America loves its own."

In an *Exclaim!* cover story that November, Kardinal said, "It's one of those things where people who don't know him will be like, 'Oh my gosh,' but I know him and I know that was said out of him being defensive. The comments about me trying to be American? Anybody with sense knows that's the antithesis of what I stand for. My whole thing is not to say that k-os is a joke or that what he's doing is a joke—because k-os runs the country right now . . . [But] the scene doesn't allow for there to be more than one chosen person at a time. All the other struggling domestic urban artists are like, 'Boy! How come this guy is the only one that gets to do this?' It creates hard feelings and it makes the scene hard for everybody to get along. They might feel that 'Oh [Kardinal's] running things,' making it hard for them to get up, or k-os is doing his thing so nobody can get up. They still like to throw you peanuts and want you to wear that Canadian flag, but the Canadian flag is only giving you lunch money. It's not just with rap—it's with the movie business, it's with anything that comes out of here."

K-os, like Kardinal, didn't like anyone telling him what he should sound like. He wanted to break the mould of what kind of music Caribbean-Canadian people were "supposed" to make, just as Kardinal wanted to break the mould of what music Canadians were "supposed" to make. "Anytime someone tells you that you have to be like somebody else, you automatically feel subjugated," k-os told the CBC's *This Is Not a Drake Podcast.* "You also feel less intelligent because you feel like what you're bringing to the table isn't good enough, especially when you're young and you're all about creating your own identity. So, yeah, I understand that. But I had Maestro and Michie Mee and Saukrates and all these people to kind of outdo. Like, imagine being around Saukrates. No one talks about that. They just talk about the arrival of this record *Joyful Rebellion.* But I actually had the same reaction that they had with the smashing of the guitar. Why do I have to be like Sauks, why do I have to be like Jelleestone, why do I have to be like Ghetto Concept, why do I have to be like the Rascalz? I just dealt with it by being myself."

Fire and Glory came and went. K-os's next album, *Atlantis: Hymns for Disco,* released a year later, debuted at No. 2 on the Canadian charts and went platinum. Kardinal's stock was arguably low. But he was still willing to take a gamble by turning down the biggest name in hip-hop: Jay-Z. It paid off.

WORKING WITH THE biggest pop hitmakers of 2003 was a gamble that did not pay off for Swollen Members. The production team known as the Matrix were hot off the runaway success of Avril Lavigne, another Nettwerk management client, and were working with Hilary Duff and Britney Spears when Swollen Members showed up in L.A.

The hook-up came via Virgin Records, who had flown the Vancouver rap crew down to L.A., gave them per diems, and paid rent for two apartments in Venice Beach: one for Madchild and Rob the Viking, where they set up a small studio, and one for Prevail and Moka Only, where the two MCs had separate suites. The only stipulation Virgin gave the band was that they couldn't sample anything. "We hadn't done that before," says Prevail. "We were old-school. We'd occasionally get session guys to play guitar, cello, whatever. But most of it was chopped and sampled. So here we are, signed to a big record deal, with a chance to make a huge impact, but we have to go back to the drawing board on the production side. [Dilated Peoples'] Evidence lived around the corner from us in Venice Beach. We're all within three blocks of each other. Rob had just started learning how to play more proficiently, and Evidence had a huge cache of live instrumentation he could access in L.A.; he knew a bunch of players. They started working on an album we weren't going to release, but just to see if we can actually make music without sampling. Everlast was very helpful. It was very organic.

"At the same time, we were working on the record for Virgin with the Matrix, who were awesome people, super talented. I was a bit more hardcore about wanting to succeed on our own terms. The Matrix, as talented as they were, approached it with quite a bit more pop appeal than what I was used to, and I was trying to wrap my head around it. There were days when the FedEx arrived and they'd ask me to grab it and it's yet another triple diamond record: 'Oh yeah, just put that in the hallway.' They had a hallway longer than my apartment with every platinum, gold, diamond record you can imagine. The top 10 back then usually had three or four Matrix productions. Absolute monsters. But we just couldn't get the one song we needed to propel us to the next level."

Virgin dropped them. Feeling flaccid, Swollen Members retreated back to Canada. To maintain the illusion of momentum, they released the tracks produced primarily by Rob, as 2003's *Heavy*. "The first week that record came out was disappointing, not what we expected," says Rob. "It was also a transitional period: album sales were deteriorating in general. We were still riding a wave of success on radio and video, and 'Watch This' was one of our most played singles, but the album only did okay. We had a tour in Australia in 2004, and Moka didn't want to go. At this point, creative differences were building up."

Moka Only split to go back to his solo career. Constant touring and being one of four minds in a band was not where he wanted to be. Instead, he put out 27 (not a typo) more records before the decade was through. His former bandmates didn't take it well. "I got a little dark," says Prevail. "I was drinking a bottle of vodka for breakfast for a month straight—not the best way to deal with it. Mad fell into a drug addiction. Things started to spiral downwards shortly after we got home. We all processed it in different ways."

"I was cocky, I was young, I was arrogant," Madchild told *Vice*. "I got introduced to Hells Angels. I always loved gangster movies. As a smaller dude, I always aligned myself with the tough guy. I have absolutely nothing bad to say about the guys—they're great guys—but it was a bad lifestyle choice for myself, the group and the label. And unfortunately, having millions of dollars from nothing, and having jewellery and cars and girls in a very short period of time and at a young age, I was looking for the next thing, and the next thing unfortunately turned into mansion parties and drugs."

"Watch This" was the first single and video. Nettwerk watched it, and quickly dropped them. Madchild was spending a lot of time in Kelowna with well-known Hells Angels—some of whom were in the video. Even for the label founded on Skinny Puppy, it was a bridge too far. "I was a little bummed out with that," Madchild told *Exclaim!*'s Andrea Woo, "because we're supposed to be living in a free country. I should be able to hang out with who I want to. It's not like I was bringing [any Hells Angels] to the [Nettwerk] office, or to any functions."

Swollen Members were determined to get back on track after the disappointment of *Heavy* and the departure of Moka Only. They spent two years making 2006's *Black Magic*, a back-to-basics record, their best since *Balance*, with real fire behind it. "Everyone was angry—which, for Swollen, is a really good place for us to be," says Prevail. "We operate the best when we're a bit jaded. That was a great comeback. It re-engaged the fans, it reinvigorated us, it got us back to what we did best: nasty underground stuff. I need mud, blood and rust once in a while." It sold well enough and got the band their fourth Juno—albeit in a fairly non-competitive year.

Behind the scenes, however, Madchild was spiralling out of control. Near the beginning of the recording process, he began a descent into opiates. It started with a Percocet at a party, which he thought was innocent enough—a painkiller, not like the heroin that was more than evident on East Hastings Street. "I'd seen *Basketball Diaries*, I'd seen *Trainspotting*," he told the *Vancouver Sun*'s Andrew McCredie. "That wasn't going to happen to me. We used to drink before shows, but I never even had a beer in my fridge back then. I tried this or that, and it just wasn't that interesting to me. I was young and single doing shows, with some financial success. I didn't need drugs or anything like that to make it any better." But he was soon taking 20 Percocets a day, whether there was a party going on or not. "Then one day someone said, 'You know, that stuff is just synthetic heroin.' I was like 'What?!' I had no idea. So I tried to get off them. I had my first experience of being dope sick. Worst feeling you can ever imagine in your life." He tried to kick them during a vacation in Dominican Republic, but upon return starting taking OxyContin, which at least didn't make him puffy. It didn't help that the rapper with the Cowboy Junkies' lyric "misguided angel" tattooed across his upper chest was also barred from entering the U.S. for three years, for reasons the band has never disclosed.

After four years of whirlwind activity, they were forced to take a break. Madchild split town. "I moved to Kelowna because I knew I could get away from my family and everyone and get deep into my addiction," he told McCredie. "At that point, I was a junkie. I was a walking zombie. I was doing 20 OxyContin 80s a day by the end of my addiction. I was 55 pounds overweight; my arm was numb. I'd look in the mirror and start crying at what I saw."

The indie rap mogul who owned 11 properties had to start selling them off to support his habit and his lifestyle. In 2007, a SWAT team surrounded his house, looking for a gang member. By 2009 he'd burned through $3.5 million and was a step away from homelessness. "It was basically time to save my life," Madchild told *Vice*. "And the tough thing about that is you don't just put your own life on hold, you put the group's life on hold, because I'm this drooling zombie and they're like, 'Let's go do this tour,' and I don't show up. I was a mess."

Prevail and Rob claimed they didn't know about it until about a year into the addiction. "As a friend and a brother and teammate and collaborator, it was such a tough thing to see, and a tough thing to stop," says Prevail. "There were times when Rob and I would do our best to do an intervention. But it's easy [for an addict] to lock the door and not let people help. The person has to really want it themselves. There's only so much exterior encouragement and support you can give; it still needs to be there, but that individual needs to want it for themselves."

Swollen Members made another record with Madchild before he finally sought help. *Armed to the Teeth*, a 2009 release, was decidedly darker and gangster-oriented than anything they'd done before. Prevail and Rob were both living in Madchild's house from 2006 to 2008. "The darkest two years of my life—of all of our lives," says Rob. "It was a really negative experience. There is a darkness about the place, and the style of music we were making was outside of what we were about. No slight against the guys we were hanging out with at the time, but it didn't seem right for our music. [Madchild] was really messed up, and lots of drama. I didn't like being in Kelowna, stuck in a place in the country, and I didn't have a car at the time. The whole thing was bad. Also, at that time, my partner was pregnant, and for most of her pregnancy I was back and forth between Vancouver and Kelowna. When my daughter was born, I was like, 'I'm not going back.'"

It was while mixing and mastering *Armed to the Teeth* that Madchild agreed to go to rehab. "He knew that shows were coming up, and he took the opportunity to get sober," says Prevail. "If you asked me 20 years ago if a guy called Madchild was going to have openness and vulnerability as their strong suit, I'd probably have said no. But he knew that if he didn't [sober up] he would die. And he knew he wasn't the only one struggling, so it was important to him to let people know about the dangers of doing something recreationally and how it can take hold so quickly. He's helped a lot of people, which I think is amazing and necessary—showing that vulnerability. I was very proud of him." Swollen Members put out three more records in the 2010s, before Madchild focused on a solo career, while Prevail and Rob started a live band, XL, with a Cuban trumpet player and a symphony flautist.

And the Toronto beef from long ago? Prevail insists there never really was one. "We were nervous, the first time we played Toronto," he says. "I'd battled Kardi in Vancouver at Richard's, and at that time we weren't on the best footing. I was nervous going to a city where he has crew, he's king. It's me, Madchild and Rob the Viking, three of the gentlest guys, and we were on high alert the whole time. As we started bumping into each other the next couple of months, while touring, we quelled our differences and realized we're happy and lucky to be Canadian MCs doing our thing. Now when we see each other, it's big hugs and high-fives."

KARDINAL WAS ALWAYS pegged to be the first Canadian MC to have an international hit—or, at least, the first since Snow. In 2008, it finally happened. But first he had to turn down Jay-Z.

The Canadian and American legends performed together at the 2006 Toronto Caribana festival. Game respects game: Jay-Z, who was then president of Def Jam, wanted to sign Kardinal to the label he'd founded in 1995, Roc-A-Fella, then part of Def Jam and riding high on the success of Kanye West. But Kardinal was cautious; he'd been burned by major label machinations before, and Roc-A-Fella was at a juncture point, with Jay-Z having returned from a short-lived retirement and Kanye being the main focus.

Meanwhile, Kardinal had been in discussions with the multimillion-selling Senegalese-American superstar Akon; he'd been invited to guest on a 2006 Akon track. The singer was about to launch his own label, KonVict, with three releases in 2008. One would be Kardinal Offishall's *Not 4 Sale*, featuring guest spots from the Clipse, Glenn Lewis, T-Pain and The-Dream.[2]

---

2   One track, "Nina," taps the same reggae sample Dream Warriors used on their hit "Ludi": Slim Smith and the Uniques' "My Conversation."

Not 4 Sale's lead single, "Dangerous," featuring Akon on the hook, was released in March 2008. It was the international hit Toronto hip-hop had been waiting for: it hit No. 3 in the U.S., top 10 in much of Europe and top 20 in the U.K. Kardinal performed on *The Tonight Show*. "Dangerous" was followed by "Numba 1 (Tide Is High)," in which Rihanna lifted the chorus of the reggae classic best known for its Blondie cover. It hit, yes, No. 1 on the German urban pop chart and was a top 10 radio hit in Israel. That same year, Kardinal appeared on a remix of "Just Dance" by another new Akon signing, Lady Gaga.

"Did I think that it would be 2008 that all this would be going on, as opposed to maybe 2004?" he said that year. "No. So to me, a couple weeks, couple months, couple years—the important thing was to try to execute what we have been trying to execute all along: to have an internationally successful project."

At the same time, Canadian response was . . . Canadian. "I literally was exploding around the entire planet except in my own country," he told the CBC. "I saw [Canada] have to play catch-up: 'Seems to be doing very well everywhere else, so I suppose we should probably support him now.' That hurt, because the first time I got signed to an American label, my first [single], the hook said, 'Everybody knows it's the T dot.' My whole narrative has been one that has taken my city and my country and put it on my shoulders. I endured ridicule for years. And then when we had this moment, we didn't even celebrate it here. Radio—I got a call from somebody saying, 'Hey, is "Dangerous" CanCon?' I was like, Why are you asking me if 'Dangerous' is CanCon?! *It's literally a number one hit around the world.* Are you telling me you're only going to play it if it's CanCon?!"

After all the independent hustle and Canadian industry insecurity and the major label drama, Canadian hip-hop had finally broken through. The year after "Dangerous," two more Toronto MCs blew up. K'naan, a Somali-Canadian MC who was discovered by Sol Guy, had an international anthem with "Waving Flag" in 2009. That same year, Drake released his third mixtape, *So Far Gone*, which was his first major step to becoming the biggest rapper in history. Kardinal had appeared on Drake's previous release, *Comeback Season*, in 2007. Kardinal's manager, Mr. Morgan, went on to run Drake's OVO Sound label. In 2013, after a chance meeting with Universal Canada CEO Randy Lennox at a Muskoka cottage party, Kardinal was hired by Universal as an A&R rep; in 2021, he became senior vice-president of A&R, all while continuing to perform and release his own music. The man who once ran the Circle was in the industry's inner circle.

"Now the kids have found a way to make it work worldwide," says Saukrates. "The building blocks were in place during the time we're talking about, that era, and gave the next generation courage and confidence to try."

"Honestly, when I go out [into the world], it's not for me to represent T dot," Kardinal told Anupa Mistry, "and I never look at it as me having the city on my back. I'm not thinking about what this shit means for our city. I'm thinking about the regular people in the barber's shop, or that I meet in the street or the clubs; that's where my influence comes from, that's where my energy derives from. That's why I never moved fully to the States. Even with the first deal, I had an apartment in New York that I used to use, but my vibe comes from here: the hate, the love, the energy, everything, the Taste of the Danforth, the Chinese New Year, the boat races, the Caribana—all of this is what made me think the way I think. That's why it's so simple to always go out and represent T dot. Anybody from this city can go out and say 'Toronto' and it's not going to be a new thing to people anymore. They'll go, 'Oh yeah, I know Toronto.' They're not going to know Toronto because of the Raptors; they're going to know because we have ill rappers, ill producers, ill directors. There are a lot of Canadians out there. We just have to further the cause and do our part."

CHAPTER 13
MUST YOU ALWAYS REMIND ME?

NICKELBACK

T ime to bring the elephant into the room: you can't talk about Canadian music in the 2000s without talking about Nickelback. *Billboard* declared them the band of that decade; Destiny's Child had to take a back seat to the Albertan boys who sold more records in the U.S. and boasted the top rock song of the decade, "How You Remind Me."

It's no secret that most music critics would rather not think about Nickelback at all. They're a match made in hell of Def Leppard, Creed and Garth Brooks. Chad Kroeger sings like a constipated Fort McMurray roughneck. Their cruellest detractors will note that breakthrough blockbuster *Silver Side Up* was released on September 11, 2001—make of that what you will.

Nickelback was also ubiquitous, ruling North American radio for a full decade. Historians can spend all the time they want writing about Arcade Fire, the Strokes and the White Stripes, but Nickelback was the actual sound of rock music in the 2000s. They sold more than 40 million records worldwide.

"People shit on Nickelback for their sound and their look," says Danko Jones, whose social connections straddle hard rock and indie rock. "I get it. I'd be on that side, too, if I didn't know them behind the scenes. I was definitely jealous, because they were making money hand over fist. But so what? So they don't play the three chords in the way you like to hear, and the singer doesn't look the way you want them to look. But I've been on the receiving end of people not liking the way I look and people hating our band because of it. I can totally empathize with Nickelback. They became such a bad name to utter, at which point the punk rock side of me says, 'Well, now I like them. Do you hate them because of the music? Or do you hate them because you're supposed to hate them and the music isn't even a factor?'"

"Nickelback are all old-school Alberta people," says country singer Corb Lund, who grew up in southern Alberta not far from Nickelback's hometown of Hanna. "My dad rodeoed with the guitar player's family." Chad Kroeger was a fan of Lund's first band, the Smalls. Both bands played more than their share of small Albertan and B.C. towns in the late '90s. "When Nickelback got big, Chad offered to remix one of our tunes, at a time when everything he was touching turned to gold," says Lund. "He did a remix and it didn't agree with us, so nothing ever came of it." The Smalls always put their live show first; not that Nickelback didn't, but Kroeger always had his eyes on bigger prizes. "Our indie hustle was booking tours," says Lund, "and Chad's hustle, from what I've heard, is that he paid super close attention to radio programming people, which for his style of music makes sense. It'd be pointless for the Smalls to do that. He was very proactive, and more power to him."

Nickelback invested some of their fortune in 604 Records, which had hits right out the gate with Theory of a Deadman and Thornley, both of which were not unlike Nickelback: highly successful, critical kryptonite and subject to ridicule. Not everything on the label sounded like Nickelback. The five women who played dour new wave in the Organ made them odd labelmates—as was Carly Rae Jepsen, who delivered the label's biggest hit in 2012. The Organ had to answer questions about their Nickelback connection in just about every interview they ever did, confirming outsiders' opinions that maybe everyone in Canada, no matter how different, actually did know each other.

In 2006, Danko Jones accepted an opening slot with Nickelback on an arena tour of Canada. The backlash from his friends on Toronto's Queen Street West was instant. "It's not like we changed our sound," says Danko. "We're the same band we were since '96, but we aligned ourselves with a band that wasn't cool, which to me just makes it high school all over again. We're in the cafeteria sitting with the losers and you [indie rockers] don't like us anymore because you're the cheerleaders? Fuck this! There was someone from Broken Social Scene who asked me, 'Why did you do that tour?' I was like, 'Fuck. You.'

"We'd never done an arena tour. We wanted to not smell a mix of beer and urine all day from soundcheck to showtime. We'd spent 10 years in shitty clubs with no stages and asshole promoters and asshole bands and drunk people. Nickelback treated us amazing and showed us how to treat an opener. We fully appreciated it. There were bands who turned that gig down, like Sam Roberts. Anyone who turns a tour like that down is either doing pretty good on their own, or they're too good to do it. We weren't too good. We were just right."

"I find myself defending them, strangely," says Corb Lund, who shared a drummer with Nickelback until the latter's career took off. "It's not my style of music, but it's hooky, big dumb rock songs. What's wrong with that? When Kiss was big, people said they were silly and that there were way better bands out there. But I fucking loved my Kiss records when I was a kid, and I suspect there will be a lot of people who, when they're older, will go back and love their Nickelback records. There's always been a place for large-scale rock for the masses."

The good news, either way, is that Canadian music didn't have to be defined by one artist. It was no longer the '80s, when Bryan Adams was the sole international face of new Canadian rock music. Nickelback may have been huge, but Canadian music was bigger.

CHAPTER 14

BAITING THE
PUBLIC

ALEXISONFIRE, BILLY TALENT,
FUCKED UP

Screaming doesn't come naturally to Canadians, in the land of Anne Murray and Dan Hill, of Sarah McLachlan and Barenaked Ladies. In the early 2000s, two things marked the most significant sonic shift in generations of Canadian music: the rise of hip-hop and the sound of young men shredding their lungs. Both were absolutely alien to an industry slow to adapt to change. Both left conservative listeners tut-tutting at award shows, "This is not music!"

Three southern Ontario bands changed this narrative. One was a group of teenagers riding a new wave of heavy metal who somehow independently broke big on MuchMusic, with arm's-length support from the industry. One was a pop-metal band who were a decade into a career of false starts, finally signed by the man who'd made the careers of Ray Charles and Aretha Franklin. One was a group of doctrinaire punks in the model of early '80s hardcore who eschewed the industry entirely, and yet somehow won the Polaris Music Prize and toured with Arcade Fire during that band's most mainstream moment.

In many ways, Alexisonfire, Billy Talent and Fucked Up couldn't be more different from each other: they were the Rolling Stones, Beatles and Stooges of aggressive music in Canada. They all received sage advice from Gord Downie. Two of them were in a long-standing and juvenile beef, with Alexisonfire playing peacemaker between the arena rock band and the prog-punk pranksters. It was also that St. Catharines band who first changed the game and blasted down doors through which others could follow.

IT WAS A NIRVANA MOMENT: something that cut through all the bullshit dominating the cultural sphere. When Alexisonfire's clip for "Pulmonary Archery" hit MuchMusic in early 2003, it was galvanizing for a new generation of Canadian rock kids. This wasn't the *Mickey Mouse Club*. This wasn't limp post-grunge. This wasn't a ska band. This wasn't even recognizable as punk rock to old people who thought they knew what that was supposed to be. This was a band barely out of high school who were playing basement shows around the Eastern Seaboard. This was a new generation of aggressive music designed to terrify anyone over 30—something rock'n'roll had long forgotten how to do. This was a genuine counterculture of a new generation.

In the video were a bunch of nerdy adolescents—spastic screamer George Pettit, 20, is wearing glasses—freaking the fuck out, windmilling their guitars every which way and spending as much time in the air as on the ground. The video is set in an abandoned mansion, in which the band is treating an empty ballroom as if it's a sweaty union hall show somewhere just off Highway 403. They look like they're not supposed to be in such austere surroundings. Even though there's no one else in the room, they look like they're crashing a party—because they are.

"It was shocking," says journalist Sam Sutherland. "It wasn't watered down. I felt like, 'This is what I see when I go to my friend's shows, but now it's on MuchMusic between Britney Spears and Stone Temple Pilots?!' I still don't understand how it happened."

But it did—across Canada, in the U.K. and in Australia. In America, not so much, even though there was a thriving scene of somewhat similar bands there. Sutherland has a theory about that. "Alexisonfire's biggest problem in America was that they were not dumb enough," he says. "If you listen to any band they would be compared to in the States, all those bands had these pristine, perfectly quantized records with really sad songs about girls who broke their heart.

"Alexis were different. Alexis made gritty, punk-sounding records. They were too good and too uncompromising. European punk audiences are more open-minded. Canadians embraced them as hometown boys and they were afforded a degree of latitude here—latitude that Billy Talent are not afforded. Billy Talent write very straightforward, shiny radio pop songs with very cool vocals and great lyrics. All credit to them. But they're not Alexisonfire."

THE SCENE THAT spawned Alexisonfire is grossly undocumented. It's far removed from what Gen Xers and Baby Boomers understand to be punk rock (which, depending on the pontificator, usually ends somewhere between *Combat Rock* and riot grrrl). The post-hardcore of the 2000s is often dismissed as emotionally stunted music for teenagers—which is really the history of rock music itself. Alexisonfire are most often compared to bands like Sweden's Refused or Austin's At the Drive-In—both of whom redefined aggressive music in that decade—but to fully appreciate Alexisonfire, there are two key bands to understand first: Hot Water Music and Grade.

Every member of Alexisonfire has a tattoo related to Hot Water Music, who formed in 1993 in Gainesville, Florida, and put out three records before signing to Epitaph in 2001. "They were the best at capturing the energy and aesthetic of the best post-punk music," says Sutherland, a millennial writer whose definition of post-punk means '90s bands like Quicksand or Helmet, not '70s holdovers Gang of Four or Public Image Ltd. "Hot Water Music stripped away a lot of the artistic posturing that goes along with the first wave of post-punk, building these ostensibly pop-punk songs without singing in a pop-punk voice. They also articulate what is, in retrospect, not toxic bro culture, but the aesthetic of 'arm in arm with my brothers in the pit singing at the top of our lungs.' For a generation of a certain type of dude—who grew up not being into sports or the sorts of activities that give you close male friends—brotherhood is front and centre when you discover this certain subgenre of punk. That was very attractive to nervous, weird kids who desired a degree of connection and wanted to get sweaty with other people." What Black Flag was to the early '80s, Hot Water Music was to the late '90s. And it's what Alexisonfire aspired to be—and became—in the early 2000s.

Just west of Toronto on Ontario's Highway 403, in Burlington, was Grade, a band credited with taking the emo genre of aggressive music and transforming it into screamo—punk with death metal vocals. "I think Grade is one of the most underappreciated punk and hardcore bands of all time," says Sutherland. "They occupy the same space as Refused: they did something incredibly innovative, and unfortunately almost everyone who followed in their footsteps sucks absolute shit. So they either get no credit because their progeny is hideous, or they're dismissed because serious music journalists don't pontificate about bands *Alternative Press* covered. But there really was no one doing the seamless integration of the screaming and singing that Grade did on [1997's] *Separate the Magnets* and totally perfected on [1999's] *Under the Radar*. The more direct descendant is [fellow Burlington band] Silverstein, who were the very commercial version of Grade and reaped the corresponding benefits. But Grade are without peer and precedent. They opened up a lot of people's minds to what was possible for a hardcore band."

When Alexisonfire eventually broke through to the mainstream, the few critics paying close attention saw it as no coincidence that a band with a screamer like George Pettit would be drinking the same Lake Ontario water as Kyle Bishop of Grade. "I saw Grade open for [Epitaph band] H2O at the Opera House in Toronto," says Pettit. "I know we share a similar melodic hardcore vibe, and I have a lot of respect for Grade, but at the time it didn't really click with me in the way people think it might have."

There was another Burlington band that struck a more direct chord. "Moneen were notorious locally," says Pettit. "They put out their first EP [in 2000], and it sounded like a nice emo record, but everyone told me their shows were mental. The first time I saw them, they were playing on the patio outside the Mindbomb in St. Catharines, and [singer] Kenny [Bridges] was on the glass roof and jumped off. I'd never seen a band perform like that before, in a heightened state of frenzy. A lot of people pantomime what they think performance is, but Kenny is on another planet. It was always a spectacle."

Moneen, Grade, Silverstein and Jersey were all pillars of the Golden Horseshoe scene southwest of Toronto: Hamilton, Burlington, St. Catharines, Niagara Falls. All four bands toured North America and Europe extensively; Jersey, originally a Grade side project, eventually signed to Virgin Records Canada. The still-booming community around Sonic Unyon Records was thriving in Hamilton, especially after the label bought a downtown building with a record store and an event space. Niagara punks coalesced around the S.C.E.N.E. festival, founded in 1995 by local punks in Revenge of the Egg People. St. Catharines' Sick Boys were also inspiring to this new wave, not just because they'd played shows with Misfits and Rancid but because they had their own label, Stumble Records, and played all-ages matinees at the Hideaway.

Documenting it all was a young record store clerk, Joel Carriere, who started a newsletter/blog called *Bedlam Society*, plugging all kinds of punk shows on both sides of the border, including ones he put on himself. At a 1998 Deftones and Quicksand show in Toronto, Carriere met Greg Below, a metal promoter and studio engineer who ran Distort Entertainment; they soon started working together. Carriere interned briefly as a regional sales rep for Polygram Records, while also working a regular retail job at Sam the Record Man in St. Catharines.

"Joel had this special section at Sam's," says Alexisonfire's Dallas Green, "where he would special-order in great punk and hardcore records. If you had an inkling about something left of centre, you'd talk to Joel. He showed me the Constantines and it blew my face off." The store was across the street from Fairview Mall, where Green worked as a movie usher. The two traded free CD promos for free movie tickets. After bonding over their love of Quicksand, Green told Carriere, "You're going to love my band." At the time, Green fronted local trio Helicon

Blue, who had put out two EPs in 2000 produced by Greg Below. They became popular enough to get 200 people out to local shows.

One night Carriere went to see a Golden Horseshoe dream bill: Moneen opening for Grade. He called Green after the first song, telling him that he had to get down there. Green left work early to catch the last few songs of Moneen. They were on Winnipeg label Smallman and about to sign to U.S. label Vagrant, home of emo poster boy Dashboard Confessional. "These were friends of friends," says Carriere, "they were our age, and they were doing something more than just drinking beer and being fine with playing your hometown."

The latter fate seemed to be the destiny for Helicon Blue. At a Toronto show opening for SoCal hardcore band Sense Field in September 2001, Helicon Blue's rhythm section didn't show up. Green borrowed an acoustic guitar from Moneen's Chris Hughes and played his first-ever solo show. Helicon Blue were through.

Watching closely was 16-year-old guitarist Wade MacNeil, known as a local gig hustler for his bands After the Hallowed Moment and Plan 9. He invited Green over to jam. They met in the bedroom of drummer Jesse Ingelevics, a classmate of MacNeil; another classmate, bassist Chris Steele from Plan 9, also joined. That's a four-piece band right there, featuring two guitarists with very different vocal styles. But MacNeil wanted one more piece for his puzzle. He called George Pettit.

Like MacNeil, Pettit was an active participant in the DIY scene, playing bass in death metal band Condemning Salem. Though Pettit wasn't the singer, he was the visual focal point. "I thought he was a maniac," says Carriere. Green was already a Pettit fan. One night Condemning Salem played the Palm Grove, a Jamaican bar across from the Fairview Mall. The next night, Pettit went to the movies, where the usher ripped his ticket and said, "Great show last night." The usher was Dallas Green.

"What do you want me to do?" Pettit asked at the first rehearsal.

"Vocals," said MacNeil.

"I can't sing."

"No, don't sing. Scream. Just yell."

"At the time," says Pettit, "you could have asked me to play oboe in a band and I'd be like, 'Sure, I'll figure it out.' That was the vibe then. Starting a band wasn't something we put thought and effort into. Everyone played in three or four different bands anyway." With nothing to lose, Pettit let 'er rip at that first rehearsal.

"I'd heard vocals like that before, but never right beside my face," says Green. "Listening to metal, I knew it was possible. I could sing, but it takes a certain kind of voice to do *that*. I never tried to write music with it in mind. I loved Converge, but I'd never known how to get it out of myself."

On the flip side, "We were also listening to a lot of ambient rock," says Pettit. "Most of us had grown up in punk, and then you get to that late-teen age and you're too old to be wearing the jacket with spikes on it, and you're like, 'You know what? I'm into other stuff.' Then you'd go to Sonic Unyon's store and buy Slint or something." Sonic Unyon artists Sianspheric, Kittens and Shallow North Dakota were also influential.

The jam sounded good enough to form a band right then and there. The name came from the documentary *Body Benders*, featuring Alexis Fire, a lactating contortionist stripper. Perhaps needless to say, the boys were still teenagers when they chose the name.

Across Lake Ontario to the north, a band formed in Toronto with an even crazier name: Fucked Up.

———————

THE FIRST TIME Damian Abraham saw Fucked Up, its teenage singer kicked him in the testicles. He responded with a choke-slam he'd gleaned from wrestling videos: the kid was hoisted in the air and slammed on the floor. The crowd, composed mostly of antipoverty activists, took issue with both Abraham's actions and his red Budweiser hat. "Fuck that Fred Durst motherfucker!" one shouted, referencing the singer of Limp Bizkit, who represented all that was wrong with male aggression in rock music in 2001.

Two gigs later, Abraham was the new singer. The original, Josh Zucker, moved to guitar, which he did not know how to play. That's Fucked Up.

The band that dared not speak its name in the media never expected they'd need to. This was a punk band that didn't want anything to do with the Warped Tour, with math rock or mall punks, with major labels, with radio. They didn't want to release anything other than seven-inch vinyl singles and vowed never to tour. By the end of the decade, they'd won one of Canada's biggest music prizes, were signed to one of the biggest American indie rock labels, made concept albums and wrote 20-minute prog epics. Abraham became a MuchMusic host, and the band opened stadium shows for Foo Fighters.

That's Fucked Up.

FUCKED UP STARTED in the fanzine culture of the *No Logo* '90s. Guitarists Mike Haliechuk and Josh Zucker put out a zine called *Quick*, which started out being about music but evolved to articulate their political awakenings. "I was a full-on anarcho-primitivist person, in environmental studies and international development at U of T," says Haliechuk. Zucker was five years younger, still in high school. "I was going to Washington and Quebec City for protests. I was learning about punk, about world trade, and me and Josh were both volunteering for [the Ontario Coalition Against Poverty] and going to jail for protests. I was in university, not writing my papers but writing 10,000-word articles on the history of primitivism for our zine. After a while, we decided we were more interested in music and thought we should just do a band that represents these ideas." One early song, "No Pasaran," references antifascist forces in the Spanish Civil War.

In assembling the rest of the band, Haliechuk's first choice was bassist Sandy Miranda. She'd been his roommate—or more of a squatter, sleeping first in the hallway and eventually the living room. Miranda was heavily involved in the local zine culture. The drummer for the first few shows was Chris Colohan, the singer for Ruination and Cursed. His next choice for drummer, Jonah Falco, was just as unusual. "Jonah lied to me when he said he knew how to play drums," says Haliechuk. "He didn't even have a drum set. He faked it until he actually could. It's not hard to play drums in a shitty punk band, so he was fine."

Zucker was initially Fucked Up's singer; when he was 13, he'd fronted a band called Youngblood that Haliechuk had seen at punk matinees at Club Shanghai on Spadina Avenue. After two shows with Fucked Up, Zucker split town for the summer for a Woody Guthrie vacation—literally riding the rails across America. Haliechuck turned to another one of his roommates, Damian Abraham, to fill in on vocals for the next few shows. "Being someone who was starved for attention," says Abraham, "I was like, 'Yes, absolutely.'"

Abraham, Haliechuk and Miranda lived in a house where the guitarist had spray-painted *fucked up* on the wall of a bathroom. A botched plumbing job had left "a toilet in an island of caulking and smashed tiles all around it," says Abraham. "It was fun, but a punk house in the most stereotypical sense of the time." Abraham and Haliechuk had met in the Kensington punk scene at a squat on Oxford Street, home to PolitiKILL inCOREct, and at the anarchist bookshop Who's Emma, both of which regularly hosted shows. Abraham was in a band, Urine Trouble, as a teenager but was mostly a fan. He and Miranda were occasional co-hosts of the CIUT show *Mods and Rockers*, run by Horseshoe Tavern booker Jeff Cohen. "I'd try and force hardcore on the radio," says Abraham of a show largely dedicated to garage rock and roots rock.

Mike Haliechuk had some actual professional experience under his belt. In his second year of university, he was recruited to play bass in Ruination, a supergroup of sorts from the punk scenes in Toronto and Chicago. He was the baby of the bunch, and was dating an older woman who lived with Ruination singer Chris Colohan. "I didn't play bass or anything," says Haliechuk. "Chris probably thought, Well, I know all these people in bands in America, I'll just get this weird kid to play bass—because who cares about bass?" The tour took him to Europe, which was fun but gruelling: nine people sharing a van, sleeping on dirt floors in squats, 40 shows in 42 days. It's part of the reason Fucked Up's initial manifesto included a vow not to tour.

The other part of Fucked Up's manifesto was to only release music on seven-inch vinyl singles. "We formed because of Dangerhouse, a '70s L.A. punk label [that only put out seven-inch singles]," says Haliechuk. "That's the entire reason Fucked Up exists. In the early 2000s, I was getting into northern soul and heavily collecting 45s. I never related to music on an LP level. It was easier to make your statement with one song, as opposed to putting a whole record of ideas out. We did one and it was fine, but then we did two or three more really quickly; they sold fast and became collector's items. We felt we could release singles indefinitely, and that's what we did for five years. It was fun and they looked cool. Once we had the design template, it was appealing to think of someone having 50 Fucked Up records in their box that all looked the same."

Though the singles came out on Vancouver's Deranged Records, Fucked Up was not looking for inspiration in Canada. "Canadian punk was weird," says Haliechuk. "You wouldn't read about it anywhere. I didn't care about the first wave. I never got into the Viletones. It wasn't part of our genesis." For him, that dismissal includes international Canadian icons D.O.A. and NoMeansNo. "I never liked either of those bands," he says. "I liked SNFU a lot—or tried to convince myself I liked them. Canadian punk was too jazzy for me. I wasn't going to like them just because they were Canadian."

Abraham took a different tack. "NoMeansNo was one of the first shows I saw," he says, "with Ultra Bidé and Alice Donut at the Opera House. I was sold for life. D.O.A., obviously, I was a huge fan. But the stuff I was into, being younger, was the Raw Energy scene [of '90s Toronto]. I still love all that stuff: Five Knuckle Chuckle, Marilyn's Vitamins, Trunk, Tirekickers."

Early Fucked Up singles flew off the shelves. File-sharing didn't hinder the band's growth at all. "We were part of the punk economy, we weren't part of the music industry," says Haliechuk. "We were selling thousands of copies of our seven-inches. People will always trade and buy punk records." That said, punk distributors at the time were used to bands putting 10 short songs on a single; Fucked Up would only have two. Some distributors turned them down because of this.

In the first three years of Fucked Up's existence they didn't play any further afield than southwestern Ontario. Everyone had day jobs: Haliechuk in a co-op grocery, Abraham as a bouncer (the Strokes' Julian Casablancas tried to kiss him at their first Toronto show, at the Horseshoe). Miranda was working at the

Showtime channel; she often wore her business attire on stage in marked contrast to the rest of the band, not the least of which was a constantly shirtless Abraham.

Crossover with the city's exploding indie scene was negligible, other than a couple of shows at the Wavelength series. There was an opening slot for Anagram at their CD release party in 2002; that gig was hyped in *Eye Weekly*, with Anagram on the cover. In February 2003, they opened a sold-out Lee's Palace show for post-riot-grrrl band Gossip; they got the gig because that band's manager had traded punk tapes with Haliechuk. "We went over terribly," Abraham recalls.

Indie rock was not ready to be Fucked Up in February 2003, but a new video on MuchMusic was about to change everything.

WITHIN A YEAR OF FORMING, Alexisonfire released the three-song *Math Sheets Demo*; the artwork was ripped from the homework of drummer Jesse Ingelevics. Greg Below, who was promoting shows with Joel Carriere, loved the demo and signed them to his management company, Distort. Below's day job was working in the studio at EMI Publishing, and he booked them to make a full-length record at the in-house studio there; he invited his boss, Michael McCarty, to see the band at Niagara Arts Centre in St. Catharines. "He thought it was insane," says Carriere, "the energy of the kids screaming. I don't think he'd seen that in that genre before. I think he saw something in them: the musicianship, Dallas's voice, Wade's voice, the nature of what the songs were about. For him to give a not very lucrative deal was no sweat off his balls either." McCarty signed Alexisonfire to EMI Publishing for $15,000. George Pettit was confused.

"Are we signing to a major label?" he asked Carriere.

"No, it's publishing."

"What the fuck is publishing?"

"Well, they're going to give you $15,000."

"Oh, okay."

Publishing is an oft-misunderstood part of the music business. It's not a record deal. It's a cash-up-front bet that the artist is writing songs that will one day earn significant royalties; it's effectively a loan against those future royalties. You can spend publishing money any way you want. Young artists often use it to record or tour. Older artists sell their publishing as a cash-out, as many classic rock acts started doing in 2020; publishing gets sold just as any marketable commodity would, which is why the Beatles' catalogue has traded hands many times. Historically, publishers traded on sheet music and the idea that other artists might cover the signee's songs. These days, publishers primarily ensure that the rights holder is collecting all royalties due to them, domestically and globally. That a mainstream Canadian publishing company saw commercial gold in a band like Alexisonfire was highly unusual in 2002.

"There were a lot of bands doing the screaming-singing-screaming thing, which obviously started with Grade," says Sam Sutherland, "but you cannot discount the genuine mystic quality of Dallas Green's voice. It was from another planet. George has one of the best proper gruff screams of anyone from that generation, and Wade ended up having this incredible, raw, Hot Water Music–ish sound. They slowly started integrating those pieces until all three were spaced out equally and used more like you would keyboard textures or guitar pedal effects."

The EMI money helped them record a full-length debut with Below, who also guaranteed them EMI distribution through his Distort label. Carriere printed up a CD sampler, and they'd all flyer outside any venue for aggressive music. "We'd sit outside and hand out records," he recalls. "We'd say, 'What's your favourite band?' 'Hot Water Music.' 'We're like that, but heavier. Hey, what's your favourite band?' 'Korn.' 'We're like Korn, but heavier.' We did that the night before the first Warped Tour we played, and then played in a tent that wasn't really a stage, and we had about 400 kids out in front waiting and going mental."

The self-titled debut came out on Halloween 2002, one year after the band formed. Jasmine White-Gluz, later of the band No Joy, reviewed it in *Exclaim!*, saying it "may just be able to save Canadian hardcore." There were still dues to pay, including a gig opening up for metal giants Disturbed at Toronto's Kool Haus. "None of us liked Disturbed's music—at all," says Carriere. "But we figured we'll probably never play the Kool Haus [otherwise], so we did it. We were capturing some older people [in the crowd], you could see it, but then some guys started calling George a faggot. Next thing I know I see 19-year-old George jump in the crowd with his mic, kicking the shit out of a 35-year-old man. Then he gets back on stage and continues on. Everyone started cheering."

"I don't remember that," sighs Pettit. "If someone had said *faggot* at a show, I would have at least said something about it. But you know what? Print that I beat him up. Let's say that: 'Oh man, I fought so many guys back in the day, I can't even remember which one!'"

Pettit was working at a video store in Grimsby when Carriere called to tell him that the band got a $20,000 VideoFACT grant for "Pulmonary Archery." Filmed at the end of January 2003 and directed by Marc Ricciardelli, who would work often with the band, it was inspired by Refused's clip for "New Noise."

"It was so tasteful for that kind of band at that moment, when everyone else was trying to be chaotic and dark," says Carriere of Refused's video. "MuchMusic wasn't touching this at the time, or any music like it. They had this thing called *PunchMuch*, where you could vote videos in. We were pretty relentless, and it got added to *PunchMuch*. We had the message board culture behind us, and the band had been touring. We got to No. 1 on *PunchMuch*, beating all the big bands. The clicks were coming from across Canada, so Much couldn't ignore us." It helped that an early adopter was MuchMusic VJ George Stroumboulopoulos, who bought a T-shirt at the band's very first Toronto show, and later often invited them on-air.

"There was nothing like us that was getting any sort of mainstream exposure—anywhere, really," says Pettit. "It was only on late-night television or secret corners of college radio. You had to stay up late to find it. Even just by being able to vote for our band on MuchMusic, that was a big deal for people. 'Hey, let's see if we can take down Justin Timberlake!' A vote for us was a vote for change as much as it was a vote for our music. We were like the reform candidate. It was a big deal."

In June 2003, the clip was nominated for Best Independent Video at the MMVAs. The band arrived on the red carpet in a Hummer. Meanwhile, MacNeil was still in high school. A U.S. tour had been scheduled around his March break. One time when he'd called in sick to school, someone saw him live on MuchMusic and ratted him out. A month after the MMVAs, Alexisonfire were booked to open a fall tour for a hot new band called Billy Talent, who'd just released their debut single, "Try Honesty."

———————

BILLY TALENT ARE A DIVISIVE BAND: there's very little middle ground on the love-hate spectrum. "I love that our band is polarizing," says vocalist Ben Kowalewicz. "Some people can't stand us, and that's the best compliment. As the late, great Gord Downie once said, 'I'd rather be a two or an eight. I don't want to be in the middle.' That's how we've always been."

When "Try Honesty" hit radio in July 2003, Billy Talent were an unknown entity toiling in Toronto clubs. Within a year, the debut album went double platinum, the band scored a Juno for Best New Artist, and they toured the country four times in increasingly larger venues. But this overnight success was 10 years in the making. The band formed in 1993 as teenagers in Mississauga, Ontario, the second-largest city in the Greater Toronto Area.

Billy Talent tracks were all over the radio and MuchMusic in the mid-2000s: bright, shiny pop-punk songs with a throat-shredding singer who was as likely to screech as he was to sing a melodic hook. Alexisonfire were not yet added to radio, and mainstream Canada had never heard anything like it. But respect was a bit harder to come by. Billy Talent's stylish appearance and youthful crowds gave the air of a teen sensation, the next wave of mall punk to be marketed by major labels and therefore resented by the underground. There was also the fact they were not kids; they were all about 27, playing music appreciated mostly by fans 10 years younger.

Kowalewicz is the make-or-break component of Billy Talent: his diction, his tone, his yelps, his screeches. But their musical chops are hard to fault; they're the type of players likely to be profiled in gear magazines. Ian D'Sa is a guitar wizard and creative arranger, whose most audible influences include Andy Summers of the Police and Tom Morello of Rage Against the Machine. The rhythm section of bassist Jon Gallant and drummer Aaron Solowoniuk is as dextrous as the Clash's Paul Simonon and Topper Headon, capable of driving aggression but informed by both Paul McCartney's melodicism and the sparse precision of reggae.

Part of the reason Billy Talent has been embraced by the Canadian music industry, if not always by critics, is that they're perfect gentlemen: polite, professional, philanthropic, grateful for every opportunity. Very Canadian. Not exactly punk rock. Except when they were asked why punks perceived them as parvenus in 2003.

"Street cred? I'm so sick of that bullshit, pompous art school world," Kowalewicz ranted in 2004 to the *Soulshine* blog. "[The idea that] if you don't record on a four-track in a basement in Guelph, you somehow aren't authentic. I have no time for that because if you want to talk about being indie, we were indie for 10 years and we were never supported by anyone else, so screw 'em. I've met the guys in other major label bands like Finger Eleven and they're total sweethearts. Just because the music they play might be different and appeals to a different fan base, it's still music and it's still art."

Caught between the sludge of modern rock and the unconventional indie rock underground, Billy Talent were in a lane of their own: old-school skills, well-crafted pop songs and deft instrumentalists, and yet screaming in tune with a new generation.

What always pushed them forward was their own confidence. "I always knew that if we could get our foot in the door, there's no way anyone could close it on us," says Gallant. "Even when we were nobodies, I always thought, Our band is good! Can't anybody see that?"

BEN KOWALEWICZ WAS always the new kid on the block. Born in Montreal, when he was in grade 6 he moved with his family to Milton, Ontario, and then to the Streetsville neighbourhood of Mississauga for high school. Eager to make friends, at a party he told a guy he played drums—"which I kind of did," he says. "He called me later and wanted to start a band. I was terrible, but we all were. After three weeks, I showed up to rehearsal one day and from the top of the stairs I heard a far superior drummer." That was Aaron Solowoniuk. Jon Gallant was the bassist. Kowalewicz was out of the band, called To Each His Own, though a month later they asked him to sing backup vocals. At a high school talent show, they saw a shit-hot guitarist named Ian D'Sa; they poached him for a new project, Pezz.

The year was 1993. The Lollapalooza lineups were a huge influence, Rage Against the Machine in particular; Pezz learned to cover that band's entire debut album, which had come out the year before. Gigs were largely at house parties, until the idea dawned on them that they could rent a PA and book a Masonic lodge or Kinsmen hall. "We met these interesting characters running these places," says Kowalewicz. "They'd charge us $500 deposit, but maybe it was $100 to rent. We'd charge enough to cover the cost of turning the lights on. It was just a matter of providing a safe place for people to come and have fun—and be kids, listen to rock'n'roll and get dirty and sweaty."

Pezz scoured Streetsville to "borrow" lumber from construction sites in order to build makeshift stages, propped up with similarly acquired milk crates. More than 300 milk crates were stored in the D'Sa family basement, which reeked of sour milk while the band practised. Two of their high school teachers, who spent summers following Yes and Rush on tour, volunteered to chaperone the gigs, attended by more than a hundred kids. This would happen at least once a month, and all profits went to the local food bank. Eventually they graduated to local pool halls. One of Pezz's first professional shows out of town was at the Sonic Picnic in Orangeville, put on by fellow teen punks Bender and featuring Sonic Unyon acts like Tristan Psionic, Treble Charger and Hayden. "Someone at that show asked us if we had any tapes, and we were like, 'Tapes! Sounds like a great idea!'" says Gallant. "We got a Fostex four-track and set it up in Ian's basement."

Two cassettes of original material resulted. As the writing developed, it married their love of '80s metal and '90s grunge. Later on, the Police and the Clash entered the mix. Canadian bands like the Gandharvas were inspirations closer to home. By the time Pezz recorded their first CD in 1998, some ska was also seeping in, largely through their friends in Guelph's Flashlight Brown, a ska punk band signed to Montreal's Stomp Records. That band's bassist Fil Bucchino introduced Pezz to playing dominoes, exclaiming "Watoosh!" every time he slapped one down—hence the CD's title, Watoosh! There was no musical consistency to the album, just the sound of a band trying to find their feet.

"Every song showcases where we were at musically at that time," says Kowalewicz. "There's a lot of pop-punk and hard rock and Sloan-y, Thrush Hermit–esque vibes, and a track with a Radiohead-ish, ambient, trippy, drum thing." There's even a tossed-off cover of the Tragically Hip's "New Orleans Is Sinking" tacked on the end. "We used to do that song when we were playing bad rock bars where people didn't like us," says Kowalewicz. "We'd start that off, get a big cheer, then we'd be like, 'Fuck you!'"

Watoosh! was recorded at a jingle studio owned by a friend of Alanis Morissette; a surprised and starstruck Kowalewicz met the global superstar in the studio's kitchen while making tea. She stuck around for a session and offered encouraging words. That's more than they got from the press: the album got a review in *Now* magazine and a story in their local *Mississauga News*, and that's about it. There were a few gigs, including a short tour with Rusty. Nobody wanted to sign or distribute the band, and not for a lack of hustling. They got form letters from all the labels except Warner Canada, whose A&R rep Steve Jordan wrote them a personal note: "You guys are really good. I can tell you put a lot of work into your playing and what you do. But you sound like the Red Hot Chili Peppers, and we already have the Red Hot Chili Peppers. It might behoove you to go and try and find your own sound." Pezz took that advice to heart.

Their high school follies appeared to be coming to an end—along with the name Pezz, after a cease-and-desist from an American band with that name. Gallant played with a Celtic pub band that paid him $500 a week for three nights' work, which put him through university. He left Pezz for three months, and they played a handful of gigs without him. ("Luckily for me, I didn't end up as a Pete Best story," he says.) D'Sa studied animation at Sheridan College and then took a job in Montreal. Solowoniuk got a job at the Chrysler plant in Oakville; a numbing pain in his legs was soon diagnosed as multiple sclerosis. Kowalewicz had the shittiest job of all: at the Toronto airport, emptying septic tanks from airplanes. Morale was low. "We were going to break up," says Kowalewicz, "not because we hated each other, but just because of life."

Then a break came. Someone at the Stardust Billiards in Mississauga got Pezz booked at the El Mocambo in downtown Toronto. "In our mind, we'd made it!" says Kowalewicz. "We were jumping up and down. We played, and it was terrible, obviously; we were opening for a blues band." But they got to know booker William New, who ran the long-standing Elvis Monday night, a Toronto tradition featuring unknown bands and no cover. They became his "cancel band," available at the last minute whenever another act bailed. Those gigs got them the attention of Yvonne Matsell of Ted's Wrecking Yard and eventually Jeff Cohen and Craig Laskey at the Horseshoe.

By then they were called Billy Talent, after a character in the 1993 novel and 1996 film *Hard Core Logo*, a Canadian cult hit directed by Bruce McDonald about a reunited punk band's final tour of Western Canada. "It was one of the greatest rock'n'roll movies I'd ever seen," says Kowalewicz. "If you were in a band and in high school in the late '90s, *Hard Core Logo* was something you had to see. Billy

Talent is the character betraying his friends to sign with a big American band. Only Canadian bands can truly understand that. But we chose it because I love the name Jane's Addiction, and I thought Billy Talent would be a great name. It wasn't because of the character; it's because it sounded cool, and it was part of that movie."

When D'Sa's animation contract expired in Montreal, he went on EI and started playing guitar every day, determined not to give up on his dreams. One of the first songs he wrote in this period was "Try Honesty," which gave him a new sense of purpose. When he returned to Toronto, he convinced his bandmates that Billy Talent should take one more shot. They maxed out Solowoniuk's credit card and recorded what became known as the Green EP in Burlington, at the studio where Grade had made all their records. The release show was scheduled for September 11, 2001. That obviously got postponed. A week later, promoter Dan Burke booked Billy Talent to open for one of his favourite bands, the Japanese garage-rock sensation Zoobombs, whose live show was a must-see event in the early 2000s. That in turn led to a last-minute opening slot for Sparta, a band that formed in the ashes of At the Drive-In, one of the main influences on Billy Talent's new sound. They only got that gig because the American band Thursday got stopped at the border. Score another one for the "cancel band."

Kowalewicz stopped shovelling shit at the airport and got a gig as a promo guy at modern rock station CFNY, a largely unglamorous job that involved handing out concert tickets and sweeping floors. He befriended veteran DJ Dave Bookman, who perhaps saw in the young singer some of the broadcaster's own endless enthusiasm and hyper-nerdery. Eventually Kowalewicz was promoted to a producer on the nightly *Live in Toronto* show. There he met A&R rep Jen Hirst, who worked for the ill-fated Song Corp. (That label soon went bankrupt and almost took down a large chunk of the Canadian music industry with it.) He invited her to see Billy Talent at their NXNE showcase at the 360 Club, a legion hall on Queen Street West. When she interviewed for a job at Warner Records shortly after, she was asked who she would sign tomorrow, if she could. "Billy Talent," she said. They responded, "Who?"

But Billy Talent were making impressions on Toronto's other industry movers and shakers. Steve Hoffman, who worked for Rush's management, recommended the band to two Atlantic Records A&R reps who were in Toronto to check out a side project for Shane Told of Silverstein. Billy Talent met the U.S. reps at the band's rehearsal studio and auditioned. Now Atlantic, a division of Warner Music Group, was interested, which bolstered Jen Hirst's case with her new Warner Canada bosses. She offered Billy Talent a $10,000 demo deal at Warner and brought in Gavin Brown as producer, who'd just worked with another new band, Three Days Grace.

"Once one person does that, it's like flies on shit," says Gallant. "We met with everybody. We were getting these offers and had no management. Luckily for us, we met the right people who could guide us. We're still with our lawyer and our agent. We got the lawyer first, Chris Taylor. Chris got us better deals than we would've by ourselves. At this point we're 27-year-old men, fully formed working adults, and can't believe we're in this situation because we've been a band for 10 years already." The band who could never get an indie record label to call them back now had offers from Island, Elektra, Atlantic and Warner—all except Island were under the Warner umbrella, which was important to them because they wanted to remain loyal to Jen Hirst.

Atlantic flew them down to New York City to make a pitch. They were put up at the Hudson Hotel in midtown Manhattan and ate Kobe beef for the first time. They met legendary label head Ahmet Ertegun, who'd signed Aretha Franklin and Led Zeppelin, in his office on his 79th birthday. "You know what I want for my birthday?" Ertegun asked the dumbstruck Canadians. "Billy Talent!"

Nonetheless, they took meetings with other labels while there. "It was probably the greatest time in my life," says Kowalewicz. "We actually did that thing where [Atlantic] called later and said, 'Have you guys made a decision yet?' 'Hmmm. We're not quite sure.' At that time, [the label] had more money than God, so we flew back [to Manhattan]. There was a little pub down the road from the Hudson, really dingy, called the Coliseum. We'd do all our meetings during the day and then get absolutely shitfaced drinking Guinness and whisky. We'd tell all the label reps to meet us there and pick their five favourite songs on the jukebox. It kept them on their toes. If they played David Bowie, we'd be like, All right." At the end of one night at the Coliseum, Kowalewicz managed to somehow dislodge a construction site dumpster on castors, which then rolled down a hill and landed on top of a car. The Canadian band left an apology note on the dash of the crushed vehicle.

A major deal wasn't a guarantee of anything; it was a leg up, and the band still had to hustle. In the fall of 2002, they were the first band of four on the MTV Campus Invasion Tour; headliners were past-their-prime I Mother Earth and Thirty Seconds to Mars, a band whose fame was primarily due to the presence of actor Jared Leto. Billy Talent flyered their own gig before the doors opened, enticing people to enter early. Significantly more exciting was a Canadian arena tour with Sum 41—whose average age was about five years younger than anyone in Billy Talent—and old friends Flashlight Brown.

Billy Talent's self-titled debut album was recorded in Vancouver at the end of 2002 with producer Gavin Brown and released in September 2003. Just before its release, the band headed to the U.S. for a series of Lollapalooza dates. It was the first time the tour had happened in six years, and the time before had been a Chicago-only event. Headlining was Jane's Addiction; also on the bill were Audioslave, featuring members of Soundgarden and Rage Against the Machine. For these '90s kids, it was a dream. From there, they went on a U.S. tour with '70s punk vets the Buzzcocks. That audience was not ready for the new wave. "We'd get spit on," says Gallant. "Shit thrown at us every night. We just plowed through it. The Buzzcocks were amazing guys. They didn't know us, but they treated us with respect. Pete Shelley hit on Ben a whole bunch."

"We learned our chops," says Kowalewicz. "It's very difficult, as a frontman, to put on a good show when you're standing one foot away from people who are literally spitting on you for 45 minutes. You learn to play for fans who are there, but you realize it's the band versus the audience. We learned not to take it personally if people don't like you, and it was motivation to try a little bit harder."

A lot of lessons were learned in public. On their first trip to the U.K., they had a slot at the Reading Festival. The night before the gig, they tagged along with Sum 41 to the Kerrang! Awards, a hard rock event presented by the popular music magazine. They ended up in a cab with Paris Hilton en route to their hotel and stayed up all night drinking with the Black Keys and Jet. Their set was at noon the next day. It did not go well. "With every snare hit, my head wanted to explode," says Solowoniuk. Between songs, they took turns barfing offstage. The *NME* reviewed their set with the headline "Billy Talent's Sick Debut." It was meant literally.

Back home in Canada, however, "Try Honesty"—the song that Ian D'Sa wrote to convince his bandmates not to give up—was a smash hit on radio.

ALEXISONFIRE DIDN'T KNOW how popular they'd become until they toured with Billy Talent in September 2003. Their debut album had gone gold by then. As the tour finished at the Croatian Cultural Centre in Vancouver, Alexisonfire played to more than 1,000 people for the first time. The next night, however, they crossed the border into Washington and played to only the bar staff.

Alexisonfire came out in the U.S. on Equal Vision, a reputable metal label, but touring was a very DIY affair, booked by MacNeil. "We played in off-the-grid weird spots, anywhere there was a room," says Pettit. "There was a lot of living on peanut butter sandwiches and sleeping in the van and waking up in the desert being cooked alive." They ended 2003 at the Kool Haus in Toronto, the site of the ill-fated Disturbed show only a year earlier. This time Alexisonfire were opening for their friends in Moneen at the 2,500-capacity venue.

Early 2004 was spent writing and recording the second record, *Watch Out!* Alexisonfire were no longer teenagers, and the new songs reflected that. "Without completely talking trash about the first record, it's a little too free in the writing," says Pettit. "We were like, 'Here's a part, here's a part, here's a part, here's a part—okay, jam all that together. Have we hit the three-minute mark? Great, that's a song.' On the second record, we were more concise. 'Hey, that part's good, we can do that again.' Writing songs more traditionally—with choruses."

The lyrics also reflected a maturity. Many were about healing, not grievance. "The idea of delving into lyrics on either of those records is cringey for me," says Pettit. "Even pictures of me at 19 have a holy-shit degree of embarrassment about it. Having said that, I was really into Joan of Arc, the band, at that time. Tim Kinsella's lyrics were so Dadaist, madness. No one was writing like that, throwing a line like 'gas-station egg-salad sandwich' in the middle. In some [early] songs, I was trying to do that kind of stream-of-consciousness thing. On the second record, there was more emphasis on topical songs."

Many of Pettit's peers trafficked in outright misogyny, endemic to a genre performed entirely by sweaty, shirtless boys who loved *Fight Club*. Alexisonfire had all the same aggression but not the misogyny. "On the first record," says Sam Sutherland, "there is a lot of lovelorn stuff, like, 'This is a .44 calibre love letter straight from my heart.' But George actually reads books and doesn't sit around thinking about how it sucks that a girl wasn't nice to him once."

"There were bands I would consider misogynist," says Pettit, "or at least had a different relationship with their fans in terms of whether they were willing to fuck as many of them as they could. I was always fairly repulsed by that. On the Warped Tour, there were these new wave young emocore bands who had T-shirts that said stuff like *How my nuts taste, bitch?* Whereas I grew up at a very young age having a copy of *Penis Envy* by Crass, or *Less Talk, More Rock* by Propagandhi. Growing up in Grimsby, it was widely known that people were homophobic, and Propagandhi introduced to me the idea of homophobia as an evil. The bands we were playing with on Warped, they didn't know *Less Talk, More Rock*. I still make it a point on stage to say, 'Alexisonfire shows are a safe place regardless of your gender or your identity or your orientation or your race. This is for everybody.'

"There are a lot of women in our audience, and I've always liked that," he continues. "The hardcore scene wasn't always the most inclusive place for women. A lot of women in the scene had a really tough time and dealt with that from all angles. As much as there were a bunch of progressive ideas there, a lot of people fell back on old tropes and ridiculous shit. I'm grateful that we were never that sort of band."

Watch Out! came out in June 2004 and debuted in the Canadian top 10; it went gold three months later. It opens with "Accidents," which right away signals that bigger, better things are ahead, starting with an actual melodic hook—something entirely lacking from the debut. Shortly after its release, they showed up at the MuchMusic Video Awards in an ambulance, in keeping with the theme of the "Accidents" video, in which Green and MacNeil play paramedics. They didn't win an award, but they did take advantage of the free bar before headlining a show further east on Queen Street at the Opera House. "The boys didn't really drink much at the time," says Carriere, "but they got pretty drunk that night, enjoying the moment. There were 800 kids at the show, and it was chaos. The band was sloppy, laughing. George crowd-surfed in a rubber dinghy. Steele's bass was unplugged for half the set, but it was so chaotic we hadn't noticed until someone finally plugged him in. I wrecked the downstairs of the Opera House wrestling with people and had to pay to fix and repaint it later. People at that show will forever remember it."

The scrappy hardcore band who'd crashed the party were now bona fide video stars. Naturally, that came with some backlash—though not much, all things considered. "I was so worried they were going to fuck it up," says Sutherland. "But it was better. It was anthemic in a way that felt earned and authentic. There was a rare sense that they had succeeded on their own terms."

"A lot of the Canadian hardcore community thought we were dicks," says Green. "Everybody thought we were making money, but all the money we made was put into the bank so we could keep touring down in the States, playing for nobody, which costs money."

That year they toured the U.K. for the first time. Though they were booked at the Reading and Leeds Festivals, they arrived with no expectations at all, only to find that the entire tour had sold out. Britain and the rest of the world beckoned in ways that the U.S. didn't. They returned to the U.K. twice more in the next year and also went to Australia and Japan. There was a tour of the Canadian Maritimes in the winter, with Jersey, playing halls holding anywhere from 100 to 1,000 people. Jersey's drummer, Jordan Hastings, would soon be a part of the Alexisonfire story. 2004 ended with their first headlining show at the Kool Haus, with the Constantines as one of the opening acts.

FUCKED UP WENT to the U.S. for the first time in September 2004. "We played at Chicagofest and there were people there from bands I loved watching us," says Abraham. "Prior to that first tour, I didn't think anyone actually liked our band. It felt like we were doing our own thing. Then we went on this tour, and people were singing along. Not every show—there were some doozies. But when the shows were good, we thought we should maybe keep putting out records."

On that same tour, they played the Knitting Factory in New York City, at a Viacom party for the Adult Swim cartoon network. It was put together by the singer from punk band Charles Bronson, who booked the Toronto nobodies. The main venue featured the archetypal 2004 bill of the Rapture, Har Mar Superstar and Radio 4, with DJ Danger Mouse. Fucked Up were playing in the basement, where the catering was. As soon as the band started playing, a food fight broke out. "They called the cops on us and security shut us down in the middle of our set while we kept playing," says Abraham. "Then they were throwing gear at us. 'Get the fuck out of here!' Amps, guitars and then this one road case I caught and I'm like, 'What is this?' I stuck it in the van and we drove off. We got to a rest stop, I opened up the case and it was a Technics 1200 turntable—which is still my turntable to this day. I hope it wasn't Danger Mouse's."

In 2005, with no full-length album in sight, Fucked Up started making mixtapes, a practice far more common in hip-hop circles than punk. Cassettes sold only at live shows, they came out every few years for the rest of the decade, featuring live tracks, demos, interview snippets, tracks from friends' bands, diss tracks ("How to Rob an Indie Rock Superstar") and some ridiculous covers.

On the first one, they tackled Kelly Clarkson's ubiquitous 2004 pop anthem "Since U Been Gone." Abraham asked Steve Lambke of the Constantines to sing on it; he had a part-time job at the College Street record store Soundscapes, where the gregarious Fucked Up frontman often hung out. Lambke had never heard the Clarkson song, but was game for anything. "No one was talking to each other," says Lambke, "or if they did it was, 'What's this guy doing here?' That kind of vibe. I'm being asked to do something, I don't know what it is, and if I did I probably wouldn't think it was cool and wouldn't have done it—and everyone hated each other. It was this insignificant thing that could have been fun but kind of wasn't."

When the mixtape came out, Haliechuk wrote liner notes that mocked Lambke's vocal performance. Abraham was furious. "You motherfucker!" he yelled. "These are my friends. You can't do this shit." That night Fucked Up played a show at CineCycle, the back-alley venue on Spadina; it was their fifth Toronto show in a row to be shut down by cops. "No violence, just crowding," says Abraham. "And because cops were dicks, and we were in DIY spaces in the Entertainment District, where they have a beat to enforce. It was constant. It wasn't fun."

A couple of days later, at a band meeting in advance of their first European tour, Abraham quit. They didn't let him leave. Instead, they decided to go on tour with a friend known only as Beav, let Abraham cool off and then reinstate him when they got back. "They went above and beyond to keep my baby ass in this band," says Abraham. "If it was me, I'd be like, 'Fuck it, leave.'" Despite his precarious position, Abraham was their spokesman in their first major piece of press, in *Vice* magazine, while Fucked Up was in Europe.

Meanwhile, on the tour itself, "something insane happened at least once a day," says Haliechuk. "It was a disaster. The first day, our driver was a 15-year-old Dutch kid who got his licence the month before. He was smoking, dropping lit cigarettes through the hole in the gear shift, almost going into the engine. The door of the van fell off when we crossed borders." The tour had been booked by someone who didn't seem to notice that two gigs were separated by a 26-hour drive. "It was literally impossible to make the show the next day," says Haliechuk. "We slept on the side of the highway in Sweden one night. We slept on the lawn of the defence ministry in Paris. This was before Mapquest. We'd be given a binder with 30 maps: 'Have fun figuring out where all the shows are!'"

The shows themselves were modest, populated by the same 20 or 30 people who will show up if there's a punk show happening in any small European town. Shockingly, the band broke even. "You could do it cheaply," says Haliechuk. "Fucked Up has never lost money on a tour. That's something we instituted from the beginning: we're not going to do a tour that loses money. We never had to pay out of our pockets to do stuff. That felt silly. We didn't have ambitions as a band. We thought it was cool to put out seven-inches and if someone wants us to play a show, they can figure it out for us. I do remember having a pouch of cash, full of 15 different currencies. I'd sleep with it in my shirt every night. That's how we did our books."

Back home, they continued to bait the local scene, which at the time was enraptured with the term Torontopia—a DIY movement detached from any commercial aspirations, instead prioritizing art, collaboration, community and spontaneity. Central to this was the Blocks Recording Club, co-run by Steve Kado and featuring his friend Owen Pallett. Fucked Up put out "Ban Violins," a jab at both the Hidden Cameras song "Ban Marriage" and the ubiquity of Owen Pallett on records by Jim Guthrie, the Hidden Cameras, Arcade Fire and others. They even claimed Pallett played on the song, which was taken at face value by the press, thereby validating the prank.

Rather than taking offence, Pallett was delighted by the mischief. Kado approached Fucked Up at a Wavelength show about putting out a single or EP on Blocks. "I think he thought we were cute in this punk historian way," says Haliechuk. "Here we are, becoming a global punk sensation, playing a little Wavelength show, and some little indie rock impresario says, 'Oh, this is cool, it reminds me of punk bands I was into before indie rock.'"

"Steve Kado came to my house, and it was super tense," says Abraham. "Years later, he told me, 'We didn't know if you guys wanted to fight us or what.'

The rhetoric had been so amped up. We were anti–indie rock. We were trying to get this into confrontation. From our point of view, we were trying to be playful. There's more of that in hardcore." Kado suggested Pallett play on Fucked Up's next record; Pallett soon came to visit Abraham as well.

"He was so cool and the opposite of what we expected," says the singer. "We thought everyone would have a chip on their shoulder in the Torontopia scene, but they were doing the exact same thing we wanted to do. Not sonically but community-wise and team-building. We were all in it together."

Or were they? "We left the country, came back with our credibility and weren't interested in sharing it with indie rock kids," counters Haliechuk. "We'd play those shows every once in a while, but our big output in Toronto was when we'd do our own international punk fest, which we did every year."

Fucked Up's annual Halloween shows at Sneaky Dee's, beginning in 2005, featured their favourite hardcore acts from around the world. "It was really awesome to get to the point where all your fantasies came true, all your favourite bands and friends from all over the place," says Abraham. "Fifteen people would stay at my apartment, and we'd go to record stores around the city. It was that Torontopian idea of building your own paradise. That was the weekend it felt like we'd done that."

One of the guests that first Halloween were Toronto punk legends the Viletones. They were on stage ready to play and no one could find singer Steve Leckie—he'd left the venue without telling anyone. What had once been the most dangerous band in Toronto, 30 years ago, sheepishly packed up their gear and left the stage. It was the Fucked Up era now.

Just as the Viletones once taunted polite Toronto with a singer who called himself Nazi Dog, the otherwise progressive Fucked Up were not above a crude, provocative prank. In the inherently political world of the local music scene, their target was the biggest mainstream Toronto rock band of the mid-2000s: Billy Talent.

IN THE FALL OF 2005, Fucked Up had a show with Alexisonfire side project Black Lungs at Queen West venue the Bovine Sex Club. "We had friends who partied there and became glam people," says Abraham. "It's not our scene, but it was such an awesome venue for shows. It was a thing to be asked to play. It didn't happen to bands like us. It felt like we were not in our world. It was a bar, not an all-ages space. This place had a sound tech and bouncers."

After the Black Lungs set, a bunch of the crowd went outside to cool off and/or smoke. When Fucked Up took the stage, the outside crowd tried to return, only to be told the club was at capacity. Altercations with the club's bouncers broke out. Meanwhile, Ian D'Sa of Billy Talent arrived with some friends and was waved through; he'd been going there since the club opened and knew the bouncers personally. That inflamed the situation. "The lineup started yelling at me," says D'Sa. "I didn't say anything, walked in, didn't pay attention to who was on stage—I wasn't there to see the band. I walked right to the back, to see my friends in Alexisonfire, and hung out for an hour or two and then left."

Meanwhile, on stage, says Haliechuk, "We were watching our friends be choke-slammed by bouncers as they tried to get into the club, physically smashed into the floor. Soon after, the bar shut down the show and called the police."

"As I was leaving," says D'Sa, "some of the kids were following me and yelling at me down the street. I told my buddy, 'Don't pay attention.' But he's a bit of a hothead, so he turns around and gives them the finger. We get in a cab and I'm like, 'Why'd you have to do that?' A few days later there was an article in *Eye Weekly*, an interview with Fucked Up where they call me a slick, douchebag poser. I'd never even met these people! It was so bizarre to me. It was such a Larry David moment."

That article, written by comedian Nick Flanagan, quoted Haliechuk calling Billy Talent "assholes" and banning them from any future Fucked Up shows. Eight months went by, and in June 2006 Billy Talent put out their second album, with the song "Where Is the Line?" Singer Ben Kowalewicz told interviewers it was about Queen Street punks.

Damian Abraham saw this and was perplexed. He called George Pettit of Alexisonfire, a mutual friend. "There's no fucking way that's about us," said Abraham.

"No, that pissed them off," said Pettit, referring to the *Eye Weekly* article. "They were super bummed out. They liked your band."

"So they wrote a dis song about us?"

"Yeah, it's probably about you guys."

Abraham, the professional wrestling fan who was also obsessed with rap rivalries, had been waiting for something like this. "I was like, 'It's on! Let's go to the studio right now!'" They quickly wrote and recorded "The Line" and put it on their next mixtape in July 2006; it soon surfaced online.

It opens with Abraham declaring, "We're going to make a cheeseburger out of this beef!" before launching into a seething screed: "Ska punk! Skanking pickle! I knew you were fake from day one . . . 'Try Honesty?' Try licking my balls!" If that wasn't enough, Abraham seals the deal with a spoken outro: "I wouldn't want people that buy your fucking records to buy our records, people that buy your records are deaf, and fucking deaf and idiots and date rapists and

447

homophobes . . . people who like you are worse than fucking Nazis . . . they're shit eaters, they can eat. my. shit."

"I look back on some of those lyrics, and they're my favourite lyrics ever," he says. "There's nothing horrible in there, just the most mean, cutting disses. I was a fat, insecure kid, and now I could take shots at rock stars." It's pointed out to him that he did, in fact, call Billy Talent's fans date rapists, among other things. "Did I say that?" he chuckles, humbled. "Okay, that hasn't aged well. But I hated their fans, hated the band. To me they were a jock band. It was born out of real hate and vitriol." It wasn't the first time Abraham came to regret some of his choices: he once titled a song "In Praise of School Shooters" on a little-heard solo project. Now a father of three, he confesses, "I'm not happy I put that out there."

Billy Talent insisted that "Where Is the Line?" was written six months before the Bovine Sex Club incident. They were hurt and angry at Fucked Up's response. "I listened to it once and it made me want to vomit," says Gallant. "It was so hurtful." Kowalewicz refused to listen to it. D'Sa, the main target of the beef, says, "Somebody sent it to me again recently, and I'm like, Wow, those guys were really angry. At the time I thought, Okay, this is juvenile, and I tried to pay it no mind—but I'm not going to lie, it got under my skin. We've never talked about it. I've been in rooms with those guys and we've never spoken about this incident. Never received an apology, which I was kind of hoping for, but it's in the past. Alexisonfire are the nice guys in between. I remember George saying, 'This is a giant misunderstanding. I don't get it. They're the biggest nerds ever. You guys would actually really get along.'"

"WHERE IS THE LINE?" was a deep cut on *Billy Talent II*, an album packed with five singles, four of which hit the top 10 on Canadian radio. The album went to No. 1 at home and in Germany. It was a huge step up artistically. It remains the band's biggest-selling record and fan favourite.

Opening track "Devil in a Midnight Mass" boasts a speaker-shredding riff that sounds like a buzzsaw cutting through a hive of bees. The martial rallying cry of "Red Flag" is a proto-Parkland/Greta Thunberg youth anthem. "Surrender" is a mid-tempo pop song in the vein of R.E.M., uncharacteristic for that time. One of the album's biggest singles was one of the last songs written for the record, "Fallen Leaves." Outside the studio in Vancouver's Gastown, in Pigeon Park, were etchings of leaves on the sidewalks, in memory of overdose victims, on streets where the city's world-famous heroin problem was more than visible. The metaphor became obvious. "We found out that a couple of friends of ours who are living there ended up getting badly hooked, so we wrote that song about their struggles," says Kowalewicz. "Luckily, they cleaned themselves up and turned their lives around. But at the time, we wrote it about friends lost into the enchanted world that leads to nowhere."

Returning producer Gavin Brown was a huge part of the album's success, but there were signs that the relationship was fraying. "Gavin did a really good job on our first record," says D'Sa, who took a co-producer credit on *Billy Talent II*. "He made us unique enough to stand out from other bands at the time. He was the one who made me realize what we're capable of sonically." On the second record, among other disputes, Brown wanted to ditch "Red Flag," which became a live favourite for decades later.

"As much as it wasn't always pretty and perfect, all the little conflicts brought the best out of the records," says Kowalewicz. "The biggest songs we've ever had are from those records. He helped harness and focus us." Among other triumphs, Billy Talent headlined their hometown hockey arena, the Air Canada Centre, for the first time (of many) in February 2007.

But America was not to be. Billy Talent's U.S. prospects took a dive when they delivered their second record to Atlantic. Their new A&R rep, who'd signed Death Cab for Cutie and James Blunt, told the band, "I don't hear a Green Day single."

"They never worked that record at all," says Gallant. "They didn't like any of it." In Canada, the album almost went gold in the first week of release. More important, it went to No. 1 in Germany.

Canadian bands are always told to sign directly to a U.S. label, so that they're a priority in the biggest English-speaking market, and the rest of the world in turn sees them as not just a regional Canadian thing. Billy Talent are the rare exception: it was Warner Germany that fell in love with the records and put their marketing muscle behind them. The press and MTV Europe jumped on board. So did one key promoter, who was distraught that the band couldn't afford to fly over for a tour he had booked, so he went back and renegotiated higher offers, while also tour-managing the band himself to save money. He hooked them up with a top 10 German punk band, Beatsteaks, for a series of opening slots that served as a solid introduction to German audiences. "Every single one of their fans ended up liking us," claims Gallant.

Subsequent headlining tours in Germany and Austria kept getting better and better to the point where touring choices became obvious. "We could play for 20 people in Oklahoma or play for 1,000 in Vienna," says Kowalewicz. "Where you gonna go?" By the end of the decade, Billy Talent's name got large-type billing on major German festivals like Rock am Ring; they headlined alongside the Killers and Korn, playing prime slots in front of 75,000 people. No new Canadian rock band since Saga, in the '80s, could say the same—and Saga wasn't multiplatinum at home.

At home, at Quebec City's Festival d'été in July 2006, Billy Talent set an attendance record: 105,000 people topping a bill with Alexisonfire and Social Distortion. The festival sent them a $2,000 bonus, which they donated to charity.

The third album—called, yes, *Billy Talent III*—was even stronger, although their American record label didn't think so. Despite being produced by Brendan Benson—Pearl Jam's preferred producer and the sonic architect of Bruce Springsteen's comeback—Atlantic was lukewarm at best on the final product, rejecting the single "Rusted by the Rain" and wanting to bump the album's release by a year. Billy Talent wasn't having it. They had commitments in Canada and Europe, which were more important anyway. They asked to be released from their U.S. contract, remaining with Warner for the rest of the world. Roadrunner Records, the U.S. label that had broken Nickelback, agreed to put it out in America with only a week's notice. It still managed to crack the top 40 of Billboard's Top Rock Albums in 2009, while going top three in Germany, Austria, Switzerland, Finland and No. 1 in Canada.

AFTER ALEXISONFIRE HAD two gold albums under their belt, the Juno Awards deemed them eligible to be nominated as Breakthrough Group of the Year in 2005. The band went to Winnipeg for the ceremony and won the award, beating former tour mates Death from Above 1979. But they felt pretty out of place.

"Two tables over from us was Burton Cummings," says George Pettit. "I grew up with the Guess Who in my house. [*Hockey Night in Canada's*] Ron MacLean was there. It was weird. We were watching the red carpet of people arriving, and Gord Downie was asked who he was excited to see—and he mentioned our band's name. I wasn't a huge Hip fan at that moment in my life, but when I was a kid I had all the cassettes. They are what they are: a cultural force, a part of Canada, ingrained in history. And now he said my band's name—that was surreal. But we felt like outsiders, for sure. We were very much in a van and touring in the punk indie world, and that world doesn't cross paths with the Juno world too much."

In between tours, Dallas Green quietly put out a solo EP called *The Death of Me*, credited to City and Colour (a reference to his first and last name). He posted the tracks to MySpace. Sam Sutherland, then a 16-year-old high school student in his first band, boldly emailed Green out of the blue and asked if he wanted to play their CD release party. "We were not friends, but he was an accessible person in the punk community," says Sutherland. Surprisingly, Green agreed, even though there was no guarantee of being paid. "It was dead silence when he played," Sutherland says. "He played with the mic three feet away from his mouth; he has an opera singer's internal organs. I don't even know if the mic was on, but he filled the entire room. When it was over, he was like, 'Cool, man, this was fun. I like getting to play my solo stuff.' We didn't make any money. I'm almost positive we didn't pay him."

City and Colour was a respite from the raucous nature of Alexisonfire shows, which were starting to get out of hand. "People would get in fights at shows," says Pettit. "The violence didn't make it an inclusive environment, so if someone was fighting, I'd stop the show and accost the people doing it. Usually I found a way to bring [the show] back [on track]. And nothing fires a crowd up more than when you're yelling at them at the top of your lungs. They liked it. I would kick [the bruisers] out of the show, and then we'd kick into a song and everyone would be pumped by the whole experience."

"People were crowd-surfing, jumping up and down, singing and going nuts," says Carriere, "but it wasn't violent. It was positive. Back then, if you went to see Snapcase or Hatebreed shows in Buffalo, it would just be too violent. Or the punk shows in St. Catharines, like the Sick Boys, were full-on drunk fests with sprayed beer everywhere. Seeing the connection Alexis had with kids in a safe environment where the shows were run by the book, seeing the crowd's enthusiasm, was awesome."

One night at Red's in the West Edmonton Mall was a bit different. "We were going across Canada with Rise Against," Pettit recalls. "The security at the show were being violent toward the crowd all night. I thought it was unnecessary. People were crowd-surfing, and [security would] bring them down, push them out of the way or punch them. I had to stop the show a few times and tell them to get it together. 'What are you doing? You're going to harm someone. These people aren't doing something wrong. We want them to crowd-surf.'

"*After* the show, a couple of security guards were roughing up a young man. Dallas came over to them and said, 'What the hell are you guys doing?' One of them put Dallas in a headlock, while another grabbed his arm and started working on it like a pretzel. Everyone from the tour piled out of the backstage and we confronted security. Mall security stepped in, so now there's these guys standing around with batons. Rise Against were touring with a guy known only as Wild Card: he was in the Air Force, a helicopter mechanic, this big guy who looks like a football player. Now he's in there, too, and we didn't know where Dallas was. Someone threw a drink from a balcony and it hit Sean [McNab] from Jersey, who was our tour manager at the time. The beer hit him and spilled on a security guard, and then the security guard clocked Sean in the face.

"Eventually we all loaded out as quickly as possible and got our shit in the van. Then the whole security staff is standing behind our van. Lucky for us, this police officer rolls up. I went over and said, 'Hey, can you please stay here, because this group of guys want to kill us.' He did, and we got the hell out of there. It was in the paper the next day, and they talked to everyone but us, and we sounded like horrible people. Stuff like that would always happen."

There was one show left in that leg of the tour in Vancouver. Drummer Jesse Ingelevics decided he didn't want to play it. He booked a flight home, and tour manager McNab saw him leaving the hotel with all his stuff. McNab confronted him. "Uh, you can't just leave, we have a sold-out show in Vancouver tomorrow."

"I gotta go home," replied Ingelevics. "I got stuff to take care of." He was married with kids, and his life path had become abruptly evident that one night. Alexisonfire cancelled the next show and drove home, but not before calling Jersey's Jordan Hastings to ask if he wanted to spend two days learning the band's catalogue, followed by three days of rehearsal and then a 28-date European tour. Hastings has been in the band ever since.

Alexisonfire then took two months off to write new material. They threw out all existing song ideas they had lying around to start fresh. As a stopgap, they put out a split EP with Moneen, each band covering the other's songs, on Joel Carriere's new label, Dine Alone. He and the band had parted ways with Greg Below and Distort. Dine Alone was a huge success right out of the gate: its first full record, released in November 2005, was City and Colour's official debut, *Sometimes*. Buoyed by the single "Save Your Scissors," the album went platinum. "That record cost us next to no money, which is awesome for a new label's first release," says Carriere. "We made our money back after we sold 50 copies."

But how did a solo acoustic song from a guy in a hardcore band get airplay on corporate rock radio? Joel Carriere says simply, "There was an audience that liked his voice." But of course there's more to it than that. "We got maybe 60% of the Alexisonfire audience," he continues, "and the other 40 probably hated his solo stuff. Then we had a new audience. We made a really cool video, shot all around St. Catharines, and it did well. I'd taken what I'd learned over the last five years and did a distribution deal with Universal. At the time, everything wasn't so corporate. I could go in there and talk with people without having to pay some kind of ser-vice fee. It was very collaborative and everyone wanted us to succeed. And tech: Dallas's first versions of City and Colour were all traded on Napster. So when we launched, we had that audience, plus the Alexis audience, a lot of stuff working in our favour. And we had no investors—it was just us."

Green also sang lead on the single "The Grace" by a studio project called Neverending White Lights (other singers on the album were from late '90s CanRock mainstays Our Lady Peace, the Watchmen and Finger Eleven). "The Grace" became a top five radio hit and a MuchMusic smash.

Along with Alexisonfire's "Accidents", and the City and Colour single, "We had three songs that were top 10 at rock radio at once," says Carriere. "Dallas's voice was on three different tracks that had three different vibes across Canada. I'd hear those songs back to back sometimes." Dallas Green was no longer the pretty voice in the weird punk band that somehow had become popular; he was a legit mainstream star.

Perhaps in part because of that, Alexisonfire felt they still had a lot to prove, and they poured that energy into their third album, *Crisis*. "I wanted to make a more serious record," says Pettit. "When you're young and playing in a heavy band and suddenly you're in this new funny world of MuchMusic, your first instinct is to make a joke of it." Hence the cartoonish pulp-fiction, pastel cover art on *Watch Out!*, designed by a tat artist from Tatamagouche, Justin Winstanley. In contrast, the cover of *Crisis* features a black-and-white news photo of a man suffering from frostbite; the internal images, and the title track, document the 1977 "white death" blizzard that crippled the Niagara Region and western New York with more than two metres of snow, howling winds and bitter cold, killing 31 people. Take that, mall punk.

The music maintained the anthemic triumph of earlier work with more dynamics, guitar textures and piano. Unlike many of their peers in aggressive music—many of whom were recording one guitar string at a time, Def Leppard style, to achieve certain harmonic effects—Alexisonfire recorded as live and raw as possible. "When you're at a concert, there is reverb and craziness and playing pristinely is not the point," says Pettit. "I have a lot of respect for people who record electronically, but when it comes to playing in a rock band, you need to hear the room. We were like that with gear, too. There were lots of people using the newest things, and their guitar gear looked like the hull of a nuclear sub. Whereas Dallas and Wade were playing these antique Gibsons through big, heavy old amps. We used heavier-gage strings: more rumble, more from the hips. That's what we sound like. At a show in Paris, someone came up and said, 'I hate screamo music. But you guys have balls.' I want the bass to come through on our records, as opposed to what other people were doing."

The album opens with "Drunks, Lovers, Sinners and Saints," beginning with Wade MacNeil, screaming, "This is from our hearts!" "That song in particular," says Pettit, "is about making art and not artifice, about performing from a place of sincerity and not because you saw someone else do it." The rest of the album is filled images of drudgery and disarray, of hollowed-out cities and societal rot, countered by earnestness and escapism akin to Springsteen: "This Could Be Anywhere in the World" is essentially "Born to Run" for the so-called "scene kids" of the 2000s.

"A lot of people have had those lyrics tattooed on them," says Pettit. "Dallas and I collaborated on the lyrics; we grew up very differently, in different households, but that song probably hit with so many people because everyone can relate to the idea of being from a city that they don't care for at some point or another, or feeling that they've been wronged by a place."

Crisis came out in August 2006 and debuted at No. 1 in Canada. Again, it was not just a coup for the band but for Carriere's Dine Alone Records, who'd achieved something Arts & Crafts and other celebrated indies had not. Leading up to the album's release that summer, Alexisonfire once again joined the Warped Tour across North America, which that year featured an unusual number of Canadian bands: Billy Talent, Moneen, Sum 41, Silverstein, Protest the Hero and the Black Maria. Alexisonfire then spent the next two years on the road, feeling they had to seize every opportunity that came in the wake of their commercial and artistic triumph. "It was nonstop," says Hastings. "Most places we would hit two or three times, like Australia specifically. The rooms were getting bigger there; it was up there with Canada and the U.K."

That came at a cost. "It wasn't good for us," says Pettit. "Four-fifths of the band were drinking too much and acting out—fairly cliché rock'n'roll lifestyle stuff and making bad decisions. A little too free. We could have handled ourselves better." While the rest of the band was partying, Green wrote acoustic material that became the second City and Colour album. In 2008, when he was ready to put it out, he called a band meeting and read the riot act.

Recalls Pettit, "He was sober and we weren't. We were fucking animals. A lot of drinking, blacking out. He was taking care of us. That was probably a pretty lonely time for Dallas at that point. He wanted us to get it together and take it seriously. The shows weren't necessarily suffering, but it wasn't going to last. At the pace we were going, someone would get hurt or something bad would happen."

FUCKED UP WERE ready to grow up. They started on their first full-length album, 2006's *Hidden World*, five years after the band's first gig. Finally ready to make a bigger statement, this collection of songs proved they were much more than juvenile punk purists with a profane name. Fucked Up signed a deal with American indie label Jade Tree, which had started as a D.C. hardcore label but had the most success with so-called emo-punk bands like the Promise Ring and Joan of Arc. It was a tiny, yet significant, step closer to the mainstream—not just the label, but the music itself.

"It was a big stylistic jump for us," says Haliechuk. "Our seven-inches were tight studies of an aesthetic, like what a punk record would sound like in the '70s.

Seeing us, we were these dirty, weird scuzz people. Then we put out this grandiose record. It was five years of learning about stuff, about life. We still didn't have any ambition to be an amazing live unit. We didn't practise that much, and we didn't care about our live show, really. The record hit people because of what it was about rather than what it sounded like or the feeling. That record is about weird stuff, dense with ideas."

"My songs were all about religion," says Abraham. "Mike's songs were all about plants and rocks. I was just winding up my degree in women's studies at the University of Toronto, and I was having my norms and perceptions and assumptions blown away daily. I was reading a lot of Chomsky; I find him very soothing. I'm not going to pretend I got into Chomsky as an intellectual pursuit; it was entirely because of Propagandhi. And Chumbawamba did a split with him, a spoken word record. That's probably the most academic Fucked Up record, because I was still in school."

It was the band's first experience with both a record contract and deadlines. "We got 10 grand to record it, which seemed like a lot but quickly disappeared," says Haliechuk. "That was two straight weeks of recording 14 hours a day, rushing to get it done, and having to call the label and asking for another couple thousand dollars. That's why it sounds so fast. We were rushing against a budget." They were also rushing to write new songs, despite having five years' worth of singles behind them. Only "Baiting the Public" reappeared on *Hidden World*. "We were confused, up to the point where we recorded it, about what was going to go on this record," says Haliechuk. "It definitely wasn't written as an LP statement, 10 songs that will sit together. It just happened."

For audiences who had only heard the band's name before, *Hidden World* was a sprawling introduction to a hardcore band whose screaming singer had plenty to say about Gnosticism and the Christian crusades, with guest appearances ranging from CBC-friendly Owen Pallett to commercial screamo king George Pettit. For the hardcore faithful, it was a betrayal of a very limited aesthetic.

"It was a micro stylistic shift in the grand scheme of things," says Haliechuk. "We had this period from 2006 to 2010, this transition where we lost our diehard fans and gained a lot more casual fans, which leaves you in this no man's land of appeal, with just as many people who despise you as they once loved you. And a bunch more people who will go to your show but maybe not next time. When you're sleeping on people's couches and playing for the same 50 people in every city, you're making really close friends all over the place. Once you realize those people don't like your band anymore, it's alienating on a personal level."

For Abraham, who had always taken a dogmatic approach to his sense of punk history, it was doubly difficult. "Every time someone gets mad at Fucked Up for 'changing our sound' or 'selling out,' I'm like, 'Yeah, dude, I get it. I'd be right there with you, too.' After you've been in a band for a prolonged period of time, you realize it would be weird to sentence someone to playing the exact same thing for their whole career."

Hidden World was launched at co-op venue Tranzac Club, with Montreal's AIDS Wolf and Toronto's Uncut and Wyrd Visions; proceeds went to the lobby group Sex Professionals of Canada. In the first of an accelerating list of media coups, Fucked Up landed on the cover of *Eye Weekly*; Abraham and Miranda were pictured holding sparklers that obscured certain letters in the band's name.

Among the stranger side effects of that exposure is that drummer Jonah Falco had to tell his parents what his band was actually called; he'd been dodging their questions for five years. "He had to tell so many lies," laughs Abraham. "He had to lie to get into the band [about playing drums]; he had to lie to his parents about being in the band. When we'd go on tour, he'd say he was sleeping over at a friend's for the weekend. We were like, 'Dude, you're in university. You don't need to lie to your parents! Just go!' Jonah had told his dad that we had changed the name and was so freaked out that whole week that his parents would find out."

By 2007, everyone was ready to quit their jobs and commit to the band full-time— which was a fairly easy decision, as only Miranda had a full-time job. Booking agents came calling. A lawyer offered to find them a better record deal. Their notoriety got another boost when they appeared on MTV Canada.

The idea of Fucked Up appearing on television, especially at that point in their career, was absurd. But the newly launched music television station—which had faced regulatory hurdles for more than 20 years in order to compete with MuchMusic—only appeared on certain cable packages and was willing to do just about anything to get viewers and notoriety of their own. So they invited Fucked Up to play live on-air at five p.m., the after-school slot, at the station's studios inside the Masonic Temple, a.k.a. the former Concert Hall on Yonge Street. Fucked Up told all their friends, who showed up—and fucked things up.

In the clip, it's hard to tell exactly what went wrong and when. It looks like a typical punk crowd of moshers and crowd-surfers, until one of them appears to be carrying a large plate of glass. "Someone ripped part of the stage off," says Haliechuk. "Officially we got blamed and were presented with a bill. I think legally they had to charge somebody, but there was never anyone saying we had to pay it." *Vice* magazine claimed the band had been "banned" from the station, which the station was quick to rebut. "In no way, shape or form was Fucked Up banned from MTV," a senior producer told *Vice*. "We fucking loved it so much we put the performance up [online] everywhere. I would like to see any other station have the balls to have them on."

Eighteen months later, MTV put their own balls to the wall. Fucked Up were invited back, and "that time we actually did do a fair amount of damage and did dangerous things," says Haliechuk.

There were discussions with the station about how best to stage a performance that wouldn't emulate the first. "We said, 'Well, we're not just going to do a normal thing, because that would be a bit of a sell-out look, to now be polished and playing on the stage. We want to do something weird,'" says Haliechuk. "All they could think of was, 'Why don't you do a show in the bathroom?' Which was ill-conceived, because you can't even really get a camera in there."

The day of the performance, they went to a Fred Perry apparel shop, who gave them anything they wanted as long as they wore it on-air. For unrelated reasons, Henry Rollins was in the MTV studio that day and they got to meet a hero. Before their one-song set, one of the VJs visited the band's dressing room.

"You guys going to fuck up the bathroom today?"

"I don't know, maybe."

"Yeah, man, fuck it up," the VJ told Fucked Up. "It's getting replaced anyway. Just fuck it up."

The band crammed into the bathroom, with Sebastien Grainger of Death from Above 1979 there to scream along and add to the mayhem. Falco's drums were in front of a urinal. Within seconds of beginning "Twice Born," Abraham thrust his mic stand through the ceiling, tore down a tile and smashed it over his head. "Kurt Cobain R.I.P." was spray-painted on the walls (odd, since it was neither the Nirvana leader's birthday nor the anniversary of his death). Someone kept turning off the bathroom lights, resulting in a dark screen on the TV feed.

"In the first chorus of the song," says Haliechuk, "you can see an amp fall on me, and I'm like, 'I'm outta here,' and pushed my way through. I just left and watched the rest of the show from the dressing room. I wasn't going to get a $400 shirt wrecked. It was actually very dangerous. The hallway was full of kids and the room could have blown up. Damian filled one of the sinks with lighter fluid and was about to light it on fire, and meanwhile we'd brought a fucking motorcycle full of gasoline in there."

"I didn't want the fucking motorcycle in there!" Abraham counters. "That was a Mike thing, some kind of nod to *Class of 1984* [a youth-gone-wild film shot at Toronto's Central Tech in 1983]. Why would you put a motorcycle in the bathroom?! My thing was to fill all the sinks with lighter fluid and then throw matches so that there would be flashpots. But as soon as I saw the motorcycle, I decided to just leave the lighter fluid where it was. Then MTV found it and was like, 'They were going to burn down the building with lighter fluid!' Clearly none of the people at MTV had ever tried to set something on fire with just lighter fluid."

At first, and privately, MTV was thrilled. "The VP came down and said, 'That was such good TV.' Which it was, I'm sure," says Haliechuk. Publicly, however, the hammer came down. The band got a bill for $10,000 and were banned from the building. "Later that same VP was quoted in *blogTO* about walking through the 'carnage' and saying things like, 'I can't believe what they did!' says Abraham, still incensed more than a decade later. "We were like, 'You motherfucker! You kept telling us this is what you wanted. We gave it to you!'" The same day they got the bill, they were dropped from a scheduled appearance on the MTV teen drama *Skins*. But all press is good press, and it drew attention to the landmark album Fucked Up had just released on October 7, 2008.

The Chemistry of Common Life took more than a year to make, in between the band's now-constant touring schedule—127 dates in 2008 alone—which took them to Europe multiple times, including a U.K. tour with Gallows, as well as extensive U.S. jaunts, including SXSW showcases in both 2007 and 2008. In August 2008, Fucked Up got a last-minute call to open for Iggy and the Stooges at Massey Hall, which Haliechuk and Falco missed because they had stayed in Europe for a vacation after a tour. Filling in for them was the band's studio engineer, Jon Drew of Uncut, and Ben Cook. Cook was a Toronto friend they'd encountered on a U.K. tour, where he sat in with them for several dates. Cook was soon the newest member of Fucked Up and its third guitarist.

Cook was a child actor (*Goosebumps*, *Road to Avonlea*) who formed the hardcore band No Warning in 1998, playing the same kind of shows Fucked Up did in the early days, although No Warning went much further. They toured Japan and were briefly managed by Treble Charger's Greig Nori, which led to Cook co-writing with Sum 41 and Hedley. No Warning was also courted by Limp Bizkit[1] and put out a record on a label run by nu-metal band Linkin Park. No Warning broke up in late 2005.

Cook didn't play on *Chemistry*, but he hung out in the studio, watching as Zucker and Haliechuk layered as many as 50 guitar tracks on a single song, à la Billy Corgan. Though the bed tracks were recorded live, Haliechuk spent much of his time building walls of sound. "*Hidden World* was 70 minutes of shrieking guitars and speed and yelling. The follow-up needed to be more diverse," he says. "I was writing a lot of it at my house with a looping pedal. We'd have 20 pedals in the studio, experimenting with what the sounds could be like. The guitar amps would be 10 at once, chained to each other. There were acoustic guitars hung on the walls of the studio, and the strings broke because there was so

---

1   A message left by Fred Durst on Cook's answering machine later appeared on a Fucked Up mixtape.

much sound when I was playing. That gave me a real boost. I wanted an insane guitar record."

On top of recording and touring, Haliechuk spent any remaining time in 2008 dealing with lawyers, as the band had to buy out their contract with Jade Tree. Fucked Up claims the label did nothing to promote *Hidden World* during an eight-month tour; the label eventually stopped returning their emails. The band was courted by several labels and opted for indie giant Matador, whose most popular acts—Pavement, Yo La Tengo, Interpol, Cat Power—were hardly on the same sonic page as the hardcore band. Being on Matador would expose the band to a whole new audience. It didn't come easy. "The Matador contract was 300 pages," says Haliechuk, who was effectively the band's manager. (He used the alias David Eliade for all managerial duties.) "It took a year to parse through and get in a good enough position to sign it."

Upon *Chemistry*'s release, Fucked Up were on the cover of *Exclaim!* with the headline "Will Fucked Up Kill Each Other?" The story by Sam Sutherland details an inner-band fistfight at Heathrow Airport and multiple attempts by Abraham, Haliechuk and Miranda to leave the band. Haliechuk is portrayed as the sonic architect and is quoted as saying, "If it were up to me, we wouldn't tour or really play at all."

"We all want to be a different band," Abraham told Sutherland. "I don't think it's a good show unless kids are going crazy. For Mike, he wants people to be like, 'Oh, I really like what you did with your pedals there.'"

The article made much fuss of the guest list on the record: it opens with a flute solo—a flute solo! On a hardcore record!—by Jonah Falco's mother, the jazz artist Jane Fair. Alexisonfire's Dallas Green sings on one track. Tom Wade-West, who plays French horn on the record, was Abraham's and Falco's high school teacher. Katie Stelmanis, formerly of riot grrrl band Galaxy and soon to be reinvented as operatic electro artist Austra, sings an incongruous duet with Abraham. Max McCabe-Lokos of Deadly Snakes and Michael Armstrong of King Cobb Steelie also guest. That month, Fucked Up was also on the cover of the *NME* in Britain, a rarity for a Canadian band of any stripe. (Since Godspeed, only Avril Lavigne, Hot Hot Heat and Arcade Fire had made the cut.) A bloodied and shirtless Abraham was pictured looking stunned standing in a record shop aisle with the headline, "Our Shows Are Orgies of Destruction."

A few days after the MTV bathroom incident, Fucked Up headed to New York to play a 12-hour gig at a store in Manhattan (which, among other things, featured Moby joining them for a cover of "Blitzkrieg Bop"), before a headlining slot at the Bowery Ballroom and another show in Brooklyn the night after that. Their New York stock was rising. A month later, the *New York Times* reviewed the album and compared it favourably to *Who's Next*, without ever mentioning the Toronto band's name.

Everything that came after is a bit of a blur for the band: five years of nonstop touring and recording, including five dates in China in March 2009, booked by a friend from the U.S. Midwest who moved there to study martial arts. The gigs in the authoritarian country weren't totally authorized.

"We took a boat from Osaka to Shanghai, a 48-hour ferry ride on rough seas," says Abraham. "Everyone on the boat, except for the crew and Jonah, were throwing up. Luckily we paid for first class, which meant we had bunkbeds in a room. Originally we were supposed to be sleeping in the main area, which was just mats on the floor with sleeping bags—so people are just rolling into each other's vomit all night." Upon arrival at the Shanghai port, they had to convince customs that it was a total coincidence that the only white people on the whole boat were also Canadians. It somehow worked. "That night we played in Nanjing in some weird-ass bar full of military soldiers, expats, hanging out with sex workers," says Abraham. "We brought a busload of people who had won a contest through Converse in China. But the bus broke down on the outskirts of the city, so we had to take cabs to the city with all these contest winners.

"Some people knew who we were in Shanghai, but we mainly played to expats," Abraham continues. "Some people knew us through YouTube. A lot of people had seen our MTV performance. We'd show up at clubs and the owners would be like, 'Please don't smash everything.' Most of the local bands would use that as a practice space. The clubs were like community centres. There was no way I'd be destroying that drum kit—that would be an asshole thing to do."

All the touring was taking a toll on Abraham in particular, and small wonder— the singer routinely cut open his forehead on stage, not unlike the professional wrestlers he loved so much, and subjected himself to all kinds of physical abuse. That dated back to their very first gig. "The first time we played Planet Kensington," he says of his 2001 debut, "I'd be in the bathroom psyching myself out. 'They fucking hate you. Let's do this shit.' Then I went out there and was a freak, unhinged completely. I was taking it out on myself. People were moshing, and I'd throw myself at their legs and knock them down. I'd jump on Jonah's drum kit while he was playing. Eventually the wrestling stuff came on my radar, and I started bleeding on stage and that side of things took over. I thought, I'm going to hurt myself either way, and if there's a lot of blood, it's more spectacular than if I'm smashing myself up on Jonah's drum kit.

"The most dangerous thing I ever did on stage was in Brighton. Our roadie, as a joke, put a jar of peanut butter on stage. I was thinking of [a legendary '70s performance by] Iggy Pop and so I covered myself in peanut butter. I was walking through the audience. No one could see what it was, because the lights were purple and red. People were opening their mouths and I'm dropping peanut butter in their mouth from my hand. Then it hits me: fuck, people die from this shit! I stopped the song. 'Yo, everybody, I'm covered in *fucking peanut butter*. If you are allergic to peanut butter, please leave and I will give you a full refund. *Oh my god*, I can't believe I did this!' I could have killed someone. I also once climbed up on scaffolding at Coachella in 2009, where I covered the whole audience in blood. I was bleeding from the head, busted open, it went everywhere. Couldn't stop the bleeding. We only played Coachella once—go figure. I look back and that was all a panic reaction, dealing with the anxiety of being on stage through self-harm. Probably not the healthiest thing to get into."

For Abraham, everything came to a head in 2009 in Europe. By that point, he was cycling on and off antianxiety medication; he'd go off them while writing lyrics at home and back on while touring. "A lot of my anxiety is around travel and the lack of security from day to day," he says. "Now we were doing these European tours with very little sleep. A perfect combination for mental health issues to arrive." In Holland, he was unable to get a refill on his medication and started to panic. He'd been offered weed before but thought it was "some hippie magical bullshit," he says. "I turned to Sandy and Josh backstage in Rotterdam, and said, 'Can I smoke that joint with you guys?' I did, and it was the best night ever. All my anxiety went away immediately. I realize this sounds like a 'do drugs' ad, but for me, it gave me something else to help deal with the tour stress, other than hurting myself on stage."

Back home, the larger Canadian media finally figured out what Fucked Up was all about. Though they had lots of media supporters—*Exclaim!*, *Eye Weekly*, Ben Rayner at the *Toronto Star*, George Stroumboulopoulos—few editors and producers took the band seriously. But in June 2009, eight months after its release, *The Chemistry of Common Life* landed on the shortlist for the Polaris Music Prize, pitting it against mainstream albums by Joel Plaskett, Metric, Great Lake Swimmers and new international star K'naan. This was not an award that Alexisonfire or Billy Talent were ever even longlisted for. (City and Colour, however, was longlisted twice, in 2008 and 2016.)

No one expected Fucked Up to win. The band themselves didn't really care; Haliechuk didn't bother to show up, staying with his girlfriend in Chicago. The day before the September gala, Abraham wrote a piece for *Torontoist* website:

"The scene we came out of has forever been ignored by the Canadian music industry and, as a result, has had to find a home outside of the 'CanCon' world. Southern Ontario hardcore bands have, for years, managed to tour the world and inspire legions of people and yet never once had one been on the cover of *Now*, featured on MuchMusic or awarded a grant. Career Suicide (from Toronto) has managed to self-finance two successful tours of Japan, there are bands throughout Europe and America doing covers of No Warning (also Toronto), seeing a homemade Left for Dead (Hamilton) shirt has become so common on tour that it doesn't really even faze me now and—for better or worse—Grade (Burlington) invented the entire genre of screamo. Yet, until very recently, none of these bands received any sort of acknowledgement within the Canadian music scene. So, for us, the prospect that one day we would be nominated for something like Polaris would have been completely laughable."

The next night at the gala, the band performed "Son the Father," joined by Justin Small and Katia Taylor of Lullabye Arkestra. Other than Abraham stripping down to underwear and socks, mayhem was minimal, although the band was on edge: the gala was held in the Masonic Temple, which still housed MTV, and so Fucked Up was technically banned from the venue. They were frisked every time they went in and out of the building; venue security even frisked Abraham's infant son upon entry, "like he might be smuggling in a weapon," says the punk papa. "What did they think we were going to do?! We didn't have a motorcycle in our pockets. We were there just to be the circus sideshow; we didn't think we'd walk away with the prize."

And then—they won. "We'd been a band for eight years at that point, so what's shocking anymore? But that was shocking," says Abraham. "I remember Jonah driving me to the afterparty. He called his dad to tell him he'd be late bringing the car home because *we fucking won*, and his dad was so unimpressed: 'Did you change the name yet?'" Fellow shortlisters Metric were far from charitable. The next day they tweeted, "Wow, pop-core takes the Polaris prize! Surprise!"

At that time, the prize came with $20,000. The band announced to a still-stunned post-gala press conference that they would be using it to fund a charity single to benefit three organizations advocating for missing and murdered Indigenous women—not a hot topic in 2009. The RCMP didn't release their much-cited report on the issue until 2014, and the final report of a national commission wasn't delivered until 10 years after Fucked Up won the Polaris. "This is an undocumented, underreported crime that's been going on for years," Abraham told *New York* magazine. "And while this [money] is for Canadian organizations, the same sort of thing is going on at the U.S.-Mexico border, with Mexican women going missing, and in Australia, with Aboriginal women there."

The single itself was hardly weighty: it was an all-star cover of Band Aid's "Do They Know It's Christmas," featuring guest vocals from Yo La Tengo, GZA, Ezra Koenig of Vampire Weekend, Bob Mould, Tegan and Sara, Andrew W.K., Kyp Malone of TV on the Radio, comedian David Cross and Broken Social Scene's

Kevin Drew. It seemed like another Fucked Up prank, but it wasn't; all those people were legit fans and down for the cause.

As for the Polaris's effect on Fucked Up's career, they might have got a few festival gigs out of it, and now the CBC had to figure out a way to say their name on-air. But most of their international success had happened before Polaris came calling. "For a band who had the proper infrastructure in place, it would have been a way bigger deal," says Haliechuk. "We still didn't have a manager or anybody to contextualize it. We were six weirdos thinking we just won an award and got some free iPods. It was just another weird thing that happened that week. Winning the Polaris was on the same level as Iggy Pop playing one of our songs on his radio show; those two things were equal to us."

A year after the Polaris win, in the summer of 2010, Fucked Up got an offer from the most mainstream Canadian band to emerge from the indie scene of the 2000s: Arcade Fire was touring their most accessible record, *The Suburbs*. The social connections were only one degree of separation apart. Abraham knew of Richard Reed Parry, because Parry used to work at Who's Emma in Kensington Market in the late '90s; he also volunteered for Food Not Bombs. "Years later, when Arcade Fire blew up, it was like, 'Holy shit, it's the Food Not Bombs dude!' So I always rooted for that band," says Abraham. At a Toronto Island show in the summer of 2010, Parry and drummer Jeremy Gara suggested to Abraham that they tour Europe together.

"I think we had very different ideas of what this tour would look like," says Abraham. "We were on tour with one of the biggest bands in the world. This was not going to be like the Gallows opening slot we did. We were the worst. We showed up late to every single show. It was two weeks, and a lot of off days, which makes sense because you have to travel. But we were like, fuck that, we're a punk band! We'd book a show in Italy and have to drive from Germany to Italy and then back to Switzerland.

"I was also at my weirdest on stage, where my thing was to smash full cans of soda on my head. The very first set, I covered all of Arcade Fire's gear with Coke. We had a crazy party backstage with all our friends at another show. But they were cool as fuck to us. They were super nice and treated us really well. Some of their crew liked us a lot, but some of their crew fucking hated us—which was understandable.

"It was like the law of diminishing returns with the audience. The first night was in Madrid. I went into the crowd afterwards, and someone handed me a bagful of weed and everyone was high-fiving me, and I'm like, 'This is going to be awesome.' The next night wasn't quite as good. Next night, not good. To the point where the last night of the tour, in Munich, there was a woman in the front row, screaming, with her fingers in her ear, for the whole set. A friend of mine was standing behind her. After the set, he told me what she was screaming: 'Make them stop! Oh god, make this band stop! Please god, make this band stop!'

"It was such a study in contrasts. You're on tour with a band who's becoming one of the biggest bands in the world. There is incredible catering. 'Wow, we're in it, we're doing it.' Then you get in the van after the show and you're like, 'No, no, we're not.'"

ALEXISONFIRE TOOK A much-needed break in 2008 to spend time on their own projects. Wade MacNeil released his debut as Black Lungs, featuring Pettit on guitar. *Send Flowers*, which featured more piano than guitars, was as much a departure from Alexis as City and Colour, with traces of country, classic rock and Nick Cave balladry. It appealed primarily to Alexis fans. City and Colour's *Bring Me Your Love*, released three months later, went platinum and featured the single "Sleeping Sickness," a duet with the Tragically Hip's Gord Downie.

When Alexis reconvened in January 2009 to work on the fourth record, the chorus of the first song, "Old Crows," boasted, "We are not the kids we used to be." And yet, despite the band's strength in Canada and their live draw across Europe and Australia, they decided to take the least appealing option in front of them: the Warped Tour. They'd done it before, for a few days or few weeks at a time, but the 2009 offer was for a gruelling two and a half months.

The Warped Tour began in 1995 for SoCal punk and third-wave ska acts; by 2009 it featured all manner of metal music as well as hip-hop, with a supposedly egalitarian approach to set times, which were different every day, encouraging fans to arrive early. One of many potential downsides for the bands was driving for 12 hours to find out they had an 11 a.m. slot to play in front of a handful of kids.

Manager Joel Carriere recalls, "The boys said, 'Whatever you do, please don't put us on the fucking Warped Tour.' I'm like, 'Guys, I get it. That shit is fucking hard.' It was changing at that time, too. The Warped Tour from '95 to the early 2000s was unbelievable. Then it just went to shit. They lost venues. Music culture was changing. Then we get offered the entire tour and it's a decent fare. Then we're like, 'Oh, fuck.' There's no other tour in punk culture. We don't really fit on energy-drink tours with Shadows Fall. I said to them, 'The fee is good. We're not going to lose money. I don't know what to say. I'm torn as well.' They said, 'Fuck, let's just do it.' I probably should not have presented it and not have done it."

"There were elements that were interesting and fun, and there were elements that were really hard," says Pettit. "Every day you wake up in a parking lot somewhere and you don't know where anything is. The vast majority of the bands playing, you just hate them. It's weird and horrible and alienating for a long period of time. That said, we made lots of friends and have fond memories of certain things. I got to see Flipper and Fear. I saw Talib Kweli from side stage. We saw Q-Tip in Salt Lake City. We shared a bus with Shad and his DJ. That was a wonderful experience. His DJ would set up at the back of the bus and Shad would freestyle. There were some fun moments, but also dismal times when I was sitting in the merch booth, sunburnt and pissed off and kind of drunk and starting to get aggressive with people.

"Every time we did the tour we lost money, and this was the year we were actually getting paid; we got to that echelon of bands that makes money on the Warped Tour," says Pettit. "Then we did our year-end wrap-up, and we lost $8,000 doing that tour, a tour that almost killed us and that we hated." It was particularly rough on Green, who was doing better in the U.S. as City and Colour than he was in Alexisonfire.

In Canada, Alexisonfire were one of dozens of acts booked to play the 2010 Winter Olympics in Vancouver. They were the only act, however, who got shut down mere seconds into their first song. The stage was at the bottom of a natural amphitheatre: not an ideal venue for a general admission audience at an Alexisonfire show. Twenty seconds into the opening song, the barrier collapsed and the crowd surged toward the stage. Pettit stopped the show immediately, called for calm and commanded everyone to take several steps back. The show was over. "When we felt it was safe to leave the stage and things had calmed down," says drummer Jordan Hastings, "we went to the medic tent because we heard there were a lot of kids with serious injuries. There were a bunch of compound fractures, bones sticking through skin. It looked like a scene from a war movie, just chaos, with people running around trying to attend to all these people. It was horrible."

The next month the band headed out on a cross-Canada arena tour with Billy Talent and Against Me! On the last night of the tour, at Toronto's Air Canada Centre, Alexisonfire were double-booked: they'd been asked to perform "Tom Sawyer" in front of Rush as they were inducted into the Canadian Songwriters Hall of Fame. "We played the ACC, packed up and had a second setup of gear at the Rush thing, hauled ass over there, got on stage in the nick of time and played," says Hastings. "We met them after, and I remember shaking Neil Peart's hand and blacking out—because I was so taken aback. I asked Wade after, 'What the hell did he say?' I was so starstruck. 'Oh, he just said you did a really good job and he thanked us for being here because he's also from St. Catharines.' 'Holy shit, I don't remember any of that!'"

By the end of the summer of 2010, just before his 30th birthday, Dallas Green announced he was out. He'd been burning the candle at both ends for the last five years, juggling two successful bands. His bandmates were upset but hardly surprised. Nor could they be bitter: Green agreed to another six months of touring before the announcement was made official, followed by a formal farewell tour. "Touring and not having two feet on the ground to deal with your shit, all that came to a head," says Carriere. "Dal can go out and do this acoustic stuff and not worry about anyone. He's in charge of his own career and not worrying about four other people fighting and complaining about stuff. He was sick to his stomach for six months and depressed and didn't want to break up the band. All five of those guys are strong personalities, and that's what makes it so charming. It wasn't like anyone was fighting and hating each other. More than anything, Dal was just mentally fatigued."

MacNeil was determined to keep the band going: the rapper P.O.S. was considered as a replacement, after MacNeil saw him fill in on guitar for Underoath. MacNeil flew to Texas to court Jim Ward of Sparta and At the Drive-In, who was interested but had just launched a restaurant. Then MacNeil himself was approached by U.K. band Gallows with an offer to replace singer Frank Carter. He accepted the offer, and Alexisonfire was officially finished. "At that point," says Hastings, "we thought, Okay, replacing one guy—maybe. Replacing two guys—no. We decided to hang it up."

There was still the farewell tour, however: 15 dates in the fall of 2012, in the U.K., Australia, Brazil and Canada, culminating in a hometown show at Copps Coliseum on December 30. "It was an emotional day," says Carriere. "It was an unbelievably powerful show. That was the first arena we'd ever headlined. I remember bawling during the last song, out of happiness. I had a lot of other [Dine Alone] things on the go, so I didn't feel like it was the end for me, and to be honest I didn't think it was the end of the band either. It was a special moment. It was so wild walking around; everyone was teary-eyed and wearing Alexis merch. It was neat to see this effect we had on people. It wasn't passive. It wasn't ever background music. We were in the foreground all the time. You had to pay attention. They struck a chord with a lot of people, and you could see that that night."

"It was moody but uplifting," says Pettit. "It felt like everything was going to be okay. I took the bus to that show; I lived walking distance to the Coliseum. My wife and my son were there. My family, lots of people, Daniel Romano. It was a positive way to end the band. Then we went our separate ways for a good year with minimal contact." MacNeil was with Gallows. Chris Steele backpacked around the world. Hastings went into the food business. Pettit, the master of crowd control, trained to become a firefighter.

BILLY TALENT NEVER had side projects. They never considered calling it quits. Having a multiplatinum commercial cushion helps, of course. But the inseparable band of brothers faced their biggest challenge when drummer Aaron Solowoniuk's multiple sclerosis began to worsen.

He'd been fighting it ever since Billy Talent signed their record deal in 2003. He didn't go public with it until after the success of *Billy Talent II* in 2006. "I felt like if I told people we'd be 'the band with the guy who has MS,'" he says. "I didn't want it to be the first thing people know about Billy Talent. MS is such a weird, invisible disease. I had kept it secret because I didn't want to be treated any differently. Back in the van-and-trailer days, I'd travel with a portable fridge filled with needles; I'd plug it into the lighter. I had to give myself three needles a week. I just made it work; my dream was to play drums in a rock band. I had one moment when I got up and walked off stage, but I could manage the symptoms. I knew there were 24 hours in a day, and I had two hours where I needed to play drums, so I made sure I had enough rest and food and energy to do that when I needed to." On Boxing Day 2006, Billy Talent organized and headlined a show called FUMS at Toronto's Phoenix club, with Alexisonfire and Moneen, one of many events they hosted in the coming years to benefit the MS Society of Canada. Solowoniuk also helped organize FUMS events in Germany.

In 2015, working on demos for a new album, the drummer suffered from crippling pain. "He was struggling just to move," says Gallant. "He would be so involved in the thought process of trying to get his body to work that he couldn't retain information anymore. He was just thinking about how his legs aren't even working. He's so good at hiding it that it wasn't until it was completely obvious that we all clued in. We played a string of summer shows to make some money. At the end of the set, we'd do 'Red Flag,' where the opening drumbeat has two kicks and two snares; I was playing and listening and thinking, He's not playing the kicks. A week later we were at the studio practising, just he and I, and I was like, 'Is everything okay? Things didn't sound good at the London show.' He said, 'I can't feel my legs.'"

"Of those eight shows that summer," says Solowoniuk, "one show was great. The other seven I was scared to get on stage. I didn't know if I'd be able to finish, and it was now in the era of everyone in the audience filming all the time. I thought I'd have an episode and people would film me failing. That compounded everything." In the studio, for months, the band watched him walk with a cane and barely be able to get himself off a bench, while the drummer assured his friends that he'd soon get out of it. "We didn't know what was going to happen," says Gallant. "Eventually it came to the point where he said, 'Let's do this record with someone else.'"

The someone else was Jordan Hastings of Alexisonfire, who easily slipped into the role with Solowoniuk's encouragement in the studio. The drummer who'd saved Alexis in a pinch a decade earlier was now doing the same for Billy Talent. When the album, *Afraid of Heights*, was released, both drummers were in all the press materials. At an Air Canada Centre show in February 2017, Hastings surrendered the drum chair to Solowoniuk for two songs, an emotional reunion to the delight of fans. The band also covered the Tragically Hip—seriously, this time—performing "Nautical Disaster" for their ailing friend, Gord Downie. For the encore, they had another trick up their sleeves: a reunited Alexisonfire.

"We went, 'Thank you, good night,' left the stage, and then Alexis came out and played five songs," says Kowalewicz. "At first the audience was confused: George came out and was stomping around, then slowly, one by one, the rest got on stage. It wasn't until they started playing that people understood what was happening. They lost their minds. The people there will remember that forever."

THAT YEAR, IN 2017, Alexisonfire decided to permanently reunite—as much as the rest of their other professional and personal commitments would allow, anyway. Shortly after the stunt at the Air Canada Centre with Billy Talent, Alexis booked five shows at the Danforth Music Hall, with surprise opening acts. One night featured both Billy Talent and Fucked Up. Ben Kowalewicz approached Damian Abraham for a little chat.

"Hey man, I just want to talk to you about *that song*," said the Billy Talent singer, referring to "Where Is the Line?"

"Oh. Yeah," said a sheepish Abraham.

"Our song, I swear to God, it's not about you guys at all."

"Oh, really?"

"Yeah. I'm really sorry."

"Why are *you* saying sorry?! I'm the one who should be apologizing!"

Hatchets were buried that day between the two singers. "Now I've gotten to know Billy Talent," says Abraham, "and I have a lot of respect for them. I've had nothing but positive experiences with them—as people. Now I regret 'The Line'— and that one line [at the end] on a lot of levels. Not because it wasn't fun, but because I didn't know them, and I made these assumptions based on the idea that these people were caricatures. Even people who are total assholes to me, I can see their insecurity. Especially with people in music, you can see how every bad review cut, every time they were dissed in the press. I remember talking to Gord Downie, and he'd say, 'Yeah, I don't get along with [a certain] band because they dissed us in an interview.' I was like, 'Wow, you, the most important Canadian musician, still has that insecurity, so I guess we all have it.' He told me, 'Lead singers have to wear it differently. You don't have anything to protect you out there, and all the shit comes toward you.' When you talk to someone in a band, especially the singer and they're an asshole, you can tell it's self-defence, the wall going up.

"Which goes back to why I regret that song even more, because Ben is not that dude. Ben from Billy Talent has every *right* to be that dude, but my experience with him—and everyone's experience with him—is that he's an awesome person I'd never thought he'd be, based on my assumption of how a rock star should act and behave. I have friends in bands who definitely live up to those stereotypes, but Ben is certainly not one of them."

And it was Alexisonfire who finally brought them together.

CHAPTER 15

WEIRDO
MAGNETS

KID KOALA, BUCK 65,
CARIBOU, CADENCE WEAPON

Weird Canada: it's the name of an MP3 blog founded in Edmonton in 2009, championing the stranger corners of Canada's musical landscape. The online fanzine was an inheritor of sorts of CBC Music's *Brave New Waves* radio show, which aired from 1984 to 2006 and brought genuinely alternative music to big cities and remote regions across the country, changing the lives of many listeners who couldn't believe they were hearing this on the national broadcaster. "There's nothing wrong with your radio," went the show's slogan. "Maybe it's you." Some *Brave New Waves* listeners became musicians written about in this book.

The name Weird Canada was a reminder that there's always been an underbelly to English-Canadian culture that's either taken for granted or shovelled under the snow. Weirdos abound in the frozen north. Norman McLaren. Syrinx. Michael Snow. Western Front. David Cronenberg. General Idea. Marian Engel. Nash the Slash. Mary Margaret O'Hara. John Oswald. Alanis Obomsawin. Kathleen Yearwood. Mecca Normal. Guy Maddin. Hundreds more, even before you start including the inherently outré cultural class of Quebec. The Festival International de Musique Actuelle de Victoriaville has been a magnet for avant-garde freaks of all stripes since 1984; the MUTEK festival was founded in 2000, making Montreal a world destination for abstract electronic music.

The four artists in this chapter aren't avant-garde per se, but they certainly could be construed as such within their chosen genres of music. Kid Koala was a hip-hop turntablist whose much-hyped debut album sounded more like a vaudeville radio play than a club banger. Buck 65 was a rapper who sounded like he recorded in a rural Nova Scotian shack using tracks lifted from static-ridden radio signals. Caribou was an electronic musician whose primary inspiration was a terrifying psychedelic rock opera by a Greek film composer, which he found on vinyl at the side of a dirt road. Cadence Weapon was a teenager when Kid Koala, Buck 65 and Caribou were putting out their first records; the Alberta rapper's debut landed him deals with leading labels in Britain and the U.S., as well as a spot on the inaugural Polaris prize shortlist.

These were artists to whom Bryan Adams and Sarah McLachlan meant nothing. Their music didn't sound like Canadian music was "supposed to"—whatever that's supposed to mean—even though they hailed from all corners of the country: Vancouver, Halifax, Hamilton, Edmonton.

Two of the four used Montreal as a brief vector; another lived there his entire adult life. Two of them made deals with their mothers that they had one year to give an artistic life a shot before going back to school. Three of the four were championed publicly by Radiohead. Three of the four had roots in hip-hop and then busted that genre wide open. Three of the four were launched by British labels, one of them a major. One of them has a PhD in math. None of them played guitar.

They all broadcast signals from unknown sonic places, creating abstract soundscapes, exploring what B.C.-born Montrealer Tim Hecker later called "an imaginary country."

IN FEBRUARY 2000, Eric San, a.k.a. Kid Koala, was one of Canada's most internationally acclaimed musicians, though he had yet to release his debut album. He'd opened for the Beastie Boys in arenas. He had worked on Damon Albarn's yet-to-be-released Gorillaz project. Radiohead were fans. He was the envy of the thriving turntablist scene in the Bay Area. He was the only non-Brit on hip U.K. electronic label Ninja Tune, which had signed him in 1996 based on a mixtape.

But until 2000, he had nothing to show for it except an out-of-print cassette full of unauthorized samples. The turntablist trend of the mid-'90s was waning. Younger DJs were nipping at the heels of the 26-year-old Koala, namely fellow Montrealer (and future Kanye West tour DJ) A-Trak, who'd won the DMC World DJ Championship in 1997 at age 15.

So what was Kid Koala going to produce? Would it be the next game-changer to succeed DJ Shadow's *Endtroducing*? An album filled with successors to "The Adventures of Grandmaster Flash on the Wheels of Steel" or Terminator X's "Contract on the World Love Jam"? Or something more like Coldcut, the DJ duo who founded Ninja Tune? Could it even be the kind of record to finally put Canadian hip-hop on the world stage?

It was none of those things. When Kid Koala's *Carpal Tunnel Syndrome* came out, it played more like Negativland's avant-garde audio collage, made by a thrift-store dumpster-diver obsessed with ancient comedy records and the Muppets. It wasn't music to dance to. It didn't provide visceral thrills or jaw-dropping technique. It wasn't commercial and wasn't trying to be cool. It wasn't going to be whatever you thought it was going to be. It was made by a second-generation Chinese-Canadian from Vancouver who lived in Montreal, played in a jam band and had a degree in children's education. It was odd. It was Canadian.

ERIC SAN GREW UP IN VANCOUVER, the son of a geneticist and an accountant, both from Hong Kong. He studied classical piano from the age of four. Later, he went record shopping at Odyssey Records with his older sister. On one trip, the clerk was playing a DJ's mixtape featuring scratching, and the 11-year-old San was intrigued. "I could tell it was live," he says. "It was swinging. It wasn't something on a computer spit out of a grid. There was a funk to it." He asked what was playing. The clerk started pulling out records for him to hear and showed him the basics of scratching.

At home, his dad's hi-fi was off-limits. His sister, however, had an all-in-one moulded plastic turntable, which San quickly started destroying. Regular records proved to be tricky, causing the needle to skip. Instead he started sourcing flexi discs from magazines found at the Salvation Army. A friend who worked at A&W brought him hamburger wrappers (unused) to use as slipmats underneath the records. "I realized I could scratch fast without jumping the needle," he says. "The other thing that was a fluke was that the erase head didn't work on my cassette player, so I could record a beat, rewind and record over it," essentially two-tracking without the benefit of playback; he wouldn't know if his scratching was in sync until he listened to the take. "I learned how to stack and layer stuff to create strange new things," he continues. "I wasn't old enough to get into clubs. There wasn't the internet to teach me. This was all just by ear."

He started saving his paper route money to buy a mixer. His sister's friends DJed high school parties, and though they weren't scratching, he got to study their equipment up close. The Sans then moved to Rockville, Maryland, outside Washington, D.C., during his final years of high school. It was the late '80s, and DJs were still accompanists to MCs, not instrumentalists in their own right. "It wasn't like I had professional aspirations. I was just a superfan," he says. He was using the name Kid Koala, a nickname he earned because of his family's affinity for Koala Springs fruit soda, which his mom bought in bulk.

San applied and got into NYU to study animation, but he couldn't afford to live in New York City. He went instead to McGill to study early childhood education—because his dream job was always to work on *The Muppet Show*.[1] He fell in love with Montreal's wealth of record stores and got a gig at campus bar Gerts, which had him moving four crates of records on a hand truck up and down a hill from his residence for each gig. "I would try to scratch now and then, but that wasn't what that crowd needed," he says. "It was a college crowd. I remember mixing Cypress Hill and some Black Crowes or Porno for Pyros and Public Enemy. I'd try to get some weird mixes in there. But really, they just wanted to hear 'Red Red Wine' by UB40 over and over. The turntables were behind a batting cage, because the kids were wicked with their requests. 'How come you haven't played "Red Red Wine" yet?' 'I JUST PLAYED IT!' 'Ah, I was in the bathroom!'"

Koala met another scratcher, DJ Devious, and they started preparing for battles: competitions where DJs would perform short routines full of technical pyrotechnics and unexpected moves to wow judges and win cash and/or equipment. Like an Eddie Van Halen contest for DJs, basically. After six months of practising, Koala and Devious entered a contest in Toronto sponsored by York University station CHRY. They were the only Montreal crew to be accepted.

"Our car broke down in Kingston," he recalls. "Then we had to find a rental. But I was under 25 and they wouldn't rent me a car. We could only get a giant cube U-Haul. It took a few hours to figure that out. I called them and said we're late and would miss soundcheck. We were stuck in Toronto in traffic listening to it on the radio. They were broadcasting live from some community centre near Jane and Finch. 'Still no sign of Kid Koala and DJ Devious!'" The duo was disqualified.

Back home they got a gig at the Savoy, above the Metropolis club on Sainte-Catherine Street, where live musicians would often sit in. Some of them formed a jazz-funk band called Bullfrog, which Koala joined as a turntablist—not a common sight in the scene. Though he entered and won a DMC DJ competition at the Dome nightclub, Bullfrog became his main focus.

"Bullfrog was doing three nights a week at one point," he says, and they were playing jazz festivals and clubs across the country. "I cut my teeth playing live, learning to recover from needle skips. It wasn't like, 'Hey, here's five minutes to show off everything you can possibly do'; it was like, 'Can you tastefully find a way to help give this song what it needs?' That became my steady gig, even though I

---

[1]   He's said he wants *The Muppet Movie*'s "Movin' Right Along" played at his funeral.

was still in school during the day." In his not-so-spare time, he worked on his solo scratch routines.

Upon graduation, his mom got him an interview with the Vancouver School Board. He wanted to focus on music. A deal was cut: if he wasn't making money from music by the end of the year, he'd come home and interview for a job. A year later, he had a record deal and went on his first North American tour.

One of his heroes was the U.K. DJ duo Coldcut, whose first single "Say Kids, What Time Is It?" playfully collected dozens of samples, from Doug E. Fresh to Ennio Morricone to *The Jungle Book* to James Brown. Their landmark track was an official remix of Eric B. and Rakim's "Paid in Full." To promote their new Ninja Tune label in 1996, Coldcut's Jon Moore came to Montreal for a gig with his side project, DJ Food. Koala got the opening slot. He wanted to have a demo ready, but had only finished one and a half sides of a cassette of rough mixes. He accompanied the promoter to the airport, thrilled to meet his heroes. Moore asked the promoter if he'd heard Coldcut's new *Journeys by DJ* mix yet; he hadn't, but there was no CD player in the car. Koala happened to have it on cassette.

"I was fanning out on them like crazy," he says, "and they were jetlagged and probably wondering, Who is this kid? Why'd you bring him?" He kept asking about certain techniques. When the cassette flipped to the second side, Koala was horrified to realize that one of his own rough mixes was on there. "Had I been sitting in the front seat," he says, "I would have immediately hit eject the moment I realized the auto reverse kicked in." Intrigued, the British DJs insisted on listening to it over Koala's protests, and asked him for a copy by the end of the ride. Jon Moore was doing a set at record store Disquivel and asked Koala to open with a five-minute set. "Then Jon started playing and started handing me records. 'Hey, Matt [Black]'s not here and he's the one that usually does the scratches, so why don't you do them.' He was playing white-label Ninja stuff and Coldcut stuff that wasn't out yet. I guess because I'd been listening to them since the '80s, it was intuitive to me where the drops were. There were a few moments during the set where it was like we had practised."

A few months later, he finished his tape, *Scratchcratchratchatch*, and made 100 copies, which he left on consignment at Montreal record shops. He barely sold any. But Coldcut offered him a record deal with Ninja Tune and asked him to finish an album in six months' time. They then took him on tour around the world, where he played a 20-minute opening set each night.

"In Toronto, I sold 250 cassettes—and that's all I'd brought for the whole tour," he says. Most of the shows were in rock clubs. At Wetlands in New York City, the venue was supposed to provide three turntables. Koala showed up to find only one. The promoters scrambled to get two more, while patrons were lined up outside. When they arrived, Koala asked if they also had a table to set up on—they didn't understand why he'd need one. The Wetlands gig proved memorable for another reason: he met future collaborator Dan the Automator, who'd just made the Dr. Octagon record with Kool Keith.

At legendary L.A. rock club the Troubadour, Koala was approached by David Byrne's manager. He immediately froze; *Scratchcratchratchatch* opens with a track called "Emperors Crash Course in Cantonese," which sampled the most obvious signifier of Chinese culture at the time in Western music, 1987's *The Last Emperor* theme by Byrne and Ryuichi Sakamoto. "It won an Oscar; everyone knows the song," says Koala. "It's not a deep cut or anything." Byrne's manager didn't say anything about it, so Koala gave her a tape and said, "Play it for David. He might recognize the first couple of minutes!" A few months later, Byrne was quoted in *Raygun* magazine talking about how much he loved it.

Ninja Tune reached out and asked Byrne if they could put it out officially; Byrne agreed. "I couldn't believe it," says Koala. "Normally, you have to say 'contains elements of' or whatever because it's one of many elements. But I just wrote 'contains *The Last Emperor*.' No elements—it's in there in its entirety." Other samples, including one of Björk, couldn't be cleared, so Ninja Tune put out an edited version of *Scratchcratchratchatch* on a 10-inch single renamed *ScratchHappyLand*.[2]

Word spread beyond the Ninja Tune scene. The Jon Spencer Blues Explosion—who'd worked with Dan the Automator—asked Koala to open two sold-out New Year's Eve shows in 1997 at the Metro in Chicago. He was to go on between opening blues act the North Mississippi Allstars and headliner Spencer. "The stagehand had a fold-out table with my turntables on them," he recalls. "They carried it out on to the middle of the stage, and people started booing the turntables. They were sharpening their fangs. I knew it was going to be a rock show, so I'd already tailored my set for that with some hard scratching. I went out there and I did okay. But mostly I just remember the turntables being booed."

Koala was getting press all around the world but had only finished five minutes of his promised album. "The panic was kicking in," he says. "I didn't actually know how to make an album. I'd made this one mixtape, and I play classical piano. It took me awhile to figure it out. And on that first mixtape, I'd exhausted all my bag of tricks. All my battle routines were featured there. I didn't have anything else."

Even small talk from friends about the album's progress sent him into a spiral of self-doubt. Photoshoots for *Rolling Stone* and "artists to watch" lists didn't help, nor did the fact that Ninja Tune had opened a North American office in Montreal.

---

2   The full version was made available years later on Bandcamp.

"While I imagine certain people thrive on that kind of attention, I was learning that I wasn't one of them," he says. "Ever since I was a child, I did my most creative work when no one was paying attention." At one point he even considered repaying his advance to Ninja Tune.

But gig offers kept coming in. Koala was a big fan of the Beastie Boys and of their keyboardist, Money Mark. He ordered a Money Mark 10-inch single in the mail, but it never arrived. So he wrote to him again and included a copy of *Scratchcratchratchatch*. A month later, the phone rang early one morning.

"Hey, is this Eric?"

"Yeah."

"Hey man, it's Mark, what's up?"

Koala thought it was Mark Robinson from Bullfrog. "Hey, when we gonna get together and rehearse?"

"Uh, I don't think you know who this is."

"Yeah, it's Mark."

"It's Mark from L.A."

"I don't know any Marks in L.A."

"Yo, it's *Money* Mark. I dug your tape. I'm really into it. I wanna know if you want to play turntables in my band while we're touring with the Beasties."

He joined the Beastie Boys' *Hello Nasty* tour in 1998, pestering them the whole time for tips on recording technique. The next year, Money Mark, Mike D and Kid Koala appeared on the debut by Handsome Boy Modeling School, a project by Dan the Automator and De La Soul producer Prince Paul; Koala can be heard scratching up a storm on the lead-off track "Rock n' Roll (Could Never Hip Hop Like This)." Dan the Automator also enlisted Koala to help with Del tha Funkee Homosapien's Deltron 3030 project and with Damon Albarn's Gorillaz. The latter became a huge pop hit when it finally came out in 2001, selling more than seven million records. But Koala, a huge comic-book nerd, got the biggest thrill from working with Gorillaz' Jamie Hewlett, who was best known as the creator of *Tank Girl*.

Slowly but surely, Kid Koala's long-awaited debut was coming together, thanks in part to the thousands of records he picked up while crate-digging on tour. He worked dawn until dusk, listening to at least 10 records a day to find bits that might work in a song: drum breaks, bass lines, horn bits and lots of spoken word pieces. "I probably listened to over 2,000 records," he told *Exclaim!*'s Dimitri Nasrallah. "The more information I had, the less I knew how to deal with it. At its core, I just wanted to make something I hadn't heard before."

He eventually had an eureka moment when he finished "Fender Bender," an audio play about two unintelligible, arguing motorists, set to lounge funk. "For the first time in ages, I was having fun working on music again," he says. "At one point I said to myself, 'Fine, if this is going to be a weird record, I'm gonna make a record that will be weird *forever*.' The further it went into the realm of strangeness, the more I was able to unlock myself out of that writer's block, and that fear."

One of the first samples heard on the record is from *Revenge of the Nerds*: "We're nothing but the nerds they say we are," which then gets cut up into micro bits and spliced over off-kilter free-jazz drums. "Roboshuffle" and "Like Irregular Chickens" sound exactly as one might imagine they would. "Music for Morning People" is a caffeinated flurry. There are no recognizable samples on *Carpal Tunnel Syndrome*. That's because, in the demo stage, the original opening track had to be scuttled because a certain sample couldn't be cleared. Though there are plenty of funky moments throughout, it's more like John Oswald applying his plunderphonics to *Sesame Street*.

"I like all kinds of music," Koala told *Exclaim!*'s Prasad Bidaye when the album came out. "I also buy a lot of comedy records and children's stuff from the Salvation Army and places like that. Records that have been driven over with Tonka trucks and stuff. But I'll buy it even if it's crap, because it's 50 cents and I can usually get two or three copies of it to play with." It's impossible to imagine where exactly he found a recording of someone saying, "You know something, Scratchy? You got a problem." Or "And that, of course, is what he deserved for pretending to be a musician when he was only a butcher!"

That's what Kid Koala felt like—a butcher. Someone who made a weird little record that wasn't in the same league as his Ninja Tune labelmates. But DJ Food's Strictly Kev told him, "You're really created something else. It's No. 1 in a field of one." Later that year, Coldcut's Matt Black came to Koala's London gig and approached him after the show with a superlative analogy: "You know, *Scratchcratchratchatch* was like your *Meet the Beatles!*, but *Carpal* is your *Sgt. Pepper*. You are a true son of Coldcut." At those words from his musical hero, in a true Hollywood moment, young Kid Koala started to tear up.

Radiohead were big fans of both the Kid Koala record and Handsome Boy Modeling School, and in the fall of 2000 they invited the latter to open the only three North American shows on the *Kid A* tour: New York, Toronto and L.A. Kid Koala joined them for the latter two. At the Greek Theatre in L.A., Koala was loading his gear in when he was approached by a stranger.

"What's that sticker?"

"It's my pass to get in."

"Why, you a tech or something?"

"No, I'm just going to cut up some records before the show."

"So that gets you into the show?"

"Yeah."

"I'll give you $5,000 for it."

"Whatever, you don't have $5,000."

The man reached into his pocket and pulled out a wad of cash.

"Forget it, you're probably going to steal Jonny [Greenwood]'s guitar or something and I'm going to get into all kinds of crap. Whatever, dude."

"Okay, so this is not $5,000, but I'll also give you this watch!"

Kid Koala was then invited on Radiohead's 2001 tour as the sole opening act. "One night at dinner I told Thom Yorke this story. He said, 'Well, you took the money, right?' I'm like, 'No!' He's like, 'Next time, just take it and then tell security.' I was broke, too. I could have bought a new computer with that money!"

While working on his next album, *Some of My Best Friends Are DJs*, Koala was approached by ECW Press to write a graphic novel, based on his album artwork and the animated video for "Fender Bender." The result was *Nufonia Must Fall*, a wordless comic for which he composed a short soundtrack of piano miniatures. Björk was shown the project and asked him to open for her in Toronto in September 2003—replacing Dolly Parton, who had to cancel.

The publisher asked him if he would go on a book tour—which he thought would be impossible, to talk about a book without words. So to promote both his new album and the book, he put together a cabaret-style seated show called Short Attention Span Theatre. His old roommate Krista Muir opened the show as a character called Lederhosen Lucil, with two other DJs acting as his band: Montreal's P-Love and San Antonio's DJ Jester. "It was about the idea that because I'm on Ninja Tune, people think [I make] dance music, which it isn't," he says. The tour was a way to "provide a context for that. A track like 'Skanky Panky' or something, I couldn't do it by myself live because of the multitracks. But if we are all standing in a row, the idea was to set up like a traditional band: a drum riser with two turntables on it, so all the drums that night were coming from there. Then all the 'vocals' were coming from the front, and the keyboard, guitar, bass from another spot. To me, it made it more clear what you're watching."

That tour—and pretty much every project he's done since—has set Kid Koala far apart from what people expect from a turntablist. "If I'd stayed in the battle circuit, I'd have a different outlook," he says. "But I played in bands. Touring with Money Mark, he'd play a ballad like 'Cry,' and what can you do on turntables that is tasteful enough to help the vibe without ruining the tension of the song? It caused me to approach it differently and dig for different records to scratch, or eventually cut my own tone records. Touring with Radiohead, the most powerful moments were these quiet moments that weren't all anthem rock. You could hear a pin drop, and there's 20,000 people there. That's the type of stuff that had my head spinning. How do you do that? How do you bring a turntable show into that kind of effect?"

It was then that Kid Koala developed one of his best-loved routines, a deconstruction of Henry Mancini's 1961 hit "Moon River." He first designed it for his parents' wedding anniversary; it's his mom's favourite song. She wanted all her children to meet them in Hawaii for a vacation, so Koala booked a gig there to cover his flight. "I knew they'd show up to the gig, so I did this ["Moon River"] routine for my parents," he says. "It was bold, because it was in the middle of this banging hip-hop night. I had to stop the show: 'Sorry, everyone, my parents are here. If this is not your vibe, go get a drink, but I'm going to dedicate this next routine to them.' I did it, and everyone went nuts. I thought, What's going on?" Though he's never recorded it, "Moon River" became a staple of his live sets—to a fault, sometimes. Though he still loves it, he says, "Even now, it could be three a.m. in some crazy nightclub scene, and I'll get some super aggressive person yelling, 'Play "Moon River"!' Are you kidding me? It's like 'Red Red Wine' all over again."

On *Carpal Tunnel Syndrome*, there is a song called "Drunk Trumpet," in which he manipulated a trumpet sample to create a new melody, a nod to his father's love of jazz. After the record came out, Koala took a trip to New Orleans and had "a life-altering experience. My father, one of the first of his records he ever played for me was a Preservation Hall Jazz Band record. He said, 'If your travels ever take you to New Orleans, you have to go to Preservation Hall and witness this music live.' It's true. You go and it's a tiny room: no amps, no mics. People breathing into their instruments, singing into the air, nobody's phones are out. It's the gift of that energy for the people in the room. It's a spiritual experience. I went to a few different clubs and kept hearing 'Basin Street Blues.' It brought tears to my eyes. I grew up listening to Louis Armstrong, but to actually be there, walk through the streets and hear that music live, I thought I'd start my next record with 'Basin Street Blues' but on turntables."

That presented considerable challenges. "I didn't know any trad jazz players [in Montreal], and none of the DJs I knew were interested in exploring that avenue. How do you do a walking bass line? You find a bass note that's hitting A flat, and I scatted the whole bass line. Then taking that note and learning how to scratch and bend it into the scat, which took me weeks to do. And then doing that with every other layer: trombone, etc. Eventually it all came together. That track took six months, just to get my bends right. That was a fun study for me." The track was the first single and video from his 2003 album, *Some of My Best Friends Are DJs*.

Preservation Hall artistic director Ben Jaffe saw it and loved it. He called Koala to say so.

"You nailed it. You caught the vibe."

"Really? I've only been to New Orleans once, but I've been listening to your music since I was a kid."

"You should come down and play with us."

"You're Preservation Hall. What do turntables have to do with this music?"

"I don't know, but I feel strongly that you should come here and show these cats how you do it."

"*At* Preservation Hall? Aren't you supposed to be preserving something?"

"We'll make it work somehow."

At the gig, the band had set up a screen in the corner of the venue and started the set by playing the video. By the end of it, they started playing along. "They lifted it up even higher, and I was literally crying my eyes out," says Koala. "Then they brought me on stage; my turntables were there. They turned to me, said, '"When You're Smiling" in B flat!' and started playing. I'm like, What?! I haven't had that much fun playing music in my life. I learned more in 32 bars of trading licks with [saxophonist] Charlie Gabriel than I had DJing by myself for 10 years. It was a real conversation. There are no parts, in a way. 'Whaddya got? Here's what I got.' And you just try and keep up. There were elements of that in Bullfrog. But with Preservation Hall, it's trad jazz, and everyone knows all the songs. If you land on the same note, you had to get out of each other's way and go down a third. I had to pinch myself."

It went a lot better than, say, the time on the Radiohead tour when Colin Greenwood asked him to replicate the horn parts on "The National Anthem." "We were in Baltimore and I had to find some skronk records and figure out how to keep it in key," he says. "Those guys all had in-ear monitors, but I couldn't hear anything. And it was the first song! It was the loudest possible crowd noise you can imagine. I was mostly watching Phil [Selway]'s snare drum to keep time. But it was exciting. I did that for the rest of that tour."

Another odd collaboration was set up by the Festival International de Musique Actuelle de Victoriaville, the avant-garde festival in Quebec's Eastern Townships. Koala was hooked up with Martin Tétreault, a veteran of Montreal's avant-garde scene who had been manipulating turntables in ways entirely unrelated to hiphop tradition, more in line with Christian Marclay's sound experiments. "I didn't know much about him before that," says Koala. "He came to rehearse at my studio. He has these old Califone turntables you'd find in elementary schools, with built-in speakers. He plugged into dual volume pedals, which I thought was advanced. He would take tiny clips of something, like one note from a classical record, and did kind of a dog-paddle scratch, and doing an opposing thing on the pedals, and it would sound like reversed but clipped. You couldn't do that with a traditional scratch setup. It sounded like the *Exorcist* soundtrack or something.

That blew my mind. We went to the festival, and I'd never encountered an audience who was that open, sonically. The crazier we could get it, the more they were into it. It's not just about decibel or frequency; it's almost like they're sound spelunkers, where they've heard every sound. 'You can't surprise us.' So when you can, they get really excited. They go to hear the sound they can't hear anywhere else. I didn't understand that crowd existed; maybe it only exists at that festival. But there was a full room of them." A recording of the 2005 performance was released in 2007.

Kid Koala's next two releases were comparatively conventional next to everything he'd done to that point. *Your Mom's Favorite DJ*, which came out in 2006, was both a natural progression from the first two records and a throwback to *Scratchcratchratchatch* in its more straight-up funkiness. There were three rock-based pieces on it with Beastie Boy associate Dynomite D; that led to a new band, the Slew.

In 2009 the Slew put out a self-titled rock album recorded with six turntables, with the intention of sounding like Public Enemy's Bomb Squad producing Black Sabbath. They toured that year with the rhythm section of Australian rock band Wolfmother. At the live show, there were no click tracks, no DJ headphones—just custom-built, shock-resistant risers for the turntables, which were run through Marshall stacks. "We're jumping around and breaking needles with records flying all over the place," Koala told the *Georgia Straight* in 2009. "It's supposed to be like that. Things fall apart and you just have to learn to roll with it." Almost 10 years after *Carpal Tunnel Syndrome* came out, Kid Koala was finally delivering the kind of visceral thrills people had been expecting.

His career has since taken many turns: a blues album, a soundtrack to a kids video game, film soundtracks, ambient works, puppet shows and more. The span of his creative pursuits, and his oddball approach to different disciplines, is firmly rooted in Montreal. "I travel all over the world and I always come back here," he says. "Musically, there is that open-mindedness. I know DJs in some bigger cities who if they tried to do a left-field night and didn't have a packed bar within two weeks, they would cut you off and just start playing whatever radio music gets people in the bar—obviously. Here there are a lot of places to play but a nurturing attitude.

"Some of my New York DJ friends were like, 'Where do you come up with this stuff?!' 'Uh, Montreal.' Even back in my record-digging days, there was a wide palette of records to chop here. The taste in music was always wide: psych-rock, jazz, folk, anything you wanted. You'd find all this stuff in record shops or flea markets. There's an adventurous audience here that appreciates everything from crazy electronic music to circus arts and everything in between. You see the same people at this vernissage or this record launch or this restaurant opening. People appreciate all that. It's small enough that there isn't that competitive nature. Everyone supports it all. Which is rare."

———————

IT'S A GUARANTEED "gotcha" trivia question: name the first Canadian hip-hop act signed directly to a major label.

Maestro Fresh Wes? Michie Mee? Dream Warriors? Someone from Toronto, right?

Nope. It was MCJ and Cool G—from Halifax.

In 1989, Maestro became the first Canadian rap artist to have a top 10 hit, with "Let Your Backbone Slide," thanks largely to a push from Attic Records, the independent label who happened to distribute the tiny New York City hip-hop label that had signed him. Michie Mee and Dream Warriors didn't put out their debut albums, on majors, via smaller imprints, until 1991.

The same year as Maestro's success, Capitol Records Canada signed MCJ and Cool G, who by then had relocated to Montreal. Their debut album, *So Listen*, came out in 1990, tapping into the trend of new jack swing. It didn't have any radio hits, but it did make a small splash on MuchMusic.

Anyone surprised that Halifax had a hip-hop scene dating back to at least 1986 either a) doesn't give the Maritime town enough credit in general and/or b) is ignorant of the complex history of Africville, the Halifax neighbourhood settled by former enslaved American in the 1840s.

MCJ and Cool G were in one of the city's first rap crews, New Beginning; also on the scene were Care Crew and Down by Law, the latter featuring mainstay Jorun Bombay and MC J-Roc, a.k.a. actor Jonathan Torrens, who later played a satirical version of himself on the hit show *Trailer Park Boys*.

Much like every Canadian city at the time, there was no hip-hop on Halifax radio except on a local campus station, Dalhousie's CKDU, which had one hip-hop show. For 11 years, that show was hosted by Rich Terfry, a.k.a. Stinkin' Rich, a.k.a. Buck 65. He played all kinds of hip-hop: new, old, mainstream, underground—and his own.

In 1997, Buck 65 recorded *Vertex*. It was made in one 48-hour period solo: Terfy was the sole rapper, producer and turntablist. It wasn't hip-hop as much as it was sound collage, a mix of the New York City illbient scene, underground film and late-night campus radio, all narrated by a guy who sounds like William S. Burroughs's slightly less annoying nephew. He dresses like an old man, works at a magazine store and raps, "I don't act hard and waste time with irrelevance / or underestimate the audience's intelligence / I do what I do with skill and sincerity / I am what I am, not a fraud or a parody."

"*Vertex* is one of my all-time favourite albums," says rapper Cadence Weapon. "The day I bought that record, a world of possibility opened up to me. Then I saw, oh my god, he makes his own beats *and* he does the cuts. He was one of the first people I heard rapping with a Canadian voice. Even him just being from Halifax, I'd never heard any rappers from Canada who wanted to do something that was outsider art. He was wilfully strange in a way that totally opened up the way I thought about rap. He's making references to David Lynch movies and stuff—not the kind of touchstones rappers had in Canada, or anywhere else. He was the only person doing stuff like this in 1998."

Buck 65 was born and bred in hip-hop, but as his profile got bigger, he busted genres wide open. Radiohead loved his 2000 song about losing his mother to breast cancer. In 2002, he signed a major label deal and put out an album of four 15-minute songs not dissimilar to *Vertex* (though with better production). His first hit single, in 2003, had a banjo in it. His second major label album featured Tortoise as a backing band. Wicked and weird, no apologies—befitting a guy who in 2000 told *Exclaim!*, "What makes Halifax different is that we make records out of fishing line and chicken bones and coal and driftwood and dog shit. How do you expect our music to sound?"

RICH TERFRY CLIMBED a tree to listen to hip-hop. That was the only way he could pick up the 33-watt campus radio signal from Halifax. He lived 40 kilometres north, in rural Mount Uniacke. When he arrived at Dalhousie University to study biology, he started doing fill-in slots on CKDU's show *The Bassment*. Eventually the regular host stopped showing up, and the slot went to Terfry, calling himself DJ Critical. He made sure to submit his playlists to *College Music Journal*, which meant he got promos sent to him. "Everyone was sending me their demos to play on the show," he says. "For as remote as we were in Halifax, it was well established."

He released his first cassette, as Stinkin' Rich, in 1993, but got his first break as a rapper when Sloan put out his seven-inch single and then a cassette on their Murderecords label in 1994—one of two hip-hop acts on the label, alongside Hip Club Groove. The two collaborated often. The latter's album title, *Trailer Park Hip Hop*, became prophetic: both in Terfry's later mélange of folk, country and hip-hop and also rapper Cory "Cheklove Shakil" Bowles's later involvement in *Trailer Park Boys*. (He played Cory.)

"There was a really good hip-hop scene, and a lot of it was high quality," says Terfry. "A lot of that you can attribute to Jorun, who is a hero of Canadian hip-hop music. He's still not as recognized in Canada as he is abroad, but he's the real deal and always was. He set the bar and produced probably half the acts out there."

When Terfry started performing and recording as Buck 65—starting with 1996's *Weirdo Magnet*—he had a built-in network to tap into via his campus radio show. He was aware of similar outsiders in nearby Maine: the rappers Sole and Alias, who soon moved to San Francisco and started the label Anticon. Buck 65 fit in perfectly with the Anticon aesthetic, as did Terfry's work in Sebutones, with Haligonian beatmaker Robert "Sixtoo" Squire.

Many in the concentric circles around Anticon were involved in Scribble Jam, an annual event in Cincinnati. "Everyone converged there," says Terfry. "My first one was '98 and I went three or four years in a row. There was great networking, decent enough crowds, and the event had good press coverage."

The festival entered mainstream discourse as part of Eminem's origin story; the future superstar lost a championship freestyle battle there to Chicago rapper Juice in 1997. Unfairly or not, Scribble Jam became associated with nerdy kids obsessed with hip-hop authenticity, placing doctrinaire importance on freestyling, turntablism and breakdancing as fundamental tenets of hip-hop culture, while simultaneously developing abstract experimentalism on a parallel course to innovations in mainstream hip-hop. It was the perfect place for Buck 65.

"One of the first years I went, I met a lot of people from [L.A.'s] Freestyle Fellowship, from that camp and various splinters, and a lot of people from San Francisco. It was certainly more diverse than a lot of the crowds I was playing for at that point. But no doubt about it: there were a lot of weird white kids there." Buck 65 started selling records through Anticon and other mail-order distributors. "It wasn't just a couple here and there," he says. "We were moving quite a bit."

Then came Len. The Toronto band, whose Marc Costanzo had gone to school in Halifax, had a worldwide top 10 summer hit in 1999 with "Steal My Sunshine." The accompanying album featured Buck 65 trading turntable cuts with DJ Mr. Dibbs of the 1200 Hobos on two tracks; DJ Moves of Hip Club Groove was also involved. Len was a fluke one-hit wonder; no one was scouring the liner notes to learn more about their collaborators.

Buck 65's next move was a sharp left turn: a full-length collaboration with jazz drummer Jerry Granelli, of the Vince Guaraldi Trio, with whom the rapper toured in Europe. His profile got a lot higher when his 1999 album, *Man Overboard*— made shortly after his mother died—was reissued in 2000 by Anticon. Influential U.S. critic Robert Christgau, among others, gave it a rave review. But it was when Radiohead started name-dropping Buck 65 in interviews that "my phone started ringing like crazy," he says. "That's the reason I ended up having a career at all."

When the British band played Montreal in August 2001, they let it be known they wanted to meet him. He got a backstage pass. They weren't just fans; they wanted to help. "One of the first things they asked was, 'What do you have going on in the U.K.?' They hooked me up with their publicist."

By this point, he had amassed a lot of unreleased material. In 2001 he made an album called *Synesthesia*, as a quick tour-only release. Before that, on New Year's Eve 1999, he had performed an entire set of new songs at Halifax's Marquee Club, which became the album *Square*. Recording with Charles Austin in 2000—while the engineer was also making Joel Plaskett's *Down at the Khyber*—Buck 65 started to move away from his exclusive use of samples. He had already removed samples of Metallica and Neil Young from the Anticon reissue of *Man Overboard*.

"I was starting to hear stories of my friends getting caught and sued, which was scaring the daylights out of me," he says. "I figured I had to go deep and start filtering things and chopping them up to stay in the clear. I was trying to use a lot of obscure Canadian sources: dollar-bin records; weird, experimental electronic things. I used a record called *Canadian Electronic Music*, probably a Canadian Talent Library thing, those types of labels."

He was now touring the U.S., Australia and Europe. The response in Paris in particular flabbergasted him. "How did these people know who I was?" he still wonders. "Folks there don't need marketing. People there are raised with so much weird art. I was seeing way bigger crowds in French cities than I was in Calgary." He rarely played Toronto, the centre of the Canadian music industry. "Maybe because hip-hop was historically a distinctly American phenomenon, and the TO scene was robust enough, with its own gravity, that if you were involved in it it probably meant a lot to make it there," he says. "But I never gave it a whole lot of thought. It was important to me to make some waves in New York and L.A. I don't think I was even bothering to send anything to anyone in Canada, at all."

He did get a Toronto lawyer, Chris Taylor, because labels were starting to sniff around. The most interest came from the U.K., where regional Warner head John Reid became Buck 65's biggest fan. Reid lobbied Warner Canada to go see him perform at the Halifax Pop Explosion. "Then at one point, there was this real shuffle at Warner," says Terfry. "A lot of people lost their jobs, but [Reid] was promoted and was chair for all of Europe. I was thanking my lucky stars, because he was my biggest champion—and now he had a bigger job." In 2002, Buck 65—the rapper from a country that rarely signed hip-hop artists to major label deals—signed to Warner internationally, although the U.S. opted out.

The first thing Warner did was release *Square*, along with reissues of *Man Overboard*, *Vertex*, *Synesthesia* and his first two records, *Weirdo Magnet* and *Language*

Arts. Back in the days of physical music promos, critics who had never heard of Buck 65 now had six of his records show up in their mailbox from Warner—and none of them were yet his official Warner debut.

Buck 65 moved to Europe—first to Paris, in 2002, then London. He was hardly down and out, drawing 500 people a night in both centres. "Warner was paying my rent, which was sweet," he says. "The idea was to be over there, work, meet people, play shows. I played a lot of festivals." He was also writing. Instead of documenting his new surroundings, he found himself writing a lot about home—both lyrically and in his musical choices. "I loved every minute of being there, but there was a bit of homesickness in a way," he says. "It made me nostalgic for my rural roots. Halifax is not a metropolis, and before that I grew up in a small town. It made me appreciate my upbringing and the music I remember hearing when I was a kid, music that was in the air.

"There was an English bookstore on a street where I lived, called the Village Voice," he says, speaking of the Left Bank neighbourhood. "I went in one day and saw a Nick Tosches book called *Where Dead Voices Gather*. It's about old-timey music, the talking blues. I knew one of his rock biographies, knew I liked his writing, and bought it based on the cover. I read it really quickly and loved it." Its influence soon seeped into his music.

Living in France shaped his approach to performance, out of necessity. "If I was in some small city outside Paris, looking out at the crowd, these people didn't understand a word I was saying—and what I do is so lyric heavy," he says. "I knew I had to entertain these people somehow." Inspiration came from 90 years earlier. He noticed that Charlie Chaplin iconography was still everywhere in France, so he started renting Chaplin's movies from an Irish video store in Montparnasse. "I studied them to learn how to be expressive not just with my face but with my body," he says. Discovering Belgian singer Jacques Brel was another revelation, particularly his 1964 live album recorded at Paris's Olympia theatre. "For my money, he's the greatest performer ever," says Terfry. "After I'd been in France awhile, I figured I'd channel some weird combo of Charlie Chaplin and Jacques Brel."

Making him a little less homesick in Paris was Leslie Feist, who moved there around the same time Terfry did in the fall of 2002. They'd met through everyone's mutual friend, Brendan Canning, whom Terfry knew via Len. "There were other expats of various stripes around, too," he says. "Chilly Gonzales. CocoRosie. Jarvis Cocker was there, I'd see him at this record store I went to; he was in there every time. There was this funny community of outsiders there."

In the summer of 2003, he found himself surrounded by Canadians at La Route du rock festival in St. Malo, France. The Yeah Yeah Yeahs were headlining, but also on the bill were Caribou, Hot Hot Heat and Feist's friends in Broken Social Scene. "At one point in my set, I could see this panic in the crowd, a lot of movement. It dawned on me that it had begun to rain, and people were trying to seek shelter. In French, I said, 'Don't leave, I promise the rain will stop by the end of the next song'—as if I had the power. It was the luckiest thing in the world: it did stop, and people just freaked out. There was even a story about it in the local paper the next day. I went out of my mind a bit during that performance. It was transcendent." Backstage he was greeted by high-fives all around from the fellow Canadians. "It was a moment that cemented this thing that was happening for Canadians in Europe. We kinda stole the show."

Leslie Feist in particular dug his moves. She was about to shoot a video for her song "One Evening" and enlisted Terfry to be her partner in a ballroom dancing routine. Though they were Parisian neighbours, the video was made in Toronto. "She rented a dance studio and we rehearsed and rehearsed," he says. "The day before we shot it, we ran into someone we knew in Kensington Market, and we said, 'Check this out!' Leslie and I started doing this synchronized dance routine, and this small crowd gathered. People didn't really know who she was at that point; her [Let It Die] record wasn't out yet." Within a year, she'd be one of the most recognizable new faces of Canadian music.

Terfry returned to Halifax to make the record he'd decided to call *Talkin' Honky Blues*, inspired by the Tosches book. Charles Austin, formerly of the Super Friendz and now of experimental band Neuseiland, was once again in charge of the session. A key component was Dale Murray on pedal steel, of local roots rock band the Guthries—"a real ringer, from another planet," says Terfry. "I wasn't going to be able, legally and financially, to sample the way I did before, so I needed musicians in the studio." He did, however, anchor "Wicked and Weird," on which Austin plays banjo, with a sample from pioneering female rock band Fanny.

Pedal steel, banjo, cinematic soundscapes that were more Ry Cooder than RZA—was this even a hip-hop record? *Talkin' Honky Blues* arrived at the same time Americans were combining country music and hip-hop with beaucoup de fromage: Bubba Sparxx, Kid Rock, Cowboy Troy. Those artists were aiming at state fairs in the American South; it was never clear exactly for whom Buck 65 was aiming. And he wasn't an ingenue; he was a 28-year-old man. "Although I had been making music for close to 15 years, this was going to be an introduction for a lot of people. I felt like I had to stop and think a bit about my whiteness. There was also a conscious thought that I have to put out a real authentic showing of myself and who I am, straight up. Look no further than the title."

Things were going very well in France: the country's primary music mag, *Les inrockuptibles*, named *Talkin' Honky Blues* the No. 2 album of the year for 2003.

While hanging on to his Paris apartment, he rented one in New York City after finally getting a U.S. deal, with V2, home of the White Stripes. The *Village Voice* put the album on their year-end list. But his live show was the main attraction.

"Some of my peers in those years had videos that got played on MTV, people like Atmosphere—they took it to a next level," he says. "That was never me. When it really started cooking, the tours that were happening through the U.S.—where I really wanted to prove it—were really amazing. I was playing in front of 1,000 or 1,500 people, headlining in Tucson or Albuquerque. It didn't last super long; people are fickle and there are a million different factors. But it was as good as I could dream of it being. I didn't aspire to cross over. For the scene I wanted to be a part of, and in the places I wanted it to happen, it was happening."

Then he shot himself in the foot. In a 2004 interview with heavy metal magazine *Kerrang*, Buck 65 was quoted as saying, "I now hate hip-hop. The more I've educated myself about music, the more I've grown to hate it. I don't use that word lightly either . . . The people behind hip-hop don't know anything about music theory or have any appreciation for other kinds of music outside hip-hop. I challenge anyone to show me a case where there's actual musicality."

While *Kerrang* was unlikely to be read by actual or potential Buck 65 fans, the quotes did spread on message boards, and the backlash was furious. It was one thing for Terfry to evolve and make different music than on early fan favourite *Vertex*, but he was now shitting on the entire genre of music that birthed him. He tried to explain it away by saying the interview was conducted under duress, backstage at the end of a long tour. He claimed the interviewer was provoking him by calling him a sell-out, and Terfry pushed back with facetious statements. He wrote to *Exclaim!* to explain himself. "No hint of irony or role-playing or intelligence came across in the story," he wrote. "Now I just look like an idiot. I take it back. I don't really believe any of that."

But he wasn't about to make a throwback record to prove his bona fides. Instead, he hired the jazzy post-rock band Tortoise. He had met drummer John Herndon at a show in Ann Arbor, Michigan, where the Tortoise member was staying with in-laws for Thanksgiving. Outside the venue after the show, they got to talking. "As he was leaving, he said, 'Well, uh, if you ever want to, uh . . .' and he made a drumming motion as he started walking away," says Terfy. "I was like, 'Whoa, whoa, whoa, are you serious about that?' When I was making *Vertex*, I was listening to [Tortoise's] *TNT* album a lot. I wasn't going to let him walk away. I grabbed him and said, 'If you're serious about this, let's do it.'" Three months later, they were in Tortoise's studio making the next Buck 65 record.

Terfry showed up with nothing prepared, the first time he'd ever written to music first. One song, "Le 65isme," features a highly unusual, syncopated beat.

"That was Herndon," says Terfry. "For as much as [Tortoise] understood that I was a hip-hop guy, they did not want to loop drum parts. They were strictly against that. On that song in particular, he's playing so hard. Watching his face turn red with the veins bulging out of his arms, while being so precise with a timing that's so off-kilter—it blew my mind. It was one of the most awesome musical performances I've ever witnessed. That [beat] was his first idea; out of the blue, he just started playing that." The two parties only got to play live together once, at the Calgary Folk Festival; in 2005, Tortoise toured with Bonnie Prince Billy instead, whose record they made immediately after Buck 65's.

His U.S. label, V2, wasn't sure what to do with him. Instead of releasing *Talkin' Honky Blues*, they had assembled a compilation of new songs and rerecordings of early material. They put him on tour with Moby and got him booked on many of the same festivals as the White Stripes. They also got him the weirdest gig of his life, which lasted less than one song.

It started out as a favour. Terfry lived on the same block in New York City as his label. He'd often hang out, "mostly freeloading, stealing people's lunch," he says. One day the president of the label asked him to meet with a promotions manager about something big.

"Look, uh, sorry to bring you in here," said the manager, "but a bunch of us just came back from this conference in Florida where radio people all come together. There's a big station in D.C., a big tastemaker, that will be celebrating a big anniversary, and they were throwing a show at the 9:30 Club. To promote the show they're going to play 'Wicked and Weird' so many times. And if they start playing you, others in the region will pick it up.'

Terfry was suspicious. "What's the catch?"

"Well, you'll be opening for [nu-metal band] Papa Roach."

"Oh, Jesus, this is a bad idea. This will not work. Look, I will do this. But I'm telling you now, it will be a disaster. So if I'm right, next time we talk about an 'opportunity,' take my word for it. Do we have a deal?"

"Okay, deal."

"It was the worst night of my life," Terfry recalls of the D.C. gig. "I tried to think what song of mine might get these people on my side. I started with the song '463,' because it has a guitar in it. It couldn't have been more than 20 seconds before they turned on me. So vicious. At the club, there was a door right off the stage that took you to a fire escape. As I'm trying to get to the end of the song, I was literally packing my gear as I'm performing. I had a fairly simple setup, with rented backline so I didn't have to bring a turntable. I finished the song, said, 'Fuck you guys,' grabbed the bit of shit I had and walked right out, straight to the train station. I was back in my [New York] apartment by 11 o'clock that night. The label was sympathetic. They had a local salesperson at the show who backed me up. It was totally brutal."

Whether it was remnants of the *Kerrang* backlash or general head-scratching at Buck 65's musical direction, reviews for *Secret House against the World* were mixed. "I almost took it for granted that I would put out a record and it would get good reviews," he says. "Starting with *Vertex*, it was one record after another. When the *Secret House* reviews came out, I was caught off guard. I mean, I was playing with these great musicians. Chilly Gonzales was on that record as well. So if people liked the records I made with my amateur friends, when they heard me working with these world-class musicians, I expected people to love it."

It didn't help when V2 folded shortly after. "I wasn't dropped," says Terfry. "They just went out of business." The love was gone at Warner, as well; they dropped him everywhere but Canada, where he remained for three more records, including 2007's unmistakably hip-hop *Situation*, made with Halifax DJ Skratch Bastid and with an appearance from Edmonton's Cadence Weapon.

In 2008, he took a day job as the host of CBC Music's new national afternoon program, *Drive*. He wasn't allowed to program the music himself—because of course that would be too wicked, too weird.[3]

———————————

HAMILTON, ONTARIO, IS known as a steel town, a rock'n'roll town. It's where promoter Harold Kudlets first brought Ronnie Hawkins, and later helped his backing musicians become the Band. It's where Crowbar held court and spawned the northern blues legend King Biscuit Boy. It's the town Teenage Head dubbed Frantic City. In the '90s it was the home of scuzz rockers Junkhouse and the grunge scene around Sonic Unyon Records. Today it's the proud home of the Arkells.

But in the 2000s, Hamilton's best-known export was a math nerd from the nearby leafy small town of Dundas, who had a life-changing moment as a teenager watching an international techno legend from Windsor, Ontario, play in someone's Hamilton basement. By the end of the decade, recording first as Manitoba and then Caribou, Dan Snaith was collaborating with members of the Sun Ra Arkestra, DJing for nine hours at a time, stacking vocal harmonies over Silver Apples grooves and using Tibetan singing bowls to anchor his dance tracks. Every story written about his career makes sure to point out that he did all this while getting his PhD in math. But the most important thing about his journey is

———————————

3   That changed in 2020, when Polaris Music Prize founder Steve Jordan became senior director of CBC Music, and granted DJs more autonomy.

the music he made along the way, and how he became the first Canadian artist to make significant waves as an electronic artist while selling hundreds of thousands of albums.

DAN SNAITH'S FATHER was a math professor and Morris dancer who once published a surrealist novel. His mother and grandfather were also math professors; his sister and brother-in-law joined the family trade. Snaith was born in London, Ontario; his family moved to Dundas when he was 10 years old. Everyone he knew, no matter their age or taste in music otherwise, loved Pink Floyd. His grade 7 girlfriend took LSD in gym class. He took piano lessons from Ron Willmot, who used to play in a prog-rock band. Willmot had an arsenal of organs and synths lying around. When he saw that Snaith was an apt pupil, he encouraged him to transcribe keyboard solos by Rick Wakeman of Yes. Everyone around him, it seemed, was a bit weird.

"Growing up in an academic family, I learned to have an appreciation for things on the periphery of culture," he says. "Math professors are definitely some of the weirdest people you'll ever meet—they're eccentric in a way that isn't easy to categorize, because one person will be a concert pianist, and the next person will only wear 'Weird Al' T-shirts. Everybody's doing something strange. My dad liked that I was a bit of an eccentric in the same way that he probably was." By the time Snaith was 15, he was wearing tie-dyed shirts with dolphins on them, trading prog-rock bootlegs at school with friends who didn't mock the math nerd with a ginger mullet and square glasses.

His brain was cracked open when his friend Koushik Ghosh loaned him a copy of the Orb's 1992 ambient dub album *U.F.Orb*. "I had zero context for it; nobody else in my school or town would listen to this kind of music," he says. "I was used to complicated solos, and this was just repetitive, weird music with spoken-word loops going on forever. It was very hard for me to wrap my head around."

Soon after, he bought a four-track and obtained a sampler from his high school. Why did his school even have a sampler? "To this day, I have no idea," he says. "It was a fantastic music program, run by Ms. Johnston, who left our high school to go to Cornell University to become head of music education there. She knew I wanted to spend all my time doing music, and she gave me the keys to the place. There were lots of instruments, the obvious ones, and I found this dusty old sampler that had eight seconds of memory. I knew nobody knew it was there. I took it home, which I was allowed to do, but I never brought it back and no one ever noticed."

His friends were all into Lollapalooza music and the local Sonic Unyon scene. Snaith hated all that but wanted to play with his friends—even though their band was called Kaptain Hairdo. Snaith spent most of his time in that group playing organ, holding long notes and wondering when he was going to be allowed to break out his Wakeman chops (never). "We'd play once a year at the school's battle of the bands," he told *Pitchfork*, "and all the Grateful Dead and Metallica dudes would be like, 'That was the worst shit I've ever heard, get the fuck out of here!'"

Koushik was the main tastemaker in that circle of friends, partially because his brother, Himadri, was one-half of techno duo Teste, who put out a single called "The Wipe." "There are some circles in techno today where that is considered a total classic," says Snaith. "There's this U.K. techno guy Surgeon, and that's his favourite track ever. Koushik would say things like, 'Yeah, my brother's off DJing in Germany this weekend.' We're like, 'What are you talking about?!' Then he wouldn't explain anything more, because he's kind of a secretive guy."

Teste travelled in the same circles as Richie Hawtin of Windsor, Ontario, whose Plastikman project became internationally acclaimed and associated with the pioneering rave scene in nearby Detroit. Though Hawtin played huge parties around the world, one night he played a house party somewhere in Hamilton. "It was exactly what you'd picture of someone's basement," says Snaith. "That was my first experience of club music. I fell in love with [Plastikman's 1994 album] *Musik*. It was like nothing I'd ever heard before. I knew from Koushik that this was not recorded in a big fancy studio."

Snaith's dad had a computer. Snaith had that sampler from the high school. He knew a guy, Matt Didemus in Hamilton, who had a Mini-Moog synth, and maybe if he could borrow that, he could put it all together and start making dance tracks.

Didemus's synth was heavily coveted; Snaith and company had seen it when Kaptain Hairdo played a battle of the bands gig at Hamilton's Corktown club; Didemus and his friend Jeremy Greenspan were there with their Pink Floyd–ish space rock band, called the Drone. Years later, those two formed Junior Boys. "People don't know this about Jeremy, but he's a shredding guitar hero," says Snaith. "He's amazing. While I was practising Keith Emerson keyboard solos, he was practising guitar solos. He and Matt were from the other part of town; we knew them from parties." The future Junior Boys also DJed one of the only electronic nights in town, at one of the only venues that would have them: a chicken-wing joint called Joe Buttinski's.

Snaith didn't know anything about Hamilton's underground history: about the psychedelic proto-punk of Simply Saucer; about Brian Eno recording parts of his ambient records at Daniel Lanois's Grant Avenue Studio with Jon Hassell, Michael Brook and Harold Budd; or about Lanois's pre-U2 work for Canadian pop stars that was more interesting than it gets credit for: Spoons, Luba, Parachute Club, Martha and the Muffins.

He did, however, know the trippy shoegaze psychedelia music of Sianspheric, who were a pillar of the Sonic Unyon scene. He'd stay up late listening to DJ Paul Verma on campus station CFMU. "He'd play ambient music, ambient techno. It was a window into another world," says Snaith. Among other things, he heard Legion of Green Men, from nearby Burlington, who were signed to Richie Hawtin's Plus 8 label. "At two in the morning, I remember this moment so vividly, I heard my own music come through the radio. I'm sure no one was listening, or a handful, but it's the most intense happiness I've ever got from music."

As Snaith got more into electronic music, he and his friends found common ground in artists like Stereolab, Tortoise and Neutral Milk Hotel. The real glue was 666 (The Apocalypse of John, 13/18) by Aphrodite's Child, a Greek band featuring future film composer Vangelis and vocalist Demis Roussos. It's a 1972 double album rock opera based on the Book of Revelations. Snaith knew Vangelis because of the music for Chariots of Fire and Blade Runner, and wasn't a fan, but this was far removed from that—or anything else. "That's still one of my favourite albums ever, and it's one of the weirdest records in the world," he says. "We found it on the street out in the country near my friend's house. We put it on, listened and thought, What on Earth? The track titled with just an infinity symbol—that one gave us all nightmares. It sounds like someone locked in a room. It's horrible, completely insane. I always loved that music."

After high school, Snaith split for the University of Toronto to study—take a wild guess—math. It turned out to be a more creative pursuit than he initially imagined. A calculus class set him on a new path. "It was a revelation, because it was totally different than anything I'd done before," he says. "It was all self-directed: they gave you a problem and you had to deal with it. All of a sudden, there was this analogy with creating music. Math was now creative in the same way. It was about being intuitive and exploring an idea until something became clear."

He was also discovering jazz by the book: specifically, The Penguin Guide to Jazz Recordings, which he went through methodically, listening to every entry. The HMV store on Yonge Street had a generous return policy at the time: anything could be returned for no reason at all, as long as you had a receipt. Every single day, Snaith would buy eight CDs, burn and return, rinse and repeat. No one at the store batted an eye; it was entirely in line with store policy. "They'd be like, 'You've got the entire recorded work of the Beatles here. You didn't find anything that you liked?' And I'd be like, 'No, these are all rubbish, sorry.' And I did the same with John Coltrane." The jazz he loved most was all from the psychedelic era: Alice Coltrane, Pharoah Sanders, Sun Ra, Albert Ayler.

He started DJing house parties at his apartment at 218 Beverly Street, and in 1999 he got a club night a five-minute walk away at We'ave, across from the Art Gallery of Ontario and where Leslie Feist ran a weekly cabaret night. He and his crew, which included Koushik, called their DJ night Social Work, playing a diverse mix of '70s psychedelic R&B, Madlib-style hip-hop and the trend of broken beat. They wanted to transform the lava-lamp vibe of the room, working with artist friends to drape different fabrics everywhere and make large origami cranes. One night there were Ziploc bags full of water, suspended from the ceiling, with waterproof LED lights inside. Five hundred people showed up to their first gig. The numbers eventually swelled to 800 people spread between three floors of the venue: "Total fire hazard," says Snaith.

For the summer of 1999, he got a job in Bristol, U.K., at a Hewlett-Packard math lab. There, he went to a festival and saw the post-rock band Fridge, featuring Kieran Hebden, who'd just released a solo project called Four Tet. Snaith could hear a similar affinity for jazz in Four Tet, and approached Hebden to exchange contacts; six months later, he invited the Brit to play a Social Work night in Toronto. "Almost nobody knew who he was; even in the U.K., he was very underground," says Snaith. "I didn't get the sense that this would sell any tickets. It was just an excuse to hang out. He'd never travelled internationally to DJ, so he thought it would be fun. He arrived at our house. We put our phone numbers on the flyers, just being a bunch of idiot college students living together. The phone rang the night before the party, and someone asked to talk to Kieran. I got on the phone, and it was Kevin Drew, who said, 'Explain what's going on here! Who are you? Who has flown Four Tet over here? What's going on?' He was totally mystified. We just did it for the love of doing it, and we had made enough money from the last party to pay for a plane ticket."

It turned out to be a wise decision: not only did the Hebden connection lead to Snaith getting a deal with Four Tet's label, Leaf, but Hebden became his lifelong friend, neighbour and sounding board.[4] The man behind the esoteric Four Tet also taught Snaith a valuable lesson that night at We'ave. "We expected him to play artists like [jazz harpist] Dorothy Ashby and clear the floor," Snaith told writer Denise Benson. "Instead he showed up with banging tunes. He played 'Intergalactic' by the Beastie Boys and had the newest Armand Van Helden test pressing couriered to his flat in London before he left. Rightly, he figured that we were basically a party for university students. That really challenged what I valued in music. Up until that point, I valued the esoteric and the difficult—I was

---

4   It's through Hebden's Canadian connections that Four Tet ended up sampling Sharon, Lois & Bram on his 2001 track "No More Mosquitoes."

a snobby elitist, basically. Getting to know Kieran was a big part of me coming to understand that pop music, at its best, can be amazing and radical and subversive."

With a record deal in hand, Snaith now had to choose a name. "I wanted a name that evoked Canadian-ness," he says, "and Manitoba is a lovely word." Snaith was a fan of the ecstasy-drenched Edinburgh duo Boards of Canada—who named themselves after the National Film Board of Canada filmstrips they watched as schoolchildren, while their dad helped build the Calgary Saddledome. "Part of the idea for the name I got from them, which as a Canadian is a weird second-hand way to come at it," says Snaith. "I definitely did feel that a lot of the music I liked was coming from the electronic music hub cities of the world, but there's some-thing about my music that connects to my nostalgia [for] growing up in big open spaces, in a wintry landscape, and Hamilton as a particular place. I looked more locally for a name, but in the end I literally picked one off a map."

Following an October 2000 EP, *People Eating Fruit*, Manitoba debuted in March 2001 with the album *Start Breaking My Heart*. The opening track is called "Dundas, Ontario." One night, DJ Patti Schmidt played it at the beginning of CBC Music's *Brave New Waves*, and Richard Reed Parry jolted out of bed. "I had tingles," recalls Parry, who had just started the instrumental band Bell Orchestre, not yet with Arcade Fire. "I sat up and thought, This is all I want to make. It was like taking a really warm bath, instantly. It was not trying to be slick or trying to hide the wires, to mask itself. But it was also banging and interesting and really beautiful. The whole thing is two four-note riffs. Some part of my brain knew I was listening to a totally unique perspective, and I wanted to listen to anything he did. Shortly after, he was interviewed on *Brave New Waves* and was talking about the Zombies as one of his big influences. He was talking about deeply psychedelic music."

Start Breaking My Heart drew obvious influence from Four Tet and Boards of Canada—and Scott Herren's Prefuse 73 was a contemporary, debuting the same year—but there were harps and flutes and elements of psychedelic folk, while the beats owed a debt to contemporary hip-hop innovators like Timbaland and Madlib. It was clear that Snaith's eclectic taste included a lot of so-called spiritual jazz, not the easy-listening lounge that was populating a lot of electronic music at the time (St Germain, Mr. Scruff). In an electronic scene that had been averse to melody for years, Manitoba tracks had critics comparing Snaith to Brian Wilson—which says a lot more about the low bar for melody at that point in time than Snaith's songwriting skills. Above all, the music felt loose and hand-assembled—because it was.

Snaith was aiming for "a good amount of sloppiness," he told *Tape Op* maga-zine in 2003. "The melodies come easily, but getting music to sound sloppy is harder than one might think. I don't use MIDI at all. All the melodies and samples I record are all slightly out of time—like a real band would be. I've found that most people making electronic music see this grid in the program they're using and they're scared as fuck to put anything in that doesn't land on that grid. The way things miss being in perfect time is often what gives the music some sort of human or emotional feeling. By quantizing everything, you lose all of that. The other thing that makes [my music] end up sounding sloppy is putting a lot of layers in with lots of things going on in the background all slightly out of time, or out of tune, to make things sound a little bit messier."

Start Breaking My Heart got rave reviews everywhere, and with that came offers to play shows. "In 2001–'02 there was very little software that would enable you to do that," he says. "I found it super frustrating, coming from a background where I played instruments live." Instead he mostly played DJ sets, including three dates on an eclectic *Exclaim!*-sponsored bill in April 2001 opening for Afrobeat band Antibalas and the Hidden Cameras.

Snaith's high school friend Ryan Smith, of Kaptain Hairdo non-fame, was in Toronto playing with the Russian Futurists, led by Matthew Hart from Peterborough. Originally a solo bedroom electro-pop project, the Russian Futurists' live show consisted of four guys seated, playing keyboards on a project table while swigging beer, with Hart in the centre singing. That band's debut, *The Method of Modern Love*, got British press and accolades from Blur and R.E.M., though it remained obscure in Canada. Hart lived next door to Snaith and Smith on Hogarth Avenue, off Broadview in Toronto's east end. "We were both enjoying this weird time, where someone would send us reviews of our records in some esteemed publication," says Snaith. "The people who loved Matt's first record were really evangelical about it. I love it."[5]

Ryan Smith knew that Snaith wasn't happy with Manitoba's live setup. He told him that if he ever wanted to start a band to let him know. As Snaith started working on *Up in Flames*, Manitoba's second record, that offer got a lot more tempting. He didn't want to make the same album twice. Hebden turned him on to the self-titled 1968 debut by Silver Apples, a synth-drum duo that predates the similarly groundbreaking work of German band Can. "It still sounds like the sound of tomorrow to me, but it has those amazing folk melodies over the top of it," he says. That sent him back to the music of his youth: "Grateful Dead, Pink Floyd, Jimi Hendrix, Doors—that was the mainstream music in high school. I loved that music; it was all around me. Making *Up in Flames* came from those influences, as

---

5   The Russian Futurists later toured with Caribou; in 2013 Hart became the long-running morning host on new Toronto radio station Indie88.

well as Stone Roses, My Bloody Valentine, early Mercury Rev." He had already started moving in that direction on some B-sides from *Start Breaking My Heart*, including the track "Tits & Ass: The Great Canadian Weekend."

He was now living in the U.K., as of September 2001, working on his PhD in math at Imperial College London. It was clear the new music could not be presented live with just a laptop. Snaith invited Smith to London to work on a plan; they shared a one-bedroom apartment with drummer Peter Mitton and Snaith's girlfriend (and later wife). The trio rehearsed for a month and then debuted at London's 100 Club, with psychedelic projections and a lot of backing tracks, including vocals—because Snaith was not at all convinced he could sing in public, and *Up in Flames* vocalist Koushik was not touring with them. All three members wore bear masks, adding to the surrealism and playing up stereotypes of the Canadian wilderness. Snaith mostly played a second drum set on stage—an instrument he'd never seriously played before, and the added percussive attack drew from his love of the 1999 Boredoms album *Vision Creation Newsun*, which had two drummers driving the band into ecstatic overdrive. He wanted to be as far as possible from the standard solo artist laptop setup—commonly derided as "DJ checking his email."

The 2003 album was well received, albeit with some befuddlement. "Something must have happened to Manitoba's Dan Snaith," wrote Mark Richardson in *Pitchfork*. "Seriously, I can't remember hearing this stark a contrast between consecutive albums in a long time, maybe ever." *Up in Flames* no doubt alienated some electronic purists, with its overt rock influences, but it blew open the appeal of Snaith's music. It was also infinitely better than the hipster hoax known as Animal Collective.

It did attract some unwanted attention. One day Snaith got an email from Handsome Dick Manitoba, a singer from the early punk days of New York City. Dick fronted the Dictators and once got beaten up for anti-trans heckling of performer Jayne County. In 1999, he opened a bar on Avenue B, called Manitoba's. The American punk felt that Snaith's project was some kind of copyright infringement. Snaith laughed it off and didn't respond. He did, however, check in with a lawyer, who assured him he had nothing to worry about.

One night, on tour with Four Tet and Prefuse 73 in Detroit, the Manitoba crew was surprised to somehow find a Dictators T-shirt mixed in with their merch. It turns out the punk band was also in Detroit that night. "It felt like some kind of veiled threat—I guess?" laughs Snaith. "I have no idea." Later on the same tour, a private investigator showed up at an L.A. gig and served Snaith with a subpoena. This time, lawyers told him it would cost $500,000 to fight the case, and he might not even win. "I thought, Whoa, this guy is for real. We didn't even reply. Maybe we should have, but his character through the whole process didn't suggest a dialogue would've solved the problem." It wasn't worth the time, money or mental energy, so Snaith changed his name right before the release of the third album, *The Milk of Human Kindness*, which was very much a continuation of *Up in Flames*.

The album—and reissues of the first two—was credited to Caribou. The name came to him during an acid trip while camping in Canada, which surprised no one who wrote about Snaith's psychedelic influences. He was quick to distance his music from drug culture, however. "I'm always sober when I make music, and it's very rare that I do drugs at all," he told writer Jesse Locke. "The process of making music, for me, is about getting lost in a world of sound. I can imagine that makes it appealing [for other people] to do drugs and then listen to [it]. I like having clarity of mind when making music. I'm sure drugs can be a valuable tool for creativity, but it gets fetishized a lot. I'm not interested in the machismo associated with it, like, 'Oh man, we did so many drugs and then made this record.' Who cares? Either you made a good record or you didn't."

Drummer Peter Mitton left the band to become a CBC producer; Brad Weber, of Kitchener-Waterloo band Winter Equinox, was recruited after his band opened for Caribou in Hamilton. For *The Milk of Human Kindness* tour in 2005, Snaith offered the opening slot to a new Hamilton band comprised of old acquaintances: Junior Boys, led by Jeremy Greenspan and Matt Didemus.

At a 2003 tour stop in Hamilton, Greenspan had given Snaith a CD with just one song on it, "Birthday," a track that was very much a throwback to early synth pop like New Order, set to a syncopated, stuttering funk then in vogue in U.K. electronic circles. "I thought it was cool," says Snaith, "but it's hard to explain now—when the '80s retro synth sound is everywhere—how at that point it was diametrically opposed to everything else going on. Stylistically, I didn't think I could get anyone interested in it. It was both retro and forward-looking, but the reference points were so different from what I heard anyone else talking about."

Greenspan knew that Junior Boys had little to no chance of getting attention in Canada, so he moved to the U.K., where his sister was a philosophy student. One of her classmates was known professionally as Kode9, an early dubstep[6] artist, who ran a label and message board called Hyperdub. "Birthday" was posted on the Hyperdub message board, and a buzz started building. "This was a time when a track had a following on the internet before it did in the music industry," says Snaith.

Junior Boys landed a record deal of sorts: a fan formed a label to release "Birthday" as a single. After the 2004 release of debut album *Last Exit*, Junior Boys

6   The term dubstep meant something very different at the time, far removed from later artists such as Skrillex.

were picked up by Domino Recording Company and became part of the wave of Canadians getting international attention that year. They weren't the only other Hamiltonians in the mix. Snaith's high school friend Koushik, whom he credits with getting him out of his teenage prog-rock rut, was signed to L.A. hip-hop label Stones Throw, home of Madlib.

Along with the name change and overdue talk of a Hamilton electronic scene, much of the press about Caribou in 2005 revolved around Snaith's recently completed PhD. He patiently tried to explain his thesis, "Overconvergent Siegel Modular Symbols," to journalists, to no avail. "It's such a cumulative subject that I can't even explain one of those words without you taking a bunch of courses," he told *Pitchfork*'s Ryan Dombal. "I can't even really remember how I made an album and finished the PhD at the same time. It seems like insanity in retrospect, and it was. But I just kept at it."

For his next project, the 2007 album *Andorra*, Snaith took a slight left turn. He'd become more interested in songwriting, as opposed to loops and layers and jams. There were conventional verses and choruses and stacked harmonies, as heard on the lead-off track "Melody Day"—a song that finally warranted the hyperbolic Brian Wilson comparisons, though Snaith was more likely to talk up the Zombies than the Beach Boys. There was even a ballad, "She's the One," sung by Greenspan.

With his profile growing, he wanted a new label for North America and went with Merge Records, best known for being run by '90s indie rock icons Superchunk—a band his high school friends probably thrust on him as a teenager and which Snaith likely hated at the time. It was the label's other acts that appealed to him. "I knew [Merge's] music through Magnetic Fields and Neutral Milk Hotel," says Snaith, citing the same artists that drew Arcade Fire's Win Butler to the label. "Those two artists were two of my favourite things in the world. I knew Superchunk to some degree, but Mac [McCaughan] and Laura [Ballance] were so enthusiastic straight off the bat. They've been such wonderful allies all these years, and trusted me to do whatever. Musically I'm often out of step with other acts on the label, but that's not an issue."

By far the biggest twist in Caribou's career came in September 2008, when *Andorra* won the Polaris Music Prize. One of the 11 jurors picking the winner that year was Denise Benson, the Toronto club DJ to whom Snaith gave his very first demo in 2000. "It was very surreal," says Snaith of his Polaris win. "Everyone says they don't expect to win, but I was genuinely in shock when it happened. I always had a conception that I was an outsider and a weirdo, and a lot of my heroes operated on the fringes when they were making their music. That was a point when I felt my music was moving more toward the mainstream than I ever expected it would, and being listened to more broadly."

The next year, he was invited to play the All Tomorrow's Parties festival in New York City, curated by Flaming Lips. For the occasion he assembled the 15-person Caribou Vibration Ensemble, which included Kieran Hebden, Sun Ra saxophonist Marshall Allen, Born Ruffians' Luke Lalonde, original Manitoba drummer Peter Mitton and Koushik. When Snaith sat behind the kit, there were four drummers on stage. He put out a live recording and resurrected this project on a couple of other occasions. As triumphant as that was, he was getting ready to shift gears yet again.

With Greenspan, Snaith had started going to clubs again to hear dance music; for the few years before that, his appreciation of that culture had become entirely cerebral. One night in 2008, he went to see Junior Boys play on a bill with early '80s post-punk dance band Liquid Liquid. Afterwards they all went to see Detroit DJ Theo Parrish, who spun an incredibly eclectic and eccentric set that nonetheless kept the crowd moving no matter what left turns they were being served.

"It was so diverse, challenging and fun—it was this amazing social experience as well, which is obviously a big part of what club music is all about," he says. "When I first got into dance music with the Warp [Records] stuff [like Aphex Twin and Autechre], it was about being obtuse and clever, but when I came back to it, it was more about the trajectory through disco, the sexier side of dance music more than the intellectual side."

It also made him question his music's place in the modern world. "Aesthetically, *Andorra* was very much indebted to the 1960s," he says. "Looking back on that, I'm proud of it for a number of reasons, but I also thought, Hang on, I'm not making music in the 1960s. When people were making those records, they weren't being conservative and looking backwards, they were trying to make the most progressive, modern-sounding music they could." He set out to do the same.

After he turned 30, the man who never imagined he would become a singer didn't want his lyrics to be somewhat random evocations of emotional expression; he wanted them to have some personal resonance. He had friends going through divorces. He had an in-law who was in an abusive relationship. His grandparents died. All of that went into writing what became his greatest achievement, 2010's *Swim*, an album that featured his greatest pop song up to that point—"Odessa," later covered by Sarah Harmer—as well as some of his trippiest and most danceable tracks. It was much less dense than previous records. True to its title—inspired by Snaith's interest in swimming lessons—the sounds were amorphous and aquatic.

"I love this idea that some people think of dance music as being very restrictive—you have to have this kind of beat, a certain range of beats per minute, and blah blah blah," he says. "But it's almost like if you satisfy those requirements, then *anything* else goes. The dance music that I like, it's quite liberating to think that as long as the music's rhythmic and propulsive in a certain way, then I can put Tibetan bowls and a harp in this track and I can still play it in a club. I really like that idea."

It seemed poised to merely do a bit better than *Andorra*: at that point, Caribou was a successful niche artist, had been around for almost 10 years and was unlikely to experience a massive growth in audience. But as the tour got longer, the audiences got bigger.

Then Radiohead came calling, offering him an opening slot on their *King of Limbs* tour in 2012. When he began headlining his own shows again, it seemed like a whole new crowd. "Not only did *Swim* sell more copies"—close to 300,000—"but it connected with people who were very different from me," he says. "With previous records, I'd play a show and look out and think the audience and I can talk about records by Can, the Zombies and the Boredoms because we have a lot in common and are around the same age. But with *Swim* there were 18-year-olds freaking out in the front row. I was in my mid-30s and the whole thing was magical to me. It shouldn't have worked. It shouldn't have connected with people, but it's very affirming that I put myself into it and it did work in this way that I didn't expect it to."

No one, least of all Snaith himself, could have predicted the migration pattern of Caribou.

▄▄▄▄▄▄▄▄▄

THERE'S A TROPE in Canadian hip-hop that there is so-called real hip-hop and then there is "hip-hop that white people like." Some of that music is made by white artists: Buck 65, Classified, the Peanuts & Corn crew from Winnipeg and most of rap québ, including regional superstar Loud. Some of it is made by Black artists, like genuine pop crossover k-os or arts journalist Shad (who ties with Caribou for having been on more Polaris prize shortlists than any other artist).

Then there's Rollie Pemberton, a.k.a. Cadence Weapon. When he was 19, he came out of nowhere—Edmonton—and made a record that sounded like nothing else in Canada; it came out on a Toronto indie rock label and he toured North America with solo violinist Owen Pallett. Pemberton was a nerdy Black kid who wrote reviews for *Pitchfork*. He is named after his grandfather, who immigrated to Canada to play for the Edmonton CFL team; his father was a pioneering hip-hop DJ in town, and his uncle was a popular local funk musician.

"I wasn't trying to rap like anyone else," he says. "Being a rapper in Canada, everyone was trying to rap like they were from New York. They would use American accents and rap about the same stuff. It was so transparent that they were faking. I thought, Man, it would be so lame if I tried to do that. I mean, I'm from Edmonton! I wanted to fuck shit up. I saw myself as a punk. All my friends were people in hardcore bands and making electronic indie rock and stuff. People who had a more confrontational way of making music. I wanted people listening to think, What the fuck is this? That was my main purpose."

ROLLIE PEMBERTON WAS three years old when Maestro dropped "Backbone" and 12 when the Rascalz' "Northern Touch" made history. He started rapping in 1999, when he was 13. He sold some CD-Rs of his material in high school and snuck into clubs underage to check out the local rap scene.

Yes, there was a local rap scene in Edmonton. "There were a few different crews," he says. "The Low Budget Affiliates were like hosers, hard-partying dudes. They had a record called 6 Bucks a Six-Pack. To me, one of the most important rappers from Edmonton was a guy called Touch, of the Dangerous Goods Collective. He had a group with DJ Nato called the Representatives. Nato now records all of Merkules's stuff—one of the biggest rappers in Canada now, with millions of fans purely off social media and YouTube. One of the other big groups was Politic Live. You had to be a part of the Edmonton rap scene to know [any of] this. There were a lot of interesting people who maybe didn't know the business side or know how to promote themselves, or they were making non-commercial music."

Yet definitions of commercial rap music were changing. In the U.S., Timbaland and the Neptunes were making the most sonically adventurous pop music in a generation. In the U.K., rapper Dizzee Rascal put out Boy in da Corner in 2003, which introduced the world outside London to a subgenre known as grime, which sounded like hip-hop from the 22nd century. It won the Mercury Prize that year, beating Coldplay and Radiohead. When it arrived in North America in 2004, Pemberton instantly sensed a kindred spirit. "The first time I heard Dizzee Rascal, I went to Listen Records in Edmonton," he says. "They had it playing over the sound system, and I was kind of repulsed, but it was recognition—because it sounded like my shit. It was too similar. I started listening to it more and had to give it props because it was truly unique. I always look for the unique thing over the most technically proficient thing. The most innovative thing. I want something new."

In January 2004, he left town to study journalism at historically Black Hampton University in Virginia. But he was too distracted by his music. "I had this nagging feeling that I had to put out this album soon before someone else did something similar," he says. "I was very paranoid about it." In Virginia, he worked on what would become his debut, Breaking Kayfabe. When he came home for the summer, he nearly lost everything.

"My mom's boyfriend at the time had been using the computer where I'd made most of my music, for gaming," says Pemberton. "He got a virus on it and it crashed the computer and everything got erased—including my album. I had to cobble things together from files I'd sent to my girlfriend at the time, and to my friend over instant messenger. They were sending me back all these MP3s and weird files, and I had to Frankenstein it all back together. Whenever you hear the beat change in a song, that's a new part I had to add. It had a cool effect, because it was a very strange and uncommon structure of songs, but that was a necessity, because I'd lost parts of the original sessions. But I ended up with some of the illest parts of the album. It was a blessing in disguise."

He went back to Virginia in the fall of 2004, but his heart wasn't in it. He dropped out in January '05. "My mom was like, 'Okay, you have a year to figure [a music career] out, and if you haven't, then you have to go back to school.' I thought, I'll be damned if I'm going back to that shit."

In advance of the album, Pemberton put out a mixtape in early 2005: *Cadence Weapon Is the Black Hand*. The originals were heavily influenced by U.K. grime but not too precious to include a Falco sample. There were also unofficial remixes of Gwen Stefani, Beastie Boys and M.I.A. To promote it, he took advantage of his side hustle as a writer. He was already writing reviews for *Pitchfork* and on his own blog. Among bloggers at the time, it was common courtesy to have a blog roll, linking to other blogs covering similar ground. He sent his song "Oliver Square," about a nondescript shopping centre in downtown Edmonton, to Matthew Perpetua's *Fluxblog*, the biggest MP3 blog at the time. After the track was posted, positive responses started flooding in. Pemberton was invited to remix a track by the much-hyped U.K. grime act Lady Sovereign and caught the attention of Toronto label Upper Class, who had managed to get international press for Toronto electro-pop act the Russian Futurists. "It was reviewed on *Pitchfork* and I started doing mail order, sending CDs all around the world," he says.

Hometown reaction, on the other hand, was muted. "They didn't really get it; they thought I was super weird," says Pemberton. "I was this teenager sneaking into their events, and suddenly I became the biggest artist in that scene. It seemed to annoy a lot of people. But I was getting a lot of respect from other rappers in the Prairies, like the Peanuts & Corn crew in Winnipeg. [Label head and producer] mcenroe was one of the first people to really encourage me to make more music." He cites mcenroe's Hip Hop Wieners album and associated rapper Birdapres as key inspirations.

"That was a scene I related to, because they also were not trying to be from anywhere else. They were true to themselves. And also Saskatoon, they had a couple of labels: Clothes Horse Records, run by Soso, and another label run by Factor Chandelier; it was weird, strange music. I thought Saskatoon had a more popping scene than Edmonton. People had their own ecosystem and they were selling records locally and on the internet. There were all these message boards and websites like Hip Hop Infinity or Ughh.com. Our records would get reviewed, and we didn't have to do the Toronto thing or the mainstream thing. That was the world I existed in before the rest of Canada heard about me."

Contrary to common perceptions of the Prairie town, "our scene was not insanely white," says Pemberton. Indigenous crew War Party were from Maskwacis (Hobbema), just south of town. MC Advokit of the Non-Status crew and DJ Creeasian (later a dancer for A Tribe Called Red) were also visible on the scene. "And there were a lot of Black people: the Politic Live crew, Touch, me and Conspiracy, a super strange character whose brother was [Toronto MC] Mindbender."

A key ally in Edmonton was Nik Kozub, formerly of Luke Doucet's Veal and now commanding the Vocoder-heavy live electro group Shout Out Out Out Out. "They were the on-call party band of Edmonton," says Pemberton of the supergroup of sorts that included members of local favourites Whitey Houston and the Wet Secrets. Kozik had recorded Pemberton's uncle, Brett Miles, and his band Magilla Funk Conduit; in early days, a young Cadence Weapon used to join them on stage at the Sidetrack Café and rap. The MC was also a fan of Dietzche V. and the Abominable Snowman, later shortened to DVAS, who made Chromeo-esque synth R&B. "They were playing super old vintage synths on stage, where he had to put a floppy disc in between tracks," says Pemberton, who later hired them to work on his 2012 album, *Hope in Dirt City*, which also featured Brett Miles on saxophone.

Breaking Kayfabe came out in December 2005 on Upper Class. It slowly gained steam over the next few months. There were few, if any, North American artists tapped into the U.K. grime scene. Between that and the novelty of an Edmonton rapper, Cadence Weapon got a fair amount of press in Canada. His first introduction to U.S. audiences was in the spring of 2006, when Islands brought him on their first tour; that band was riding a wave of anticipation after the breakup of its much-loved predecessor, the Unicorns.

Pemberton was a Unicorns fan; he saw them play at Red's in West Edmonton Mall, where they did a cover of "P.I.M.P." by 50 Cent. "That Islands tour was awesome," he says. "I didn't make any money. The tour was good because I got a lot of, uh, *exposure*"—he laughs, referring to the eternal music biz promise that usually adds up to nothing. "But that was back when it actually *was* decent exposure. It was absolutely worth it. I played all over North America to big audiences every night. It was a trial by fire. I had basically barely played live before that. They took a chance on a guy with a super weird record, and it helped a lot. We all got along great. But during the tour, [drummer] Jamie [Thompson] quit. We got through the last few shows, but I remember Nick [Thorburn] collapsing at a show in Kansas, on stage; he was crestfallen. I realized that touring is really hard on you."

It was with Islands that he played the El Rey club in Los Angeles, where he was seen by Anti- Records, the label—home to Tom Waits, Nick Cave and the Weakerthans—that soon signed both Islands and Cadence Weapon. While it was a successful and reputable label, it wasn't necessarily the best choice to break Pemberton out of the indie rock circle he was in. Neither was touring with his friend Owen Pallett, whose music seemed the total opposite of Cadence Weapon's.

"I was performing a lot for indie rock audiences or audiences where rap is not their number-one thing," says Pemberton. "Back then, after my first four songs of a set, I'd say, 'Okay, everyone, I'm a rapper. I'm rapping over these songs. I know you've maybe never heard rap before and I might be the only Black person in the audience. But you're gonna like it, it's gonna be okay. So when I say *this*, you say *that*.' It was baby steps, every day of my life for five fucking years. No comprehension or appreciation for rap music. I was the only Black person pretty much anywhere I went. It was very difficult."

He also had trouble connecting with other rappers at home. "In Canada, other rappers will not be friendly," he says. "This is why our scene is not as good as it could be. There's constant backbiting and competition and negativity, typically coming from the Toronto scene. In my career, other than Peanuts & Corn, who were always great to me, I've always had to do my own thing because people didn't want to fuck with me. Or they didn't get what I was doing."

The U.K. was a different story. He was courted by Rough Trade—he would have been the first hip-hop act signed to the legendary indie label—but went instead with Big Dada, the hip-hop imprint of Ninja Tune, home to Roots Manuva, Ty and Diplo. "In 2008, I played over 100 shows, and most of them were in Europe. I was playing all kinds of European festivals, and all over England extensively, Glastonbury. I was getting lots of props, really good press. The Big Dada connection felt really good, because Roots Manuva felt like a contemporary to me."

Brits had been historically supportive of off-beat Canadian hip-hop, championing the Dream Warriors in 1991 before anyone in North America did, even in Toronto. "I love the Dream Warriors," enthuses Pemberton. "They are really great people. When I came on the scene, they gave me props. They understood that I was in the lineage with them. We don't, as a country, have the musical vocabulary to explain something that's new. That's something I felt early in my career: that I was doing something that didn't exist before and people were disturbed by it, frightened by it, confused by it and polarized by it, in all corners. It did get attention around the world and blew up more than even I expected it to, but I still feel like in Canada it's not clearly articulated that I made it easier for some people who came after me."

His first release for Anti- and Big Dada, who had distributed *Breaking Kayfabe*, was 2008's *Afterparty Babies*. It flopped. It opens with a doo-wop song, later covered by Great Lake Swimmers. Much of the album isn't drastically different than the debut, and yet it was perceived at the time—shortly after the Kanye West and Daft Punk collaboration—as some kind of techno makeover, maybe for as shallow a reason as the song called "House Music." *Now* magazine in Toronto gave it one star (or one "N," as per their rating system) in an archetypally asinine Tim Perlich review: "Whether it's a matter of Cadence Weapon having too many bloggers email him that his *Breaking Kayfabe* album was a work of genius or wasting too much time touring with [Owen Pallett], *Afterparty Babies* suggests that former *Pitchfork* writer Rollie Pemberton has lost the plot. The boring beats and throwback rhyme flow (circa '92) [are] weak even by Edmontonian standards." It goes on to compare it to comedian Tom Green's Juno-nominated Organized Rhyme.

Though his new labels got him a lot of gigs, they both dropped him when the record didn't sell. "It was career suicide," says Pemberton. "The central irony of hip-hop is the way it's made allows it to be the most creative, innovative music possible, because it consumes all other genres. It's a sponge for everything. You sample everything. It's referential and you're always sharing ideas and it's a conversation between different generations of rap. At the same time, people in hip-hop are some of the most conservative in the music world—and why? They're not open to new perspectives, new voices. Once something has been prescribed as part of the canon, you can't divert from it.

"For someone like me who came into the game saying, 'Fuck everything that came before me; I'm going to do what I want,' people hated me. In the rap scene, they thought I was making noise garbage music. I didn't look hip-hop and I only played with white rock bands, so I wasn't part of the conversation. Whereas in Britain they understood right away and I was playing to big crowds. I was plugged into some of the U.K. grime artists like Jammer. I went to his basement, which is considered a sacred place in U.K. rap. They recorded me there and I signed my name next to Dizzee Rascal and Wiley on the stairs. It felt really cool to be respected as part of that lineage, but I wasn't seen the same way in Canada."

His hometown threw him a curveball: he was chosen to be the poet laureate of Edmonton between 2009 and 2011. He started spending time in Montreal, and moved there in 2011. A comeback record, 2012's *Hope in Dirt City*, was another reinvention, a career highlight, and it landed him back on the Polaris shortlist, competing with Drake, Feist and his new Montreal friend Grimes. When *Breaking Kayfabe* celebrated its 15th anniversary in 2020, he says, "People came out of the woodwork, telling me how influential it was. Such an outpouring of positivity. I was surprised. It was a cool record and people liked it at the time, but I didn't have an idea of whether it would be remembered.

"I was like, 'Guys, this is outsider music that people thought was so weird back then. Now it's normal.'" The next year, the 35-year-old won the Polaris for his album *Parallel World*, making him the second-most celebrated artist in the prize's history, after Caribou—and ahead of Drake.

CHAPTER 16
DRUNK CLOWNS
OF THE VICTORIAN ERA

HOT HOT HEAT, WOLF PARADE,
THE UNICORNS, BLACK MOUNTAIN

B less the pawn shops of British Columbia. In the 1990s, the province with the most hippies per capita was somehow rich with discarded synthesizers. Several of them found their way into the hands of four key bands with roots in Vancouver Island. They didn't use them to make Skinny Puppy–style industrial music, nor slick pop music. Each one employed those rusty synths in a garage aesthetic that injected new life into so-called indie rock.

Two of them, Wolf Parade and the Unicorns, are better known as bands who helped put post-Godspeed Montreal on the map—which is kind of remarkable, given both bands' ramshackle trajectories. Another band, Hot Hot Heat, played it straight, had chart hits and brought the pre-fame likes of Franz Ferdinand and the Killers on the road as opening acts. The final one, Black Mountain, boasted a Victoria veteran who started out in a teenage speed-metal band signed to Slayer's label and later enlisted an analog synth collector who relished the chance to resurrect the days of keyboard-heavy hard rock.

"For a long time, nobody had a keyboard in a band; you might as well have a flute or something," says Wolf Parade's Arlen Thompson. "All the keyboards were these '90s, really crappy digital Korg M1s and [Yamaha] DX7s, which nobody knew how to actually program, with this artificial, glassy sound to them." That changed when the punks started playing analog synths, inspired in part by British bands like Stereolab and Add N to (X) and by American bands Trans Am and Six Finger Satellite—none of them near the mainstream. "You could still buy a lot of these synths for relatively cheap; they weren't a hot vintage buy yet," says Thompson.

The Unicorns' Nick Thorburn and Alden Penner found their Roland Jupiter-4 synth and TR-707 drum machine in their hometown of Campbell River, in the remote northeast corner of Vancouver Island. "Both are miraculous finds in a small town like Campbell River," says Thorburn. "Those two pieces of gear ended up defining our sound." That sound made them one of the buzziest and most beloved indie bands of 2004, directly paving the way for their friends in Arcade Fire.

Spencer Krug of Wolf Parade grew up in Penticton, in the B.C. Interior. As a teen, he found a Roland Jupiter-4 synth at a pawn shop, which he traded for $20 plus "a shitty knock-off hollow-body guitar that I probably got for 100 bucks. I went with my father, and he was mad because I didn't haggle and make a straight trade, wasting 20 bucks. The irony now is that the keyboard is worth thousands of dollars. I still have it."

Victoria multi-instrumentalist Paul Hawley "bought a Juno-6 for 300 bucks," says Arlen Thompson, who played in earlier bands with him. "He put it through a guitar amp, and it had this wild sound to it." Hawley then handed it to his bandmate Steve Bays, and Hot Hot Heat was born.

Bays had resisted the Juno-6 at first. "I thought keyboards were so lame," he says. "I was more into Don Caballero and Tortoise, bands where the drummer was the star." But he took to his new role instantly and soon became the focal point. At the time, Hot Hot Heat was one of many projects for its members; none of them expected it to be a real thing. Until it was.

"Victoria was split into camps," says Wolf Parade's Dan Boeckner. "Hot Hot Heat was really going against the grain by actually committing to a career in pop music and being professional—being on time and not destroying things. Then there was this whole other world that had a completely different vision of performance, which was more post-modernist, the idea of a drunk clown. That was the Victoria thing. Wolf Parade took that surrealist aesthetic and put it into our early stuff."

"Victoria was a competitive environment," concurs Bays. "It was a self-sustained ecosystem, because it's expensive to get off the Island. Whenever a band would leave it would be, 'Whoa, that's crazy.' The bar was really high. I went to so many shows to see local bands that were mind-blowing. I played with millions of bands after that, and I still stand by those local bands from Victoria."

After Hot Hot Heat recorded its first demo with future Black Mountain drummer Josh Wells, they got a review they couldn't ignore. It came from a man known only as Wazzle, a local Victoria character who worked at Ditch Records. "He was a well-known nudist and often dressed in women's clothes," says Bays. "His bedroom was filled with stuffed animals, wall to wall." One day Bays ran into Wazzle on the street.

"Steve!" exclaimed Wazzle. "I just heard your Hot Hot Heat demo!"

"Oh, that's great, man, what did you think?"

"During the first song, 'Fashion Fight Pods,' I just dropped my pants and started *masturbating immediately*."

Every band on the Island would kill to have had a review like that. Maybe the Juno-6 helped.

IN 2005, LCD SOUNDSYSTEM released the single "Daft Punk Is Playing at My House," an era-defining song that captures the excitement of rock kids getting into dance music, with fuzzy '80s synths and disco beats. In the '90s, LCD's James Murphy had done sound for synthy Sub Pop prog-punk band Six Finger Satellite before discovering dance music. His first underground hit was producing the Rapture's "House of Jealous Lovers" in 2002, which, post-Peaches, set a tone for the rest of the decade. Meanwhile, Daft Punk became actual pop stars, Grammy winners and Kanye West collaborators.

It's not known whether or not Daft Punk, a French house music duo, ever played a punk rock basement party in North America. But the Rapture sure did—including one at Steve Bays's house in Victoria, long before they signed to Sub Pop, moved to New York City or even met James Murphy. A few years later, both the Rapture and Hot Hot Heat were buzz bands at the forefront of a hot musical trend.

British Columbian punk has always been closer to its cousins in California—spiritually, musically and geographically—than to anything else. That was true of D.O.A. and NoMeansNo in the early '80s, and it was true of the Victoria punks of the late '90s. The San Diego scene in particular, with bands like the Locust and Drive Like Jehu, was a mecca. Connections were made, which is how the Rapture, who formed in San Diego, ended up playing a Victoria house party.

Drummer Arlen Thompson went to California with his band, Honeysuckle Serotina, when he was 18. "We had this idea that we were going to [go to] L.A. and make it," he laughs. "We lived out of a van in Santa Monica, trying to get gigs and the attention of a record label—or something. We had no idea what we were doing. Completely ridiculous, but it was fun." That lasted several months.

When he came back, he formed Detroit Death Watch, a band where future Hot Hot Heat drummer Paul Hawley played guitar. "In Victoria, eventually you play in a band with everybody you know, and you're at a point where you're dating everyone else's ex-girlfriend," he says. "Nobody really got any attention. Daddy's Hands was the first band to ever get any kind of press, when they made some kind of top 10 list" in British avant-garde bible *The Wire*.

Daddy's Hands didn't sound like anyone else on the West Coast at the time.

They didn't have a vintage synth, but they did have saxophone. They didn't look like anyone else either: bandleader Dave Wenger was known to play a gig in a dress, swimming flippers and a gas mask. He also had a homemade mask made from a woman's nylon stocking (with a mouth hole cut out) and covered with fake fur; two button eyes completed the ensemble. "It was very, very upsetting to look at," says Dan Boeckner, "really unpleasant." Yet Steve Bays describes Wenger, a handsome six-foot-two guy, as a "Christ-like figure" in the scene, and his band as "melodic, punk, weird, catchy, cutting-edge, emotional but still standoffish." Josh Wells of Black Mountain says, "Daddy's Hands were definitely way out of the canon of what most people were doing at the time. They didn't sound like a rock'n'roll band in any way, really. They were closer to the Cramps or Tom Waits, with a volatility to their live show that really scared people. They were extremely intense and prone to weird, sometimes violent outbursts. You never really knew what you were going to get. They were very confrontational. They really didn't want people to like them—and yet people loved them."

Dave Wenger had started in a thrash band called Moral Decay, then a mid-'90s Victoria hardcore band called M Blanket, "which Jawbreaker must have heard and ripped them off," claims Bays. Dan Boeckner's first formative live music experience was seeing M Blanket play in Duncan, B.C., in 1995; he later became Wenger's roommate in both Victoria and Vancouver. M Blanket's Chad Jones moved to Montreal, reinvented himself as hushed solo artist Frankie Sparo and was one of the first signees to Constellation Records. Stephen McBean, later of Black Mountain, was a huge fan of M Blanket, with whom his punk band Gus often shared bills; they covered each other's songs.

M Blanket folded after morphing into the heavier, denser, Slint-like group Ache Hour Credo. Wenger's next project was completely different from everything else he'd done. "Daddy's Hands, to me, started the Canadian indie rock sound—and I mean that in the best way," says McBean. "They completely influenced [Frog Eyes'] Carey Mercer, Spencer Krug, so many people. Dave was a very charismatic frontman. He had a lot of power. In the mid-'90s, things were a bit stuffy in the punk scene, politically. Daddy's Hands made dance music. He loved Captain Beefheart and James Brown. There was some crude humour and an artiness, letting loose a bit. Dave would turn in his grave if I said 'carnival punk,' but it was really refreshing at the time. It was a little less by the numbers."

After putting out two cassettes, Daddy's Hands split for Vancouver in 1998; Wenger moved to Montreal a year later, an early migrant from Vancouver Island to that city: the rest of his band soon followed—as did Frankie Sparo, Wolf Parade, the Unicorns, Arcade Fire's Sarah Neufeld and others.

Hot Hot Heat were one of the only ones to stay.

POLYMATH STEVE BAYS was in several bands as a drummer, bassist or singer. Since the age of 14, he had been a promoter, booking bands he wanted to see so he could study them up close. Most, including his own bands, were part of the then-new punk trend of emo, although he also had a straight-up metal band with 3 Inches of Blood's Cam Pipes. Musical trends in town were tied to what worked live.

"The Achilles heel for every show promoter was the PA," says Bays. "It was so hard to get vocals on top of the volume, especially in the '90s when it was noble to be loud. It was like, okay, people won't even hear the vocals, so we'll get into quirky time signatures." If the music wasn't prog metal, it usually had a groove, with an obvious debt to hometown heroes NoMeansNo or to Gang of Four, the British band who laid the much-emulated template for post-punk dance music on 1979's *Entertainment!*

"When you have a shitty PA in a super echoey gym room, the only way you know if people like your band is if people are moving," says Bays. "The better the band, the more the room is like a sauna. When I started singing, it was such a struggle to hear my voice on top of the music, so I always sang at the top of my range, which is where I could get the most volume."

But for the first two years of Hot Hot Heat, Bays wasn't the singer—Matt Marnick was. They became popular enough to sell out the Starfish Room in Vancouver, play in Alberta and tour down the West Coast with gloomy Vancouver new wave band Radio Berlin, featuring Josh Wells on drums. "We opened for the Locust at [San Diego's] Ché Café, which was the coolest place to play there at the time," says Bays. "We brought 100 demos with us and sold them all that one night." But Marnick was done: his enthusiasm was waning, while drummer Paul Hawley's was waxing. "Paul wanted to take over the world," says Bays. "Matt's drive was not the same, and I was somewhere in the middle." While that intra-band drama was playing out, Bays started a solo project: writing straight-up pop songs, playing all the instruments and recording them on his hard drive.

In the early days of file-sharing, users' personal libraries were visible to anyone who chose to browse online. Andy Dixon, who had put out Hot Hot Heat singles on his label, Ache Records, was poking around in Bays's music folders when he stumbled across something titled "new songs." He loved them and wanted to put them out. Surprised, Bays then played the songs for Hawley, who suggested they immediately break up the band and focus on this instead. They didn't bother changing the name. Hot Hot Heat was no longer a weird punk band; they were a pop band with Bays singing.

They also finally had a guitarist: Dante DeCaro, another local punk who knew the prog-pop discography of XTC inside out. A few new songs were recorded locally and sent around to labels as a demo. Sub Pop invited them to open for Liars in Seattle; after seeing the live show, the label offered to put out an EP.

Steve Bays and bassist Dustin Hawthorne were living together, in a former crack house that reeked of cat urine, and where Victoria police had recently shot four dogs on the lawn. Seven people lived there in total, paying $100 a month in rent each. Bays was 21 and had just been offered a job as creative director at a local TV station; he'd studied digital art in school and considered that his most realistic career option. But even his practical parents urged him to focus on music for a while.

"From that point on, I took the band really seriously," he says. "We stopped going out to bars, didn't chase girls, didn't drink. We just stayed home, drank tea all day long. We had a VCR with the Beatles' *Anthology*, which is seven or eight tapes, and we'd watch it over and over again in the background. I saw a quote recently that called Hot Hot Heat 'the most caffeinated band of the 2000s,' and I thought, Yeah, there was definitely undiagnosed ADHD mixed with a love of caffeine and general anxiety. It was a ball of nerves. Plus, all four of us could have been bandleaders. We all had strong emotions and opinions and drive and dreams and goals."

Sub Pop suggested Chris Walla of Death Cab for Cutie as a producer; it would be one of his first professional gigs. Two tracks from the demo, "Le Le Low" and "5 Times Out of 100," were combined with the Walla session for an EP, *Knock Knock Knock*. Released in early 2002, it hit like a bomb: few other bands in Canada sounded this different, this bold, this dressed for success. In the very first song, Bays seemed to be taunting his elders: "Where's all your passion gone? / Where's all your fashion gone? / Where's all your magic gone?"

Bays's voice was a stumbling block for many; to say that he's yelpy would be an understatement. On the stuttering chorus of "Le Le Low," he sounds like a chicken. But the music was thrilling, like the weirdest mix in the world between NoMeansNo and Platinum Blonde. There were more musical ideas and hooks in one Hot Hot Heat song than in most contemporaries' entire albums—a notable exception being fellow British Columbians the New Pornographers. "In the early 2000s, it felt like melody was finally cool again," says Bays. "There was a new brand of punk that wasn't called indie rock yet—a nice period where everything felt undefined."

Sub Pop could tell they were about to blow up. Right after the EP's release in early 2002, Hot Hot Heat played L.A., opening for (long-forgotten) labelmates Arlo on a bill with Jenny Lewis's Rilo Kiley. "We were first on the bill, and it was wall-to-wall slammed, people losing their minds," says Bays. "Then the place cleared out after we played." At a show in Seattle with Mudhoney, the other opening act was the Shins, who told the Victoria band that the EP was in constant rotation in their van. Along with Iron & Wine, the Shins are often given credit for revitalizing Sub Pop as a major force in the 2000s; oft forgotten is that Hot Hot Heat, who arrived on the label in between both those acts, sold just as many records as either of them. For a moment they were second in sales only to Nirvana's *Bleach* in the label's history.

It helped that Hot Hot Heat looked like total rock stars. For starters, Bays's curly locks made him look like he stepped out of the cover of *Frampton Comes Alive!* Hot Hot Heat were all skinny boys who bought their jeans from the women's section of the Gap, accessorizing with studded belts and thrift store fashion. Drummer Paul Hawley, the most devout Beatles disciple in the band, suggested they wear dress shirts and ties, because it had worked for the Fab Four.

Though they had music ready for their full-length debut, Bays did not have the lyrics ready; he wrote some on napkins on the ferry from Victoria to the Vancouver studio. They were working with Jack Endino, who recorded many of the early Sub Pop records, including Nirvana's. On the album's biggest single, Bays says, "I thought I would replace the word *bandages*, that I could come up with a better word than that, but there just wasn't enough time." He was also too lazy to bring his Juno-6; he assumed there were synths at the studio. There were not. He played a lot of piano and organ instead, which gave the album more of a garage-rock sound than initially intended. "But 'No, Not Now' and 'Talk to Me, Dance with Me' had to be on synth, so we used this shitty Korg Trinity, where I tried to simulate a Juno sound—not very well," he says. "And those ended up being two of the biggest songs on the record." The process was fast: recorded in six days, mixed in one day and a few songs remixed on one other day. The entire record cost $7,000.

When they went to play it for Sub Pop, Bays had a sinking feeling, largely because of his own vocals. "I just thought it was so awful," he told writer Cam Lindsay. "I think just because it was so naked, and it still is when I listen to it now. The bare minimum of tracks, the vocals are super loud, there's not much to hide behind. But I think to the average ear that was refreshing at the time."

As Hot Hot Heat was about to explode, another Victoria resident, Dan Boeckner, was about to ship off to Montreal. "Dan did not seem like he was from Victoria or even Canada," says Bays. "He was like the crazy exchange student where you couldn't tell if he wasn't aware of local norms or if he was just next level, and maybe he wasn't socializing because he knew he was better than everyone. He was a lone wolf and very intimidating."

DAN BOECKNER HAS spent much of his life travelling: his later bands Handsome Furs and Operators made a point of playing corners of Asia and eastern Europe where few North American bands ever ventured. He's moved between Vancouver, Montreal and southern California several times, before being pulled back to Montreal, the city where he formed Wolf Parade, which he calls, with some authority, "the most liveable city in North America."

Part of his wanderlust comes from growing up in Lake Cowichan, B.C. (population: 3,000). "It's a two-hour drive north of Victoria," he says. "It's not remote, but it takes effort to get there. It's not on the way to anywhere." It was a depressed logging town with high unemployment. "Cocaine was the main drug at my high school," he says. "These guys would see their parents go work in the bush, and a cool thing for the parents to do on the weekend was do an eight-ball and get completely shit-hammered in the backyard."

When he was 16, a bus route opened between Lake Cowichan and Duncan (population: 5,000), 20 minutes down the highway. It was there that a window opened to the rest of the world for Boeckner, at a skateboarding shop that stocked magazines and CDs, adjacent to a Chinese grocery store run by the same family, the Chows. Boeckner read the music mags obsessively and imagined what the music sounded like before asking the Chows to order a record. Boeckner's "very first band would play what we thought Guided by Voices sounded like." Punk, hip-hop, Aphex Twin: all soon became accessible. Few bands ever came to his town, mostly Victoria hardcore acts, such as Gus with Stephen McBean of Black Mountain. The first show Boeckner ever saw was in Nanaimo: the Smugglers, with future CBC Radio 3 host Grant Lawrence, and the Evaporators, featuring Nardwuar the Human Serviette. In Cowichan, Boeckner formed Say Uncle, whose gig at a Victoria curling rink impressed a young drummer named Arlen Thompson. "I remember this super skinny dude from the Duncan-Cowichan area, just going nuts," says Thompson.

Boeckner moved to Victoria the day after graduating from high school. He went to university for political science and history, and started writing songs on a four-track. Despite living in a squat with Dave Wenger of Daddy's Hands, he didn't connect to the local punk scene and was ready to reject what he called the "aesthetic fascism" that came with post-hardcore.

"I started playing country music a lot," he says, "because I learned how to sing." He got some help from his neighbour: Carolyn Mark, a saucy country singer originally from Sicamous (population: 2,500) in the Interior. In the '90s she had a cowpunk band, the Vinaigrettes, and later collaborated with Neko Case and became one of Canada's best songwriters of the 2000s. But in 1998, she was starting her solo career and hosting a weekly hootenanny at Logan's, which had begun in the early '90s. Boeckner played many of Mark's hootenannies, including a few where he sat in with Toronto band the Sadies. He hung out at Mark's house quite a bit, "because her house was nicer. At our place, the bathroom literally fell through the rotted floor into the basement where our rehearsal space was. She kind of adopted me."

Victoria may have seemed exotic to him when he lived in Lake Cowichan, but a bigger city now beckoned. Between 1997 and 1999 he bounced back and forth between Vancouver and Victoria; on the mainland, sometimes with Wenger, he lived in "two famous punk rock squats," one run by the band Submission Hold, the other the centre of the local riot grrrl scene.

It did not go well. "I developed a pretty severe drug problem," he says. "Opiates and speed. It was a very personal, quiet thing, but it got bad. Heroin was very, very cheap. Speed was really cheap. The Downtown Eastside is just awash in that. Combine that with a limited amount of economic possibilities. Everyone I hung out with was poor. We were all working-class people, with a few exceptions: some grew up extremely privileged and somehow drifted down into the dirt with the rest of us. It became fashionable, in this circle, to do the most nihilistic things they could think of, which inevitably is going to be opiates. A lot of people died. I needed to get the fuck out of there. I went back to Victoria and got my shit together." He was there long enough to meet some potential new bandmates, before he and his girlfriend decided to take a Greyhound bus to Montreal in the summer of 1999.

Boeckner fell in love with Montreal; his girlfriend did not. They were flat broke and fought constantly. "We lived on Parc Avenue across from the hospital in a completely dilapidated, empty giant apartment," he says. "I dumpster-dived for food." There were other Victoria expats in Montreal, from the Daddy's Hands crowd. But nothing was happening for Boeckner, and he headed back to B.C. To earn enough money to pay for a bus ticket, he got a job as an extra in a video by Québécois metal legends Voivod. "I love that band," he says, "but that was not the best era of Voivod."

Upon returning to Victoria, he started Atlas Strategic; John Pollard from Daddy's Hands was the sax player. Their very first gig? Opening for Modest Mouse, a gig that Hot Hot Heat had been angling to get. "I just bullshitted my way in," says Boeckner. "I really wanted it, even though I wasn't that familiar with Modest Mouse." The gig was at a strip club called the Ice House, and soundcheck took place during regular hours. The 22-year-old's introduction to the big time was being heckled by horny old men who were upset at the racket. As for the show itself, "I had a shaved head and was extremely excited about being very physical on stage," he says. "I was flinging myself around and fucking with the audience. I have no idea how it sounded."

Modest Mouse's Isaac Brock thought it sounded great. The two men hung out all night. When it came time to part, Brock asked for Boeckner's number. The Victorian had neither a landline nor a cellphone; he gave him the number of the Bent Mast, the restaurant where he worked slinging cheeseburgers. Brock did call and offered Atlas Strategic the opening slot for a Modest Mouse tour, which kicked off with two sold-out shows at the Crystal Ballroom in Portland in front of 1,400 people each night. "I was terrified," says Boeckner. "We were super green and annoying." The next night was at the Warfield in San Francisco on September 10, 2001. They woke up the next morning to find out that, among other world events, the tour was cancelled. In 2002, Brock invited the band on a full West Coast tour with his solo project, Ugly Casanova. He was very interested in signing them to Sub Pop, for which he was doing some A&R work. Meanwhile, Hot Hot Heat had just put out their Sub Pop debut.

In L.A., after a show at the Troubadour and a party at the Roosevelt Hotel, Boeckner called his mother. "We had a strained relationship for about a year before that point," he says. "I talked to her for two or three hours—which I later had to pay hundreds of dollars for. The Troubadour was a venue she and my dad knew because Neil Young played there, so she was very, very happy. We broke through, it was beautiful." He went back to Victoria at the end of the tour. Two days later, his dad told him he needed to come home to Cowichan Lake immediately. When he arrived, his parents were just returning from the doctor's office.

"She had systemic lupus from the time I was six until her death," says Boeckner. "Taking immunosuppressants gave her fatal liver cancer. She was in remission for lupus, started feeling unwell. By this point she was familiar with many ways her body could fail her, but this was new. So she went to the doctor, who told her she had terminal cancer and then she died [a week later]. We didn't even call anyone. We didn't know what to do. Her body was in the house for days. We had a wake, then a funeral, and then I left for Montreal. That was the dividing line in my life."

He wrote a song called "This Heart's on Fire," with the lyric, "I am my mother's hen / And left the body in the bed all day / we don't know what to do." Atlas Strategic split up, and Boeckner quit his restaurant job. A friend he'd recently met in that kitchen became key to his new life in Montreal.

SPENCER KRUG HAD landed in Victoria in 2000, where he started playing with a new band called Frog Eyes. While working at the Bent Mast restaurant, he met "this weird, super sarcastic, funny punk, and we hit it off. Right away we started talking about starting a band someday." The punk, of course, was Dan Boeckner.

Krug grew up in Penticton, near Kelowna, and started playing in bands when he was 11, with friends of his older sister. In high school, he joined a band called the Friendly Ghosts and then a ska band, the Two Tonne Bowlers, who once opened for the Smugglers and Evaporators. Upon graduation, he bounced between Vancouver and Calgary, including a stint at Vancouver Community College to study music. While there, he lived in a house with six other musicians and artists, including Dan Bejar of Destroyer, who was just about to put out *Thief*. "All those guys were like, 'Have you heard Dan's record? He's singing his poetry. It's weird, but cool.' We'd never heard anything like it."

Krug and his girlfriend drove to Montreal in the summer of 2001, having never been there before but knowing they'd at least find several West Coasters. Coincidentally, they moved down the street from Boeckner. Krug enrolled in music and creative writing at Concordia and started four-tracking. He had no intention of performing the material live. "The idea was foreign and absurd," he says. "I was way too nervous to even think about it." In Montreal's Mile End, he placed CDs of his recordings, credited to Sunset Rubdown, in the Distroboto machines, which were old cigarette machines repurposed to sell music, zines, arts, crafts; every item was $2.

Reconnecting with Boeckner, the Victorians talked about starting not one but two bands, in which they'd back each other up. They did not have much equipment. "Our first setup was the Jupiter-4 [keyboard] and a guitar run through a primitive digital audio converter coming out of computer speakers," says Boeckner.

Alex Megelas of Grenadine Records was booking the Jupiter Room on St. Laurent; he had signed a Belgian band called Melon Galia ("they were like the direct-to-video version of Stereolab," says Boeckner) and needed an opener. A mutual friend suggested Boeckner and Krug, who immediately accepted the gig. But they had no drummer and no name. Their choice for drummer was obvious: Victoria scene staple Arlen Thompson, who'd moved to Montreal in 2001 to go to Concordia.

As for the name, Krug thought he had it: "Guys, I've figured out the best name for the band: the Unicorns!" Boeckner turned to him. "Uh, that's already a band. *From our town.*"

The two started brainstorming for an alternative. "When Atlas Strategic opened for Modest Mouse, there was another band on the tour called Mice Parade," says Krug. "Every night of the tour, Dan would introduce his band as some other kind of animal parade: 'We're monkey parade!' or whatever. Back then there was that style of airbrush paintings that you'd see on the side of Dodge vans, and they'd be titled things like *Spirit of the eagle* or *Spirit of the wolf*. They passed one on the highway one day, so he introduced [Atlas Strategic] that night as Spirit of the Wolf Parade. I liked the name, but it was a bit long, so we shortened it."

They had one rehearsal before the Jupiter Room show. Boeckner felt electrified: "I'd never had another experience like that. The songs completely came alive." While they didn't think much of the headliner, they did form an immediate bond with the other opening band, Arcade Fire. Some other Vancouver Islanders showed up, who had tried unsuccessfully to crash a Cat Power show earlier that night—they were ones who'd already staked a claim on the name Unicorns.

THE UNICORNS WERE definitely real, though much of their story is hard to believe.

"It didn't make any sense how badly they wanted to be taken seriously," says Richard Reed Parry of Arcade Fire, "contrasted with how *not* serious it came across. It was phenomenal."

In the space of 18 months, the Unicorns transformed from a band who once spent an entire show motionless in sleeping bags to midwifing Arcade Fire's success to having the Yeah Yeah Yeahs beg them to stay together after turning down a multimillion-dollar deal. All this happened to a band who were prone to onstage fistfights, whose one and only album was about how much the two core members hated each other. They formed in high school in tiny Campbell River, B.C., on northern Vancouver Island. One of their last gigs was at Orson Welles's house in L.A. for a debutante's birthday party. In between is one of the most unusual stories in the history of Canadian music.

NICK THORBURN GREW UP in Prince Rupert, near Haida Gwaii and the Alaskan border. When he was 14, his family moved to Campbell River, a working-class industrial town where he was bullied relentlessly. Music was his salvation. He went to punk shows in nearby Courtenay, seeing Vancouver's Submission Hold and an early version of Hot Hot Heat. When he was in grade 12, Thorburn noticed a kid two grades below, wearing a plaid skirt and a T-shirt that said *Share the Power*. His name was Alden Penner.

Thorburn was obsessed with music; Penner actually knew how to play it. "I didn't have a guitar or any skills," says Thorburn. "When Alden asked if I played music, I lied and said yes." They quickly agreed he should just sing. "We did these youth centre, rec centre shows," says Thorburn. "I was really trying to do a Peter Murphy thing, because Bauhaus was my vibe. The bassist was a punk guy. The drummer was into funky stuff. Just a criss-cross of styles. I was paranoid that I was a terrible singer. I quit out of total fear of being exposed as a fraud." In 1999, upon graduation, he split for Montreal to study film. A friend from Cortez Island had told him the city was a paradise for people like him.

Montreal was everything he hoped it would be. "My head exploded," he says. "Every night, it was outrageous." He put up an ad to start a band. Chloë Lum responded. She was a visual artist who was about to start Da Bloody Gashes with her boyfriend, Yannick Desranleau. She needed a roommate; Thorburn needed an education. "She was really cool and really rock'n'roll," he says. "She had all these records and gave me a really quick, total musical education, took it up to the next level and turned me on to so much. I'd go to shows as much as I could. I didn't have any money. Nothing. I also didn't drink. My costs were low. There was this thing at Concordia called the People's Potato, which was free vegan food. I would eat that every lunchtime and take leftovers for dinner. It was perfect and cheap." Thorburn's film career got off to a rocky start. For his student project, he was determined to make a movie with Corey Haim.

The Toronto-born troubled Hollywood child star (*Edison Twins*, *Lost Boys*) had reportedly moved to Montreal. Thorburn saw an opportunity. He hit the phone book and started calling Haims. The second one was the actor's uncle, who offered to pass along the message.

"Great!" Thorburn responded. "We met at a party a few nights ago and really hit it off. I'm a young filmmaker who'd like to talk to him about my next film."

"Okay, I'll give him your number and maybe he'll call you."

One minute later Thorburn's phone rang. It was Haim, confused but curious. "I kept up the facade for 20 seconds," says Thorburn, "and then I said, 'Look, I gotta level with you. We didn't meet. I just wanted to work with you.' He was really impressed and moved by the gesture and the effort. I didn't know what would happen. He agreed to do the movie."

Thorburn now needed to raise money for what might be more than just a short student film. "It was scandalous, but I did a benefit show at the Jailhouse [club] called Save Corey Haim, implying that he was dying and we had to raise money to save him," he says. "We raised all this money to fly him in, even though he was coming in for a wedding; he actually lived in Toronto. It all didn't turn out so well, ultimately.

"The film was about me trying to get Corey Haim to be in my film. It was all non-synch sound and I was into experimental stuff, so there were sock puppets. It was a chaotic mess. There was a final scene I'd envisioned where he'd sit down at a diner and tell me he couldn't be in the film. Ultimately, he showed up really late and there was a guy with him who was really freaky. He wanted me to come to his car and give him the money. Everyone on my little crew was like, 'Don't do it, he'll just leave.' It got really weird." The director of photography then smashed the camcorder tape with all the Haim footage and demanded a kill fee; Haim later threatened to sue. The film was rescripted and ended up being just about the initial phone call.

Thorburn returned to Campbell River in the summers and reconnected with Penner. They played a few shows on the Island, hitchhiking with their gear, and one at Ms. T's Cabaret in Vancouver. In the fall, Thorburn returned to Montreal and tried to coax Penner to join him, while they wrote songs by emailing sound files back and forth.

One night at an experimental improv jam—of which there were many in Montreal at any given time—Thorburn saw a drummer play a kit with his foot on the snare drum. "He was amazing and doing some crazy shit. I wanted to befriend him." This was Jamie Thompson.[1]

Thompson grew up in Guelph, Ontario, making music in a scene that included Royal City and Gentleman Reg, in whose band Thompson played alongside Tim Kingsbury (later of Arcade Fire). He fell in love with Montreal before he moved there. "I'd taped this old NFB movie about a drummer named Guy Nadon, called *Le roi du drum*, and watched it 100 times," he says. "He played on garbage cans and had this weird successful-slash-unsuccessful career. I developed this really romantic notion of Montreal as this exotic place that was cool in a way I didn't understand." It was. "When I moved here in 1999, the rent was almost nonexistent. I paid $150 a month."

After meeting Thorburn, Thompson moved into an apartment with him above a butcher shop at St. Laurent and Pins, and then underneath him in the Fattal Lofts in St. Henri, a building that *Maisonneuve* magazine described as "infamous in Montreal for their cheap rent, custodial negligence and infestations of misfits, artists and crust punks." During the day, Thompson busked in Metro stations to make rent. At night, he played in a live house music band, Gazelle, who were big enough to play a major outdoor stage at the Montreal Jazz Festival that year, in front of tens of thousands of people. He backed up Spek of the Dream Warriors for a while. Above him, Nick Thorburn and Richard Reed Parry paid $600 for an enormous space as well as access to a concrete jam spot in the building, dubbed the Bread Factory.

Alden Penner came to visit several times from the West Coast, while he and Thorburn pieced together the *Unicorns Are People Too* EP, which was mostly Penner's guitars with Thorburn's drum programming. "That was the best creative

---

1   No relation to Wolf Parade's Arlen Thompson.

situation for Nick and Alden," says Thompson, "because as soon as they had to be in the same room together, things got more difficult." Nonetheless, Penner soon moved into the Bread Factory. Some of the Unicorns' earliest Montreal shows were in another loft, where Chloë Lum lived, above the club Barfly on St. Laurent. Brendan Reed, later of Arcade Fire, was an early Unicorns drummer; he set his cymbals on fire at one show, opening for the Microphones. Another drummer was Michael Makhan, the co-owner of St. Laurent vegan restaurant Aux Vivres.

Thorburn sent demo CDs to every promoter in town. But he didn't have any money for postage, so he'd put packages in the mail without stamps—addressed to himself, with the promoter as the return address. "We'd write these letters that were like hostage negotiation letters," says Thorburn. "Not with clipped out letters, but the tone was very forceful. 'Trust me, you have to do this.' The kind of brash hubris only a 21-year-old can have."

Sometimes it worked: in May 2003, upstart promoters Blue Skies Turn Black started giving them opening slots for Metric, the Walkmen and one of the band's heroes, Texan outsider artist Daniel Johnston. But the Unicorns burned a bridge with the big boys early on. In April 2003, they were begging to open for Cat Power, whose show was put on by the big promoter in town, Greenland Productions.

"We had no bona fides," says Thorburn. "They're like, 'No.' We tried to will it into reality, so we showed up early during soundcheck and started loading our stuff in through the back door of Theatre Outremont. We started eating Cat Power's rider. Her tour manager walked in. 'Uh, what the fuck are you doing?' 'Oh, we're playing, Greenland said we're on the bill.' She's like, 'No, you're not on the bill. Get out of here.' That was our promotional attack. We wanted this to exist so badly. I also wanted to have fun. There was a prankish, impish component to it. 'Why do we have to be so serious about all this? Let's just fuck around a little bit.' That was the MO for the early days."

TWO MONTHS AFTER the Cat Power incident, the Unicorns started recording their debut album. "It was made in our practice space, the Bread Box, this concrete box inside the Bread Factory," says Richard Reed Parry, who had by then recorded the Arcade Fire EP in Maine and was also working on his own band, Bell Orchestre. "The whole thing was made using my instruments: some synths, an amp I had, a glockenspiel, an Echoplex. I was like, Huh, someone's getting really creative with my stuff! That lit a fire under me."

Local sound tech Mark Lawson volunteered to help them put it together. "We basically won the lottery when Mark Lawson got involved," says Jamie

Thompson. "He had all this know-how and put all this effort into crafting a record that sounded pretty good. I think we spent $300 total to make that record, and most of that was for renting mics."

Jamie Thompson wasn't yet officially in the band during the recording; he also fell ill, so Penner played some of the drum tracks. "I wasn't sure I wanted to be in the band," says Thompson. "I got an offer to play in a cover band that was very highly paid. I probably could have made more money doing that than being in the Unicorns, ultimately. It was steady, shitty work. But I made a decision: I'm going to literally sell all my belongings and go on tour." Thompson had other concerns and terms upon joining a band that had once played a gig at the Mile End Greek pub Pasalymani's dressed in sleeping bags and performing a puppet show.

Thorburn booked a show at the Jupiter Room in the summer of 2003 where neither of his bandmates showed up—which was fine with him. "Jamie and I were at loggerheads a lot," he says. "Jamie has a very strong personality. Brilliant human being. I felt a little threatened. Alden had maybe double-booked, but we got in a fight and broke up temporarily. I was outside the Jupiter Room and saw two guys panhandling, so I offered them $10 each to come on stage and be my backing band." What should have been disastrous turned out to be a turning point: Gary Worsley, who ran local noise label Alien8, was there and intrigued. By the end of the night, he wanted to sign the Unicorns—whoever that might be. The three original members put aside their differences and took the plunge.

Alien8 didn't do indie rock. They specialized in abrasive electronic music, both locally and internationally. "I don't know what they thought of us," says Thorburn. "I think they saw the playful, experimental side. We were into all that stuff, too: Merzbow, Phÿcus, Brian Damage from Unireverse. A lot of drills, buzzing and true industrial sounds. We were influenced by that, but we were also into Simon and Garfunkel. We were really trying to fuse those two. They courted us by taking us to Aux Vivres, and we split the cheque when the bill came. I was like, Oh, is this how the record biz works?"

The album eventually sold almost 100,000 copies. "I think we recouped," Thorburn deadpans.

It was time to break out of Montreal. In July 2003, they had a show booked at Clinton's in Toronto, with Constantines side project Woolly Leaves and comedian Nick Flanagan. They bought a used Honda Civic for $200, from a guy who warned them that it needed a ton of work and needed to be certified. "We said, 'Okay, no problem!' and immediately drove to Toronto," says Thorburn. "We had to pull over every 30 minutes because it was overheating. The last leg, we had to push it on the side of the 401. It took us 12 hours to get from Montreal to Toronto." (It's normally a six-hour drive.) Miraculously, they made it to the show.

The only other rock band on the Alien8 roster was Soft Canyon, the new project for Andrew Dickson, from the much-beloved garage band Tricky Woo. The two bands embarked on a national tour—which should have been a great gig, except that Soft Canyon was a psychedelic country-rock band that didn't sound anything like Tricky Woo, and whose album had a lukewarm reaction. Turnout across the Prairies was low. And the Unicorns' Honda Civic fared only marginally better than it did on their Toronto trip.

But there was no turning back. All three were committed to the road, come hell or high water. The next 18 months was full of both.

On the West Coast, they spent some time at home in Campbell River and, with some parental help, bought an '80s RV camper van in Victoria for $2,000, as a low-rent touring bus for the broke band. "It immediately started falling apart," says Thorburn. Exhaust fumes easily penetrated a hole in the floor. The heat didn't work, so the windows had to remain up. Carbon monoxide poisoning was a serious concern. Nonetheless, it became the Unicorns' touring vehicle for three straight cross-country trips.

"We drove that RV from Victoria to Halifax to Victoria to Montreal," says Jamie Thompson of the fall of 2003. "Touring in that thing in the winter in Canada, you'd be sitting with a blanket over you, shivering, blowing steam while wind came in the cracked manifold in your face for a 20-hour drive from Edmonton to Winnipeg. We left it parked somewhere in Montreal. We left the doors open so that homeless people could live in it for a while." The shows were sparsely attended: 15 people, maximum. Most of them came from local campus stations, after the band sent all the station managers CDs with a unique typewritten note.

The album, *Who Will Cut Our Hair When We're Gone?*, was released in October 2003. It was deeply melodic and based in pop songcraft, and it was deeply weird. The synths sounded like they were barely being held together. The guitars were scrappy indie rock. The live drums and drum machine were mostly rough; Thompson only plays on a couple of tracks, and it's pretty clear which ones. Yet everything also sounded carefully planned: the dynamics, the directed tempos, the instrumental choices. "I Was Born (A Unicorn)" became an immediate set highlight: in part because it's driven by a relentless Thompson beat, in part because of a three-chord riff with West African overtones, in part because of the dance breakdown in the middle, in part because Thorburn and Penner don't just trade lines but get into an argument while doing so ("'I write the songs' / 'No, I write the songs!'").

American campus radio loved it. Will Butler of Arcade Fire was working at Chicago station WNUR at the time. "People were losing their shit over it," he says. "WNUR was deeply committed to being weirdos. We played Lightning Bolt.

We were playing '70s minimalism, like Terry Riley. We were on the early Rapture train; with later Rapture, we were like, 'Bah. This is essentially a hit.' But the Unicorns threaded the needle. They were just weird enough. The music director would write a little review on the sticker of every CD, and on this one he said something like 'the possibilities of pop music but it's experimental.' The Chicago nerds thought it was amazing." Reaction across the continent was similar, among snobs and non-snobs alike.

At the Pop Montreal festival a couple of weeks before the album release, the Unicorns tried to put their CD in the hands of as many bands as possible. It worked. Hot Hot Heat invited them to tour in November. Though they were fellow Vancouver Islanders of the same generation, there were no previous social connections. Hot Hot Heat was, well, hot at the time.

The Unicorns saw a great opportunity—until they learned that Metric had been added to the bill. "We were really pissed," says Thorburn. "This was going to be a big break, and now we were first of three on the bill and our [guarantee] went down. We were only getting $100 a night. Hot Hot Heat were doing a victory lap and were in celebration mode. We were tagging behind in this RV that was barely able to get to the next town, waking up to frozen bottles of water in the van."

Jamie Thompson enjoyed himself a bit more. "I watched their set almost every night," he says. "Such joy: [drummer] Paul [Hawley] and [singer] Steve [Bays], especially, were so fucking psyched to be doing that. Their positivity was infectious to me. It made us feel like we were supposed to be there. Whereas a month earlier we were playing to 10 people in Regina. Psychologically to me, the tour felt right. It felt like what should be happening."

The crew was a different story. Thorburn recalls, "One of the last shows we did with Hot Hot Heat, the tour manager came back from dinner and was like, 'Oh, that lobster was so delicious.' We were starving, and we were like, 'Do you have our meal buyouts?' He just callously laughed in our face and said he'd used it toward his lobster dinner. This was after touring with these guys for three weeks. The tour ended with two nights at [Toronto's] Opera House. We were always pissing people off. We did something on stage, I don't remember what it was, and we got kicked off the tour on the second-last night. Their merch guy opened for them instead."

HOT HOT HEAT's full-length Sub Pop debut, *Make Up the Breakdown*, came out in the fall of 2002. They toured the U.S. with New York City band the Walkmen, who had formed in the ashes of Jonathan Fire*Eater, an early Hot Hot Heat influence; the two bands alternated headlining spots on tour. They also headlined a tour with

Franz Ferdinand, a new Scottish band who'd released only one single, "Take Me Out," which Bays sang with them on stage every night. It soon became one of the defining rock songs of the decade, a perennial dance floor favourite.

In Las Vegas, another new band, the Killers, opened for Hot Hot Heat; the Nevadans were already a huge fan of the Victorians. Two years later, when the Killers' debut came out, a *Spin* review of their set opening for the sleepy Stills—headline: "Stills Chill, Killers Kill"—praised singer Brandon Flowers for having "the undeniable charisma of Hot Hot Heat's Steve Bays."

Despite the touring opportunities, *Make Up the Breakdown* was not an instant smash. "It did okay," says Bays. "We would have pockets where we had a fan base, and other places where there was no one there and we'd be opening for some crappy band who was huge 10 years ago. It was hard to figure out where we sat between the mainstream and the underground, and back then it was more important to people that there was a distinction. It was a delicate balance."

Hot Hot Heat had been on the cover of *Exclaim!* when the album came out in 2002; in September 2003, they became one of the only pop acts to ever appear on the cover of *Maclean's*, Canada's newsweekly. It wasn't exactly an in-depth profile: it was a 200-word blurb, part of a larger top-30-under-30 package with the headline: "Red, Hot and Cool: They're Young. They're Talented. These Canadians Are Changing Our World."

The band only had a one-record deal with Sub Pop and were eager to look elsewhere. They signed with Sire Records, which, like Sub Pop, was under the Warner umbrella; *Make Up the Breakdown* then got a second marketing push. Needless to say, Sire had a much bigger budget and a stronger presence in Europe. When the single "Bandages" was initially released in Britain around the time of the U.S. and U.K. invasion of Iraq, it was charting on BBC Radio 1—until it got pulled for political reasons. The broadcaster received complaints that the song was somehow insensitive to soldiers. And yet the White Stripes' "Seven Nation Army" was a massive radio hit at the same moment.

Once Sire came on board, U.S. radio didn't have any problems with the song. In 2004, 18 months after the BBC ban, "Bandages" and "Talk to Me, Dance with Me" were No. 1 and No. 3 at influential L.A. station KROQ, during the week Hot Hot Heat played in front of 50,000 people at the station's annual Inland Invasion show. The theme that year was Flashback to the Future, a lineup stuffed with '80s bands and very few current artists. Third on the bill, right before Duran Duran and the Cure and after Echo and the Bunnymen, were Hot Hot Heat. The billing upset a Bunnyman. Bays overheard that band's Ian McCulloch talking shit about the young Victoria band backstage, "because he was so pissed that he had to open for this band he didn't know or didn't like."

There was a rotating stage at the amphitheatre, "so that as one band played their last chord, the stage would start revolving and the next band starts, on the same stage," says Bays. "No pause between bands." Hot Hot Heat were set up and playing dice, waiting for Echo and the Bunnymen to finish. The head of their management company came to see them as they packed up their game. As they did so, they could hear the Bunnymen finish "Killing Moon" with McCulloch issuing a throwdown to the Canucks, closing his set by yelling into the mic, "Try and top that!"

As the crowd cheered, the manager said, "I think you guys should open with 'Bandages.'"

"What? No. Obviously that's the closing song."

"No, you want people to know who your band is, and everyone knows that song."

With seconds to spare, as the stage was turning, they took his advice and immediately launched into "Bandages." "Everyone stood up in the audience, tens of thousands of people dancing," says Bays. "It was so wild. It was such a blur. I don't remember anything else about the show." Somewhere at the corner of the stage, no doubt, sat a very sad Bunnyman. He'd been topped.

Other vets were kinder. Backstage at a festival in San Francisco, drummer Paul Hawley ended up having lunch with Stewart Copeland and Dave Grohl, both of whom effusively praised his playing. Near the end of the touring cycle, however, Hot Hot Heat lost a unique element when Dante DeCaro announced he was quitting.

The band had been on tour for three straight months when an offer came to play on BBC TV's *Later . . . with Jools Holland*. Accepting the gig would mean extending the tour. "Dante was such a homebody, and he just hated it," says Bays. "He was like, 'There's no way I'm doing it.' At this point we were on Warner U.K. They said it was the equivalent of playing *Saturday Night Live*; if you play it, you'll be a household name in the U.K. They offered to fly him home first-class and fly him back three or four days later.' He refused. Warner was so pissed that they ended up dropping us. Not immediately, but we were essentially shelved." Bays was angry but wasn't going to pull rank. "Music is like sex: if one person isn't into it, it's totally creepy," he says. "I wasn't going to convince him. Talking to him near the end, he said, 'Do you hate me for quitting? Am I making a mistake?' I said, 'I can't tell you. I can tell you that I think it's an idiotic move, but you gotta do what you gotta do.'"

The split was as amicable as possible. DeCaro stuck around to make the next record, 2005's *Elevator*, before heading back to rural Vancouver Island. "We knew that would bide time and give us time to try people out," says Bays. "I'd always hoped that he would change his mind, but he didn't. I kept wondering what he would do with himself. Here was a guy who wrote these crazy guitar parts, he should be used for something. He was living in Shawnigan Lake, living in a barn on his mom's property for a while. He always had a Discman on him, and he was obsessively listening to Bob Dylan. He sent me some solo recordings, and I thought it was awesome, but I felt he needed the drive of someone willing to sell themselves a little bit. I think he was cheesed out by the prostitution of being a touring musician."

Within a year, DeCaro resurfaced with another group of Victorians signed to Sub Pop.

THE UNICORNS' STOCK was rising while they were on tour with Hot Hot Heat in the fall of 2003. On November 11, *Pitchfork* gave the album an 8.9 rating. It appeared on several year-end top 10 lists. *Vice* magazine, staffed by Montreal pranksters infiltrating Brooklyn hipster circles, declared the Unicorns "the best band in the world." In December 2003, they were the top seller at the U.S. online music retail outlet Insound (the indie rock equivalent of Amazon at the time). They spent the first four months of 2004 touring the U.S. extensively, with venues selling out and increasing in size with each return visit. Unlike every other ladder-climbing careerist indie rock band, the Unicorns were wildly unpredictable.

"Alden and I were big practisers, and Nick wasn't," says Jamie Thompson. "When we first started, Alden and I could keep it really steady. Nick would sometimes lose himself, but it created this interesting approach. We couldn't just nail our songs perfectly every night, so it had to open up. We could just show up and improvise. Maybe we'd just make weird noises until someone started playing a song. Nick got tighter obviously, just touring and touring. It made us unflappable. We had so many weird things happen—because we created a situation where weird things *could* happen."

That extended to their dealings with the press. They claimed to be Scientologists, or that Thorburn and Penner met while nose modelling. All these claims were taken at face value, especially at *Pitchfork*, which ran a rambling, nonsensical and lengthy transcript of a conversation. (One headline, from *Prefix* magazine: "We Spent an Hour with These Guys and Didn't Find Out Dick.") On stage, the heterosexual band all wore pink, which—four years before the advent of Pink Shirt Day—led to speculation that they were gay. When asked directly in the press, they would neither confirm or deny, which was understood to be a tacit admission, not unlike Ricky Martin or Michael Stipe's public stances. "In the early 2000s," says Thompson, "any straight guy would deny it right away." "I think we're all fairly straight," says Thorburn now, when asked to clarify. "But hey, it's a spectrum, baby!" Meanwhile, some zealous fan started posting extremely detailed erotic fan fiction online called "Uniporn"; assumed to be yet another prank, it was too weird even for the actual Unicorns.

Ever savvy, they also knew that few things drive media attention more than a beef: Beatles vs. Stones, Blur vs. Oasis, Tupac vs. Biggie. In one early 2004 interview they took shots at fellow Montreal band the Stills, who were signed to *Vice*'s new record label, "exposing" the band's ska past and exclaiming, "Fuck the Stills!" The Unicorns' manager, Dan Seligman, soon got a call from *Vice*'s Suroosh Alvi, who told him point blank, "Don't bite the hand that feeds you." To make amends, the two bands played shows together in Cleveland and Baltimore.

"At the end of the night [the Stills] were like, 'Hey, that wasn't cool,'" says Thorburn. "We apologized and we moved on and after that we were friendly. Only Oliver [Corbeil], the bass player, kept a grudge going. Everyone else realized it was just playful poking."

Adding to the unpredictability was roadie Max Groadie, part of a planned posse that never really took shape. "I had read that Toni Braxton had gone bankrupt because she had a 60-person entourage that travelled with her all the time," says Jamie Thompson. "For some reason, I said to Nick, 'We should do that!' We could show up in town and find the weirdest people and eventually have a 60-person entourage of the craziest people anyone's ever met."

They made a list of all their favourite freaks, starting with a guy named Bill, who was down on his luck and washing dishes in Victoria. He didn't know anything about music, never mind tuning guitars, but they hired him and dubbed him Max Groadie. Sound tech Mark Lawson became his boss and minder. Because Groadie wasn't much of a roadie, he started developing characters that became part of the show. "He had this one character, King Cobra," says Thompson. "He found a pair of fake leather pants at a thrift store. He'd be topless and had a big Elvis pompadour wig and a cane with a dragon on it. He would come out and just heckle us, or whatever."

"Whatever" took a turn toward the particularly strange at the Knitting Factory in New York City, in May 2004 at a gig with the still-unknown Arcade Fire. The Unicorns had just paid themselves for the first time in six months; until then, all money had gone straight to food and gas. They were selling out shows and selling tons of merch, and Dan Seligman gave them a big cash payout before the first of two Knitting Factory shows. Thorburn bought a new guitar. When he went on stage, he left the rest of the money in the backstage area. When he got off stage, it was gone. At least he had his new guitar.

The next night things got weird. Max Groadie came out in his topless get-up and asked the crowd, "Who's going to crowd-surf me?" People cheered. Groadie continued, "Okay, who's going to KILL ME?"

"It was like, What the *fuck*?!" says the normally nonplussed Thompson. "It was super awkward. Then he took a bear-bottle of honey he had shoved down the back of his pants, poured it all over his chest and said, 'Who's going to crowd-surf me now?' Everyone's like, 'Nooooo!' He said, 'Fine,' then turned around and hugged Nick—and got honey all over his guitar. We started the next song, and Nick couldn't play. It was his older guitar, thankfully, and so he just smashed it. He got off stage. Me and Alden were still playing, and we think, 'Okay, I think that's that. Good night, everybody!'

"Backstage there was this documentary film crew from New Orleans who'd come to some shows. I got off stage, and everything was chaos. I played mediator a lot, because Nick and Alden genuinely hated each other. I was trying to calm down, and there was a camera in my face. 'Can you get the fuck outta here?!' I found out later it was Kurt Braunohler, the comedian. He'd just answered a Craigslist ad to help work on a documentary. I don't know where any of that footage went, by the way. We just never heard from them again. We didn't have time to think about it."

"Max Groadie was the linchpin, or the scapegoat," says Thorburn. "His role was to funnel and pour all of our anger and frustration onto him—we weren't yelling at him, but we were encouraging him to be destructive. He was our impish mascot and would go on stage and do disruptive things that would antagonize the audience—and the headlining band and the venue. There are lists of people we had to apologize to. We could easily have just said, 'Sorry, that's Max Groadie, our crazy roadie. We can't contain him, but we'll try harder next time.'

"At one show he took Thousand Island salad dressing from Ben Kweller's backstage area and spit it into the front row of the audience. The tour manager, who is now Arcade Fire's tour manager, made us apologize to Kweller's guitar player. She said, 'You know, he asks for this salad dressing every night. It's the one thing on his rider. He finally got it tonight and you guys spewed it into the crowd.' People were so mad. We did a show for the CBC and Max Groadie came on stage and started ranting about how the CBC was a secret society. The show was entirely unusable and wasted all this time and money. It never aired.

"We never understood what consequences were, because we were falling up while fucking around," Thorburn continues. "It was working. We weren't malicious. We weren't trying to hurt anybody. We just wanted to be playful with the nobility of rock'n'roll, which we thought was stupid. These bands from that time like Interpol or the Futureheads and all these pretentious British rock bands who were so self-serious. I mean, fuck you, this should be fun—why not be crazy with it? I'm glad we got that out of our system at 21 or 22. I think you're supposed to be a little irreverent and impish at that age. But you gotta do it before you're 25. After that, it's just a bad look."

None of this scared Arcade Fire. They were more than excited to accept an offer from the Unicorns to open an American tour in June 2004. They'd just finished recording *Funeral*, had just signed to Merge Records and were ready to take on the world. But the Unicorns had also stepped up their game. "It was the first time I'd seen a band become a real band," says Richard Reed Parry. "When we met them at the first show of our tour, they'd been on the road for many months. They were burning. People were so stoked to see them, and musically it was just so awesome. They'd transformed themselves. They were still a weird indie band, but it wasn't scrappy and art-schooly anymore. It was really heavy and saying something quite profound—while still totally irreverent. I was jealous. And there were only three of them. Nothing beats that."

At the Milwaukee stop, they played a bar where the stage had a gear-loading door directly behind it that led to the street. In the middle of a Unicorns song, a stranger opened the door, poked his head in and looked around. The crowd started laughing; when the band noticed, they invited him in but told him he had to rap if he wanted to stay to see the show. "Nick ushered him up to the microphone," recalls Parry, "and then he just started freestyling—in Spanish, like a baller, and he loved the attention. He totally killed it, and they went with it."

This attitude endeared them to risk-takers in every town. "We ended up with a lot of celebrity fans, people in comedy and film, especially in Los Angeles," says Jamie Thompson. Fellow Canuck Michael Cera, a 16-year-old actor on the show *Arrested Development*, was vocal about the Unicorns being his favourite band. "It wasn't just that we built a big following in terms of crowds—they weren't huge shows, necessarily," says Thompson. "But the key people got into it at the right time."

The irony of their success and onstage chemistry is that the two principals fought constantly and quite literally. "I mean, we'd made a concept album about how much we hated each other and wanted to break up," says Thorburn. "We were ready to call it quits before we even started playing the game."

"Nick and Alden were already fist-fighting—like legitimately fighting, not a stage thing—back when we were still opening for people at Casa del Popolo," says Thompson. "Usually Alden would get Nick into a submission hold, because Alden had a bit more natural aggression. Nick has a different aggression. I'd usually just try to keep the energy of the show going and keep playing. But occasionally I'd go break it up. One time in Chicago, I broke up a fight with them and then Nick tried to fight me, so I picked him up and threw him over a couch. It wasn't a fair fight between me and either of those guys, really."

"We were thrust into this position where we were constantly working and we had the stamina for it—or Jamie and I did," says Thorburn. "We embraced it. Jamie and I had fights that final year as well, and sometimes on stage. But for the most part, it was Jamie and I versus Alden, or Alden and Jamie versus me. It was this weird triangle where we were trying to consolidate power. Alden wasn't happy playing bigger shows. Jamie and I relished it: why not have this be as big and fun and exciting as it can possibly be? And use this platform to do something different? And if nothing else, to entertain ourselves, like projecting *My Dinner with André* behind us as our light show."

Things got bigger and more exciting when they went to Europe for the first time in August 2004. Someone who worked for XL Recordings was a big fan and offered to be their driver in the U.K., pro bono. At that time the label was known for Badly Drawn Boy and the Prodigy (later on as home to Radiohead and Adele). The Unicorns were big fans of the U.K. grime records XL was putting out by Dizzee Rascal and Wiley. They took a meeting at the label's office with CEO Richard Russell.

"They made us an absurd offer," says Thompson. "I won't speak numbers, but it was a ridiculous, stupid offer, an insane amount of money." It was just to license the debut outside of North America, with an option on the next two records. Penner was dead set against it. He didn't provide any reasons.

That European leg ended in Paris—badly. "We ended up breaking up on stage that night," says Thorburn. "I smashed a microphone stand into this brick wall and chipped the wall and the venue refused to pay us. There was this big kerfuffle. Geoff Travis of Rough Trade records was there and was like, 'I need to sign this band.' He came backstage and was like, 'Get back together. I like it.' We thought, Fuck it, let's do it."

"The Rough Trade deal was maybe 10% of what XL had offered us," says Thompson, "and Alden was like, 'That's great! Let's do that!'"

Penner had become obsessed with the DIY philosophy of Fugazi and their main mouthpiece, Ian MacKaye. Manager Seligman gave MacKaye's phone number to Penner and told him to just call him. Which he did, repeatedly. Penner wanted the band to start booking their own shows and charging a cap of $5 at the door, like Fugazi did. To pacify him, Thompson and Thorburn let him book three shows in Vancouver and Victoria at the end of the September tour, places where he'd have some connections.

"Needless to say, those Vancouver and Victoria shows didn't go that well," says Thompson. "But Alden doubled down. I would understand if we were being chewed up by the machine. But Dan Seligman was our manager, and he's maybe the best person I've ever dealt with in the entire music industry. He didn't tell us to do anything. I don't care if his title is 'manager' and there's a history in the music industry of managers being horrible. Alien8, same thing: run by two guys, they weren't a problem. Our booking agent was one guy. Our publicist was a one-person operation at the time, while taking care of his sick mother. We did all-ages shows all the time."

After yet another North American jaunt, the Unicorns went back to Europe, beginning in London with an official Rough Trade showcase at Barfly in Camden. It was packed with a who's who crowd. Onstage tension was high.

"There was some weird technical glitch on stage with a rented synth and we ended up not really playing a show, just making noise and screaming at each other," says Thompson. "We went backstage, sitting on a couch, no one's looking at each other. Then Karen and Nick from the Yeah Yeah Yeahs came in and were like, 'Guys, that was so great! We loved it!' We're like, 'You loved *that*?!'" The two bands had never met before; the Yeah Yeah Yeahs were just finishing the tour cycle for their breakthrough debut. They all retired to the New Yorkers' hotel room, where they drank and talked for two hours about how to manage internal conflicts. The Unicorns were urged not to break up and left that night with an opening slot for the American stars at a sold-out gig in London a few nights later. But because they dallied on accepting the offer, the Unicorns ended up third on the Yeah Yeah Yeahs' bill, playing right after the club's doors opened to a tiny fraction of the 3,500 ticketholders. "The writing was on the wall," says Thorburn. "You could only put us back together so many times."

It wasn't the ideal time to tour the other side of the world. But they had six dates in Australia booked for December 2004 with one odd stop en route: the 16th birthday party for the daughter of Russian aristocrats held at an L.A. mansion once owned by Orson Welles. "It's weird, but Alden was super into doing that," says Thompson. "It seemed against anything he would have wanted to do." The girl's family paid for the band's flight and hotel room on top of their fee. While there, the Yeah Yeah Yeahs invited them to a dinner party with Beck, who wanted the Unicorns to open for him in Montreal on his next tour. Back at the hotel, however, the Unicorns decided once and for all to split.

That clarity made the Australian dates somewhat easier, even though Penner and Thorburn didn't speak once during the two weeks there. "We flew there and had five days off in Melbourne," says Thompson. "Everyone had their own hotel room, which was the height of luxury. The people we worked with there were amazing. Then we went back and played a huge sold-out show in Houston, three times the size we had before, maybe 1,000 people. More people than had ever come to see us in the States, bigger than L.A. or New York. We kept telling people it was our last show—and nobody believed us. Nick got annihilated, wasted. We snuck a bunch of kids in the back of that show, and they came up on stage and danced. Nick disappeared after, and so did Alden."

"There was a bootleg recording of that gig floating around, and it's horrifying," says Thorburn. "I was just gone. I knew it was the end. It was a funereal air in the room. Very dark and very negative. We left Houston and we both went back to Campbell River; we might even have been on the same plane but did not speak. Then [Penner] called me a week later and said, 'I can't do this anymore.' I said, 'Okay.'"

"I was really interested in the dynamic between Nick and Alden," says Thompson. "Nick does film stuff. He put out a graphic novel. If you said, 'We need someone to design a toothbrush!' Nick would probably be good at that. He's a super creative, visionary guy. He's not an obsessive, music-specific guy. He was more of a frontperson and wanted that attention. Alden was really obsessive, had a very introverted approach to things. He might want to go live in a cave and just play guitar. That's an interesting mix of guys."

On December 28, 2004, 14 months after their debut was released, a message was posted on the band's website: "The Unicorns are dead R.I.P."

IN THE TIME it took the entire Unicorns story to unfold, and while their friends in Arcade Fire were gearing up to take over the world, Wolf Parade were quietly howling to themselves in Montreal. No one had heard their debut album until the fall of 2005, but they had an American record deal before they'd even spent a full year together as a band.

There were relatively few Wolf Parade shows in 2003, mostly loft parties, a gallery in St. Henri, Lederhosen Lucil's Soiro Bizarro festival and a pop-up art space in Chinatown. Another B.C. friend, Hadji Bakara, was asked to join, playing modular synths he'd bought with money made from tree planting that summer. At Bakara's debut Sala Rossa show, opening for Arcade Fire, his textural electronic fuckery included a theremin—though all the audience heard were bowel-rupturing bass tones. An EP was recorded directly to Krug's computer using very primitive technology, and CDs were burned to sell at Cheap Thrills near McGill.

Arcade Fire bonded deeply with Wolf Parade. Both bands felt like total outsiders in the Montreal music scene. Both were primarily playing for the same group of Anglo arrivistes. Both shared a mischievous sense of humour as well as a dogged determination. Whether or not they were sharing a bill, they were always heckling at each other's gigs. Arcade Fire took Wolf Parade on the newer band's first out-of-province gigs. During a transition period in Arcade Fire's lineup in 2003, Boeckner played bass on some short tours to Toronto and New York City.

Keeping tabs from a distance was Isaac Brock of Modest Mouse, on whom

Boeckner's Atlas Strategic had left a lasting impression. Brock's A&R gig with Sub Pop was going well, after he tipped them off to the Shins. In early 2004, he came to Montreal. A show was booked at Spencer Krug's apartment above Barfly; money made from the cover went to pay their rent. Brock showed up with Sub Pop staffers, only to meet a classic case of Montreal exclusivity. "Whoever was working the door said, 'You guys aren't on the list'—the place was rammed," says Boeckner. "So they were standing in this shitty hallway staircase until they could get in. At that point we played two more songs and then the police shut it down."

Undaunted, Sub Pop soon offered them a deal. Brock took them on tour with Modest Mouse in the summer of 2004, just as his band was finally achieving a mainstream breakthrough, with the single "Float On." That album, *Good News for People Who Love Bad News*, sold more than a million copies by the time Wolf Parade joined them in August for a two-week East Coast tour. Until then, their biggest audience had been at La Sala Rossa; now they were playing the Bowery Ballroom in New York City and hockey arenas in suburban Pittsburgh. "We were total babes in the woods," says Arlen Thompson. "Everything was held together with spit and tape. Still is, in a lot of ways." The band didn't have a manager—then or for the next six years.

They drove to Portland to start making their record with Brock. It was the beginning of a long, strange process. "Here's a good microcosm of how fucked up it was," says Krug. "We all lived in Montreal, and Isaac Brock lived in Portland. We were piling into a van and driving from Montreal to Portland, scraping together gas money and eating Taco Bell the whole way, just to get to the studio and start recording. It didn't occur to us to ask the label for help. We got there and Isaac had forgotten that we were showing up; he expected us a couple of days later and had to call in a few favours to start the session. No one knew what they were doing: we'd never made a record before, and Isaac had never produced a record before. I don't want to shit-talk that guy at all, he tried his best, but looking back it was a lot of people trying something new."

The studio was also new, run by a guitarist who had joined the second incarnation of the German band Faust. "The studio had a bunch of gremlins in it," says Arlen Thompson. "There was also no seating. No functioning bathrooms. I'd never played to a click track before. It was a difficult session." Bakara felt like a kid in a candy shop, with access to Faust's synthesizers, and spent an entire day trying them all out instead of tracking. One day when Thompson and Krug were the first ones in the studio, they wrote the opening track, "You Are a Runner and I Am My Father's Son," in an hour.

In general, time and money were not well spent. "The first hotel we stayed at, for a week or so, was amazing," says Boeckner. "Then we got moved to a less amazing hotel. Then at the end, we were all staying in the same room in a budget motel across from the university. We were overbudget, overtime. We weren't in charge of the budget, though. When we were in the studio, things like a pile of food and a box of margarita glasses would arrive from the Mexican restaurant next door."

When tracking was finally finished, the band split for Vancouver, stopping at the Sub Pop offices in Seattle en route to beg for gas money, which someone from the label fetched from an ATM. There were shows in Victoria and Vancouver, as well as a session for CBC Radio 3. "Victoria was exciting; Vancouver was hilarious," says Arlen Thompson. "Two bands opened up: Chet, and the Countless Jibes, this band made up of Zulu Records employees, a 10-piece band doing improvised Krautrock jamming. They both took up so much time that we only got to play three songs before we got the hook at 12:30."

Bakara and Thompson then drove down to L.A. for the band's next gig at the All Tomorrow's Parties festival, while Boeckner and Krug flew directly there to mix the record and share a hotel room with Brock. "We were at a studio where Guns N' Roses were doing sessions for *Chinese Democracy* in the same complex," says Boeckner. Wolf Parade's own record seemed to be just as troubled as Axl Rose's opus, which didn't come out for another four years. Brock's initial mixes didn't go down well. "Spencer and I both thought it was so wrong, so bad," says Boeckner. "It was a combination of slick and half-assed. It didn't sound like us."

Frustrated, they headed to All Tomorrow's Parties, which was being held on the RMS *Queen Mary*, a World War II ship that was once one of the largest in the world. Fellow Sub Pop signees the Constantines were there, as well as Peaches, on a bill curated by Modest Mouse and featuring the Flaming Lips, the Shins and Sufjan Stevens. Their friends in Frog Eyes had a gig in L.A. and came to hang out with some other Victoria friends; 13 people in total were crashing in Wolf Parade's one room on the boat. Wolf Parade played at two p.m. on the main stage, while the weekend's headliner watched.

"We were playing 'Shine a Light' and Lou Reed was watching us play," says Boeckner. "I was playing the classic Velvet Underground strumming pattern and feeling very self-conscious. It was an amazing experience. We saw the Cramps, who were the best thing at the whole festival. We were given a ton of booze. At night we started wandering around the ship causing trouble. There was a seance in the Winston Churchill ballroom, where someone in our crew carved a Ouija board into an old table. Then it got thrown off the boat. They had a museum section we were fucking around in. Our room itself got trashed.

"I remember passing out and waking up the next morning, and our booking agent was like, 'What the fuck did you guys just do?!' It wasn't Mötley Crüe–style chaos, just surrealist idiocy." The *Queen Mary* management begged to differ. "We've had the Sex Pistols *and* Mötley Crüe stay on this boat," they told the band, "and you are the only guest whose reservation we've had to cancel."

From there, they had a tour booked on the way back to Montreal: a totally unknown Canadian band without an album out, making $100 a night, playing to 40 people at the most, sleeping in the van. Except when they didn't. In Tucson, the promoter invited them to crash at an art gallery. Thompson crawled into a bed, which in the morning he discovered was part of the gallery's window display.

"I woke up in my underwear with all these people walking by on the street outside the window," he recalls. "We played our worst show ever in St. Louis. It was at the end of the tour; we felt like it was the end of the band. We arrived and were trying to figure things out with printed MapQuest directions. The St. Louis skyline was hollowed out, the skyscrapers were partially demolished. It looked like *Mad Max* or something. We played a really weird venue. Two people came out. The opening bands were terrible. We were so pissed off we drove [16 hours] home afterwards straight from St. Louis to Montreal. No one was talking."

Once home, Wolf Parade were determined to salvage the situation. Brock went incommunicado for a while. When he got back in touch, he told them he'd lost an entire reel of tape with three songs on it. (It didn't resurface until 2020.) Eschewing their patron, they took the tracks they did have to Montreal's new Breakglass Studios, run by Jace Lacek of the Besnard Lakes. Boeckner redid some vocals, two of the three missing tracks were recut, and Lacek ended up mixing nine of the album's 12 tracks. "Shine a Light" was rerecorded and mixed entirely in Krug's loft, a new spot in Mile End called 100 Sided Die, an art studio and occasional performance space run by Chloë Lum and Yannick Desranleau, whose surrealist gig poster work under the name Seripop had become commonplace on the Plateau. They practised there at full volume with their new band, AIDS Wolf.[2] A picture of Wolf Parade taken at 100 Sided Die was the lead picture in the February 2005 issue of *Spin* magazine touting Montreal as "the next big scene." ("Canada is now officially cool!" it proclaimed.)

Even when Wolf Parade's record was finally done, Sub Pop couldn't fit it into their release schedule until September 2005, which left the band broke and with a lot of time on their hands. In April, they opened triumphant shows for the white-hot Arcade Fire, three each in Montreal and Toronto. A stopgap EP on Sub Pop came out in July, with two album tracks and two B-sides. There was a tour of Scandinavia, where the band was getting national radio play based entirely on

---

2   A third contemporary "wolf" band from Montreal, We Are Wolves, led to plenty of jokes in the press in coming years.

tracks uploaded to the CBC Radio 3 website. Joining the band on that tour was guitarist Dante DeCaro, who'd recently left Hot Hot Heat but decided he was not yet done with rock'n'roll; he was replacing Bakara, who had academic commitments. Despite being burnt out from his previous band's whirlwind pop career, DeCaro cast his lot with Wolf Parade and stuck around.

Back home, Spencer Krug spent his downtime compiling the best of his four-track recordings as Sunset Rubdown on a debut album, *Snake's Got a Leg*, out on Global Symphonic; he also joined Frog Eyes for a European tour where they backed up Destroyer. Arlen Thompson had a part-time job in the A/V department of Concordia, while Dan Boeckner went back to work as a telemarketer at a medical company, couch-surfed and eventually fled to Taiwan for almost four months to hang out with a girlfriend teaching ESL. There, he worked a lucrative part-time job under the table but wasn't able to take the money out of the country in cash, so he landed back in Montreal flat broke.

Two weeks before the album, *Apologies to the Queen Mary*, was released in late September, the band went to the CMJ festival in New York City. Wolf Parade played a packed Bowery Ballroom on a Sub Pop showcase with the Constantines and Chad VanGaalen. Boeckner wore a T-shirt touting one of the most politically incorrect band names ever, '70s Toronto punk band Battered Wives. As is always the case with Wolf Parade, things got strange. "I hit the Sub Pop bar tab," says Boeckner, "then blacked out and came to, very far away from the Bowery, alone at a table with Emily from Metric, eating Lebanese food. I had no idea how I got there.

"That was also the weekend we destroyed our potential for a career in the U.K.," he continues. "The *NME* wanted to do a feature on us. We had no experience with industry festivals. We were very green. I thought playing a festival meant you had access to see bands. But industry festivals are for industry people, and you're kind of shuttled around between venues and press. To 26-year-old me, that was unforgivable. I was very angry. The *NME* reporter asked us how we liked being at that festival, and we told her, 'It fucking sucks! This is bullshit. This is corporate. This is in the service of middle management.' She told us, 'What I want to hear is that you're having a really good time at CMJ.' In retrospect, she was trying to help us in her own way, but for a band like us, it was totally the wrong thing to say. We became completely uncooperative with the interview and the photo shoot. And they were like, 'Fuck these guys. They don't want to play ball, so fuck 'em.' It was pretty childish, but whatever."

Arcade Fire invited Wolf Parade on a North American tour, as a victory lap to end the *Funeral* tour cycle. In Vancouver, Boeckner reconnected with Alexei Perry, with whom he'd worked as a telemarketer in Montreal. They'd harboured secret workplace crushes while in other relationships, but now Boeckner was ready to take a plunge. He was already living out of a duffle bag, and caught the first plane back to Vancouver at the end of the tour to be with Perry.

In early 2006, Wolf Parade went to Europe beyond just Scandinavia. "Total fucking disaster," says Boeckner. "[The tour] was 14,000 U.S. dollars in the red by the time we were finished. We were staying in hostels, not sleeping, flying to Spain then back to England, sleeping in an unheated practice room in Bristol by the sea in the middle of December and getting locked in at night and getting pneumonia. The routing was awful, the guarantees were bad, and it was winter. We all went crazy." When it was done, their U.K. booking agent offered them three arena shows opening for the incongruous Kings of Leon. They immediately fired him and went with their Scandinavian agent for all of Europe.

In the U.S., *Apologies* garnered high praise and a devoted audience. Like Arcade Fire, the music was earnest and anthemic, but Wolf Parade delivered more visceral rock'n'roll thrills, with Krug's and Bakara's keyboards adding an unusual, often prog-like undercurrent. In an era where indie rock got more conformist as it got more popular, Wolf Parade were accessible to any Springsteen fan and yet thankfully too weird to be co-opted into lifestyle-accessory branding. It was both endearing and frustrating that the band was often their own worst enemy.

"We'd get on stage and just play as hard as we could, until the songs would naturally fall apart—or gel into something else," says Boeckner. "When it worked, it really worked. But when we played Coachella in 2006, we wrapped Spencer's analog keyboard in foam or something; it was left out in 90 degree heat, detuning all the oscillators right before we played for the biggest crowd we'd ever played for. We were broke, so we couldn't spend any money on equipment. Our gear was objectively terrible. The whole band had Peavey amps for a really long time, well into our career. Those things are punishing: solid state, and sound like total fucking garbage. But we tried to use that as an aesthetic."

"Nobody told us anything," says Krug of the management-free band. "We didn't know what the fuck we were doing."

STEPHEN MCBEAN DIDN'T know what the fuck he was doing until he was 35 years old, in 2004. That was when he and long-time musical partner Josh Wells ditched their band and their sound, beginning anew, putting aside years of false starts. They were ready to conquer mountaintops.

Their previous band, Jerk with a Bomb, was understandably having trouble getting traction post-9/11. That band's third album, 2002's *Pyrokinesis*, was the best thing they'd done to that point, though it largely fell on deaf ears. What should have been thrilling gigs were letdowns. McBean got to open for one of his favourite bands, Royal Trux, in London, Ontario—to an audience of five people. He got to play punk mecca CBGB in New York City, where the band was paid $27—which didn't cover their $45 bar tab.

"It was bleak," he recalls of Jerk with a Bomb's final year. "But the final nail in the coffin was when we played at 7th St. Entry in Minneapolis"—the small club attached to First Avenue, "home to Prince's *Purple Rain* and the Replacements. We played New Band Night, and the band before us was a funk metal band doing a cover of the *Inspector Gadget* theme. I mean, you can play a big show to a lot of people and [the vibe is] not happening and it can burn you out for days. Then you play a show for one person and it's the best thing in the world. But something about that night and waiting to play after this band—and we had driven from Edmonton, because we couldn't get shows in Saskatoon or Winnipeg—my brain was just like, I don't want to fucking do this. I had no positive thoughts at all, just: fuck this."

Drummer Josh Wells agreed. By the time they got back to their Vancouver base, they were ready to give up. Instead, McBean wrote a song called "Rock'n'Roll Fantasy." Jerk with a Bomb changed its name to Black Mountain, and they made one of the greatest rock'n'roll records of the decade.

NO ONE ELSE in this book was in a speed metal band in 1981. Stephen McBean was raised in Kleinburg, Ontario; his family moved to the Victoria area when he was 10. The local punk scene was hopping, with the likes of NoMeansNo and the Dayglo Abortions. McBean was 12 years old when he played in Jerk Ward; he was 16 when he was in Mission of Christ. The latter was signed and dropped by Metal Blade Records, home of Metallica and Slayer, before even making a record. But hey, they were still teenagers. McBean moved to Vancouver in 1990 and started what he calls an "angular hardcore band," Gus, where he crossed paths with a band called Pebble. Pebble's drummer was really good. His name was Josh Wells.

Wells, too, was relatively new in town, having been born in Chicago, raised in Victoria, Alberta and Toronto before landing in Vancouver in 1990. They moved in together with other members of Wells's darkwave band Radio Berlin, in a house at the corner of Frances Street and Commercial Drive. They started a new band, Ex Dead Teenager. McBean was flirting with acoustic music for the first time in his life, experimenting on his four-track, making music he describes as a cross between Billy Bragg and Sebadoh. Someone asked him to play live; the idea of performing without a wall of amplifiers terrified him, so he enlisted Wells to play stand-up snare at the first show billed as Jerk with a Bomb.

"We only played three shows over the course of a couple of years," he says. "I was 26, 27, and questioning whether I wanted to be in a band anymore. Which had been on my mind since I was 16: 'Oh, this is my last band, for sure.' Then our friend Paula asked if [Jerk with a Bomb] wanted to do a record. She had an inheritance or something. We recorded it, but she didn't end up putting it out, so I put it out myself. That was *Death to False Metal*."

They hit the road in 1999, booking themselves across North America, 25 shows in 10 weeks. Lots of days off. Lots of confused audiences when this acoustic duo showed up to play hardcore punk venues. "Which was fun for a while, until we ran out of money and couldn't eat," says Wells, who also toured in a similar ramshackle style with Radio Berlin at the time, including a West Coast jaunt with early Hot Hot Heat. "But Steve and I didn't really care about anything other than touring and playing music. We had jobs and would quit them to go on tour, lose all our money, then come home and get another job." Two more albums followed, each one increasingly dark and paranoid, rife with the kind of dystopian ennui that inspired Vancouver writers William Gibson and Douglas Coupland. In McBean's lyrics, he was often searching for sanctuary from structural oppression, finding refuge in the arms of friends, lovers and hydroponic helpers.

Wells started juggling keyboard duties with his drumming. On 2002's *Pyrokinesis*, they added bassist Christoph Hofmeister. Amber Webber, of psych-folk trio Dream on Dreary, joined on vocals at select local dates. "She was really, really, really shy then," says McBean. "We sang together, and it was so effortless. It was such a welcome addition to my ears, to not have to hear my nasally voice." With Webber in mind, McBean introduced new material to showcase her.

"We felt like we had improved a lot," says Wells. "But our tours and shows were getting much worse. That was when we truly questioned whether trying to do music as a living was just completely foolish for us, because it clearly wasn't working." *Pyrokinesis* sold even fewer copies than 2001's *The Old Noise*.

But the idea of a new band with Webber and Hofmeister was appealing. Wells had also left Radio Berlin. "We went from, 'This sucks, we are terrible,' to not doing anything and getting bored and just doing it again," says Wells. McBean booked some time at local studio the Hive, run by Colin Stewart. Hofmeister pulled out right before the session; McBean decided to use it to make a solo record, credited to Pink Mountaintops. Wells and Webber contributed. It was made in 10 days. Not that different musically from Jerk with a Bomb— mostly slow, loping rhythms, somewhere between Pink Floyd and Jesus and Mary Chain—the self-titled Pink Mountaintops record displayed a raunchier, less-serious side of McBean, on songs like "I (Fuck) Mountains" and the Stooge-ish "Sweet '69." Webber showed up to sing a gorgeous duet, "Tourist in Your Town."

The album closes with a "Sister Ray"–ish cover of Joy Division's "Atmosphere." If this record alone marked McBean's new direction, it would be more than enough. But he had more work to do with Wells.

The former jerks with bombs started recording the new band, Black Mountain, in their practice space underneath the Argyll Hotel at Hastings and Abbott. "It was this big, really high ceiling, cavernous jam room," recalls McBean. "I don't think we had monitors, so everything was done with headphones." Colin Stewart loaned them an eight-track and a mixing board. McBean played most of the bass parts, later overdubbed by their friend Matt Camirand, who was playing in Sub Pop glam band the Black Halos.

What they achieved on their own in that hotel basement sounded better than most other rock records released that decade—or any other. "There were a lot of people later who said, 'How did you get that sound? It sounds like a band in a jam room.' Which it was," says McBean. "We didn't have a lot of gear. We experimented. Most of the sound stems from Josh having an old Gretsch kit, knowing how to tune it properly and how to hit the drum in the right sweet spot every time."

"Both Steve and I had done tons of home recording," says Wells, "all with very minimal gear. I had an eight-track cassette player since I was a teenager and always messed around with that. But I didn't know anything beyond plugging one thing into another and turning it up."

"Modern Music" opens the album with a garage-rock, two-chord jaunt, where a saxophone dances like Daddy's Hands around a Josh Wells beat that tumbles all over the place, in ways only Deerhoof's Greg Saunier would ever dare to do inside the confines of a rock song. On every chorus, the song collapses into a complete free-jazz mess while McBean exclaims in a fey affectation, "Oh, we can't *stand* your modern *music*! Oh! We feel *afflicted*!" In between choruses, there's a sing-songy count, "1,2,3, another pop explosion / 1, 2, 3, another hit recording." At the end of the final chorus, there's a quick squeal of feedback before the entire mess clicks into a rock-solid Sabbath riff for a 20-second romp to the finish line.

Much of *Black Mountain* is joyous, raucous, the sound of a band in love with their favourite music and not at all worried about what they may or may not be ripping off. "No Satisfaction" sounds a lot like the Velvet Underground via the Vaselines; "No Hits" sounds like Iggy Pop fronting the German band Can. The songwriting deserves fair criticism for being record-collector rock, and some of it sounds thrown together quickly; that's because it was. "'No Satisfaction' was probably written in a minute," laughs McBean. "No one was listening, so it seemed funny to me."

Black Mountain was the sound of a guy in his mid-30s discovering unself-conscious pleasure. It was also an escape: all members were involved in social work in the opiate-ridden Downtown Eastside, some at the Portland Hotel Society working on housing issues, some at InSite, North America's first legal supervised injection site; Webber worked in a seniors' home. When dealing with very real pain at work, rock'n'roll should be a release.

"When I was in bands as a teenager, [music] was all from the gut; we never questioned it," says McBean. "It rips or it doesn't. You hit your 20s and you think you have it all together, but you look back and you were just a weird, whiny ball of dough. When I started Jerk with a Bomb, I really wanted to learn how to write songs and all that exciting stuff. After a while, I wanted to let go of the preciousness of songwriting. I got a little tired of playing punk and metal and thrash bands my whole life. I didn't want to do *that*, but I didn't want to do *this* either. One of my old punk friends probably said, 'Why don't you just write a riff again, you fucking loser?!'"

Living in Wells's house at the time was synth player Jeremy Schmidt, who played in Destroyer-adjacent band the Battles (not the NYC band signed to Warp) and had a long-running solo synth project called Sinoia Caves. "I got him to play on four songs, to just make some noise," says Wells. "He invented some cool parts. Some of that was already there; I was playing it on the demos. But he came up with more elaborate atmosphere. Then we decided we should integrate him into the band. After that, his parts became totally integral."

So did Webber, whose feminine presence was a welcome break in the sonic sausage party, her quavering alto the cool glacial river running down the side of Black Mountain. "We told her she should sing on everything," says Wells. "Part of the foundation of Black Mountain was a shift in perspective. We didn't want it to be a singer-songwriter thing anymore. A lot of the lyrics were more universal, and less 'I'm a sad guy.'" Even though Pink Mountaintops drew from the same well as Black Mountain, it became clear that the latter was a band while the former was not. "Although I played on both," says Wells, "for the Pink Mountaintops record, I was just 'Oh, why don't I just do this.' Whereas with Black Mountain, we were both constructing arrangements together. And especially after the record, it was a real band, not a project or a collective."

Though McBean had worked for local record store and regional distributor Scratch Records, there wasn't a lot of external interest—except for the label that eventually signed them, Jagjaguwar. McBean had sent them the Pink Mountaintops demo, which they liked. Though the American indie label had been around since 1997, it was just beginning to get a profile with artists like Oneida, Okkervil River and Julie Doiron; in 1999, they became partners with Indiana label Secretly Canadian, then known for Antony and the Johnsons. McBean was finally going to be on a label where his music might be heard.

Pink Mountaintops came out six months before *Black Mountain*, in the summer of 2004. "At first Jagjaguwar weren't sure they wanted to put out two new bands and wanted me to just make it one thing," says McBean. "I was like, 'No, it's gotta be two bands!' It was all in fun, but it was definitely designed to see if people would pay attention." Pink Mountaintops didn't set the world on fire, but it did get enough attention that Black Mountain arrived with mild fanfare on campus radio and the blogosphere. "It was having fun with creating some sort of myth," says McBean. "At the time there was also the whole thing that all the music press, especially in England, they were like, 'Every band from Canada is a collective!' From Godspeed to Arcade Fire to New Pornographers." With Camirand also fronting Blood Meridian, and Jeremy Schmidt's totally obscure Sinoia Caves, Black Mountain could join the list of so-called Canadian "supergroups," full of people no one had ever heard of. It's possible Amber Webber was mistaken for her twin sister, Ashley, who played bass in actual buzz band the Organ.

Black Mountain met with incredibly divisive reviews: it was either one of the greatest rock records of the decade or lazy pastiche. *Pitchfork* gave it an 8.3 rating and a "best new music" designation. Black Mountain were on an American tour with Brooklyn psych-punk provocateurs Oneida, when their American booking agent, Adam Boyce, called them.

"You won't believe who called," Boyce told McBean.

"Uh, I don't know, the Make-Up?"

"No, Coldplay."

"Huh. Well, we'll never hear from them again."

"Well, if they call back, what should I ask for?"

The subsistence-living musician wasn't sure how to respond. "I don't know, $500 a night?"

Coldplay did call back, and offered five times that much. Black Mountain joined them for 17 arena dates across North America. "We were playing for a crowd that probably didn't want to hear us, and we weren't particularly interested in making them happy either," says Wells. "We did whatever we wanted to, made some money and had a good time. We brought some friends along and partied every night in our weird little room. By the time we opened the door, everyone in the arena would be gone. It was completely absurd, but I'm happy we did it. It let us see what big production looks like, which prepared us for festival stages. Saying yes to stuff that seemed highly suspect can help."

Though not necessarily big with the Coldplay crowd, Black Mountain attracted all kinds of fans of all ages. "After we played on *Conan O'Brien*, the next two weeks we were in the Midwest and there was definitely a lot of rocker dads showing up," says McBean. "Bellingham, Washington, for some reason, has a lot of—maybe just crazy people—but old hippie vets and libertarian types, dudes in their 70s who claim they saw Hendrix."

Europe took to Black Mountain particularly well. "We did really well in Italy," says McBean. "It rules to tour there: the food, the wine, laid-back. You'll play in some warehouse in a farmland area and there's no one there and you think, Who's going to come to this? Gigs start later there, and at gig time all these people show up. When we play in Germany, freaks will come out who saw Kraftwerk. And Britain has always been a bizarre place. It's the last bastion of the printed music press. We were lucky when we first came out that the British press really liked us, generally, and they didn't cast us out—they've been very supportive over the years. A lot of the journalists there are hippie guys in their 60s who saw the Pistols and T. Rex."

The band's success was vindication for years spent in the trenches. "It was fantastic," says Wells, without hesitation. "I had been waiting my whole life to play in front of people. I was 30. Steve was 35. It's not like we were young and overwhelmed by it. We were like, Finally, we get to do something that seems worthwhile."

WITHIN A YEAR of releasing their debut album, Wolf Parade had a fairly loose commitment to what was now a professional band. Spencer Krug and Dan Boeckner started devoting almost as much time to their respective solo projects. Krug fleshed out Sunset Rubdown into a full band and started a new project: yet another Canadian indie rock supergroup, Swan Lake with Dan Bejar of Destroyer and Carey Mercer of Frog Eyes. ("The three most annoying male vocalists in Canada!" snarked one CBC host.) Bakara left to finish his PhD.

Boeckner started writing with his spouse, Alexei Perry, in a synth duo called Handsome Furs, heavily influenced by au courant Swedish duo the Knife. "I called the booking agent," says Boeckner, "and told him I had another band with nothing out, but could he book us 500-euro-minimum-guarantee shows in Scandinavia? We toured by train and then recorded an album." Sub Pop released Handsome Furs' *Plague Park* in May 2007. Handsome Furs toured deep into eastern Europe, Russia, China and Southeast Asia over the next few years.

It was in Hungary that one of the weirdest chapters of the Wolf Parade story took place, but Boeckner wasn't even there. It involves a medical fraud, a drunk explosives expert, a cast of extras in 17th-century costumes, a terrible Led Zeppelin cover band and an aborted duel in hot-air balloons. No, really.

It starts with their friend Matt Moroz, who had briefly lived at 100 Sided Die and did the artwork for *Apologies to the Queen Mary*. He was broke and looking for work. A mutual friend from Victoria was living in Hungary, working as a video editor for William Nelson, an engineer and homeopath, who had a "training centre" in Victoria. Nelson had patented a radionic machine that allegedly cured cancer; he made a small fortune selling these $20,000 devices before being busted by the U.S. FDA on fraud charges and chased out of North America.

Now in Budapest, Nelson pursued a peculiar passion, under the name Desiré Dubounet. "[Their] view of gender is that they are not transgender, but the best parts of both man and woman," says Thompson. "[They are] a nonbinary person who is extremely free," adds Boeckner, with "a wife and a Romanian lover, and a passion for making films about lizard people," a.k.a. "reptoid humanoids," based on the writings of the anti-Semitic conspiracy theorist David Icke. Dubounet paid Hungarian network television to screen these films late at night—and paid well. Moroz figured he had nothing to lose and went to Hungary to work for Dubounet as a camera operator.

While there, Moroz emailed Wolf Parade and pitched them on the idea of using Dubounet's resources to film a video for "I'll Believe in Anything." The only cost to the band would be the 35mm film stock. The concept involved a duel in hot-air balloons, filmed by a DOP in a third balloon. All of this appealed to the band's sense of adventure and the absurd—although neither Boeckner nor Krug could make it to the shoot, due to commitments to Handsome Furs and Sunset Rubdown. Thompson, Bakara and DeCaro all flew to Budapest. The only professional on set was cinematographer Samy Inayeh, who was flown in from Toronto. He thought the whole thing was nuts, especially the balloons.

"So, do you have any insurance?" he asked, three days before the shoot.

Moroz was taken aback. "What do you mean? What's insurance?"

"This Arri 35mm movie camera is worth $1 million."

Luckily, the weather rendered the insurance issue moot. A storm was imminent, and no company would rent them balloons. Thompson suggested they instead duel with cannons at a location that hosted war re-enactments. Arrangements were made.

"The first day of the shoot was at this castle in the city centre of Budapest," says Thompson. "We had these crazy 17th-century costumes on, full makeup, everything. All these extras. At one point, we heard that something happened with the finances and there was no money. We had to get in vans, all the Canadians, and take as much money as we could out of our bank accounts, in Hungarian currency, so we could actually pay the extras before they realize that they've stood around for 10 hours and could not get paid. We were running around from bank machine to bank machine in full 17th-century garb. But we got all the footage we needed.

"The next day we go out to the field to do the duel. The worst weather. Pouring rain. We start the day in my friend's car, picking up people and stuff. We get the pyro guy, who was this super old, grizzled, ex-military Hungarian dude who is grumpy as fuck. He gets in the vehicle, we get out there, it's raining and gross. I say, 'Before we start firing these cannons, can we just see one go off so we know how loud it's going to be?' The pyro guy gets this explained to him in Hungarian, and grumbles, 'Okay, I'll show these guys.'

"He has this little bomb thing and he's close to a ditch. He takes his cigarette and lights the explosive in his hand. We could all see him get this *oh fuck* moment. The wick burns down incredibly fast and the whole thing blows up right in his face. He's cursing and swearing, his face all red. He goes to a restaurant with the Hungarian PA and downs six shots of Jägermeister and two beers—at seven in the morning—then comes back and gets on with the day. The whole day the crew was cracking up because I guess he was just cursing us in Hungarian in the crudest possible terms. So we were firing cannons, and I had to chase around a chicken"—for reasons that can't be explained until one sees the video. "Samy is saying, 'There is no way this would even come close to happening in Toronto. There are no rules here. There's no first aid person on set. No nothing.'

"Then we had one more day and everyone was leaving on the same day back to Canada. We ended up at Desiré Dubounet's bar and saw [their] band play. [They're] the most bizarre human being who's walked the Earth, bar none. To see [them] in person after watching [their] movies, to be in [their] presence was totally weird. [They] had this cover band, a normal, shitty bar band only fronted by this six-foot-tall American presenting as a woman, singing Led Zeppelin—terribly. But in their mind, they're the greatest interpreter of Led Zeppelin of all time. Super surreal. We hung out and got super trashed."

Trashed enough that the next morning, Moroz's girlfriend took the wrong bag to the airport on an earlier flight—the bag with Thompson's passport in it. Eight hours of panicked confusion later, Thompson managed to get hold of his friends and have the bag sent back to Budapest so he could leave the country the next day. "That video shoot is indicative of Wolf Parade's entire career arc: rolling, absurd disaster," says Boeckner. "And we ended up with a pretty good video."

Meanwhile, Boeckner and Krug turned more of their songwriting focus to Handsome Furs and Sunset Rubdown respectively. Both bands put out better records in 2007 and 2009 (Sunset Rubdown's *Random Spirit Lover* and *Dragonslayer*; Handsome Furs' *Plague Park* and *Face Control*) than Wolf Parade's 2008 album, *At Mount Zoomer*. There were no gigs at all in 2009, before Wolf Parade returned with the much better *Expo 86* in 2010. But they realized that the live shows were not as tight as they should be, especially for a band that had been around for seven years.

"No one was being their best—myself included," says Boeckner. "There were different visions of how to move the band forward—or if we even should." The lack of management was also becoming an issue. "We just had a booking agent and pure chaos, trying to manage ourselves," says Krug. "We never even had tour managers. We'd just use common sense."

But not common cents; what eventually did Wolf Parade in was the most mundane issue of all: taxes. "Owing a bunch of tax money in the U.S., you just have no fucking idea how to start it," says Krug. "Canadian taxes, too—to be honest, our bank account was seized by the Canadian government. We found ourselves in a financial bird's nest. Arlen tried to tackle most of it, because he's the most pragmatic of all of us. He eventually crumbled under the confusion. Dante tried to pick up the thread and fucked it up even more. And the band was falling apart emotionally at the same time, so it made sense to just announce an indefinite hiatus."

HOT HOT HEAT'S 2005 album *Elevator* was going to be produced by Rick Rubin. They hung out a bit, but the band balked when they learned that the renowned producer made Weezer write 100 songs before entering the studio—and even then only showed up at five p.m. each day to check in on the progress. Instead, they went with Dave Sardy, who'd made one of their favourite songs in recent years, "The Rat" by the Walkmen, which Steve Bays had sung live with that band when they were tour mates. Hot Hot Heat purposely wanted to avoid getting lumped in with the Rapture and LCD Soundsystem. "We really wanted more emphasis on the songwriting rather than a style," Bays told a reporter that year. "We paid a lot of attention to aesthetics on that last record, and it had that whole '80s new wave retro feel. [This time] we didn't want a record that only hipsters would buy."

Elevator spawned some radio singles, and the band continued to tour with new guitarist Luke Paquin. But by 2007, recording the album *Happiness Ltd.*, the wheels were starting to fall off. "We did our record at Mushroom Studios in Vancouver," says Bays, "but the label 'didn't hear a single.' They wanted us to work with Rob Cavallo, who was *coincidentally* VP of A&R at Warner at the time." Cavallo is most famous for recording Green Day's *Dookie*, elevating that band to superstar status. "The label thought we should pay him $45,000 per song and do a couple of songs. I whipped out this song, 'Let Me In,' in a day on GarageBand, and people liked it. At that point it was called 'Change My Mind' and the chorus was in a minor key, kind of goth-pop."

On the day of recording, Cavallo told Bays, "I think you should change it from a B minor to a D major."

"But that changes the whole vibe! The whole song is about building up to that chord."

Cavallo shook his head. "No."

Bays protested. "This is the best song I've ever written, trust me!"

"No, trust *me*: this is *not* the best song you've ever written."

"Then why is it the single? Why are you here? Are you just taking our money and running?"

Bays caved nonetheless. In the end, it didn't matter: *Happiness Ltd.* didn't do any better or worse than the first two records, selling more than 250,000 copies in the U.S., a number most bands would kill for. But Bays could see the writing on the wall. "When we first signed to Sire, we went to [parent company] Warner in Burbank. On the left wall of the lobby were all these gold and platinum albums, floor to ceiling, which was inspiring, and on the right was a banner with a pic of a crowd rushing the stage when Hot Hot Heat played the Troubadour [in L.A.]. It was so cool.

"But in 2007, I walked in and it was all T-shirts on the wall, because they thought T-shirts and ringtones were the future. They had such a sick lineup [of radio and publicity people] when we signed with them, but by 2007 everyone had either quit or was let go and the place was run by interns. The only reason we ever wanted to be on a major was to have a recording budget and work with good producers."

Hot Hot Heat turned down a $500,000 advance for their next record and asked to be let out of their deal. The day Bays left the label's office for the last time, he could hear his own music coming from the art director's office, but couldn't place it at first. It was the unreleased demos for *Elevator*.

"How come you're listening to these?" he asked.

"Oh, I prefer these over the album," responded the art director.

"Wait, you prefer the demos I made for free over the $300,000 album we just made?"

"Yep."

Bays knew then that he'd just made the best decision of his life.

"Then I locked myself in a room," he says, "and studied engineering and production and mixing by reading *Tape Op* and listening to YouTube videos and podcasts." He produced the next Hot Hot Heat album, 2010's *Future Breeds*, and became an in-demand producer when the band went on hiatus shortly afterwards.

BLACK MOUNTAIN'S EARLY attempt to follow up its debut was abandoned; everyone felt it was too rushed and instead turned to side projects. There was another Pink Mountaintops album. Matt Camirand's roots rock band Blood Meridian signed to V2. Sinoia Caves put out its debut record. Wells and Webber started an excellent duo called Lightning Dust. Black Mountain then regrouped, recorded *In the Future* and released it in February 2008 to wide acclaim and a spot on the Polaris prize shortlist. *Wilderness Heart* followed in 2010, as did two more Pink Mountaintops records, including 2009's *Outside Love*, featuring Sophie Trudeau of Godspeed You! Black Emperor. 2016's excellent *IV* again landed Black Mountain on the Polaris prize shortlist, though Webber and Wells left the band shortly afterwards. Lightning Dust continued, and Wells became a key member of Destroyer, both as live drummer and producer of 2017's *ken*. McBean and Schmidt carried on the Black Mountain name, with members from their new base in Los Angeles.

In 2019, to the confusion of many fans of Vancouver rock bands, Black Mountain put out a record called *Destroyer*. They turned down an offer to open for Deep Purple.

AFTER THE BREAKUP of the Unicorns in December 2004, Nick Thorburn didn't want to face a Montreal winter. He went to L.A. and urged drummer Jamie Thompson to join him. They started plotting a new band, Islands. They knew what kind of baggage they carried. "I didn't want to be that joke that isn't funny after awhile," says Thorburn. "Something that really bothered me about how the Unicorns were framed was that it was whimsical and quirky. 'They play toy instruments!' These things that weren't true. We were playing synthesizers from the '70s and drum machines from the '80s—those aren't toys. But that was the narrative and it irked me. I hated bands that were 'adorkable.' I really wanted to make serious music that could move you but also make you laugh. When Jamie and I started Islands, we wanted to try some things. Some of those things were to write explicitly sad songs or romantic or emotional songs, and that's what I've tried to do ever since."

First, however, came a hip-hop project.

With Steve McDonald of Redd Kross and future Red Hot Chili Pepper Josh Klinghoffer, Thorburn and Thompson started backing L.A. rappers up live. This evolved into something they called Th' Corn Gangg, which didn't exist past two SXSW performances and one sold-out L.A. gig. "My great regret in life was not doing more Corn Gangg stuff," says Thompson, "because that was an amazing project."

Instead, focus turned to Islands demos, also done in L.A. with Steve McDonald. Though happy with the results, Thorburn and Thompson wanted more of a Montreal vibe. They returned to the Unicorns' birthplace and invited their friends: all but two members of Arcade Fire, most of Bell Orchestre and Wolf Parade, Snailhouse's Michael Feuerstack, Jim Guthrie, bassist Patrice Agbokou. The debut, *Return to the Sea*, came out on the short-lived Equator Records, a label founded by Matt Drouin, a high-school startup wunderkind. They turned down an offer from Universal, because Drouin, who was now Metric's manager, could get them more money from Canadian granting agencies than the major label was offering as an advance. And yet, says Thorburn, "I never received a single dime or saw a single royalty statement from Equator."

Beck kept in touch, and the offer still stood to open his Montreal show at the Bell Centre, which would be Islands' official live debut. The band, all clad in white, featured Feuerstack, Agbokou and two string players who'd never played a rock show before. Jim Guthrie was also on board. Says Jamie Thompson, "For me, growing up in Guelph, that was like Paul McCartney joining the band. It was a huge deal."

The debut was well received, the tour well attended; there was also a tour opening for Hot Hot Heat. But by then Jamie Thompson was exhausted and wanted out. He'd assumed financial and managerial duties since Islands' inception, as well as tour managing, and it all got to be too much. He left in the spring of 2006, just a few months after *Return to the Sea* came out. "In high school, I figured I'd be an unknown jazz musician who died penniless, like all my heroes," he says. "When success came, I was determined that no one was going to take it away. I'd be on the phone, doing emails and spreadsheet work, and we're on a bus and everyone else is having the time of their lives, drinking and partying, and there was more and more shit falling on me. We'd do wild things, and I'd have to talk to the cops all the time—and I'm not a huge fan of talking to cops."

One night in Providence, Thorburn led the crowd out of the club and played the encore with acoustic instruments in an adjacent basketball court; people stuck around to play a game afterwards. Good times. The next night in Manhattan, the same stunt didn't fly and led to the promoter telling Thompson that they wouldn't be paid. "While everyone else is having this wild, transcendent experience on the streets of New York, I'm talking to cops and finding out we're not getting paid," he says. "I had to put gas in the bus and pay this guy and that, and it got more and more stressful. In L.A., Nick had been taping smoke bombs onto the headstock of his guitar and lighting them off at shows. The person at [influential California promoter] Goldenvoice came up to us and said, 'We've heard he's been doing this thing. We're telling you right now, if he lights off a smoke bomb, you're not getting paid and Goldenvoice is never working with you again. Just so you know.' I went back and said, 'Dude, you have to not do this.' But he has an antiauthoritarian thing, and now I'm the heavy. He ended up doing it, and the woman chewed me out like crazy afterwards. That was it for me."

Around the same time, Alden Penner re-emerged in Montreal with a five-piece called Clues, co-founded with Brendan Reed, an early Unicorns drummer.

They put out one record on Constellation in 2009 before packing it in. He surfaced again in the Hidden Words, a conceptual project based on Bahá'í texts, at a time when he was reconnecting with his faith. It was primarily a three-piece with violinist Marie-Claire Saindon and Jamie Thompson, with whom he'd reconciled over a long and apologetic phone call. After releasing one Hidden Words album on Bandcamp in 2011, *Free Thyself from the Fetters of the World*, "he had some family issue and had to go away," says Thompson. The album has since disappeared from all online platforms.

Improbably, the Unicorns reunited in 2014. Or perhaps it had been prophesied: the last thing they released was a single called "2014" in 2004. Penner was in a better emotional and musical space; his 2014 solo album *Exegesis* was deservedly acclaimed. Penner and Thorburn had talked occasionally over the years about doing something, but the ice finally thawed when an invitation from Arcade Fire came to open some key dates on the *Reflektor* tour. Uncharacteristically, Penner agreed to six shows and signed all the contracts before telling his bandmates. "Which is hilarious, but that's life," says Thompson.

Penner told the *Kreative Kontrol* podcast, "It's not really a cash grab or based on any sort of nostalgia coming from those who've been calling for it for a long time. It feels like a point in my life where it'd be nice to honour that friendship. It's never too late to do that sort of thing, even though it might feel that way as you get older."

"We hadn't played in 10 years," says Thompson. "We rehearsed in L.A. for a couple of days before. On the first song on the first day, we just counted in and played it perfectly. It was super normal, very casual and natural for us to be playing a huge show like that." There were two shows at the Forum in L.A. and three at the Barclays Center in Brooklyn, followed by a hometown show headlining the Metropolis as part of Pop Montreal. Offers flooded in to keep it going, including one from the *Pitchfork* festival. Thorburn says, "Alden and I couldn't come to a resolution about how to perform live, the scale of the live show, and Jamie's involvement, so I turned it down."

Is there not a certain beauty, Thompson is asked, about burning so brightly before imploding and then having a brief, triumphant return? "Yeah," he laughs. "But I'm over 40 now, and there would also be a beauty in being able to buy a house."

DAVE WENGER OF Daddy's Hands occasionally performed in Montreal between 1999 and 2006, though he struggled with self-sabotage and alcohol—a battle that worsened after his beloved bassist, Emily Bauslaugh, with whom he had a long and complicated on-and-off relationship, died of a heroin overdose in 2002. He bounced around between Victoria, Vancouver and Montreal. At Pasalymani's, the anything-goes Mile End bar where the Unicorns felt most at home, Wenger hosted a cabaret night called Charter Cruise, which involved a Casio keyboard programmed to play ersatz versions of Daddy's Hands songs while Wenger played guitar, sang and heckled his audience. "Like a cruise ship act," says Boeckner, "but extremely upsetting."

Relations between Boeckner and his teenage idol were strained. "He treated me like a little brother—which I was, for many years," says Boeckner. "I met him when I was 15. When I started writing my own songs, he'd give me a pat on the head and be condescending. When Wolf Parade started getting attention—or even just playing shows—I had a couple of interactions with him where he was really bitter and cruel about it. I have to be honest: the guy was a fucking ass-hole, in the way that self-absorbed alcoholics are assholes. There was a very good part of Dave, a part that people want to be around, because he's charismatic and fun and could be incredibly kind to people. But the flipside is that he could be extremely cruel. Then he totally softened. He stopped drinking for a period, and in my last couple of interactions with him, he was extremely kind."

In May 2005 in Victoria, with the rest of Daddy's Hands and Black Mountain's original bassist Christoph Hofmeister—whose very first teenage band was with Dan Boeckner in Lake Cowichan—Wenger finished a new album in Victoria, *Welcome Kings!* It was recorded by Carolyn Mark's bandmate, Tolan McNeil, and released in 2006 on a small label run by Dante DeCaro. On Wenger's final trip back to Quebec, the 33-year-old wrote to his father in Victoria, saying, "I'm going back to the city that I love, and that loves me back."

That November, at three a.m. on a rainy night on St. Laurent just north of Rachel Street, Dave Wenger was struck by a car and killed. The car raced away; the driver was never found. "I waited for that call for 12 years, but I didn't think he would go like that," his brother Matthew told the *Globe and Mail* in a feature-length obituary. "There were a number of different ways he could have gone, and we could go on blaming ourselves. This way, there is no blame."

His friends and peers were devastated. So were those who were once intim-idated by him, but nonetheless inspired. "I was too shy and uncomfortable showing my weakness and vulnerability to get too close to Dave [Wenger] and Dan [Boeckner] and Carey [Mercer]," says Steve Bays. "Whenever I felt like there was a club I maybe wasn't invited to, I just didn't want to be there. The last time I saw Dave, he was backstage at a Hot Hot Heat show at the Commodore, and he was singing 'Goodnight Goodnight,' poking fun at me. I'm like, 'Ha, ha, I get it, it's a simple lyric.' But at the same time it was cool just to be acknowledged by him, because I really looked up to his music."

"For as much as Daddy's Hands inspired me," says Boeckner, "and how I don't think my career would've taken the same path without them, there is a dark side to that coin. At a certain point, you're not just at your local bar saying, 'I'm going to piss off 75% of the people in this bar, and the 25% who are my friends are going to laugh and love this.' You can do that at Thursday's Bar and Grill in Victoria, but when you go to the next town, everyone is like, 'Why are these people being assholes?' The career self-sabotage got wrapped up in that: Fugazi ethics through the lens of wanting to be a Dadaist irritant. That aesthetic leads to incredibly talented people who are constantly sabotaging themselves."

CHAPTER 17
CROWN OF LOVE

ARCADE FIRE

E motions were raw in the summer of 2004. The U.S. was fighting wars on two fronts. It had been three short years since the first large-scale foreign terrorist attack on North American soil (of the post-settler era, anyway). Ten years after the economic ennui of Generation X, it was clear that each successive cohort was going to be worse off than their parents. The political fault lines that would define at least the next two decades were firmly in place. And popular music didn't have much to say about any of it.

Arcade Fire's *Funeral* is not a political record; it is, however, a zeitgeist record. It's filled with tales of escapist magic and wonder, of young adulthood, of generational trauma, of seeing through hypocrisy, of refusing to be blinded by fear. It's about harnessing your own strength, about refusing to sleep in, about drawing from your community, about how "power's out in the heart of man / take it from your heart, put it in your hand." It's an emotional journey filled with both sorrow and ecstatic release. All the feels. People wept tears of joy at Arcade Fire shows. That didn't happen for the Strokes.

Arcade Fire became a sensation the week *Funeral* was released. Thankfully, they had a live show to back it up and were wired for longevity. The listeners of the world were on their side; they'd been primed for something like this to happen. By September 2004, it wasn't surprisingly to anyone that the greatest new band in the world came from Canada.

During their ascent, Arcade Fire's closest peers were Vancouver Islanders living in Montreal and a bunch of Guelphites who turned Toronto music on its head. Arcade Fire recorded in the studio of another mysterious Montreal band who had changed perceptions of Canadian music forever. Their genetic makeup was presaged by a power-pop band from Vancouver, an anthemic and amorphous large Toronto band and a queer orchestra with a flair for the unusual. Arcade Fire itself comprised people from Toronto, Ottawa, Guelph, Courtenay, Houston and the south shore of Montreal via Haiti.

Arcade Fire was a band from everywhere and nowhere. On the eve of their mainstream breakthrough, Will Butler was asked, "Are you an American band or a Canadian band?" He paused and then the Texan said confidently, "We're a Montreal band."

TO UNDERSTAND ONE of the most successful Canadian bands of the 2000s, one has to take a long walk around corners of American musical history.

Win and Will Butler were both born in Truckee, California (just outside Reno, Nevada), 30 months apart: Edwin in April 1980 and William in October 1982. Their father was a geologist from Maine, whose family moved there from England in the late 1600s. Their mother, Liza Rey, descends from an equally long lineage from Utah. Through Rey, the Butler boys are connected to a deep thread of American history.

Liza Rey's mother, Luise King Driggs, sang in a Utah family band that evolved into the King Sisters, a popular attraction in a travelling variety show that traversed the American west in the 1920s. Considered a precursor to the Andrews Sisters and other close-harmony vaudevillians, the King Sisters toured with Horace Heidt's orchestra; in San Francisco, King met a Cleveland guitar player named Alvino McBurney—who had changed his last name to Rey when he moved to New York City.

Alvino Rey, the Butler boys' grandfather, is credited as one of the first to build electric pickups for both guitar and banjo, and as one of several key figures developing the pedal steel guitar. He worked with Gibson designing its electric guitar and was possibly the first electric guitar player heard on U.S. national radio. In the 1940s, he invented a precursor to the vocoder he called "the singing guitar," later Sonovox, and even later known as a talk box, used by Peter Frampton, Joe Walsh and others.

In 1939, he and Luise moved to Hollywood, where he became a bandleader on national radio. Their children, including Liza Rey, were part of a children's vocal group that did backup sessions at the Capitol Records building for Frank Sinatra and Doris Day. In the 1950s, Alvino Rey played with Juan Esquivel's band

and released solo records as part of the new hi-fi stereo trend. Though Rey had hits under his own name, his employers were always more famous—including his wife.

In the 1960s, the King Sisters had their own national television show, featuring extended family members and on which Rey, and his Sonovox, played a starring role. The show ran for a year in 1965, went into syndication and returned in 1969 for another year before the family moved to Utah, embracing the Kings' Mormon roots. When Luise King died in 1997—shortly after the entire King family headlined Utah's sesquicentennial celebrations—she was the subject of a feature *New York Times* obituary, detailing her rich life full of American music history.

Daughter Liza Rey played the harp professionally, getting a master's degree in performance while moonlighting in rock bands. Inspired by early Joni Mitchell, Liza led her own quintet, made several records and played festivals.[1] The Butlers moved to Houston in 1985, when Edwin Butler Sr.'s job got transferred. Liza put her professional music on pause, though enlisted her preteen sons into a neighbourhood band that played "La Bamba" and "Lean on Me" at local schools. That community was a Houston suburb called the Woodlands—fodder for many Win Butler songs later in life.

WIN BUTLER'S TEENAGE dreams of escape were reflected in his musical choices, mostly U.K. acts of the '80s: the Cure, New Order, Depeche Mode. He liked Nirvana as much as any '90s child, but the only current album to really capture his imagination was Radiohead's *The Bends*. By extension, that became younger brother Will's first contemporary love as well, after a childhood immersed in the Beatles and classical music.

The elder Butler left the Woodlands in high school to attend Phillips Exeter Academy, an elite boarding school just north of Boston, known for educating presidents' children and celebrated authors. Before arriving, he was given a guitar from his grandfather, to fend off anticipated boredom in his new environs. His new peers immersed him in Bob Dylan, Bruce Springsteen and Neil Young, but the Cure's "Just Like Heaven" was the song he first performed in public, at a school assembly.

Upon graduation in 1998, he went to Sarah Lawrence College, a small, prestigious university just outside New York City, with a laissez-faire approach to curriculum. Filmmaker Jordan Peele was a classmate. After a year, Butler realized he was spending all his days four-tracking, which made the tuition hard to justify. He called his former Exeter classmate Josh Deu, who attended Concordia

---

1   Decades later, when her sons took her to see Joanna Newsom, Liza was delighted to see a woman succeed at what she'd been trying to do 30 years earlier.

University in Montreal, and the two decided to decamp to Boston, hoping to find a rhythm section there.

Instead, Butler found campus radio, and a whole new world opened up to the Texan raised on MTV's definition of alternative. He heard Magnetic Fields and Neutral Milk Hotel and was enchanted. "I had associated indie music with having an excuse to be crappy," he told writer John Cook. "Like, 'Oh, we didn't spend much money, that's why it sucks.' Whereas [campus radio discoveries] were like, 'We didn't spend that much money because—who cares? We write really good songs.'" He went to see Magnetic Fields in Boston in 2000 at one of the few shows they played to support their landmark album *69 Love Songs*. "When I left the show, I could sing 10 of their songs after hearing them once," he says. "It was the first time I had physical contact with people I thought were as good songwriters as anyone, as opposed to just listening to stuff that happened in England in the '80s. It's a very different scenario."

In Boston, Butler worked at a shoe store. (He's a size 15.) Otherwise, he and Deu spent all their time writing songs: they had little money, little else to do, and shared a bedroom. It was a gruelling, self-directed apprenticeship. Butler had very high standards for himself and others, tossing out song after song and being let down by other musicians he met, who were either too flaky or too technically minded—usually Berklee students. He didn't know what he wanted, and he didn't know how to get it. But he knew he wasn't going to get it in Boston.

After a year, Deu wanted to go back to Concordia, in a city Butler knew absolutely nothing about. Nonetheless, Butler enrolled first at Concordia and then at McGill, with a major in religious studies and a minor in Russian literature. In Montreal he discovered everything he thought New York City would be but wasn't. "When I was in New York," says Butler, "all I found was people not from New York [saying], 'I want to be in a famous band.' I was like, 'Your band is not going to be famous.' I felt like I was in a never-ending industry showcase. When I got to Montreal, all of our first shows were at weird modern dance shows or at someone's loft where we'd play records and dance afterwards. And rent was so incredibly cheap."

Butler and Deu hung around the practice rooms in McGill's music department, hoping to find a drummer. Butler, standing six foot five and sporting a Texan hat, stuck out. A jazz student approached him in the cafeteria and asked him what he was doing there. He said he played a bit of piano, a bit of guitar, and was looking for a drummer. "Yeah, well, a lot of people play a little piano, a little guitar," she taunted. She gave him her number and told him she might know some drummers, but not at the university. Days later, Butler saw her singing jazz at a Concordia art opening. He was intrigued. He knew he had to make music with this woman.

RÉGINE CHASSAGNE WAS born in the southern-shore suburbs of Montreal, the daughter of Haitian immigrants. They had fled the country separately in the early '60s, under the bloody reign of "Papa Doc" Duvalier and his killing squads, the Tonton Macoute, who murdered 60,000 people in a population of four million. Her mother came back from market one day to find her cousins and friends killed in what was known as the Jérémie massacre. Her paternal grandfather was kidnapped and executed at the Fort Dimanche prison.

The parents met after arriving in the U.S. and moved to Montreal together when her father, Stanley, got into Concordia to study math, followed by a master's in biology; he mostly worked with statistics. Her mother, Alice, studied Spanish literature and worked several jobs, one of which was as a secretary in Concordia's engineering department. Régine Chassagne was born in 1977. She and her younger sister were brought up to appreciate everything they had, to always remember where they'd come from. Chassagne was the kind of Catholic school kid who actually enjoyed wearing a uniform, so that she didn't have to worry about what to wear and could concentrate on learning.

Music was her primary passion. She taught herself to play Mozart on piano when she was four. "The piano was my friend," she says. "In my neighbourhood there weren't any friends my age. I didn't know any musicians. For me it was such a privilege to meet a musician, and I would grill them: 'You play drums? You play music? Tell me everything!' When I was young, I would think that in the best world, I would hang out with musicians. It was a very naive way of thinking. I always took music very seriously, because it was not something that was obvious. I didn't have a lot of CDs"—her first cassette was Billie Holiday, at age 14—"so everything I heard was very important. Any music that I don't understand, I'm automatically interested, because I have to figure it out. I would tape songs off the radio, like Charlie Parker. When I was 16, I heard Arvo Pärt on the radio. I didn't know what it was, but I stopped and stayed in one position for 25 minutes, because if I moved there would be [radio] static and I just wanted to listen. I would drink the sounds and try to remember every detail, playing them in my head, trying to reproduce what I'd just heard until I could hear it again."

At CÉGEP,[2] Chassagne answered an ad in the school paper placed by a medieval band, playing music of 12th- to 14th-century France and Spain, called Les Jongleurs de la Mandragore. "I was really interested, because it works on a completely different aesthetic than any modern music," she says. Chassagne was in the band for six years; she can be heard on their 2001 debut CD. They played in shopping malls and at corporate Christmas parties—because in Quebec such

---

2   Quebec's unique postsecondary, pre-college/university system, the equivalent of grades 12 and 13.

music doesn't seem all that unusual. Chassagne also performed solo gigs, just voice and percussion.

Music was clearly her passion, but for what she calls "self-imposed practical reasons of needing to provide income for the family," she got a communications degree from Concordia. She worked three jobs to put herself through school, and after graduating in 1998 she enrolled at McGill to study vocal jazz. Her mother died in 1999, at age 51, when Chassagne was 23. If she was a serious student before-hand, the tragedy firmed her resolve. "My mom took difficult job after difficult job, just to work, so to me music was never a hobby," she says. "I didn't want to be in a band to be cool and make friends. It was a serious thing." When she encoun-tered Win Butler in the hallways of McGill, she realized she'd never met anyone who seemed as serious about music as she was.

He invited her to his apartment to jam. She didn't want him to think it was a date, so she purposely dressed down and brought a bunch of musical prophy-lactics: her medieval instruments. "I wouldn't ever have thought of [being in a rock band]," she says. They hit it off immediately, writing several songs that night, including "Headlights Look Like Diamonds." A few weeks later, they went to see Ang Lee's film *Crouching Tiger, Hidden Dragon*. It wasn't supposed to be a date: they both promised to bring a friend each, and then purposely didn't invite them. Chassagne's social circle was primarily francophone; she didn't realize the subti-tles for the Chinese-language film might be in French. They were. The Texan did not speak or read French. Chassagne whispered translations in his ear through the entire film. Afterwards they went to a party with her friends, where she insisted Butler keep his Texan hat on. They've been a couple ever since.

Her role in Arcade Fire was unclear at first. There were three American guitar players—third member Tim Kile was from New Hampshire—and her musi-cal background was decidedly different from theirs. But the musical polyglot soon gelled with the Texan new wave guy. "At first it was really clashing," says Chassagne, "but then we started being influenced by each other and knew what the other one was going to do. It was very intense, because we were falling in love at the same time." In late 2001 they all went to Boston to record a demo, *Winter for a Year*. Tagging along was Butler's younger brother, Will, who had just graduated from Phillips Exeter. Chassagne picked up drumsticks for the first time in her life, playing on a track called "In the Attic."

Sean Michaels saw Arcade Fire at a battle of the bands around this time, two years before he launched one of the first MP3 blogs, *Said the Gramophone*. "Régine may have played organ on one song, but mostly wandered around the stage in deely bobbers," he recalls. "Win wore a cowboy hat and had a beat-up acoustic. It was the original lineup with Josh Deu and Tim Kile. Josh is even more

Texan charm, à la *Friday Night Lights*, than Win was: good sense of humour, kind of a jock thing. He and Win would argue about politics or music, and he could go round for round with Win in a way I'm not sure any of the other later band-mates did. The band had more of a twang in those days, like a mystic country rock band. Definitely not a new wave band. I loved them. I signed up for their mailing list."

Shortly after, that lineup fell apart. "Josh had this intuition that he needed to do something else," says Butler. "It's not like we broke up or anything." They remained close: some songs they co-wrote appeared on *Funeral* (earning the ex-bandmate a Juno for songwriter of the year); he animated the 2005 video for "Laïka"; Butler was best man at Deu's 2004 wedding.

Butler put up posters around Montreal's Plateau neighbourhood looking for new bandmates, which cited New Order, Debussy, Pixies, Arvo Pärt, Neil Young and Motown as influences. Very Montreal.

Dane Mills, Brendan Reed and Myles Broscoe answered the call, and a new chapter of Arcade Fire began. Chassagne played some accordion and occasionally poked her head out from behind a curtain. Arcade Fire was still quite folkie at this point, with a lot of what Butler called "aggressive joy." A review in the *McGill Daily* called them "the musical equivalent of a Chinese fire drill. An upright bass was exchanged for a tambourine and a steel drum, and again for an accordion, as keyboards and guitars were switched among the band members with impressive inconsistency." This lineup played sporadic gigs in 2001 to '02, mostly in lofts.

"At early shows," says Sean Michaels, "a common shtick was that all the song titles were written on pieces of paper stuck to the wall. They'd ask the crowd what they should play next, and then they'd rip that paper off the wall. At one show where Win and Brendan lived, they had apples hanging from strings, and you could tear down an apple and eat it. It's not like they had a bunch of money, where it's like, 'Everyone gets a glow stick!' They figured out how much money they could make at a show, and then taking 30 of those dollars and spending it on a stunt—it was part of the joy. It wasn't just a Montreal thing, because Hidden Cameras did stuff like that, too."

One early fan was Richard Reed Parry—though the Concordia student's first impression was less than stellar. "They played in my electronic art class, and I thought, Who are these American assholes?" says Parry. "It was Tim Kile, Josh and Win. They were supposed to be doing an interactive electronic art presen-tation; Josh was in my class. Instead, he called in his buddies to sing a folk song, which I didn't like very much, on acoustic guitars. The electronic portion was these Christmas lights that blinked at a certain part of the song and a non-working video installation that Win had made. I was really unimpressed."

Parry played in a band called the New International Standards. Butler came to see them play and told them how much he liked it. Shortly afterwards, Parry saw them at one of Chloë Lum's matinee loft shows above Barfly. "It was great—really great," he says. "It kind of freaked me out how much I liked it. I was sick for a few days after that." He also realized that he'd answered an ad Butler had placed looking for a roommate. "Great place above a bar, which means you can make noise all the time," it read. By the time Parry called, new Arcade Fire drummer Brendan Reed had taken the place, located above a queer bar at the southwest corner of St. Laurent and Bernard. Parry moved in with a band called the Unicorns instead. But within a year he was recording Arcade Fire's first EP.

RICHARD REED PARRY and his sister, Evalyn, travelled around Ontario as Morris dancers.[3] They grew up in Toronto; their mother, Caroline, was a poet, their father, David, an academic and founder of Friends of Fiddler's Green, a group dedicated to the folk music and dance of the British Isles. The Parry kids were also in a children's choir on albums by Eric Nagler and Sharon, Lois & Bram; the Parry parents and their friends were often in those artists' backing bands. Friends of Fiddler's Green and David Parry both put out records on Stan Rogers's record label.

"We were a musical family, but I was never taught how to play anything and we didn't sit around jamming or anything," says Parry. "We were just 'doing' music. We had a show that we'd do at the Tranzac Folk Club in Toronto every year, the Parry Family Winter Solstice Show."

The Parrys moved to Ottawa when the kids were teenagers; Richard went to the arts-focused Canterbury High School. Upon graduation, he spent two years in Ottawa writing what he says were "absurdist outdoor theatre plays," then moved to Toronto to work at Food Not Bombs, with future Hidden Camera and civic activist Dave Meslin. The summer before he moved to Montreal to study electro-acoustics and dance at Concordia, his Ottawa band Big Fish Eat Little Fish went on a national tour—or rather a few scattered dates from Nova Scotia to northern B.C., with a lot of time off in between.

At Concordia, he was commissioned to score a dance piece, and to do so he formed Bell Orchestre with violinist Sarah Neufeld and drummer Stefan Schneider; Parry played upright bass. Trumpeter Kaveh Nabatian and French horn player Pietro Amato were soon added. The first time Bell Orchestre played a rock show was after a dance performance, when they rushed to Win Butler's loft to open for

---

3   It's likely they danced with a young Dan Snaith of Caribou.

Arcade Fire. Parry was doing double duty that night: also on the bill was his other band, the New International Standards, led by Tim Kingsbury.

Kingsbury grew up in the same scene that had given birth to Royal City and Jim Guthrie, in Guelph, Ontario. There, Kingsbury and Unicorns drummer Jamie Thompson backed up Gentleman Reg, part of the original Three Gut Records crew. He went to school in Ottawa, living there from 1997 to 2001, playing in John Tielli's band Clark with drummer Jeremy Gara, as well as in Yellow Jacket Avenger with Geoffrey Pye. His first cross-Canada tour was backing up Calgary songwriter Aaron Booth. Kingsbury left Ottawa for Montreal, where rent was cheaper, though work was hard to find—and the furnace in his apartment was prone to breaking down in the winter. He worked at the venerable St. Laurent grocery store Warshaw, where he contemplated giving up on music and becoming a butcher. In May 2002 he saw Arcade Fire play at a loft in Griffintown, on William Street near Guy, south of downtown near the Lachine Canal.

"I was totally shocked at how much I liked it," he says. "It was way quieter than it [became], Anita Fust was playing harp, and there was no real PA at this loft. Win was singing through his guitar amp. Brendan [Reed] was really striking to me; he and Régine were really fun to watch, and Win was hard to ignore. And I had the songs in my head afterwards, which doesn't happen often." He'd be in the band by the end of the year.

WIN BUTLER AND Régine Chassagne spent the summer of 2002 at the Butler family compound in Maine. In August, they were joined by the rest of the band, as well as Will Butler and, briefly, original member Tim Kile. Richard Reed Parry was invited to record what became the band's first proper EP. "I liked the band, and I liked them as people," Parry says. "It felt like we were cut from a similar cloth. We were all excited to be doing stuff that was real—and not school."

And yet it's somewhat miraculous that anything at all came out of the session. For starters, there was no mixing board. "We had very little equipment," says Parry. "I was the experienced one because I'd taken one course at school in how to record. I had a tape machine—and Win was really excited to know someone with a tape machine. We cobbled together a few microphones; some were Win's mom's. But we didn't have monitors; we were plugging computers into guitar amps. It was rough. It wasn't a band that jammed a lot, or even rehearsed. There was nothing routine about it, fairly chaotic."

Everyone took jobs in the local tourist town, Bar Harbor. "Win and Will worked in a fancy hotel; Régine worked in a different fancy hotel," says Parry, who worked in a pizzeria. "A couple of other guys were helping out Win's dad, tending the field." The non-Butlers stayed in a second cabin on the property; recording took place in the barn. It was a tight living situation, and the personal relationships were nowhere near strong enough to be sustainable. There was a lot of time spent at the beach. The band didn't feel their opinions were respected by the headstrong Win. "The band was a mess in Maine. It was a total disaster," says Parry. "Too much intensity. There were two halves of the band that weren't talking to each other, and I was the only one talking to both. It was not what I was expecting."

It was difficult to record drums and capture any live intensity, which was especially frustrating on a live favourite like "No Cars Go." "When we were in Maine listening to it," says Win, "we just thought, Oh god, this sucks. After working on it for a while, I went back to that song after assuming that it wasn't going to be on the record, and I thought, Well, it's not worse than anything else."

The EP didn't come out for another six months. The band did a weekend tour in Ontario, which included a gig at the Embassy Hotel in London, Ontario, where they shared the bill with the New International Standards; both were opening for a local frat funk band called Grand Poobah. Win suggested the two Montreal acts pool their resources and share a set, trading songs. "In typical chaotic, stupid fashion, we did that, and it was a mess," says Kingsbury. But he and Parry often hung out at the Arcade Fire loft to jam.

"It wasn't consciously forming a band," says Parry, whose musical focus was with Bell Orchestre at the time. "It was more enjoyable just to dick around and play rock music. There were so many ideas flying around, and it felt good—which it doesn't always, playing rock music. It can often be a fate worse than death, in some ways, trying to start a rock band from nowhere. It can feel so silly."

Kingsbury had been writing to his friends at Three Gut Records in Toronto, hoping to get the New International Standards an opening slot for one of its acts. Royal City had a show at La Sala Rossa on December 1, with a Toronto band who'd just put out their second record and had never played Montreal before: Broken Social Scene. The New International Standards were added to the bottom of the bill, but the band soon fell apart when co-founder Annesley Black left town. (She's now an award-winning composer in Berlin.) Butler told him to keep the gig and play it with Arcade Fire instead, suggesting they could once again combine their sets. "But we only had time to learn one of my songs," says Kingsbury. "It was clear to me that it was not designed to be a backing band."

Not that Arcade Fire songs were easy or less demanding. Butler and Chassagne never wanted to settle for "good enough." "I found the Arcade Fire challenging in a way that playing with other people had never been," says Kingsbury of his earliest days in the band. "Often I'd play something and be happy with it and look around and no one else would be nearly as excited as I was. I'd just shrug and move on, and eventually I'd find something way better than what I would have originally settled on."

Now in the band, Kingsbury got Arcade Fire another gig: in Ottawa in February 2003 opening for his old band, Clark, in which Jeremy Gara was still the drummer. The Ottawa crowd, composed largely of Wooden Stars disciples, was largely unimpressed with Kingsbury's new band. "They came across like they were trying way too hard," says Samir Khan, who played with Gara in both Kepler and Weights and Measures. "I felt bad for Tim. He seemed, to me at least, to be a unit of dignity within a crowd of, like, eager-to-please acting students." After the show, Kingsbury stayed at Khan's apartment.

"What did you think?" Kingsbury asked Khan.

Diplomatically, he responded, "I liked what you did in the band, but I'm not sure I get it."

"Yeah, that was a sloppy show for us. We can do better."

"Right, well, I thi—"

"Win thinks we're going to make a real go of this. Like get on *Letterman* or something."

Khan had to suppress a literal spit take, to avoid splattering red wine all over his kitchen wall, and then laughed, "That dude better get a plan B!" (Years later, telling this story, Khan adds, "I've been eating delicious, delicious crow ever since.")

Arcade Fire got a better reception in Toronto, where they played the El Mocambo, opening for Jim Guthrie at his release show for *Morning Noon Night*. They opened their set in the middle of the floor, stomping and singing and capturing the talkative crowd's attention immediately. It was an unusual move in the historic Toronto club, but something they often did at Montreal loft shows. "The most straightforward way to make people not talk was just to be in the audience," says Butler. "You'll feel like an asshole if you're talking and the singer's right next to you. If the audience doesn't buy in, then you're fucked to begin with."

They were almost fucked before they even got to the show. Butler had recently bought a mini school bus, which had an extraordinarily leaky gas tank and no heat. They ran dry on the on-ramp to the Don Valley Parkway from Highway 401, blocking traffic until they could get help. And yet they kept the bus for future gigs. When driving, "Win would put on these huge bearskin gloves up to his elbows," remembers Sean Michaels. "The band would be desperately asking people [on message boards], 'Anybody want a ride to Toronto?' They were trying to raise funds to pay for the trip in that gas hog."

The EP release show was on the first day of spring, March 21, 2003, at Casa del Popolo, the 100-capacity venue co-owned by Mauro Pezzente of Godspeed, who did sound that night. Will Butler came up from Chicago, planning to take a semester off and stay until the fall. Parry joined them on stage, as did violinist Marika Anthony-Shaw, harpist Anita Fust and a violinist remembered only as Adam (who later performed with Alden Penner of the Unicorns). Arcade Fire were suited up in dress shirts and ties for the first time. Opening the show was synth-pop/hip-hop trio Parka 3 and piano-and-tap-dancing duo Kosher Dill Spears and Big Gold Hoops—not at all an unusual bill in Montreal at the time.

The tiny bar was jammed and sweaty; so was the stage. As was the band's nature, there was a lot of instrument-swapping. Drummer Brendan Reed reached his breaking point. "I was nostalgic for an earlier time," he told a French magazine. "People were in and out of the group too much and it was feeling like a backing band. During one of the last songs, I might have come in early on a verse, and Win walked back while we were playing and said, 'You messed everything up,' or something. I think he was joking, but it was so hot up there, and I felt caged in by harp strings and bodies and so I pushed the drums out of the way so that I could get off the stage. The violin player was in front of me, and I guess the cymbal hit her hand, or somehow she was pushed in a way that damaged her violin." Reed stormed off stage. Only those in the first few rows were able to tell what was going on. But it was a transformative moment in Arcade Fire's career: an end and a beginning.

Brendan Reed was not just a bandmate; he was also Win's roommate, which made things awkward. That week they took a long walk, talked it out and decided to dissolve the band—or that version of the band, as it was obvious Win and Régine would continue. There was a gig booked at the Jupiter Room two weeks later, which both Reed and Dane Mills agreed to play. Reed didn't show up; Mills quit 10 minutes beforehand. Chassagne realized she'd have to be the drummer that night. Morale was low, to say the least. "We were fucked," remembers Will Butler. "Then Wolf Parade played and it felt like something was alive." It was the opening band's first gig ever, and Win Butler was blown away, even from the first few notes he heard through the bathroom walls. His attitude about the night changed immediately. Arcade Fire were about to become an entirely new band.

They had to. The EP had underwhelmed some observers who had foreseen big things. Sean Michaels was one. "Before Arcade Fire released anything," he says, "it felt like they were going to be a big deal, and the song that was going to do it was 'Headlights.' The live version of 'Headlights' was their closer, their signature, and people felt, Oh yeah, this is going to shoot them into the stratosphere. And it didn't. The recording didn't sound that good. There was a lull after that. People wondered what was next."

Richard Reed Parry was slowly seduced into the fold. "I was on the fence," he says. "I didn't know what my role would be; it felt like too many cooks. I went out for dinner with Win and Régine and said, 'I can't really do this. You don't need me. You should tour with just the two of you and a boom box. I would go see that.' Then we'd drift in and out of each other's musical orbit, for random reasons. I was at their house one day while they were jamming. No drummer. They were working on 'Wake Up' before it was a finished song. I wrote the vocal part of the outro, and everyone was like, 'Great! That's the part.' It was like, 'Whoops, I'm in the band.' On the EP I was an outside voice. Now we were hanging out with an unfinished song and I had an impact on it."

"'Wake Up' was written in reaction to the band breaking up," says Butler. "We wanted to do something that was louder than anything we'd done before, very bombastic. At least, I did. It was written as an opening song." Other material followed that was in more of a rock direction: "Laïka," "Power Out." "Crown of Love," which begins as a waltz before morphing into a disco stomp by the end, debuted at La Sala Rossa, with Butler playing the grand piano at the back of the room while the rest of the band was on stage, with the audience in between.

The presentation became more formal: the band now dressed in white dress shirts and black ties, looking like undertakers, doorstep missionaries—or the Sadies. "The clothes are more for us than the audience," said Butler in 2004. "It's more for our own headspace, to make it special. It's important for me to put on clothes that I'm not already wearing. It puts you in a different mode." For Chassagne, there had never been any distinction between the animated way she usually lives her life and the way she performs on stage. "For me, I don't think about 'theatrical,'" she said in 2004. "For me, it's not something that I put on. It's not much of a game or a character." Win was now primarily playing electric, not acoustic, guitar. Will Butler and Parry developed a routine during "Laïka" that involved one of them wearing a motorcycle helmet, which the other attacked with drumsticks as a percussion instrument.

With new material and a new direction, the only problem was that they didn't have a drummer; Chassagne didn't want the position. In the spring and summer of 2003, they played with a guy they remember only as "other Tim," with whom they didn't gel personally or musically. There was an Ontario swing opening for former Royal City drummer Nathan Lawr, starting at the Rivoli in Toronto. Though it was Lawr's tour—he'd just released an excellent debut as a singer-songwriter, *The Heart Beats a Waltz*—he wisely decided to flip the bill and have the Montrealers close each show. Not that they were winning everyone over: "I want to punch this band," one woman at the Rivoli was overheard saying.

"The show at the Ford Plant [in Brantford] was in front of 12 kids," says Will Butler. "I remember a couple of really young kids being there and their faces just being blown off. In Guelph we played the Black Mustard restaurant; it definitely felt like the audience was like, Uh, what's up? And at Call the Office in London, literally no one showed up. We played 'Wake Up' and 'Power Out' and stopped. It was just Nathan and his one friend in the audience. Even Andy Magoffin, the sound tech, left." That was followed by a brief swing of the northeastern U.S. that included a gig with Devendra Banhart and Xiu Xiu in Cambridge, Massachusetts. The school bus finally died in Boston when the gears gave out. No one remembers how they got home.

That jaunt was the end for drummer Tim, but the band forged ahead with recording plans. The most attractive option was the Hotel 2 Tango studio, operated by members of Godspeed You! Black Emperor. It had just opened up to commercial clients in 2004, after Godspeed went on hiatus. "We were coming out of the Godspeed scene," says Will Butler, "and while there were aspects of it that were annoying and silly, that's why we recorded at the Hotel—it was also the only place to record. We thought, Oh, we gotta do our thing underneath the Godspeed water tower."

Engineer Howard Bilerman had first heard of Arcade Fire through his friend Scott Chernoff of Molasses. Chernoff worked with Tim Kingsbury at PSL, the same call centre that employed Richard Reed Parry, Bobby Beaton of the Gruesomes, Michael Feuerstack of Snailhouse and Mike Moya of Godspeed.[4]

Chernoff gave Bilerman a copy of Arcade Fire's EP and said, "Do you want to hear the next greatest band in the world?" Howard laughed him off.

"I thought it was a band who did have more of an identity than others but that hadn't really found their sound yet," he says. "A few weeks later I got an email saying that they wanted to come to the studio to record two songs. I told them I'd like to see them play beforehand. I had a suspicion that it would be more difficult to record than other stuff and I wanted to know what I would be faced with. I went to Win and Régine's kitchen and they played 'Wake Up.' I was just knocked on my ass. It was such a huge leap from everything I had heard on the EP."

Win Butler and Régine Chassagne got married in a sugar shack north of Montreal in August 2003, the morning after a massive blackout on the Eastern Seaboard. (Quebec was unaffected, being powered by its own hydroelectric grid.) The ceremony was scored by Parry and performed with several auxiliary Arcade Fire members. Among the guests was 95-year-old Alvino Rey, one of the last times Butler saw his grandfather, who died in February 2004.

Shortly afterwards, they went to Hotel 2 Tango to record "Wake Up" and

---

4   Wolf Parade's Dan Boeckner and the Unicorns' Nick Thorburn later worked there as well. "Everybody there used the copy machine to make posters," says Kingsbury. "The woman who ran the joint, Andrée, only hired artists. She tried to spread out the work as much as possible. She was very subtle about it."

"Power Out" for a planned seven-inch. The latter was done with a drum machine; Arlen Thompson of Wolf Parade was brought in to play "Wake Up." He'd never heard the song before. Win told him the first part was like the Ronettes' "Be My Baby" and the second part was like Iggy Pop's "Lust for Life" (though it's more like "We Will Rock You" and then "You Can't Hurry Love"). The string players on "Wake Up" were culled from the Constellation Records roster: Jessica Moss of A Silver Mt. Zion and Geneviève Heistek of Hangedup.

When it was done, Butler asked Bilerman if he knew any drummers able to play a couple of gigs coming up, including an Ontario weekend. Bilerman said he knew about 20 drummers, but they were all in multiple bands already. But having recently picked up the sticks again to play on a Silver Mt. Zion record, he threw his own hat in the ring. "I didn't hear anything for a week, even though we were recording the whole time," he says. "It was like asking someone to the prom and having them tell you, 'Hmmm, I'll get back to you'—even though the prom might be next weekend. At the end of the recording session, they asked me if I was serious about my offer, and I said absolutely."

Will Butler went back to Chicago for school. Dan Boeckner of Wolf Parade filled in for a few gigs, including a Pop Montreal show opening for Hawksley Workman. "It was definitely not our show," says Kingsbury, "and we'd never played a room anywhere near that big. We were playing 'In the Backseat' and we could hear people talking. At one point, Win stamped his foot and yelled really loud. The whole room got quiet—for 10 seconds." At the end of the set, Boeckner taunted the headliner's crowd by saying into the mic, "Up next: troubadour poet Hawksley Workman!"

With Bilerman in the band, Arcade Fire scrapped the seven-inch idea, unhappy with the version of "Power Out" and returning to the studio whenever possible to finish the rest of an album. As studio manager at the Hotel, Bilerman booked Arcade Fire into any holes in the schedule. When he was away with A Silver Mt. Zion for a short tour, Arcade Fire set up in the studio for a week. They also did plenty of tracking in Butler and Chassagne's loft. It was all done on old-school tape—and on both eight-track and 16-track.

It got more than a bit confusing when it came time to mix. "We did a lot of recording when Howard was gone, and we're not good at labelling what track was what," says Butler. "It would have been impossible for a third party to come in, because it was so unprofessional. Like halfway through the tambourine track, Régine's vocals might come in. The mixing/mastering period was so hard. You lose a lot of perspective. 'Haiti,' which turned out to be one of my favourite songs on the record, almost didn't make it on there. We were so depressed with the way it sounded." Chassagne's vocals on "Haiti" were recorded on a Dictaphone in the bathroom with the lights off; the lyrics were too personal for her to perform in front of people.

On the other hand, Chassagne had no trouble nailing her vulnerable vocal on "In the Backseat," a song about the death of her mother and her aunt; it had first been attempted for the EP. It's the closing track on *Funeral*, and her vocals are all the more remarkable because they're incredibly raw: as she hits the impossibly high notes at the end, her voice isn't doubled or laden with effects like every other modern vocalist's, nor is it turned into a big Céline Dion moment, despite it being such an emotional climax. It's pure and beautiful.

Parry didn't mind the chaos. "Bouncing between environments and not having a plan and trying things to see what happens and moving forward without fussing too much—that's the best way to do things," he says. "I find anything more organized than that to be stressful. I love Tom Petty records, but I have zero interest in doing 70 takes of a song. I don't have that bone in my body. I like to capture a more raw, Holy Ghost, one-time-only kind of thing."

"If we only had two days to do two songs, we'd quickly set up three mics on the drums," says Bilerman. "Whereas on 'Wake Up,' we had eight mics on the drums. It gives the record this weird mixtape feeling, because no two songs were recorded the same way. Also, the songs were being recorded immediately after being written—or at least immediately after I learned how to play them—so they all had this freshness."

The album's imperfections were what many people loved about it, and Parry agrees. "Arlen came in never having played 'Wake Up' before," he says. "There's a cool thing in the feel where he lost the beat and flips it at a certain point. I don't think it's conscious, but it's permanently in the DNA of the song now. That's part of the magic of the record. It hasn't been endlessly toned. It has charming things in it that make you feel alive. There are lots of particular things that wouldn't make it on to one of our records now."

Arcade Fire was just as ramshackle out of the studio as they were inside. Bilerman recalls a show in Guelph, at the Ed Video artspace, with local teenage band the Barmitzvah Brothers. At the end of the night, "everyone had left, but we hadn't loaded the van yet," he recalls. "I was like, 'Where is everybody?' The backline was packed and ready to go, and there was this hat box in front of it, the first thing you see in the middle of the stage. As I walked closer, I noticed that it's the merch float, and it's overflowing with $20 bills. I'm like, 'What trusting soul would leave what is easily $1,000 in cash unattended on the stage? Guys, put this in a bank right away!' That, to me, is a perfect metaphor for that time in the band: impressing people to the point where you're rolling in dough, but leaving a lot of dough innocently unattended. That distills 2003 Arcade Fire to me perfectly."

Now on board was violinist Sarah Neufeld, a close friend of Parry. She grew up outside Courtenay, B.C., on the northern tip of Vancouver Island, where she started learning violin at age three with the Suzuki method. As a teenager, she decided to learn a bunch of Jimi Hendrix solos on guitar. When she went back to violin, she was drawn to jazz; she moved to Montreal in 1997 to study electro-acoustics at Concordia. That's where she met Parry, who shared her interest in modern dance and in bands like the Rachel's and Penguin Café Orchestra. She never had ambitions to play in a rock band. But she loved Arcade Fire, loved play-ing with Parry, signed on in the fall of 2003 and soon became an integral part of the new sound.

Two of *Funeral*'s most beloved tracks were written in the middle of the pro-cess in early 2004. "Rebellion (Lies)" was introduced in February at a show with the Hidden Cameras at a pop-up gallery in Montreal's Chinatown. A month ear-lier, on January 9, Arcade Fire played their first headlining show in Toronto at Sneaky Dee's. Parry recalls, "That was the first show where it felt like, whoa, this is bonkers." On what *Now* magazine described as "the coldest night of the year," the 300-capacity room was sold out with a lineup down the block—the first time that had ever happened to Arcade Fire, even in Montreal. Owen Pallett joined them on stage, despite never having heard several of the songs. They debuted a new song called "Tunnels," which opens with a soft pulse, with Chassagne on drums and Bilerman on guitar, that slowly evolves into a soaring vocal refrain and a disco stomp. The crowd lost their mind, giving the band a Hollywood moment in which a brand new song goes over like gangbusters. Maggie MacDonald of the Hidden Cameras shrieked at them to play it again. Sarah Liss concluded her five-star live review in *Now* by reporting that "the screaming audience was practically in tears when the band left the stage."

In the studio, "Tunnels" opens with a twinkling piano sound before a ragged guitar introduces the main melody, doubling another piano track. "I really wanted that piano to feel like stars or a cloud over the whole thing," says Parry. The guitar sounds slightly out of focus—with good reason. Win recorded it as an overdub, not with the rest of the band. He did a take, loved it and thought he was done. Then Bilerman realized he had turned on the wrong channel: not the one for the mic on the guitar amp but for a vocal mic across the room. They decided to keep it. The cumulative effect is cinematic, like a curtain lifting or a camera slowly tightening its focus. The final version of the song is a composite of three different mixes, later assembled by mastering engineer Ryan Morey, in a way that gradually opens up the sound.

The album's biggest radio single, "Rebellion," had a unique snare sound for a reason. Bilerman had someone in the band operate the tape machine while he was playing drums. They did a few takes until one felt right. But the snare mic wasn't plugged in.

"That's the take!" said Butler.

"Absolutely not, we can't have a song without a snare in it," retorted Bilerman.

"But that's the one with spirit, that's the take," insisted Butler.

They overdubbed Chassagne playing just the snare. The final sound is a combination of that and the ghost of Bilerman's original through a hi-hat mic.

The strings were recorded at the Arcade Fire loft. Owen Pallett and Michael Olsen of the Hidden Cameras came in from Toronto, to join Neufeld and Parry. Each track was doubled, so they sound like a string octet. Contrary to popular belief, Pallett was not the arranger, though he's played that role for many other artists since. Chassagne had very clear ideas about what she wanted— and loved every minute of the session. "That was one of the best days of my life, having all these strings in my house, in my living room," she said shortly before the record came out. "Because I played drums on ["Crown of Love" and "Tunnels"], I knew when and how it was going to speed up, so I was conducting them all. I was in wonderland! I couldn't have been happier. It was like my birthday times 1,100. So fun."

So much about *Funeral* was unconventional. On "Tunnels" there is not one hook but three: the main instrumental theme—introduced on piano and guitar, reappearing as wordless vocals at the end—the main vocal melody and the guitar melody underneath the verse. Other than the New Pornographers, most acts of the day might repurpose some of those elements for separate songs; Arcade Fire layered them all into one. The second song, "Laïka," opens with four bars of an upside-down drum beat laced with sleigh bells, then four bars of a fractured funk riff played by a guitar with an Asian tonality, then four bars of an accordion melody. When the vocals enter, they're doubled by the bass. "Power Out" sounds like New Order playing the Clash's "London Calling" until Men without Hats show up with a glockenspiel melody lifted from "Safety Dance." The song closes with an eight-bar melody that soon became a set-ending audience chorale, à la U2's "40."

Despite all the curious arrangements and sonics underneath *Funeral*'s melodies, they were designed for impact. It was as if the band was singing along to their own songs before they had a massive audience to do so.

There was a spiritual element to this for the band, most of whom had performed in church as children. Parry, who was raised Quaker, says, "There's something greater than you when there's a bunch of you assembled. That idea of a spirit moving through a group. It's not just a bunch of dudes playing guitar solos. Something happens that can't be named. That's kind of the prize." Arcade Fire shows were cathartic for both band and audience. The joyous release was crafted to connote euphoria. "The shows where the music is an emotional catalyst, that's the best thing," says Parry, "when you come home from a show and feel like you can climb a building. If one person in the audience is super inspired to go off on their own and do something exciting, it would make my day."

When Kingsbury first joined the band in October 2003, he and Butler took a walk up Mount Royal in the heart of the city.

"If there was a band where you could have their kind of career right now, what band would that be?" asked Butler.

"Probably Calexico." Kingsbury had seen the Arizonan band the night before and was blown away. They struck him as a well-respected, creatively inspiring band that had reached a reasonable level of commercial success.

Win paused. "Huh."

"Why, what were you going to say?"

"U2."

ALVINO REY DIED in February 2004 at the age of 96. It was a real blow: Win Butler had been in frequent contact with his grandfather in the previous five years. "He was so sharp, so there mentally," says Butler. "I'd ask him a lot of questions. At the wedding he gave his speech and had everyone in stitches. He got the biggest reception. Great comedic timing."

"He was cooler than anyone I ever knew," said Chassagne in 2004. At the funeral, Chassagne and the Butler brothers performed "Abide with Me," accompanied by mother Liza Rey on harp. The service ended with a recording of "My Buddy," an endearing but eerie song Alvino recorded in the 1940s, using his ghostly Sonovox. Win had never heard it before and was entranced. A few months later, Arcade Fire released it as the B-side to their debut single.

The album was now going to be called *Funeral*, in tribute to Alvino Rey; to Parry's aunt, who died a month later; to Chassagne's grandmother, who had died just before the wedding; and to David Parry, who had died when Richard was 17. Chassagne had also lost her mother, when she was 23.

The band wasn't sure who would release it. At one point, Win considered starting a new label with Jenny Mitchell of the Barmitzvah Brothers. But bigger names soon came to bite. The San Francisco–based label Absolutely Kosher had first heard the Arcade Fire EP when Xiu Xiu brought a copy back from the Cambridge show; Arcade Fire played two shows with another Absolutely Kosher act, hot critics' favourite the Wrens, in New York and Montreal. Label owner Cory Brown flew to the band's hometown to talk to them. There were also negotiations with Toronto's Paper Bag Records.

But it was a hometown label that seemed to make the most sense: Alien8, who had handled the unexpected runaway success of the Unicorns in the past four months. That band managed to capture the imagination of campus radio, bloggers and new music websites in the U.S. Their success seemed like an attainable goal for Arcade Fire. It didn't matter that the rest of Alien8's roster consisted largely of Japanese noise artists and Montreal avant-garde electronic musicians.

While contemplating options, Arcade Fire were invited to play the Canadian Independent Music Awards with Bif Naked and D.O.A.'s Joey Shithead, part of industry schmoozefest Canadian Music Week in Toronto. They played two songs at the ceremony, held at the Phoenix, but arrived with zero expectations. Backstage, the band was approached by legendary Montreal music mogul Donald K. Donald, who'd launched the careers of April Wine, Corey Hart, Sum 41 and others. He sauntered up to the band looking like a cartoon character of a record executive. No one in the band recognized him—because why would they?

"You guys got a record contract?"

"Nope!" responded Parry.

"You got a record?"

"Yep, ten bucks!"

The mogul paid up, took a copy of the EP and walked away. That was the extent of Arcade Fire's interaction with the mainstream Canadian music industry.

They packed up and played a show in the basement of an activist screenprinting shop, Punchclock, run by Parry's former Toronto roommates, with opening act Jon-Rae and the River from the Blocks Recording Club. The audience illuminated the stage with flashlights. It was a somewhat secret show, promoted only on the Stillepost message board. The next time they played Toronto it was at the 600-capacity Lee's Palace. "Every time we played Toronto, I felt like I was playing drums in the Beatles," says Bilerman. "The audience would double every time, and in very short succession. And they'd be so into it, whereas Montreal was more reserved. 'How excited should we get?' Playing Toronto was the real litmus test."

Bilerman had one important label connection, but he was somewhat reluctant to use it. He had been friends with Mac McCaughan and Laura Ballance, who run North Carolina's Merge Records, ever since the first time their band Superchunk played Montreal, in 1993. Over the years, they crashed on Bilerman's couch when in town, and he taped their local live shows. When talking with Win about label options, the singer brought up Merge, because they'd put out life-changing records by Magnetic Fields and Neutral Milk Hotel. Parry was a big fan of Spoon, one of Merge's more recent success stories. Bilerman mentioned his personal relationship with the label, with the caveat that it certainly didn't guarantee anything but at least would ensure an envelope would get opened.

Humble Howard felt weird about, in his words, "profiteering from my friendship with [Merge]. But there was also self-interest: having a record I worked on come out on Merge would be a huge deal for me." He sent the label a DVD of some live footage, which they couldn't view because of a formatting error. He sent them another package with rough mixes of the record. He didn't hear back immediately and assumed the worst. Merge was having a particularly busy year, in part because they were planning a week-long 15-year anniversary party in July.

Meanwhile, Alien8 was very interested. In April 2004 the band signed a deal with them over dinner at Mondo Fritz, next door to Schwartz's on St. Laurent. The next day, Merge responded with strong interest. The band was in an uncomfortable position, legally and ethically, but their dream date was calling. They asked McCaughan and Ballance to come to Montreal to chat, but the former had a newborn and the latter was pregnant. So Butler, Chassagne and Parry drove 13 hours down to Durham, North Carolina, to meet them.

The band was buzzing with nervous energy, Chassagne constantly tapping and drumming in the label's office and at dinner at Lantern, owned by McCaughan's wife. The next morning, they met again at the office. The band said they were ready to sign. "Don't you want to think about it for a few days?" asked Ballance. Publicist Martin Hall had to stop himself from kicking her under the table. They signed a contract with Merge on April 30 and had to break the news to Alien8. "They told me later that if they put it out, it would have killed them," says Butler.

Funeral was guaranteed to be more than just another Canadian indie record. Merge had—and still has—a boutique reputation similar to Sub Pop and Matador, in terms of a certain quality standard. It can guarantee that certain radio programmers and critics will at least listen to their releases.

"All I'd ever hoped for when making *Funeral* was that it would be as important to people as the first Violent Femmes record is to me," said Bilerman, who was born in 1970. "Which is: every kid grows up listening to their parents' music, until one day in grade 8 art class someone plays 'Blister in the Sun' for you and you find music that understands your human condition and you don't feel alone. To me, that was the bar. If I was going to be in this band doing double duty as drummer and recording, I wanted it to be one of those records."

Merge put out a seven-inch single of "Tunnels," backed with Alvino Rey's "My Buddy," on June 8, 2004. The label still had not seen the band play live. That month Arcade Fire did their first American tour, opening for the Unicorns. They skipped a South Carolina date to play the Cave in Chapel Hill instead, a tiny venue where Win's head scraped the ceiling. The stage was beside the front door. A very pregnant Ballance stood in the doorway, watching the audience, witnessing waves of smiles and joy ripple through the crowd with each successive song. By the end of the show, she was trembling.

The rest of the tour was like an evangelical tent-revival campaign through the U.S. This band was not detached and cool, like the Strokes. They weren't ironic, like the Unicorns. They had uniforms and stage gimmicks, but they weren't the Polyphonic Spree (the Austin choral rock band dressed in angelic robes) or Tilly and the Wall (the Omaha band with a tap dancer as a percussionist). Arcade Fire was a seven-piece band that played with fiery fervour and, best of all, the songs backed up the bluster.

New fans showered the band with money at the merch table. At a show in Washington, D.C., where fellow Montrealers Chromeo were also on the bill, Arcade Fire sold 250 copies of their EP; the club held 300 people. The initial run of the EP was 500 copies; by July 2004 it had sold 3,000 copies. At one point in the tour, looking at the wads of cash strewn around a hotel bed, Arcade Fire felt like they'd robbed a bank. They could certainly afford hotels, but there were no wild rock'n'roll adventures in them.

Arcade Fire and the Unicorns would drive for two hours after each gig to find a cheaper hotel in the middle of nowhere, en route to the next gig. "We'd always stay at Comfort Suite motels, because we had a card and we'd get points on that," says Kingsbury. "We'd often get a big room. Two people would sign in, and then we'd sneak everyone else through the back, with air mattresses."

"We were touring in two vehicles, a van and a car, so we could do the cross-border fake out" on the way into the States, says Parry. Half the band and sound tech Sharon Levinson had American parentage, so that half drove the van with instruments over the border. "The van was listening to *Dune* as a book on tape. After a show, it was like, 'Okay, who wants to listen to *Dune*?'"

Both Arcade Fire and the Unicorns were conspicuous sights, especially in the deep South. It didn't help that Parry had to endure constant physical comparisons to the title character in *Napoleon Dynamite*, an instant cult hit film released that month. In Birmingham, Alabama, he was walking around town with the Unicorns' Nick Thorburn before the show. "Nick was dressed in pink, I was in my show clothes, and some locals definitely thought there was something not right," says Parry. "We were trying to avoid getting beat up. The band started without me; I made it in time for the second song. It was a bit hairy."

When the tour was over, Arcade Fire headed back to North Carolina for Merge's anniversary festival, alongside Destroyer, M. Ward, Spoon, Crooked Fingers and others. Being the label's newest signee, they opened the festival on a Wednesday night at a small bar, with Sebadoh's Lou Barlow opening for them. It was an early show; afterwards, stragglers stuck around for Merge karaoke, where Butler and Chassagne sang the Magnetic Fields' "Born on a Train." Raves about their non-karaoke performance rippled through the weekend. The band themselves were not convinced their lives would change much in a month's time; Butler was musing about writing record reviews as a side hustle.

Sarah Neufeld went tree planting in Oregon. Will Butler left the continent for the summer, going to Prague on a research grant for six weeks to learn about Czech rock of the '80s and '90s. "Not the '70s stuff that was super provocative, like Plastic People of the Universe," he says, "but the generation after that, like Už jsme doma and Psí vojáci. I only had to write a two-page summary. Most people were doing stuff for their theses, but I was doing mine just for the hell of it."

The Unicorns and Arcade Fire both played the Hillside Festival in Guelph in late July for their biggest crowds ever: 1,500 people in a packed tent for each set. A week later, they were invited by Sloan to be on a bill alongside Sam Roberts, Buck 65, Constantines and more. Arcade Fire were the second band of the day, after Death from Above 1979. *Exclaim!* editor James Keast recalls hearing the opening notes of "Wake Up" and then watching everyone who had been milling around the park make a beeline for the front of the stage. The band whose debut record wasn't out for another month was already a must-see act, regardless of their place on the bill.

That summer, advance copies of *Funeral* were circulating to press and retailers. Word of mouth from the Unicorns tour had built up anticipation. But the band was largely oblivious. In an interview for an *Exclaim!* cover story in August 2004, Win said, with uncharacteristic modesty befitting his Mile End milieu, "I think the record is an improvement over the EP. Some people might say the EP is better, but that's a load of crap. The singing on this is a lot better, for both of us. I definitely think there's progress, and that's what keeps me moving. We're figuring some things out. I don't know if it ever feels like, Oh, sweet, we've done something really awesome."

"For me, I'm always at square zero trying to get to square one," said Chassagne. "For me, I haven't achieved anything yet. This is a start."

THE START GOT rocky really quickly when Howard Bilerman left the band mere weeks before *Funeral*'s release. On the drive back to Montreal from the Sloan show, Bilerman shared a vehicle with Kingsbury; when he dropped him off, Bilerman told him, "I think that was my last show with the band." It had been coming for a while. "Win is pretty much exactly 10 years younger than I am," says Bilerman. "I was 34 years old with a 24-year-old boss. That didn't feel so great. If we were all just poker buddies, that's fine, but it was a power balance, which is the only time age would factor into the conversation."

Bilerman had been reared on the ethos of Steve Albini and his friends on Constellation Records, where every business decision a musician makes is an ethical quandary. It was clear that Arcade Fire were about to enter a different arena (and eventually actual arenas). On top of that, Bilerman was expecting his first child, and Hotel 2 Tango had just opened to commercial clients. At a crossroads in his life, he chose the more stable option. It was awkward, but all parties agreed it was for the best.

When interviewed for the 2004 *Exclaim!* cover story, Bilerman already knew he was out of the band, though that news was not yet on the record. "I saw it instantly in Win that music is in his blood," he said. "And it's always refreshing to meet a band—and I'm talking about all of them—who care more about making music than being successful at making music, who are working on music and living up to the responsibility that I think should be involved in putting out a record. I also definitely saw some impatience. Sometimes Win gets very obsessed over wanting things to happen right away, and I don't think it's a negative thing as much as it is that he's young and eager."

Reflecting on his choice in 2016, Bilerman said, "You know that joke about how someone asked John Lennon, 'Do you think Ringo is the greatest drummer in the world?' He said, 'Ringo's not even the best drummer in the Beatles.' I felt like I was the third best drummer in Arcade Fire. I was a stand-in. Most of the songs on *Funeral* were written before I joined. Once it was all recorded, we started to practise and it just didn't feel like there was any chemistry there. It was frustrating. Win and I had a lot of talks, and eventually decided that they should find a new drummer—because shit was going to get out of hand, really quickly. And I don't think I have the constitution to be in a band—at least at that time. I had these incredibly uncompromising beliefs about how you should proceed. I would get these weird fight-or-flight responses to stupid things."

Funeral's official launch was held at the Salvation Army Citadel in downtown Montreal on September 25, 2004: Bilerman's 34th birthday. He was invited to play it. "I didn't want to do it for a variety of reasons," he says. "Instead I went to the country with Silver Mt. Zion. We had a big dinner and a campfire where we recorded the song 'Hang On to Each Other.' It may or may not have been a ploy by that band to get me out of town for my birthday."

At the release show, Wolf Parade's Arlen Thompson and Bell Orchestre's Stefan Schneider sat in on a couple of songs. The rest of the night featured the only person the band considered as a potential touring drummer: Jeremy Gara, who was well known to Kingsbury and Parry from their Ottawa days. Gara came up in that city's punk scene but could play just about anything and was a renowned pinch-hitter. He was still in Kepler with Samir Khan and often played with Jim Bryson and Michael Feuerstack. That summer he was hired by Maritime, a band featuring members of American emo staples the Promise Ring and the Dismemberment Plan. They were touring in Europe when Gara got a call from Kingsbury asking if he was available to do a tour. "Then the *Pitchfork* review came out," says Gara, "and I thought, This is going to be longer than I think it is."

"HOW DID WE GET HERE? Ours is a generation overwhelmed by frustration, unrest, dread and tragedy. Fear is wholly pervasive in American society, but we manage nonetheless to build our defenses in subtle ways."

Those are the opening lines of *Pitchfork*'s review of *Funeral*, which ran two days before the album's retail date. Writer David Moore approaches it like a literary essay, praising the emotional content of the record, using words like *catharsis* and *enlightenment*. The review laments the "self-imposed solitude" of the *Bowling Alone* generation, leaving them "politically and spiritually inert" and therefore ready to embrace music like this. The philosophy, which is considerably lofty for a record review not written by Greil Marcus, plays better than the writing about the actual music. Regarding "Power Out," Moore writes, "The fluidity of the song's construction is mesmerizing."

It's strange to think a record review like this could launch a band's career—especially a review written by someone who only ever wrote a total of 12 *Pitchfork* reviews over four months and then disappeared. There's no soundbite, like Jon Landau writing, in 1974, "I have seen rock'n'roll's future and its name is Bruce Springsteen." It's entirely likely most people didn't even read Moore's review and simply looked at the score on the top right of the page, where *Pitchfork* gave *Funeral* a 9.7 rating.

Since the website's inception, *Pitchfork* has been pilloried for the idea that music can be evaluated down to the decimal point—as if that's any more or less absurd than a regular 10-point or five-star scale. Even the magazine's founder and many of the early writers admitted that the scoring was an elaborate joke, one that obviously backfired as the site developed actual clout.

Pitchfork did not give out perfect scores often. It did for Radiohead's *Kid A* in 2000 and Wilco's *Yankee Hotel Foxtrot* in 2002. Both those records were part of a general critical consensus; *Pitchfork* wasn't breaking any ground in singing their praises. Also in 2002, however, writer Matt LeMay gave a perfect score to *Source Tags & Codes*, the major label debut of Texan band . . . And You Will Know Us by the Trail of Dead. It did not help: the review became an albatross, an example of blogger hype in the new era of music criticism. Both reviewer David Moore and Ryan Schreiber, the site's founder and editor, wanted to give *Funeral* a perfect 10. But they also didn't want to burden it with too much expectation.

"We started to understand the gravity of the 10.0 beyond what it meant just to us," said LeMay in 2020, after Fiona Apple got the first perfect score in a decade. "A lot of the conversation became more about the score than about the music. I found it often had a negative effect on how these records were perceived by readers."

If anything, the site was usually cautious; it gave the Strokes' 2001 debut a 9.1. Reviewing Broken Social Scene's *You Forgot It in People* in 2003, in language that would suggest a perfect score, Ryan Schreiber gave the record a 9.2; 10 other records that year rated higher, though none higher than 9.5 (the Wrens). On *Pitchfork*'s year-end list for 2003, the No. 1 record was the Rapture's *Echoes*, which received a 9.0 upon its initial review—that's one decimal point lower than Frog Eyes' *The Golden River*, an album not deemed worthy of the year-end top 10.

Point being: 9.7 was a big fucking deal. And it was for a record that *Rolling Stone* didn't get around to reviewing until three months later. *Pitchfork* was credited with breaking Arcade Fire and became an inseparable part of the band's narrative.

Win Butler called his brother. "The *Pitchfork* review just came out," he told Will. "We should probably upgrade our website plan."

"We got a lot of overage charges that September," remembers Will. "This was back when you would put up a low-quality, 20-second clip of an MP3 because you didn't want people to steal it. But even that was killing us."

Merge had ordered a first run of 10,000 copies; orders placed in the summer had not been unusually high.[5] Within hours of the *Pitchfork* review, the number of orders went into the stratosphere and the record was instantly out of print. It wasn't easy to reprint. The artwork was complex, involving a foil-stamp that needed time to dry, plus a die-cut sleeve that had to be assembled by hand. The insert was an unusual shape, formatted like a booklet, signed by each member as if it were a contract, a promise of sorts to the listener. All of that added up to a two-week turnaround on print jobs.

A hit record that's unavailable makes for good word of mouth, but it also made Merge look like amateurs. It likely meant plenty of online pirating those first few weeks. All parties could have agreed to put out a streamlined standard jewel case packaging—but both band and label held the ideal that if something

---

5   As a point of comparison, the first run of Magnetic Fields' *69 Love Songs*, on Merge, was 7,500. It also sold out instantly.

can't be done right, it shouldn't be done at all. Further, distributor Touch and Go didn't want to print a glut, worried that this was just a fad. You know, like Trail of Dead.[6]

One fan made sure to snap up an early copy the week it came out. Merge's Mac McCaughan sent the band an email that read, "We just got a note from the manager of Tower Records in New York. Bruce Springsteen just walked in there to buy a copy of *Funeral*."

JEREMY GARA HAD two and a half rehearsals with Arcade Fire after he got home from Europe. At the Montreal release show, Wolf Parade's Dan Boeckner heckled them loudly from the back of the room. After a show at the Black Sheep Inn in Wakefield, Quebec, with the Hilotrons, they then headed to the Butler farm in Maine to rehearse further with Gara and try to write some new songs. They played a low-key show in nearby Bar Harbor while they were there. Rave reviews from the outside world kept pouring in.

Arcade Fire's official coming-out party was the CMJ Marathon in New York City, where every year the industry scouted the next big thing. *New York Times* music critic Kelefa Sanneh already knew that would be Arcade Fire, so he pitched his editors on a profile. A review in *Pitchfork* was one thing; a large profile in the *New York Times* right after your debut record was another.

In New York, the band took Sanneh to some Turkish baths, where they explored the acoustics by serenading him with a five-part chorale. They were photographed in the middle of the street in the Lower East Side, Chassagne spinning her umbrella horizontally. They played three gigs: one at the Strokes' home turf, the Mercury Lounge; another at the Museum of Television and Radio to be broadcast on KEXP in Seattle; and the other at the tiny Arlene's Grocery, where Sire Records' Seymour Stein—who'd signed all the CBGB acts in the '70s, as well as Madonna and k.d. lang—could be seen chatting up McCaughan from Merge. The next day Stein took him out for breakfast and told him to "write a number on a piece of paper," hoping—in vain—to buy Arcade Fire's contract from him, as if it was McCaughan's to sign away. Like all Merge contracts, the band and label split profits 50/50 after expenses.[7]

---

6   Before signing to Interscope and releasing the 10.0-rated album in question, Trail of Dead were on Merge. *Source Codes* sold 130,000 copies, which was considered a disappointing number for Interscope, but would be a major success for Merge.

7   This is known as a "net 50" deal, a royalty rate approximately four times what major labels offered at the time. And Merge had plenty of experience with majors trying to poach its artists, including Superchunk itself.

After New York, Arcade Fire headed back to Maine to prepare for the upcoming tour, which started at the Halifax Pop Explosion in early November, playing the Marquee with the Organ. Parry's sister Evalyn, a playwright and performance artist, was also playing the festival; he accompanied her for a set in which she was dressed as a giant tampon. And then things got wild.

Arcade Fire shows in Ithaca, Boston and New York that were supposed to be headlined by the Hidden Cameras had the bill reversed. David Byrne came to see them at the Bowery Ballroom in Manhattan and raved on his blog. That boost fuelled a 35-day tour with 28 dates throughout the U.S., ending with three shows in Vancouver and Victoria. Though they did not have a manager, they did have a major booking agent, Billions, that they'd met on tour with the Unicorns in Chicago. Jeremy Gara was the tour manager; he had the only cellphone in a van for seven people—eight when Will took a few days off school to join them. Martin Hall at Merge was fending off most press requests, while Gara, who'd only been in the band for two months, fielded calls from an American music industry that was suddenly very interested in this ramshackle Montreal band.

"Even though we had a bubble, a self-contained world, it was pretty easy [for someone] to bust into," said Gara in 2007. "We didn't say no to anything. We were friendly. We definitely made time to meet everyone who wanted to meet us, but it wasn't until we got exhausted that we realized we should put up a bit of a curtain. It was exhausting, but it was worthwhile, and it helped inform the decisions we've made since then. Just meeting everyone in the entire world of the music biz and realizing, I don't want to work with any of these people! I *thought* I wanted to say no, but now I *know* I want to say no. There was so seldom a time when everyone was not agreeing fully about that whole side of things. Everyone was on the same page: 'Yeah, that dude *was* an asshole!'"

"We never discussed it," says Parry. "We were just of a similar mindset: earnest and doing the thing for the love of the thing in a pure way, but also realizing that we're negotiating this circus. We had a healthy fear of the grossness of the biz world. Though Win was more of a 'Motown is the answer' dude: not fearful at all of being commercial, of being a mainstream commodity. We didn't see eye to eye on that, but not in a problematic way. We both connected on loving [Cyndi Lauper's] *She's So Unusual* but also on [Pixies'] *Doolittle*. We didn't really connect on Fugazi; Win's not a fan.

"I don't think Win ever identified with any kind of indie rock scene," Parry continues. "He didn't grow up seeing indie rock bands or hardcore bands. It was so not his culture, whereas Tim and Jeremy and I were so of that. He always resented being lumped into that category, because he thought of himself as being in the Beatles or Motown or the Cure. I remember him having a fight with [someone] from Constellation at some party. They were talking about the Clash, and [this person] said, 'I'm embarrassed to say that the first Clash album I discovered was *Combat Rock*.' Win was like, 'That's an incredible album! That's what's wrong with your record label, is that you're ashamed of anything. Fuck. You.'"

Owen Pallett opened the U.S. shows in January and February 2005, and joined them on stage as second fiddle. KROQ in L.A. put "Power Out" and "Rebellion" into rotation; pockets of the U.S. soon followed suit. One dollar from every ticket sold went to Partners in Health, a global health charity working in Haiti, to which the band gave plenty of vocal and financial support in the coming years.

At the Bowery Ballroom in New York, David Byrne joined them on stage for a cover of Talking Heads' "This Must Be the Place (Naive Melody)." In the audience was David Bowie, who had reportedly bought boxes of *Funeral* to give out to friends. Their presence only fuelled media interest—and Bowie's star wattage led to Byrne signing his occasional correspondence with the band as "the other DB." "That Bowie/Byrne thing was mega fuel for fire, no pun intended," says Parry. "That became such a headline. It was a torch-passing gesture from two of the most respected veterans of artful rock music."

Then it was off to the U.K. and Europe, where *Funeral* had only just been released on the Rough Trade label. As in North America, the reviews of the live show were ecstatic; it certainly helped that the Canadian band sounded more European than American. Selling merch for them was Montreal friend Sean Michaels, who was at school in Edinburgh. "It was a confusing mix of them playing small clubs in some cities to larger venues in London, where Björk or Jarvis Cocker would be in attendance," he says. "It was almost a dysmorphia of this band that was on a small and local scale suddenly and abruptly transitioning into a shared international discourse. It was so exciting, it was just bewildering. And then you start to think this happens all the time, but it really doesn't."

Arcade Fire's live performance was, for Britain in particular, a shot in the arm after years of shoegazing acts. Will Butler in particular had become a focal point: not just because he and Parry were hammering each other while wearing motorcycle helmets on "Laïka," but because he'd be wrapping Parry in duct tape or wrestling him while attempting to play. As the venues got bigger, Will could be found scaling the scaffolding with a floor tom in hand and repeatedly tossing it in the air upon returning to the stage. Outside the aggressive music scene, there had been no real element of chaos in mainstream rock music for a long time. "Will is not on *Funeral* much," says Kingsbury. "Which is why I think when we toured, he became the energy of the band—because he was just trying to figure out what to do."

Will learned early on what the limits were. "The Commodore Ballroom [in Vancouver] was one of the first shows where we played to 1,000 people," he says, not having been at Hillside. "It was a big step up. We were doing 'Laïka' and I picked Richie up, held him upside down and dropped him on his head. It really hurt him, really bad. It was like, Oh, that was a mistake. Oh right, we *are* physically hurting each other. We don't have to do that. It was the end of an era."

At the first London show, they met Scott Rodger, a manager whose sole client was Björk. He showed up the next night in Amsterdam, hit it off with the band and ended up sleeping on their tour bus for a few days. Björk was a huge inspiration to everyone in the band—not only her music, but the way she did her business, chose her projects and held everything to a high creative standard. Rodger was responsible for ensuring all her unusual ideas make some semblance of financial sense. He soon signed on with Arcade Fire. "Getting a manager happened at the exact right time," says Gara. "If we'd even waited another week or two, we would have killed ourselves. It was at a point in the tour where it was calm enough to talk to him. If he had come in the middle of the American leg, we would have been out of it. But in Europe we had a tour manager and could actually talk about this kind of thing."

Rodger was very committed and hands-on from day one. When the band played Coachella in April 2005, he was their guitar tech and only crew member other than sound tech Sharon Levinson. The Coachella gig became legendary, heralded years later as one of the most historic performances in the festival's history. It was the band's first large festival appearance anywhere. "It was a fun show, ridiculously chaotic," says Kingsbury. "The energy was good, but the sound was crazy. We played 'Power Out' into 'Rebellion,' and at one point Will was smashing a cymbal around the stage and somehow spliced one of Win's guitar cables. The guitar just cut out, although we didn't figure that out until later, when we found the spliced cable on the stage."

Seven years into its existence, Coachella had become the primary festival in America, drawing plenty of L.A. celebrities and being written about on gossip and style websites as much as in the music press. It was the place to be seen for musicians and audience members alike. Arcade Fire's 2005 set became the single most important gig of their career.

Not that they were remotely prepared. "We were still carrying everything around in Tupperware," says Will. "The summer before, Régine and I jury-rigged a system. We'd wrap this beautiful old '60s Guild bass in a blanket and put it on top of everything [in the van], because an actual hardwood case would cost $200. We had a Prophet 600 [synth] and I made a case for it out of wood that people left on the curb, and bought hinges from Home Depot. We had a Tupperware and baggie system [for cables] that we used well past Coachella. We first got roadies in the U.K. in the spring of 2005, two lovable young dunderheads who were extra hands. We had a tour manager there, too, because we were in a bus and crossing borders. But in North America, Jeremy was our tour manager. It totally destroyed him, both having to tour manage and the psychic weight of having a bag with tens of thousands of dollars [in merch money] in it beside his drum throne." In June 2005, Will graduated from Northwestern and finally moved to Montreal.

After Coachella, Arcade Fire were offered the cover of *Spin* magazine in June 2005. They turned it down and asked for a rain cheque; they were wary of more hype and knew the tour was about to wind down. The decision was met by facepalms across the board: no Merge artist had ever been offered the cover of *Spin* and they were turning it down? Publicist Martin Hall got a series of calls the afternoon of the decision, one after another from people further up the *Spin* masthead until finally the publisher called. The answer was still no. Other than Ani DiFranco (who actually did appear on the cover of *Spin*), no other popular artist had pushed back so hard against media demands since Nirvana criticized *Rolling Stone* on the cover of that magazine itself.

They did agree to a *Spin* article. Writer Caryn Ganz tried to capture why this band and this record had seized the imagination of so many people. "*Funeral* seemed to resonate as Americans grappled with war, hurricanes and a general sense of anxiety," she wrote. "With their sophisticated emotional palette, Arcade Fire paint in broad strokes, updating teenage angst for the yuppie-goth *Six Feet Under* era." That HBO show about a family of undertakers was one of only two times that decade that Arcade Fire allowed a song ("Rebellion") to be licensed to film or television.[8] The band loved *Six Feet Under* so much they also agreed to write a song, "Cold Wind," for the closing scene of the series finale, which aired in August 2005. It got nominated for a Grammy.

The exhausted band took off June and July, playing only Lollapalooza in Chicago and Hillside in Guelph on the same weekend. Bell Orchestre finally released their debut album on Rough Trade Records in August. The last two weeks of August were spent at festivals in Asia and Europe; Butler and Chassagne celebrated their second anniversary while flying from Japan to Portugal. In September, the CMJ festival coincided with Fashion Week in New York, where David Bowie had invited Arcade Fire to back him up singing "Wake Up" for the event's TV special. The next day Arcade Fire—who at that time the previous year were playing Arlene's Grocery in the Lower East Side—were now headlining at Central Park, where Bowie joined them for "Wake Up" and his 1971 song "Queen Bitch." The touring cycle ended in November in Boston; after

---

8   The same song was used in *The Black Donnellys*, a TV show co-created by Paul Haggis; the band
     had met the Academy Award–winning Canadian director through his work in Haiti.

the show, they brought a trash bag back to the hotel room filled with merch money: $40,000.

Then U2 called. The Irish superstars were on their Vertigo tour and had been using "Wake Up" as their walk-on music, right after the lights went down. They wanted to bring Arcade Fire with them to Japan, South America and Australia. "I wouldn't want any other group to support us ever again," Bono told the media. The Canadians agreed to do only Ottawa and Montreal on the weekend of American Thanksgiving, so they wouldn't have to travel.

When the lights went down right before the Arcade Fire set, they brought some walk-on music of their own: U2's "Where the Streets Have No Name." Thousands of fans rushed to take their seats, worried about missing U2, only to see Arcade Fire take the stage.

THAT'S HOW IT ALL STARTED. The band bought a church in November 2005, an hour south of Montreal in a town that happened to share Win Butler's middle name: Farnham. There, they recorded *Funeral*'s follow-up, *Neon Bible*, and also worked on a score for a movie by the director of *Donnie Darko*. Upon its release in March 2007, *Neon Bible* debuted at No. 2 on the Billboard charts. Music legends and Hollywood continued to be enthralled by Arcade Fire. In the 2008 presidential election, they played Obama campaign rallies in swing states—including a North Carolina stop with their Merge Records associates in Superchunk—and then played the Inauguration Ball in D.C. for campaign volunteers. In 2010, *The Suburbs* debuted at No. 1 in both the U.S. and the U.K. On February 13, 2011, at the Grammy Awards, Barbra Streisand stumbled over the word *suburbs* after she opened the envelope to announce Album of the Year. Arcade Fire became the first Canadian band to win that award and the second independent artist to do so in living memory, after Alison Krauss with Robert Plant.

"What the hell?" were Win Butler's first words into the mic, after beating Eminem, Katy Perry, Lady Antebellum and Lady Gaga for the award. "I just want to thank the city of Montreal, Quebec, for taking us in, giving us a home, a place to be a band." Twitter lit up with variations on the theme of "Who the hell is Arcade Fire?!" *The Suburbs* went on to win Album of the Year at the Junos and the Brit Awards, as well as the Polaris Music Prize. When accepting the Juno for Group of the Year, Win said, "I want to shout out the bands we came up with, from Royal City to Hidden Cameras to the Unicorns, Wolf Parade and all the amazing Canadian bands."

Then U2 came calling again, this time wanting Arcade Fire to open a massive outdoor show in Moncton. They agreed, in part because it allowed them to do something they'd always wanted to do: play SappyFest in adjacent Sackville, the festival started by Julie Doiron and run in part by Steve Lambke of the Constantines. The lineup that year included Owen Pallett, Gara's former employer Jim Bryson, the Weakerthans' John K. Samson, Constellation Records' Sandro Perri, Nathan Lawr's Minotaurs and new Montreal acts like Little Scream (Richard Reed Parry's future wife) and Grimes. Arcade Fire's slot on the schedule was under the alias Shark Attack, but their presence was a poorly kept secret—their tour bus was more than a bit conspicuous on the streets of the tiny New Brunswick town.

Barbra Streisand and the world now knew their name. But this was the Arcade Fire on home turf among peers.

CONCLUSION
WE BUILT
ANOTHER WORLD

B y 2005, Steve Jordan had spent 10 years as an A&R rep, primarily for Warner Music Canada: signing bands, trying to sign bands, funding demo deals. But it became increasingly clear to him that a new generation of musicians was finding ways to work around the limitations of the Canadian music industry. There should be a way to celebrate that, he thought. So he quit his job and founded the Polaris Music Prize, modelled on Britain's Mercury Prize for music and Canada's Giller Prize for fiction. More than 200 writers and broadcasters would vote on a long list and then a shortlist; 11 of those jurors would choose a winner.

The first Polaris shortlist, announced in June 2006, showed off a new Canada. Some of the artists, like Broken Social Scene and Metric, had radio and video support; most did not. Some, like Sarah Harmer and the New Pornographers, had been recognized earlier by the Junos; most had not. Half the list was composed of debut albums. Two (Cadence Weapon, K'naan) were by hip-hop artists. One, (Malajube) by a francophone rock band. One, the Deadly Snakes, was a garage-rock band who'd been ignored by the Canadian industry and had broken up just before the September 2006 gala. Two (Wolf Parade, Owen Pallett) had direct connections to Arcade Fire. The winner was Pallett, a solo violinist on a tiny co-operatively run record label whose CDs were hand-assembled art projects. This wasn't the Junos. Or the MuchMusic Video Awards.

Polaris quickly developed a reputation of picking left-field winners that prompted the industry and the general public to scratch their head. Pallett's win was followed by Patrick Watson, Caribou, Fucked Up and Karkwa before Arcade

Fire's *The Suburbs* became the first obvious winner—for perhaps the only time in the prize's history.

"When Caribou won in 2008," says Jordan, "I remember a veteran of the industry, saying, 'You've really cocked it up this time, Steve. Nobody cares about this band, nobody's heard of it.' First of all, that's the goddamn point. Second of all, I went to Tower Records in Dublin six months after the win, and I saw two front racks of Caribou product and I heard Caribou playing in the store—loudly! I went up to the cash and said, 'Hey, you guys really like Caribou, eh?' 'Fuckin' A, mate, he played Electric Picnic and there were 10,000 of us losing our shit.' That's what Polaris was about: repatriating what was happening and saying, 'No, this is internationally important.'

"Not to get too patriotic," continues Jordan, who later became head of CBC Music and fired Randy Bachman, "but Canadian music is awesome—and not in a way that mainstream media says it's awesome. I went to Iceland Airwaves [festival] in 2001 and went to every record store in downtown Reykjavík, including whatever the national equivalent of Walmart would be. Not only did every store have a Godspeed section, but they'd also have a Constellation Records section. In 2001! The cognoscenti all know what the reach of that band is, but the average person who considers themselves aware or who would look at a Polaris shortlist and say, 'I've sort of heard of them'—these people don't realize the reach of artists like that." Godspeed won the Polaris 15 years after they'd first had rave reviews in Europe and the U.S. and were still treated like an underground novelty act in the Canadian mainstream—a mainstream from which they were perfectly happy to exist independently.

Thirty-five of the 42 artists featured in this book—the seven exceptions are largely hip-hop and aggressive music acts—have been at least on a Polaris longlist. Seven of them (Owen Pallett, Caribou, Fucked Up, Arcade Fire, Feist, Godspeed, Cadence Weapon) have won the main prize; four others (Peaches, Broken Social Scene, Kid Koala, k-os) won the Polaris Heritage Prize, celebrating records made before 2005. The music made in the first six years of the 2000s casts a long shadow.

One band cast the longest shadow of all. And not only because its singer stands six foot five.

"THE WHOLE TIME FROM 2004 TO 2011, I would be ribbed about Arcade Fire," says Broken Social Scene's Kevin Drew. "It was my dad's favourite thing to do. 'Huh, saw Arcade Fire on TV last night with Bowie. Pretty cool!' 'Oh look, Arcade Fire just played in front of thousands of people!' 'Read another article about Arcade Fire!' Always rubbing it in my face. In 2011, we were going on our last tour before our hiatus. We were going to South America for a few shows. Pops picked us up and drove us to the airport early in the morning. We're on the highway beside the airport, and he says, 'Oh, look at that!' We look up and there's this beautiful private jet just about to land. He goes, 'Is Arcade Fire in town this weekend?'"

Drew first saw Arcade Fire in early 2003 and was a huge fan. By the time *Funeral* came out in September 2004, Broken Social Scene was "on our own path by that point, and their path was shooting off to the stratosphere," he says. "It was very annoying to witness for anyone with an ego. It wasn't all, 'Oh, aren't they great!' There was a lot of backroom chatter about the success of Arcade Fire. But *Funeral*: how can you compete with that? It was an incredible, stunning album. And *Neon Bible*: such a phenomenal, dark piece of blood. I adored them."

He was far from the only peer to feel competitive. Tegan and Sara's *So Jealous* had a release date of September 14, 2004, the same day as both *Funeral* and Stars' *Set Yourself on Fire*. "I remember thinking, Oh, fuck," says Sara, who first saw Arcade Fire open for Hawksley Workman at Pop Montreal in the fall of 2003. "I specifically remember knowing that their record would haunt me. I knew it was going to be fabulous and that everyone would freak out over it. That's the only time in our career where I had a really competitive feeling about another band. I used to dream about that band and feel stressed out by them. I loved them! I was a fan, but I knew we'd never be able to compete. We would be overshadowed."

Her premonition turned out to be true, even though *So Jealous* ultimately proved to be a major breakthrough for Tegan and Sara: going gold in Canada, landing them major festivals, radio play and opening slots for new American superstars the Killers. "But Arcade Fire were on the cover of every magazine, and we were inside," says Sara. "Who got the cover of *Exclaim!*? Arcade Fire. We played Coachella for the first time that year [2005], and we played before Arcade Fire. When we were finished our set, the crew was like, 'Okay, get off now.' Like, 'Get out of the way. We're about to be legends.' The whole album cycle, I just felt like, *GODDAMMIT*. We'd feel excited about getting something, and I'd look on *Pitchfork* and it would be, 'David Bowie comes to see Arcade Fire!' I'm like, Well, I should just kill myself. What the fuck?! It felt like I was living in the shadow of their exciting career.

"Obviously I feel differently now; we're all running a marathon, and we're all still in it," Sara continues. "Feist is another person like that. I remember feeling the compulsion to run when I saw her in real life, just terrified of her, desperately wanting her approval. This is true of Emily Haines, too. I'd see these girls and I felt like the nerdiest nerd. One time I saw Leslie in an airport. In my mind she looked like her press shot, with some leather jacket and perfectly worn-in boots. I probably was wearing pants with one leg shorter than the other because my girl-friend and I always rode bikes. I had short hair and felt like a 20-year-old twinkie lesbian. I was not cool. Any time I'd see those people I thought, Oh god, let the earth swallow me."

International reviews of drastically different Canadian bands often compared them to each other, just as every New York City band experienced five years ear-lier. "As we were blowing up and doing well," says Arcade Fire's Richard Reed Parry, "people were already combing for the next Arcade Fire. There was buzz to be capitalized on, and you could see it. Bands that had only been together for three months, there would be all these A&R dudes going to their first show. That is hell. That is the death of bands. Give them a minute to be a band! It was so desperate. The Strokes broke right out of the gate [in 2001], then people wanted to find the next Strokes. Then our band was its own thing and *not* the next Strokes, and then it became, 'What is the next Arcade Fire?' Then it all turned into a burning gar-bage fire."

"Whether you like Arcade Fire or not, they drove pseudo-commercial indie rock, or guitar-based music, in a completely different direction that would have both excellent repercussions and terrible repercussions," says Dan Boeckner of Wolf Parade. "Like Talking Heads or Skinny Puppy or any other band who would move the needle. The fact that all those ideas were cooked up in this weird petri dish of a city, and that the city is as much a character in their story as they are per-sonally—that's incredible to me. Even if you're too cool to like Arcade Fire, you have to recognize that's a huge coup.

"I was on the inside," continues Boeckner, who is close friends with the band and who briefly served as their bassist. "Their best decisions were to not worry about what anyone thought—which hurt some people in this community, person-ally and emotionally, but it's a double-edged sword. I think they had to do what they had to do. The train was leaving the station."

Inherent in an Arcade Fire backlash is also the "crabbuckit" that k-os sang about the same year *Funeral* came out: the band made exponentially more money than most of their peers, evidenced by the fact that they could afford to match $1 million in donations to Haitian relief in 2010, on top of millions more they've raised for Partners in Health. "I mean, what would *you* do with that amount of resources?" asks Boeckner rhetorically. "I've seen so many bands who have as much stored up in the war chest for doing something cool, or trying something absurd, and then completely fucking blow it. Arcade Fire take risks with the resources they have. They also donate a lot of money! I know all the things that people could throw at Arcade Fire and criticize the way they handled their ascension, but I think with enough years behind it, none of those things are egregious or terrible to me."

Toronto musician Hawksley Workman moved to Montreal in 2017. "I realized how hot-button the issue was of talking about Arcade Fire with people in Mile End," he says. "All the middle-age guys who were part of the scene when all the world was looking to Montreal are all still there. Who got famous and who didn't—that's all quite raw there. Arcade Fire is like a tattoo on that part of the city that will never go away. Some people show off that tattoo proudly, and some people are embarrassed by it."

"What it means to be a band from Montreal did change as a product of all that," says Efrim Menuck of Godspeed, who grew up in Toronto and moved to Montreal in 1991. "There is a regional truth here that wasn't conveyed. I'm not Québécois. I've lived in Montreal for a gazillion years, and a lot of my civic pride is around [how] Montreal is hard to understand. You can't assume you get it because every now and then you spend a weekend here.

"I remember when the Wolf Parade crew arrived [from Vancouver Island]," he continues, "and they all moved into the block around my apartment and they started calling it Little Victoria. I'm not putting anyone down, but they came as a unit and didn't learn French. They just kept their weirdo Victoria punk thing. They didn't assimilate, ultimately, you know?" He laughs. "That is a different story than what Godspeed lived. Especially because half of Godspeed is Québécois Montreal. A lot of what was getting represented as Montreal [in 2005] was just people who happened to live here."

Which, of course, could also be said of New York City or London or any metropolis that attracts cultural migrants. "Absolutely," Menuck concurs, "but New York and London are New York and London, know what I mean? All Montreal has going for it is that it's a weird city. I still don't fucking get it. I'm still constantly surprised by the flowers that grow here—and the flowers that don't."

"That time in Montreal was a really weird, special era," says Arlen Thompson of Wolf Parade. "Everyone had time to sit at Café Olimpico and drink coffee for three hours every day. I work now as an electrician and I try to describe this stuff to people who went to trade school after high school. I say, 'Oh, in my 20s I hung out with all these people and went swimming and made records and collaborated with artists and lived like people who were retired.' And many of these people have gone on to do exceptional things, whether it's writing novels that win Gillers or making records that win Grammys or being nominated for Oscars or working on the Large Hadron Collider. This group of weirdos came together from different areas of Canada and the United States, who lived in this laissez-faire hipster Disneyland that was Mile End. Montreal was a make-your-own-fun world, a real DIY spirit. The commercial side of things was very secondary."

That's why it's all the more shocking how successful many of these unconventional artists were, from Montreal or otherwise, based primarily on online press and word of mouth. "What I remember about that time is that if you got an amazing review on *Pitchfork*, like more than 8.5, it would correlate to you selling 100,000 records, like the Unicorns," says Howard Bilerman, who recorded *Funeral*. "That was the next stratosphere. I mean, some people signed to Matador or Merge or Thrill Jockey were already selling those numbers. But what *Pitchfork* at that time did was elevate bands no one had heard of to being bands selling 100,000 records and being able to play all around the world. That power is gone now. I know bands who have been lauded by *Pitchfork* in the last few years who are only selling 5,000 records, and that's disheartening. I'm the beneficiary of getting royalties from a record that did really well at a time when people were still buying records."

Murray Lightburn of the Dears says, "We're one of the bands who had this Indiana Jones thing, with the ball rolling down and the door closing. The bands on the other side of the wall are fucked. We grabbed our hat and got through at the last minute. If you are starting a band now, it's fucking hard."

Natalia Yanchak adds, "There are artists who have millions of plays on Spotify, and then they go play a show and they can't get a single person to come. And yet streaming metrics have so much value." Live performance was a key element for almost all the acts in this book. No one was phoning it in. Now, arguably, that matters less and less. "How many followers you have dictates whether or not you're playing a festival—that's literally how these things are being curated," Lightburn says. "Never mind whether or not you can play or you're a good band or whether anyone even knows your name."

Allan Reid, the former Universal A&R rep who now runs the Juno Awards, says streaming metrics are not that different from the days of tracking illegal downloads. "When it's free, are you actually converting those people to fandom? Nowadays you hear about bands who stream three million times, but you learn that it's because they were on one popular playlist. Does that mean you have three million fans? No. Did those people become fans of your music, or was it like hearing a song on the radio once by chance?" The Canadian acts who became popular during the file-sharing era have proven that they weren't flashes in the pan.

"For a band to have a breakthrough record now—how does that even happen?" says Bilerman. "Records I really care about have been announced, come out, get favourable reviews and don't correlate to a career. It's scary. The time we're talking about here in music was the last gasp of being able to climb the ladder. Honestly, even in the middle of all that, I thought that notion had died 10 years before.

The big-font artists on festival posters in 2001, 2002—Wilco, White Stripes, Strokes—it felt like those guys were the last people off the island." Bilerman played in a popular *band* and he's citing other popular *bands*. After 2005, as economic challenges grew and the cost of real estate squeezed all creative pursuits—particularly rehearsal space—bands became endangered species; solo artists were the only acts truly flourishing.

The industry changed quickly with the death of physical product, which can be pegged largely to the rise of the iTunes store, followed by the dawn of streaming. "Things shifted quickly in 2005 to '07," says Ian Ilavsky of Constellation Records. "We pressed 15,000 copies of [one 2009] record, and I don't think we sold more than 4,000. We made some huge over-pressing errors, and that was in close consultation with our distributor." The vinyl resurgence was a drop in the bucket compared to income lost from CD sales. Live music became the primary source of income for most musicians—and luckily, new Canadian artists were able to deliver, whether it was the unconventional unpredictability of Tanya Tagaq or straight-up, sweaty rock'n'roll like Japandroids.

But, of course, all the artists quoted above are people who grew up with the indie rock mindset, whose formative musical discoveries happened before the internet, who aren't necessarily hard-wired for the streaming world. Starting with Drake and the Weeknd in 2010, it became incredibly obvious that there were other routes to success—and that being identifiably Canadian was never going to be considered a hindrance again. Over the next decade, independent artists as diverse as Grimes, Lido Pimienta, Alvvays, Kaytranada, Pup, U.S. Girls, the Halluci Nation, Bahamas, BadBadNotGood and Daniel Caesar thrived internationally, while July Talk and Arkells filled arenas at home. And those artists are the tip of the iceberg.

It's safe to say that most, if not all, of those artists took direct inspiration—musically and strategically—from the Canadian music made specifically in 2000 to 2005. None of them lacked confidence in the idea that their music, as Canadians, belonged in the larger world, and the world had no trouble believing them. Lots of interesting Canadian music comes out all the time—*why wouldn't it?* It's long beyond time to dump bullshit colonial self-owns like the phrase *world-class* and accept the concept as a given.

And yet artists today face myriad challenges encountered by no other generation of the modern era: plummeting revenue, societal contempt for working artists, infinite competition for audience's attention and a real estate crisis that impacts creativity in general. It's imperative to get even more innovative about making impossible things happen, on any and every scale.

"The methods of distributing and accessing music are different now, but the strongest thing we had [in 2000] was the community and the sense of fun," says Tyler Clark Burke of Three Gut Records. "I feel like another Three Gut could start next week. Everyone wanted to hang out together. It really did feel like a family, and we even had a house where we all lived together at different points. Someone could start a magical community of people who do fun stuff that excites people in a totally different way."

"The fact that so many of us came out with this big sound that we wanted to create and be joyous—people were ready for it," says Kevin Drew, whose breakthrough album arrived a year after a cataclysmic moment in North American history, called *You Forgot It in People*. "They were ready for anthems. They just didn't know it. People should remember that right now. It's time for anthems again."

ACKNOWLEDGEMENTS

This book is dedicated to the memory of Gord Downie, without whose legacy this book would literally not have been possible. He might have enjoyed this one. Here's to streets ahead and the never-ending present.

I continue to be in eternal debt to Jason Schneider and Ian A.D. Jack, my co-authors on this book's predecessor, *Have Not Been the Same*. I'm not convinced any of this would have happened without them. Ian fosters new generations of young musicians and brings light to their world. I once again thoroughly recommend Jason's 2009 book, *Whispering Pines*, which I regard as the first chronological installment of a trilogy that concludes with the book you now hold in your hands. All three books wouldn't exist without the faith of ECW Press editor Michael Holmes: thank you for 20 years of belief.

Thank you to my most excellent peers for their first drafts of history, for writing with such passion and poetry, particularly those from whose research I borrowed heavily in this text: Stuart Berman, Prasad Bidaye, Lorraine Carpenter, Del Cowie, Cam Lindsay, Sarah Liss, Anupa Mistry, Josh Ostroff, Ben Rayner, Tabassum Siddiqui, Sam Sutherland. Please write (more) books. I want to read them.

The following writers read an early draft, and went far beyond the call of duty with their suggestions: the most excellent Mary Dickie, Sean Michaels and Carl Wilson. Thanks also to those who helped with research or by reading certain passages, including Colton Eddy, Gordon Krieger and Tanis Rideout. I'm frankly in awe of the heavy lifting done by copy editor Crissy Calhoun and proofreader Jen Knoch. Thanks also to ECW's Shannon Parr, Jen Albert and Claire Pokorchak.

For other assistance: Aaron Brophy, Jesse Brown, Tyler Clark Burke, Keiko Devaux, Dalton Higgins, Kim Juneja, Emmanuel Madan, Richard Reed Parry, Dan Seligman, Laurel Sprengelmeyer, Joseph Shabason, Reg Vermue, Liz Walker. Thank you as well to all managers and publicists who helped facilitate these interviews. RIP Joni Sadler.

For life-saving photo assistance, thank you to Jeff Harris, Atsuko Kobasigawa, David Leyes, Lisa Moran, Mike Olsen, Julie Penner, Christina Rentz and Frank Yang.

Thank you to my fellow 2021–22 journalism fellows at University of Toronto's Massey College for clearing my head after this monumental project, especially atop Gros Morne Mountain: Rebecca Collard, Patrick Egwu, Wency Leung and Jonathan Montpetit. With Emily Mockler and the junior fellows, you all provided "a soft place to land" and plot new chapters.

I'd like to nominate *Exclaim!* magazine's founders, Ian Danzig and Atsuko Kobasigawa, to the Order of Canada for their service to this country's culture. James Keast nurtured several generations of Canadian music writers at *Exclaim!*, including me, who all owe him a great debt. The Hillside Festival in Guelph embodies so much of what I love about music; thank you to Sam Baijal and all its staff and volunteers—long may it run. Thank you to Nicholas Jennings, for his 1997 classic *Before the Gold Rush*, and to Dave Bidini for 1998's *On a Cold Road*. Both men's eternal curiosity, intergenerational history and ongoing work continue to inspire me. May the *West End Phoenix* continue to rise.

Two books published in 2011 were ideal models for the book you now hold in your hand: Dan Charnas's *The Big Payback: The History of the Business of Hip-Hop* and Will Hermes's *Love Goes to Buildings on Fire: Five Years in New York That Changed Music Forever*. Re-reading those while writing this book was incredibly daunting; I can only aspire to achieve that kind of mastery.

I've never publicly acknowledged the debt that *Have Not Been the Same*—and therefore this book as well—owes to Peter Biskin's 1998 book, *Easy Riders, Raging Bulls: How the Sex-Drugs-and-Rock 'N' Roll Generation Saved Hollywood*. Gina Arnold's *Route 666: On the Road to Nirvana* was and is also a model. While writing *The Never-Ending Present*, the following biographies were inspirations: Bob Mehr's 2016 book, *Trouble Boys: The True Story of the Replacements*, and Sylvie Simmons's 2011 book, *I'm Your Man: The Life of Leonard Cohen*. Barney Hoskyns's *Lowside of the Road: A Life of Tom Waits* is exemplary unauthorized bio writing.

This book was written during a pandemic, in a state of heightened mental anxiety and upheaval, personally and globally. I'm frankly amazed it exists. It was largely a solitary affair. So for historical support, personal and/or professional, eternal gratitude to (in addition to all mentioned above): Wilma Aalbers, Mark Agnew, Jon Bartlett, Denise Benson, Stuart Berman, Geoff Berner, Alan Berry, Dave Bidini, H. Chris Brown, Melanie Buddle, Sam Cino, Dave Clark, Heather Corscadden, Nick Craine, Jen Cutts, David Dacks, Tawny Darbyshire, Douglas Davey, Chris Dempsey, Cynthia Dennis, Mary Dickie, Jonny Dovercourt, Drew Edwards, Stephen Evans, Kate Fenner, Sue File, Bretton Fosbrook, Yuani Fragata, Vicki Fraser, Geordie Gordon, Kate Greenaway, Candace Gritter, Marion Gruner, Sheila Gruner, Jim Guthrie, Jon Halliwell, William Hare, Martin Haynes, Tanya Hobbs, Brian D. Johnson, Steve Jordan, Karl Kannstadter, Samir Khan, James Keast, Tim Kingsbury, Rolf Klausener, Erik Kucher, Nathan Lawr, Grant Lawrence, Sarah Lazarovic, Liisa Ladouceur, Greg Lettau, Maggie MacDonald, Max MacDonald, Michael MacDonald, Kelly McCullough, Stephen McGrath, Michael McLarnon, Fiona (Wall) McPhaden, Glen McQuestion, Lewis Melville, Shawn Micallef, Cheryl Misener, Jenny Mitchell, Patricia Mora, Paul Mora, Lisa Moran, Janet and Melanie Morassutti, Erin O'Connell, Michael O'Connell, Tristan O'Malley, Angie Pajek, Sandra Patrick, Julie Penner, Barb Petek, Simon Racioppa, Aaron Riches, Kate Richmond, Anicka Quin, Geoff Roberts, Patti Schmidt, Tab Siddiqui, Tannis Slimmon, Sarmishta Subramanian, Liz Sullivan, Dianna Symonds, Samantha (Armstrong) Teney, Dean Therrien, Patricia Treble, Brendan Wall, Paul Wells, Bill Whitehead, Carl Wilson, Dave Withers, Victor Wolters. Many more: if you think you belong on these pages, you do. You have all helped lift me up; when I know why I'm happy, it's because of you. Anne Kingston RIP. Bless all the Barclays, Kuntzes, Spitzers and Blocky Cube. Big up the Flaming Glass.

James Rocchi was a personal and professional inspiration to me for half my life, a brilliant melonfarmer who never hesitated to tell people how much he loved them and believed in their talents. I'm half the writer he was and I'm blessed to have been his friend. Goodbye, pork-pie hat. RIP.

When I first met Helen Spitzer, she was a fellow campus radio DJ and writer, wearing a T-shirt with Destroyer lyrics ("Stay critical or die") she had screenprinted herself. She led me to several pivotal events in this book, and infinitely more in real life. And so this book is for mass romantic Montreal nights, for Torontopian Track and Fields, for Dog Day Afternoons, for Mergefests, for CMJ Canadian brunches in Brooklyn, for telling me to try honesty. It's for everything gained, everything lost, and everything she taught me. This book is of course for our young lion, but even more so for her, and for a lifetime of non-musical memories—the good ones.

I feel it all. I believe in the good of life.

SELECTED SOURCES

For the complete endnotes, please visit https://www.michaelbarclay.ca/heartsonfire-endnotes.

INTERVIEWS

All interviews were conducted by the author in 2020–21 unless otherwise indicated.

Damian Abraham

Steve Bays

Geoff Berner

Howard Bilerman (2004, 2020)

Ian Blurton

Dan Boeckner

Jim Bryson

Buck 65

Basia Bulat

Tyler Clark Burke

Linda Noelle Bush

Will Butler

Win Butler (2004, 2007, 2010)

Torquil Campbell

Brendan Canning

Joel Carriere

Stephen Carroll

Ro Cemm

Régine Chassagne (2004, 2007, 2010)

John Collins

José Contreras (2016)

Kim Cooke

Evan Cranley

Jonny Dovercourt (2006)

David Drew

Kevin Drew (2003, 2020)

Ian D'Sa

Kathleen Edwards

Leslie Feist (1999, 2004, 2017, 2020)

Frazey Ford

Jon Gallant

Jeremy Gara (2007)

Gentleman Reg (2002, 2004, 2009, 2020)

Joel Gibb (2002, 2004, 2013, 2020)

Gonzales (2008, 2020)

Dallas Good

Jim Guthrie

Mike Haliechuk

Sarah Harmer (2000, 2001, 2004, 2020)

Jordan Hastings

Ian Ilavsky

Danko Jones

Steve Jordan

Steve Kado (2006)

Kid Koala

Tim Kingsbury (2004, 2007, 2010, 2020)

Trish Klein

Ben Kowalewicz

Spencer Krug

Steve Lambke

Trevor Larocque

Nathan Lawr

Murray Lightburn

Corb Lund

Maggie MacDonald

Stephen McBean

Doug MacGregor (2001, 2020)

Efrim Menuck

Sean Michaels

Amy Millan

Lisa Moran (2005, 2020)

Carl Newman

Owen Pallett (2004, 2006, 2010, 2014, 2020)

Richard Reed Parry (2004, 2007, 2010, 2020)

Samantha Parton

Peaches

Rollie Pemberton

George Pettit

Mauro Pezzente

Joel Plaskett (2007, 2010, 2016, 2020)

Prevail

Matias Rozenberg

Sara Quin

Tegan Quin

Allan Reid

Aaron Riches (2000, 2001, 2005, 2020)

Sam Roberts

Rob the Viking

John K. Samson (2007, 2010, 2021)

Saukrates

Dan Seligman

Katie Sketch

Justin Small

Dan Snaith

Aaron Solowoniuk

Charles Spearin

Justin Stayshyn (2004)

Sam Sutherland

Jason Tait

Arlen Thompson

Jamie Thompson

Nick Thorburn

Bry Webb (2001, 2005)

Josh Wells

Mandy Wheelwright

Andrew Whiteman

Carl Wilson (2014)

Hawksley Workman (2001, 2020)

Natalia Yanchak

FREQUENTLY CITED SOURCES

Abraham, Damian. "Episode 35: Dallas Green," *Turned Out a Punk* podcast, July 8, 2015.

Benson, Denise. *Then & Now: Toronto Nightlife History*. Three O'Clock Press, 2015.

Berman, Stuart. Stubermania.tumblr.com.

Berman, Stuart. *This Book Is Broken*. House of Anansi, 2009.

Berman, Stuart. *Too Much Trouble: A Very Oral History of Danko Jones*. ECW Press, 2012.

Brainwashed.com/godspeed.

Burns, Todd L. "Win Butler," Red Bull Music Academy, October 3, 2016.

Callender, Tyrone. "Northern Touch at 20," CBCMusic.ca, January 31, 2018.

Carpenter, Lorraine. "Glummer Girls," *Exclaim!*, June 2004.

Carpenter, Lorraine. "Profane Peaches," *Exclaim!*, October 2003.

Carpenter, Lorraine. *Lost in the Plot*. Invisible Publishing, 2011.

Clay, Joe. "Beautiful Colours Everywhere," *The Quietus*, October 30, 2014.

Cook, John, Mac McCaughan and Laura Ballance. *Our Noise: The Story of Merge Records*. Algonquin Books of Chapel Hill, 2009.

Cowie, Del. "Man on Fire," *Exclaim!*, November 2005.

Dey, Claudia. "An Interview with Leslie Feist," *The Believer*, July 1, 2013.

Dombal, Ryan. "Caribou: 5-10-15-20," *Pitchfork*, September 30, 2014.

Dombal, Ryan. "Destroyer's Dan Bejar Serenades the Apocalypse," *Pitchfork*, January 14, 2020.

Dwyer, Nick. "Peaches," Red Bull Music Academy, 2011.

Fontana, Kaitlin. *Fresh at Twenty: The Oral History of Mint Records 1991–2011*. ECW Press, 2011.

Harper, Ty. "Episode 1," *This Is Not a Drake Podcast*, January 14, 2021.

Kaplan, Ben. "The Measure of a Band," *National Post*, April 2, 2009.

Lechner, Alysa. "Pissing People Off," *Vice*, July 22, 2014.

Liss, Sarah. *Army of Lovers: A Community History of Will Munro*. Coach House Press, 2013.

Lyons, Patrick. "Cue Fake Drums," *Stereogum*, January 23, 2020.

Mansuy, Anthony. "Children, Wake Up," *DumDum*, September 22, 2014.

McCredie, Andrew. "Swollen Members' Madchild Riffs on the Drug Addiction That Nearly Killed Him," *Vancouver Sun*, August 27, 2012.

Meter, William V. "She's a Very Kinky Girl," *Spin*, June 23, 2003.

Mistry, Anupa. "Kardinal Offishall," Red Bull Music Academy, October 10, 2016.

O'Kane, Josh. *Nowhere with You: The East Coast Anthems of Joel Plaskett, the Emergency and Thrush Hermit*. ECW Press, 2016.

Ostroff, Joshua. "Metric's System," *Exclaim!*, July 2003.

Parco, Nicholas. "Tegan Quin on the Legacy of *The Con* and How Tegan and Sara Almost Broke Up while Touring It," *New York Daily News*, November 1, 2017.

Powers, Devon. "Taking Measurements," *PopMatters*, October 13, 2004.

Pratt, Greg. "Nazi Baiting and Hardcore Raging," *Exclaim!*, September 24, 2012.

Rayner, Ben. "Cons' Prose," *Toronto Star*, December 7, 2009.

Siddiqui, Tabassum. "Questionnaire: Emily Haines," *Exclaim!*, October 2006.

Spitzer, Helen. "Poster of a Woman," *Nuvo*, February 20, 2018.